Britain's Birds: a guide to

see *pages 6–7* for more

Status/conservation designations in Britain, Ireland and Europe

Easy reference to similar species

Status summary including seasonal changes

Range map including migration routes

Habitat summary

Key ID features including flight patterns

Detailed text highlights crucial ID features

All distinctive features shown

Comparison species shown to scale

At-a-glance comparison tables where appropriate

All regular subspecies described

Unrivalled selection of high-definition photos

Photos give a feel for typical habitat

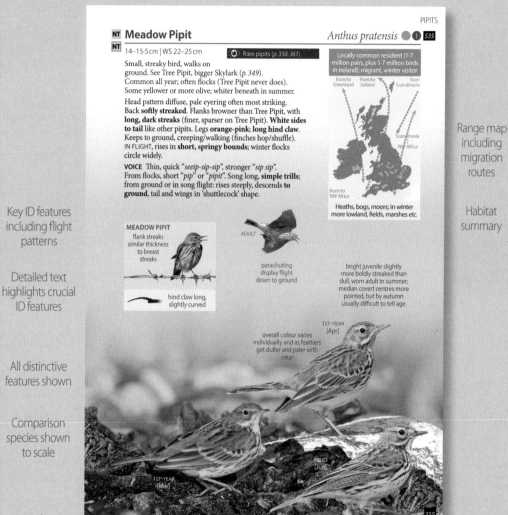

PIPITS

NT **Meadow Pipit**   *Anthus pratensis* ● ❶ 535
NT

14–15·5 cm | WS 22–25 cm   ↻ Rare pipits (p.358-361)

Small, streaky bird, walks on ground. See Tree Pipit, bigger Skylark (*p. 349*). Common all year; often flocks (Tree Pipit never does). Some yellower or more olive; whiter beneath in summer.

Head pattern diffuse, pale eyering often most striking. Back **softly streaked**. Flanks browner than Tree Pipit, with **long, dark streaks** (finer, sparser on Tree Pipit). **White sides to tail** like other pipits. Legs **orange-pink; long hind claw**. Keeps to ground, creeping/walking (finches hop/shuffle). IN FLIGHT, rises in **short, springy bounds**; winter flocks circle widely.

VOICE Thin, quick "*seeip-sip-sip*", stronger "*sip sip*". From flocks, short "*pip*" or "*pipit*". Song long, **simple trills**; from ground or in song flight: rises steeply, descends **to ground**, tail and wings in 'shuttlecock' shape.

Locally common resident (1·7 million pairs, plus 1·7 million birds in Ireland); migrant, winter visitor

from/to Greenland   from/to Iceland   from Scandinavia

Scandinavia
NW Africa

from/to NW Africa

Heaths, bogs, moors; in winter more lowland, fields, marshes etc.

MEADOW PIPIT
flank streaks similar thickness to breast streaks

ADULT

parachuting display flight down to ground

bright juvenile slightly more boldly streaked than dull, worn adult in summer; median covert centres more pointed, but by autumn usually difficult to tell age

hind claw long, slightly curved

1ST-YEAR [Apr]

overall colour varies individually and as feathers get duller and paler with wear

ADULT [Jun]

1ST-YEAR [Mar]

355

BRITAIN'S BIRDS

An identification guide to the birds of Britain and Ireland

Rob Hume, Robert Still, Andy Swash, Hugh Harrop and David Tipling

WILDGuides

PRINCETON

press.princeton.edu

Published by Princeton University Press,
41 William Street, Princeton, New Jersey 08540
In the United Kingdom: Princeton University Press, 6 Oxford Street,
Woodstock, Oxfordshire OX20 1TR
nathist.press.princeton.edu

Requests for permission to reproduce material from this work should be sent to
Permissions, Princeton University Press

First published 2016

British Library Cataloging-in-Publication Data is available

Library of Congress Control Number 2016930332
ISBN 978-0-691-15889-1

Production and design by **WILD**Guides Ltd., Old Basing, Hampshire UK.
Printed in China

Published under license from RSPB Sales Ltd. to raise awareness of the Royal Society for the
Protection of Birds (Charity registration England and Wales no 207076, Scotland SC037654).
For all items sold Princeton University Press will donate a minimum of 40 pence to
RSPB Sales Ltd, the trading subsidiary of the RSPB. All subsequent sellers of this book are
not commercial participators for the purpose of Part II of the Charities Act 1992.
www.rspb.org.uk

10 9 8 7 6 5 4 3 2 1

FSC
www.fsc.org
MIX
Paper from
responsible sources
FSC® C005748

Contents

Introduction

This is a complete and authoritative photographic guide to the wild birds of Britain and Ireland. It covers all plumages likely to be recorded of every species accepted onto the British and Irish lists up to the end of March 2016, including rarities. It also covers a few species that have recently been identified but not yet officially added to the lists. Many other species have been recorded as escapes from captivity or introductions, and a number of these have bred in the wild. Those that seem most likely to become established or lead to confusion with regular species are included, either with the relevant species or in a separate section at the end of the book (p. 522). While primarily an identification guide, the book also presents up-to-date population estimates for regular breeding, wintering and migrant birds, and, for rarities, a summary of the number of records. For the increasing number of species that are of conservation concern, information is included on their status based on current knowledge and assessments up to January 2016.

At the end of the book is a complete list of all the species on the British or Irish lists, presented in scientific (taxonomic) order. Uniquely, this list summarizes the conservation status and relevant EU and domestic conservation legislation relating to each species (see p. 524). This will be useful to birdwatchers, conservation managers, landowners and estate managers and local authorities alike, and has been verified by experts at Biocensus ecological consultants and the RSPB.

Producing this book has been an ambition of **WILD**Guides for many years, but without the help and advice readily offered by so many people this ambition could not have been fulfilled. Without the photographs, in particular, this project could never have been completed. Although the majority of the images were taken by the authors, bird photographers from all over the world have enthusiastically offered their images: the photographs themselves stand as testament to the quality of their work, and the outstanding collection of pictures presented reflects their very considerable skill and countless hours of dedicated effort. Most of the photographs were taken in Britain or Ireland and include, where possible, images of individual rarities that have been recorded. The photographers are acknowledged individually at the end of the book (p. 541), and details are given of who took each of the images. A special mention must go to the staff at the Agami Photo Agency in the Netherlands, since without their invaluable and enthusiastic assistance the project would inevitably have stalled.

Each regular breeding, wintering and migratory species has a map, annotated where appropriate to show the destination of birds migrating to, from or through Britain and Ireland. The maps have been adapted from base maps kindly supplied by BirdLife International, the international authority on the range and status of wild birds.

This book has evolved considerably during its preparation. New rarities have been discovered, new decisions made that affect the British and Irish lists, and new identification criteria continue to be proposed and tested for difficult species. It is intended that the book will be updated and revised to reflect future changes in status and new records. But it would also be extremely valuable to have input from readers in other ways: if you have suggestions that would help improve the book's accuracy or ease of use, they would be very welcome. While the authors have done everything possible to ensure accuracy, should you find errors or omissions please contact **WILD**Guides.

Using this book

The book will help birdwatchers at any level of experience and expertise to identify what they see, using a simple step-by-step approach. You should be able to find a bird by looking at the contents list or the following gallery of thumbnail images, and turning to the relevant section if you know roughly what you are looking at – a duck, a wading bird, a woodpecker, or a small songbird. Possibilities can then be narrowed down using the group introductions. These give a brief overview of the species within each section, and subdivisions help further to narrow down the possibilities (and to highlight other options that might need to be excluded).

Alternatively, you can scan through the book to find the likely group or pinpoint the bird that looks like the best fit. However, it is essential to read the text and check the maps and status details in conjunction with looking at the photographs. One of the most common causes of misidentifications is jumping to a wrong conclusion without checking all available facts. The book contains more than 3,200 photographs and presents an incomparable set of images of British and Irish birds, so browsing and finding those that look most like your bird will be a rewarding experience – but it is all too easy to go wrong.

Once you find a likely answer to your identification problem, check all the material on the pages – is the bird in the right location, in the right habitat, at the right season? Is there a commoner, or more likely, alternative? One feature might seem just right, but is it overruled by others – the tail colour, the wingbar, the bird's size, or the shape of its bill? A single feature is never as reliable as an overall assessment.

Checking the texts and pictures against the bird as you watch it can be invaluable, but you may not have time: it is better to concentrate on the bird while you can. Taking photographs can be invaluable and enjoyable but again may reduce the time you have actually watching and enjoying the bird. Making notes and sketches, if you can, helps you look at each part of the bird more closely and systematically (you cannot write down the colour of the legs or bill, or undertail coverts, without looking at them first!) and to build up an overall assessment of what it looks like, how it behaves and how it calls or sings.

The birds in this book are deliberately arranged to allow close comparison of similar species (rather than appearing in strict taxonomic order, as in the list at the back of the book (*p. 524*)). This guide begins with water birds (those that habitually swim) and then moves to seabirds (from Gannet through shearwaters, gulls and terns to auks). It then covers waterside birds, including those conventionally termed 'waders' (or shorebirds), followed by herons and egrets and 'crakes and rails' (including Moorhen and Coot). Following these are the grouse and partridges, pigeons, owls and birds of prey, and a mixed group including kingfishers, cuckoos and woodpeckers, before the large and varied grouping known as Passerines, or perching birds.

As well as showing all the species that have been recorded in the wild in Britain or Ireland, details are provided of all the subspecies (or races) known to have occurred – as well as distinctive plumages, where relevant. Some birds that may be seen apparently 'wild' (even though most are introduced or escapes from captivity) are briefly described in the relevant section for comparison, or are listed at the back of the book (*p. 522*).

The photographs – many taken especially for this book – have been carefully selected to enable detailed comparisons to be made of birds in similar poses and similar lighting. In designing the pages, close attention has been paid to ensuring that the images are scaled appropriately. When trying to decide on a bird's identity, it is important to bear in mind that colours can be affected by many factors, such as bright sunlight, dull conditions, or reflections from water.

There is an abundance of books, regular journals and magazines catering for all degrees of interest and experience, and many organisations to consider joining. You can learn much more, become involved in conservation or bird survey work and support conservation locally and internationally, by joining a local bird club, a Wildlife Trust, the RSPB (the Royal Society for the Protection of Birds), the BTO (the British Trust for Ornithology) or the WWT (the Wildfowl & Wetlands Trust) or their Scottish, Welsh and Irish equivalents.

The Species Accounts

The species accounts that follow are divided into 30 broad sections, each with an introduction summarising the number of species recorded and their key identification features.

Most birds you are likely to encounter are wild and native, or indigenous. A few have been introduced, and some have 'escaped' from captivity and begun to breed: many 'escapes' are one-off occurrences but brief details are included of those that have bred 'in the wild' and might become established, just like the Greater Canada Goose, or Little Owl. The various categories are listed and explained on *p. 524*.

Technical jargon is avoided and everyday terms are used in the book, but a few specialist terms will help – for example 'pale tips to the greater coverts' is more precise than 'spots on the wing'. Sometimes judging relative lengths of tail, wingtip and tertials, for example, must be attempted – so knowing such feather groups is interesting, informative and invaluable. Where they are important to specific identification in a particular group (e.g. waders, gulls and buntings), these terms are explained in the introduction to that group. As far as possible each species account is presented in a consistent manner, as shown by the annotated page below.

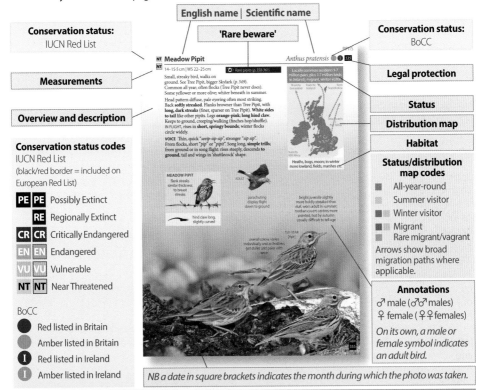

English name | Scientific name

Conservation status:
IUCN Red List

'Rare beware'

Conservation status:
BoCC

Measurements

Legal protection

Overview and description

Status

Distribution map

Habitat

Conservation status codes
IUCN Red List
(black/red border = included on European Red List)

PE	PE	Possibly Extinct
RE		Regionally Extinct
CR	CR	Critically Endangered
EN	EN	Endangered
VU	VU	Vulnerable
NT	NT	Near Threatened

BoCC

🔴 Red listed in Britain

🟠 Amber listed in Britain

ⓘ Red listed in Ireland

ⓘ Amber listed in Ireland

Status/distribution map codes

⬛ All-year-round

⬛ Summer visitor

⬛ Winter visitor

⬛ Migrant

⬛ Rare migrant/vagrant

Arrows show broad migration paths where applicable.

Annotations
♂ male (♂♂ males)
♀ female (♀♀ females)

On its own, a male or female symbol indicates an adult bird.

NB a date in square brackets indicates the month during which the photo was taken.

🕐 'Rare beware' and using the accounts

Always read the **status** and **habitat** preferences. You may find that, for example, a 'yellow' wagtail is likely to be a Grey Wagtail (or a passing harrier more likely to be a Hen than a Montagu's) at certain times of year; or that the brown owl in an Irish wood is probably a Long-eared, not a Tawny Owl. Although any bird can occur almost anywhere, overwhelmingly often the bird you see will be the one that should be there, in that habitat, at that time of year. Nevertheless, be aware; similar species are referenced for comparison, and a **'rare beware'** symbol indicates rarer possibilities and/or birds of captive origin. For the rare species emphasis is given to those plumages that have been recorded in Britain or Ireland, or are most likely. A few species are included that have been reliably identified but are not yet officially included on the British List.

English and scientific names

Each species has a common **English name** and *scientific name* (in italics).

- English names vary between authorities. This book uses those names recommended by the British Ornithologists' Union Records Committee (BOURC) and adopted for the Irish List, as they are best known to most people. Local English names for species are shown (in brackets) if the name is in frequent usage.
- The scientific name consists of two words – the first refers to the genus, which classifies those species that are closely related, the second refers to the species. The combination of these two words is unique to a species and applicable worldwide. A species can be variable in appearance and voice across its range and often these variations are classified as subspecies (or races). These races are identified using a third word and are covered in the relevant species accounts. In some cases where scientific names have changed as a result of recent taxonomic research the former name is included in brackets to prevent confusion.

NB a ◆ symbol after a name indicates that the species has only been recorded in Ireland.

Measurements

The length (bill-tip to tail-tip laid out on a flat surface) and wingspan of the species are given as a range, (with male and female separate if appropriate). NB A very long bill or tail feathers, can give a misleading indication of size in some cases; and a slim bird that is the same length as a rounded one may look much 'smaller' in reality.

Overview and description

A summary of general appearance and behaviour leads into detailed notes on different plumages (where relevant) according to age, sex and time of year. Important or diagnostic points are highlighted in **bold**. Descriptions begin with ADULT MALE in breeding (summer) plumage as the basis for comparisons, followed by WINTER MALE, FEMALE, and young birds:

- JUVENILE indicates a bird with feathers grown for its first flight.
- 1ST-WINTER indicates a bird that has undertaken its 1st-winter partial moult. Subsequent age definitions vary according to species, some being almost indistinguishable from older individuals when just one year old, while others take several years to mature.

The term 'ADULT' on its own may be taken to mean that sexes look alike; similarly, summer/winter plumages will be the same unless specified.

Where useful, a description of the bird IN FLIGHT follows, and an approximation of its calls and song. While vocalizations can be essential, writing them in words is difficult – they serve as useful *aide mémoires* if you have heard the bird already, or give a good impression of what to expect.

Annotations

Short notes highlighting key features, those relating to flight are in blue text.

Conservation status, legal protection and Irish records

- Species (or races) on the Red or Amber list, as a Bird of Conservation Concern (**BoCC**) in Britain or Ireland (see *p. 525*), are indicated by an appropriate colour-coded dot.
- Species listed by the International Union for Conservation of Nature (IUCN) as Threatened or Near Threatened, globally or in Europe, and that are on the **IUCN Red List** (see *p. 526*) have a colour-coded square. Squares with a black border indicate the European Red List status.
- Species afforded **legal protection** are indicated by a black square with a number referring to the page on which information regarding that species can be found.

Status

The **Status** box indicates how common (or otherwise) the species is in Britain and Ireland, with an estimate of the population, and the time of year it is seen. Birds referred to as 'migrants' travel to and from Britain and Ireland, or pass through or close by, on an annual cycle.

- **Rare migrant**: >1,000 records in total, or usually >100 recorded each year.
- **Very rare migrant**: >300 records, or >50 recorded each year.
- **Vagrant** describes a species that is off its usual migration route. The area of origin for these species is given. Area modifiers are as follows: N = North, E = East, S = South, SE = South-east, NW = North-west, NE = North-east, C = Central. NB N Europe includes Scandinavia. Numbers of records are given in close approximations (*e.g.* <5, <100).

Distribution map and habitat

Maps for all regular breeding, wintering and migrant species show summer, winter or all-year-round distribution, and typical migration routes where relevant. A box below the map gives most likely **habitats** in which to find a species. For rare migrants and vagrants this information is given in their **status** box.

The types of bird

This gallery of thumbnail images of typical birds from each group should allow you to go quickly to the relevant pages when trying to identify a bird.

'WATER' BIRDS   Swans | Geese | Ducks

Swans *pages 17–20*

Geese *pages 21–31*

Shelduck *page 32*

Ducks (dabbling)
pages 36–47

Ducks (diving)
pages 48–69

Ducks (sea)
pages 60–69

'WATER' BIRDS   Cormorants | Divers | Grebes

Cormorants *pages 74–75*

Divers *pages 76–78*

Grebes *pages 80–85*

'WETLAND' BIRDS Herons | Bitterns | Egrets | Spoonbills | Ibises | Cranes | Storks

Herons, Bitterns	**Egrets**	**Spoonbills, Ibises**	**Cranes, Storks**
pages 240–243	*pages 244–246*	*pages 249, 241*	*pages 247–248*

BITTERN

IBIS

STORK

'SEA' BIRDS Auks | Gannet | Shearwaters/Petrels | Storm Petrels

👁 RARE SEABIRDS

Auks	**Gannet**	**Shearwaters/ Petrels**	See *pages 98–101* for other very rare seabirds that are different in form from those shown here.
pages 165–172	*page 88–89*	*page 90–95*	

Storm Petrels
pages 96–97

'SEA' BIRDS Gulls | Terns | Skuas

Gulls (larger)	**Gulls (smaller)**	**Terns**	**Skuas**
pages 118–141	*pages 106–117*	*pages 142–155*	*pages 156–164*

'WETLAND' BIRDS Plovers | Waders

Snipe	Plovers (smaller)	Plovers (larger)	Stone-curlew
pages 218–220	*pages 182–184*	*pages 187–192*	*page 177*

Sandpipers	'Peeps', Calidrids	Waders (larger)	Curlews / Godwits
pages 209–211	*pages 194–201*	*pages 202–208*	*pages 212–215*

Avocet and Stilts	Oystercatcher and Turnstone	Phalaropes	◉ OTHER WADERS
pages 180 and 181	*pages 178 and 179*	*pages 216–217*	See *pages 192–193* for coursers and pratincoles

'WETLAND' BIRDS Crakes | Rails

Moorhen / Coots	Rails	Crakes	Corncrake
pages 256–257	*page 258*	*pages 259–261*	*page 255*

BIRDS of PREY, CUCKOO   Eagles | Buzzards | Kites | Hawks | Falcons | Cuckoos

Eagles
pages 294–296

Kites
page 304

Osprey
page 300

Harriers
pages 305–309

Buzzards
pages 298–303

Hawks
pages 313–315

Falcons
pages 316–325

Cuckoos
page 328

'NIGHT' BIRDS   Owls | Nightjars

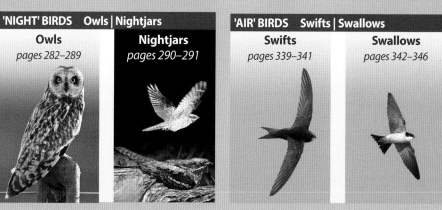

Owls
pages 282–289

Nightjars
pages 290–291

'AIR' BIRDS   Swifts | Swallows

Swifts
pages 339–341

Swallows
pages 342–346

'GAMEBIRDS'   Pheasants | Partridges | Grouse | Quail

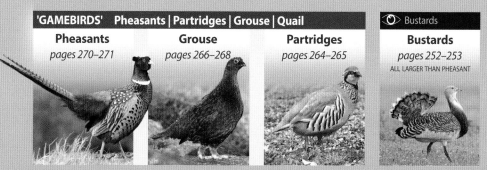

Pheasants
pages 270–271

Grouse
pages 266–268

Partridges
pages 264–265

Bustards

Bustards
pages 252–253
ALL LARGER THAN PHEASANT

11

'COLOURFUL' BIRDS

Kingfishers
page 327

Parakeets
page 332

Bee-eaters
page 330

Roller
page 331

Hoopoe
page 329

Oriole
page 371

DOVES and PIGEONS

Doves
pages 278–280

Pigeons
pages 275–277

👁 SANDGROUSE

1 species: extremely unlikely vagrant, related to pigeons – *page 274*.

🕐 AMERICAN LANDBIRDS

See *page 510* for vagrant landbirds from America. All of these are either from, or bear a close enough resemblance to, groups shown here. Using this initial guide and subsequent pointers should enable you to find these species.

WOODPECKERS

Woodpeckers
pages 335–337

Wryneck
page 334

'PERCHING' BIRDS Crows | Shrikes

Jay
page 472

Crows
pages 464–471

Magpie
page 473

Shrikes
pages 456–463

'PERCHING' BIRDS

Larks
pages 348–353

Pipits
pages 354–361

Wagtails
pages 362–365

Dipper
page 367

Wren
pages 369–370

Accentors
pages 368, 375

Starlings
pages 372–373

Thrushes
pages 378–387

Nuthatches
page 452

'Creepers'
page 453

Waxwings
pages 374–375

Chats
pages 388–402

Warblers ('reed')
pages 405–413

Warblers (other)
pages 414–435

Crests
pages 436–437

Flycatchers
pages 439–442

Tits
pages 444–451

Sparrows
pages 476–477

Finches
pages 478–494

Buntings
pages 496–509

WILDFOWL

Water or waterside birds, some freely using both water and dry land habitats nearby, often feeding on land and resting or roosting on water, safe from predators.

3 swans: 1 resident, 2 widespread but local winter visitors; 1 'escape'.

14 geese with several distinct races: 2 introduced residents that breed, 1 native breeder that is also widely introduced and a winter visitor; 5 regular winter visitors; 6 rare; also some 'escapes'.

2 shelducks: only 1 regular.

41 ducks: 20 frequent, others rare or irregular; 15 breed (2 introduced); 1 summer visitor, others mostly increase in abundance autumn–spring; several escapes likely.

Swans (*pp. 17–20*) large, white; swim, upend, walk and feed on open ground, but lack agility. Fly straight, powerfully. Mute Swan all year, widespread; two 'wild swans' mostly November to March at a few regular sites.

MUTE SWAN

MUTE SWAN

Swan ageing/sexing

Swan sexes alike except male heavier, and in Mute Swan larger knob on bill. Juveniles dull, become whiter during first year; dull bill gradually gains adult colours.

MUTE SWAN

Geese (*pp. 21–31*) introduced Canada and Greylag Geese all year; wild, migratory geese spend the winter mostly in north and in East Anglia. Large, sociable, water/waterside birds, obvious farmyard goose shape; may form big flocks (most at traditional sites), dramatic and vocal in flight. Sexes alike; juveniles differ slightly until spring.

'Grey geese' are grey-brown: check bill/leg colours, wing patterns, subtleties of shape, head-body contrasts. Juveniles less neatly barred.

Other geese are black and white on head, neck and chest: check patterns. Juveniles duller, less neat.

Shelducks (*pp. 32–33*) intermediate between ducks and geese; walk freely on mud or dry land but always close to water. Sexes almost alike; juveniles differ in plumage.

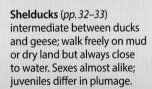

CANADA GOOSE

GREYLAG GOOSE

SHELDUCK

DUCK ID
BREEDING MALES: overall pattern and shape
FEMALES/JUVENILES: size/shape | bill + leg colours | upperwing pattern | belly colour

Ducks (*pp. 34–69*) mostly 'surface feeders', 'diving ducks' or on the sea. Males brightest in winter, when easily identified; females, juveniles and males in summer more difficult. Check bill and leg colours, wing pattern and colour and, on females, presence or absence of white belly. Upperwing may have long central stripe, or a patch of colour and bars on hindwing ('speculum'). Records of rarer birds are bedevilled by escapes from collections (see *pp. 16*), and confusing hybrids.

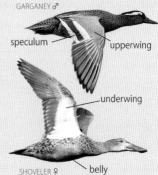

GARGANEY ♂

speculum | upperwing

underwing

SHOVELER ♀ | belly

SURFACE FEEDERS swim with slightly raised tail on open water or amongst flooded vegetation, or paddle in muddy shallows; some feed on land, often at night. Flight fast, agile, with quick take off from water or land.

Some feed by upending

GADWALL ♂

MALLARD ♂ + ♀

RED-BREASTED MERGANSER ♀

'Sawbills' (Red-breasted Merganser, Goosander, Smew) elongated, with long, serrated bills.

TUFTED DUCK ♂

GOLDENEYE ♀

DIVING DUCKS rounder-backed, tail low, and dive from the surface while swimming. Some drift in flocks by day, others dispersed when feeding, in flocks when asleep. Some stand at the water's edge, others can barely walk. Flight low, straight, fast but less agile than surface-feeders, with pattering run at take off; settle onto water, not dry ground. Some diving ducks (such as eiders and scoters) are essentially marine, occasional on inland waters, often ones and twos amongst commoner species.

POSSIBLE CONFUSION GROUPS
Coots, grebes, divers, auks and cormorants all swim. **Coots** are round-backed, short-tailed; **grebes** round-bodied, almost tailless; **divers** long-bodied, short-tailed, dagger-billed; **auks** squat, dumpy, small-winged; **cormorants** longer-tailed, hook-billed.

AUK *pp. 166–170*

COOT *p. 257*

DIVER *pp. 76–79*

CORMORANT *pp. 74–75*

MERGANSER (duck) *p. 58*

GREBE *pp. 80–84*

Moult sequence in ducks (Mallard)

Juvenile from fledging until autumn; look much like adult females.

JUVENILE
JUL–SEP
[Jul]

ADULT ♂ BREEDING
OCT–MAY

| 1st moult | 2nd moult |

1ST moult
JUVENILE → 1ST-WINTER
JUL–SEP: males start to develop adult colours.

2nd moult
1ST-WINTER → 1ST-SUMMER
DEC–APR: protracted full body moult.

NB **1ST-WINTER** (first breeding plumage from SEP–APR) and **1ST-SUMMER** (first non-breeding plumage from MAY–AUG) birds generally very similar to adults, the differences being mainly in feather wear and fringe colours that indicate retained juvenile feathers.

| 3rd moult | 4th moult |

3rd moult
1ST-SUMMER →
ADULT BREEDING
AUG–NOV: full body moult, timing adult, brings the bird into breeding condition; thereafter following the **adult yearly (4th/5th+) moult cycle**.

4th moult
ADULT BREEDING →
ADULT NON-BREEDING ('ECLIPSE')
MAY–JUL (♂); JUL–AUG (♀): includes wing feathers, birds flightless JUN /JUL.

5th moult
ADULT NON-BREEDING →
ADULT BREEDING
AUG–NOV.

ADULT ♂ NON-BREEDING ('ECLIPSE')
JUN–SEP

Females look the same year-round; males in 'eclipse' similar to females, increasingly easy to tell apart by late winter.

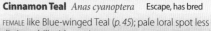

ADULT ♀
ALL YEAR

Escapes and introductions

Several related species of ducks, geese and swans may occasionally be seen as escapes (from ornamental collections) and introductions (released in the hope that they will breed and add interest to indigenous bird life). Some have bred (Category E* species, listed on p. 523).

Shown here are some of the more frequently encountered escapes that look similar to naturally occurring (wild) species and which may cause confusion. If a rare bird, or one that is of questionable identity, is encountered, the possibility of an 'escape' should always be considered.

Cinnamon Teal *Anas cyanoptera* Escape, has bred

FEMALE like Blue-winged Teal (p. 45); pale loral spot less distinct; bill wider at tip.

MALE **rufous brown**, black bill, **red eye**.

Trumpeter Swan
Cygnus buccinator
Like Whooper Swan (p. 19); **black bill**.

Escape, has bred

Ross's Goose *Anser (Chen) rossii*
Like small white Snow Goose (p. 31); **small, grey-based bill**.

Bar-headed Goose
Anser indicus
white head crossed by two black bars.

Emperor Goose
Anser (Chen) canagica
Blue-grey, **dark bars**; white head, hindneck; orange legs.

Possible vagrant

Escapes that have bred

Mute Swan

Cygnus olor   527

140–160 cm | WS 200–240 cm

Huge and white; the familiar swan that comes for bread.

ADULT white, often stained reddish/olive on head and neck; **bill uniquely orange-red, black knob (biggest on old males) and tip**. JUVENILE dull grey-coffee-brown, wings whiter; increasingly patched white with age (Whooper/Bewick's Swans (*pp. 18–19*) paler, drabber); bill grey, black tip, no knob. Legs grey-black. Neck often in sinuous 'S'-curve, can be raised straight; bill and long, flattish head typically down-tilted (generally more horizontal in Bewick's and Whooper Swans). Neck thin or thick, ruffled. Wings often more or less arched (dramatically in threat). **Tail slim, pointed, angled up** (shorter, held low, squarer, less tapered in Bewick's/Whooper Swans). IN FLIGHT, told by head/bill shape/colour, rhythmic, **whooping wing noise**.

VOICE Calls frequently, mostly quiet grunts, hisses and reedy, weak or squeaky trumpeting.

Common and widespread resident; introduced (historically) (74,000; 6,000 breeding pairs)

Sheltered sea coasts to inland waters, wetlands, grassy fields

ADULT ♂
bill orange-red with black knob
(biggest on old male) and tip

ADULT ♀

JUVENILE
bill grey with black tip,
no or small knob

downtilted
head

pointed tail

ADULT ♂

EN Bewick's Swan

Cygnus columbianus ● ❶ 527

115–130 cm | WS 170–195 cm

Smallest swan, still large, but size of isolated birds difficult to judge. Generally shy and wild, usually in flocks.

ADULT white, sometimes stained on head; bill long, wide, slightly dished on top, **rounded yellow patch** short of nostril; pattern unique to individuals. JUVENILE **plainer, greyer** than Mute Swan (*p. 17*), whiter with age; **bill pattern like adult**, black and pale cream/grey, often pink, even raspberry red; base becomes yellower over winter. Legs black (rarely brown or yellowish). Long, heavy bill typically horizontal, on shapely, rounded head. Neck thick/goosy, or thin and sinuous – feeds with neck in loopy-caterpillar 'S'. Tail shorter, held lower than Mute Swan.

VOICE Yapping, **honking, whooping notes**, less bugling than Whooper Swan; usually single or double notes (Whooper Swan often three or four). In flight, wings lack hum of Mute Swan.

from Arctic NE Russia

Freshwater, marshes, wet and ploughed fields

WHOOPER SWAN
all ages have diagnostic pale 'wedge' on bill (yellow in adults)

BEWICK'S SWAN
yellow on bill is rounded patch; extent varies (may join across top or form isolated patches)

'Tundra' Swan race *columbianus* (vagrant from N America (<5 records) Bill has minute yellow spot: demarcation between yellowest 'Tundra' Swan and blackest Bewick's (race *bewickii*) difficult to judge.

ADULT

Whooper Swan

140–160 cm | WS 205–235 cm

Large, angular, wild swan. Only slightly smaller than Mute Swan (*p. 17*) but most similar to smaller Bewick's Swan. Large, **wedge-shaped head and bill** on long, upright neck when alert; **bill typically held more horizontal** than Mute Swan (neck curved when relaxed).

ADULT white (stained dark in summer). Yellow on bill forms **long triangle** either side, joining across base. Bill has a longer, flatter profile (less concave) than Bewick's Swan. JUVENILE like Bewick's Swan, less brown than Mute Swan. Bill has adult pattern, **pointed wedge of whitish** or cream with dark pink/grey tip, slowly becoming pale yellow as winter progresses.

VOICE Like Bewick's Swan but more **bugling or clanging**, deep, nasal, **often** three/four notes (Bewick's Swan usually one/two). Flock chorus noisy, confused and varied. In flight, wings do not give musical throb of Mute Swan.

At a distance the longer, more upright necks of **Whooper Swans** (six birds in the background) are distinctive compared to the shorter, more sinuous necks of **Bewick's Swans** (two birds in left foreground).

Scarce and local winter visitor; numerous at a few traditional areas (14,500, mostly Nov–Mar). Rare breeder (22 pairs)

from Iceland

Freshwater, wet fields, marshes, occasionally on coasts

although smaller than in Whooper Swan, the bill of **Bewick's Swan** can appear surprisingly long and heavy when seen close up

JUVENILES

(dark bill)

(pale bill)

BEWICK'S SWAN

WHOOPER SWAN

diagnostic pale 'wedge'

ADULT

Swans in flight

Direct flight powerful, straight, in shapeless groups (Whooper Swans often in 'V' or wavy line). Head/neck outstretched, tail short. Descend with wings stiffly arched, body angled, legs lowered, to splash-down on water or short run on land.

MUTE SWAN

IMMATURE **Mute Swan** has strongest contrast: dark coverts/ pale hindwing.

MUTE SWAN

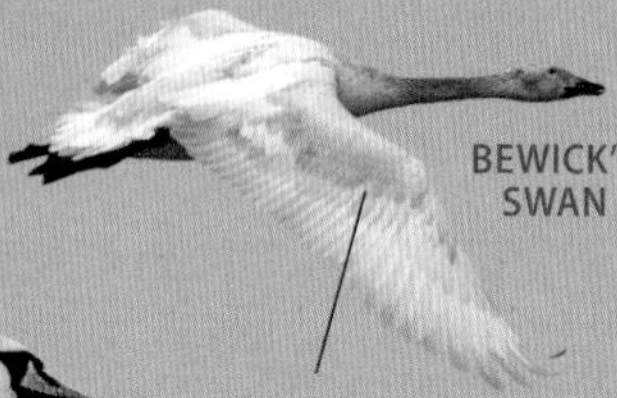

ADULT swans have all-white upperwings.

BEWICK'S SWAN

MUTE SWAN
(p. 17)

huge; head/bill best visual features but loud humming throb of wingbeats distinctive

IMMATURE **Whooper** and **Bewick's Swans** upperwing relatively uniform.

BEWICK'S SWAN
(p. 18)

WHOOPER SWAN
(p. 19)

smaller than Whooper Swan, with shorter neck – but hard to judge

huge, rangy, with fine-pointed head

Geese in flight

White-fronted Goose
Quick, agile, in lines/'V's.
Adult **belly distinctively
marked** (though beware,
as juvenile is unmarked).
Sharp, bright, laughing
calls with yodelling 'catch'.

Pink-footed Goose
In long lines, 'V's or
masses. Head and neck
short and dark.
Nasal, bubbly, deep
chorus interspersed with
high "wink-wink".

Bean Goose
Relatively long-necked and
long-winged; dark.
Nasal, deep double- or
triple-note calls.

Greylag Goose
In lines, 'V's or a
shapeless mass.
Head large,
chunky and pale.
Coarse, clattering,
cackling chorus.

darkest
underwing

underwing
paler than on
Bean Goose

palest
underwing

JUVENILE

GREYLAG GOOSE (p. 27)

BEAN GOOSE
(p. 28)

**PINK-FOOTED
GOOSE** (p. 29)

**WHITE-FRONTED
GOOSE** (p. 30)

upperwing
pale bluish-grey
contrasting with
dark trailing edge

upperwing
dark, mid-grey
towards tip

black
wingtips

upperwing
largely mid- or
pale blue-grey

upperwing
mid-grey
on outer part

SNOW GOOSE (p. 31)
Very distinctive black-and-white
wings in the white form most
often seen in Britain/Ireland.

**BARNACLE
GOOSE**
(p. 26)

white
forehead

white
'collar'

BRENT GOOSE
(p. 24)

grey-
brown

**GREATER
CANADA
GOOSE**
(p. 22)

grey,
patterned

grey,
plain

white chin

Barnacle Goose
Neat, narrow-winged, pale greyish,
upperwing steely-grey with blackish
edge; black neck and chest
Sharp, barking, yappy calls.

Brent Goose
Dumpy, dark, thick-necked.
Obvious white stern and tail.
Short, deep, rolled,
rumbling calls.

Greater Canada Goose
Very large and long-necked. Big white
stern against black tail. Upperwing
dark brown, chest very pale; black
neck. Deep, honking calls.

Greater Canada Goose

Branta canadensis 527

80–105 cm | WS 155–180 cm

Big, long-necked, striking, approachable; dramatic in large flocks.

Browner than other geese, barred paler, with **white chest**. **Unique black 'stocking' on neck, white 'chinstrap'**. (Barnacle Goose has black over chest, more white on face.) **Black bill and legs**, big white stern. JUVENILE very like adult but duller, less sharply patterned.

VOICE Loud, deep, full honks, including double "*ar-hunk*".

There are many races of Canada Geese, recently split into two species, Greater Canada Goose and Cackling Goose, each with a number of races, which may occur in Britain and Ireland as natural vagrants. **Beware, however, that these forms also turn up as 'escapes'**. Additionally there is overlap in size and plumage detail such that the groups are best treated as a cline. The basic differences between 'Canada' and Cacking Geese are summarised below; the differences in the recorded races are detailed opposite.

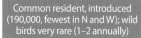

Common resident, introduced (190,000, fewest in N and W); wild birds very rare (1–2 annually)

Mostly lowland lakes, gravel pits, grassy river valleys, some estuaries

IN FLIGHT, huge, even against Greylag Geese (*p. 27*), dark, long-necked, black tail obvious.

Canada Geese typically fly as a close flock

CANADA GEESE: Less inclined forehead, longer bill, long-necked

large-bodied

CACKLING GEESE: Steep forehead, stubby bill, short-necked

small-bodied

NB Canada Goose race *parvipes* is intermediate in form and plumage

'ATLANTIC' CANADA GOOSE
race *canadensis*

white 'chinstrap'

black neck

Greater Canada Geese races

The resident, naturalized population is known as 'Atlantic' Canada Goose (race *canadensis*). Vagrants from N America are very rare and generally smaller forms that differ in their head and bill characters: note carefully the extent of pale/white on base of neck and chest, as well as size and structure – though all these features are variable and overlap between races and sexes (males average 5% larger than females).

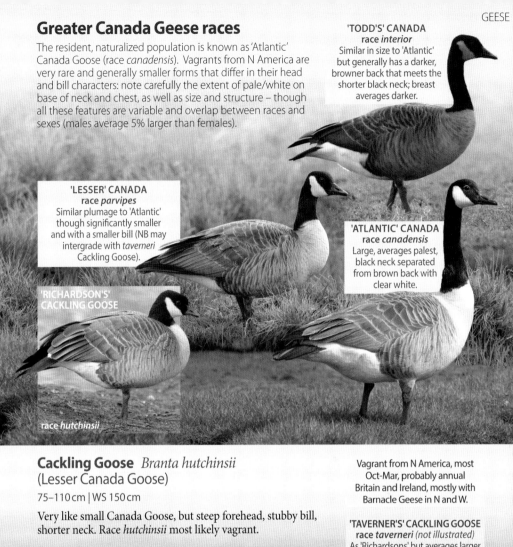

'TODD'S' CANADA
race *interior*
Similar in size to 'Atlantic' but generally has a darker, browner back that meets the shorter black neck; breast averages darker.

'LESSER' CANADA
race *parvipes*
Similar plumage to 'Atlantic' though significantly smaller and with a smaller bill (NB may intergrade with *taverneri* Cackling Goose).

'ATLANTIC' CANADA
race *canadensis*
Large, averages palest, black neck separated from brown back with clear white.

'RICHARDSON'S' CACKLING GOOSE

race *hutchinsii*

Cackling Goose *Branta hutchinsii*
(Lesser Canada Goose)

75–110 cm | WS 150 cm

Very like small Canada Goose, but steep forehead, stubby bill, shorter neck. Race *hutchinsii* most likely vagrant.

Vagrant from N America, most Oct-Mar, probably annual Britain and Ireland, mostly with Barnacle Geese in N and W.

'RICHARDSON'S' CACKLING GOOSE
race *hutchinsii*
Paler breast, often with a golden wash; 5–10% have dark stripe under chin.

'TAVERNER'S' CACKLING GOOSE
race *taverneri* (*not illustrated*)
As 'Richardsons' but averages larger and darker, with a more rounded head (similar to paler breasted *parvipes* Canada Goose, with which it may intergrade). 40–75% have dark stripe under chin.

'RIDGWAY'S' CACKLING GOOSE
race *minima*
Smallest, with small bill, short neck and relatively long legs. Variable, but typically darkish brown with purplish sheen on breast.

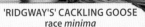

23

Brent Goose

Branta bernicla 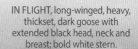 **527**

55–62 cm | WS 105–117 cm

Small goose (length of Mallard (*p. 38*) but looks bigger), swims and upends in saltmarsh creeks, even around seaweedy rocks, grazes on fields, parks.

Generally **very dark with white back end**. Three races occur – 'dark-bellied', 'pale-bellied' and Black Brant (see *opposite* for last two). 'Dark-bellied' race *bernicla* dark brown-grey. **Black head, neck, chest** contrast sharply against browner belly (depending on angle and light). Small **white patch** high on side of neck. Plain greyish back, **big white stern**. Flanks barred pale; **dark on belly extends between legs**. JUVENILE has pale bars on wings, no neck patch until midwinter.

VOICE Deep, rolling croaks, "*grr-r-unk*", with conversational character; loud, quick, even chorus from big flock.

Locally numerous winter visitor to coastal areas (Oct–Mar): 'dark-bellied' 91,000 (most in NE, SE, S); 'pale-bellied' 41,500 (38,000 of which in Ireland). Black Brant rare but annual vagrant (10–15/year).

'Pale-bellied' from Canadian Arctic

'Dark-bellied' from Eurasian Arctic

Coasts, saltmarshes, muddy creeks, grassy pastures, arable

flies in irregular flocks, but small groups form lines and 'V's

IN FLIGHT, long-winged, heavy, thickset, dark goose with extended black head, neck and breast; bold white stern.

'DARK-BELLIED' BRENT GOOSE
race *bernicla*

white patch on side of neck

ADULT

striking white rear-end   dark behind legs

Red-breasted Goose 527
Branta ruficollis
VU **NT**
54–60 cm | WS 110–125 cm

Striking, but 'disappears' surprisingly easily in large flocks of birds. Basically black and white with **bold panels of deep rust-red** on head and neck; black chest against white belly; **broad white flank stripe**.

IN FLIGHT, easily overlooked in Brent Goose flocks; white wingbars, white belly.

Vagrant from Asia: <100 records (Britain), Oct-Mar. Bedevilled by 'escapes'; usually with Brent or White-fronted Geese. Marshes, pasture.

ADULT

PALE-BELLIED BRENT GOOSE (race *hrota*)
paler on body; contrast between **black breast and pale belly**; flanks whitish with greyer bars, a few darker ones at rear. Pale belly, no black between legs.

BLACK BRANT (race *nigricans*)
Vagrant from N America/E Siberia: (300 records (<50 Ireland), complicated by intergrades/hybrids.

Neck patches typically **broad and bold, meet in front**; back darker; belly darker, head slightly larger than 'dark-bellied' Brent Goose; **shining white flank patch**, broken by bars on lower edge, two or three dark bars at rear. Black on belly extends behind legs.

'PALE-BELLIED' BRENT GOOSE
race *hrota*
ADULT

BLACK BRANT
race *nigricans*
ADULT

neck patches large; meet on front

strong contrast between breast and belly

pale behind legs

prominent white flanks
dark behind legs

'DARK-BELLIED'

JUVENILE

'PALE-BELLIED'

pale behind legs

dark behind legs

JUVENILE

Geese in flight *p.21*

Barnacle Goose

Branta leucopsis  527

58–70 cm | WS 120–142 cm

 Emperor Goose (*p. 16*)

Small, clean, immaculate goose, **lacking any brown**.

At long range, bright pale grey with sharp vertical divide against black front. Black neck widens into **black 'breastplate'**, contrasting with white belly. Large **white/yellowish face patch** surrounds black eyeline. Back neatly barred. Bill short, deep, stubby; bill and legs black. JUVENILE duller, barring above less regular.

VOICE Barking calls, vary in pitch "*kaw*"; yapping flock chorus.

Very locally numerous winter visitor (90,000 (40,000 on Islay, 32,000 Solway, 5,500 Ireland), Oct–Apr). Introduced resident population, mostly in England (2,700)

from Greenland

from Svalbard

Barnacle Goose skeins generally form long lines

Estuaries, coastal meadows, saltmarsh; lakes, gravel pits

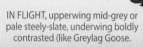

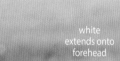

IN FLIGHT, upperwing mid-grey or pale steely-slate, underwing boldly contrasted (like Greylag Goose.

white extends onto forehead

black 'breastplate'

Greylag Goose

74–84 cm | WS 149–168 cm

Obvious 'farmyard goose' form. Approachable introduced flocks; winter migrants wilder.

Large, big-headed, heavy build, **pale brown** with **large, pale orange bill** (paler at tip). **Legs pale pink** (some pale to bright orange, at least in introduced flocks). Low winter light gives strongly contrasted buff/brown effect, **breast pale**; prominent white rear-end. Some have white near bill or black spots on belly, but not like smaller, small-billed White-fronted Goose (*p. 30*). (Juvenile White-fronted Goose which lacks white or black markings, has smaller bill, orange legs, darker wings.)

VOICE Noisy; clattering, clanging or cackling chorus from flock – "*kya-gaa-gaa*" or "*ang-ang-ank*".

Locally common resident, many introduced populations (46,000 pairs, 225,000 in winter). Wild immigrants mostly Scotland (85,000, Oct–Mar); native breeder (3,200 pairs, most Scottish islands)

from Iceland

IN FLIGHT, **underwing strikingly contrasted** (like Barnacle Goose). **Pale blue-grey upperwing** much paler than Pink-footed Goose (*p. 29*). Dull white uppertail, with mid-grey central band.

ADULT

Meadows, farmland, lakes and gravel pits

Greylag skeins can be lines, 'V's, or shapeless.

on water, large, bulky; head upright, tall or squat; tail raised revealing white stern (see *p. 14*)

ADULT

Bean Goose

Anser fabalis race *fabalis* race *rossicus* **527**

69–88 cm | WS 140 cm–174 cm

Big, dark goose, similar to Pink-footed Goose but longer head/bill profile; slimmer than Greylag Goose (*p. 27*). Difficult to find amongst commoner geese, especially Pink-footed Goose.

Rich brown, **dark head/paler breast**. Dark **back neatly barred** (JUVENILE scaly). Flanks same tone as back (darker on Pink-footed Goose). 'Taiga' race *fabalis* has long, largely **orange bill**, longer neck than Pink-footed Goose. 'Tundra' race *rossicus* has shorter bill with **narrow orange band**, bulging black base. Shorter, dark neck contrasts with chest, as on Pink-footed Goose. **Legs orange or yellow-orange**, but pink/orange hard to judge in dull light.

VOICE Calls lower than White-fronted and Pink-footed Geese, less clattering than Greylag: "*ung-ung*" or "*yak-ak-ak*".

Rare winter visitor (mostly Oct–Apr), most at a few localized sites in Scotland and East Anglia: 'Taiga' (400), 'Tundra' (320)

from Arctic NE Russia

Rough, rushy fields, wet pastures, arable land

PINK-FOOTED GOOSE
variable pink band
on small bill

'TUNDRA' BEAN GOOSE
race *rossicus*
bill shorter, thicker than *fabalis*,
longer than Pink-footed
Goose; black with narrow
orange band; shorter
neck than *fabalis*

bulging;
open
'grin'

'TAIGA' BEAN GOOSE
race *fabalis*
long, largely orange
bill; longer neck than
Pink-footed Goose.
Some birds hard to
assign to race

straight

ADULT

IN FLIGHT, upperwing dark.
Tail dark; narrow white 'U' above,
narrow pale tip. **Underwing
dark** (much paler on Greylag and
Pink-footed Geese).

race *rossicus* has shorter, darker neck
than race *fabalis*, contrasting more
with chest (like Pink-footed Goose)

**'TUNDRA'
BEAN GOOSE**
race *rossicus*

ADULT

ADULT

flank 'thumbprint'
same tone as back

Pink-footed Goose

Anser brachyrhynchus ● **527**

64–76 cm | WS 137–161 cm

Familiar goose form; small bill and head and barred grey back give neat appearance. Often in large, crowded flocks.

ADULT has **round, dark head, short neck**; **short, dark bill** with narrow pink band; **contrasted pale buff chest**. Back dusky blue-grey, less brown than Bean Goose. Legs dull **pink** to darker purple-pink. Upperwing has extensive grey, darker than on Greylag Goose (*p. 27*). JUVENILE drabber, browner than adult, but dark bill rules out young White-fronted Goose (*p. 30*). Needs care to separate small-billed 'Tundra' Bean Goose within Pink-footed Goose flocks.

VOICE Deep, nasal, gabbling chorus from flock, with frequent distinctive, high, sharp "*wink-wink*" interspersed.

IN FLIGHT, uniformly paler back/upperwing, greyer back, darker flank than Bean Goose; pink legs usually distinct (orange on Bean Goose).

Locally abundant winter visitor: (360,000, Sep–Apr)

from Iceland

Fields, coastal marshes, lakes

underwing paler than on Bean Goose

ADULT

Pink-footed Goose skeins can be lines, 'V's or shapeless, though tend to be more 'clumped' and changing in form than Greylag Goose skeins

the shape and amount of colour on the bill varies between individuals in both Bean and Pink-footed Geese

ADULT

ADULT

flanks with 'thumbprint' darker compared to back

JUVENILE

ADULT

White-fronted Goose

Anser albifrons race *flavirostris* **527**

64–78 cm | WS 130–160 cm

Lesser White-fronted Goose

Boldly marked lively, agile goose
(easily leaps into flight); two distinct races.

ADULT European race *albifrons* mid-brown; buff neck and breast;
long **white stripe** along flank. **White forehead blaze** with
straight, vertical edge in side view. Belly has variable **black bars**
and blotches, occasionally solid. Bill pale **pink**; legs rich orange.
Greenland race *flavirostris* darker, 'oily' brown, black belly bars
often more extensive. Bill **orange** with paler tip (hard to judge
orange/pink in poor light). Upperwing dark; subtle grey less
obvious than on Pink-footed Goose (*p. 29*). JUVENILE lacks white
face and black belly bars: puzzling if alone, best told by leg/bill
colour and dark wings with little grey. Develops white forehead
by late winter.

VOICE High, laughing, yodelling with a catch in the middle:
"*kyu-yu*" or "*lyo-lyok*". Flock chorus high, yapping/yodelling.

Winter immigrant (Oct–Mar):
European race in S, rare (2,000,
lost from most traditional sites);
Greenland race in N and W
(22,000 incl. 9,000 in Ireland)

from Greenland

from Arctic NE Russia

Estuaries, pastures; Greenland
race estuaries/islands, rushy
fields, moors

IN FLIGHT, ADULT plain
greyish underwings,
distinct black barring
on belly; JUVENILE plain
beneath except white
vent; orange legs help
if discernible.

ADULT

JUVENILE

'GREENLAND'
WHITE-FRONTED GOOSE
race *flavirostris*

bill orange
with pale tip

dark markings on
belly more extensive
than on *albifrons*

ADULT

'EUROPEAN'
WHITE-FRONTED GOOSE
race *albifrons*

ADULT

juveniles lack white on face
and dark barring on belly

JUVENILE

Snow Goose

Anser (Chen) caerulescens

65–75 cm | WS 133–156 cm

Chunky goose: ADULT **pure white** (commonest form) with **black wingtips** (grey patch on leading edge); bill, feet red-pink. Dark form ('blue goose') **white head, dark blue-grey body**, paler wings. JUVENILE pale brownish with dark eyeline, dark bill, grey legs.

Very rare migrant from N America: <10 per year (>100 records Ireland), most Oct–Mar. Released/escaped birds (180 Britain) widespread (even breeding). Marshes, pasture.

👁 Ross's Goose (*p. 16*). Beware hybrids involving Greater Canada (*p. 22*) and other geese, often with white heads and dark legs

ADULT

ADULT
white form

ADULT
dark form

VU
EN

Lesser White-fronted Goose *Anser erythropus* 527

56–66 cm | WS 115–135 cm

Like small, neat White-fronted Goose but less barred above, less black beneath, chunkier head, shorter neck and smaller bill.

ADULT **white on forehead that curves back above eye**. **Bill bright pink**. Obvious **yellow eyering** even at distance (weak on White-fronted Goose). JUVENILE lacks white on forehead but has **yellow eyering**. Small bill has **pale nail** (dark on young White-fronted Goose). Hard to find, especially juveniles: search flocks for forehead splash first, then eyering/bill.

Vagrant from N Europe: <150 records (<5 Ireland), Oct–Mar. With White-fronted Geese or Bean Geese (p. 22). Pasture.

white blaze on forehead

white curves back above eye

ADULTS

no eyering

yellow eyering

WHITE-FRONTED   LESSER W-F

JUVENILES

dark nail

pale nail

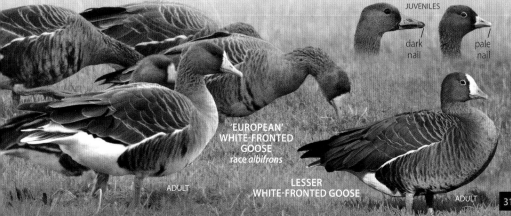

'EUROPEAN' WHITE-FRONTED GOOSE
race *albifrons*

LESSER WHITE-FRONTED GOOSE

ADULT

ADULT

Shelduck

Tadorna tadorna ● ● ⓘ 527

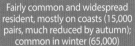

Fairly common and widespread resident, mostly on coasts (15,000 pairs, much reduced by autumn); common in winter (65,000)

to/from North Sea + S Baltic

Coastal marshes, lagoons, estuaries, inland gravel pits, wet meadows

55–65 cm | WS 100–120 cm

Striking adults unmistakable: juvenile puzzling but unlike anything else. Big, heavy, long-legged duck, at home on dry ground, mud or water.

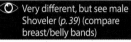

👁 Very different, but see male Shoveler (*p. 39*) (compare breast/belly bands)

ADULT strikingly **bright white**. Bold black head, **long black bands** along back, **orange-brown band** around front of body. **Bill vivid red**, MALE's with big basal knob. FEMALE has whitish face/cheek marks. Legs clear pink. JUVENILE has long-legged, short-billed, big-bodied look of adult, but is gangly. **Largely white**; brownish bands along back, dark brown back of head and neck (white around eye and lower face). **Pinkish bill, greyish legs**. Vaguely resembles Egyptian Goose.

VOICE Wings whistle in flight; calls variable, whistling notes and deep rhythmic "*ga-ga-ga-ga-ga*".

IN FLIGHT, deep-chested, heavy; broad dark trailing edge and black tips to white wing.

JUVENILE

Egyptian Goose

Alopochen aegyptiaca

Parks, lakes, reservoirs

63–73 cm | WS 110–120 cm

A peculiar bird (not always recognised as a goose).

Pale; olive-brown back, greyer or **rufous** towards rear, pale chest. Pale crown, **dark neck ring and mask**. Bill small, pink and black; legs rather long, red-pink. JUVENILE no mask.

VOICE Monotonous, repetitive, rhythmic bark or babble in alarm, various hissing and gagging notes.

ADULT

IN FLIGHT, **white forewing** remarkably striking.

grey type has pale head and weaker mask

ADULT

Juvenile plumage similar to adult, but more drab; lacks clear head pattern

Ruddy Shelduck 527

Tadorna ferruginea

58–70 cm | WS 110–135 cm

Obvious shelduck shape/size, rich **orange-brown with pale head**; black bill and legs. MALE has black neck ring; FEMALE whiter face.

IN FLIGHT, big **white patch at front of black wing**, above and below (beware Egyptian Goose); black rump/tail.

note head pattern, as other similar shelducks wander free from collections

Vagrant from Asia: most Jul-Oct. UK birds perhaps escapes. Estuaries.

Regularly occurring ducks in flight

RED-BREASTED MERGANSER (*p. 58*)

♀

GOOSANDER (*p. 59*)

♀

SHELDUCK (*p. 32*)

♂

♂

MALLARD (*p. 38*)

♂

♀

GADWALL (*p. 40*)

♀

SHOVELER (*p. 39*)

♂

♀

GADWALL (*p. 40*)

♂

PINTAIL (*p. 41*)

♂

♀

TEAL (*p. 42*)

POCHARD (*p. 49*)

POCHARD (*p. 49*)

♂

GARGANEY (*p. 43*)

♀

GARGANEY (*p. 43*)

♂

♀

TEAL (*p. 42*)

♂

WIGEON (*p. 37*)

♀

WIGEON (*p. 37*)

♂

♀

♂

AMERICAN WIGEON (*p. 44*)

♀

BLUE-WINGED TEAL (*p. 45*)

annual North American vagrants

SMEW (p. 57)

♀ ♂

GOLDENEYE
(p. 56)

♂

SURF SCOTER (p. 68)

♂

LONG-TAILED
DUCK (p. 60)

♀ ♂

VELVET
SCOTER
(p. 62)

♂

COMMON
SCOTER
(p. 63)

♂

KING
EIDER
(p. 66)

♀

♀

♀

EIDER
(p. 64)

♀

See also Ring-necked Duck (p. 53)
and Lesser Scaup (p. 52).

1st-winter ♂
KING EIDER
(p. 66)

SCAUP (p. 51)

♂

♀

1st-winter ♂
EIDER
(p. 64)

♂

TUFTED
DUCK
(p. 50)

♂

EIDER
(p. 64)

TUFTED
DUCK
(p. 50)

♀

FERRUGINOUS
DUCK (p. 53)

♂

KING
EIDER
(p. 66)

♂

35

Identifying female dabbling ducks

Female surface-feeding ducks can look very similar. On birds flying overhead, take note of underwing patterns, underwing/body contrast.
On standing birds check overall shape, bill size and colour, head shape, belly colour and leg length.

identification of speckled female dabbling ducks				
	Shoveler (*p. 39*)	Mallard (*p. 38*)	Gadwall (*p. 40*)	Pintail (*p. 41*)
Bill	orange; **spatulate**	diffuse orange and brown	sharp orange sides	grey
Legs	orange		orange (pale)	grey
Throat	buff		white	
Belly	brown		sharp white	blended white

TEAL (*p. 42*): shown here for size comparison; averages 30% smaller than the other ducks shown below.

SHOVELER

PINTAIL

dark underwing

GADWALL

white

MALLARD

brown

TEAL

SHOVELER

spatulate

PINTAIL

grey

grey

MALLARD

blue wing patch

brown

bright orange

white wing patch

GADWALL

white

pale orange

Wigeon

Anas penelope   **527**

43–50 cm | WS 72–85 cm

> American Wigeon (*p. 44*)
> Falcated Duck (♀) (*p. 522*)

Short-legged, **short-billed**;
noisy flocks graze on land or swim, rising as one when
disturbed. Smaller than Mallard (*p. 38*), bigger than Teal (*p. 42*).
Grey legs and bill always instant clue.

MALE blue-grey; **black-and-white rear-end**. Head **red-brown
with pale forehead**; body slightly paler (Teal darker overall).
Pink breast, striking on sleeping birds. **White forewing** may
show (thinner line on Teal). 1st-winter male lacks white
on wing; summer male like female but **redder**; **white wing
patch**. Colourful/patchy intermediates in autumn (grey legs/
bill helpful). FEMALE barred/spotted, not streaked like Mallard/
Gadwall/Pintail, grey-brown to **tawny**; greyer head, variable
smudge behind eye. **White belly**, **plain flank**.

VOICE Distinctive: male explosive whistle, "*whe-ooo*" or
"*whew!*"; female low growl, "*ra-kraa*". Chatty flock chorus.

Locally common winter visitor
(470,000, most Sep–Mar); rare
breeder (400 pairs) in far N

from Iceland

from Scandinavia

from Siberia

Estuaries, lakes, wet meadows

IN FLIGHT,
fast; tapered,
swept-back wings;
short, pointed tail.

FEMALE grey forewing;
dark hindwing;
lacks white

♀ / 1ST-WINTER

♂

MALE striking
white
forewing
(grey in 1st-
winter)

♂ MAY—OCT

SUMMER MALE has some
grey feathers on back

short grey bill
with black tip

BREEDING MALE has
distinctive head
pattern and black-
and-white rear-end

♂ NOV—APR

crisp white fringes to wing coverts
and very fresh feather edges
indicate ADULT FEMALE

♀ [Dec]

Browner, barred type, showing
individual variation. Tertials lost
through early moult. Some feather
edges old and worn.

1ST-SUMMER ♀
[Mar]

37

Mallard

Anas platyrhynchos ● 527

50–60 cm | WS 81–95 cm

◉ Black Duck (*p. 44*)

Familiar, wild or semi-tame.
Surface-feeding, upends, sometimes dives; frequent on dry land.
MALE pale, lengthwise brown bands; black-and-white rear-end.
Head **green** (blue/purple gloss) above white ring. **Bill yellow;
legs bright orange**. In summer like rusty female; **yellow bill**,
green-black cap and eyestripe, mottled rufous chest.
FEMALE dull **yellow-brown, streaked blackish**; 'V'-shapes
on flanks; nearly **white tail** helps at long range. Head more
or less striped; bill brown, marked with orange/yellowish.
Legs bright orange. Belly dark, underwings white. JUVENILE like
skinny female, blacker crown, streaked (less spotted) breast.

VOICE Quiet quack, nasal whistles from male. Loud, short
quack and long, coarse, descending series from female.

Common and widespread
resident (100,000 pairs) and
winter visitor (650,000)

from
N and
W Europe

Watery places from coast to high
moors, town parks

IN FLIGHT, large, long-necked, long-
winged; wingbeats mostly below
body level. **Dark blue hindwing**
with two parallel **white stripes.**

white
edge

♀

♂

SUMMER MALE loses strong
colours and pattern, may
look greyish or more
rusty; head greyer than
female's, bill remains
yellow

♂ JUN–SEP

♂ OCT–MAY

orange legs

♀

Shoveler

Anas clypeata **I** `528`

44–52 cm | WS 73–82 cm

◉ Blue-winged Teal (*p. 45*)

Big, large-headed with long, heavy bill. Feeds/rests in water or shallows at water's edge, not wandering far over drier land.

Long body, shoulders low in water; head low, well forward, **broad bill** striking. Upends, showing markedly long wing points. On land, more 'tear drop' shape, tapered to high tail, than deep-bellied Mallard. MALE head blacker than Mallard, **yellow eye**, black bill, **white chest**. Flanks red-brown, **black-and-white rear-end**. SUMMER/AUTUMN/JUVENILE MALE striking, more like female, often redder; greyish head with variable **upright whitish crescent** on face. Yellow eye on adult, dark on juvenile. FEMALE pale, streaked; **dark belly**, **orange legs** like Mallard (Gadwall (*p. 40*) and Wigeon (*p. 37*) have white belly). JUVENILE more finely marked.

VOICE Calls weak, male a nasal "*too-took*", female a quiet, hoarse quack. Taking flight, wings make loud whoosh.

Scarce breeder (1,000 pairs) and fairly common winter visitor (18,000, most Aug–Apr)

from Iceland

from N and W Europe

To S Europe

Lakes, reservoirs, saltmarshes, coastal lagoons

white edge absent

grey forewing

♀

SUMMER MALE gradually develops white crescent on face, which becomes more striking in autumn

blue forewing

♂

IN FLIGHT, MALE **forewing pale blue; no white line at rear**; FEMALE white underwing/dark belly, like Mallard.

♂ MAY–AUG

white foreparts/dark reddish flank unique

♂ SEP–APR

orange legs

♀

`39`

Ducks in flight *p. 34*

Gadwall

Anas strepera ● ❶ 527

46–56 cm | WS 78–90 cm

Much like Mallard (*p. 38*): squarer head, steep forehead, slim bill; long-bodied.

Square **white patch** on innerwing: triangle or diamond on swimming bird; smaller on juvenile, more like Wigeon. MALE grey (lacks Wigeon's blue), **black rear-end** (no white). Head buffish, back streaked black with pale edges; tertials may create pale patch. Face pale, almost silvery in autumn; **black bill** looks 'stuck-on'. SUMMER MALE like female, bill orange on sides, but sharper contrast between grey head and brown breast, blacker rump, retains chestnut and black on wing. FEMALE **like Mallard**, but **belly white** (obvious in flight). Head paler, greyer or buff; tail dull. Well defined orange side to bill; **legs orange-yellow**. Slim, narrower-winged in flight. JUVENILE has mottled belly, finely streaked (less spotted) breast.

VOICE Quiet quacks, frequent nasal "*nhek-nhek*" from male; very vocal in displays from late summer on.

Common and widespread resident (100,000 pairs) and winter visitor (650,000)

from Iceland

from W Europe

Watery places from coast to high moors, town parks

IN FLIGHT, upperwing looks dark with obvious white square on hindwing close to body; FEMALE has white belly.

♀

♂

♂ MAY—SEP

more solid blackish feather centres than Mallard

orange sides to bill

♀

white on wing often hidden

black bill

♂ OCT—APR

Pintail

51–62 cm | WS 79–87 cm

Large surface-feeding/grazing duck, like Mallard (*p. 38*) but more elegant; longer neck but body quite deep and heavy.

MALE lead-grey (duller, darker than Wigeon (*p. 37*), not bluish). **White breast** not so brilliant as Shoveler's (*p. 39*), often stained. Head dark with **white stripe**. Stern black, yellow-buff patch (white on Wigeon). **Legs grey; bill bluish with black stripe**. Long tail spike easy to see even at long range but plumage unlike Long-tailed Duck (*p. 60*). SUMMER/AUTUMN MALE can be puzzling: very pale, blurry buffish with soft bars and streaks, dark chequering above, becoming patchy grey; plain gingery head against long, blue-sided, black bill. FEMALE much like Mallard but finely marked with lacy loops and streaks; head **plainer buffy-brown. Bill grey; legs grey** (never orange).

VOICE Male whistles, female gives short, low quacks.

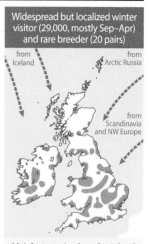

Widespread but localized winter visitor (29,000, mostly Sep–Apr) and rare breeder (20 pairs)

from Iceland

from Arctic Russia

from Scandinavia and NW Europe

IN FLIGHT, distinctive, with long white line along trailing edge. Long wings, long tail, slim neck reasonably obvious.

Mainly estuaries, but also inland floods, wet meadows, lakes

♀

♂

♂ JUL–OCT

plain head

becomes very white on neck and body in autumn

♀ slim grey bill

white neck stripe

♂ NOV–JUN

buff flank patch

Teal

Anas crecca ● Ⅰ 527

34–38 cm | WS 53–59 cm

👁 Rare teal (*p. 45*)

Small, agile; groups in flight
recall waders with twists and turns; near-vertical take-off.
Often on muddy watersides, hidden in weeds, or flooded
willows; upland moors in summer.

MALE compact; often looks dark (but bright in low winter sun).
Darker grey than bigger Wigeon (*p. 37*), slimmer bill;
white stripe along body. Black-edged **mustard-yellow triangle**
on stern. Head dark; glossy green panel, edged buff, behind eye.
Bill and legs black. FEMALE/SUMMER MALE coarsely mottled (less
streaky than Mallard (*p. 38*) or Gadwall (*p. 40*)). **Whitish streak
beside tail**. JUVENILE like female but more finely streaked.

VOICE Often heard from 'invisible' birds on marsh or reservoir:
male's high, sharp, ringing whistle, "*cree*" may not bring 'duck'
to mind; female has low, gruff, nasal quack.

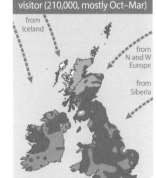

Scarce breeder (1,400 pairs) and
common and widespread winter
visitor (210,000, mostly Oct–Mar)

from
Iceland

from
N and W
Europe

from
Siberia

IN FLIGHT, **central wingbar broader
than hindwing line; flashy grass-green**
between stripes eliminates Garganey.

Moors, waterside thickets; in
winter lakes, pits, estuaries

broad midwing
stripe; flash of
green

♂   ♀

dark, with pale
triangle at rear

dabbles in shallow water/wet mud
(Wigeon graze on drier grass)

SUMMER/JUVENILE MALE like female,
often with dark cap and pale face;
any grey vermiculations indicate
that it is a male.

white streak near tail

horizontal white stripe

♂ OCT–APR

pale triangle

Garganey

Anas querquedula  ● ● I 527

37–41 cm | WS 59–67 cm

👁 Rare teal *(p. 45)*

Almost as small as Teal,
distinctive in spring, harder in autumn.

MALE **white crescent over eye**. Head and chest warm brown.
Pale, drooping feathers over wing. FEMALE/JUVENILE like Teal but
larger, paler, more obvious flank spots. Dark cap, stripe through
eye and band across cheek; long whitish stripe over eye (thin
in middle), whitish upper cheek line. Clear **white spot by bill**.
AUTUMN MALE like darkish female, head marks stronger, white chin.
In autumn, pick out by head pattern and dark olive hindwing
patch (brilliant green on Teal).

VOICE Infrequent: spring male has curious dry rattle; female
has nasal "*ga ga ga*" and weak quack.

IN FLIGHT, male forewing pale blue; female milky-grey spilling onto outerwing
(dark on Teal). Garganey has **equal parallel white stripes** (unequal on Teal;
cf. Mallard *(p. 38)*). Contrasted blackish edge to forewing beneath.

Rare summer visitor (<100 pairs
breed), scarce migrant
(most Mar/Apr and Aug/Sep)

1 via Iberia
2 via Italy
To
sub-Saharan
Africa

Freshwater habitat, wet meadows

dull dark band
between two
white lines

♀

♂

pale streak near tail
very weak or absent

1ST-WINTER ♂

Spring birds often favour tall,
flooded vegetation.

stripy face
♀

drooped back feathers

♂

Rare dabbling ducks

American Wigeon *Anas americana*

48–56 cm | WS 76–89 cm

Distinctive 'wigeon' form and pattern. MALE told from Wigeon (*p. 37*) by **white forehead and crown** above **dark head band**, pale purplish/pinkish body. FEMALE/IMMATURE/ECLIPSE MALE difficult to pick out and identify. Generally slightly more contrast between greyer head and more orangey body than female Wigeon, and hint (or more) of male's dark head band/pale forehead (but some Wigeon very similar).

IN FLIGHT, axillaries ('wing pit') entirely white (greyer on Wigeon). FEMALE whitish upperwing bar broad, (narrow on Wigeon). Good strategy is to wait patiently for bird to flap.

white

UNDERWING
greyish

WIGEON

narrow bar

AMERICAN WIGEON

broad bar

UPPERWING

1ST-WINTER ♂

♀ WIGEON

usually warmer brown and no hint of an 'eyepatch'

♀

♂

Vagrant from N America: >500 records, 10–15 per year, most Sep–Mar. Usually with Wigeon. Freshwater, estuaries.

Black Duck *Anas rubripes*

53–61 cm | WS 85–96 cm

Like female Mallard (*p. 38*) but darker (though beware 'farmyard' types) with contrasting paler head/neck, **yellowish bill**, orange legs.

IN FLIGHT, underwing white, hindwing patch bluish-purple-greenish with **no white lines**.

MALLARD

BLACK DUCK

♀

white underwing

white lines

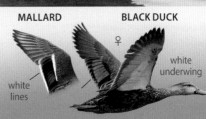

♂

dark edges to tail (white on Mallard)

Vagrant from N America: <50 records (<20 Ireland), Oct–Mar; some long-stayers. Freshwater.

Green-winged Teal
Anas carolinensis
34–38 cm | WS 53–59 cm

Vagrant from N America: 20–60 per year, most Sep–Mar. Freshwater.

MALE very similar to Teal (*p. 42*) but **vertical white band beside chest**; lacks pale buff edge to green head band. FEMALE like Teal (may have stronger facial stripes and pale spot by bill) and very similar to other, even rarer species.

GREEN-WINGED TEAL

♂

usually buff bar above green

TEAL

♂

white bar above green

vertical white band

Blue-winged Teal
Anas discors
37–41 cm | WS 58 cm

Vagrant from N America: <300 records (<150 Ireland), most Sep–Mar. Freshwater.

👁 Cinnamon Teal (♀) (*p. 16*)

MALE distinctive: **white face crescent**, spotted tawny flank, white patch near black stern. OTHER PLUMAGES difficult: look for **broken pale line over eye**, white eyering, **white spot against bill** in front of **plain cheek**, white chin, relatively heavy blackish bill, **yellowish legs**.

Females and juveniles of the rare teals are similar to Teal (*p. 42*) and Garganey (*p. 43*). The wing and head patterns are important features for identification.

GARGANEY
grey patch; two whitish bars

TEAL
green patch; midwing bar widest

BLUE-WINGED TEAL
blue forewing

BAIKAL TEAL
dark hindwing, white line at rear

slightly spatulate bill

white crescent

♀

♂

Baikal Teal *Anas formosa*
39–43 cm | WS 55–60 cm

Vagrant from Asia: <10 records (1 Ireland), Nov–Apr. Occasional escapes. Freshwater, estuaries.

MALE unmistakable: **black/ white/buff/green patterned** head. OTHER PLUMAGES like Teal (*p. 42*) and Garganey (*p. 43*), **dark-bordered whitish face spot**, slight pale streak beside tail.

GARGANEY
pale spot; cheek band

TEAL
pale spot absent or subtle at best

♀ ♀

BLUE-WINGED TEAL
white spot against plain cheek; heavy bill

BAIKAL TEAL
dark-bordered white spot; cheek plain

♂

45

Red-crested Pochard

53–57 cm | WS 85–90 cm

Big, bulky, large-headed; generally a surface-feeder.

MALE colourful, **fuzzy orange crown**, sharply defined black neck and breast; body pale brown and white; bill long, **pink-red**. Summer male browner; **bill red**, head two-tone dark cap/pale brown cheeks. FEMALE dusty pale brown; large head brown with darker eye patch, **lower half pale buff-white**; bill grey with pink patch near tip. Female Common Scoter (*p. 63*) similar but darker with dark bill (and all-dark wings in flight).

VOICE Quiet and insignificant, but squeaky "sneeze" in display.

Rare Eurasian vagrant and scarce introduced breeder in Cotswolds (300 pairs), occasionally elsewhere; number of true wild birds hard to determine.

Reedy lakes, pits and reservoirs

IN FLIGHT, **broad white band** along full length of wing.

white edge to forewing

♂

white wingbar (rules out scoters)

♀

♂ APR–SEP

like high-crowned Common Scoter with pale bill band

♀

'fuzzy' crown

red eye and bill

white flank obvious at long range

♂ OCT–MAR

Mandarin

Aix galericulata

41–49 cm | WS 65–75 cm

Small and unobtrusive duck, often in/near trees.

MALE unmistakable: dark, **broad white band over eye** beneath long, rusty crest overlying back; lower face a broad golden-buff fan; **unique upright 'orange peel' 'sails'**. FEMALE very dark, breast finely streaked white, **flanks boldly spotted**; blunt, thick crest above fine **white 'spectacle'**, white chin, small grey bill.

VOICE High, squeaky whistle in flight.

Long-established introduction: scarce (3,000 breeding pairs), mostly in the south; rare wanderer elsewhere

Wooded lakes, rivers, park ponds; nests in holes in trees

IN FLIGHT, small, fast, direct; upperwing dark with thin white trailing edge.

spotted flanks

distinctive 'sails'

thicker patch behind eye

Wood Duck *Aix sponsa*

47–54 cm | WS 66–73 cm

Occasional escape (though possible vagrant from N America).

MALE multicoloured like Mandarin but lacks 'sails'. FEMALE like Mandarin but has thicker white patch behind eye, buffer flank spots.

Ruddy Duck

Oxyura jamaicensis

35–43 cm | WS 50–55 cm

Small, round-backed, large-headed duck with long, stiff tail (often flat on water, inconspicuous until raised).

MALE bright coppery-red with bold black cap, nape and neck **enclosing white face**; bill blue. WINTER MALE dull, dark, with black cap and **stark white face**, grey bill. FEMALE dull, face less striking, dark with pale line over eye and **pale cheek, crossed by dark band**. Wings plain dark brown. Confusion possible with Smew (*p. 57*), larger female Common Scoter (*p. 63*), and much bigger, paler Red-crested Pochard (*p. 46*).

VOICE MALE has low croak in display.

Introduced; formerly widespread, mostly Midlands and south but progressively being eradicated: 40 left, including 10 females; likely to be extirpated in 2016

FORMER RANGE

Reed-fringed lakes and ponds

IN FLIGHT, usually low, fast, direct, no agility.

♀

dark bill (in winter)

ADULT WINTER ♂

Males raise their tail and head high in display and patter the bill against their breast feathers, expelling air in a spray of bubbles.

White-headed Duck EN 528

Oxyura leucocephala EN

43–48 cm | WS 55–65 cm

Occasional escape though possible vagrant.

Like Ruddy Duck; bill **bulges at base**. MALE pale rusty-brown, **head white**, small black cap, collar; no white under tail. IMMATURE blackish head. FEMALE grey bill; black crown; white face, dark band; body finely barred.

dark cap

dark cheekband (may be weak)

sloping bill

rounded back

bold face pattern

tail often held flat

♀

♀

white face

blue bill

white head

♂

♂

Pochard

VU
VU

Aythya ferina ● **I** 528

42–49 cm | WS 67–75 cm

Redhead, Canvasback (*p. 54*),
Ring-necked Duck (♀) (*p. 53*)

Sleepy diving duck, often rests
by day with smaller, more active Tufted Ducks (*p. 50*).

Sleek, rather round-bodied, round-headed with **sloping
forehead**. MALE pale grey, **dark at both ends**; head rich red-
brown, bright in good light, eye red; pale blue-grey band across
dark bill. FEMALE/JUVENILE trickier; greyish, darker front and back.
FEMALE brown on breast and stern, diffusely **mottled brownish
on grey body**; head pale brown, **whitish eyering and around
bill and throat**, pale stripe curls over cheek; long, grey bill with
pale central band. JUVENILE browner than female, darker cap,
paler cheeks, whitish beside bill and on chin can be puzzling
(see female Ring-necked Duck (*p. 53*)).

VOICE Infrequent: MALE gives nasal "*wha-oo*" in display;
FEMALE a purring growl.

Scarce breeder (600 pairs); fairly
common and widespread winter
visitor (38,000, mostly Aug–Apr)

from
E and W
Europe

Mainly gravel pits, reservoirs
(winter); breeds on reedy lakes

IN FLIGHT, broad, pale grey panel along
spread wing; lack of white safely excludes
Tufted Duck and Scaup (*p. 51*).

♀

♂

all have deep-based,
tapered bill with
pale band

rather pale,
pattern obscure

♀

♂ JUL–SEP

JUVENILE

pale body with
dark head/neck
and rear-end

♂

Tufted Duck

Aythya fuligula **I** 528

40–47 cm | WS 65–72 cm

Lesser Scaup (*p. 52*), Ring-necked Duck (*p. 53*)

Buoyant, round-headed diving duck; with tuft on head; smaller than Coot (*p. 257*).

MALE distinctive black and white (bright purple gloss on cheeks). **Head and breast black** (unlike Goldeneye (*p. 56*)), back black (unlike Scaup), **sides bright white**. Droopy 'tuft', yellow eyes. FEMALE dark, plain-chocolate brown, **'bump' or slight tuft on back of head** (rules out Scaup); flanks paler in winter, belly white. Bill slim, grey, **broad black tip**. FEMALE/SUMMER MALE/JUVENILE may have white facial marks, often sharply defined but rarely as extensive as on Scaup. Often whitish under tail (less bright/extensive than Ferruginous Duck (*p. 53*)).

VOICE Loud, rough growling notes; bubbling whistles from displaying males.

Fairly common and widespread breeder (7,500 pairs) and winter visitor (110,000, most Sep–Apr)

from Iceland

from N and W Europe

IN FLIGHT, long white stripe along wing (grey on Pochard (*p. 49*)).

Lakes, reservoirs, pits, rivers, occasionally on the sea

Flocks of Tufted Ducks, common on inland waters, are worth checking for unusual species.

♂ JUN–OCT

♀

some FEMALES can have 'Scaup-like' white patches above the bill; the hint of tuft is always the 'give-away' feature

♂ SEP–MAY

Scaup

Aythya marila ● Ⅰ 528

42–51 cm | WS 71–80 cm

👁 Lesser Scaup (*p. 52*), Ring-necked Duck (*p. 53*)

Lesser Scaup (*p. 52*), Ring-necked Duck (*p. 53*)

Similar to Tufted Duck and Pochard (*p. 49*): combines pattern of both with Pochard's shape/size; strong, leaping dive. Broader beam, wider bill than Tufted Duck, larger head rounded, no trace of 'tuft'.

MALE **pale in middle, black both ends**, flanks **white**; grey back excludes Tufted Duck. FEMALE paler ginger-brown than Tufted Duck, greyer back (like Pochard). Forehead steep; **small black spot at tip of broad bill** (wide band on Tufted Duck). **White blaze on face** higher over bill than any Tufted Duck. In summer, pale **ear patch**. JUVENILE needs care, especially inland – **larger**, broader than Tufted Duck, **rounded head**, wider bill. White face diffuse, but **ear patch** good clue.

IN FLIGHT (see also *p. 52*), white wing stripe excludes Pochard.

flocks at sea are highly unlikely to be Tufted Ducks or Pochards; Scaup is typically a marine duck, but very localized

Scarce and declining winter visitor, mostly on N, NW and NE coasts (5,000, Sep –Apr)

from Iceland

from N Europe

Offshore, estuaries, occasional inland

♀ white wing stripe ♂

IMMATURE ♂

JUVENILE

all have domed forehead; smooth, curved nape

JUVENILE bill has smudgy triangular dark tip unlike adult, but less sharp band than Tufted Duck

white ear patch in summer

♀ MAR–SEP

♀ SEP–MAR

black head, white flank rules out Pochard; grey back rules out Tufted Duck

♂ SEP–JUN

Rare diving ducks

Regular scrutiny of wildfowl flocks might eventually result in the discovery of a rare bird. Lesser Scaup, Ring-necked Ducks and Ferruginous Ducks all tend to be found associating loosely with Tufted Ducks and Pochards on inland waters. Rare sea ducks such as Surf Scoters and King Eiders become mixed with close relatives, and finding them is a challenge.

Lesser Scaup *Aythya affinis*

38–45 cm | WS 60–65 cm

Small 'scaup'. MALE like Scaup (*p. 51*) with coarsely-barred grey back, white flanks, **small bump/'tuft' on back of head**. FEMALE like small, dark Scaup, tiny tuft on head; greyer back and less black on bill tip than Tufted Duck (*p. 50*). Beware hybrids (*p. 55*).

> Vagrant from N America: <200 records (<50 Ireland), most Oct–Mar. Usually with diving duck flocks; a few long-stayers. Freshwater.

hint of tuft more like bump at rear of crown above indented nape

♂

♀

Scaup and Lesser Scaup identification

FEMALES

peak at back of crown

rounder head higher on forehead

distinct tuft on nape

white face small or obscure

small black nail on bill

LESSER SCAUP

small black nail on bill

SCAUP

broad, dark bill tip

TUFTED DUCK

IN FLIGHT, white **wingbar only on innerwing**).

♂

SCAUP outer part of wingbar white

LESSER SCAUP outer part of wingbar greyish

♂

SCAUP head 'peaks' at front

♂

LESSER SCAUP head 'peaks' at rear

♂

Ring-necked Duck
Aythya collaris
37–46 cm | WS 65–70 cm

MALE like smart Tufted Duck
(*p. 50*), high-peaked head (no tuft) and grey (not white) flanks
(outlined in white and with **white front peak**); white ring on
bill. FEMALE like Tufted Duck but whitish around bill extends to
chin, throat; eyering and 'spectacle' line; banded bill like male
(see juvenile Pochard (*p. 49*), Redhead (*p. 54*)).

Vagrant from N America: 10–15
annually (>300 records Ireland),
most Sep–Mar. With Pochard/
Tufted Duck flocks. Freshwater.

IN FLIGHT,
broad, grey wing
stripe extends to
end of wing.

white stripe **TUFTED DUCK**

pale band on bill

grey flank
with white 'spur'
at front

subtly
distinctive
head pattern

NT ## Ferruginous Duck
Aythya nyroca
38–42 cm | WS 60–67 cm

Vagrant from E Europe:
<500 records (<50 Ireland), most
Sep–Apr, declining. Freshwater.

IN FLIGHT, **wide white band** on
wing; male has white leading edge.
White belly shows well.

528

Small, smart diving duck, like sleek, bright female
Tufted Duck (*p. 50*) with slender bill.

MALE glossy mahogany-brown, back dark; **white under tail** edged
black. **Eye white**. Bill grey, soft pale band. FEMALE browner with
dark eye. Smooth, peaked head shape (higher than Pochard
(*p. 49*)). **Upperparts always unmarked**: grey bars indicate
hybrid (*p. 55*). Female Tufted Duck may show white under
tail but rarely so sharp or bright. JUVENILE as female but
all-grey bill, dark cap/paler rear cheek, dark eye, duller/
faintly spotted white under tail.

white belly
patch

wide white
wing stripe

head shape changes,
from quite low to
distinctive high peak

white eye

dark collar
(hard to see)

dark eye

Very rare diving ducks from North America

Bufflehead

Bucephala albeola

32–39 cm | WS 55–60 cm

Tiny. MALE white with black back; head dark, iridescent, with **broad white band** behind eye and around nape. FEMALE small white panel behind eye, browner body.

Hooded Merganser

Lophodytes cucullatus

42–50 cm | WS 75–80 cm

MALE unmistakable: black head with **fan-like**, black-edged, white crest, white chest, tawny flank, **black bill**. FEMALE/ IMMATURE grey-brown, pale 'saw bill', dusky face blending into wide, fanned, tawny crest.

Redhead

Aythya americana

44–51 cm | WS 65–70 cm

Like large, dark Pochard (*p. 49*) with rounder head, steep forehead/**bulging forecrown** when resting, cocked tail.
MALE has **golden eye**, pale grey bill with broad black tip beyond diffuse pale band. FEMALE has dark cap, plain, pale face, more uniform body than Pochard, whiter under tail.

Canvasback

Aythya valisineria

49–56 cm | WS 70–80 cm

Like large, long Pochard (*p. 49*) with **long, all-black bill** sloping up towards high crown. MALE very pale grey with dark-face. FEMALE greyer than Pochard.

like Goldeneye (*p. 56*) with white cheek

big white nape

BUFFLEHEAD

Vagrant from N America: <20 records (plus escapes) (<5 Ireland), Oct–Mar.

'fuzzy' crest, dark face

HOODED MERGANSER

Vagrant from N America: <10 records (plus escapes) (<5 Ireland), Oct–Mar.

dark cap; 'steep' forecrown

REDHEAD

golden eye

upright forehead

Vagrant from N America: <5 records (1 Ireland), most autumn–winter.

POCHARD both sexes have pale areas on the bill

CANVASBACK

long, sweeping black bill

black bill

N American vagrant: <10 records (Britain), winter.

black foreparts angled against grey

Hybrid ducks

Ducks interbreed more than most birds, mainly in captivity. Resulting hybrids differ according to which parent is male, and female progeny are generally less obvious than males. They usually show obviously mixed features, but may look remarkably like a third species. Many combinations occur: this sample shows both subtle and obvious results. Hybrid possibilities must always be borne in mind when identifying rare wildfowl, especially Ferruginous Duck (*p. 53*), Redhead and Lesser Scaup (*p. 52*).

Mallard × Pintail

Male combines colours and shape of both parents, clearly differs from either.

Shoveler × Gadwall

Body largely like male Gadwall but peculiar head pattern incorporates Shoveler green.

Wigeon × American Wigeon

Intermediate, or closer to one parent; pale head with dark band, grey body frequent.

Tufted Duck × Pochard

Like dark Scaup with a tuft, or Lesser Scaup with a uniform back; larger black bill tip.

Tufted Duck × Ferruginous Duck

Like Ferruginous Duck but with a duller eye colour and a tuft; or Tufted Duck with dark flank.

Pochard × Ferruginous Duck

Like Ferruginous Duck but often reddish eye, greyer body, white under tail reduced.

Tufted Duck × Ring-necked Duck

Like Ring-necked Duck but with a tuft on the nape; grey flank lacks white peak at front.

Scaup × Tufted Duck

Both sexes like Scaup but with more black on the bill; male darker, with a tuft.

Goldeneye

Bucephalus clangula ● ❶ 528

↻ Barrow's Goldeneye (*p.67*)

40–48 cm | WS 62–77 cm

Rounded duck, dives feverishly, elusive, but groups sleep with heads back, long tails raised, or display actively (males throw heads back and call).

MALE **white** (brighter than Goosander (*p. 59*); black, green-black head; **white face spot**. Eyes yellow, legs orange. FEMALE **dark, grey, round-backed**. Dark head; low, round nape; **triangular bill**; white collar. White wing markings often hidden. Bill grey with orange band; eyes yellow or white. JUVENILE like female but neck darker; male develops white body and face patch during winter.

VOICE Rarely heard. When displaying males make ratchety, clock-winding "*nhair-nhairr*" sounds; female deep growls. Wings (especially adult males') whistle loudly in fast flight, often heard before birds are seen.

Fairly common and widespread winter visitor (20,000, Sep–Apr); rare breeder in far N (<200 pairs)

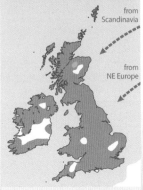

from Scandinavia

from NE Europe

IN FLIGHT, MALE innerwing largely white, outer black; FEMALE innerwing white crossed by two dark bars, belly white; JUVENILE like female but only one dark wingbar.

Sea coasts, lakes and reservoirs, even small, cold upland pools; nests in holes in trees, nestboxes

♀   ♂

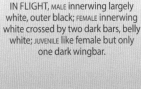

grey body (looks dark at distance)

very dark, peaked head

short triangular bill

♀

round white face spot

contrasting black-and-white body

♂

Smew

Mergellus albellus 528

38–44 | WS 56–69 cm

Lively, alert, small-headed diving duck; often elusive (even under flooded waterside bushes or in reeds).

MALE **predominantly white**, flanks pale grey; **black eye patch**. Close up, black nape beneath white crest, fine chest lines, black back, grey rear (white much more 'up front' than Goldeneye, Goosander (*p. 59*)). Crest can be raised, pushed forward extravagantly. FEMALE lead grey, small head **red-brown, lower third white**; blacker around eye. Steep forehead, small grey bill echo male's shape; crest splayed upwards against wind. Smaller and shorter-billed than Goosander, more extensive white on face (like winter male Ruddy Duck (*p. 48*) but white on wings). JUVENILE like female but redder head without dark eye patch; males develop white during winter.

Rare/scarce, local winter visitor (usually 100–200/year, Nov–Mar); occasional influxes, mostly in S

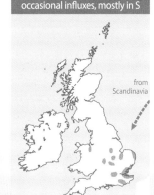

from Scandinavia

Lakes, reservoirs, flooded pits

IN FLIGHT, MALE **piebald**, white around chest (curiously like Shoveler (*p. 39*)); FEMALE wings white in front, white lines across back; JUVENILE like female but less white.

♀

white forewing

white underside

♂

lead-grey body

white patch
♀

body white with
black marks

♂

NT Red-breasted Merganser

Mergus serrator 528

52–58 cm | WS 67–82 cm

(◔) Hooded Merganser (*p. 54*)

Scarce and local breeder (2,200 pairs), mostly on coast in N and NW; widespread but uncommon and local in winter (8,000)

Extravagant diving duck, drakes with splendid patterns, dramatic shapes. Often stands at water's edge (more upright than Goosander); shows white belly (often stained orange), vivid orange legs. Nests on ground (Goosander in tree holes) and more marine than Goosander, often pairs, sometimes scores/hundreds.

MALE darker than Goosander, white band along wing above **grey flanks**, black/white foreparts, **orange-brown chest**. White collar beneath green-black head; **long crest** clusters into wispy, bristly points. Eye red; bill **bright red**, slender. FEMALE elongated, rather heavy-bodied, like Goosander but smaller, browner, **drabber** in dull light. Dull pale breast merges into orange-brown neck, paler gingery head blending into throat. Less weighty, double-pointed crest. Bill slim, slightly upswept (hint of a smile), pale red. **VOICE** Insignificant, deep growl.

IN FLIGHT, innerwing white, crossed by black bars (MALE) or black line (FEMALE) (usually clear white on Goosander).

from Iceland

from N Europe

Breeds near coast, estuaries; in winter mostly on sea

♂ MAY–OCT

long, slim profile

♀

♂

Ducks moult in summer; males in subdued 'eclipse' plumage look more like contrasty females but keep their upperwing patterns.

spiky, pale head

slim bill

♀

brown head fades into pale body

red eye

white collar

slim bill

♂ NOV–MAY

dark chest

Goosander

Mergus merganser ❶

58–68 cm | WS 78–94 cm

⟨◉⟩ Hooded Merganser (p. 54)

Big, long-bodied, long-billed diving duck, obvious amongst commoner species. Red-breasted Merganser only likely confusion, but see Great Crested Grebe (p. 80). Frequently stands on bank, revealing bright red legs.

MALE **white/pale salmon-pink** (some intense pink, others pure white, yellowish in evening light). Large **green-black head**, bulbous forehead, dark eye, black back. Bill thick-based, strongly hooked, deep plum-red. SUMMER MALE like female with bigger white wing patch. FEMALE pale, **clean grey**, whitish breast; **sharp divide against red-brown head** and upper neck. Well-defined **white chin patch**. Long red bill. Rounded, drooping crest (paler, more ragged in summer), raised in 'anvil' shape in courtship. Belly often stained orange. JUVENILE like female with stripes from bill to eye, duller bill, less white on wing; young male develops white erratically over late winter. **VOICE** Croaking flight note.

IN FLIGHT, long, heavy, head outstretched (fast, direct); innerwing white, outerwing black.

Scarce and local breeder in SW, Wales and N (2,600 pairs); more common and widespread in winter (12,000)

from N Scandinavia

from NE Europe

Breeds near rivers; winter mostly bigger lakes, reservoirs, rivers

♂ JUL–OCT

Male Goosanders in summer 'eclipse' plumage still look big, heavy and thicker-billed than Red-breasted Mergansers.

♀

deep-based bill

neat white chin

sharp contrast between head and body

♀

dark eye

deep, dark bill

♂ NOV–JUL

white breast

Long-tailed Duck

Clangula hyemalis 528

VU
VU

♂ 49–62 cm (incl. tail 10–15 cm); ♀ 39–47 cm | WS 65–82 cm

Small sea duck. Complex plumages often puzzling, but recognisable character. Auk-like, thickset, squat, or humped rear/tail down; head large, rounded; **bill short, deep** triangle.

MALE long, whippy tail feathers (see Pintail *p. 41*, but no real confusion: Long-tailed Duck does not stand on mud or grass). WINTER MALE **white with dark brown bands**, broad breast-band, grey flanks; two-tone dark head patch; bill dark with pink band. SUMMER MALE darker, streaked rusty-buff and black, head and breast very dark; pale face patch, white eyering. WINTER FEMALE dark above, pale below, white head with dark cap, **dark smudge on cheek**; bill grey. SUMMER FEMALE darker, bigger dark cap and cheek marking, finer whitish line back from eye and white neck patch. JUVENILE (sometimes solitary, sometimes inland) like female, but face greyer, **whitish around eye**, more extensive **dark cheek** – work out by elimination (nothing else fits), dumpy shape, triangular beak, frequent diving with **wingtips splayed**.

VOICE Male gives frequent, nasal, yodelling "*ar-ar-ardl-ow*"; quiet "*gag*" notes.

Scarce and local winter visitor, mainly to N and E coasts (11,000, Aug–May; declining)

from N Europe

Offshore, sandy bays; occasional inland

JUVENILE

dark ♀

light ♀

♂ AUTUMN

head patterns variable but males can always be told by the pink tip to the bill

♀ NOV–APR

♂ NOV–APR

♂ WINTER

♀ WINTER

IN FLIGHT, wings very dark, rump **dark with white** sides, recalling Guillemot (*p. 166*).

long, straggling flocks fly low over sea, often with Common Scoters

white stripe tapers behind eye

white collar

white spectacle

white flank

♀ MAY–JUN

grey face

♂ MAY–JUN

61

Velvet Scoter

Melanitta fusca ● ❶ 528

VU

51–58 cm | WS 79–97 cm

⟨◉⟩ Rare scoters (*p. 68–69*), Harlequin Duck (♀) (*p. 68*)

Big scoter, associates with Common Scoter. Angular, wedge-shaped head recalls Eider (*p. 64*) but bill slimmer; tail short.

ADULT MALE **black**, with broad **white hindwing panel**, white 'tick' under eye. Bill has yellow side panels, black top. Legs red (blackish on Common Scoter). FEMALE dark, same stark **white wing panel**, reddish legs. Face very dark, hint of pale spot near bill and pale cheek, or typically whiter cheek spot and pale patch near bill (see female Scaup *p. 51*). Bill deep-based, tapers (slightly upwards) to slender tip. JUVENILE like female with well-marked face, whiter belly. All tend to hide white wing panel at rest (thin line at best, hard to see at long range), so watch scoter flocks to catch frequent wing-flapping, when Velvet Scoters' shiny white marks flash brightly.

Scarce and declining winter visitor (3,000, most autumn-winter), mostly to NE coast

from Scandinavia

Offshore, bays; rare inland

IN FLIGHT, shows prominent **white hindwing panel**.

♀

♂

two white patches on head

♀

IMMATURE ♂

curved yellow patch on bill

♂

white wing patch (does not always show when swimming)

Common Scoter

Melanitta nigra ● **I** 528

44–54 cm | WS 70–84 cm

◉ Black Scoter (*p. 69*)

Combines heavy body with long, pointed tail, slender neck, elegant shape. On sea in long, ragged groups, showing on rising swell; often raises head and tail. Sits up from water with lowered head, to flap wings.

ADULT MALE **black** with **paler outerwing**, yellow patch on top of neat, wedge-shaped bill beyond basal bulge. Dusky wingtips show when flapped on water, better in flight. **immature male** brown at first, gaining black in blotches. FEMALE dark, obscurely barred, **blackish-brown cap**, **dusky-buff cheeks**, darker near bill/under eye and on throat (less pale than female Red-crested Pochard (*p. 46*), male Ruddy Duck (*p. 48*)). Summer birds have worn, pale, ragged patches on back.

VOICE Whistled, piping notes and growling note from female.

Common passage migrant and winter visitor (100,00); rare breeder in N Scotland and NW Ireland (<100 pairs, declining)

from Iceland

from N Europe and W Siberia

Nests near moorland lakes; winters at sea, mostly in big sandy bays or well offshore; rare inland in winter

IN FLIGHT, lacks white but outerwing paler, as if slightly translucent over dark sea.

♀

♂

Scoter flocks trail across the waves, rear following rise and fall of leaders in 'roller coaster' effect; look for white wing patches revealing Velvet Scoters (at least eight here!)

♀ MAY–OCT

FEMALE in summer has pale edges above; pale face patches, cheek fades whiter by winter

♀ OCT–APR

♂

Slim, pointed tail (often raised clear of water).

Ducks in flight *p. 35*

NT
VU

Eider

Somateria mollissima 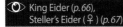 race *mollissima* race *faeroeensis* **I** 528

60–70 cm | WS 95–105 cm

King Eider (*p. 66*),
Steller's Eider (♀) (*p. 67*)

Big, long, heavy sea duck.
Wedge-shaped head, short, often cocked, tail. No common
duck much like it, but immature/summer males can confuse.
MALE black and white, salmon-pink breast; **white back**,
flank spot; black body; sea-green patch on nape. **Long white
wedge** beside long grey bill. Breast fades paler/yellower.
SUMMER MALE **piebald**, blacker face, browner breast, darker back.
Pale greenish-grey bill blends into pale line over eye and cheek.
IMMATURE MALE rather similar or very dark with whiter breast,
mottled above. (Beware farmyard Mallard types (black/brown
with white chest) – look for obvious head/bill details.) FEMALE
rich brown, **barred** not streaked; dark at distance, rufous close
up; striking crosswise barring over flanks, chequered/barred
back. Pale **brown wedge beside bill** (which has pale 'blob'-tip).

VOICE Passionate cooing "*aa-ooh*" from male and guttural
"*gak-ak-ak-ak-ak*" from female.

Locally common breeder,
particularly in N (60,000, though
declining)

Sea coasts and islands; rare inland

IN FLIGHT, MALE white in front/on top, black behind/
beneath; FEMALE hindwing dark with or without
double white line like Mallard (*p. 38*);
JUVENILE plainer, greyer brown.

IMMATURE ♂
[Apr]

♀

♂

FEMALES show considerable
variation in overall colour: rufous,
sandy or greyish

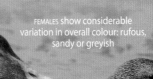

♀

Winter FEMALE is darker than
summer; females in Shetland (race
faeroeensis) are darker and more
finely barred than southern ones
(race *mollissima*); all become darker
with wear (pale edges reduced).

♀

♂ of northern race *borealis* from Arctic N Atlantic (recorded very rarely) has orange-yellow bill and small white tuft on back.

♂ of Nearctic race *dresseri* (Atlantic N America, recorded once, Ireland) has longer, rounded facial lobe; small white tuft on back; green line under eye.

British/Irish race
mollissima/faeroeensis

Northern race *borealis*

Northern race *borealis*

Nearctic race *dresseri*

♂ JUL–SEP

IMMATURE ♂
[Apr]

♂ OCT–JUN

Rare sea ducks | Eiders and goldeneye

King Eider *Somateria spectabilis*

55–63 cm | WS 87–100 cm

Rare associate of Eider (*p. 64*) flocks; beware odd Eider plumages. male immediately obvious but female difficult. MALE blacker than Eider with deeper salmon breast; **head bluer**, with **red bill**, bulging **orange frontal shield**. IMMATURE MALE like Eider but **bill reddish and frontal shield yellow**. FEMALE rusty, neatly marked with bars and chevrons. Close-up, look for tiny **'sails'** on back, 'smiling' dark gape line, shorter facial wedge against **smaller bill with dark tip** (pale on Eider).

IN FLIGHT, WINTER MALE like Eider but less white on upperparts; bill colour best clue; FEMALE as Eider (headshape only real difference).

Vagrant from Arctic: <300 records (<25 Ireland), average 5/year plus returnees, all months. Invariably with Eider flocks on coast.

EIDER

KING EIDER

STELLER'S EIDER

To identify FEMALE eiders, concentrate on the head shape, bill profile and shape of the gape.

IMMATURE ♂

IMMATURE ♂

bill colours developing

pale, plain head

curved gape line

♀

hint of a tuft

unique head and bill unmistakable

♂

NT **Barrow's Goldeneye**

Bucephala islandica

44–54 cm | WS 77–83 cm

Very like Goldeneye (*p. 56*). MALE has more black above, bold **kidney-shaped** white face patch on heavier head. FEMALE larger than Goldeneye with **heavier nape**, rounder crown, shorter bill.

GOLDENEYE

extensive white on forewing

no dark bar

♂ ♀

little white

♂

dark bar splits white

BARROW'S GOLDENEYE

GOLDENEYE

♂

rounded face patch

kidney-shaped face patch

heavier nape; smaller bill; 'rounder' crown than Goldeneye

♀

white spots

♂

black 'spur'

Vagrant from Iceland/Nearctic: <5 records (1 Ireland), Oct–Apr. Coasts, freshwater.

♀

VU **Steller's Eider** `528`

Polysticta stelleri

42–48 cm | WS 68–77 cm

Very small eider. MALE unmistakable: pale yellow-buff with black back and stern; head **greyish-white** with black neck ring, **dark nape spot**. FEMALE/IMMATURE dark brown, faintly barred; bill thick, plain grey, without 'lobes' of Eider (*p. 64*); spike-like tail.

♀

♂

1ST-YEAR ♂

IN FLIGHT, MALE boldly and distinctively patterned; FEMALE dark with two white lines on hindwing, recalling Mallard (*p. 38*), and white underwing flash.

1ST-YEAR ♂

♀

♂

Vagrant from Arctic: <20 records (Britain), Sep–Mar. Coasts.

Rare sea ducks | Scoters and Harlequin Duck

Surf Scoter *Melanitta perspicillata*

45–56 cm | WS 75–85 cm

Big, bulky scoter; dives with open wings (like Velvet Scoter
(*p.62*); Common Scoter (*p.63*) more often with wings closed).
MALE bulky-headed, **black** with big **white nape patch** and
forehead triangle. Bill swollen, boldly patched black, white
and orange. FEMALE like Velvet Scoter with double facial spots,
sometimes hint of nape patch; bill more **deeply triangular** with
hint of darker basal patch. **Wings all-dark**, so check heads, not
flapped wings, to find one, then check wings to rule out Velvet
Scoter.

FEMALE may lack pale nape patch: plain
wing unlike Velvet Scoter, requiring
patience until bird flaps or flies

IMMATURE ♂

Vagrant from N America:
>500 records (<200 Ireland), all
months. In scoter flocks. Coasts.

Harlequin Duck

Histrionicus histrionicus

38–43 cm | WS 65–68 cm

MALE blue-grey with **white patches**,
rusty flank; OTHER PLUMAGES scoter-
like, dark brown with smudgy pale
face patch, bright **white ear spot**,
all-dark wing.

Vagrant from N America/Iceland:
<20 records (Britain), Oct–Apr.
Coasts.

White-winged Scoter
Melanitta deglandi
50–57 cm | WS 78–95 cm

Vagrant from N America (race *deglandi* (1 record)) or E Asia (race *stejnegeri* (1 record)). Coasts.

Usually with Velvet Scoter (*p. 62*).
MALE *DEGLANDI* has **angular 'step'** on **pinkish-red bill** and **yellowish ridge**; white eye patch sweeps upwards. MALE *STEJNEGERI* **high basal knob** on **largely red bill**; **bulging crown** (forehead concave on Velvet Scoter; on *deglandi* sweeps up to peaked crown); eye patch upswept. FEMALE *DEGLANDI* bill **bulges**, like Surf Scoter; told by white wing panel. FEMALE *STEJNEGERI* bill flatter from crown to tip. (NB race *stejnegeri* sometimes treated as a full species, **Stejneger's Scoter**.)

race *deglandi* ♀

race *deglandi* ♂

SCOTER ID MALES: bill pattern and shape; FEMALES: head pattern and bill shape

MALES

slight bulge

yellow

VELVET

bulge

pink

WHITE-WINGED
race *deglandi*

1ST-WINTER ♂

ADULT small 'knob'

pink-red, with yellow ridge

WHITE-WINGED
race *stejnegeri*

yellow

grey-black

COMMON

yellow

BLACK

NT ## Black Scoter
Melanitta americana
44–54 cm | WS 70–85 cm

Vagrant from N America: <20 records (Britain), Sep–Apr. Coasts.

Very like Common Scoter (*p. 63*), with which generally found.
MALE has big, wide, **domed yellow patch** at base of bill.
FEMALE has **'bump' on bill base** with some yellow streaks.

♀

♂

FEMALES

slightly concave

VELVET

concave

WHITE-WINGED
race *deglandi*

straight

WHITE-WINGED
race *stejnegeri*

convex

flat

bill black

COMMON

'bump'

BLACK

some yellow

CORMORANTS, DIVERS and GREBES

Highly specialized water birds, unable properly to walk on land; divers slide onto waterside nests, grebes occasionally stand upright at the water's edge, cormorants often stand out on ground or perch. All swim and dive under from surface, reappearing far away, sometimes hard to follow.

3 cormorants: 1 widespread, 1 marine, 1 very rare.

5 divers: 2 breed locally but are widespread in winter, 1 other regular, 2 very rare.

6 grebes: 2 breed commonly, 2 are rare and restricted, scarce but more widespread in winter, 1 regular but declining migrant, 1 very rare.

CORMORANT ID   face pattern | crest shape | bill size | underparts colour | habitat

Cormorants (*pp. 74–75*) are long-bodied, long-tailed, hook-billed waterbirds; swim low with head up and tail flat on water and always dive from surface. Fly well, Cormorant occasionally soaring high, or gliding down (often several in unison) to settle with precision. Shag more strictly marine, braving roughest surf on rocky coasts, Cormorants equally at home inland and on big rivers, often in treetop roosts and breeding colonies. Both often perch with their wings widely spread.

SHAG

When diving, rolls forwards in the water; Shag more often with a forwards leap.

Cormorant and Shag often stand with wings open: may help in the digestion of large fish but probably mainly to dry feathers.

SHAG

CORMORANT

Ageing/sexing

Sexes alike; juveniles browner than adults, gaining full colours after two–three years.

CORMORANT

POSSIBLE CONFUSION GROUPS

Diving ducks (such as Red-breasted Merganser) small and slim; **grebes** much smaller, pointed bill tips; **auks** squat, dumpy, small-winged; **divers**, from smaller to similar size, have pointed bills, slimmer head/neck profile, short tails.

AUK
pp. 166–170

DIVER
pp. 76–79

CORMORANT
pp. 74–75

MERGANSER (duck)
p. 58

GREBE
pp. 80–84

DIVER ID
SUMMER PLUMAGE – distinctive: head colour | throat pattern/colour | back pattern
WINTER PLUMAGE – all much alike: size | bill shape | head/neck /flank patterns
IN FLIGHT – can be difficult: neck shape | size | wingbeats

Divers (*pp. 73, 76–79*) have dagger-like bills; webbed feet. Grebes have pointed bills; broad, flat lobes on unwebbed toes, more like Coots (*p. 257*); cormorants have all four toes webbed.

Two divers breed on Scottish lochs (Red-throated Divers fly with quacking calls, to feed on the sea; Black-throated Divers stay on big lochs with islands). All more widespread autumn to spring (Black-throated Diver scarcest of regular three; White-billed and Pacific Divers extremely rare). Red-throated Divers locally numerous but divers usually in ones and twos. All scarce inland but might linger on a large reservoir.

Ageing/sexing

Sexes alike; winter and breeding plumages differ, and juveniles resemble winter adult but are separable at close range by detailed head pattern and shape of pale feather edging/barring on back.

RED-THROATED DIVER

JUVENILE

ADULT WINTER

ADULT MOULTING FROM SUMMER INTO WINTER

ADULT SUMMER

Divers submerge from the surface, with a smooth, low, forward roll.

ADULT SUMMER

RED-THROATED DIVER

GREBE ID
SUMMER PLUMAGE – distinctive: size | bill shape | head pattern | neck colour
WINTER PLUMAGE: – size | bill shape | head pattern
Beware 'intermediate' plumages in autumn and spring

Grebes (*p. 72, 80–84*) are smaller than divers. Largest is Great Crested Grebe, widespread on lakes, large rivers, often on sea. Head pattern, dagger-like bill rule out ducks. In flight, long and slim; trailing feet; white in wing rules out divers. Takes off with run, lands with breast-first splash. Little Grebe smallest, common on lakes and rivers, scarce on sea; brown or dark, no white on foreneck. Skitters across water. Calls distinctive spring trills and less obvious whistling notes.

Slavonian Grebe (rare nester in Scotland, rare on coasts in winter), Black-necked Grebe (rare nester, scarce or rare on lakes and coasts in winter) and larger Red-necked Grebe (declining and rare, autumn and winter) all much scarcer.

Ageing/sexing

Sexes alike; winter and breeding plumages; juveniles distinctive but 1st-winter resembles winter adult, separable by smudgy head/neck patterns with hint of summer colour.

GREAT CRESTED GREBE

JUVENILE

ADULT WINTER

ADULT WINTER

Flight infrequent, low, fast, lacking manoeuvrability.

Grebes swim buoyantly and dive frequently.

ADULT SUMMER

GREAT CRESTED GREBE

71

Cormorants, divers and grebes in flight

Grebes migrate yet look inefficient fliers, low down, stretched out, with quick beats. Divers have longer wings and a more powerful progress. Cormorants are rounder-winged and have long, broad tails rather than narrow, trailing feet.

CORMORANT (*p. 75*) in flight, head extended, neck kinked; long, broad tail and wings (geese have shorter tails (see *p. 21*)), lengthy glides. May fly high over water (Shag low) or land, often in synchronized groups; can soar high up. Wings hunched/bowed, often in long glide, rolling to lose height.

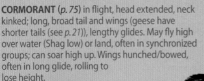

ADULT SUMMER

JUVENILE

SHAG

IMMATURE

CORMORANT

ADULT SUMMER

ADULT SUMMER

SHAG (*p. 74*) in flight like Cormorant but quicker action; usually low over sea, going round headlands/islands rather than over them. Deeper rear body, straighter neck.

ADULT

ADULT WINTER

WINTER GREBES IN FLIGHT

GREAT CRESTED GREBE
Long, thin neck, big trailing feet; large white wing patches.

RED-NECKED GREBE Much less white than Great Crested Grebe, stockier shape	**BLACK-NECKED GREBE** Long, slim wings with broad white rear edge
LITTLE GREBE Little or no white on dull brown wing	**SLAVONIAN GREBE** Rounded wings, white rear edge and shoulder

Winter grebes

GREAT CRESTED GREBE (*p. 80*)
long **pinkish bill**; distinct dark cap; **white above eye**; head shape **slightly 'horned'**; white cheeks and dark on hindneck narrow

RED-NECKED GREBE (*p. 81*)
long **yellow bill**; dark cap merges into dull white cheek below eye; **dark on hindneck broad**, smudging onto foreneck

BLACK-NECKED GREBE (*p. 82*)
short, slightly upturned bill; **steep forehead**; dark cap usually merges into white cheek creating 'comma' shape

SLAVONIAN GREBE (*p. 83*)
short, straightish bill; shallow forehead; dark cap usually very distinct from **white cheeks**

LITTLE GREBE (*p. 84*)
dull, buff and brown; darker, round cap

RED-THROATED DIVER SUMMER

typically drop-necked profile

BLACK-THROATED DIVER
SUMMER

straight, 'tube' neck

WHITE-BILLED DIVER
SUMMER

GREAT NORTHERN DIVER
SUMMER

RED-THROATED DIVER
WINTER

BLACK-THROATED DIVER
WINTER

not safely identifiable in flight

PACIFIC DIVER
WINTER

GREAT NORTHERN DIVER
WINTER

very big; long wings

very big; very heavy head/bill

WHITE-BILLED DIVER
WINTER

Winter divers

WHITE-BILLED DIVER (*p. 79*)
pale head, pale, uptilted, angled bill

GREAT NORTHERN DIVER (*p. 78*)
dark cap broken by white around eye; cap/hindneck **darker than/same tone as** back; no white flank patch

RED-THROATED DIVER (*p. 76*)
'button' eye in pale face; **cap/hindneck much paler and narrower** than other divers

BLACK-THROATED DIVER (*p. 77*)
dark cap to eye level; **cap/hindneck paler than back; white flank patch**
(cf. Pacific Diver *p. 79*)

Shag

Phalacrocorax aristotelis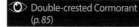

68–78 cm | WS 95–110 cm

👁 Double-crested Cormorant *(p. 85)*

Locally common coastal resident (32,000 pairs breed, 110,000 in winter); rarely inland

Similar to Cormorant; requires care, usually distinctive. Swims like Cormorant, very buoyant. Often **large flocks at sea**, often in ragged lines, thin, upright, stick-like necks below bulbous round heads. Often dives with **upward leap** (Cormorant rolls forward).

ADULT dark green-black, except **bright yellow gape** and chin (no white). In spring, **forward-curled crest** unique; **slim bill, steeper forehead** (bump) than Cormorant, rounder head, thinner neck give snaky look. JUVENILE dark brown; **whitish chin spot**, eyering; develops paler underside but little white except vent, no dark breast-band/pale belly. Legs pale, sometimes yellowish. Often worn, pale panel on wing.

VOICE Grunts and cackling alarm at nest.

IN FLIGHT, like Cormorant but quicker; usually low over sea, not high up or over land (going round headlands). Neck less kinked, wings set farther back.

Sea coasts (breeds on cliffs); rarely reservoirs/large rivers

ADULT BREEDING

JUVENILES

CORMORANT

white chin spot

SHAG

ADULT NON-BREEDING

ADULT BREEDING

brown breast

SHAG
white chin spot, thin bill

JUVENILES

CORMORANT
yellow skin around thicker bill

Cormorant

Phalacrocorax carbo races *carbo* and *sinensis* **I**

77–94 cm | WS 121–149 cm

Double-crested Cormorant (p. 85)

Big, distinctive waterbird.
Long bill; **broad wings**; **long, rounded tail**. **Stands upright**, often with **spread wings**, or more horizontal in odd, contorted poses. Swims low, **bill uptilted**; rolls into dive (Shag 'leaps'); often alone, occasionally scores in 'feeding frenzies'.

ADULT **blackish**, white chin, **white thigh**. Variable whitish crown, neck plumes. Continental and many S/E English birds white-headed in spring. ADULT WINTER white face dull, yellow skin obvious. JUVENILE black-brown, **whiter beneath** by winter, whitish chin, yellow face; later darker, or dark breast, whiter belly. OLDER IMMATURES mottled black, orange-yellow facial patch, pale bill, whitish face (Shag has less yellow, darker below eye).

VOICE Calls low, deep, guttural or cooing notes.

Common and widespread resident (14,000 pairs); and winter visitor (37,000)

from N and W Europe

Coasts, inland waters

Races *carbo* and *sinensis* ('Continental') may be difficult to assign to race; *sinensis* whiter head (dark crest) earlier in spring. Check bare skin behind gape: *carbo* angle 38°–72°; *sinensis* 65°–110°, so 'square' shape (around 90°), with white patch parallel-sided, less fan-shaped, indicates *sinensis*.

race *sinensis*

race *carbo*

ADULT

IN FLIGHT, neck extended; **long, broad tail**.

ADULT BREEDING

birds from SE England and the continent may have white heads in spring

ADULT BREEDING

ADULT NON-BREEDING

IMMATURE

variable but extensive white front

Divers in flight *p. 73*

Red-throated Diver

Gavia stellata Ⓘ 528

55–67 cm | WS 91–110 cm

Scarce and local breeder Scotland (1,300 pairs); winters at coast (17,000, Sep–Mar); rare inland

from Iceland

from Svalbard

from Scandinavia

Long, low diving bird; smallest diver but overlaps with Black-throated Diver. On water, **upright, straight neck** (Black-throated Diver more sinuous), **head and bill uptilted**, **bill tapered** to **straight upper edge**.

ADULT **dark, white breast**. Head/neck grey, fine lines on sides and nape; **narrow dark throat** widest at bottom. Bill black, eye dark red. ADULT WINTER, grey back flecked white; flanks whiter, mottled, can form rear patch as on Black-throated Diver. Breast and foreneck white, **bare white face around dark-button eye**; narrow dark cap and hindneck. JUVENILE/IMMATURE similar to adult winter but browner on foreneck, cheeks.

VOICE Loud quacking "*kwuk kwuk kwuk*" in flight in summer; summer calls include wailing "*eeaaooow*" and remarkable fast, rhythmic duetting between pairs.

Breeds on lakes, feeds at nearest coast; winters at sea, bays, estuaries

WINTER

IN FLIGHT, elongated, **narrow-winged**: long wings dark above, white beneath, narrow dark flank line; head/**bill slightly drooped**, smallish feet trailed. Wingbeats quicker, deeper than other divers.

typical 'drop-necked' flight profile

ADULT SUMMER APR–NOV

1ST-WINTER DEC–FEB

sloping forehead; white mark in front of eye

pale almost to back of neck

ADULT WINTER AUG–MAR

Black-throated Diver

Gavia arctica ⬤ Ⓘ `528`

63–75 cm | WS 100–122 cm

👁 Pacific Diver (*p. 79*)

Medium-sized diver.
Bill **dagger-shaped, horizontal** (compare Red-throated Diver).
In summer, head and neck large, almost inflated. From rear,
body narrow, neck narrower than **bulbous head** (body wider,
neck more uniformly thick on Great Northern Diver (*p. 78*)).

ADULT immaculate; grey head, blacker face, striped neck,
black throat patch. Breast white; patch of white bars on back.
ADULT WINTER dark, vaguely like huge Guillemot (*p. 166*).
Greyer nape slightly paler than back (reverse of Great
Northern Diver); dark cap to eye. Front edge of hindneck
extends as faint, dark forward point. **White rear flank patch**
usually visible. JUVENILE/IMMATURE browner, scaly, head paler,
greyer but pattern still useful; **white flank** distinctive.

VOICE Calls loud wailing scream/squeal and loud, rising,
whistling series in summer.

Rare and local breeder N Scotland
(200 pairs); scarce UK coast in
winter (500); rare inland

from
Scandinavia

Breeds on large lakes with islands;
winters offshore

IN FLIGHT, long, straight: **neck thick,
hardly drooped**; large feet trail.

WINTER

typical straight-necked
flight profile

ADULT SUMMER
FEB–OCT

1ST-WINTER
JAN–APR

cap and hindneck
paler than back

well-defined
white cheeks/
front half of neck

ADULT WINTER
OCT–MAR

white patch

77

VU Great Northern Diver

Gavia immer 528

73–88 cm | WS 122–148 cm

White-billed Diver (*p. 79*)

Biggest regular diver; see other divers. Bill **deep dagger** shape (not slim/straight/hooked); forehead often has 'bump' before crown.

ADULT **head black**; breast white. Back **chequered with white** (barred patches on Black-throated Diver (*p. 77*)). ADULT WINTER recalls Cormorant (*p. 75*) but never on dry perch; tail tiny. Bill grey/whitish, **dark upper edge** (Black-throated Diver's thinner). White eyering, throat; **cap and hindneck blacker than back** (reverse of Black-throated Diver); black half-collar. Back barred (squarer bars, less scaly, than Black-throated Diver). Flank dark. JUVENILE/IMMATURE scaly above, browner head, head/neck pattern much as adult winter.

VOICE Calls sometimes heard away from breeding range in summer, especially quick, laughing sequence; also loud wails.

Scarce winter visitor (3,000, Aug–May); few summer in far N; rare inland

from Iceland

from Greenland

Mostly on sea, in sandy bays, estuaries

IN FLIGHT, big, heavy head barely drooped, large protruding feet. Long, centrally-set wings; dark flank band. Wingbeats whippier than smaller divers, but big bill and bulk best clues.

WINTER

immatures in winter-type plumage occasionally seen in summer

1ST-WINTER JAN–APR

'bump' on forehead

cap and hindneck **darker** than back

bill thicker, less bluish than Black-throated Diver

ADULT WINTER OCT–MAR

back covered with white squares (oval patches of white bars on Black-throated Diver)

ADULT SUMMER APR–OCT

Pacific Diver *Gavia pacifica*

60–63 cm | WS 109–122 cm

Vagrant from N America: <10 records (1 Ireland), Nov–May. Coasts.

528

All plumages as Black-throated Diver (*p. 77*) but lack white rear flank. Head more rounded, steeper forehead above smaller bill. Shows slight dark 'chinstrap' and dark vent band in winter.

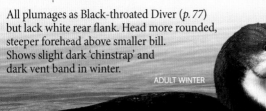

ADULT WINTER

chinstrap

no obvious flank patch

no chinstrap

ADULT WINTER

white rear flank patch

BLACK-THROATED DIVER

NT **White-billed Diver** *Gavia adamsii*

VU 77–90 cm | WS 135–150 cm

Very rare migrant from N Siberia: <400 records (<20 Ireland), most months; in N some in late spring. Mostly in far N and NW islands, very rare farther south. Coasts.

528

Massive diver, like Great Northern Diver, but bill deeper, more sharply angled up to sharp tip (Great Northern's less extreme). **Head and bill raised** like huge Red-throated Diver (*p. 76*). ADULT bill **pale yellow/ivory** against black head. ADULT WINTER/ IMMATURE **top of bill dark only at base; tip all pale.** Diffuse pale patches on rear cheek around dark cheek mark, narrow dark band on hindneck.

in winter plumage, some Great Northern Divers have a very pale bill, but the less 'upturned' shape and dark ridge and tip should distinguish them from White-billed Diver

ADULT SUMMER

GREAT NORTHERN DIVER

1ST-WINTER

1ST-SUMMER

Great Crested Grebe

Podiceps cristatus Ⓘ

46–51 cm | WS 59–73 cm

Vaguely duck-like water bird; slim neck, tailless shape; sleek or dumpy, size hard to judge. Neck withdrawn into shoulders or upright; broad-based, silvery-white (distant 'L'-shape on water). Dagger-like bill unlike any duck. Frequently dives from surface. Often in sizeable flocks. Rarely on land; cannot walk.

ADULT black crest; broad, rounded, **chestnut frill**; white face. White face and foreneck; white underside. ADULT WINTER **shiny white neck** obvious. Thin black cap and line from bill to eye, **separated by white** (solidly dark on Red-necked Grebe). Bill pinkish, dark tip. JUVENILE nondescript pale fawn, whiter chest, black-and-white stripes on head at first. IN FLIGHT, white patches at front and rear of narrow wings. Fast, direct; gangly neck; large, trailed feet drooped. Settles chest-first, feet trailing.

VOICE Summer calls loud, croaking or nasal. Chicks' persistent loud, whistling "*pli-pli-pli*" common wetland sound in summer.

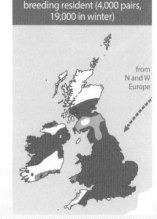

Widespread but localised breeding resident (4,000 pairs, 19,000 in winter)

from N and W Europe

Lakes, reservoirs; sea coasts outside the breeding season

JUVENILE

1ST-WINTER
AUG–MAR

thin black cap; white above eye

ADULT WINTER
AUG–MAR

ADULT SUMMER
MAR–JUL

Red-necked Grebe

Podiceps grisegena ● 530

40–46 cm | WS 55–60 cm

Similar to larger Great Crested Grebe and smaller Slavonian Grebe (p. 83). Bill heavy (slight drooped effect) with variable **yellow base**; relatively **thick neck**; eyes dark or yellow, not red. Often dives with slight 'leap', unlike smoother Great Crested Grebe. Often solitary, or one or two with other grebes.

ADULT black cap, short tuft at back. Grey face edged white, **rusty-orange neck and chest** (lacks white breast of Great Crested Grebe). Bill **yellow-and-black**. ADULT WINTER **black cap extends to eye**. Cheeks smudgy grey or duller white than Great Crested Grebe or Slavonian Grebe (smaller but can be tricky); white 'hook' on ear coverts. **Foreneck greyish** or rusty buff, chest whitest. JUVENILE bill paler, striped face. IN FLIGHT, like Great Crested Grebe but less white on innerwing.

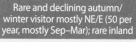

Rare and declining autumn/winter visitor mostly NE/E (50 per year, mostly Sep–Mar); rare inland

from W Europe

N American/NE Asian race *holboellii* (vagrant, 1 record (Britain): Sep) larger, with bigger bill than regularly occurring race *grisegena*.

Mainly along sea coasts, harbours; rarely reservoirs

JUVENILE
JUN–NOV

dark cap extends below eye (unlike Great Crested Grebe); cheeks dull white (Great Crested and Slavonian Grebes bright white)

ADULT WINTER
SEP–FEB

autumn adults and juveniles, in 'in between' plumages, more or less rusty on neck; juveniles retain some black and white striping on head

ADULT SUMMER
MAR–SEP

Black-necked Grebe

Podiceps nigricollis ⬤ ❶ 530

28–34 cm | WS 45–50 cm

Smallish grebe, much like Slavonian Grebe; marked seasonal changes. Buoyant on water, between long dives.

ADULT **mostly black**; only flanks coppery-red. **Drooping** golden-yellow fan behind eye. In spring (Feb/Mar) acquires yellow fans, **peaked crown**, dark head, while still white on chest and flank. ADULT WINTER similar to Slavonian Grebe, but bill **faintly upturned**, dark-tipped; steeper forehead, high crown peaked in middle; **deeper black cap**. Dark crown/pale cheek contrast can be sharp, but typically cheeks dusky, whiter 'hook' on rear cheek; **broad dark nape**, grey foreneck (silky white on Slavonian Grebe: but see bigger Red-necked Grebe (*p. 81*)). Cherry-red eyes catch sun at remarkably long range. JUVENILE striped on head; in winter loses stripes but retains orange-buff wash over face/neck. IN FLIGHT, white hindwing line extends to outer half but no 'shoulder' spot as on Slavonian Grebe.

VOICE Weak trills and rising whistles; silent in winter.

Rare, local, erratic breeder (50 pairs), scarce migrant and winter visitor (130 birds per year)

from
S Scandinavia
and
E Europe

Breeds on freshwater lakes, winters on coast and a few lakes/reservoirs

striped face

JUVENILE

ADULT SUMMER
APR–OCT

TRANSITIONAL FROM SUMMER TO
WINTER PLUMAGE

BLACK-NECKED
GREBE

SLAVONIAN
GREBE

BLACK-NECKED GREBE

dark bill
slightly upturned

often shows hint
of brown on face
and neck

ADULT/1ST-WINTER
SEP–APR

Slavonian Grebe

Podiceps auritus ● ❶ **530**

31–38 cm | WS 46–55 cm

Medium-sized grebe with marked seasonal changes in plumage: readily identified in summer, more tricky in winter.

ADULT underparts and **neck deep rusty-red**. Head black with broad, flat or raised wedge of golden-yellow each side. Bill small, **straight**, dark with pale tip (bigger and yellow-based on Red-necked Grebe (*p. 81*)). ADULT WINTER similar to Black-necked Grebe but fairly low crown, straight bill. Blackish above, whitish below. Cap black, peak at rear, **sharply defined** against white face (slight 'hook' at back of cap, white cheeks **almost meet on nape**). Whitish mark ahead of cherry-red eye. Bill grey; dark band, whiter tip useful in good light, even at long range. JUVENILE striped head; stripes disappear during winter leaving dusky marks on face, resembling Black-necked Grebe.
IN FLIGHT, white hindwing patch, restricted to inner half; usually small whitish 'shoulder' spot.

VOICE Rather insignificant whinnies in summer.

Scarce winter visitor/migrant (1,100 birds per year); very rare breeder in N (20 pairs)

from Iceland

from NE Europe

Breeds on freshwater lakes, winters around coast (harbours, estuaries)

striped head

JUVENILE

ADULT SUMMER
MAR—JUL

high crown, more black on face

flatter crown, more white on face

COMPARISON OF 'BLACK-AND-WHITE' GREBES IN WINTER PLUMAGE

'fuzzy'

sharp contrast

BLACK-NECKED GREBE

SLAVONIAN GREBE

pale area

BLACK-NECKED GREBE

bill straight, **pale tip**

SLAVONIAN GREBE

note pink line from bill to eye

ADULT/1ST-WINTER
JUL—MAR

Little Grebe (Dabchick)

Tachybaptus ruficollis Ⓘ

23–29 cm | WS 40–45 cm

◑ Pied-billed Grebe

Widespread and locally common resident (7,500 breeding pairs) and winter visitor (16,000)

Smallest, brownest, roundest and most dumpy grebe, with cork-like buoyancy. Often sits on water's edge, occasionally stands upright on short legs. Compare with Black-necked Grebe (*p. 82*); winter/juvenile head pattern can be contrasty, but brown/buff not black/white.

ADULT **very dark**. Blackish cap, back and breast; **chestnut-red face**; pale yellow spot at base of short bill. Flank feathers spread to reveal rich orange-buff. ADULT WINTER paler, browner, more contrast between dark back and buff flanks and dark cap and pale cheeks/whitish throat (less black-and-white than other small grebes (*pp. 82–83*). Pale bill with **whitish basal spot**. JUVENILE dark face and cap, striped cheeks; short, stout bill unlike other small grebes. IN FLIGHT, wings dull dark brown; longer necked and trailing dark feet when skittering across water.

VOICE Loud, sudden whinnying trill – characteristic waterside sound in summer. Various short, thin, puzzling whistles from juveniles. Short pipes and trills in autumn/winter.

Breeds on lakes and rivers; winters on coast and lakes

JUVENILE

JUVENILE (moulting)

often shows strong contrast on head, but brown/buff, not black/white

ADULT/1ST-WINTER SEP–MAR

ADULT SUMMER APR–SEP

Double-crested Cormorant *Phalacrocorax auritus*

70–90 cm | WS 95–130 cm

Vagrant from N America:
1 record (Britain), Dec.
Freshwater.

Very like Cormorant (*p. 75*) and difficult to identify in immature/winter plumages. Size, bill shape between Cormorant and Shag (*p. 74*); rather long tail.
ADULT has orange facial skin but **no white**. IMMATURE has **orange face**, breast paler than belly, reverse of Cormorant.

CORMORANT

DOUBLE-CRESTED CORMORANT

SHAG

bare patch broad and rounded beneath chin

stripe of pale skin in front of eye

IMMATURE

ADULT WINTER

Pied-billed Grebe *Podilymbus podiceps*

31–38 cm | WS 45–62 cm

Vagrant from N America:
<50 records (<20 Ireland), most months. Freshwater.

Medium-small grebe with large, 'frog-like' head, deep, sharp, arched bill. Dark brown, with darker crown, whitish stern.
ADULT has black chin and white bill with **vertical black band**.
ADULT WINTER/IMMATURE have paler throat, bill dull grey, lacking the sharp black band.

1ST-WINTER

ADULT SUMMER

SEABIRDS

Seabirds include the shearwaters and petrels and the Gannet, which are covered below, as well as cormorants, auks, gulls, terns and skuas, which are treated in separate sections. Some of these are much more strictly marine than others, but those introduced below are all true seabirds, only rarely driven inland by gales. Sexes alike; age groups identifiable in Gannet.

16 shearwaters and petrels (plus 2 identified only to species pair/group): 4 breed and are widespread, 4 regular migrants (2 from Southern Hemisphere), others rare or very/extremely rare.

1 gannet: a very local breeder but wanders widely around coasts.

SHEARWATER ID size and shape | upperpart colour | underpart colour | head pattern
SMALL PETREL ID rump pattern | upper/underwing pattern | tail shape | wing shape

Gannet

Gannets (*pp. 88–89*) are big, long-winged and easily seen from a great distance over the sea. They fly magnificently in gales and dive to feed from a height, or go in at an angle, from the air. Gannets breed in a few big colonies, mostly on islands, but are widespread offshore.

GANNET

Other species

Many birds live on or close to the sea for some part of their lives. Gulls, terns, skuas, cormorants, divers and grebes, as well as many ducks and geese, can all be seen on the sea, while many waders fly over it. Almost anything can be seen flying over the sea, from migrant swallows to birds of prey: so not every bird you see over the waves will necessarily be a 'seabird'.

Rare seabirds

2 albatrosses; 2 frigatebirds; 1 tropicbird
True seabirds roam widely over the oceans and inevitably some travel far from their normal geographical range. The chance of seeing a rare seabird is very small, but always there. The main problem in identifying them is often that they fly by once and disappear, never to be seen again.

Ageing/sexing

Sexes alike. Juveniles (early autumn) very dark; in next year most become paler with whiter belly; over subsequent years, variable rate of progress through chequered stages to adulthood.

Shearwaters and petrels

Large group worldwide, 'tubenoses', with tubular nostrils to excrete excess salt and exploit highly developed sense of smell, vary from giant albatrosses to tiny sea-going petrels.

The **Fulmar** is most widespread, easiest to see by day at cliff-ledge nests, and most gull-like because of grey and white colouring.

Shearwaters (*pp. 91–95*) are slender-winged, sea-going, usually seen low over the water. Manx Shearwater breeds around UK, coming to land only at night, but is seen widely around coast or from ships. A black-and-white, long-winged cross-shape low over the sea, it tilts from wingtip to wingtip, sometimes in long lines, or feeding in irregular packs.

Other shearwaters are rare. Balearic Shearwater, a threatened Mediterranean bird, feeds in the English Channel in late summer. Sooty Shearwater is big and dark (recalling a skua); Cory's Shearwater, brown and white, is more gull-like, with a languid, rolling action in calm weather but high, steeply banking, bounding climbs in gales. Great Shearwater is similar but more contrasted, less likely from the coast.

Petrels (*pp. 96–97, 100–101*) are smaller seabirds. Two are regular, others rare, best sought on boat trips or from exposed headlands. Leach's Petrels breed on remote islands, are generally scarce at sea, but come close inshore during autumn gales. Storm Petrels breed more widely and likewise come to land only at night, but are generally less frequent from southern coasts, more likely from ships/long-distance ferries. Search constantly with binoculars, low over waves.

DISTANT SHEARWATERS

Fulmar – good baseline for comparison/generally most familiar

Cory's/Great Shearwaters – large, slim-winged, relaxed action

Fulmar – big head/tail

Sooty Shearwater – dark, slim-winged, heavy-bellied

Manx, Balearic Shearwaters – small; narrow wings, fast action

LARGE

FULMAR (default)

MEDIUM

SMALL

CORY'S SHEARWATER

FULMAR

SOOTY SHEARWATER

MANX SHEARWATER

Gulls fairly bowed wings, round tail, relaxed flight

Fulmar white head/grey tail, stiff wings, flap-and-glide

Storm petrels tiny, dark, erratic flight

STORM PETREL

See also skuas (*p. 158*), terns (*p. 142*)

GREAT BLACK-BACKED GULL

FULMAR

RESTING SHEARWATERS

Shearwaters will rest on the sea (especially Fulmar) where they may initially be thought to be gulls – apart from the 'tubenose' diagnostic of the group, shearwaters generally have closed wings that are barely longer than their tail.

87

Gannets moult wing feathers semi-continuously and three generations of feathers may be seen at once: moult may even be asymmetrical. Individuals develop at different rates, so plumages are very variable and ageing difficult.

JUVENILE/1ST YEAR (fledging to following April or May)
A few one-year-olds as dark as juveniles, even in July.

brown

no dark feathers

ADULT

trailing edge all white

ADULT (4–5 years+)
Almost half at the end of their 4th year already look adult; very few retain dark feathers in their 5th year.

TYPICAL 1-YEAR-OLD
Some remain this dark well into second year.

white

dark feathers on back

3RD-YEAR
Typically has a few dark secondaries (not all black) and one or two dark tail feathers, some small black marks on back/scapulars.

LATE 1ST-YEAR OR 2ND-YEAR
Some second years more boldly chequered with white.

trailing edge and scapulars with dark marks

Less advanced 3rd years have 'piano key' hindwing, variable black-and-white patches on back, black tail feathers; more advanced individuals, close to adult.

Gannet

Morus bassanus ● Ⅰ

85–97 cm | WS 170–192 cm

Big, elegant, dramatic seabird with heavy head, sharp bill, slim pointed tail, long wings. Best northern hemisphere substitute for albatrosses in strong wind.

◐ Black-browed Albatross (*p. 98*); possibly other seabirds – see *p. 86*

ADULT **gleaming white**, **black wingtips**: easy even at great range. Head golden-buff or yellowish. Bill dagger-like. JUVENILE dark, copious white spots give grizzled greyish look. Older IMMATURES **chequered with black and white patches**: striking two- to three-year-old piebald with yellow head. Near-adults have dark feathers on trailing edge, dark central tail, otherwise like adult. IN FLIGHT, flies steadily, singly or in lines, well above sea, or glides close to waves; periodically circles and **plunges**. Flight is controlled even in gale: long glides, steep banks; head/neck extended, held higher and bigger than **spiky tail**. Immature gulls (especially Great Black-backed Gull (*p. 128*)) may confuse, but wings more bowed, head and tail short, different rhythm.

VOICE Calls at colony have strange, repetitive, mechanical effect in constant guttural chorus.

Locally abundant resident (260,000 pairs, including 33,000 in Ireland (breeds Jan–Oct), plus many non-breeders); common summer/autumn migrant; thinly spread around coast all year

At sea/offshore; breeds at scattered colonies, most on islands

splashes from plunge-diving Gannets can be visible at a great distance

Gannets swim high in the water, big and white, pointed at both ends: ADULT like a distant swan unexpectedly at sea (for JUVENILE on water – see *p. 86*).

A Gannet will periodically circle and then plunge vertically, entering the water with a splash. Closer to the surface, it may slip in at an angle, with little or no splash.

EN Fulmar

Fulmarus glacialis ● ● race *glacialis*[1]
see p.525

43–52 cm | WS 101–117 cm

Gull-like but **cannot stand** or walk, sitting or shuffling at best. Evocative seabird, around coastal cliffs much of year. On cliffs, white 'blobs' scattered on broad, grassy ledges. On sea, swims high in water, head and tail up, leaning forward.

Breeding pairs are more loosely scattered than most cliff-nesting seabirds.

Locally common breeder (540,000 pairs, including 39,000 in Ireland, Nov–Aug); present all year, widely offshore

Sexes alike; no seasonal changes. Pale **grey and white**. Grey upperwing, dusky tips (**no black**), whitish patch beyond joint. Plain **grey rump and tail** (unlike any gull). Head white or yellowish-white, **dark eye patch**; bill stubby. Underwing white with **dark rim** (less marked on northern birds – *see inset*). IN FLIGHT, wings rather stiff, slightly whippy beats, held quite straight (angled in glides on clifftop air currents). Masterful glides over sea in strong winds; heavy in flat calm.

VOICE Tuneless, loud, throaty, choking, cackling notes from ledge.

Offshore/at sea; breeds on coastal cliffs (few inland in N)

no black on wingtip

pale patch

Scarce northern birds darker overall, smoky brownish-grey with pale wing patches more striking.

thickset; long, straight wings

swims high, tail up

NT Sooty Shearwater

Puffinus griseus **1** **529**

40–50 cm | WS 93–106 cm

Balearic Shearwater (*p. 95*); possibly other seabirds – see *p. 86*

Only likely to be seen in flight. Looks angular, dynamic, all-black at long range (see Arctic Skua (*p. 158*)). Quite heavy, long-bodied; long, sharp, narrow wings set centrally, often held angled at bend (like half-size juvenile Gannet (*p. 89*)).

Large, pot-bellied, **narrow-winged, dark** smoky-brown shearwater with slightly paler hindwing and largely **pale underwing** that gives silvery-whitish flash in good light: beware others in silhouette and especially dark Balearic Shearwater (*p. 95*) (smaller with shorter, blunter wings; shorter tail; faster flight action) and dark skuas (*pp. 156–164*).

Scarce but regular migrant Jul–Sep (few thousands per year)

from/to S Atlantic

Offshore/at sea, often most numerous North Sea, off headlands

Heavy-bellied, narrow winged. In stronger wind, few flaps low down between long, high, curving glides, belly to wind.

stout body

all-dark above

pale underwing band

in calm winds, flies low; 3–7 quick, stiff-winged flaps between glides of 3–5 seconds

pale underwing band

sexes and age groups look alike, as in other shearwaters

GREAT SHEARWATER

white above tail

blackish cap and bill

pale head and bill

GREAT SHEARWATER

dark marks on underwing

CORY'S SHEARWATER

all-white underwing

two dark spots

more distinct 'W' effect across wings than Cory's Shearwater

SCOPOLI'S SHEARWATER

single dark spot

white along inner webs of primaries

Great Shearwater
Puffinus gravis
43–51 cm | WS 105–122 cm

At sea/offshore

Rare summer migrant (50–100 per year, most in SW, sporadically hundreds or thousands)

Big shearwater: usually far out at sea. Exclude Fulmar (*p. 90*), Cory's Shearwater and smaller, faded Manx Shearwater (*p. 95*) (white rump sides can give illusory patch over tail).
Dark brown and white, sharp (blackish at distance). White patch above tail more obvious than almost all Cory's; beneath, dark belly/wingpit patches may be visible – best way to rule out Cory's Shearwater. Moulting birds in autumn show ragged whitish midwing. IN FLIGHT, wingbeats stiffer, quicker than Cory's Shearwater (recalls Fulmar) but equally variable

from/to S Atlantic

Cory's Shearwater Ⓘ
Calonectris borealis
50–56 cm | WS 118–126 cm

At sea/offshore

Rare/scarce (erratic) migrant in late summer/autumn, most in SW (usually few, occasionally 100s)

529

Big (size of Lesser Black-backed Gull (*p. 126*)), relaxed, heavy-bodied shearwater. Brown and white. Pale back/dark wingtip, slight dark band across innerwing creates weak 'W'. Tail narrow (unlike gulls), whitish marks above base. **Head dull**, more or less hooded; **bill thick, pale yellow** (good mark against dark water). Underside clean white; underwing white with thick dark hind edge and tip. IN FLIGHT, lethargic in calm, three or four slow, even, shallow downbeats (often as bird turns, giving weaving effect) between glides on **bowed wings**. Wind induces more active flight, in gale **high, towering climbs**. Juvenile Gannet (*p. 86*) bigger, longer, sharper bill and tail.

from/to Macaronesia

Scopoli's Shearwater *Calonectris diomedea*
44–49 cm | WS 117–135 cm

Vagrant from Mediterranean: <5 records (Britain), Jul–Aug. At sea.

Like Cory's Shearwater but more distinct 'W' effect across upperwing and typically less solid black wingtip beneath, with **white 'fingers' along inner webs of primaries** usually more distinct; **single dark spot on white primary coverts** beneath wing (two on Cory's Shearwater).

GREAT SHEARWATER

CORY'S SHEARWATER

Balearic Shearwaters sometimes associate with Manx flocks.

Shearwaters dive for food and sit on the sea in rafts, Manx Shearwaters are often offshore near breeding colonies in the evening.

MANX SHEARWATER

little/no foot projection

blackish upperside

feet protrude

white 'hook' behind cheek

dark flank

white flank mark

BALEARIC SHEARWATER

uniformly brown above

thick bill, bulging tip

dull underparts, dark vent

heavy build

BALEARIC SHEARWATER

white vent

white belly

dark mark

diagonal band to dark patch on hindwing

MANX SHEARWATER

brown vent

faint pale 'hook'

feet protrude

dark flank bar typical

slim bill underwing clean white

white over eye

often silvery hindwing

tiny bill

clean white below

MACARONESIAN (BAROLO) SHEARWATER

YELKOUAN SHEARWATER

Manx Shearwater
Puffinus puffinus ● ● Ⓘ 529

30–35 cm | WS 71–83 cm

Far the commonest
shearwater. Smallish, slim,
tapered body; stiff wings.

Offshore/at sea; breeds on
offshore islands in N and W
(300,000–370,000 pairs, including
37,000 in Ireland)

Locally abundant breeder;
common migrant around coast

Blackish (fades browner), **white below**. Dark cap, white lower
face; white flanks show beside rump. IN FLIGHT, narrow wings and
long body give dark cross-shape, low over water: **alternates black
and white** as bird banks over. Wingbeats **quick, flicked, between
glides** – in wind, almost all glides, with higher, banking turns
on wingtip. On migration, groups/long, thin lines; in summer,
near colonies (visited at night), evening gatherings offshore, often
settling on water.

VOICE Chorus of guttural croaks, laughing notes and deep
cooing calls at colony at night

VU Yelkouan Shearwater *Puffinus yelkouan*

30–35 cm | WS 70–84 cm

Vagrant from Mediterranean:
1 record (Britain), Jul. Offshore. 529

Small shearwater; slender form, appearance more like Manx than drabber Balearic Shearwater, but
plumage features variable. Flank bar, underwing diagonal, dark vent, blurred neck sides helpful.

CR Balearic Shearwater
CR
Puffinus mauretanicus ● Ⓘ

34–39 cm | WS 78–90 cm

Offshore/at sea

Rare: summer/autumn migrant;
non-breeding summer visitor in S

Highly threatened
Mediterranean equivalent of Manx Shearwater; migrates to
feed in Biscay/English Channel in late summer.

Like **thickset, browner** Manx Shearwater, **dusky brownish
beneath**, dark under tail; bill grey. IN FLIGHT, fast, with quick
wingbeats, looks a little dumpier than Manx Shearwater with
heavy belly, shorter tail and **projecting toes**. Sooty Shearwater
(*p. 91*) bigger, with longer, slender, angled wings.

from/to
Mediterranean

Macaronesian (Barolo) Shearwater *Puffinus baroli*

25–30 cm | WS 58–67 cm

Vagrant from Atlantic islands:
<100 records (<25 Ireland), May–
Sep. Offshore; occasionally in
Manx Shearwater colonies.

Small, squat shearwater. Black and white; black cap above eye,
leaving **white, disk-like face**. Smaller, shorter-winged than Manx
Shearwater; may show whitish bar across rear wing, or silvery hindwing. IN FLIGHT, clearly a
shearwater (but see Razorbill (*p. 167*)), but **more wingbeats, shorter glides** than Manx; bowed
wings may resemble Common Sandpiper (*p. 211*). May settle briefly with raised wings.

VOICE Higher than Manx Shearwater: penetrating, rhythmic "*pi-pi-pi-poo, pi-poo*".

MANX SHEARWATER

BALEARIC SHEARWATER

Rare Storm Petrels (p. 101)

STORM PETRELS

pale upperwing band

dusky
underwing

forked
tail

LEACH'S PETREL

white
bar

square/
round tail

square tail;
projecting toes

STORM PETREL

plain
upperwing

pale
upperwing
band

WILSON'S PETREL

STORM PETREL

white
bar

dark
underwing

WILSON'S PETREL

yellow
webs

Leach's Petrel

Oceanodroma leucorhoa

18–21 cm | WS 43–48 cm

Offshore/at sea; breeds at a few colonies in far N and W, May–Sep (48,000 pairs)

Scarce and very local summer visitor; scarce autumn migrant

Breeding sites more far-flung than those of Storm Petrel, but more likely inland or blown inshore after autumn gale.

Most likely to be seen IN FLIGHT. Sooty brown, **paler band across innerwing** reaches front edge (brightest, greyest on juveniles). **White rump** relatively small (rarely absent), often broken by central dark band (sometimes just smaller notch). Upperwing band often obvious; **underwing all-dark**. Bigger than Storm Petrel. **Wings long, pushed forward and angled**; tail forked or notched (hard to see); tail shape/rump patterns very variable. Flight erratic, sudden turns or rising twists. When feeding, stalls or hangs into wind, foot-patters; in gales may patter along beach.

VOICE Visits nesting burrow at night, when gives a long, high-pitched purring, punctuated by higher double note.

Storm Petrel

Hydrobates pelagicus

15–16 cm | WS 37–41 cm

At sea/offshore; breeds on islands in N and W, May–Sep (100,000 pairs in Ireland, 26,000 in UK)

Locally common summer visitor; scarce migrant; very few in winter

Tiny, delicate, martin-like seabird with white rump.

Most likely to be seen IN FLIGHT. Smoky brown-black, except **bold white rump** wrapping around each side. Weak, fine pale wingbar above (on juvenile) and broad **white band along underwing** (key feature). Wings curve back, like broad House Martin (*p. 343*) with rounder tips; tail **wide and rounded**. Easy, smooth, rolling, swooping, twirling action depending on circumstance; often seen from ships, flying over or beside wake or more directly alongside. More likely than Leach's Petrel from headlands in summer, near breeding areas, usually well offshore but also from ferries.

VOICE Visits nesting burrow at night, when gives prolonged, slightly squeaky, rolling purr, punctuated by short, deeper note.

Wilson's Petrel *Oceanites oceanicus*

16–18·5 cm | WS 38–42 cm

Very rare migrant from Southern Oceans: >600 records (>250 Ireland), Jul–Oct. Mostly in the SW. Offshore/at sea.

Only likely to be seen IN FLIGHT. Mixes characters of Storm and Leach's Petrels, with **round** or concave tail (slightly 'dished' so raised sides give concave effect), **wide grey upperwing band** not quite reaching leading edge (does so on Leach's Petrel); **all-dark underwing** and big, broad, **wrap-around white rump**. Long legs trail beyond tail (can be withdrawn, so beware). Larger than Storm Petrel; wider, paddle-shaped wings, smoothly rounded on leading edge, tapering back to point in direct flight; trailing edge straighter than on Leach's Petrel. Flight Swallow-like and low, bouncing, skipping feeding flight with wings raised. Variation in size influences flight action. **Yellow webs between toes**, usually show best in photographs and unlikely to be seen well in the field.

Rare seabirds | Albatrosses, frigatebirds, tropicbirds

Watching seabirds from headlands, especially during strong winds, can be exciting. Rare birds may appear almost anywhere but are, naturally, unpredictable: a 'once in a lifetime' rarity may suddenly appear and be gone within minutes, never to be seen again. A disciplined assessment of all features – size, shape, flight action, plumage patterns – has to be attempted if possible!

Gannet (p. 89) to scale

NT **Black-browed Albatross**

Thalassarche melanophris

80–95 cm | WS 200–235 cm

Only likely flying over sea. Bigger than Gannet (*p. 89*); stout-billed, round-headed, **square-tailed** (like giant Fulmar (*p. 90*)); very long, slender wings. White with black back/upperwings and **dusky tail** (check immature Gannet, adult Great Black-backed Gull (*p. 128*)). Underwing crucial: **broad white band, narrow black trailing edge, broader black leading edge.** Bill yellow/orange. Black eyebrow. IMMATURES darker bill tip, greyish collar, dusky underwing masking pattern.

Vagrant from Southern Oceans: <50 records (15 Ireland), most months. Offshore/islands.

dark tail-band (unlike Great Black-backed Gull)

ADULT

broad black leading edge to underwing

BLACK-BROWED ALBATROSS

IMMATURE

ADULT

extent of white on underwing increases with age

dark bill tip

EN **(Atlantic) Yellow-nosed Albatross**

Thalassarche chlororhynchos

90 cm | WS 200–210 cm

Albatross shape/actions; look for **black bill with a yellow stripe on ridge** and **narrow black margins to the underwing.**

Vagrant from Southern Oceans (1 record (Britain): Jun; on coast). Usually at sea

blackish bill

ADULT

narrow black leading edge to underwing

(ATLANTIC) YELLOW-NOSED ALBATROSS

Magnificent Frigatebird
Fregata magnificens
90–114 cm | WS 215–245 cm

Absolutely lives up to its name: fantastic, huge, long-winged seabird with **long forked tail** (much more extreme than a kite's; may form single thick spike); long, hooked bill. MALE **black** with **red throat sac**. FEMALE **white chest**; IMMATURE **whitish on head**. Flies with **angled wings**; able to soar to great height over sea or adjacent land, or chase other birds/flying fish over waves.

Vagrant from America: <10 records (<5 Ireland), Jun–Dec. Most on coast but storm-driven inland.

VU Ascension Frigatebird
Fregata aquila
85–105 cm | WS 205–230 cm

Very similar to Magnificent Frigatebird and only told by subtle differences; the two species practically indistinguishable at sea. JUVENILE (both British records) has white on belly that just extends onto inner part of underwing (white restricted to belly on Magnificent Frigatebird).

Vagrant from South Atlantic: <5 records (Britain), Jul. On coast.

Red-billed Tropicbird
Phaethon aethereus
45–50 cm (plus streamers of 46–56 cm) | WS 100–115 cm

Like large, stocky tern (*pp. 144–152*) with **thick red bill**, **very long, flexible, central tail spike**. White upperwings with dark bars; **black on wingtips**.

Vagrant from tropical seas: <10 records (Britain), Mar–Sep. Coast/offshore.

ADULT ♂

sooty brown-black

MAGNIFICENT FRIGATEBIRD

whitish head and belly

black underwing

JUVENILE

JUVENILE

white belly patch expands onto underwing

ASCENSION FRIGATEBIRD

white plumage   ADULT

black outerwing wedge

RED-BILLED TROPICBIRD

99

Rare seabirds | Petrels and storm petrels

More than 50 'Soft-plumaged Petrels' recorded in British and Irish waters; was split into three species (**Soft-plumaged Petrel** *Pterodroma mollis* (Southern Ocean), **Fea's Petrel** *P. feae* (Cape Verde and the Desertas Islands) and **Zino's Petrel** *P. madeira* (Madeira)). Only a few were identified (all as Fea's Petrel), but this itself is now split into **Fea's Petrel** and **Desertas Petrel** *P. deserta*. **Zino's Petrel** is smallest overall; bill shape like small Fulmar's; **Fea's Petrel** bill looks stout, deeper; **Desertas Petrel** deepest; differences both in length and depth less than 3 mm, near-impossible unless trapped. Records are referred to as Fea's/Desertas Petrels.

l to r: **Desertas, Fea's and Zino's Petrels**

white stripe

NT Fea's Petrel 529

Pterodroma feae

33–36 cm | WS 86–94 cm

A shearwater-like bird with fast, sweeping, gliding flight, angled wings. Looks dark grey and white, with **subtle dark 'W' across upperwings**, light **grey rump/tail**, dusky breast-side smudge. Look for **dark eye patch** and thick black bill.

Vagrant from Atlantic islands: <10 records, plus <100 (most Ireland) not specifically identified, Aug–Sep. Offshore.

Fulmar (p. 90) to scale

dusky above

dark around eye

big, stout, pale-headed

FEA'S PETREL

EN Capped Petrel

Pterodroma hasitata

40 cm | WS 98–105 cm

Only likely to be seen in flight, out to sea. Large petrel with white forehead, **black cap/nape** above full **white collar**, **white rump; underwing white with black diagonal bar and trailing edge.**

Vagrant from Caribbean: <5 records (Britain,: Mar (1850), Dec (tideline corpse).

white collar

CAPPED PETREL

black stripe on underwing

EN Frigate Petrel 529

(White-faced Storm Petrel)

Pelagodroma marina

20 cm | WS 41–44 cm

Grey, black and white storm petrel with **white underside, dark cap and mask, wide, paddle-shaped wings.**

Vagrant from S Atlantic: 1 historical record (Britain), Jan.

tiny; greyish

dark cap, black mask

FRIGATE PETREL

Madeiran Storm Petrel 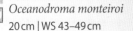 `529`
Oceanodroma castro

NT ## Cape Verde Storm Petrel
Oceanodroma jabejabe

VU ## Monteiro's Storm Petrel
VU *Oceanodroma monteiroi*

20 cm | WS 43–49 cm

Like Leach's Petrel (*p. 97*); tail less notched, **white rump narrow, 'U'-shaped**; feet do not project beyond tail. Upperwing bands short of front edge; less elegant feeding actions than Leach's – head-up, wings fanned, tail spread.

NT ## Swinhoe's Petrel

Oceanodroma monorhis

18–21 cm | WS 45–48 cm

Dark-brown petrel; size, shape as Leach's Petrel (*p. 97*); **white outer primary shafts**. Most trapped ashore, identified by biometrics/ DNA testing. At sea, hard to separate from other dark-rumped petrels, including rare dark-rumped Leach's.

Vagrant from NW Pacific: <10 records (<5 Ireland), Jul–Aug. All but one tape-lured and trapped; other unidentified *Oceanodroma* petrels recorded spring, summer, autumn.

Black-bellied Storm Petrel

Fregetta tropica
White-bellied Storm Petrel

Fregetta grallaria

20 cm | WS 46 cm

Small petrels with dashing, shearing flight. **White rump joins white underside and underwing**. Black (or smudgy) belly stripe indicates Black-bellied Storm Petrel; white belly could be either species. Black-bellied has larger hood than White-bellied.

Vagrant from S Atlantic: 1 record (Britain), Sep (not identified to species).

Madeiran, Cape Verde and Monteiro's Storm Petrels are now treated as separate species, based on breeding seasons, moult and detailed morphological differences; identification in the field not yet possible.

Vagrant from Atlantic islands: <5 records not specifically identified (1 Ireland), Jul–Sep. At sea.

MADEIRAN STORM PETREL (GROUP)

square tail

short pale upperwing band

dark underwing

Leach's Petrel (*p. 97*)

rump usually pale

long pale upperwing band

forked tail

forked tail

pale primary marks absent

SWINHOE'S PETREL

pale primary marks

plain upperwing

white underside with or without dark stripe

BLACK-BELLIED STORM PETREL

A species pair that can be near-impossible to identify: the only British record is undoubtedly one or the other, but it was not possible to determine which.

GULLS and TERNS

Water/waterside birds, web-footed, long-winged, rather short-legged; only gulls agile on foot.
Sexes alike, but summer, winter and several immature plumages differ.
26 gulls, (several distinct races): 7 breed; 19 migrants / winter visitors – 6 regular; 13 rare / vagrant.
18 terns: 5 breed; 13 summer / passage migrants – 1 regular, 12 rare / vagrant.

GULL ID   time of year | size | leg length | bill shape | bill and leg colour | back colour |
head pattern | detailed wing/wingtip pattern | age and the effects of moult

Gulls (pp. 106–141)

Some are adaptable and opportunistic; gulls of some kind
are likely almost anywhere, ranging over all kinds of open
countryside, even onto high peaks in summer. Common
species – Black-headed, Common, Lesser Black-backed, Herring
and Great Black-backed Gulls – are associated with shores of
mud, sand and rocks, harbours, playing fields, meadows, car
parks, and watery places inland, including reservoirs on which
thousands gather to roost.

Eight have dark hoods in breeding plumage, others are white-
headed from January to August. 'Hooded' gulls lose most of the
head colour, while white-headed ones become streaky-headed,
in non-breeding plumage. Breeding plumage can be acquired
in mid-winter and lost in late summer. Smaller 'hooded' species
generally breed on marshes; larger white-headed gulls tend to
nest on cliffs and islands, increasingly on roofs.

Kittiwakes are marine, breeding on coastal cliffs, and ledges (not
roofs or chimneys) on seaside buildings; flocks rest on beaches
in summer.

Gull ageing/sexing

Sexes are alike but male gulls
have larger heads and bills
than females (and in some
different body lengths affect
the wingtip projection beyond
the tail). There is a progression
from juvenile to adult through
intermediate plumages that
become increasingly easy to
identify. Smaller species may
become mature within two
years, larger ones in four or five
years (see *pp. 104–105*).

Possible confusion species

Immature gulls could be
confused with skuas (*p. 158*).

TERN ID   size / structure | bill shape / colour | head pattern

Terns (pp. 142–155)

Most are grey-and-white, black-capped '**sea terns**' or duskier,
shorter-tailed '**marsh terns**'. **Sea terns** dive from the air for
food and are most common on the coast; some are migrants
at inland waters. Common Terns also breed inland (where they
dive infrequently). **Marsh terns** include Black Tern, a frequent
migrant, and two rarities, all dip-feeders, flying into
the wind, picking from the surface,
rarely properly diving.

'MARSH TERNS': short bill,
broad wings, notched tail

BLACK TERN

COMMON TERN
Bill to tail length: 31–35 cm
Weight: 110–140 g

'SEA TERNS': long bill,
narrow wings, deep tail fork

COMMON TERN

Tern ageing/sexing

Sexes alike; summer, winter
and juvenile plumages differ;
fully mature in two to three
years. Ageing after juvenile
can be difficult or impossible
due to a complex moult
strategy that has individuals in
overlapping plumage types.

HERRING GULL
JUVENILE MOULTING
INTO 1ST-WINTER

uppertail coverts
tail
rump
tail-band
lower back
back
nape
crown
scapulars
lesser coverts
median coverts
greater coverts
tertials
(slide forward underneath scapulars as wing is straightened)
secondaries
P1 P2 P3 P4 P5 P6 P7 P8 P9 P10
alula
primary coverts
primaries (10)

HERRING GULL
ADULT SUMMER

Primaries are moulted in sequence, P1 to P10; these numbers help describe patterns with precision

trailing edge

Notch on trailing edge shows where innermost primaries (P1 and P2) have been shed, at the onset of moult. (NB only one primary (P1) shed on left wing.)

P3 P4 P5 P6 P7 P8 P9 P10

'mirror'
primary tip

wingtip projection
A: beyond tertials
B: beyond tail

primaries
tertials
scapulars
A
B
tail
vent/undertail coverts
greater coverts
median coverts
lesser coverts
back
nape
crown

HERRING GULL
JUVENILE MOULTING INTO 1ST-WINTER

ADULT WINTER
ear covert spot

BLACK-HEADED GULL

eyelids
hood

ADULT SUMMER

GULLS AND TERNS: RELATIVE SIZES
Bill to tail lengths show relative sizes but underestimate differences in the 'bulk' of gulls. A Lesser Black-backed Gull is only a few centimetres shorter than a Great Black-backed Gull, but side-by-side the Lesser Black-backed Gull may seem barely 'half as big' as the Great Black-backed Gull, and may indeed weigh only half as much.

LITTLE TERN
Bill to tail length: 25 cm
Weight: 50 g

BLACK-HEADED GULL
Bill to tail length: 40 cm
Weight: 200–300 g

GREAT BLACK-BACKED GULL
Bill to tail length: 70 cm
Weight: 1,800 g

Moult sequence in gulls

Like other birds, gulls renew their feathers in a regular sequence of moults, producing distinct plumages. Because they are big and strongly patterned, the process is easily appreciated; it is summarised here for a gull that takes four or five years to reach maturity (Herring Gull) and one that takes two years (Black-headed Gull).

Herring Gull

2ND-WINTER
SEP–MAR
[Jan]

1ST-WINTER
SEP–APR
[Jan]

2nd moult
1ST-WINTER → 1ST-SUMMER
Partial moult of head and body feathers; wing and tail feathers now a year old.

(Herring Gulls moult few feathers and simply fade paler)

1st moult
JUVENILE → 1ST-WINTER
Head and body feathers replaced

JUN JUL AUG SEP OCT NOV DEC J   MAR APR MAY JUN JUL AUG SEP OCT NOV DEC   EB MAR APR MAY JUN J
1ST-WINTER
JUVENILE   1ST-SUMMER   2ND-WINTER   2ND-SUMMER

3RD CALENDAR YEAR
→

3rd moult
1ST-SUMMER → 2ND-WINTER
Prolonged complete moult of head, body, tail and wing feathers. Bill colour progressively changes with age.

1ST CALENDAR YEAR   2ND CALENDAR YEAR
←   →

JUVENILE
JUN–AUG
[Aug]

1ST-SUMMER
MAR–OCT
[Jun]

JUVENILE/1ST-YEAR primary feathers have pointed tips; tail feathers are rounded. All later stages have rounded primary tips and squarer tail feathers. On large, pale-eyed gulls, juveniles have dark eyes; becoming paler in the second year.

Black-headed Gull

JUVENILE
JUN–AUG

1ST-WINTER
JUL–APR

1ST-SUMMER
APR–SEP

FLEDGLING
MAY–JUN
in nest, fledging into juvenile plumage

1st moult
JUVENILE → 1ST-WINTER
New head and body feathers replace juvenile brown.

2nd moult
1ST-WINTER → 1ST-SUMMER
Gains variable hood, wing and tail markings fade, feathers up to a year old.

JUN JUL AUG SEP OCT NOV DEC JAN FEB MAR APR MAY
1ST-WINTER
JUVENILE   1ST-SUMMER

1ST CALENDAR YEAR   2ND CALENDAR YEAR
←   →

JUVENILE

1ST-WINTER

1ST-SUMMER

7th moult
3RD-SUMMER → 4TH- WINTER (ADULT)
Complete moult: head and body.

8th moult
ADULT WINTER → ADULT SUMMER
Partial moult: head and body.
This sequence is repeated throughout the gull's life. NB Some may be recognisable as **4th-winter** and **4th-summer** (some brown in the wings, often dark bill markings), but the sequence becomes **adult summer** (breeding), **adult winter**, repeated.

5th moult
2ND SUMMER → 3RD WINTER
Prolonged complete moult.

ADULT WINTER
SEP–MAR
[Oct]

3RD-WINTER
SEP–APR
[Jan]

6th moult
3RD-WINTER → 3RD-SUMMER
Partial moult of head and body feathers only.

4TH CY

3RD-WINTER

ADULT SUMMER
MAR   APR   MAY
FEB
JAN
ADULT WINTER

DEC

NOV
OCT
SEP
AUG
ADULT SUMMER

ADULT SUMMER
no brown in wings;
new white head
feathers from January
onwards

SEP OCT NOV DEC JAN FEB MAR APR MAY JUN AUG JUL SEP OCT NOV DEC

3RD-SUMMER

4TH CY

5TH CY+

2ND-SUMMER
FEB–OCT
[Jun]

4th moult
2ND-WINTER → 2ND-SUMMER
Partial moult of head and body feathers only.

3RD-SUMMER
MAR–OCT
[Jun]

3rd moult
1ST-SUMMER → 2ND-WINTER (ADULT)
White head with dark spot; bright red bill and legs; wing feathers new.

NB Most **2nd-winters** are indistinguishable from **adults**. However, a few may be identified by dark markings on the primary coverts.

ADULT SUMMER – hood may appear as early as January; bill and legs darken; wing feathers become worn.

2ND-WINTER (ADULT)
ADULT SUMMER
MAR   APR

4th moult
2ND-WINTER (ADULT) → ADULT SUMMER
Partial (spring) moult: head and body.

5th moult
ADULT SUMMER → ADULT WINTER
Complete (autumn) moult.
This sequence is repeated throughout the gull's life. NB intermediate plumages spring and autumn, with white faces/incomplete hoods.

2ND-WINTER (ADULT)
AUG–MAR

JUL   AUG   SEP   OCT   NOV   DEC
2ND-WINTER (ADULT)

2ND CALENDAR YEAR

3RD CY+

JAN
ADULT SUMMER

FEB
JUN
ADULT SUMMER
JUL
DEC
NOV
OCT   SEP
ADULT WINTER

ADULT WINTER

105

Black-headed Gull

Chroicocephalus ridibundus ● ❶ 533

35–39 cm | WS 86–99 cm

👁 Rare 'hooded' (*p. 112–113*), Slender-billed (*p. 137*) Gulls

Small, quarrelsome, 'white' gull. **White flash on wingtip/dark beneath.** Feeds on beaches, fields, tips, reservoirs, roofs, car parks.

Mature when two years old. ADULT SUMMER **dark brown hood**, fades paler; **plum-red** legs and bill. ADULT WINTER white head, **black ear-spot; red legs, bill. White face** in spring and late summer. IN FLIGHT, **long white triangle** on wing; black trailing edge; **white stripe** against **grey-black underwing.** JUVENILE tawny-brown, silver-grey. Black streaks on white wing flash (on some, more black isolates white spots), **white underwing stripe** more striking. Dark diagonal band on innerwing; tail-band. Underwing grey, sometimes silvery. 1ST-WINTER white head and neck, dark ear-spot; back grey. 1ST-SUMMER patchy hood; wing markings browner.

VOICE Calls strident, shouted, screaming or grating – "*krree-arr*", "*karr*", abrupt "*kek*" or "*kekek*".

Locally common (170,000 pairs, including 40,000 pairs Ireland); abundant and widespread winter visitor (2.2 million birds)

from Iceland

from Scandinavia NW and E Europe

to W Africa

Almost anywhere, breeds from coasts to uplands

1ST-WINTER

black streaks on white forewing

distinct white stripe on leading edge

ADULT SUMMER

ADULT WINTER

patchy, blotchy brown

ADULT WINTER

JUVENILE

1ST-SUMMER

1ST-WINTER

wingtip black with white streak on lower edge

ADULT SUMMER

Mediterranean Gull

Larus melanocephalus

37–40 cm | WS 94–102 cm

Compare Black-headed Gull, Common Gull (first-year) (*p. 115*). Size of Black-headed Gull but **thicker, blunter bill**.

Mature when two or three years old. ADULT SUMMER **white wingtip, black hood**, white 'eyelids'; **red bill contrasts** with hood (dark on Black-headed Gull). ADULT WINTER grey around eye, nape. IN FLIGHT, **white wingtip, white underwing**. 1ST-WINTER resembles same age Common Gull but **paler back, dark behind eye**, white 'eyelids', bulbous dark bill; stiffer flight. **Blackish wingtip** (unlike Black-headed Gull); **pale midwing**; bill blackish, buff/orange/red at base. 1ST-SUMMER dark areas browner; **midwing/back all pale** (Common Gull has darker back). 2ND-WINTER upperwing **pale grey right to tip, black streaks** (see Little Gull (*p. 110*)); **white underwing**.

VOICE Distinctive loud, nasal "*yaa-uh*" or "*ee-ow*".

Scarce summer visitor (600 pairs, including 5–10 pairs Ireland), migrant, winter visitor (1,800 birds); increasing

from Europe

Mostly coastal, nearby pools, fields, marshes

1ST-WINTER

ADULT SUMMER

white streaks, unlike Common Gull

2ND-WINTER

ADULT WINTER

JUVENILE

blackish bill, legs; brownish head, breast; scalloped back

ADULT SUMMER

plumage faded pale; darker in autumn

ADULT MOULTING INTO WINTER PLUMAGE

1ST-WINTER

ADULT WINTER

Kittiwake

Rissa tridactyla ● ❶

37–42 cm | WS 93–105 cm

Medium-small gull, **very short legs**. Awkward on flat ground (summer flocks on sand, rock platforms). Brilliant flier, high shearing loops in gales. Catastrophic decline in recent years.

Mature when two years old. ADULT SUMMER **legs blackish** (few brown); bill yellow; eye black. IN FLIGHT, **black wingtip triangle**, **outerwing paler**, underwing white. White head looks longer than tail. ADULT WINTER **grey nape, ear crescent**. JUVENILE **black collar, band** on wing: **black 'W'** in flight (see Sabine's Gull, Little Gull (*p. 110*)). Inner primaries pale (juvenile Little Gull's streaked); back grey (dark brown on juvenile Little Gull). 1ST-SUMMER **faded wing markings**, drab. Underwing white (dark band on Sabine's Gull). Two-year-old like adult or dusky head in summer, bill black at base and/or tip, black in primary coverts.

VOICE Loud, wailing, nasal, rhythmic "*kitti-a-waike*" (even from migrants inland in spring); long, high, whining notes.

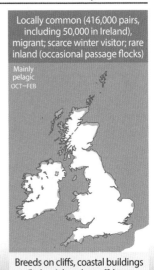

Locally common (416,000 pairs, including 50,000 in Ireland), migrant; scarce winter visitor; rare inland (occasional passage flocks)

Mainly pelagic OCT–FEB

Breeds on cliffs, coastal buildings (ledges); beaches, offshore

1ST-WINTER

ADULT SUMMER

ADULT WINTER

JUVENILE

prominent black wingtip

black zigzag across wings

sharp collar

ADULT WINTER

JUVENILE

yellow bill (no red spot)

ADULT SUMMER

Sabine's Gull

Xema sabini

30–36 cm | WS 80–87 cm

Small gull; striking **black, grey, white triangles** on wing in flight. See Kittiwake, Little Gull (*p. 110*). On water, dark, slim, tapered; closed tail (especially juvenile) forked, spread tail sharply triangular. Head dove-like; bill fairly short, thick. Quick, agile: broad, angled wings give great manoeuvrability; shearing flight in gales. Picks from surface while swimming.

Mature when two years old. ADULT SUMMER **hood lead-grey** bordered black, bill black, **yellow tip**; wingtip black with large **round white tips to primaries** (smaller with wear). ADULT WINTER blackish nape band. JUVENILE/1ST-WINTER crown, chest sides, back grey-brown, scaly buff edges; wingtips, tail-band black. IN FLIGHT, **triple-triangle wing** at all ages (immature Kittiwake has black band, dull trailing edge, drabber in first-summer). **Dusky band beneath wing** (unlike Kittiwake). Intermediate plumages, dark nape/neck/chest patches, but **wing pattern remains the same**.

VOICE Insignificant sharp "*kik*".

Rare coastal migrant (100–150, rarely up to 600 per year), very rare inland; mostly autumn but occasional spring/summer.

from Arctic Canada and Siberia

At sea; rarely storm-blown inland

clear white triangle

dusky underwing band

ADULT SUMMER

ADULT WINTER [Oct]

note: primary tips worn away

JUVENILE

1ST-SUMMER [Jun]

Sabine's Gull has a complete moult in early-mid winter followed by a partial one (head/body) in spring, more like some terns and skuas than most gulls

JUVENILE

white primary tips worn away

ADULT WINTER

ADULT SUMMER

NT # Little Gull   *Hydrocoloeus minutus* **I** **533**

24–28 cm | WS 62–69 cm   ◑ Ross's Gull

Slim, lightweight gull; copes
well over sea even in gale, feeds like Black Tern (*p. 142*), dipping
head-to-wind over water. See Kittiwake (first-year) (*p. 108*),
Mediterranean Gull (*p. 107*).

Mature when two or three years old. ADULT SUMMER **black hood**.
ADULT WINTER blackish cap, ear-spot; pink legs. IN FLIGHT, pale grey
upperwing, **white trailing edge and tip**; **underwing blackish
with white rim**. 2ND-WINTER black streaks on wingtip; patchy
underwing. JUVENILE dark above, white below; **dusky hindneck
onto chest sides** (see Black Tern). IN FLIGHT, **blackish 'W'** on
wings joins across back (Kittiwake has grey gap); dark hindneck
(thin collar on Kittiwake). 1ST-WINTER back/rump grey; dark
streaks on inner primaries (Kittiwake's whiter); outer primaries
striped (solid black on Kittiwake).

VOICE Calls insignificant "*kik*", "*kek*".

Scarce migrant, mostly autumn/
early winter (small numbers but
100s in few favoured places).

from
E Europe

Offshore, coastal lagoons; scarce
on inland waters

ADULT
WINTER

ADULT
SUMMER

1ST-WINTER

JUVENILE

1ST-WINTER

black under far
wingtip often
shows

no white eyelids;
no red on bill

ADULT SUMMER

ADULT WINTER

very short legs

EN Ross's Gull *Rhodostethia rosea*

29–32 cm | WS 73–80 cm

Mature when two years old. Dove-like; long wings; **tail wedge-shaped or pointed**. ADULT SUMMER pale pink and grey, **black ring** outlines same hood shape as Black-headed Gull (*p. 106*). **Upperwing pale, white trailing edge**; underwing grey, white rear edge. ADULT WINTER, nape grey; tiny ear-spot. 1ST-WINTER dark 'W' above resembles same age Little Gull, Kittiwake (*p. 108*); **dark trailing edge to outerwing behind long finger of white**; grey underwing band.

ADULT SUMMER

1ST-WINTER

ADULT WINTER

Easily overlooked as Little Gull.

1ST-WINTER

1ST-SUMMER gains black neck ring.

round head, short dark bill

Vagrant from Arctic: <150 records (<20 Ireland), most Jan–Feb, but most months. Coast, beaches, adjacent lagoons.

ADULT WINTER

short legs

NT Ivory Gull

Pagophila eburnea

41–47 cm | WS 100–113 cm

Mature when two years old. Size of Common Gull (*p. 114*); pigeon-like, short legs, long wings. ADULT **wholly white** except black eye, legs and **grey bill with yellow tip**. JUVENILE/1ST-WINTER **scattered blackish spots. Dirty/sooty face. Legs black** (rules out albinistic Common Gull, but not albinistic Kittiwake (*p. 108*)).

Vagrant from Arctic: <200 records (<20 Ireland), all months, most Nov–Feb. Coasts.

1ST-WINTER

ADULT SUMMER

ADULT SUMMER

1ST-WINTER

long, broad wingtip

some birds more heavily spotted on wings

Note: white individuals of other gulls occasionally appear, so bill and leg colours vital to confirm identification.

Rare 'hooded' gulls from North America

Three gulls from North America are exciting finds, most likely in flocks of common smaller gulls, including lake or reservoir roosts. Bonaparte's Gull resembles a dainty Black-headed Gull (*p. 106*); Laughing and Franklin's Gulls are black-hooded like Mediterranean Gull (*p. 107*) but much darker grey above.

Laughing Gull *Larus atricilla*

36–41 cm | WS 98–110 cm

Mature when two years old. **Upperparts slaty-grey**; bill long, 'drooped'. ADULT SUMMER hood black, white eyelids (see much paler Mediterranean Gull (*p. 107*)); bill and legs dark red. ADULT WINTER white head, grey crown, ear covert patch (see Franklin's Gull). IN FLIGHT, white trailing edge; **black wingtip triangle**; white primary tips wear off in summer. 1ST-WINTER/SUMMER grey back, brown on upperwings, outerwing blackish (like Common Gull (*p. 114*)), black trailing edge. Black tail-band, grey tail sides outline white rump. **Grey breast-band and flanks**. Bill blackish; legs dark grey.

2ND-SUMMER

ADULT WINTER

1ST-WINTER

white eyelids

long, heavy, black bill

dingy on breast, unlike Franklin's Gull

1ST-SUMMER

white eyelids incomplete behind eye

ADULT SUMMER

ADULT WINTER

1ST-WINTER

<250 records (<50 Ireland), all months. Most on coast; beaches, lakes.

Bonaparte's Gull *Chroicocephalus philadelphia*

31–34 cm | WS 79–84 cm

Mature when two years old. Like small Black-headed Gull (*p. 106*). Upperwing as Black-headed Gull; **underwing white.** ADULT SUMMER **hood black, bill black.** ADULT WINTER **pink legs, black bill.** 1ST-WINTER/SUMMER upperwing like Black-headed Gull, but inner primary coverts paler, outer ones edged dark; **blacker diagonal bar and trailing edge; underwing white with long, dark trailing edge. Bill black, legs pink.**

ADULT WINTER

ADULT WINTER

BLACK-HEADED GULL

ADULT WINTER

BONAPARTE'S GULL

1ST-WINTER

1ST-WINTER

small head and bill, like Little Gull (*p. 110*)

ADULT SUMMER

ADULT WINTER

<300 records (<100 Ireland), all months, most autumn. Coasts, inland waters.

Franklin's Gull *Larus pipixcan*

32–36 cm | WS 81–93 cm

Mature when two years old. Size of Black-headed Gull (*p. 106*). **Dark grey** above. IN FLIGHT, **white trailing edge spreads across tip;** black tip beneath like Kittiwake (*p. 108*) **but white spots.** Tail has grey centre. ADULT SUMMER black hood; bright red bill, legs. ADULT WINTER **dark half-hood, white forehead and eyelids.** 1ST-WINTER neck, flanks **pure white.** 1ST-SUMMER grey above, black wingtip beyond **thin white line,** tail with **grey centre.**

ADULT SUMMER

1ST-WINTER

thick white eyelids meet behind eye

white breast

ADULT WINTER

2ND-WINTER/ ADULT WINTER difficult; adults often show more white in wingtip

2ND-YEAR birds difficult to tell from adults

2ND-WINTER

in winter, all ages, dusky hood remains prominent

1ST-WINTER

<100 records (<20 Ireland), most May–Aug, Nov–Jan. Most coastal; beaches, lakes.

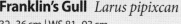

Common Gull

Larus canus ● ① 533

40–46 cm | WS 100–115 cm   ◁◉▷ Ring-billed Gull (*p. 116*)

Medium-sized, between
Black-headed (*p. 106*) and Herring (*p. 124*) Gulls. ADULT **darker**
than British Herring Gull, **bolder white patch** between grey
back and black wingtip; **white wingtip spots** rule out Kittiwake
(*p. 108*). **Eyes dark**. Bill greenish, variable dark band in winter;
no red spot. Legs green.

Mature when three years old. ADULT SUMMER head white;
ADULT WINTER head streaked, sometimes dusky hood.
IN FLIGHT, wide white trailing edge, two 'mirrors' join as **big
white patch within large black tip**; more black below than
Herring Gull. JUVENILE dusky brown head, breast, upperparts.
1ST-WINTER majority lose most brown on back and flanks.
IN FLIGHT, upperwing **blackish tip**, grey midwing; **broad black
band on tail** (see Herring Gull). 2ND-WINTER small white wingtip
spots; variable dark band on dull bill (see Ring-billed Gull
(*p. 116*)).

VOICE Calls typically high-pitched and squealing, "*keeea*",
"*klee-u*" and long, laughing, wailing "*ke-ke-ke-kleee-a kleee-a*".

Locally common summer visitor
(50,000 pairs, including 1,600
pairs Ireland), migrant; common
winter visitor (700,000)

from
Iceland

from
Scandinavia
and
NW Europe

Breeds moors, lakes; in winter,
grassy fields, shores, reservoirs

ADULT WINTER

dark band on
bill variable   ADULT WINTER

Larger Russian race *heinei*
probably regular in winter; darker
back; paler eye; more extensive
black in wingtip.

dark eye

bold white
patch

yellow bill
(no red spot)

ADULT SUMMER

yellow-green legs

sharp
tail-band

neat
tail-band

NB: outer
primaries still
growing

hindwing
bar

large white
'mirrors'

JUVENILE

1ST-WINTER

2ND-WINTER

ADULT SUMMER

wingtip dull
black

dark bill tip
or band

2ND-WINTER

neat round
head, slim bill

grey back

1ST-WINTER

JUVENILE

neat wing
covert pattern

by 1ST-SUMMER, grey back darker
than bleached wings (see
Mediterranean Gull (p. 107))

Ring-billed Gull *Larus delawarensis*

41–49 cm | WS 112–124 cm

Much like Common Gull (*p. 114*): **paler back**, less white against wingtip; fractionally larger, back rounder; **thicker bill**; broader wings, but sharper tip. Mature when three years old. ADULT crucial features: pale back; **yellow eye** (hard to see at long range due to dark ring); **thick bill with sharp black band** (Common Gull often has band on thinner, duller bill; bigger sub-adult Herring Gull (*p. 124*) has black or black/red band on heavier yellow bill). IN FLIGHT, can look strikingly pale; big black wingtip, **small white 'mirrors'**.

1ST-WINTER like Common Gull but **paler**, more contrasted wing, **paler midwing panel and inner primaries**. **Tail-band less clear-cut**, dark wedges towards base, outer edge barred. **Bill thick, pink** (yellower with age, some by late winter); black tip. 2ND-WINTER like adult; more black on wing, small white 'mirror'; variable **blackish marks** on hindwing and tail tip (rare on Common Gull).

Vagrant from N America: 15–30 per year, all months, most Oct–Mar. Estuaries, lakes.

small 'mirrors'

ADULT WINTER

RING-BILLED GULL

COMMON GULL

pale midwing panel

dark

1ST-WINTER

nape spotted, less streaked than Common Gull

bill ring looks like dark tip at moderate range

ADULT WINTER

ADULT WINTER

ADULT SUMMER

ADULT SUMMER

2ND-YEAR and ADULT paler than Common Gull; less white between grey back and black wingtip

2ND-WINTER

2ND-WINTER

COMMON GULL

1ST-WINTER

1ST-WINTER

Regular small and medium-sized gulls in non-breeding plumage

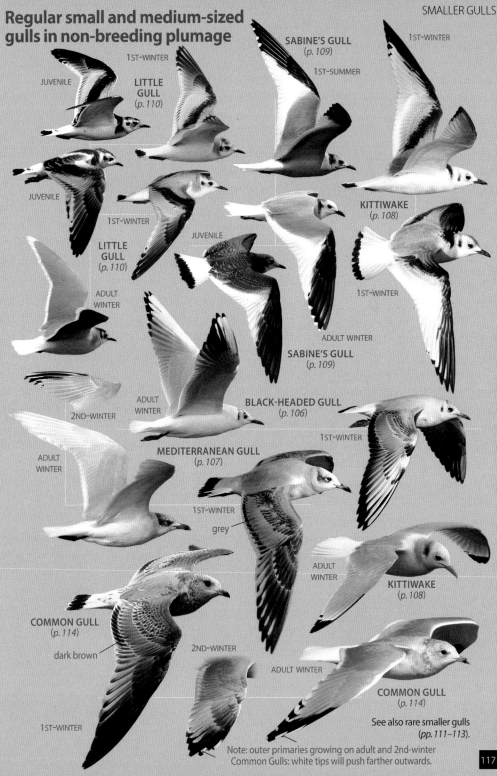

JUVENILE

1ST-WINTER

LITTLE GULL
(p. 110)

SABINE'S GULL
(p. 109)

1ST-SUMMER

1ST-WINTER

JUVENILE

1ST-WINTER

LITTLE GULL
(p. 110)

JUVENILE

KITTIWAKE
(p. 108)

1ST-WINTER

ADULT WINTER

SABINE'S GULL
(p. 109)

ADULT WINTER

2ND-WINTER

ADULT WINTER

BLACK-HEADED GULL
(p. 106)

1ST-WINTER

MEDITERRANEAN GULL
(p. 107)

1ST-WINTER

grey

ADULT WINTER

KITTIWAKE
(p. 108)

COMMON GULL
(p. 114)

dark brown

2ND-WINTER

ADULT WINTER

COMMON GULL
(p. 114)

1ST-WINTER

See also rare smaller gulls
(pp. 111–113).

Note: outer primaries growing on adult and 2nd-winter
Common Gulls: white tips will push farther outwards.

117

Larger gulls | Introduction

Large gulls are either **'dark-winged'** or **'white-winged'**. 'White-winged' gulls include difficult species and races: they are treated together in the following pages.

Adult gulls interact in spring, when each species must look and sound unique: hence they are then easiest to identify. Immatures, having no 'need' to look different, are more difficult to identify. Most gulls vary in detail but critical features remain consistent: amongst thousands of Black-headed Gulls only one or two paler ones may stand out. But Herring and Lesser Black-backed Gulls vary widely between extremes of shade and size, and young Herring Gulls' feather patterns vary greatly, too. Concentrate on the important things: primary, tertial and tail patterns, and structure. Young Herring Gulls' pale inner primaries and young Lesser Black-backed Gulls' all-dark primaries will separate them, while endless variations in detail simply confuse. For some rare gulls, however, differences in detail must be grasped. As large gulls mature, adult back colour, wingtip patterns, bill colour and leg colour come into play, making identification more straightforward.

Leucism and hybrids

Melanin darkens and strengthens feathers: black rarely changes, but white feather tips wear off. Rare individuals with reduced pigment – leucistic – look very pale. White Common Gulls suggest Ivory Gulls, pale Herring Gulls look like Glaucous Gulls, but they don't quite 'fit'. Details such as 'shadows' of darker wingtips and tail-bands remove confusion. Gulls occasionally hybridize, especially where one species is extending its range – hybrid pairs may persist, or disappear as the population increases.
Some hybrid gulls defy identification.

3RD-WINTER

3RD-WINTER

HERRING GULL (p. 124)

GLAUCOUS GULL (p. 134)

GREAT BLACK-BACKED GULL (p. 128)

1ST-WINTER

GLAUCOUS GULL (p. 134)

1ST-WINTER

1ST-WINTER

HERRING GULL (p. 124)

A young Glaucous Gull at a reservoir roost is strikingly pale, but settled amongst thousands of birds may take some finding. Look for the wingtips. Glaucous Gulls are intermediate in size between Great Black-backed Gulls and Herring Gulls (northern Herring Gulls can be as large). Iceland Gulls are closer to the smaller end of the Herring Gull range.

Glaucous and Iceland Gulls have different 'expressions', but such subtleties are hard to describe.

1ST-WINTER

GLAUCOUS GULL (p. 134)

ICELAND GULL (p. 135)

1ST-WINTER

Larger gulls | 'Dark-winged' regular adults

Adult gulls flying over may be identifiable at long range by their underwings:

Herring Gull has pale grey under flight feathers, black tips;

Lesser Black-backed Gull darker grey band under flight feathers;

Great Black-backed Gull blacker beneath with broader white trailing edge extending to tip.

The pattern of the primaries is important for distinguishing Herring, Yellow-legged and Caspian Gulls – see *p. 130*

LESSER BLACK-BACKED GULL (*p. 126*)

GREAT BLACK-BACKED GULL (*p. 128*)

CASPIAN GULL (*p. 131*)

HERRING GULL (*p. 124*)

YELLOW-LEGGED GULL (*p. 130*)

YELLOW-LEGGED GULL (*p. 130*)

NB: American Herring Gull (*p. 140*) is more difficult when adult than in immature plumages.

HERRING GULL (*p. 124*) race *argentatus* is darker than race *argenteus* with more white in the primaries – see *p. 125*

CASPIAN GULL (*p. 131*)

race *graellsii*

GREAT BLACK-BACKED GULL (*p. 128*)

NB: Slaty-backed Gull (*p. 138*) has bright pink legs.

LESSER BLACK-BACKED GULL (*p. 126*)

race *intermedius*

NB: race *fuscus* even blacker.

119

Larger gulls | Juveniles/1st-winters

Look carefully at size, wingtip patterns and contrasts,
tail-bands and tail/rump contrasts, bill shape and colour.

LESSER BLACK-BACKED GULL (p. 126)

all dark flight feathers

CASPIAN GULL (p. 131)

white head

black tail-band

AMERICAN HERRING GULL (p. 140)

YELLOW-LEGGED GULL (p. 130)

'striped' primaries

pale inner primaries

black tail

palest inner primaries

HERRING GULL (p. 124)

weak tail-band

GREAT BLACK-BACKED GULL (p. 128)

huge size

Thayer's Gull (p. 136)

dusky hindwing and wingtip

small head and bill

large head and bill

Kumlien's Gull (p. 136)

dusky wingtip streaks

ICELAND GULL (p. 135)

pale wings

GLAUCOUS GULL (p. 134)

pale wings

LESSER BLACK-BACKED GULL (p. 126)

'wavy' pale edges and pale tip

YELLOW-LEGGED GULL (p. 130)

straight pale edges near tip only

'HERRING' TYPES note structure; head shape; tertial pattern

CASPIAN GULL (p. 131)

U-shaped pale tip

longer legs than Herring Gull

'HERRING' GROUP

AMERICAN HERRING GULL (p. 140)

darker and larger than Herring Gull

'notched' pale edges

HERRING GULL (p. 124)

Thayer's Gull (p. 136)

VERY DARK

Kumlien's Gull (p. 136)

BROWN MARKS

extent of markings on the primaries grades from 'Iceland' to 'Thayer's

'ICELAND' GROUP

GREAT BLACK-BACKED GULL (p. 128)

ICELAND GULL (p. 135)

WHITE/IVORY

SLATY-BACKED GULL (p. 138)

'WHITE-WINGED' TYPES – note size and primary pattern; head, bill, legs

GLAUCOUS GULL (p. 134)

'bubblegum' pink legs

GLAUCOUS-WINGED GULL (p. 138)

Larger gulls | regularly occurring 'dark-winged' 2nd-years

Adult colours begin to develop, but look for upperwing patterns, back/innerwing contrast

white head, dark collar

CASPIAN GULL *(p. 131)*

head shape and bill shape important

dark mottled back

GREAT BLACK-BACKED GULL *(p. 128)*

two birds showing variability

dark back

HERRING GULL *(p. 124)*

YELLOW-LEGGED GULL *(p. 130)*

small dark eye in pear-shaped head

LESSER BLACK-BACKED GULL *(p. 126)*

uniformly dark primaries

often shows new pale upper tertials

long wingtips

long slim bill

back darker than Herring/Caspian Gull

bill often dark

long dull legs

long wingtips

HERRING GULL *(p. 124)*

thick bill

CASPIAN GULL *(p. 131)*

YELLOW-LEGGED GULL *(p. 130)*

bright pink legs

LESSER BLACK-BACKED GULL *(p. 126)*

GREAT BLACK-BACKED GULL *(p. 128)*

Larger gulls | regularly occurring 'dark-winged' 3rd-years

Further progress towards adult patterns, identification becomes clearer

GREAT BLACK-BACKED GULL (p. 128)
darkest back

pale grey back

CASPIAN GULL (p. 131)

wingtip pattern, head shape and bill shape important

long grey 'tongues' penetrate black

pale grey back

palest grey back

YELLOW-LEGGED GULL (p. 130)

mid-dark grey back

HERRING GULL (p. 124)

sharp black wingtip

dark eye

long slim bill

LESSER BLACK-BACKED GULL (p. 126)

dark eye

dark bill band frequent

long wingtips

YELLOW-LEGGED GULL (p. 130)

HERRING GULL (p. 124)

palest back

long legs

CASPIAN GULL (p. 131)

long wingtips

yellow legs

pink legs

heaviest bill

LESSER BLACK-BACKED GULL (p. 126)

dark grey back

yellowish legs

blackest back

pinkish legs

GREAT BLACK-BACKED GULL (p. 128)

NT # Herring Gull

Larus argentatus ● except race *argentatus* **I** 533

54–60 cm | WS 123–148 cm

Big, pale, widespread gull. Soars well; flies to roost in lines, 'V's. See Yellow-legged (*p. 130*) and Caspian (*p. 131*)

Yellow-legged Gull (*p. 130*)
Caspian Gull (*p. 131*)
American Herring Gull (*p. 140*)
Vega Gull (*p. 141*)
Thayer's Gull (*p. 136*)

Gulls, other rare large gulls and also Lesser Black-backed Gull (*p. 126*) and Common Gull (*p. 114*).

Mature when four/five years old. ADULT British/Irish race *argenteus* paler than Common Gull; pale eye, **yellow bill with red spot**, **pink legs**. Head white Jan to Aug/Sep, otherwise heavily streaked. For IMMATURE plumages see annotations.

VOICE Yelping, barking notes, strident "*kyow*", soft "*gag-ag-gag*"; loud, trumpeting display call, higher pitched than Lesser Black-backed Gull, "*kyyaa-kya-kya-ka-ka-ka-kya-kya-kyau*".

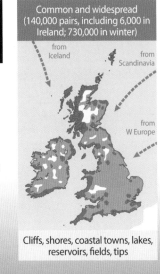

Common and widespread (140,000 pairs, including 6,000 in Ireland; 730,000 in winter)

from Iceland

from Scandinavia

from W Europe

Cliffs, shores, coastal towns, lakes, reservoirs, fields, tips

JUVENILE

increasingly pale grey above with age

ADULT SUMMER

JUVENILE/1ST-WINTER pale inner primaries unlike Lesser Black-backed Gull, but see Great Black-backed Gull (*p. 128*).

2ND-WINTER

3RD-WINTER

black wingtips, one or two white 'mirrors', white tips, which wear off in summer. Underwing pale grey

ADULT WINTER
British/Irish race
argenteus

head variably streaked dark, bill may have dark marks

ADULT SUMMER
British/Irish race
argenteus

pink legs (note: some adults from the Baltic have yellow legs – see Yellow-legged Gull (*p. 130*))

Northern race *argentatus* (frequent N/central Britain in winter) larger, darker and with less black/more white in wingtip than British/Irish race *argenteus*.

race *argenteus*

race *argentatus*

race *argenteus*

ADULT WINTER Northern race *argentatus*

extreme 'Arctic' examples are like Glaucous × Herring Gull hybrids, but too dark, or like Thayer's Gull (*p. 136*) but too big; dull bill

race *argenteus* paler grey than race *argentatus*; drab head autumn–winter

ADULT WINTER British/Irish race *argenteus*

3RD-WINTER

bill colour and pattern from first- to third-year is highly variable

2ND-WINTER

JUVENILE

JUVENILE

JUVENILE/1ST-WINTER paler than Lesser Black-backed Gull; **wider pale tips and 'notches' on tertials**

JUVENILES vary from darker to paler individuals. All become paler and more contrasted as plumage is worn and bleached by 1st-winter

125

Lesser Black-backed Gull

Larus fuscus except race *intermedius* **I** **533**

48–56 cm | WS 117–134 cm

👁 Yellow-legged Gull (*p. 130*),
Caspian Gull (*p. 131*),
Slaty-backed Gull (*p. 138*)

Locally common summer visitor;
breeds in colonies in N and W
(16,000 pairs, including 5,000 in
Ireland); widespread migrant,
winter visitor (130,000)

Smaller than Great Black-
backed Gull (*p. 128*); see
Herring (*p. 124*), Yellow-legged (*p. 130*) Gulls.

Mature when four/five years old. ADULT SUMMER dark grey above;
legs yellow. ADULT WINTER head/breast grey-brown, legs duller.
IN FLIGHT, **clear-cut black tip** above, small white 'mirrors';
dark band beneath. For IMMATURE plumages see annotations.

VOICE Distinctly deeper, throatier version of Herring Gull
(often heard from migrating flocks overhead inland).

Two races regular: British/Irish *graellsii* and darker *intermedius* (breeds NW
Europe, not always easily identifiable). Race *fuscus* (Baltic Gull) recorded but
rare: blackest, slimmest.

from Iceland

from Scandinavia

from NW Europe

to Africa

Coasts, reservoirs, fields, tips

2ND–WINTER

3RD–WINTER

increasingly **dark grey on back** with age

1ST–SUMMER

ADULT SUMMER

black wingtip
contrasts with rest
of wing (unlike Great
Black-backed Gull)

JUVENILE/1ST–SUMMER
primaries all-dark, dark trailing
edge and second dark band
across coverts (Herring Gull
has pale inner primaries, no
covert band; Yellow-legged
Gull intermediate)

ADULT WINTER
race *graellsii*

ADULT SUMMER
race *graellsii*

ADULT from autumn to
late winter variably
streaked on head and
chest, some very dark,
others remain largely
whitish; some have dark
bill-tip marks

Race *fuscus* (Baltic) migrates SE; rare in W Europe. Long-winged, small head, slender bill, short legs. Adult black above, no contrast with wingtip; almost white head in winter. **Moults only inner 1–4 primaries Oct–Nov** (other races moult all primaries May/Jun–Nov).

ADULT
race *fuscus*
[May]

Race *intermedius* (regular S Britain in winter) can be as black as Great Black-backed Gull; whiter head than race *graellsii* in winter, but not all are identifiable.

ADULT WINTER
race *intermedius*

ADULT WINTER
race *graellsii*

readily told from Herring Gull once dark grey shows on back

3RD-WINTER

2ND-WINTER

JUVENILE/1ST-WINTER tertials blackish, **narrow pale tips** (pale 'notches' on Herring Gull). Gains whiter head, dark around eye like Yellow-legged Gull (*p. 130*), blackish bill

JUVENILE

127

Great Black-backed Gull

Larus marinus ⬤⬤ I `533`

61–74 cm | WS 144–166 cm

👁 Slaty-backed Gull (*p. 138*)

Biggest, most predatory gull, most 'eagle-like' flight. Dominates other gulls, may chase roosting flocks; chooses conspicuous, exposed perches (cliff tops, sea stacks, buoys, piers). Long, bowed wings; strong, steady beats (superb soaring in wind). Massively broad head; huge bill on males. Legs long, **pale, pinkish** or whitish.

Mature when four/five years old. ADULT **blacker** than British/Irish Lesser Black-backed Gull (race *graellsii*) (*p. 126*), more white in black wingtip, which **does not contrast with rest of wing**. ADULT WINTER **head remains largely white**. For immature plumages see opposite.

VOICE Generally deepest of all gulls, loud, barking "*huh-huh-huh*" distinctive.

Locally common resident breeder (19,000 pairs, including 2,000 in Ireland); commoner, more widespread in winter (76,000)

from Iceland

from NW Europe

Coasts, reservoirs, tips

JUVENILE/1ST WINTER upperside like pale juvenile Herring Gull (*p. 124*); pale spots near tips of inner primaries

increasingly **blacker above** and whiter on head with age

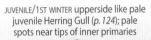

ADULT WINTER

1ST-WINTER

2ND-WINTER

3RD-WINTER

white trailing edge continues towards tip (narrower on Lesser Black-backed Gull)

no contrast between black wingtip and rest of wing (unlike Lesser Black-backed Gull)

4TH-WINTER

ADULT SUMMER

black/white contrast
obvious; size and
structure important

3RD-WINTER

blackish chequering
above

big bill, especially on
males – head/bill most
obvious features

2ND-WINTER

JUVENILE

JUVENILE/1ST-YEAR enormous; **heavy, black bill**, whiter
head than Herring or Lesser Black-backed Gulls,
boldly chequered above, whiter belly

Yellow-legged Gull

Larus michahellis ●

52–58 cm | WS 120–140 cm

Herring Gull (*p. 124*), Caspian Gull

S European equivalent of Herring Gull (*p. 124*). Adult has **yellow legs**. Upperparts **darker than British/Irish Herring Gull** (race *argenteus*), paler than British/Irish Lesser Black-backed Gull (race *graellsii*) (*p. 126*); hard to judge in isolation. Grey shades vary with conditions/angle of light.

Mature when four/five years old. ADULT SUMMER like Herring Gull; more black on wingtip, smaller 'mirrors', darker grey beneath primaries (see *p. 132*). In autumn head streaking mostly behind eye, quickly lost. ADULT WINTER big, rounded head and breast **strikingly white** (from January, Herring Gulls acquire white heads, too). Bill heavy, rich yellow, dark red spot; legs pale to bright **yellow**. For IMMATURE plumages see *pp. 132, 120–123*.

VOICE Deep, much like Lesser Black-backed Gull.

Scarce, most late summer/autumn/early winter (low 100s); very rare breeder (1–4 pairs)

from S Europe

Reservoirs, coasts, fields, tips

1ST-WINTER

2ND-WINTER

3RD-WINTER

ADULT [Oct]

Note: new outer primaries still short towards end of moult: white tips and 'mirrors' will push farther towards wingtip as feathers grow.

ADULT WINTER

'Azorean' or 'Atlantic' Gull race *atlantis*
vagrant, <10 records (<5 in Ireland): Jul–Dec)
ADULT WINTER has defined dark, streaked hood but very variable.

ADULT SUMMER

ADULTS look like this from late autumn to late summer: white-headed and dark-backed compared with typical winter Herring Gull; males, especially, have bulbous head and thick bill

Caspian Gull

Larus cachinnans ● **533**

55–60 cm | WS 138–147 cm

Herring Gull (*p. 124*),
Yellow-legged Gull

Mature when four/five years old.
Often difficult to identify.

Rare but increasing winter visitor
(50–100 per year: juveniles/first-
years from August; scattered).
Vagrant Ireland (<15 records).

ADULT SUMMER like Herring Gull, some larger, lankier, males
longer-legged. **Long, slim bill** on MALE, not distinctive on FEMALE;
slight angle on lower edge, pale greenish-yellow, dull spot, often
dark band. Long 'snout' on some (not all) gives pear-shaped
head. Flatter back, often markedly longer wingtip projection
than Herring Gull's. **White head in winter**, like Yellow-legged
Gull. Rather upright, bulk around chest/shoulders, belly hangs
down behind legs. **Long, slim legs** dull yellowish/pinkish-grey.
IN FLIGHT, large black tips on **outer six**, sometimes seven feathers
(only five/six on Herring Gull – see *p. 132*); **long fingers of paler
grey/white cut into black** (shorter, no paler, on Herring Gull).
Wing mostly white beneath. For IMMATURE plumages see *pp. 132,
120–123*.

from
C Europe

Beaches, inland lakes, tips

3RD-WINTER

1ST-WINTER

2ND-WINTER

grey/black border indented by
whitish patches or 'fingers' may
be striking

ADULT
SUMMER

pale underwing, as if reflecting light
from water or snow beneath

dark eye often
distinct

ADULT SUMMER

legs dull pinkish
or yellowish

Yellow-legged Gull and Caspian Gull Identification

Adults: Primaries are numbered according to the sequence in which they are moulted: innermost is P1, outermost P10. Details of patterns are needed to identify some of the rarest gulls.

YELLOW-LEGGED GULL

no paler patches

P5
P6
P7
P8
P9
P10

Like Herring Gull, often more black: more solid black on P5 and P6 feathers; some have complete white tip to outer feather (P10).

HERRING GULL
race *argenteus*

small pale grey patches

P5
P6
P7
P8
P9
P10

Large 'mirror' on outer feather (P10), sometimes joins tip; smaller 'mirror' on next; less black on P5 and P6; grey/black border with little paler grey.

CASPIAN GULL

whitish patches

P5
P6
P7
P8
P9
P10

Large white tip (joining 'mirror') on outer feather (P10) typical of westernmost breeding birds; large 'mirror' on P9 feather; more black on P5 and P6 feathers; grey/black border indented by whitish patches.

HERRING GULL

tail-band more solid than Herring, narrower than Lesser Black-backed

inner primaries almost same tone as outer

underwing more contrasting than Herring; Caspian has paler underwing

YELLOW-LEGGED GULL

CASPIAN GULL

back greyish

back mottled brown

inner primaries darker than Herring, more 'striped'

1st-winters

Look for head shape, bill shape, head/back/wing contrasts (see also *pp. 120–121*).

1st-winter tertial patterns

'oak-leaf' scalloped pale edges

HERRING GULL

no pale edges; pale 'U'-shape on tip

CASPIAN GULL

straight pale edges near tip

YELLOW-LEGGED GULL

head more rounded and usually not as pale as Caspian or Yellow-legged

HERRING GULL

upper tertials often replaced by new, pale grey feathers

CASPIAN GULL

YELLOW-LEGGED GULL

White-winged gulls in flight

ADULT WINTER

ICELAND GULL race *thayeri*
(Thayer's Gull) (*p. 136*)

1ST-WINTER

3RD-WINTER

1ST-WINTER
(pale)

ADULT
WINTER

1ST-WINTER
(dark)

ICELAND GULL race *kumlieni*
(Kumlien's Gull) (*p. 136*)

3RD-WINTER

ADULT
WINTER

1ST-WINTER

ICELAND GULL
race *glaucoides*
(*p. 135–136*)

2ND-WINTER

ADULT
WINTER

GLAUCOUS GULL
(*p. 134*)

JUVENILE/
1ST-WINTER

2ND-WINTER

3RD-WINTER

1ST-WINTER

ADULT
WINTER

GLAUCOUS-WINGED GULL
(*p. 138*)

ADULT WINTER
GLAUCOUS GULL

133

Glaucous Gull

Larus hyperboreus ●

63–68 cm | WS 138–158 cm

👁 Glaucous-winged Gull (*p. 138*)

Large 'white-winged' gull: size between Herring (*p. 124*) and Great Black-backed (*p. 128*) Gulls; **no black on wings**.

Generally 'heavier' than Iceland Gull; less round-bellied, **bill longer**; **longer legs**. Closed **wingtip projects less beyond tail**. Head shape and expression important, but require care: Glaucous Gull 'mean' (Iceland Gull 'gentle', steep forehead, high crown, low nape). Glaucous Gull's head can be round, but different effect. ADULT **wingtips white**. In summer white head; in winter head and breast streaked. On water, **long white triangle of tertial tips/wingtip** first clue. JUVENILE coffee-brown, barred. Wingtips pale beige/ivory, tail buff-brown. 1ST-WINTER (faded juvenile) paler, some have underparts darker than back. **Bill pink, sharp black tip** (see Iceland Gull: a few Herring Gulls similar). 1ST-SUMMER blotched white. 2ND-YEAR similar but paler eye, rounder primary tips, dark band/pale tip to bill. 3RD-YEAR gains pale grey above. For birds in flight see *p. 133*.

VOICE Much like Herring Gull.

Rare winter visitor (300–500 birds, most Oct–Apr; occasional long-stayers)

from Greenland and Arctic Canada

Harbours, coasts, reservoirs, tips

juvenile plumage fades to 1st-winter, and fades further by first-summer, when begins to develop a small pale bill tip

DARK JUVENILE

1ST-WINTER

1ST-WINTER

1ST-WINTER

2ND-WINTER

wingtip can look long and pointed

3RD-WINTER

ADULT WINTER

Iceland Gull

Larus glaucoides ●

52–60 cm | WS 123–139 cm

Size much as Herring (*p. 124*)/Lesser Black-backed (*p. 126*)
Gulls; domed head, shorter bill. Thick feathering, short legs give
dumpy, dove-like effect (longer wings most obvious on water).

Plumages as Glaucous Gull. Bill rather **short**; forehead steep;
less 'chin' when swimming. **Wingtips project more beyond tail**,
especially on first-year birds. Head rather large, round; long,
often upswept, pointed wingtip compared with broader-backed,
shorter-winged Glaucous Gull. ADULT **white wingtip**. Bill often
duller than Glaucous Gull; eye looks darker in **more domed
head**; legs often darker pink. 1ST-WINTER **black tip extends back
in point into dull base** (not sharp pink/black of Glaucous Gull).
Some 1ST-SUMMER/2ND-YEAR birds very white. 2ND-WINTER shows a
little grey above; dull bill has pale tip, dark band.
For birds in flight see *p. 133*.

Rare winter visitor (200–500 birds;
Nov–Apr)

from Greenland
and Arctic Canada

Harbours, coasts, reservoirs

Kumlien's Gull
ADULT WINTER
(well-marked)

Thayer's Gull
ADULT WINTER

Three races of Iceland Gull
have been recorded: Iceland
Gull (*glaucoides*), Kumlien's Gull
(*kumlieni*) and Thayer's Gull
(*thayeri*) (see *p. 136*).

1ST-WINTER

2ND-WINTER

3RD-WINTER

ADULT WINTER

See p. 120–121 for comparison with other large gulls

Iceland Gull complex

Includes three races, which are difficult to separate where characters intergrade.
race *glaucoides* – Iceland Gull (see *p. 135*)
race *kumlieni* – 'Kumlien's Gull'
race *thayeri* – 'Thayer's Gull', sometimes treated as full species

Kumlien's Gull – Race *kumlieni* from NE Canada (rare Britain and Ireland). ADULT **white spots on grey wingtip; grey streaks** on spread primaries. Wingtip varies from almost white (like Iceland Gull) to almost as dark as Thayer's Gull; 'average' birds distinctive. IMMATURES range from Iceland-type to darker with streaked wingtip, slight brown tail-band; more like pale young Thayer's Gull, or hybrids.

Thayer's Gull – Race *thayeri* from Arctic N America (vagrant, <5 records). Between Herring Gull (*p. 124*) and Iceland Gull in size, structure. ADULT like Herring Gull but **smaller, duller bill**; **darker eye**; steeper forehead; deeper pink legs. **Slightly darker back** than Iceland Gull. 1ST-WINTER wingtips brown, upperside more uniform than Herring Gull; tertials brown with mottled pale tips; rump/undertail broadly barred; bill like juvenile Iceland Gull but darker base. 2ND-WINTER wingtips dark brown; broad, crescentic pale feather tips. 2ND-WINTER like adult but brown tail-band. IN FLIGHT, white streaks or spots inside blackish wingtip (darkest Kumlien's similar; most have smaller, greyer marks).

ADULT WINTER

Kumlien's Gull
considerable variation

ADULT WINTER

ICELAND GULL

ADULT WINTER

Thayer's Gull

HERRING GULL

1ST-WINTER

1ST-WINTER

1ST-WINTER

1ST-WINTER

'Kumlien's' type

considerable variation

1ST-WINTER

typical Kumlien's

Kumlien's Gull

much like Herring Gull; Iceland Gull-like shape may catch the eye

1ST-WINTER

Thayer's Gull

Kumlien's Gull

pale individual   ADULT WINTER

closed wingtip like Herring Gull (Kumlien's Gull grey and white)

Thayer's Gull   ADULT WINTER

Great Black-headed (Pallas's) Gull
Larus ichthyaetus
58–67 cm | WS 146–162 cm

Mature when three/four years old. ADULT big pale gull, **broad white wingtip crossed by black band**; long, yellow legs; long, heavy, yellow bill with black/red band. 1ST-WINTER pale grey and white; black tail-band. 2ND-WINTER grey back with fewer markings, similar head and bill (blackish hood in 2ND-SUMMER), tail-band reduced, black wingtip with white streaks on primary coverts/base of primaries, small white 'mirrors'.

ADULT
WINTER

1ST-WINTER

dark mask, white eyelids

pale grey with dark mottles

pink bill, sharp black tip

black hood in summer; dusky mask in winter

1ST-WINTER

ADULT SUMMER

Vagrant from Middle East: 1 historical record (Britain), adult, May 1859, Devon. On coast.

Slender-billed Gull *Chroicocephalus genei*
37–42 cm | WS 90–102 cm

533

Vagrant from SE Europe: <10 records (Britain), May–Jun. S and E coasts. Shallow lagoons.

Mature when three years old. Pattern as Black-headed Gull (*p. 106*), but **always pale-headed**: bigger, bulkier on water; longer-legged. Long neck, extended 'snout', forward-leaning pose. Bill straight, sharp, longer than Black-headed Gull's. ADULT SUMMER **head pure white**; body flushed pink; **bill dark red to blackish; red legs**. ADULT WINTER grey ear spot.

ADULT SUMMER

1ST-WINTER

long bill

dusky ear spot

black tail-band

plain head

eye pale (often hard to see)

ADULT SUMMER

pink flush

ginger-brown markings on spread wing

1ST-SUMMER

long bill and legs pale orange

Slaty-backed Gull *Larus schistisagus*

55–68 cm | WS 135–160 cm

ADULT WINTER

Mature when four years old. ADULT much like Lesser
Black-backed Gull (*p. 126*) but legs **bright pink**, bill thick.
1ST-WINTER **thin dark centres** to tertials, **pale fringes
to brown primaries**; tail solidly dark brown;
bill dull with black tip. (See *opposite*.)

> Vagrant from coastal E Siberia,
> N Japan: 1 record Britain,
> 1 Ireland, Jan–Feb. Coasts, tips

3RD-WINTER

1ST-WINTER

bright pink legs
at all ages

Glaucous-winged Gull *Larus glaucescens*

60–66 cm | WS 137–150 cm

Vagrant from N America:
<5 records Britain, 1 Ireland,
Dec–Apr. Coasts, pools, tips.

Mature when four/five years old. ADULT looks like heavy-billed
Glaucous Gull (*p. 134*) with **dark eye, white tips and 'mirror'
on grey primaries**. In winter, head clouded grey; short legs
dark pink. 1ST-WINTER like dark, greyish, drab Glaucous Gull with
darker wingtip/tail above, same drab shade as back (paler than
back on Glaucous Gull), but bright, pale flight feathers below;
bill all-black at first. 2ND-WINTER: paler than 1st-winter,
bill still blackish; more like adult with
dark bill. (See in flight *opposite*.)

3RD-WINTER

ADULT WINTER

1ST-WINTER

GLAUCOUS GULL

darker than Glaucous

1ST-WINTER

2ND-WINTER

SLATY-BACKED GULL

two white 'mirrors' and white tips on black wingtip

GLAUCOUS-WINGED GULL

white spots between pale grey and dark grey tips, large white mirror

middle primaries have **white spot between grey base and black subterminal band**, above and below.

broad white tertial tips/ trailing edge

LESSER BLACK-BACKED GULL

AUDOUIN'S GULL

ADULT SUMMER

3RD–SUMMER

2ND–SUMMER

dark underwing with whitish central band

1ST–SUMMER

ADULT

ADULT

Audouin's Gull *Larus audouinii*

533

44–52 cm | WS 117–128 cm

Mature when four years old. Like small, slim-winged, elongated Herring Gull (*p. 124*) with sloping forehead, extended 'snout', grey legs, dark eyes. ADULT pale grey above, washed soft grey below with white head, long 'face', **black eyes**. **Stout, dark red bill with black band**; dark **grey legs**. Black wingtips, white tips and small white 'mirror'; black tips/ white underwing contrast recalls Gannet (*p. 89*) at distance. 1ST-WINTER dark above, paler face; dark flank, whiter belly. **Grey legs**, grey-green bill with large black tip. 2ND-WINTER paler, outerwing, hindwing and tail-band black; bill redder by 2ND-SUMMER. 2ND-WINTER like adult with blackish primary coverts.

JUVENILE

1ST-SUMMER

pale, plain head with white eyelids, black-tipped grey bill

ADULT SUMMER

bright white head against greyer body, dark eye and bill

Vagrant from Iberia: <10 records (Britain), May–Aug. S and E coasts. Beaches.

139

'Herring' Gulls

Circling the globe south of the Arctic 'Herring Gulls' have evolved into several species, but races/species and lines of division remain controversial. Recent occurrences suggest almost any of these can appear in Britain and Ireland, but identification of some may remain contentious.

American Herring Gull *Larus smithsonianus*

60–66 cm | WS 120–155 cm

Vagrant from N America: <120 records, mostly (<100) Ireland, most months, some long-stayers. Coastal, beaches.

Extremely similar to Herring Gull (*p. 124*): large, heavily-built. Mature when four/five years old. 1ST-WINTER generally darker than same-age Herring Gull with dark band on greater coverts; **dark brown belly**; **blackish tail**; heavily **barred rump/undertail**; usually plain, dark neck and breast sides. IN FLIGHT dark underwing coverts contrast with pale flight feathers. 2ND-WINTER dark beneath and on rump/tail but very variable, and rate of development to adult varies.

ADULT WINTER Herring Gull variably streaked; American Herring Gull often darker streaks/mask often extending onto breast sides; bill colour and dark band variable on both

4TH-WINTER OR ADULT WINTER

ADULT WINTER

HERRING GULL

4TH-WINTER

2ND-WINTER

JUVENILE Herring Gull has paler greater coverts and a paler, more streaked neck, breast and underside. Race *argenteus* smaller than American Herring Gull.

HERRING GULL

1ST-WINTER

3RD-WINTER more blackish marks on outerwing and tail than Herring Gull (even 4TH-WINTER often has isolated black spots)

3RD-WINTER

3RD-WINTER

AMERICAN HERRING GULL

HERRING GULL

VEGA GULL

ADULT WINTER

pattern of black/white on Vega Gull highly variable but most have black from P4 or P5 outwards, and pale spots between grey base and black tip on middle feathers

more solidly blackish tail, finely marked only at edges

darker greater covert band

1ST-WINTER

darker neck/breast

darker bars on rump

1ST-WINTER

HERRING GULL race *argenteus*

Vega Gull

P3
P4
P5
P6
P7
P8
P9 P10

P3
P4
P5
P6
P7
P8
P9 P10

Vega Gull   *Larus vegae* ◆

55–65 cm | WS 125–160 cm

East Asian counterpart of Europe's Herring Gull (*p. 124*) and the American Herring Gull; its relationship to other forms across North and Central Asia remains controversial but it is generally treated as a full species. Slender, 'gentle-looking' gull; high crown/nape, rather short bill, darkish eye. ADULT back darker than Herring Gull race *argenteus*. Legs dull, pale pinkish, rarely yellowish. Bill pale, greenish-yellow; most (60–70%) have no black on bill; most (90%) have red spot reaching cutting edge, on others restricted to smaller patch.

Vagrant from E Asia: 1 record (Ireland) awaiting formal acceptance. Coastal

dark spots

broad white tertial tips

ADULT WINTER

ADULT WINTER

HERRING GULLS

ADULT WINTER Herring Gulls variable, but the vast majority have a pale iris; often some black on bill

Black Tern
Chlidonias niger 533

22–26 cm | WS 56–62 cm   ⟲ Whiskered Tern (*p. 150*)

Scarce spring and autumn migrant (100s/low 1,000s: Apr–Oct). Coastal and inland waters

Smaller than Common Tern (*p. 144*); **shallow tail fork**. Flies into wind, dips to surface; flocks may fly high, circle, disappear or return to feed. Perches on buoys, posts, rafts. See juvenile Little Tern (*p. 148*).

ADULT SUMMER **smoky black** below, **white under tail**; underwing pale. Bill, legs black. In autumn mottled as black is lost.
ADULT WINTER white body, mid-grey upperparts, pale grey rump. Short black bill; **three-lobed black cap** extends onto nape; white half-ring around eye. **Dusky patch beside chest**. Legs dull reddish. JUVENILE barred brown back, dark front and back edges on innerwing; a few paler above, a few darker with paler rump (see White-winged Black Tern). **Dark chest patches**.

Regular race is *niger*; N American race *surinamensis* vagrant (<10 records (<5 Ireland): Aug–Sep): ADULT SUMMER jet-black on head/breast; for JUVENILE see *opposite*.

VOICE Call insignificant, slightly squeaky, "*ki-ki-ki*" or "*kyeh*".

from/to E Europe

from/to Africa

Harbours, coasts, reservoirs, tips

ADULT SUMMER

White-winged Black Tern   *Chlidonias leucopterus*
20–24 cm | WS 50–56 cm

Like Black Tern but a little **dumpier, longer-legged, shorter-billed**, with straighter wings and less airy, floating action.

ADULT SUMMER **black body**; **white tail, forewings**. Bill black, **legs red**. Patched white in autumn. ADULT WINTER paler than Black Tern, **almost white rump**; **no dark chest patch**; crown streaked, **dark cheek spot**. JUVENILE (most likely in autumn) like young Black Tern but **no chest patches**; back more **solidly dark brown**, wings pale grey, creating **dark saddle/pale wings**; **rump white**.

Very rare migrant from E Europe: about 15 per year, Apr–Oct, most early autumn. Inland and on coasts, mostly in S Britain but widely scattered. Marshes, lakes, coast

ADULT SUMMER

BLACK
TERN

ADULT
SUMMER

ADULT
SUMMER

ADULT
MOULTING
INTO WINTER

BLACK TERN

ADULT JUL–FEB

ADULT
SUMMER

ADULT
SUMMER

ADULT
MOULTING
INTO WINTER

ADULT JUL–FEB

WHITE-WINGED BLACK TERN

WHITE-WINGED
BLACK TERN

'AMERICAN' BLACK TERN
race *surinamensis*

BLACK
TERN

BLACK
TERN

grey crown,
dark mask

white flanks

grey flanks

JUVENILES

Juvenile 'black' tern identification

white over eye

darker back, paler wings
than Black Tern

short bill

unmarked
white chest

WHITE-WINGED
BLACK TERN

JUVENILE

long legs

pale back

JUVENILE

dusky
breast
patch

BLACK TERN

short legs

143

Common Tern

Sterna hirundo ●● **I** `533`

34–37 cm | WS 70–80 cm

Forked tail, dark cap identify as tern. **Longer legs** and bill than Arctic Tern. In flight, subtle differences in profile: see *opposite* and *p. 149*. Hovers before confident plunge; inland, often dips like Black Tern (*p. 142*).

👁 Roseate (*p. 146*), Forster's (*p. 154*), Whiskered (*p. 150*) Terns

ADULT SUMMER **scarlet bill**, black tip. IN FLIGHT, underwing has **broad** blackish outer trailing edge, **square** against **translucent patch**. In autumn **moults inner primaries** (Arctic Tern does not); white forehead; rump becomes **greyer** (white on Arctic Tern). Outer primaries replaced later, inners again before spring. JUVENILE gingery back; blackish forewing. Bill **orange**, dark tip.

VOICE Calls sharp "*kit*", squabbling "*kit-it-it-it*", long-drawn, nasal "*kierri-kierri*".

Locally common summer visitor, Apr–Oct (14,500 pairs, including 4,000 in Ireland), migrant

from/to Scandinavia

from/to W Africa

Coasts, islands, inland lakes, rivers

white forehead, black bill

1ST-SUMMER (APR–AUG) [Aug] very similar to non-breeding adult from Sep onwards

black edge against restricted translucent patch

ADULT SUMMER

spring adult has dark streak on 5th/6th primary; in summer, grey 'bloom' wears off old outer feathers, creating dark outerwing; newer inner primaries remain pale (no such contrast on Arctic Tern)

rump pale grey

browner than juvenile Arctic Tern; underwing as adult

JUVENILE [Aug]

blackish forewing, pale midwing, grey hindwing bar; only those with dark outer primaries and hindwing bar can be aged; others look like adult

JUVENILE [Sep]

usually strong black shoulder bar

back browner, forehead faintly browner and bill paler than juvenile Arctic Tern

JUVENILE (fresh) [Aug]

bll scarlet with black-tip (slightly longer, weightier, less 'spiky' than Arctic Tern's)

pale inner primaries contrast with darker wingtip

relatively short tail

ADULT SUMMER

relatively long legs

Arctic Tern

33–39 cm | WS 66–77 cm

Roseate Tern (*p. 146*),
Whiskered Tern (*p. 150*)

Very like Common Tern; very
short legs. Flight profile important – see *opposite* and *p. 149*.
Dive hesitant: hovers, half-dives, briefly hovers again.

ADULT SUMMER greyer body, whiter cheek/throat than Common
Tern; **shorter bill all deep red**. IN FLIGHT, upperwing uniformly
pale, underwing white with **narrow dark trailing edge; all
flight feathers semi-translucent**. In autumn, wingtips darker,
but no sharp contrast; does not moult primaries until winter.
White forehead Sep/Oct onwards (Jun/Jul on Common Tern).
JUVENILE ginger soon fades; **back scaled grey, white and blackish**.

VOICE Calls like Common Tern, more piping/ringing,
more emphasis on last rather than first syllable.

Locally common summer visitor,
Apr–Oct (55,000 pairs, including
3,500 Ireland; declining), migrant

from/to Arctic Canada,
Iceland and Greenland

from/to Arctic

from/to S Africa
and S oceans

Coasts, islands, offshore; scarce
inland

1ST-SUMMER

white
secondaries

translucent
primaries and
secondaries

primaries all moulted in winter so
same age with no contrast, unlike on
Common Tern

rump
white

ADULT SUMMER

short head/neck/bill;
long tail streamers; short
innerwing, long outerwing

generally more black below
eye than Common Tern

JUVENILE
[Aug]

greyer than juvenile
Common Tern;
underwing as adult

diffuse dark forewing
blends back to
white hindwing

JUVENILE (faded)
[Aug]

back greyer
than juvenile
Common Tern

red bill base on fresh juvenile
soon becomes darker

JUVENILE (fresh)
[Aug]

closed wingtip all silvery,
no contrast

relatively short legs

ADULT SUMMER

Roseate Tern

Sterna dougallii ●ⓘ

33–36 cm | WS 67–76 cm

👁 Forster's Tern (*p. 154*)

Rare summer visitor, Apr–Oct
(850 pairs, including 750 in
Ireland); rare migrant

Resembles Common Tern
(*p. 144*) but paler overall (see Sandwich Tern).

ADULT SUMMER **white, pink-flushed body without grey** (pink may
persist in autumn). Long cap tends to curve down hindneck.
Blackish stripe on closed wingtip. Tail very long. In summer, bill
black, dark **red at base**. IN FLIGHT, **noticeably pale**. Round head,
long bill; long tail; rather stiff, quick, shallow, fast beats; when
feeding often dives from straight flight without hovering.

VOICE Calls include distinct double "*chivik*".

underwing has
dusky streaks,
no blackish
trailing edge;
translucent
patch like
Common Tern

ADULT SUMMER

blackish streaks on outerwing
like Sandwich or Common Tern,
unlike Arctic Tern

to
W Africa

Islands, coasts; very rare inland

JUVENILE

similar to a very young Sandwich
Tern: scaled blackish above;
cap, bill and legs dark

JUVENILE
(more advanced)
[Aug]

JUVENILE
[Aug]

bill gradually changes from black
in spring to black with bright red
base by autumn

ADULT
[Jun]

ADULT
[Jul]

ADULT
[Aug]

Sandwich Tern

Sterna (Thalasseus) sandvicensis **533**

37–43 cm | WS 85–97 cm

👁 Gull-billed Tern (*p. 150*), Cabot's Tern (*p. 153*)

Large, very pale. Compared with Common Tern (*p. 144*), bigger, **whiter**; long, angled wings; short tail; longer, blacker bill; longer **black legs**. Over sea, very white (see Mediterranean Gull (*p. 107*)), long-winged; high-dives with big splash. ADULT SUMMER **white below**, more or less darker outer/paler inner primaries. **Bill black with pale (yellow) tip**.

VOICE Highly distinctive, loud, rhythmic, abrupt, short, tearing "*kierr-ik, ki-rink*" or "*ko-yok*". Young: high, whining "*srreee-i*".

Locally common summer visitor, Mar–Oct (118,000 pairs, including 3,700 in Ireland); a few winter

to W Africa

Sandy coasts, lagoons; scarce inland

wingtip blackish by late summer; pale after autumn moult; forehead white from June/July

ADULT WINTER

JUVENILE

slight darker 'W' on upperwings; dark corners to short tail. Trails behind adult, calling to be fed

dusky cap (becomes blacker mask/white forehead)

grey with dark scales above

blackish bill

black cap, ragged crest

JUVENILE [Sep]

blackish legs

ADULT WINTER JUL–FEB

yellow-tipped black bill

ADULT SUMMER MAR–JUL

Little Tern

Sternula albifrons ● ● **I** `532`

21–25 cm | WS 41–47 cm

Small, fast, long-winged tern: splashing headlong dives into water (real 'smack', not dip). Slightly tubby-chested; wings long, narrow, tapered: closed tail long 'spike'. Fast, direct flight; quick, regular, sweeping beats of curved-back wings. When feeding, more erratic, **frequent fast hovers**.

ADULT very pale grey and pure white; sharp black cap/eyestripe, **white forehead** even in spring. **Bill yellow**, black tip; legs yellow to orange. Long closed wingtip shows black lower edge. IN FLIGHT, **outer primaries blackish**. JUVENILE like tiny young Sandwich Tern; barred, dusky on crown, legs pale.

VOICE Quick, rasping "*kreet*" and fast rhythmic chatter "*kiereet kiereet kiereet*".

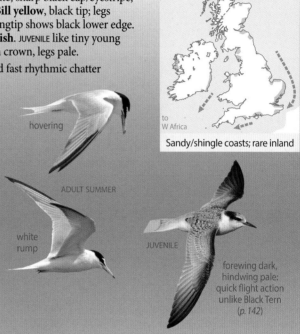

Scarce/rare summer visitor, Apr–Sep (2,000 pairs, including 200 in Ireland)

to W Africa

Sandy/shingle coasts; rare inland

ADULT SUMMER

grey rump

North American form *antillarum* (may be full species, **Least Tern**) Vagrant: 1 record (Britain) Jun–Jul, bird returning for ten consecutive years) **grey rump**; chirping, squeakier call than regular race *albifrons*.

hovering

ADULT SUMMER

white rump

JUVENILE

forewing dark, hindwing pale: quick flight action unlike Black Tern (*p. 142*)

JUVENILE

ADULT SUMMER

Regularly occurring terns in flight
(adults in summer)

GULL-BILLED
TERN
(*p. 150*)

LITTLE TERN

SANDWICH TERN (*p. 147*)

COMMON TERN
(*p. 144*)

ARCTIC TERN
(*p. 145*)

ROSEATE TERN
(*p. 146*)

WHISKERED TERN
(*p. 150*)

BLACK TERN
(*p. 142*)

CASPIAN TERN
(*p. 150*)

WHITE-WINGED
BLACK TERN
(*p. 142*)

Whiskered Tern *Chlidonias hybrida*   `533`

24–28 cm | WS 57–63 cm

Very rare migrant from S Europe: <200 records, 4–5 per year, (vagrant Ireland <25 records). Apr–Oct. Lakes, marshes, lagoons.

Like Black Tern (*p. 142*) but more robust; longer, heavier bill; longer legs; flight a little heavier. ADULT SUMMER black cap like Common Tern (*p. 144*); back, rump, tail pale grey. ADULT WINTER white below; hint of chest patch at most; bill reddish at base; without ear-lobe of Black Tern or isolated cheek spot of White-winged Black Tern (*p. 142*). **Shallower tail fork** than Common Tern, greyer rump/tail. JUVENILE like adult winter but head washed brownish; wings silvery-grey. Stronger contrast with paler wings than Black Tern, less contrast, more barred than White-winged Black Tern. By autumn, greyer back, barred scapulars; grey hindwing band like young Common Tern, but no blackish shoulder. Tail has dark spots on tip, white sides (Common Tern has pale tips, blackish sides).

VOICE Short, hoarse notes; likely to be silent in Britain/Ireland.

JUVENILE 'MARSH TERNS'

BLACK

WHISKERED

WHITE-WINGED BLACK

Caspian Tern *Hydroprogne caspia*   `533`

48–55 cm | WS 96–111 cm

🕐 Large, orange-billed terns (*p. 152*)

Very rare migrant between Baltic and S Europe: <300 records, about 5 per year, declining (vagrant Ireland <15 records), Apr–Oct. Coastal lagoons, lakes.

Huge tern; long head/neck/bill, short tail; size of large gull. Bill well-proportioned but obviously large close-up. ADULT SUMMER **gull-like** on ground; **black legs**, heavy body, **big black cap**. Bill **dagger-like, red with dark patch** near tip. ADULT WINTER cap dark, finely streaked white. IN FLIGHT, reminiscent of small Gannet (*p. 89*) with **pointed, angled wings; black under tip**. JUVENILE barred blackish above, brownish cap; nape blacker; bill orange-red with dark tip. 1ST-SUMMER like adult winter but whiter crown streaks, darker tips to primary coverts, fresh pale inner primaries, old darker outer ones, less black under wingtip.

VOICE Calls include deep, heron-like, shouted "*kree-ahk*".

Gull-billed Tern *Gelochelidon nilotica*   `532`

35–42 cm | WS 76–86 cm

🕐 Forster's Tern (winter) (*p. 154*)

Very rare migrant from S Europe: <400 records, about 3 per year (vagrant Ireland <20 records), May–Sep. Has bred once. Lagoons, marshes/wet meadows.

Resembles Sandwich Tern (*p. 147*), needs care. Feeds by dipping and hawking over drier ground, does not normally dive. Longer-legged than Sandwich Tern; **head rounder**, no crest. Legs black. **Bill stout, all-black**, shorter than Sandwich Tern's – but see juvenile Sandwich Tern. ADULT SUMMER pale grey, white below. IN FLIGHT, head short, wings long, slender; tail has shallow notch. **Rump and tail pale grey** (easy to miss). Dark outer/pale inner primary contrast like Sandwich/Common (*p. 144*) Terns; fresh primaries have **dark trailing edge** and distinct line underneath (weak on Sandwich Tern). ADULT WINTER **black patch through eye** (see Forster's Tern (*p. 154*)). 1ST-WINTER very pale, weak dark eye patch, greyish nape; rump whitish, tail palest grey.

VOICE Call low, harsh "*ker-wick*".

WHISKERED TERN

ADULT
SUMMER

ADULT
WINTER

ADULT SUMMER

ADULT WINTER

CASPIAN TERN

ADULT SUMMER

bill held more or less
horizontal in flight

1ST-SUMMER
(one-year-old)

ADULT
SUMMER

GULL-BILLED TERN

**SANDWICH
TERN**

ADULT
WINTER

ADULT
SUMMER

**SANDWICH
TERN**

ADULT
SUMMER

NT Elegant Tern *Sterna (Thalasseus) elegans* ◆

43 cm | WS 76–81 cm

Black-capped, black-legged tern, size/shape as Sandwich Tern (*p. 147*) but see Lesser Crested Tern; long, slender orange bill with redder base and paler **drooped tip**. Rump and short tail almost white. ADULT long, narrow, shaggy, drooped crest; forehead white in winter, **broad black mask encloses eye**.

rump/tail look white

ADULT SUMMER

long drooped crest in summer

ADULT WINTER

ADULT SUMMER

Vagrant from N America: <10 records (Ireland) [British records under review], May–Jul). Coasts.

Lesser Crested Tern *Sterna (Thalasseus) bengalensis*

33–40 cm | WS 76–82 cm

Smaller than Royal Tern: size of Sandwich Tern (*p. 147*); **size/structure** judgment imperative. Broader-winged than Sandwich and Elegant Terns, less extreme angularity; flies with bill more horizontal. Bill tapered to finer tip than Royal Tern. ADULT SUMMER upperparts **darker than Sandwich Tern** and Royal Tern. Bill **bright orange**, or deep orange with paler tip (paler, less red, than Royal Tern, less slender than Elegant Tern). IN FLIGHT, **rump and tail pale grey** (hard to see in strong light). Fresh primaries (autumn–winter) very pale, silvery; worn outer ones (summer) become dark.

Vagrant from Africa: <15 records (1 Ireland), May–Aug. Has bred (mixed pair with Sandwich Tern). Coasts.

rump/tail very pale grey

ADULT SUMMER

short crest in summer

extensive white crown in winter

ADULT SUMMER

ADULT WINTER

Royal Tern *Sterna maxima* (*Thalasseus maximus*)
42–49 cm | WS 86–92 cm

Big, elegant, well-proportioned tern: see Caspian (*p. 150*), Lesser Crested, Elegant Terns. Bigger than Sandwich Tern (*p. 147*), nearer Common Gull (*p. 114*) in size (vital to assess size). Long, dagger-like bill **more slender than Caspian Tern's**. ADULT SUMMER black crown, short crest. Bill **orange-red**; legs black. Upperwing similar to Common Tern (*p. 144*) (outer primaries wear to black). ADULT WINTER big **white forehead, isolates dark eye** (Caspian Tern has dark forehead).

CASPIAN TERN to scale

maxima

rump/tail white

albididorsalis

ADULT SUMMER

ROYAL TERN

Presumed African race *albididorsalis* also recorded (adult, Ireland/Wales, June): bill slimmer, more yellow-orange, compared with American race *maxima*.

ADULT SUMMER race *maxima*

white extends behind eye in winter, unlike Caspian Tern

ADULT WINTER race *maxima*

Vagrant from America: <10 records (1 Ireland), Mar–Dec. Coasts.

ADULT WINTER race *albididorsalis*

Cabot's Tern *Sterna acuflavida* (*Thalasseus acuflavidus*)
37–40 cm | WS 85–95 cm

Very similar to Sandwich Tern (*p. 147*) with a slightly shorter, thicker bill, thinner white fringes on inner webs of outer primaries and more sharply defined black nape/white crown in autumn (speckled border on Sandwich Tern).

thicker white tips to fresh outer primaries

white tips narrow/absent

SANDWICH TERN

ADULT SUMMER

CABOT'S TERN

Race *acuflavidus* (one record, Britain) has black bill with yellow tip (dark/dull yellowish tinge on juvenile), while race *eurygnatha* (Cayenne Tern) (one as yet unconfirmed, Britain) has a dull yellow to orange bill and sometimes yellowish on legs.

speckled

more solid black

bill slightly thicker than Sandwich Tern's

SANDWICH TERN

CABOT'S TERN

ADULT WINTER

ADULT SUMMER

N America vagrant: 1 record (Britain), Nov. American-ringed 1st-winter bird found dead in a wood inland. Usually coastal.

SANDWICH TERN

Forster's Tern *Sterna forsteri*

33–36 cm | WS 64–70 cm

Much like Common Tern (*p. 144*). ADULT SUMMER red bill, large black tip; red legs. tail **grey with white edge**; upperwing paler towards tip. **Underside white**.
More obvious in winter (terns being rare at that time of year, plumage more distinctive, but see Sandwich Tern (*p. 147*), Gull-billed Tern (*p. 150*)). ADULT WINTER black bill, **frosty white upperwing**, solid **black mask** behind eye. IMMATURE has weak dark tips to primaries and coverts.

COMMON TERN
dark edge to tail
silvery-white primaries

tail grey with white edge
ADULT SUMMER

ADULT WINTER

eye-catching black mask in winter

ADULT SUMMER MAR–AUG [Apr]

NB forecrown all black in full summer plumage

COMMON TERN
ADULT SUMMER
underside grey

underside **white**

ADULT WINTER AUG–FEB

Vagrant from N America: <60 records (<40 in Ireland), Jan–Mar, Aug–Dec. Coasts, estuaries.

Aleutian Tern *Onychoprion aleuticus*

32–34 cm | WS 75–80 cm

Like dark Common/Arctic Tern (*pp. 144–145*), or pale Bridled Tern, with spiky **black bill**, black legs. Neat **white forehead** reaches just over eye, black eyestripe, white cheeks and throat; pale grey underside. Underwing pale with broad **dark trailing edge to secondaries** and outer primaries, broken in centre. Rump and long, forked tail white.

black trailing edge to innerwing

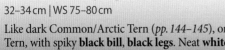

head like Bridled Tern's

ADULT SUMMER

Vagrant from N Pacific coasts: 1 record (Britain), May. Coast.

Sooty Tern *Onychoprion fuscatus*
42–45 cm | WS 72–80 cm

A large, dark-backed tern: see Bridled Tern.
ADULT long, slim, elegant; black, sooty-grey
and white. Upperparts blackish, fading
browner/greyish; **cap jet black, forehead
white** (deep/broad white 'blob', blunt over
eye in side view). **Bill long and black.**
IN FLIGHT, tail has blackish centre and
long white sides with large white tips
(less striking on Bridled Tern).

ADULT
SUMMER

strong
underwing
contrast

short white 'V'
to eye

ADULT SUMMER

Vagrant from tropical seas:
<25 records (<5 Ireland),
Apr–Sep. Coasts.

Bridled Tern *Onychoprion anaethetus*
37–42 cm | WS 65–72 cm

Slightly smaller than Sooty Tern (size of
Common Tern (*p. 144*)) but similar pattern.
ADULT upperparts paler **grey-brown**; cap black;
elongated **white forehead reaches back over
eye** in side view, a **striking 'V'** from in front.
Clearly **contrasted jet-black cap/grey-brown
back** (Sooty Tern very weak contrast at most).
Worn birds have dark trailing edge/paler
coverts on upperwing. In strong light over sea,
underparts can look dark in shade.

ADULT
SUMMER

weaker underwing
contrast than
Sooty Tern

long white 'V'
over eye

ADULT SUMMER

Vagrant from tropical seas:
<25 records (Britain), Apr–Oct.
Coasts, reservoirs.

SKUAS

SKUA ID size | tail shape | underparts pattern | rump/vent barring | underwing pattern

Island- or moorland-breeding seabirds that feed at sea and spend the winter far south of Britain and Ireland. In summer they breed in the north, but in spring and autumn (extending into early winter) may be seen widely from coasts, especially headlands. Inland records are mostly linked to post-storm displacement.

4 regular species: 2 breed; plus at least one vagrant not yet identified to species level.

Skuas (*pp. 158–164*) fly directly, low over the sea, with a relaxed yet purposeful action, and pursue other birds, especially terns and smaller gulls, to force them to disgorge and drop their food. These tightly-turning, twisting pursuits and dark silhouettes identify them as skuas at great range), but closer views are needed to separate species. Adults have distinctive tail projections but immatures can be difficult to identify in short views over the sea.

Intermediate form
Arctic Skua harassing
an Arctic Tern.

Arctic and **Pomarine Skuas** show dark and pale forms (and 'intermediate' birds), as well as distinct 1st-winter plumages (second-year birds tend to remain farther south all year), all with a pale outerwing 'flash'. Long-tailed Skuas are rare migrants but pass by a few remote north-western headlands (and may even cross overland) in larger numbers in spring. Adults do not show a fully dark plumage but 1st-winter birds are variable.

Great Skuas are bigger and heavier than the others, and have no pale-bellied forms, being dark, more or less streaked, with especially bold white wing patches. They are big enough to tackle almost any seabird, and increasing numbers may hasten declines in Arctic Skuas, already adversely affected by reductions in smaller seabirds and their small fish prey.

GULLS

A skua's smooth or barred appearance and lack of a white rump rules out most immature gulls

Ageing and moult sequence in skuas

The timing and extent of moult in skuas explain some of the variations in winter and immature plumages, mostly rare in British and Irish waters. The moult sequence over the time to maturity (3–5 years) is shown here. Juvenile Pomarine Skuas, for example, quickly moult their body feathers, then the wings and tail from February to July, unlike adults. A complete moult follows from the following July; subsequent moults are patchy in winter and spring, so immature birds in summer have variable amounts of winter plumage retained before the next complete moult in summer and autumn. Bleached old feathers alongside dark new ones create bizarre patterns. The steadily increasing tail projection is the best indication of age in smaller skuas.

POMARINE SKUA
PALE FORMS

1ST-SUMMER
(2ND CALENDAR YEAR)
NOV–JUN
[May]

JUVENILE
JUL–OCT
[Oct]

juvenile plumage

immature plumages

POST-JUVENILE MOULT

FLEDGE

W

T

HB

JUN JUL AUG SEP OCT NOV DEC JAN FEB MAR APR MAY JUN JUL

1ST
CALENDAR
YEAR

2ND
CALENDAR
YEAR

KEY: W = wing; T = tail; HB = head and body

Skua forms (in flight – see p. 164)

Arctic and Pomarine Skuas have recognisable forms (or morphs): pale and dark. However, these interbreed freely and produce a more or less continuous gradation between extremes (hence there are also 'intermediate' birds). Juveniles also show differences but they are generally much less clear cut. Juvenile Long-tailed Skuas have various forms, but adults are more constant.

Arctic Skua forms, left to right: pale, intermediate and dark

Pomarine Skuas migrating past North Uist: flocks often pass headlands in the far north-west and along English Channel coasts at the end of April/early May

2ND-SUMMER
(3RD CALENDAR YEAR)
JUL–APR
[Aug]

Years 2–(5) Immature moults are often not completed, hence the confusing array of plumages that may be encountered – most immature birds have shorter central tail feathers than adults

Adults moult their whole plumage from August (or July in failed breeders) to December, and some head and body feathers again between February and April.

Immature plumage moult cycle repeated until breeding maturity is reached within 3–5 years.

immature plumages
IMMATURE MOULT

W
T
HB

ADULT BREEDING
APR–JUN
[May]

OCT NOV DEC JAN FEB MAR APR MAY JUN JUL AUG SEP OCT NOV DEC JAN FEB MAR APR

2ND CY 3RD CY

5TH CY
+

FIRST FULL
PRE-BREEDING
MOULT

failed and non-breeders
may start in July

HB
T
W

POST-BREEDING MOULT

PRE-BREEDING MOULT

adult plumage moult cycle repeated

157

Arctic Skua

Stercorarius parasiticus ● **532**

38–41 cm (plus up to 7 cm tail projection) | WS 107–125 cm

Elegant, tapered, gull-like seabird; chases gulls, terns. Fast, twisting pursuit, dark shapes identify skuas far out to sea. Narrow tail, **white flash on outerwing**. Size as Kittiwake (*p. 108*); slimmer than Pomarine Skua. Flight relaxed, direct.

ADULT thin, **pointed tail spike**. Pale form **plain brown** above, neat breast-band, white underside. Dark form brown, dark hindwing band (less contrast on Pomarine Skua, more on Long-tailed Skua (*p. 160*)). Beware Sooty Shearwater (*p. 91*); young gulls have pale rumps. JUVENILE typically yellowish- or rufous-brown, finely barred; pale primary tips. A few solidly black. (See also *pages 162–163*.)

VOICE In diving display flights, calls loud, nasal, mewing "*waaa-ooh*" or "*mee-ah!*"

Scarce breeder in N Scotland (2,000 pairs, declining); fairly common spring/autumn migrant

↑ APR—MAY   from/to Arctic

↓ AUG—OCT

to
S oceans

Islands, coasts, rare inland

ADULT SUMMER
PALE FORM

adults are aggressive to intruders, including people at colonies

JUVENILE
see p. 162

ADULT SUMMER
DARK FORM

ADULT SUMMER
INTERMEDIATE

Mixed pairs are frequent and, as a result, gradations between the forms are recognisable at any age.

ADULT SUMMER
PALE FORM

Pomarine Skua   *Stercorarius pomarinus*

38–57 cm (plus up to 10 cm tail projection) | WS 110–138 cm

Gull-like, piratical seabird; white wing flash. Small groups in spring. Compare with young gulls (which have whiter rump/dark tail-band). Dark and pale forms, plus immature plumages.

Larger and heavier-bodied than Arctic Skua (Common Gull (*p. 114*) size) with broader wing, rounder belly. ADULT **broad tail spike** ('spoons'; may break off). Pale form darker above than Arctic Skua, breast-band/spotted flanks patchy. Dark form brown, white wing flash. JUVENILE variable from brown to black, typically darker than Arctic Skua; dark primary tips. A few solidly black. (See also *pages 162–163*.)

Widespread, generally scarce spring and autumn/early winter migrant (100s–low 1,000s a year)

↑ APR–MAY   from/to Siberia
↓ AUG–NOV

from/to
W Africa and
mid-Atlantic   APR–MAY

Coasts, offshore; very rare inland

ADULT SUMMER
PALE FORM

JUVENILE
see p. 162

ADULT SUMMER
DARK FORM

ADULT NON-BREEDING
PALE FORM

ADULT SUMMER
PALE FORM

Comparison of adult skuas *p. 164*

Long-tailed Skua

Stercorarius longicaudus

35–43 cm (plus up to 15 cm tail projection) | WS 102–117 cm

Small, slender, long-winged, deep-chested skua (weight more up-front than Arctic Skua (*p. 158*)). Note tail shape, thin white flash on outerwing. About size of Black-headed Gull (*p. 106*)/ Kittiwake (*p. 108*). Flight tern-like.

ADULT like pale Arctic Skua (no dark form); **greyer** with **blacker flight feathers**; two white shaft streaks. White breast **merges into dusky belly**, **no breast-band** (Arctic Skua has dark chest sides/breast-band, white belly). **Underwing all-dark** (pale primary patch on Arctic Skua). Tail spike very long, flexible (longest Arctic Skuas' surprisingly long). JUVENILE slender, slim; small bill. Typically greyish, often pale on head and belly, some very dark. (See also *pages 162–163*.)

Rare spring and autumn migrant on coasts; rarely flocks (10s/low 100s) in spring in NW

↑ MAY–JUN
↓ AUG–SEP

from/to Arctic

from/to
S oceans

Coasts, offshore; very rare inland

ADULT SUMMER

ADULT SUMMER

JUVENILE
see p. 162

some have darker belly, white on breast, but there is no distinct dark form

ADULT SUMMER

Great Skua (Bonxie)   *Stercorarius skua*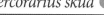

50–58 cm | WS 125–140 cm

Biggest, heaviest, gull-like, predatory skua. On migration flies low, direct; big, dark with **triangular white wing patches**. Fast, twisting pursuit of birds as large as Gannet (*p. 89*); may dive on seabird and kill it with bill. Very aggressive to people at its colonies, flying chest-high and swooping over head. Displays on ground with raised wings.

Broad-based wings, outerwing tapered to point. ADULT warm brown, pale streaks, darker cap, blacker wingtip with **wide white flash**. Many show dark cap/pale face. JUVENILE/1ST-WINTER darker, more uniform rufous below, more barred above, wing flashes smaller, especially above (see *p. 163*).

VOICE Short barking calls at colony.

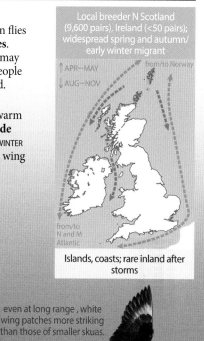

Local breeder N Scotland (9,600 pairs), Ireland (<50 pairs); widespread spring and autumn/ early winter migrant

↑ APR—MAY   from/to Norway
↓ AUG—NOV

from/to N and M Atlantic

Islands, coasts; rare inland after storms

ADULT

even at long range , white wing patches more striking than those of smaller skuas.

ADULT

ADULT

South Polar Skua
Stercorarius maccormicki

Vagrant from South Atlantic: <5 records (Britain), Oct, Feb. Coast.

Originally identified by DNA as Brown Skua *Stercorarius antarcticus*, all records now considered to be South Polar Skua. Very like Great Skua, difficult to identify; more compact, thinner bill, more uniform upperparts, usually pale neck.

JUVENILE

ADULT

Identification of juvenile skuas

PALE

DARK

short, stubby bill

small; varies from pale greyish to very dark

LONG-TAILED SKUA
(p. 160)

varies from buff bars on brown to very dark

PALE

bill slim, dull grey, black tip

'INTERMEDIATE'

ARCTIC SKUA
(p. 158)

neat, pale primary tips

primary tips dark, or fine pale tips

bill thick, pale base, dark tip (like Arctic Skua), visible at longer range

varies from buff bars on brown, to very dark with rufous bars or solidly blackish

'INTERMEDIATE'

POMARINE SKUA
(p. 159)

Adult skuas in fresh plumage have plumage patterns, tail projections and size differences that easily distinguish them. Juveniles and 1st-winter birds are much harder: although size, shape and actions may make them seem distinctive at a distance, birds seen more closely often provoke controversy. It might seem unlikely that a Pomarine Skua could be confused with a Great Skua, for example, but a very dark bird sitting on a beach can be surprisingly difficult. That in itself might help rule out the smaller Arctic Skua: but flying Arctic/Pomarine juveniles, especially in poor viewing conditions, may often be left unidentified even by experienced observers.

ochre streaks on neck and wing coverts

largest, most streaked, but dark individuals much like dark Pomarine Skua

GREAT SKUA
(p. 161)

LONG-TAILED SKUA
(*p. 160*)

generally greyer
than Arctic Skua

PALE

barred

paler birds:
blackish

whitish

PALE

1ST-SUMMER
tail spike more
pointed than
juvenile/
1st-winter

pale-barred
rump

white flash on
darkest birds

'INTERMEDIATE'

DARK

small primary flash

central tail feathers
typically rounded but
can be pointed or thin

ARCTIC SKUA
(*p. 158*)

short tail point

PALE

most are rufous-brown;
yellower/rusty head,
underside. Palest have
paler neck; broad pale bars
under tail; dark rump

DARK

rump not paler
than nape

White flash on
upperwing

**POMARINE
SKUA**
(*p. 159*)

whitish primary patch plus
second crescent on
underwing primary coverts

short, blunt,
or no tail
point

'INTERMEDIATE'

pale crescent
on wing
coverts can
be striking

palest are barred
buff across rump,
under tail; barred
underwing

PALE

PALE

rump usually
paler than nape

'INTERMEDIATE'

GREAT SKUA
(*p. 161*)

resembles dark
Pomarine Skua
but lacks pale
barring on
rump and vent

tail short: square
or wedge-shaped,
barely protruding
central feathers

large white wing patches

163

Adult skuas in flight

ARCTIC SKUA
(p. 158)

POMARINE SKUA
(p. 159)

PALE

PALE

LONG-TAILED SKUA
(p. 160)

PALE

PALE

PALE

PALE

ARCTIC SKUA
(p. 158)

DARK

'INTERMEDIATE'

DARK

GREAT SKUA
(p. 161)

AUKS

9 species: 4 breed; 1 regular autumn/winter migrant; 4 very or extremely rare.

AUK ID bill shape and colour | head pattern | underwing

Strictly seabirds, associated with cliffs and islands in summer, but out at sea at other times, auks are heavy-bodied and short-legged, often seen in flight low over the sea or swimming. In flight they look heavy, small-winged, with a fast, whirring action: high speed but little agility. On water, they sit low but are buoyant, and dive under from the surface.

Black Guillemots like small rocky islands and boulder-strewn shores, Guillemots prefer flat-topped offshore stacks and long narrow ledges on sheer cliffs. Razorbills share the cliffs but nest in small cavities. Puffins burrow into soft earth higher up or nest inside cavities in scree slopes. While the others squat upright, settled on the length of their legs, Puffins stand properly on their webbed feet and walk quite well. Little Auks are just autumn/winter migrants, flying offshore or swimming, sometimes exhausted, close inshore.

Auk ageing/moult

Juvenile Guillemots and Razorbills leave the cliff ledges half-grown, with an adult; they look like adults by the following spring.
Adults are flightless for 6–7 weeks in the autumn while they moult.
Young Puffins leave the burrow at night, alone, and young Black Guillemots also go to sea unaccompanied.

Puffins can be seen on clifftop swards and grass-grown or rocky scree slopes; Guillemots may nest on flat-topped stacks or open ledges on sheer cliffs.

NT Guillemot

Uria aalge

38–46 cm | WS 61–73 cm

Cliff-breeding seabird, nesting on open ledges. On land, upright, legs back near tail, **bill pointed**, tail short and square. On sea, long and low, short neck upright, horizontal head/bill with **neat dagger-like shape**.

ADULT **dark brown** to blackish above; white underside rounded against dark neck. Short white bar on closed wing (trailing edge in flight). **Rump dark, narrow white sides** (Long-tailed Duck (*p. 60*), Razorbill wider white sides). A few (with increasing frequency northwards) show white line behind eye ('bridled'). ADULT WINTER/IMMATURE dark on crown/nape, white face/cheeks; **dark line bisects white rear cheek**.

VOICE Calls on cliffs long, whirring notes; at sea, young bird calls with loud, musical whistle, "*plee-u*", puzzling at first.

> Brünnich's Guillemot, Ancient Murrelet (*p. 172*)

Race *aalge* breeding in N Britain is darker than race *albionis* breeding in Ireland and S Britain.

Locally abundant breeding resident (1.3 million birds); rare inshore in winter

On/off rocky coasts/cliffs in summer, offshore in winter

Guillemot colonies on flat rocks or high, sheer cliffs are noisy, busy places in summer.

IN FLIGHT, tapered both ends, fat in middle; narrow, mid-set wings, **fast, rather whirring action** over sea (not high except when visiting cliff).

JUVENILE/1ST-WINTER (juvenile initially identifiable by small size and call, but after September not safely distinguished from winter adult)

ADULT SUMMER

black

pointed bill

ADULT WINTER

white

ADULT SUMMER 'BRIDLED'

short tail

ADULT WINTER

marked flanks

ADULT SUMMER race *aalge*

Razorbill

Alca torda ● except race *torda* ● **I**

NT

NT

38–43 cm | WS 60–69 cm

👁 Brünnich's Guillemot (p. 172)

The race breeding in Britain and Ireland is *islandica*; northern race *torda*, a winter migrant, is generally larger but overlap makes recognition impossible at times.

Like Guillemot, more clearly **black and white**, **bull-necked**. Tail pointed; white underside more pointed against neck. More often in estuaries/deep bays than Guillemot. Dives often, opening wings slightly as it does so. Nests in cavities/crevices, less on open ledges/stacks.

ADULT bill **blade-shaped**, less pointed than Guillemot; **white cross-band** and **line to eye**. ADULT WINTER/IMMATURE bill blunt; all-dark on young bird; crown black; white blob behind eye but less obvious line across cheek than Guillemot. Squat, head sunk low, if tired/inshore.

VOICE Calls at nest guttural, growling "*goarrr*", harder, less whirring/musical than Guillemot.

Locally common breeding resident (164,000 birds); scarce inshore in winter

On/off rocky coasts/cliffs in summer, offshore in winter

IN FLIGHT, difficult to tell from Guillemot unless bill shape visible; a little shorter, dumpier (see Little Auk (p. 170)), cleaner white under wing. **Parallel white rump sides** (see Long-tailed Duck (p. 60)).

ADULT SUMMER

thick bill

JUVENILE/1ST-WINTER

Razorbills tend to be scattered more thinly amongst Guillemots in mixed colonies.

ADULT WINTER

white

ADULT SUMMER

long, pointed tail often raised when swimming

VU
EN

Puffin

Fratercula arctica 532

28–34 cm | WS 50–60 cm

👁 Tufted Puffin (*p. 172*)

Locally common summer resident (580,000 pairs); rare inshore in winter

Cliffs, islands; at sea in winter

Small, upright, standing/ waddling on toes (Guillemot (*p. 166*)/Razorbill (*p. 167*) rest on lower leg). Often on same cliffs as Razorbill, Guillemot, but nests in cavities or burrows into earth or detritus slopes amongst lush vegetation, often on islands.

ADULT black and white, but large, round head and bright bill unique – **pale grey disk on face; triangular red, yellow, grey bill; orange legs**. ADULT WINTER more tricky, especially when flying at long range: face much darker, bill smaller, much duller and darker, but still obvious deep shield-shape, not pointed like Guillemot or so shallow as Razorbill. JUVENILE has even smaller bill: see Little Auk (*p. 170*), but face dark, cheeks dusky, upperwing plain black.

VOICE Low, hard cooing and "*arrk arrk*" notes.

ADULT SUMMER

ADULT SUMMER

IN FLIGHT, **dark underwing**, lack of white trailing edge on top; dark breast-band; dark rear flank. Fast, whirring wingbeats

Puffin colonies may be associated with other auks or in quite different places on clifftop slopes or small grassy islands.

face becomes dusky and bill smaller and duller after breeding

JUVENILE

ADULT WINTER

ADULT SUMMER

Black Guillemot (Tystie)

Cepphus grylle

32–38 cm | WS 49–58 cm

Unlike Guillemot (*p. 166*) in many ways: hangs about rocky islets, piers, offshore rocks, boulders, harbours and sheltered Scottish sea lochs, not on ledges of sheer cliffs.

ADULT smoky black with **oval white wing patch**, striking at very long range. Underwing mostly white. Inside bill and **legs bright red**. ADULT WINTER head and body smudgy white, back barred grey-black; wing black with big, unmarked, white patch. Bill tapered to point, like small Guillemot, but **legs still red**. JUVENILE dark, barred black and white on flanks, browner on head; wing patch barred dark. 1ST-WINTER, whiter, like adult winter, but black spots/bars reduce clarity of white upperwing patch. See winter grebes (*p. 72*) for possible confusion.

VOICE High, shrill whistle, open mouth bright red inside.

Widespread but uncommon resident in N, W (38,000 pairs); rare in S in winter

Rocky shores, islands, sheltered inshore waters

ADULT SUMMER

IN FLIGHT, low, whirring, big oval white patch on upperwing and white underwing obvious, especially in summer.

ADULT WINTER

ADULT SUMMER

Black Guillemots nest as isolated pairs or small groups around rocky islets, or at the foot of larger cliffs.

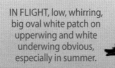

JUVENILE/1ST-WINTER

ADULT WINTER

ADULT SUMMER

169

Little Auk (Dovekie)

Alle alle

19–21 cm | WS 34–38 cm

👁 Rare murrelets (p. 172)

Rare murrelets (p. 172)

Rare/scarce autumn/winter visitor to N, E; rare in S/W and inland after gales (100s–low 1,000s)

from Arctic

Tiny, thickset, short-billed
auk: see Puffin (p. 168), Black Guillemot (p. 169). Most likely in late autumn during/after gales. Tired/storm blown bird swims with head hunched, wings slightly drooped and **flicked open as it dives**.

ADULT (rare in Britain) black, white belly; fine white streaks on closed wing. Short, stout bill and large head give frog-like effect but healthy, alert bird can be quite slim-necked. ADULT/1ST-WINTER sharply black and white, **bold black hood extending around eyes, white collar; white streaks on wing** (rules out Puffin).

IN FLIGHT, small, dumpy, with slender wings (sometimes look surprisingly long, as bird or group twists and banks, like some unknown small wader). Fast, whirring wingbeats: see Puffin which also has slim wings with dark underside and fast beats – Little Auk has quicker whirr of more swept-back wings and thin white trailing edge. Size of Starling (p. 372); even rarely caught up in Starling flocks.

WINTER

SUMMER

Offshore/at sea; rarely inland waters

JUVENILE/1ST-WINTER

RAZORBILL
(size comparison)

WINTER

LITTLE AUK

SUMMER

Little Auks in breeding plumage have very rarely been recorded in Britain in colonies of other auks.

healthy, alert birds hold their head up

WINTER

exhausted birds often droop wings, head hunched down

uses wings underwater, resting between dives with wings drooped on or just below the surface

WINTER

Auks in flight

Auks passing far offshore, low over the sea, often in strong winds, are difficult. Look for overall colour, underwing and rump patterns, and try to estimate size.

BLACK GUILLEMOT (*p. 169*)
SUMMER

PUFFIN (*p. 168*)
SUMMER

SUMMER

LITTLE AUK
SUMMER

streaked flanks — dark

white underwing and flanks

white underwing and flanks

GUILLEMOT
SUMMER

RAZORBILL
SUMMER

BRÜNNICH'S GUILLEMOT
SUMMER

short tail; feet project
SUMMER

SUMMER

short tail; feet project
SUMMER

white along bill
SUMMER

white across bill

GUILLEMOT (*p. 166*)
SUMMER

long tail; feet same length
SUMMER

SUMMER

WINTER

RAZORBILL (*p. 167*)

BRÜNNICH'S GUILLEMOT (*p. 172*)

no white behind eye

LITTLE AUK
WINTER

WINTER

BLACK GUILLEMOT (*p. 169*)
WINTER

WINTER

171

Rare auks

Brünnich's Guillemot
Uria lomvia
40–44 cm | WS 64–75 cm

Like Guillemot (*p. 166*),
blacker; **bill thicker**, pointed,
unlike Razorbill (*p. 167*).
ADULT **white streak along
cutting edges of bill** to gape;
white breast in a point against
neck. ADULT/1ST-WINTER difficult:
peaked dark head with **no
white on rear cheek** or behind
eye (cap down to beneath
eye, leaving small white face).
Flanks **clean white**. May have
chinstrap effect. IN FLIGHT
deeper body more 'rugby-ball'
shaped, less tapered; wingpits
lack dark mark of Guillemot.

GUILLEMOT
(winter)

RAZORBILL
(winter)

white

white

dark

white
along
bill

WINTER

unmarked flanks

ADULT SUMMER

Vagrant from Arctic/Iceland: <50 records (1 Ireland), Oct–Jan,
extremely rare in summer. Coast.

Tufted Puffin
Fratercula cirrhata
36–41 cm | WS 60–63 cm

Like Puffin (*p. 168*) but black
with red bill, white face,
yellowish crest.

Vagrant from N Pacific: 1 record
(Britain), Sep. Coast.

ADULT SUMMER

Ancient Murrelet
Synthliboramphus antiquus
27 cm | WS 45–48 cm

Tiny, short-billed auk with
black cap, white lower cheeks
and neck, pale bill.

Vagrant from N Pacific:1 record
(Britain), May (2 years). Coast.

ADULT SUMMER

NT Long-billed Murrelet
Brachyramphus perdix
25 cm | WS 45 cm

Like tiny Guillemot with
whitish shoulder patches, slim
bill, white cheek/throat.

Vagrant from E Asia/N Pacific: 1
record (Britain), Nov. Coast.

1ST-WINTER

WADERS

WADER GROUP ID size | leg length + colour | bill length + shape

77 species recorded: 18 breed regularly, 6 rare or irregular breeders; 7 mostly autumn–spring visitors, 5 spring–autumn visitors and 5 passage migrants; more than 40 are very rare / vagrants.

Waders are birds that, with the exception of Stone-curlew, feed on or near the water's edge, at least for part of the year. Other species do so, too: herons, crakes, gulls, wagtails, even finches and buntings.

Identifying waders (see p. 174)

All waders **walk**: they do not hop. A long, fine bill used for probing soft mud should identify a 'wader'; most birds wading into shallows and picking from water will be waders (except for herons, Spoonbill, crakes/rails and some gulls). Bill shapes and leg lengths, together with flight patterns, are invaluable in deciding which 'group' a wader belongs to. Within each group, identification of a species relies on plumage details, with many species having identifiable breeding and non-breeding plumages, as well as intermediate stages. Juvenile waders, especially, tend to have well-demarcated feather groups and feathers are often neatly marked, so learning which are which is useful.

Most are sociable, others solitary: if you see a large flock of small waders, they will not be, for example, Common or Green Sandpipers, or phalaropes. Some breed in territories, defended from others, but flock as soon as the breeding season is over.

The majority are long-distance migrants. Many waders (even of species that breed here or come in winter) 'pass through' in spring, coming from farther south, stopping briefly and dashing on northwards – usually later than might be supposed as their destination, the Arctic tundra, remains frozen until early summer. They return in 'autumn', earlier than might be expected: adults that have finished breeding or failed to breed might return in July/August, whereas juveniles often come in a second wave in August/September.

Breeding colours may be seen on migrants before they leave in spring and again, now faded or patchy as they moult, in autumn. Many waders have juvenile plumages that look like faded breeding birds.

Wader ageing/sexing

Some waders have a range of plumages; others look the same year-round.

SANDERLING

JUVENILE
JULY—JAN

moult
as adult
from FEB

ADULT

non-breeding
plumage
OCT—FEB

ADULTS

moulting into
breeding plumage
FEB—MAY

NB similar
when moulting into
winter plumage
JUN—SEP

ADULT

breeding
plumage
JUN—JUL

A roosting flock of Dunlins, Ruffs, Curlew Sandpipers and Golden Plover in breeding plumage.

Wader identification

Bill length and shape

Focus on the relative length and overall shape of the bill.

LONG, EVENLY DOWNCURVED

Curlews and whimbrels

CURLEW

LONG, STRAIGHT, TAPERED

Godwits, sandpipers (larger), snipe, Woodcock, phalaropes

BLACK-TAILED GODWIT

LONG, SLIM, SLIGHTLY UPCURVED

Godwits, sandpipers

GREENSHANK

LONG, SLIGHTLY DOWNCURVED

Sandpipers

CURLEW SANDPIPER

SHORT, STOUT, POINTED

Plovers, Turnstone

GREY PLOVER

Plumage features

Look for obvious rump, wing and tail patterns in flight.

CURLEW SANDPIPER

wingbar

rump

tail white with dark tail-band; rump white 'square'

GREENSHANK

LITTLE RINGED PLOVER

tail barred; rump white, merging with back to form a white 'triangle'

tail dark; rump dark with white sides

the relationship between wingtip and tail tip is used in identification for some species

fringe (edge of feather)

eyering

coverts

tertials

tail

wingtip

primaries   vent

'knee' – actually the equivalent of an ankle

the length of the leg above the 'knee' can be useful for identification

COMMON SANDPIPER

The types of wader

Waders, such as **Stone-curlew** (*p. 177*), **Oystercatcher** (*p. 178*), **Avocet** (*p. 180*) and the rare **Black-winged Stilt** (*p. 181*) and the vagrant **Cream-coloured Courser** (*p. 192*), are unlike anything else and easy to identify. **Pratincoles** (vagrants, *p. 193*) and the rest of the waders are distinctive as types but are often more difficult to identify to species. In these groups, sexes look alike and seasonal differences are slight.

Pratincole

Stone-curlew

Oystercatcher

Avocet

Stilt

Courser

Plovers – including 'ringed' and 'golden' types, and lapwings (pp. 182–192)

Stocky waders with short, even stubby, bills. Characteristic run-stop action, tilting to pick from the surface.

Turnstone (p. 179)
small but distinctive black-and-white bird of rocky coasts. with a short, wedge-shaped bill.

GOLDEN PLOVER
RINGED PLOVER

TURNSTONE

Sandpipers (pp. 194–211) – small to medium-sized birds of mudflats and watersides, in distinct groups (examples of each shown here). Scarcer species sometimes with similar common ones, such as Little Stints amongst Dunlins. Some breed, most are passage migrants and many winter.

With the exception of curlews and snipe, waders on this page have seasonal differences, obvious or slight, and some differ between male and female.

♂ and ♀ different

'PEEPS'
'SHANKS'
'SANDPIPERS'
DUNLIN
REDSHANK
GREEN SANDPIPER
RUFF ♀

Godwits (pp. 212–213) – bigger than 'shanks', long-legged and long-billed: pattern on spread wings key to identification. Black-tailed Godwits prefer muddy creeks or marshy places; a few breed. Bar-tailed Godwits mostly on open estuaries; breed in the Arctic.

BAR-TAILED GODWIT

Curlews and **whimbrels** (pp. 214–215) – big, gull-like, spangled brown, with long, downcurved bills. Curlews present year-round and have evocative calls. Whimbrels mostly spring and autumn migrants, a few breeding in far north.

CURLEW

Snipe and **Woodcock** (pp. 218–220) – brown, striped heads. Snipe has remarkably long beak; Jack Snipe's shorter. Woodcock feeds at night in open fields but mostly seen flying over woods at dusk in summer, or flushed from woodland floor in winter.

SNIPE

Phalaropes (pp. 216–217) – feed while swimming. Grey Phalaropes occasionally inland after autumn gales, or close inshore in rough weather, very rare in spring. Red-necked Phalaropes scarcer but breed in far north.

RED-NECKED PHALAROPE ♂
♂ and ♀ different

Distinctive 'large' waders and regularly occurring plovers in flight

AVOCET
(p. 180)

BLACK-WINGED STILT
(p. 181)

OYSTERCATCHER
(p. 178)

WINTER

STONE-CURLEW

LAPWING
(p. 187)

SUMMER

LITTLE
RINGED
PLOVER
(p. 182)

KENTISH
PLOVER

WINTER

See also American and
Pacific Golden Plovers
(p. 191).

WINTER

GREY PLOVER (p. 189)

RINGED
PLOVER
(p. 183)

SUMMER

SUMMER

GOLDEN
PLOVER
(p. 190)

WINTER

WINTER

see also
p. 204

DOTTEREL (p. 188)

WINTER

SUMMER

WINTER

TURNSTONE
(p. 179)

JUVENILE

38–45 cm | WS 76–88 cm

Secretive bird, best seen towards dusk. Like big, pale, long-tailed plover of dry fields, sandy heaths, close-cropped grass. Long-striding, hesitant walk or forward-leaning run between long, upright pauses: looks surprisingly big on open ground. In early autumn, forms loose flocks around gravel pits before migration.

At distance, **pale bill base/white face**. Pale stripes above and below eye, black-tipped bill, **white band across wing** all revealed when closer. Pale legs 'disappear' against background; squats with lower part of leg flat on ground.

VOICE Calls at dusk: loud, Oystercatcher-like pipes and sharp "*ki-vi-vi*", and Curlew-like (*p. 215*) whistles.

Rare summer visitor (400–475 pairs, Mar–Sep); rare migrant

to S Europe and N Africa

Downland, stony areas, sparse crops, heaths, grassland

Stone-curlews nest in flinty fields or on grassy heaths, often in areas specifically prepared for them or given special protection.

IN FLIGHT, white bands, spots on mostly blackish wing; plain rump/tail. Wings stiff, bowed; white beneath.

ADULT

ADULT

white stripes on head more obvious at distance than pale eye

pale band across wing

yellow legs

NT Oystercatcher
VU

Haematopus ostralegus ● I `530`

39–44 cm | WS 72–83 cm

A big, black-and-white wader, with strident calls; easily identified. Classic sight and sound of estuaries, sandy or shingle beaches, quiet lochsides and upland fields; on coast, often in huge flocks. Favours mudflats and mussel scarps, but found in all kinds of waterside habitats and damp fields.

ADULT bill obvious, more so than pale pink legs. ADULT WINTER/ IMMATURE white frontal collar, back browner, bill darker at tip.

VOICE Shrill, piping, penetrating notes, such as "*peep*", "*k-peep*", "*kip-kip-kip*" and fast, bubbling, ecstatic piping from small groups with open bills pointing down.

Common resident, migrant, most in N (113,000 pairs breed); common winter visitor (340,000)

from Iceland

from Norway

to S Europe

Breeds on coasts and upland meadows; winter estuaries, rocky, sandy, shingle shores

IN FLIGHT, **white 'V' rump and long, broad white wingbars** create 'dazzle' effect.

ADULT WINTER/ IMMATURE

1ST-WINTER

bill tip pointed or chisel-shaped

white 'collar' outside breeding season

ADULT WINTER/ IMMATURE

vivid orange bill

ADULT SUMMER

Turnstone

21–24 cm | WS 43–49 cm

Small, stocky, long-bodied, low-slung. Mixes with Dunlins (*p.196*), Sanderlings (*p.194*), Purple Sandpipers (*p.198*). Busy but inconspicuous flocks (on weed/rocks/strandline). Really does turn stones or heaves over piles of weed.

Blackish chest, white belly, **bright orange legs**, thick, strong bill tapers to point. Pattern obvious, seasonal changes marked. ADULT **black-and-white head**, **bright rusty-ginger** and black above. ADULT WINTER black breast-band, pale chest side, above bright white underparts; dark, dull back. JUVENILE neater 'V'-shaped buff fringes above, paler cheeks than winter adult.

VOICE Short, fast, clipped, rather low-pitched, or strung into quick chattering trills if flushed – "*kew*", "*tuk-a-tuk*".

Locally common, widespread winter visitor (50,000, Aug–May); scarce migrant inland

from Canada and Greenland

from Russia

from/to Morocco

from/to W Africa

Estuaries, sandy/stony beaches, rocky shores, piers/groynes

IN FLIGHT, chequered: white back and shoulder bands, wing stripe and tail base conspicuous against dark background.

ADULT WINTER

ADULT ♂ SUMMER

JUVENILE

ADULT ♀ SUMMER

1ST-WINTER

ADULT ♂ SUMMER

ADULT WINTER

Avocet

Recurvirostra avosetta ⬤ 530

Scarce summer visitor (1,900 breeding pairs, mainly E England, few inland and in NW), migrant, very locally common winter visitor (7,500, most in SW)

Coastal lagoons, shallow lakes, estuaries

42–46 cm | WS 67–77 cm

White wader with black markings. Unique **upswept bill** enough to identify it at close range; at a distance, can be 'lost' in gull flocks on shiny mudflats. Feeds in shallow water with regular sideswipes of beak; swims with tail uptilted.

ADULT bright white; curved **black bands** around white oval patch on closed wing; black cap to below eye and back of neck. Long grey legs; fine black bill upturned. JUVENILE like adult but mottled brown over white areas of upper back, black areas duller.

VOICE Calls ringing, piping, "*klute*" or "*krup krup krup*".

IN FLIGHT, strikingly white with black wingtips and forewing bar.

ADULT

white oval outlined in black

ADULT

upswept bill

JUVENILE

Black-winged Stilt *Himantopus himantopus* `530`

33–36 cm | WS 60 cm

Rare migrant from S Europe: <600 records (<100 Ireland), all months, most May–Jun; rarely breeds. Favours coastal lagoons.

Supremely elegant wader with long wings, slender body, fine needle bill and unfeasibly long legs.

MALE green-glossed black above (FEMALE browner), white below; head variably white, dusky black or grey. JUVENILE duller, paler, wide **whitish trailing edge** to wing.

VOICE Loud, frenetic calls if disturbed near nest, tern-like, "*kyik kyik kyik*"; migrants usually silent.

ADULT ♂

ADULT ♀

ADULT ♂

IN FLIGHT, **underwing black** against white body; long **white 'V'** up back. **Pink-red legs** trail far beyond tail (feet often crossed).

male and female head patterns vary: males more extreme (blackest, whitest), females more dusky, but female's head darker than male's in many pairs

ADULT ♂

JUVENILE

ADULT ♀

181

Little Ringed Plover

Charadrius dubius **I** **531**

15·5–18 cm | WS 32–35 cm

Small, brown, white and black 'ringed' plover, standing/running on freshwater margins and rough stony/sandy waste.

Rare *Charadrius* plovers *(pp. 184–185)*

ADULT similar to Ringed Plover but **plain wing**. Smaller, rounder body, long **tapered rear-end**. Small bill dark, dull pale base. Legs dull, pinkish. Close up, **yellow ring around eye** easy to see, striking on adult male, which has blacker markings than female. JUVENILE dull: shape as adult. Pale eyering sometimes visible; **upper half of head brownish**, blended buff forehead, paler area over eye (whiter stripe over eye on Ringed Plover); angular dark cheek marking (rounder on Ringed Plover). Lack of wingbar on spread wing best clue.

VOICE Good clue to presence and identity – short, abrupt, "*tew*" or "*te-u*" with downward, not upward, inflection. Song hard, rolling "*crree-a crree-a*" in low, bat-like display flight.

Scarce summer visitor (1,200 breeding pairs, Mar–Oct); scarce migrant

to Africa

Gravel pits, waste ground, shingle reservoir edges, coastal pools

generally rounded

distinct white band

RINGED PLOVER

JUVENILE

IN FLIGHT, **plain upperwing** (only finest of pale lines, no white wing stripe).

ADULT SUMMER ♂

indistinct paler area

brownish top half of head

rather pointed

yellow eyering

JUVENILE

ADULT ♀ SUMMER

black bill

ADULT ♂ SUMMER

pale pinkish/ yellowish legs

Ringed Plover

Charadrius hiaticula ● except race *tundrae*

17–19·5 cm | WS 35–41 cm

Semipalmated Plover (p. 186)
Rare *Charadrius* plovers
(pp. 184–185)

Commonest 'ringed' plover; often by freshwater, but most numerous on coast. Short bill. Typical plover run-stop-tilt-stand action. Mixes with Dunlins and others. Heavier, dumpier than Little Ringed Plover, shorter tail end but longer, deeper belly, short, bright **orange legs**.

ADULT broad **black head bands and breast 'ring'** (boldest on male), contrasting bright **orange bill** with black blob tip. Black cheek, breast-band blurred brown in winter. JUVENILE duller, dull legs, 'ring' reduced to brownish side patches, but sharp white forehead, **white band over eye** unlike Little Ringed Plover.

VOICE Loud, musical, soft "*too-ee*" or "*ploo-eep*". Alarm note shorter pipe. Song quick, rhythmic sequence of "*too looee*" notes, usually in low, waving, straight-winged flight.

Common resident (5,300 pairs), migrant (30,000), winter visitor (37,000); inland mostly Mar–Oct

psammodramus from Greenland via Iceland

tundrae from Russia

MAY ↑
AUG/OCT ↓

↑ APR
↓ AUG/SEP

from Baltic

to W Africa
to W Africa
to France and Spain

Sand/shingle, muddy estuaries, inland lake shores

ADULT SUMMER ♂

white wingbar

JUVENILE

IN FLIGHT, all ages reveal **long white stripe** on wing, black 'blob' near tip of wedge-shaped tail.

female markings more subdued than males

JUVENILE

ADULT ♀ SUMMER

black-tipped orange bill

Race *tundrae* is a winter migrant to Britain, breeding in N Eurasia; it is slighty smaller and darker than the British/Irish breeding race *hiaticula*. Ill-defined race *psammodromus*, breeds Canada – Iceland – Faeroes, migrant.

ADULT ♂ SUMMER

ADULT ♂ SUMMER race *tundrae*

yellow/orange legs

Kentish Plover *Charadrius alexandrinus* 531

15–17 cm | WS 31–32 cm

Very rare migrant from Europe, winters NW Africa: 10–15 per year (vagrant Ireland <25 records), most Mar–Jun. Sandy shores, pools, sandy 'waste' ground.

Small, pale 'ringed' plover; **incomplete breast-band (vestigial patches), dark legs**. Noticeably small; almost 'chick-like', with round head, rounded body, short, tapered rear, thin legs set well back. Runs on beach like Sanderling (*p. 194*). See juvenile Little Ringed and Ringed Plovers (*pp. 182–183*); check leg colour. MALE **rufous cap, black forehead band**, eyestripe, **black 'kidney-bean' chest patch**. ADULT FEMALE like male but dark marks **brown**. JUVENILE chest patch even paler. Bill all-dark; **legs grey to black**.

VOICE Useful, unlike 'ringed' plovers: short, hard "*pwit*" or "*bip*" or metallic "*tip*".

IN FLIGHT, wing stripe like Ringed Plover, but **white on side of short, square tail**, with central black patch.

ADULT ♂ SUMMER

ADULT ♂ SUMMER

incomplete breast-band

white 'collar'

dark bill

JUVENILE

blackish legs

ADULT ♀ SUMMER

dark legs

Rare *Charadrius* plovers

Caspian Plover and especially the sand plover pair can be difficult and Kentish Plover should also be borne in mind: a combination of size, head and bill shape and proportions and presence or absence of white collar helps, while features such as leg colour and call can be useful for some individuals. If possible, build up a complete assessment over a long period of observation.

Identification of rare *Charadrius* plovers – summary of key features						
	Bill and head	**Legs**	**Adult breeding**	**Adult winter**	**In flight**	**Voice**
Ringed Plover (*p. 183*) 18–20 cm	Blunt, two-tone	Short; orange	Black and white chest-bands	White collar. Black chest ring	White wing stripe	Whistled "*too-lee*"
Kentish Plover 15–17 cm	Small, pointed, black	Grey to black	Small dark mask, chest marks	White collar. Small dark chest marks	Wing stripe, white tail sides	Short "*pwit*"
Caspian Plover 18–20 cm	Long, fine, black; head small, neat	Long; brownish/ greenish	White over eye and throat, rufous breast-band	Poorly defined breast-band. No white collar	Short, narrow midwing stripe, dark tail	Loud "*tyup*"
Lesser Sand Plover 19–21 cm	Average, blunt, black; head rounded	Greenish-grey to blackish	Black mask, white throat, chestnut chest/breast sides	Grey-brown head, distinct chest patches. No white collar	Wing stripe, weak tail-band; feet do not project	"*chitik*"
Greater Sand Plover 22–25 cm	Long, heavy, tapered; black; head big, bulky, angular	Longest; yellow-green to greenish-grey	Black mask, white throat, chestnut chest	Grey-brown head, distinct chest patches. No white collar	Broadest wing stripe, dark tail-band; toes may project	Trill or shorter note

RE Caspian Plover

Charadrius asiaticus
18–20 cm | WS 55–61 cm

See table *opposite* for summary of key features.

JUVENILE/1ST-WINTER

JUVENILE/ 1ST-WINTER

bill distinctly pointed

legs brown-green, rather long

Vagrant from Asia: <10 records (Britain), May, Jul. Scattered. Coasts.

well-defined rufous band on chest

ADULT ♂ SUMMER

Lesser Sand Plover

Charadrius mongolus
19–21 cm | WS 45–58 cm

See table *opposite* for summary of key features.

JUVENILE/1ST-WINTER

uniform tail

WINTER

bill 'neat': 'nail' less than half total length

NB the 'nail' is the slightly bulging frontal portion of the upper mandible

'nail'

black mask over forehead

legs variable; distinctive when blackish

Vagrant from Asia: <10 records (1 Ireland), May–Aug. Scattered. Coasts

black mask over forehead; white throat; breast-band deep orange-rust

ADULT ♂ SUMMER

VU Greater Sand Plover

Charadrius leschenaultii
22–25 cm | WS 53–60 cm

See table *opposite* for summary of key features.

JUVENILE/1ST-WINTER

darker tail tip

WINTER

bill 'heavy': 'nail' half or more than total length (western race *columbinus* has smallest bill, close to Lesser Sand Plover)

'nail'

black mask; white forehead

legs usually green, long and strong

Vagrant from Asia: <20 records (Britain), Apr–Dec. Scattered. Coasts, reservoirs.

white throat; rusty-orange nape, breast-band, chest sides

ADULT ♂ SUMMER

185

Semipalmated Plover *Charadrius semipalmatus*
16–17·5 cm | WS 31–32 cm

Vagrant from N America:
<10 records (<5 Ireland),
Mar–Nov. Scattered. Mudflats.

Very difficult N American equivalent of Ringed Plover (*p. 183*): small size and **call** may draw attention. Small webs between front toes (one tiny web on Ringed Plover), rounder head, shorter stubby bill (varies; different profile on more obvious birds). Faint eyering, weak whitish stripe over cheek (bold on Ringed Plover). Thinner black chest ring. JUVENILE duller; white throat **extends beneath black face patch above point of gape** (solid dark on Ringed Plover).

VOICE Vaguely Spotted Redshank-like, rising "*chewee*".

'Ringed' plover calls at-a-glance	
Little Ringed Plover (*p. 182*)	abrupt down-inflected "*tew*" or "*te-u*"
Ringed Plover (*p. 183*)	"*too-ee*" or "*ploo-eep*"
Semipalmated Plover	rising "*chewee*"

JUVENILE **RINGED PLOVER** ADULT

dark

weak whitish stripe

narrow yellow eyering

white

ADULT ♂ SUMMER

JUVENILE

narrow black chest-band

Killdeer *Charadrius vociferus*
23·5–26 cm | WS 59–63 cm

Like large, long-tailed 'ringed' plover with **double breast-band**. Favours grassy places, sandy shores. Brown above, white below.

VOICE Call long, rising "*klu-ee*".

IN FLIGHT, blackish wings with long, wide white stripe, and **bright rufous rump** blending in to long, dark tail.

1ST-WINTER

1ST-WINTER

double breast-band

Vagrant from N America:
<100 records (<25 Ireland), most
Nov–Mar. Scattered. Coasts.

NT
VU

Lapwing

Vanellus vanellus ● ❶ 531

28–31 cm | WS 82–87 cm

Eye-catching, social, mostly dry land wader. Flocks (June onwards) lines, irregular masses, over valleys and marshes, often 'thickest in the middle', trailing behind. Slower flight than other waders, gulls, pigeons, Jackdaws.

Long, **upswept, wispy crest**. Black and white at long range, or dark green; **black chest**, **white underparts**. Close up, **rich green**; closed wing **shiny emerald, purple, bronze**; **orange under tail**; pink-red legs. MALE larger black marks on whiter face than FEMALE. WINTER MALE loses black throat; rusty-buff fringes on upperparts. JUVENILE crest short, broad buff tips to feathers above.

VOICE Calls include creaky, nasal "*pee-wit*", "*wheet*" and emphatic, strong, shrill "*pwee-y-weet*". Song wheezy, rasping in tumbling flight; ripping, throbbing wing noise.

Locally common (150,000 pairs, declining); many more autumn/ winter (640,000), declining

from N, E and W Europe

Saltmarshes, wet meadows, ploughed fields, moors, lakesides

IN FLIGHT, broadly rounded wing, **black outer half**, black-and-white beneath.

ADULT ♂ SUMMER

ADULT ♀ SUMMER

JUVENILE

ADULT ♀ SUMMER

ADULT ♂ SUMMER

long, upswept crest

black chest

pure white underparts

orange

ADULT WINTER

Dotterel
Charadrius morinellus ● 531

20·5–24 cm | WS 57–64 cm

👁 Sociable Plover (p.192)

Typical small plover shape,
unique multicoloured, partridge-like colours in summer.
Upright, long-legged, slender when alert, rounded when relaxed.
Often tame.

ADULT pale at distance, females darker than males. Blackish cap,
white band over eye forms **striking white 'V'** from rear.
Narrow white breast-band; **black belly** often more obvious
especially on female. **Yellowish legs** often 'lost' against
background or in long grass/crops. JUVENILE pale; dark cap,
white stripes over eyes meet in 'V' at back of head; weak, pale
breast-band; belly peachy-buff. Buff edges to dark feathers
above. **Yellow-ochre legs** (unlike Golden Plover (*p.190*),
Grey Plover (*p.189*), or sand plover types (*p.185*)).

VOICE Call abrupt "*pi-urr*", "*pew*" or purring note.

Rare and very local summer
visitor (420 breeding pairs, Apr–
Oct); rare migrant

to
N Africa

Breeds northern plateaux; on
migration inland fields and hills/
moors (small groups) in spring,
mostly coastal (singles) in autumn

IN FLIGHT, upperwing plain,
no wingbar, underwing whiter.

ADULT SUMMER ♀

JUVENILE

plain upperwing

Small groups ('trips') of spring migrants can 'disappear' against the
background: dark belly patches may show best.

ADULT ♂ SUMMER

prominent
white stripe

white stripe

ADULT ♀ SUMMER

white
crescent

dark belly

JUVENILE

Grey Plover

Pluvialis squatarola

26–29 cm | WS 56–63 cm

American/Pacific Golden Plovers (*p. 191*)

Solid, dumpy plover, like estuarine Golden Plover (*p. 190*) with bigger bill; easily overlooked on mudflats in harsh light but short bill unlike Redshank, godwits. Widely scattered when feeding, tight flocks at roost. More sluggish stop-start action than Golden Plover.

ADULT mottled black on grey, **white neck/chest sides**, **solid black belly** (Golden Plover has white flank stripe), white vent. Moulting early autumn birds have some black, are piebald and eye-catching. ADULT WINTER colourless, mottled dark grey, pale buff-grey, whitish below – dark in dull light, pale close up. JUVENILE browner, yellow buff spots above, like Golden Plover.

VOICE Frequent estuary sound, relaxed, plaintive whistle, trisyllabic with downslur in middle – "*tee-yoo-eee*".

Locally common and widespread migrant, winter visitor (44,000, most Aug–Apr)

from Siberia

from/to W and S Africa

Estuaries, coastal pools; rare inland

white rump

black 'armpits'

IN FLIGHT white wing stripe stronger than Golden Plover, **white rump**, unique **black 'armpits'**.

Late spring/early autumn migrants may show breeding plumage – note size next to Bar-tailed Godwit (*p. 213*).

ADULT SUMMER

1ST-WINTER

ADULT MOULTING

JUVENILE

Golden Plover

Pluvialis apricaria ❶ 531

25–28 cm | WS 53–59 cm

👁 American/Pacific Golden Plovers

Scarce and local breeder (23,000 pairs); migrant, common winter visitor (420,000)

Pointed-winged, short-billed plover; run-stop-tilt action. Often with Lapwings (*p. 187*), flocks separating in flight. Big flocks form long, wavering, fast-moving lines, often over pastures, cereal fields.

Smaller-billed than Grey Plover (*p. 189*). Small-headed; **yellowish-brown**, little contrast; scattered across fields, running and tilting forwards. ADULT **blackish face, belly**; British/Irish breeders narrow dark chest mottled white; northern breeders (spring flocks) **wider black chest broadly edged white**. Upperparts spangled black, cream, **yellow**. ADULT WINTER/IMMATURE both forms spangled yellow and black, paler below, white belly. IN FLIGHT (see *opposite*), **white underwing** and belly (show as bird settles or stretches); **rump and tail dark**; upperwing has whitish stripe.

VOICE Call loud, piping, mournful whistle, "*peeuw*"; rhythmic song given in flight over moors, repeated "*poo-peeee-oo*".

from Iceland

from Scandinavia

Moors, upland grassland; winter widespread, mostly traditional areas, meadows, fields, saltmarsh

yellow spangling on upperparts

ADULT ♂ SUMMER (northern)

ADULT ♀ SUMMER (southern)

ADULT ♀ SUMMER (northern)
ADULT ♂ SUMMER (southern)

ADULT WINTER

wingtips about equal to tail

tips of tertials well short of tail tip

JUVENILE/1ST-WINTER

Rare 'golden' plovers

American Golden Plover
Pluvialis dominica
24–27 cm | WS 55–60 cm

Vagrant from N America: 10–30 annually (<250 records Ireland), most Sep–Oct. Widespread. Marshes, pasture.

Pacific Golden Plover
Pluvialis fulva
21–25 cm | WS 50–55 cm

Vagrant from Asia: <100 records (<20 Ireland), most Jul–Aug (earlier than American Golden Plover), few spring. Widespread.

Two rare golden plovers associate with Golden Plovers and can be difficult to identify. American GP much more likely than Pacific GP. Both have dusky underwing (white on Golden). Some differences in plumage but best identified by structure, voice.

underwing white

all have dark rump and tail

AMERICAN GOLDEN

GOLDEN PLOVER

white

underwing dusky

feet do not project

feet project

PACIFIC GOLDEN

Identification of rare 'golden' plovers – summary of key features			
	Golden	American Golden	Pacific Golden
Underwing	Largely white	Dusky grey-brown	
Size/legs	Largest; legs relatively short	Slightly smaller than Golden Plover; legs long	Smallest, slim; legs long; in flight feet project beyond tail
Wingtip projection	Equals tail tip or just longer	Clearly longer than tail	Slightly longer than tail
Tertial tips	Well short of tail tip	Short of tail tip	Close to tail tip
Primary tips	3–4 visible	4–5 visible	3 visible
Voice	"*tooee*" or "*peooo*"	Double "*clu-eet*"	Definite "*tchoo-it*"

AMERICAN GOLDEN
UPPERPARTS: **coarsely patterned**
FLANK: **little or no white**
UNDERTAIL: **black**   ADULT SUMMER

GOLDEN PLOVER
UPPERPARTS: **more finely patterned**
FLANK: **white**
UNDERTAIL: **mottled black/white**   ADULT SUMMER

PACIFIC GOLDEN
UPPERPARTS: **coarsely patterned**
FLANK: **narrow band of white**
UNDERTAIL: **mottled black/white; a few like American GP**   ADULT SUMMER

1ST-WINTER overall tone **greyish**; dark cap; prominent white stripe over eye; dark in front of eye

tip of tertials fall well short of tail tip

wingtips project **well beyond tail**

dark

tip of tertials **close to tail tip**

wingtips project slightly beyond tail

1ST-WINTER overall tone yellow-brown (as Golden Plover); dark cap; yellowish over eye

smaller, slimmer, longer-legged than Golden Plover

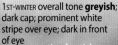

AMERICAN GOLDEN PLOVER
1ST-WINTER

PACIFIC GOLDEN PLOVER
1ST-WINTER

CR Sociable Plover
CR *Vanellus gregarius*
27–30 cm | WS 65–70 cm

Typically with Lapwings (*p. 187*); similar form but narrower wingtips. ADULT grey-brown, washed mauve/purplish; dark red/**black belly**; **black cap, eyestripe**, white over eye. Bill, legs black. ADULT WINTER dull with whiter belly. Narrow black cap and eyestripe, **broad buff-white band** over eye. JUVENILE duller, pale fringes.

Vagrant from Asia: <50 records (most old, declining) (<5 Ireland), mainly Sep–Nov. Scattered. Marshes, pastures.

IN FLIGHT, **black wingtips, broad white trailing edge.**

ADULT SUMMER

ADULT WINTER

dark cap, broad white stripe over eye

pale feather fringes

JUVENILE/ 1ST-WINTER

White-tailed Lapwing
Vanellus leucurus
26–29 cm | WS 75–85 cm

Unmistakable tall, upstanding wader, smaller than Lapwing (*p. 187*): **long yellow legs**, black bill and **plain, round head**. JUVENILE spotted on sandy-buff back.

Vagrant from E Europe: <10 records (Britain), May–Jul. Freshwater margins.

IN FLIGHT, black wingtip, **broad white midwing band; rump and tail pure white**. Long yellow legs trail.

ADULT

ADULT

plain head

black and white bands along closed wing

purplish-brown 'breastplate' in summer

vivid yellow legs

NT Cream-coloured Courser
Cursorius cursor
24–27 cm | WS 51–57 cm

Peculiar small, rounded, upright bird with plover-like actions. Looks sandy-buff. Round head; short, faintly downcurved black bill; long pale legs.

Vagrant from N Africa/Middle East: <50 records (most old), (1 Ireland), all months, most Sep–Dec. Short grassland.

JUVENILE/ 1ST-WINTER

IN FLIGHT, **outerwing black** above, and whole of **underwing black**.

'clean' head stripes

'dull' head pattern

532

ADULT

JUVENILE more barred above

long pale legs

1ST-WINTER

Pratincoles

Attention-catching birds, standing on open ground (rounded, long tail/wings, or more elongated if alert) or flying over (like brown tern, with long, forked tail). ADULT sandy-brown, white belly, blacker wingtips. Buff throat outlined black, red base to short bill. ADULT WINTER, face pattern reduced to smudge. JUVENILES (all species similar) dark spots/creamy scales on top, speckled chest. For all ages, structure and wing coloration are the best identification features.

PRATINCOLES IN FLIGHT

BLACK-WINGED

underwing black

COLLARED

white trailing edge

underwing rusty-red

contrastingly dark flight feathers

ORIENTAL

short tail

underwing rusty-red

Pratincoles – summary of key features			
	Black-winged	Collared	Oriental
TAIL/WINGTIP	**tail shorter**	**tail longer**	**tail much shorter**
BILL BASE	smaller red mark	larger red mark	
UNDERWING	all-black	rusty red in good light	
UPPERWING	**dark**, little contrast with dark flight feathers	pale, with **contrasting dark flight feathers**	darker than Collared
TRAILING EDGE	**dark**; faintly translucent at most	**white, usually obvious**	white very narrow or absent

Collared Pratincole `532`

Glareola pratincola

24–28 cm | WS 60–70 cm

Vagrant from S Europe: <100 records, (<5 Ireland), Apr–Sep, most Jun. Scattered. Marshes.

JUVENILE

1ST-WINTER

ADULT

red base to bill

Tail longer than wingtips (beware tails that are broken or not fully grown).

Vagrant from Asia: <50 records, (<5 Ireland), Apr–Nov, most Aug. Scattered. Open areas.

Vagrant from Asia: <10 records (Britain), May–Sep. E, SE coasts. Marshes.

NT
VU

Black-winged Pratincole

Glareola nordmanni

24–28 cm | WS 60–70 cm

Red area at bill base smaller than that of Collared Pratincole.

Tail falls short of wingtips.

ADULT

Oriental Pratincole

Glareola maldivarum

23–27 cm | WS 55–65 cm

Much like Collared Pratincole but **tail shorter** and wing darker above. Belly buff, less shining white.

Tail much shorter than wingtips.

ADULT

Sanderling   *Calidris alba* ● 531

18–21 cm | WS 35–39 cm   ◉ Rare 'peeps' *(p. 231)*

Small beach sandpiper:
typically at water's edge on sand, also mudflats (spring migrants, especially, briefly inland). See Dunlin (*p. 196*), Little Stint (*p. 201*): Sanderling larger; **thicker, straight bill**. Runs beside waves, picks from mud (less standing/probing than Dunlin). Mixed flocks at roost, **purer grey** winter Sanderlings stand out. Close view reveals diagnostic **lack of hind toe**.

ADULT in spring, marbled **black/rufous/white breast**: white wears off to reveal brighter colours in summer; **white below**. By autumn duller, retains rusty-red neck. ADULT/1ST-WINTER pale grey, white below, **breast hardly marked**. JUVENILE black, three-lobed spots above; black 'shoulder', streaks on chest sides; warm buff neck; **clean white beneath**.

VOICE Short, hard "*plit*" or "*twik*" lacks any 'musical' quality.

Locally common migrant, winter visitor (18,000, Jul–May); scarce inland (mostly May)

from Greenland

from Siberia

Sandy or muddy coasts

IN FLIGHT, **broad white stripe** on **dark wing**.

ADULT/ 1ST-WINTER

JUVENILES

dark spangles above

bright, 'clean' grey and white

unmarked (all plumages)

JUVENILE

ADULT WINTER

no hind toe

pale edges wear off to reveal brighter colours

ADULT SPRING

ADULT SUMMER

NT Knot

Calidris canutus

23–26 cm | WS 45–54 cm

👁 Great Knot (*p. 235*)

Distinctively medium size, medium bill, medium legs, few strong marks. Most in large flocks on few estuaries. A few on rocky shores. Stocky, size or two bigger than Dunlin (*p. 196*); smaller, lower, than Redshank (*p. 206*). Bill tapered, longer than plover's (see Grey Plover (*p. 189*)); faint down curve. **Short, greenish legs.** Feeds **slowly in close, organised groups**, even where scarce; shoulder-to-shoulder crowds where common.

ADULT pale-bright **coppery-orange**; faded orange by early autumn. ADULT/1ST-WINTER, **dull grey**, paler below. JUVENILE lacy blackish/whitish scales above; fine, pale grey lines on pale peach beneath.

VOICE Obscure, soft "*whet*" or "*nut*", as unmusical rapid chorus from jostling flocks at roost.

Locally common winter visitor, migrant (330,000 in autumn/winter, Jul–May); scarce inland

islandica from Canada and Greenland

canutus from Siberia

IN FLIGHT, white wing stripe, **pale grey rump**. Co-ordinated, tight, rolling flocks, often aerobatic, using vast amount of airspace, flashing white/smoky grey at distance.

grey rump

JUVENILE

Feeds on coastal mudflats; roosts in flocks on lagoons, spits

Race *canutus* breeds Siberia, migrant; race *islandica* breeds Canada, Greenland, winters; fractionally shorter-billed and paler beneath in summer.

drab grey

ADULT/1ST-WINTER

greenish legs

pale orange head and underside

pale grey, flushed orange below

JUVENILE

ADULT SUMMER

Dunlin

Calidris alpina except race
arctica **I** 531

17–21 cm | WS 32–36 cm

🔁 Rare 'peeps' *(p. 231)*

Benchmark for scarcer birds;
usually commonest Starling-sized wader, on coast or inland;
roosts in packed groups, with other small waders.

Long bill tapers to **downcurved tip** (long, front-heavy look).
Legs dark. Bigger than Little Stint (*p. 201*); smaller than Knot
(*p. 195*). Forward-leaning, picks more than probes; quick runs.
ADULT **black belly**; breast finely streaked; upperparts **rusty-
brown**, blackish and cream. ADULT WINTER/1ST-WINTER **mouse-
brown**, white beneath. On sparkling mud, dark chest/white
belly; in direct sun, paler, browner (Sanderling (*p. 194*)
purer grey). JUVENILE bright buff, plain-headed. Long, **cream lines
on back** (see Little Stint) increasingly mixed with new greyer
winter feathers; **dusky streaks on flanks** (unlike Little Stint,
Curlew Sandpiper (*p. 199*)).

VOICE Call thin, scratchy/'reedy', vibrant "*trreee*". Song, often
from spring flocks, develops into vibrant 'referee's whistle' which
runs down – "*shrree-ruee-ruee-we-we-we-wee wee*".

Three races: *schinzii* (breeds Britain, Ireland; common migrant);
alpina (breeds Scandinavia, Siberia; migrant, winter);
arctica (breeds Greenland, Spitsbergen; scarce migrant).

Scarce and local breeder (9,000
pairs, Jun–Jul); locally common
migrant, winter visitor (360,000,
Aug–May), declining; frequent
inland spring/autumn

Iceland *schinzii*
Iceland ↔ NW Africa

alpina
from
Norway

arctica
Greenland
W Africa

UK *schinzii*
to W Africa

Breeds moors/hills/northern
islands; all kinds of watersides,
especially estuaries, muddy
reservoir edges

UK and Ireland Dunlin migration

race	J	F	M	A	M	J	J	A	S	O	N	D
schinzii (UK)				▬	▬	▬						
schinzii				▬	▬			▬				
alpina	▬	▬	▬							▬	▬	▬
arctica								▬	▬			

Race *schinzii* small, bill variable
(♂ 23–36 mm); breeding bird
(Mar–Apr onwards) has large
black feather centres on back,
yellowish-red/cinnamon fringes;
rufous scapulars, often a few old,
winter feathers; breast streaks
quite dense, some blotches; solid
black belly.

'droop-tipped'
bill

ADULT WINTER

white underside,
streaked breast-band

black legs

Breeding male has whitish
hindneck; breeding female
browner hindneck, less contrast
with crown and back

black belly
patch

ADULT ♂ SUMMER [Jun]
race *schinzii*

ADULT ♀ SUMMER
race *schinzii*

white rump with dark central line

white wingbar

IN FLIGHT, fast-flying flocks aerobatic, flash dark and white as they rise, fall and turn.

creamy line along top of wing

females longer-billed than males; N European/Siberian *alpina* longest-billed race, but much overlap

dusky streaks on flanks

JUVENILE

JUVENILES

Dunlin races in Britain and Ireland: *schinzii*, *arctica* and *alpina*

Identifying the three races that occur is not straightforward; plumage differences are not always obvious, and vary with state of moult and wear. Breeding plumage is gained by incomplete head/body moult in spring; new feathers have broad, pale fringes that wear thinner and darker, giving variation in individual appearance, but races often distinctive in May and June. Females are larger and longer-billed than males and measurements overlap between races, so size/structure not wholly reliable. First-summer birds may also be intermediate between adult breeding and winter with grey intermixed above and less solid black patch below.

ADULT ♂ SUMMER [Jul] race *arctica*

Race *alpina* largest, longest-billed (27–36 mm); breeding plumage (later than others, Apr–May onwards) wider pale grey feather edges on back, wearing away to reveal deeper rusty-red.

ADULT ♀ SUMMER [Jun] race *alpina*

Race *arctica* smaller, slimmer, bill averages shorter (♂ 23–29 mm; ♀ 27–32 mm) than *schinzii*; breeding bird (Mar–Apr onwards) paler; back feathers with larger black centres with narrower, yellower fringes; some grey feathers in mantle and scapulars; some scapulars have narrow buffy-yellow fringes; breast streaks thinner, no blotches, on whiter background; pale feather edges on black belly.

197

Waders in flight *p. 205*

Purple Sandpiper

Calidris maritima ⬤ `531`

19–22 cm | WS 37–42 cm   👁 Great Knot (*p. 235*)

Often on wave-washed rocks with Turnstones (*p. 179*). Looks dull, but exquisite close-up. Heavy build, short legs; thick-based, slightly downcurved bill.

ADULT dark, finely streaked black below, **chequered with black and rufous fringes** above. ADULT WINTER **grey/mauve-brown**, paler feather edges. Eyering, chin white. Underside dull white; **soft grey breast**. Bill dark, **orange-yellow base**; legs dull **orange-yellow**. Early autumn adult retains rufous, cream fringes, blacker feather centres. JUVENILE (into winter) like winter adult but scaly white edges on most of upperparts.

VOICE Call weak, sharp "*quit*" or "*quit-it*".

Scarce winter visitor (25,000, Aug–Apr), rare inland; very rare breeder in far N highlands

from Greenland   from Norway

Rocky coasts, piers, groynes – not on wide, muddy shores

ADULT WINTER

IN FLIGHT, stocky but fast, direct (or leaping over breaking wave), dark with white wing stripe, **broad black rump** with white sides.

ADULT WINTER

JUVENILE

1ST-WINTER

orange-yellow base to bill

orange-yellow legs

plain head

ADULT WINTER

ADULT EARLY SUMMER

Curlew Sandpiper

NT
VU

Calidris ferruginea

19–22 cm | WS 37–42 cm

👁 Rare 'peeps' (*p. 231*)

Most in autumn, adults July/
August, juveniles later, often with Dunlins (*p. 196*), Little Stints
(*p. 201*). **Call** draws attention; **white rump** obvious in mixed
flock. Like taller, long-necked Dunlin; longer, **smoothly curved
bill**, longer legs (often hidden as it wades deeply, bill tilted down).

ADULT broad white feather tips wear off to reveal **coppery-red**,
white eyering, chin; rump mottled. In autumn, adult retains
faded red patches on dull white. ADULT WINTER grey, white below.
Clear white rump. JUVENILE cleaner than stripy juvenile Dunlin:
back has curved fringes/spangles of cream (more scaled, less
streaked than Dunlin, without stripes). Underparts pale;
bright peach chest, **unmarked flanks**.

VOICE Rich trill "*chirrup*" amongst thin Dunlin notes.

Scarce but widespread migrant;
rare winter/spring (about 740 per
year, most Aug–Oct)

from
Arctic

to
Africa

Coastal pools, estuaries,
freshwater margins

IN FLIGHT, broad white rump
catches eye in fast-flying
mixed flock (with *e.g.* Dunlin)

cap diffusely streaked,
shorter eyestripe
less contrasting

DUNLIN JUVENILE
(long-billed)

juveniles look
'cleaner', fresher
than Dunlin

back and
wings
'scaled'

streaked cap over
long, white eyestripe

dark markings

JUVENILE

peachy wash
(often very
obvious)

no markings

ADULT
EARLY SUMMER
[Jun]

ADULT MOULTING INTO
WINTER PLUMAGE [Jul]

Temminck's Stint

Calidris temminckii **531**

13·5–15 cm | WS 30–35 cm

👁 Rare 'peeps' *(p. 231)*

Must separate from Little Stint and Dunlin *(p. 196)*; **pale legs** spark excitement. Check Common Sandpiper *(p. 211)* (much bigger), and rarer species. Tiny, creeping secretively on freshwater edges, mostly spring migrants in twos and threes or single autumn juveniles.

Elongated, **long-winged**; **dull upperparts/breast** and white underparts (like Common Sandpiper). Crucially, **pale ochre/ greenish legs**. Bill faintly downcurved. ADULT irregular **blackish blotching** above (weakly edged rufous) on olive-brown. Chest finely marked in narrow band. ADULT WINTER plain brown above. JUVENILES thin, dark-and-cream feather fringes in wide, curved scales above; plain dull **grey-buff breast-band**; white throat, paler centre, like tiny Common Sandpiper.

VOICE Call useful: dry, rippled trill "*si-si-si-si-si*".

to Scandinavia

from Middle East

Pools, reservoir edges

IN FLIGHT, white wing stripe; **white sides of rump extend onto outer tail feathers** (best seen as bird takes off). Tends to go up and fly far away – that might be that, but call helpful.

ADULT SUMMER

white outer tail feathers

JUVENILE

long wings

distinct breast-band

pale yellowish legs

ADULT SUMMER

dark blotches

ADULT SPRING

pale ochre/ greenish legs

Little Stint

Calidris minuta

14–15·5 cm | WS 28–31 cm 👁 Rare 'peeps' *(p. 231)*

Smaller than sparrow/wagtail; compare with larger Dunlin *(p. 196)* and Sanderling *(p. 194)*. Dainty, quick-moving, thin-legged (often half-crouched), **bill short, straight**; **white beneath**, buffy chest patches, no flank streaks. Legs black (pale on Temminck's Stint).

ADULT (uncommon) black and rufous above, **white below**, neck/chest sides pale rusty. ADULT WINTER grey and white, dull grey feather centres, fine black bill and legs: **tiny size** essential. JUVENILE (most likely) shows two **white 'V's** from rear. Foxy mixture of rust, black and cream above (black spots isolated on paler ground as rufous fades). Streaked cap (dark centre, rufous sides) above wide whitish line, **forked** over eye.

VOICE Call helpful: short, hard "*tip*" sometimes tripled.

Widespread but scarce migrant (around 750 per year, most Jul–Oct); a few in winter/spring

from Arctic

to Africa

Coastal pools, watersides inland

IN FLIGHT, Dunlin-like pattern: white wing stripe and rump sides, grey tail (Temminck's Stint has white tail sides).

grey outer tail feathers

JUVENILE

white lines along top of wing, form 'V' at rear

JUVENILE

JUVENILE (rufous individual)

JUVENILE

JUVENILE (greyish individual)

no palmations between toes (a feature of some similar rare 'peeps')

ADULT WINTER

black legs

ADULT SUMMER

white edges to feathers obscure pattern but wear away by summer

bright, clean white beneath

ADULT SPRING

201

Ruff

Calidris pugnax **531**

♂ 29–32 cm | WS 54–60 cm
♀ 22–26 cm | WS 46–49 cm

👁 Buff-breasted (*p. 226*) and
Pectoral Sandpipers (*p. 227*)

Very rare/irregular breeder (<10 nests); fairly common migrant (low 1,000s), scarce winter (800)

Medium-sized wader, non-breeding birds like Redshank (*p. 206*), but shorter, faintly curved bill, small head, hump-backed, neat dark spots/pale edges above, legs ochre/greenish (pale reddish on breeding females, brighter red on winter males), wings with thin white stripe; calls insignificant.

Male bigger than female, **long-legs, long-neck**; female smaller than Redshank, **short-bill**. Summer birds unlike commoner autumn juveniles. MALE (rare in Britain/Ireland) extravagantly patterned; crest, flamboyant ruff. ADULT SUMMER FEMALE buff- or grey-brown, **chequered blackish**, blotched chest.
ADULT WINTER grey-brown, white belly. Short bill. Male has **whiter face**, eyering. Legs dull ochre; male's orange-yellow to red.
JUVENILE **buff**; dark, blunt bill, **ochre legs**. **Clean buff breast, back scaly** with cream fringes (unlike Redshank, Greenshank (*p. 208*), godwits (*p. 212*)).

VOICE Usually silent; low quacking notes.

from/to Scandinavia and Russia

from/to Africa

Wet meadows, freshwater margins, estuaries/creeks

1ST-WINTER ♂

ADULT ♀

Males have pale base to bill and white eyering.

wading females can be confusing until they reveal their legs

ADULT ♀

barred tertials

female Redshank-sized, male noticeably bigger

males lose their breeding finery in winter and are barred above

JUVENILE ♀

unbarred tertials

'clean' buff underparts

ADULT ♂ WINTER
JUL–FEB

JUVENILE ♀

IN FLIGHT, thin white wingbar, white rump sides form almost or complete 'V'. Flight rather slow, large-winged, relaxed.

ADULT ♂ PRE-BREEDING
MAR–MAY [Apr]

ADULT ♂ PRE-BREEDING
MAR–MAY [Apr]

ADULT ♀

striking white-headed 'satellite' males on fringes of display ground attract females' attention

ADULT ♂ BREEDING
MAY–JUN
(different colour forms)

Non-breeding, regularly occurring 'sandpipers' and snipe in flight

Whimbrel

Curlew

WHIMBREL
(p. 214)

CURLEW
(p. 215)

Black-tailed
Godwit

Bar-tailed
Godwit

BLACK-TAILED
GODWIT
(p. 213)

BAR-TAILED
GODWIT
(p. 213)

GREENSHANK
(p. 208)

SPOTTED
REDSHANK
(p. 207)

REDSHANK
(p. 206)

See also
yellowlegs
(p. 224)

GREY PHALAROPE
(p. 217)

**RED-NECKED
PHALAROPE**
(p. 216)

see also
p. 176

TURNSTONE
(p. 179)

see also
p. 176

**RINGED
PLOVER**
(p. 183)

See also
rare 'peeps'
(p. 230)

**CURLEW
SANDPIPER**
(p. 199)

DUNLIN
(p. 196)

**LITTLE
STINT**
(p. 201)

SANDERLING
(p. 194)

**TEMMINCK'S
STINT**
(p. 200)

**PURPLE
SANDPIPER**
(p. 198)

KNOT
(p. 195)

**WOOD
SANDPIPER**
(p. 209)

RUFF
(p. 202)

**GREEN
SANDPIPER**
(p. 210)

WOODCOCK
(p. 220)

See also
Great Snipe
(p. 223)

**COMMON
SANDPIPER**
(p. 211)

SNIPE (p. 218)   **JACK SNIPE** (p. 219)

See also
Spotted Sandpiper (p. 232)

Redshank

Tringa totanus **532**

24–27 cm | WS 47–53 cm

> Lesser Yellowlegs (*p. 224*),
> Terek Sandpiper (*p. 233*)

Locally common resident (39,000 pairs, declining), migrant, winter visitor (125,000)

Typical estuary/saltmarsh/poolside wader. Noisy, active, bobs head; in summer calls anxiously from posts. Medium-sized, **brown**; **bright red legs** rule out all but Spotted Redshank, winter Ruff (*p. 202*). Often silhouette on mud: dumpier than Spotted Redshank or Greenshank (*p. 208*), taller than Knot (*p. 195*). Singly/small groups; roosts in jostling flocks. Whitish stripe above eye (bolder than Ruff, weaker than Spotted Redshank). ADULT chequered black on brown. ADULT/1ST-WINTER plainer, greyer. JUVENILE buff fringes, **yellow-orange legs**.

VOICE Rich, bright, musical "*teu*" or sad "*teu-hu*"; 'bouncy' "*teu-huhu*", quicker, less even than Greenshank. Frenetic "*pit-u-pit-u-pit-u*" when flushed, "*kyip*" in alarm; rhythmic, musical "*t'leeo-t'leeo-t'leeo*" song.

white triangle up back

white hindwing

Estuaries, marshes, wetlands, river valleys

Birds from Iceland (race *robusta*) are larger, but size overlaps and any identification is unreliable.

1ST-WINTER

IN FLIGHT, **white triangle** on back, **broad white hindwing** instantly obvious. Quick to take flight. Often settles with wings raised, flashing white underside.

Note: some individuals have yellow legs and could be mistaken for Lesser Yellowlegs (*p. 224*).

pale feather edges

whole bill base red

ADULT SUMMER

JUVENILE   pale legs

vivid red legs

weak head pattern; indistinct white line above eye

plainer body than in summer

ADULT/1ST-WINTER

Spotted Redshank
Tringa erythropus ● ● ❶

29–33 cm | WS 61–67 cm

 Wilson's Phalarope (juvenile) (*p. 233*)

Scarce migrant (about 420 per year); a few present almost all year on coastal lagoons

Like slim-billed, long-legged, deep-bodied Redshank; **longer, fine-tipped bill**, **longer legs**. Wades deeply, runs/darts, upends, swims.

ADULT blackish, wide white fringes that wear away so **black** by summer; early autumn patchy black, grey and white. ADULT AUTUMN/WINTER, **pale grey** (no hint of brown), whiter below. JUVENILE browner; **brownish bars** below. 1ST-WINTER black eyestripe, **white line above eye** (widest in front, unlike Redshank or Greenshank (*p. 208*)).

VOICE Distinctive call invaluable clue: sharp, clearly enunciated "*tchew-it!*"

from/to Sweden and Finland

from/to S Europe and Africa

Shallow fresh, brackish or salt water coastal habitats

long, white oval patch on back

legs extend well beyond tail

rather plain wings

ADULT WINTER

IN FLIGHT **wings plain**, long **white oval on back** (see Greenshank). Wings arched, long-body but pot-belly, short-winged effect. Legs extend well beyond tail tip.

black head and underparts

ADULT SUMMER

distinct white line, widest in front of eye

long, slightly droop-tipped bill

ADULT WINTER

JUVENILE

brownish barring

red on lower edge of bill only

long, bright red legs

Greenshank

Tringa nebularia **532**

30–34 cm | WS 55–62 cm

◐ Marsh Sandpiper (*p. 222*),
Greater Yellowlegs (*p. 224*)

Long, elegant, greyish wader;
long, green legs. Often by freshwater, coastal lagoons, creeks,
less on open mudflats; breeds on remote bogs. **Bigger, greyer**
than Redshank (*p. 206*): see Spotted Redshank (*p. 207*). Feeds
sedately, sometimes fast runs, deep wading but generally less
quick/agile than Spotted Redshank.

Long bill **slightly upturned**, grey. Legs **yellow-green**, pale on
juvenile, grey-green in winter: 'lost' against background where
Redshank's vivid red stands out. Ruff (*p. 202*) usually has yellow-
ochre, less green, legs. ADULT streaked/spotted blackish and grey.
ADULT WINTER greyer, whitish streaks concentrated on hindneck,
white-faced, dark eye; white wing-covert edges complete.
JUVENILE pale wing-covert edges broken at tip.

VOICE Loud, **distinct**, frequent estuary sound: ringing, powerful
"*tyew-tyew-tyew*" on same note (see Redshank).

Rare and local breeder in far
N (1,100 pairs); scarce migrant
(1,000s), winter visitor (1,000)

from
Scandinavia

Breeds on peat bogs, extensive
damp forest clearings; winters
lakes, reservoirs, estuaries

IN FLIGHT,
**dark wings,
white 'V' on
lower back.**

no
wingbar

blackish
streaks

yellow-green
legs

ADULT SUMMER

whitish
head

white feather
edges broken
at tip

feather tips
unbroken white

bill upcurved,
pale at base

ADULT WINTER

JUVENILE

bright white
beneath

pale yellowish
legs

Wood Sandpiper

Tringa glareola

18·5–21 cm | WS 35–39 cm

Lesser Yellowlegs (*p. 224*), Wilson's Phalarope (*p. 233*)

Similar to Green Sandpiper (*p. 210*) but paler, less robust; can look round-bodied, yet slim neck, tail, long legs give more drawn-out effect. Long **pale stripe over eye and cheek** (short, in front of eye, on Green).

ADULT SUMMER heavily chequered. JUVENILE browner, bolder pale spotting than Green Sandpiper. Breast streaked, fades into white, without breast-band of Green Sandpiper. Bill finer than Green Sandpiper's, **legs longer, yellower**.

VOICE Call thin, high, quick, "*chiff-iff-iff*" on even note, without Green Sandpiper's down-up rhythm.

Scarce autumn, rare spring migrant; usually ones and twos (low 100s per year, most Jul–Sep)

from/to Scandinavia and Russia

from/to sub-Saharan Africa

Freshwater or brackish marshes, lagoons and shallow pools

IN FLIGHT, rises high, fast, **square white rump** against **brown wings** and back (less contrast than Green Sandpiper but clearly alike); **tail more barred**; feet project beyond tail. Underwing **dusky grey-buff**.

ADULT SUMMER

no wingbar

broad band over eye

chequered back

JUVENILE

pale yellowish legs

ADULT SUMMER

adult scattered dark spots, pale spangling on back

yellow legs

Green Sandpiper

Tringa ochropus  532

20–24 cm | WS 39–44 cm

👁 Solitary Sandpiper *(p. 235)*

Solitary Sandpiper *(p. 235)*

Compare with Common Sandpiper: bigger, darker; bright white beneath but without white 'hook' beside chest. **Plain wings, white rump**. Bobs head, swings tail up and down.

Dark head, white line from bill only to top of eye (longer on Wood Sandpiper *(p. 209)*); **dark breast-band**. Bill longer, heavier than Common Sandpiper's. ADULT greenish-brown-black above, fine pale speckling. JUVENILE clearly spotted buffish, never so chequered as Wood Sandpiper.

VOICE Tends to fly high and away if disturbed, with loud, rich, fluty, yodelling "*tluee-wee-wee*".

Widespread, scarce autumn migrant, fewer in spring; small numbers winter (low 100s / year)

All kinds of water bodies

Comparison of Wood, Green and Common Sandpipers

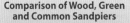

IN FLIGHT, square white rump striking; few dark bands on tail: '**black and white**' as it gets up and goes, like big House Martin *(p. 343)*. White belly, **blackish underwings**, unlike any other common wader.

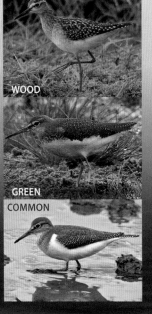

WOOD

GREEN

COMMON

very dark underwings

square white rump

dark wings, no wingbar

ADULT WINTER

white stripe only reaches eye

finely speckled

white eyering

very fine spots above

ADULT SUMMER

bright white beneath

JUVENILE

Common Sandpiper

Actitis hypoleucos

18–20·5 cm | WS 32–35 cm

👁 Spotted Sandpiper *(p. 232)*

Distinctive impression: bobs head, **swings rear body up and down**. Tail extends well beyond wingtips.

Plain sandy-olive-brown, eye-catching white below; dusky breast sides, **white 'hook' in front of shoulder**. Pale brown back unlike most common waders, most like Ringed Plover *(p. 183)*. Pale-based, straight bill; **inconspicuous greenish-ochre legs**. Size of Dunlin *(p. 196)* but slimmer, **longer-tailed**. Pale stripe over eye, pale eyering. ADULT upperside flecked blackish. JUVENILE **close bars** of blackish-brown and cream across wings, pale notches on tertials, tail sides.

VOICE Call distinctive, slight, melancholy fall in pitch and volume – "*swee-wee-wee-wee*". Song varies this into fast rhythmic trills and runs.

IN FLIGHT, **white wing stripe**; white sides to tail, rounded, dark 'blob' tip. Flies low; flicked, or fluttering, beats of **stiff, arched wings**, often giving loud, **ringing calls**.

Locally common summer migrant (24,000 pairs breed, Apr–Oct), rare in winter

from/to Scandinavia

from/to Africa

from/to Africa

Nests by rivers, lakes, mostly in upland N and W Britain and Ireland; on migration by freshwater; creeks, rocks on coast

white on underwings

white wingbar

dark tail and centre to rump

ADULT SUMMER

weak head pattern

plain back

barring on wing coverts becomes uneven with wear

1ST-WINTER

often seen in 'flicking' flight

white 'hook'

pale stripe over eye

dark bars/arrowheads above; single dark bar on wing coverts

JUVENILE

long tail

ADULT SUMMER

neat bars on wing coverts: double dark bands indicate juvenile

BAR-TAILED GODWIT

BLACK-TAILED GODWIT

square white rump; black tail

white wingbar

BLACK-TAILED GODWIT
no wingbars

white triangle up back

BAR-TAILED GODWIT

dark cap

orange wash

spotted back and wings

streaked back and wings

JUVENILE

BAR-TAILED GODWIT

BLACK-TAILED GODWIT

JUVENILE

legs long (much longer above 'knee' than Bar-tailed Godwit)

BLACK-TAILED GODWIT

plain back and wings

streaked back and wings

ADULT WINTER

BAR-TAILED GODWIT

ADULT WINTER

BAR-TAILED GODWIT

ADULT ♂ SUMMER

legs relatively short (much shorter above 'knee' than Black-tailed Godwit)

ADULT ♀ SUMMER

NT Bar-tailed Godwit

Limosa lapponica   ● ● **I** 531

33–41 cm | WS 62–72 cm

Locally common winter visitor
(43,000, Aug–Apr; declining),
migrant; rare inland

Slightly smaller, **shorter-legged** than Black-tailed Godwit, long bill slightly more upcurved; much **plainer in flight**. Feeds well-spaced on open mud, less often flocks in narrow, hidden creeks than Black-tailed Godwit.

MALE (fades by autumn) **bright coppery-red extending under tail**, little or no white, **no dark bars** (unlike Black-tailed Godwit). FEMALE paler orange. ADULT WINTER dull; fine **dark streaks** above. JUVENILE browner, **streaked upperparts**, buff chest, pale notches on tertials, more like Whimbrel/Curlew (*pp. 214–215*) at long range. Brighter, plainer chest, whiter underside, neater shape of sleeping birds help if bill hidden. IN FLIGHT (see *opposite*), dull upperwing, pale inner/dark outer half, long **white 'V' on rump**. Fast, twisting, acrobatic descents from high over estuary.

VOICE Nasal, wickering "*ki-wee ki-wee*" or "*ik-ik-ik*".

from Siberia

Muddy/sandy estuaries

NT Black-tailed Godwit
VU

Limosa limosa   ● race *limosa* ● race *islandica* **I** 531

37–42 cm | WS 63–74 cm   👁 Hudsonian Godwit (*p. 234*)

Very rare and local breeder
(50–60 pairs); locally common
winter visitor (50,000, mostly
E, S and SW)

Large, **long-legged, long-billed**, larger than Redshank (*p. 206*). Excitable groups; bill pointed down to toes, probed deeply, in mud or shallow water.

Long, straight bill, **mostly orange or pink** (Bar-tailed Godwit's dark in summer, upcurved but can be very long). Black legs **long above joint**. MALE **coppery-red**; FEMALE pale orange. Flanks white, **black bars**. ADULT WINTER **plain grey-brown**. JUVENILE (late summer/autumn) orange-buff, upperside dark with rusty fringes: like most juvenile waders, echoes adult colours. IN FLIGHT (see *opposite*), **white stripe** (longer, narrower than Oystercatcher's (*p. 178*)), **white underwing with black edges**. **Square white rump**, black-banded tail. Flight fast, deep beats of bowed wings: can look rather small; flocks manoeuvre tightly.

VOICE Quick, nasal notes; mechanical/metallic bickering when feeding/quarrelling.

islandica from Iceland

from Central and N Europe

Breeds wet meadows; migrant
on floods; winters mainly on
coast, estuary mudflats/creeks,
saltmarsh

Two races: *islandica* (Iceland) shorter bill and legs, darker breeding plumage; *limosa* (breeds rest of Europe) long bill and legs, paler but more extensive red in spring. JUVENILE *islandica* has stronger, more extensive rusty wash than JUVENILE *limosa*.

ADULT ♂ SUMMER
'Icelandic' race
islandica

ADULT ♂ SUMMER
'European' race
limosa

Whimbrel

37–45 cm | WS 78–88 cm

👁 Hudsonian Whimbrel (*p. 234*), Little Curlew (*p. 234*)

Rare breeder N isles (300 pairs), widespread but scarce migrant (3,000), rare winter (30–50)

from/to Scandinavia and Russia

from/to W Africa

Damp meadows, saltmarshes, estuaries

Smaller, darker than Curlew, stronger head pattern.

Larger than godwits (*p. 213*). Spring flocks, sometimes inland, otherwise mostly small, scattered groups on coasts.

Brown, dark streaks: greyer brown than Curlew, pale notches wear off in summer. Dark cap with **pale central stripe**, dark eyestripe, **pale band above eye**. Curlew may suggest pale over eye/dark crown, but no central line. Bill **blackish, downcurved**, usually more 'bent', less smooth curve, than Curlew.

VOICE Call diagnostic: quick, even repetition of short whistle in rippling trill: "*pipipipipipipip*". Song long whistles developing into even, sad trill.

IN FLIGHT, dark wings, inner half paler; dark tail; **white 'V' on lower back**. Darker, deeper-chested, chunkier, quicker than Curlew.

ADULT

obvious pale crown stripe

pale band over eye

plain crown (sometimes with faint stripe)

dark line through eye

bill shorter than Curlew's and distinctly 'kinked'

WHIMBREL

colder brown than Curlew

bill smoothly curved

plain 'face' with 'isolated' dark eye **CURLEW**

ADULT

NT Curlew
VU

48–57 cm | WS 89–106 cm

Numenius arquata ● ❶ 531

Scarce resident (68,000 pairs (150 pairs Ireland), declining rapidly); common winter visitor (150,000)

Biggest estuary wader, gull-like, long-winged, slower than Whimbrel or godwits (*p. 213*). Like others, in dull light on mud very dark, in bright sun paler, buffier. Feeds singly or spread out, roosts in tighter groups.

Mid- or buffy-brown. **Head plain**, or paler over eye, darker cap without Whimbrel's central stripe and dark eyestripe. **Bill long, downcurved:** MALE's less curved, shorter; FEMALE's very long.

VOICE Hoarse or barking notes; loud "*vi-vi-vi*" of alarm; clear, fluty "*cur-lee*" and "*cue-cue-cue*". Song loud, mournful, accelerating into mesmeric bubbling trill, often heard on estuaries but most ecstatic on breeding moors.

Flocks on migration form lines or 'V's, reminiscent of gulls.

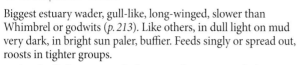

Breeds moors, river valleys; winters mostly on coast, estuaries, saltmarshes, meadows

ADULT

IN FLIGHT, like Whimbrel/Bar-tailed Godwit: dark outerwing, pale innerwing, **white 'V' up back**; long bill usually obvious.

JUVENILE

longer bill than ♂

ADULT ♀

brighter, buffier than Whimbrel

shorter bill than ♀

ADULT ♂

215

Red-necked Phalarope

Phalaropus lobatus ● ● **I** `532`

17–19 cm | WS 30–34 cm

 Wilson's Phalarope (*p. 233*)

Wilson's Phalarope (*p. 233*)

Small water/waterside bird, often swims. Smaller than Grey Phalarope (hard to judge size of lone birds); finer, all-black **needle-like bill**. Rotund; high shoulders taper to fine wingtips/tail, held clear of water when swimming. Sometimes 'spins' on water when feeding.

ADULT dark with **long buff lines**; white throat more or less surrounded by **rufous band** (brightest on female) above **dark grey chest** (no other phalarope has this grey).

ADULT WINTER like Grey Phalarope, **whiter stripes on grey back**.

JUVENILE (Aug/Sep), darker than Grey Phalarope, **more striped**; long lines of buff at first, stripes of grey/white/blackish as matures (Grey Phalarope increasingly has round grey patches within black). Pale pinkish on neck (quickly fades white).

VOICE Short, sharp "*kwit*".

Very rare summer breeder in northern isles (30–60 pairs); rare migrant (<100 per year)

to tropical Pacific (?)

Breeds on marshy pools; offshore

ADULT ♀ SUMMER

JUVENILE

IN FLIGHT, similar to Grey Phalarope, with white stripe on very dark wing; winter adults/juveniles, not safely identifiable at distance.

'mask' tends to turn down at rear

white lines on back

ADULT WINTER

fine, all-black bill

black and buff stripes on back

JUVENILE

ADULT ♂ SUMMER

dark grey chest

ADULT ♀ SUMMER

Grey Phalarope

Phalaropus fulicarius

20–22 cm | WS 36–41 cm   👁 Wilson's Phalarope *(p. 233)*

Small water bird. Does not breed in Britain/Ireland but commonest phalarope; in autumn/early winter after storms, most phalaropes seen will be Grey Phalaropes. Swims buoyantly, leaps over breaking waves; wades at water's edge, swims on sea. Thicker, broader bill than Red-necked Phalarope, but not always easy.

ADULT (very rare in Britain/Ireland) brick-red; white face, striped back (females most intense). ADULT WINTER **pale grey and white**; darker nape and crown sides, **black eye patch ('mask')**.

JUVENILE easily confused with Red-necked Phalarope: conspicuous brown/buff streaks above, soon develops broad **grey bands on back**, buff/apricot on foreneck; by late autumn greyer, blackish wings. Tiny **pale bill base**; legs tinged ochre.

VOICE Short "*pit*".

Rare but regular autumn migrant (400–600 per year); very rare in spring, winter

to tropical Atlantic

Mostly coastal, most near shore after gales

ADULT WINTER

Juvenile Phalaropes compared

'mask' droops at rear

buff lines

relatively thick bill

'mask' tends to rise at rear

grey bands

'needle' bill

RED-NECKED

GREY (moulting to 1st-winter)

ADULT ♂ SUMMER

ADULT ♀ SUMMER

IN FLIGHT, white stripe on dark wing, like long-winged, pot-bellied Sanderling *(p. 194)*.

'mask' tends to rise at rear

JUVENILE → 1ST-WINTER

JUVENILE MOULTING TO 1ST-WINTER

faint pale base to bill

ADULT WINTER

SANDERLING ADULT/1ST-WINTER

Sanderling in flight very similar but has narrower dark centre to rump/tail, lacks dark 'mask'

JUVENILE MOULTING TO 1ST-WINTER

Snipe

Gallinago gallinago   `532`

23–28 cm | WS 39–45 cm

Great Snipe (*p. 223*), Wison's Snipe (*p. 223*)

Often inconspicuous, in or near long vegetation on wet mud. Typically flies off in rolling zigzag, with noisy calls.

Very long-billed, squat, short-legged. Bill points down (even in flight). Bright brown, black, buff; cream stripes on back. Striped head: **pale central stripe**, buff over eye. **Flanks barred** above white belly. Age, sex and seasonal differences insignificant.

VOICE Loud harsh "*skaarch*"; calls (often from post or wire) rhythmically repeated "*chip-per chip-per*" spring/summer; harsh "*chip*". Switchback display flight, loud, vibrant, buzzing "*h'h'hhhhhhh'h*" made by tail feathers.

Localized, scarce breeder (76,000 pairs, declining); common and widespread in winter (1 million)

from Iceland

faeroeensis from Faeroes

from Central and N Europe

Bogs, marshes, wet moors; freshwater margins

outer tail feathers spread in dive

IN FLIGHT, **white trailing edge** to dark wing; rufous on tail. Settles with tail fanned, revealing **white tip**.

display flight

ADULT

white trailing edge

1ST-WINTER race *gallinago*

1ST-WINTER race *faeroeensis*

Snipe from Iceland, Shetland, Orkney and the Faeroes are race *faeroeensis* (shown above right), but only Faeroese birds are really distinct: redder overall, with narrower white stripes. The race breeding in the rest of Britain and Ireland is *gallinago*.

pale central stripe

broad flank bars

extremely long bill

ADULT WINTER

Jack Snipe

18–20 cm | WS 33–36 cm

Hard to see unless almost trodden on, when flies up quickly, quietly, circling briefly before dropping again (Snipe dashes away with loud call). Feeds inconspicuously; bouncy action.

Small snipe; dark, cryptic plumage; **bill not excessively long**. Two **long, golden-buff stripes** down each side; green gloss to dark feathers between. Head shows **dark central crown** (pale line on Snipe), double pale band over eye. Age, sex and seasonal differences insignificant.

VOICE Usually silent when flushed; sometimes a quiet croak.

Local winter visitor
(100,000, Oct–Mar)

from Scandinavia and Russia

Wet grassy marshes, reedbeds

ADULT/
1ST-WINTER

weaker
trailing edge
than Snipe

IN FLIGHT, wings quite long, rather straight, dark, with weak pale trailing edge; dark, pointed tail; **dark underwing** beside white belly. More useful is noticeably more 'normal' bill, not extreme length of Snipe's.

dark crown without prominent pale central stripe

JACK SNIPE

prominent pale central crown stripe

SNIPE

Typically very well hidden on the ground, long stripes down the back and along the sides mimicking grass stems; much smaller than Snipe (right) with no pale stripe down the centre of dark crown.

dark crown

long pale stripes along body

bill not remarkably long

ADULT/1ST-WINTER

Woodcock

Scolopax rusticola ● **I** `532`

33–38 cm | WS 55–65 cm

⟨**◎**⟩ Great Snipe (*p. 223*)

Rather snipe-like (*p. 218*); bigger, more barrel-shaped; different habitat and behaviour. Not often seen: usually flushed within woodland or **flying over at dusk**; feeds at night in damp fields and ditches.

Big, rusty-brown ground bird. **Long straight bill**. Pale, peaked forehead, **crosswise** black bands over rear crown. Dead-leaf patterning, close barring beneath. Sex, age and seasonal differences insignificant.

VOICE Alternate sharp, whistled "*tsiwik!*", low, croaking grunt, "*rorrk-rorrk*" during display flight.

IN FLIGHT, **rufous on rump and tail**. Wings long, broad-based, no marked pattern. Rises fast, twisting, with whoosh of wings. Flies over trees in display (roding), **calling distinctively**, pot-bellied, quick, flickering action seemingly superimposed on slower beats. Head up, thick bill angled down; feet often slightly lowered.

Scarce resident (78,000 pairs; declining), widespread winter visitor (1·4 million)

from N and W Europe

Woodland, adjacent pasture, ditches

rufous rump and tail

ADULT

ADULT

broad wing base

barred underside

black bands across head

'leaf-litter' pattern

ADULT

Rare waders

Waders the world over fall into more or less the same groups as those seen in Britain and Ireland. Most rare waders have an obvious affinity with commoner ones, but some have a different character, unlike more familiar birds.

Typical of those that 'look like European birds', and can thus be easier to put into a category, yet much harder to identify for sure, are the North American 'peeps'. These small sandpipers, such as **Semipalmated** and **White-rumped Sandpipers**, look like **stints** or **Dunlin**. If you think you have seen one, first rule out all the commoner options, then rule out even rarer ones.

For example, noticing a **Semipalmated Sandpiper** in autumn is an achievement, but you must be sure it is not an unusual-looking **Little Stint**. Then, you have to exclude **Western Sandpiper** – and, to be pedantic, the even rarer and harder **Red-necked Stint**. This takes you far into the realm of really difficult identification problems, requiring good views, long and close study, very accurate perception of plumage patterns, lots of detailed notes, and, if possible, photographs.

Spotted Sandpipers look much like **Common Sandpipers**; **Solitary Sandpipers** like **Green Sandpipers**; the two **yellowlegs** look like **Redshanks** or **Greenshanks**. But American **dowitchers** are different, combining features reminiscent of godwits, 'shanks' and snipe. At least you are more likely to notice such oddballs that 'aren't quite right' for any of the usual species. Telling the two apart – Long-billed from Short-billed Dowitcher – is an altogether different level of challenge.

Finding a difficult, rare or entirely unfamiliar wader is perhaps a little academic for most of us, but the unexpected is always possible. There is an undeniable thrill about seeing a rarity: finding it yourself and being faced with the challenge of identifying it is best of all. With most, an essential first step is to decide what age it is or at least what plumage it is in – adult summer or winter, or juvenile (autumn). Try to fix it into one of the groups on the following pages – is it a 'shank', a 'peep', a godwit, or maybe a snipe? Look at the common birds within that group. Does your mystery bird fit any of those? If not, then look at the rare options and try to work through the book to the best available possibilities. Ruling out what the bird is **not** is as important as trying to decide what it is.

As with any other rarity, the importance of long, close, detailed observation cannot be overstressed. Taking notes and making sketches undoubtedly fixes features in the mind many times better than taking a quick photograph (vital as that might be). If nothing else, completing a sketch (however basic) means you have to look at every part, and check again to make sure you have it right. Train yourself to look in detail, over a long period of time: it is surprising how often a second visit, or a later, better view from a different angle, or with better light, brings a slight change of mind. As you watch, the more you build up a complete and accurate picture of what your bird is. But be sure to check the book, especially the tables of crucial features for difficult groups, to be certain you do not miss the one tiny detail that might clinch the identification.

Greenshank (centre) with rare Marsh Sandpiper and Lesser Yellowlegs

Marsh Sandpiper: from SE Europe, typically a spring vagrant, often in breeding plumage.

Lesser Yellowlegs: from N America, typically an autumn vagrant, often long-staying.

List of vagrant waders

Some 41 species of wader have been recorded as vagrants in Britain and/or Ireland from Europe, North America or Asia. A number of these are covered earlier in this section, and the remaining 28 are included here. All the vagrants are listed, by group, in the table below, cross-referenced to the relevant page.

Charadrius plovers	Caspian Plover (*p. 185*), Lesser Sand Plover (*p. 185*), Greater Sand Plover (*p. 185*), Semipalmated Plover (*p. 186*), Killdeer (*p. 186*)
Vanellus plovers	American Golden Plover (*p. 191*), Pacific Golden Plover (*p. 191*), Sociable Plover (*p. 192*), White-tailed Plover (*p. 192*)
Courser	Cream-coloured Courser (*p. 192*)
Pratincoles	Collared Pratincole (*p. 193*), Black-winged Pratincole (*p. 193*), Oriental Pratincole (*p. 193*)
Tringa sandpipers	Marsh Sandpiper (*p. 222*), Lesser Yellowlegs (*p. 224*), Greater Yellowlegs (*p. 224*)
Snipe	Great Snipe (*p. 223*), Wilson's Snipe (*p. 223*)
Dowitchers	Long-billed Dowitcher (*p. 225*), Short-billed Dowitcher (*p. 225*)
Small *Calidris* sandpipers	Pectoral Sandpiper (*p. 227*), Sharp-tailed Sandpiper (*p. 227*), White-rumped Sandpiper (*p. 228*), Baird's Sandpiper (*p. 228*), Stilt Sandpiper (*p. 229*), Broad-billed Sandpiper (*p. 229*), Long-toed Stint (*p. 231*), Least Sandpiper (*p. 231*), Semipalmated Sandpiper (*p. 231*), Western Sandpiper (*p. 231*), Red-necked Stint (*p. 231*), Great Knot (*p. 235*)
Other sandpipers	Buff-breasted Sandpiper (*p. 226*), Upland Sandpiper (*p. 226*), Spotted Sandpiper (*p. 232*), Terek Sandpiper (*p. 233*), Grey-tailed Tattler (*p. 235*)
Godwit & curlews	Hudsonian Godwit (*p. 234*), Little Whimbrel (*p. 234*), Hudsonian Whimbrel (*p. 234*)
Phalarope	Wilson's Phalarope (*p. 234*)

Marsh Sandpiper *Tringa stagnatilis*

22–25 cm | WS 55–59 cm

Like tiny Greenshank (*p. 208*); clearly slighter overall, **fine, straight, dark bill** and long, slender legs (approaching stilt-like effect). Delicately built, high-standing. Compare size with other waders (critical). ADULT clearly spotted black on buff. ADULT WINTER dark cap, white stripe over eye, less streaked. JUVENILE has broad buff lines on upperpart feathers.

VOICE Call important "*kyew*" or "*kyu-kyu-kyu*", higher, quicker, weaker than Greenshank.

IN FLIGHT, pattern like Greenshank with **dark wings**, even longer **thin white wedge** on back; toes project more beyond tail.

fine, straight, dark bill

MARSH SANDPIPER

ADULT

GREENSHANK

thick-based, upturned, two-toned bill

ADULT (moulting wings)

needle-fine bill

plain above

black chequers above

ADULT WINTER

long, greenish legs

streaks and spots on chest

ADULT SUMMER

Smaller than Redshank (*p. 206*).

Slender, long-legged and small

Vagrant from Asia: <150 records (<10 Ireland), all months, mostly spring. Widespread.

Very rare migrant/vagrant from N Europe: <800 records (<20 Ireland), mainly autumn, few spring. Widespread, most N and E coasts. Marshes, rushy ground.

NT **Great Snipe** *Gallinago media* `532`

NT **Great Snipe** *Gallinago media* `532`

26–30 cm | WS 43–50 cm

Difficult to find, see, identify. Migrants often in drier areas than Snipe (*p. 218*) (but tired Snipe can appear anywhere).
ADULT obvious snipe; coarsely marked, 'marbled' effect: loopy **white tips to wing coverts**. Long, crescentic **bars across flanks and under belly** (see Snipe). Bill a little shorter, thicker than Snipe's. JUVENILE narrower stripes above, narrower bars below.

VOICE Short insignificant "*brad*" and rush of wings on rising.

GREAT SNIPE — white-edged dark panel
no white edge
SNIPE
barred
white

IN FLIGHT, **blackish midwing panel, edged white** each side, extending to leading edge around primary coverts; weak white trailing edge. Head/neck held quite straight. Spreads tail to reveal large triangular **white corners** (slightly less white on juvenile).

JUVENILE

SNIPE | GREAT SNIPE

Snipe 14 (12–18) feathers, narrow white tips; Great Snipe 16 (14–18) feathers, **outer four white** (adult), **white with dark bars** (juvenile).

SNIPE

1ST-WINTER

SNIPE
mostly white
slightly broader
AXILLARIES: **dark < white**

Wilson's Snipe *Gallinago delicata*

23–28 cm | WS 41–44 cm

Vagrant from N America: <10 records (1 Ireland), Oct. Marshes near coast.

Very like Snipe; ideally requires close views/photographs of raised wing and tail to assess fine details (see *inset right*).

VOICE Calls "*scaipe*" when flushed.

Outer tail feather with 2–3 dark bars = Snipe; Wilson's/minority of Snipe 4+ bars.

1ST-WINTER

WILSON'S SNIPE
extensive black barring
slightly narrower
AXILLARIES: **dark ≥ white**

Compared to Snipe, Wilson's Snipe has axillaries with thicker dark bars, a darker, more extensively barred underwing, and a slightly narrower white trailing edge

Rare American waders: Yellowlegs

The two yellowlegs are difficult to identify. Redshank and Greenshank must be ruled out, as they sometimes have yellow legs. Plain, dark upperwing rules out Redshank (*p. 206*); square white rump also rules out Greenshank (*p. 208*). Wingtips project beyond tail unlike Wood Sandpiper (*p. 209*), which also has a dark cap and broad pale stripe over eye. Yellowlegs are easiest to tell apart in breeding plumage; winter birds are plainer, juveniles more spangled above. Size and structure are hard to judge on lone birds; voice is a useful clue.

REDSHANK
(*p. 206*)

GREENSHANK
(*p. 208*)

GREATER YELLOWLEGS

LESSER YELLOWLEGS

Lesser Yellowlegs
Tringa flavipes

23–25 cm | WS 65–67 cm

Bill **short** (slightly longer than head), **fine, straight**, all-dark; wingtip **well** beyond tail. ADULT underparts plain. JUVENILE breast diffusely streaked. IN FLIGHT plain secondaries and primaries.

Greater Yellowlegs
Tringa melanoleuca

29–33 cm | WS 65–70 cm

Bill **long** (much longer than head) **slightly upturned**, pale at base; wingtip **just** beyond tail. ADULT spotted on chest, barred on flanks. JUVENILE more streaked on head and chest. IN FLIGHT, secondaries and inner primaries with fine spotting.

Vagrant from N America: <500 records (<150 Ireland), most Aug–Dec. Widespread. Freshwater, estuaries.

Vagrant from N America: <50 records (<20 Ireland), most Aug–Mar. Widespread. Freshwater, estuaries.

unmarked

spotted

ADULT SUMMER

ADULT SUMMER

Calls at-a-glance	
Redshank (*p. 206*)	Ringing "*tyew yew-yew*", fading away
Greenshank (*p. 208*)	Loud, even-paced "*teuw-teuw-teuw*"
Lesser Yellowlegs	1–4 weak, hesitant "*tew*" notes
Greater Yellowlegs	3-4 piercing, rhythmic notes: "*peu-peu-pew*"

GREATER YELLOWLEGS

short wingtip

bill longer than head

bill about as long as head

LESSER YELLOWLEGS

long wingtip

JUVENILE

JUVENILE

Rare American waders: Dowitchers

Long-billed Dowitcher
Limnodromus scolopaceus
27–30 cm | WS 48–50 cm

Vagrant from N America: <400 records (<150 Ireland), most Sep–Oct, fewer Apr–May. Mostly coastal. Freshwater, saltmarsh.

Short-billed Dowitcher
Limnodromus griseus
25–29 cm | WS 48–50 cm

Vagrant from N America: <10 records (<5 Ireland), Mar–Oct. Coast. Freshwater, estuaries.

The rare Long-billed Dowitcher (**LBD**) and very rare Short-billed Dowitcher (**SBD**) have a distinct shape – like an oversized Knot (*p. 195*) with a snipe-like bill but longer, green legs. The two are extremely hard to separate. Bill length varies with age and sex, and overlaps considerably between the species; only extreme individuals can be identified with certainty using this feature alone. They are best distinguished by call, though a suite of other features, depending on age, can assist identification.

SBD

LBD

IN FLIGHT, both species have long white triangle on back, white trailing edge.

Dowitcher calls

LBD – Short, sharp "**kip**", "**keek**" or "**kyip**", often confusingly two or three quick notes

SBD – Fast, double or triple, slightly rattling "**tudu**" or "**tududu**"

JUVENILES: TERTIAL + SCAPULAR: **pattern and colour**

LBD

SCAPULARS: **neat, rusty fringes/notches**
TERTIALS: **plain dark grey with narrow fringes pale/rusty**

JUVENILE

SBD

JUVENILE

SCAPULARS: **irregular markings**
TERTIALS: **dark with rufous bars/blotches; fringes rufous/buff**

ADULT SUMMER: UNDERSIDE: **colour**; CHEST SIDES: **shape of markings**

LBD   CHEST SIDES rufous with **dark bars**   BACK slightly 'concave'

ADULT SUMMER   UNDERSIDE **rufous**

SBD   CHEST SIDES rufous with **dark spots**   BACK subtly rounded, less 'concave'

ADULT SUMMER   UNDERSIDE **whitish**

WINTER: Plumages near-identical; SBD may show more specks/bars on lower breast; best identified using call and shape features

BILL/HEAD LENGTH RATIO:
≤ 2 indicates LBD | ≈ 1·5 indicates SBD

BLACK/WHITE (B/W) TAIL BARS RELATIVE WIDTHS:
B > W indicates LBD
B = W may be either species
B < W indicates SBD

FOREHEAD gentle slope indicates LBD

LBD

FOREHEAD steeper indicates SBD

SBD

BILL slightly downcurved towards tip

BREAST 'clean' indicates LBD

BILL thicker, usually more downcurved

BREAST 'dirty' indicates SBD

LBD

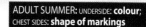

225

NT Buff-breasted Sandpiper *Calidris subruficollis*

18–20 cm | WS 43–47 cm

Like Dunlin (*p. 196*)-sized, rounded juvenile Ruff (*p. 202*) but clearer buff. **Small round head**, short dark bill, **mustard-yellow legs**. ADULT buffy-brown with pale eyering, black-grey-buff scaled upperparts, buff underparts, spotted neatly on chest sides. JUVENILE paler beneath than adult, scaled whitish above.

VOICE Usually silent.

JUVENILE

IN FLIGHT, plain above on long, pointed wings, and **dark on the rump without white sides**. Dark-edged white underwing obvious.

rather plain head

bight scaling above

JUVENILE

JUVENILE

bright yellow legs

Vagrant from N America: 10–60/year; <500 records, Ireland, May–Jun, most Aug–Oct. Freshwater, grassland.

Upland Sandpiper *Bartramia longicauda*

28–32 cm | WS 50–55 cm

Small, pale wader with long body, **longish tail, short, fine bill**, medium-short **pale legs**. Two **dark stripes on head**; neatly marked cream feather edges and notches on tertial fringes.

VOICE Usually silent.

IN FLIGHT, dark wing and rump.

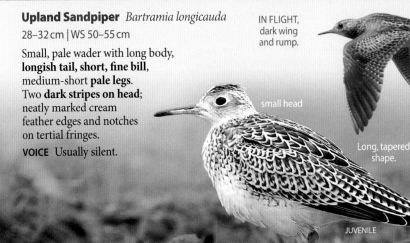

small head

Long, tapered shape.

long tail (extends beyond wingtip)

JUVENILE

bright yellow legs

Vagrant from N America: <70 records (<15 Ireland), Sep–Oct. Mostly on coast. Grassland.

Pectoral Sandpiper *Calidris melanotos*

19–23 cm | WS 43–47 cm

Usually bigger than Dunlin (*p. 196*), smaller than Ruff (*p. 202*). **Streaked** breast-band against white belly, **pale legs**. Creeps or squats in wet vegetation, mud, edges of reedbeds. Bill thick, medium-length, **faintly curved**, like Ruff, but pale base. ADULT breast-band, white belly; dull back. JUVENILE rusty cap; back **scaled like young Ruff, pale 'V'**; neck/breast finely streaked, **ending sharply against white belly** – breast-band most distinctive head-on. Legs **yellow-ochre** to greenish-yellow.

VOICE Call trilled "*krrrt*".

DUNLIN   PECTORAL SANDPIPER

obvious   faint

ADULT SUMMER
IN FLIGHT dark-centred rump, thin white wing stripe.

ADULT SUMMER

streaked breast against white belly

stout bill: slightly decurved with pale base

pale 'V' on back

JUVENILE

clean white belly below breast-band

yellowish legs

Very rare migrant/vagrant from N America: 50–175 per year, Apr–Dec, most Jul–Nov. Scattered. Marshes.

Sharp-tailed Sandpiper *Calidris acuminata*

17–21 cm | WS 36–43 cm

Like Pectoral Sandpiper, pale-legged, but ADULT has **rufous cap**, **spotted chest**, 'V'-shapes on flanks. JUVENILE pale buff to bright orange-buff on chest, streaks only on sides/throat.

VOICE High, short notes repeated, "*shilip-sheep-sheep-ip*".

Vagrant from Asia: <50 Records (<10 Ireland), few winter–spring; most Aug–Oct. Freshwater.

rufous cap

ADULT

spotted

bright rufous cap

streaks onto flank; whitish breast

breast streaks diffuse; no breast-band

JUVENILE MOULTING TO 1ST-WINTER

JUVENILE

White-rumped Sandpiper *Calidris fuscicollis*

16–18 cm | WS 38–40 cm

Like Dunlin (*p. 196*) but short-legged, long, sleek. Bill short. Legs black.
ADULT AUTUMN/WINTER greyish; scattered black-centred feathers above. JUVENILE like slim Dunlin, pattern more like Little Stint: white 'V's on back, stripe over eye.
Chest streaked, belly white (lacks dark marks, golden/buff look of young Dunlin).

VOICE Call sharp, thin "*tjeet*".

Vagrant from N America: <500 records (<150 Ireland), most Aug–Oct. Freshwater, estuaries.

IN FLIGHT, **white crescent above tail** (narrower than Curlew Sandpiper (*p. 199*)).

CURLEW SANDPIPER
JUVENILE

WHITE-RUMPED SANDPIPER
ADULT

grey replaces black-centred feathers after breeding

pale base

round, pale feather edges above

JUVENILE

wings very long; extend beyond tail

ADULT

Baird's Sandpiper *Calidris bairdii*

14–17 cm | WS 40–43 cm

Long, low, short-legged shape; longer wings than White-rumped Sandpiper.
ADULT WINTER dull, a few black spots above. JUVENILE buffier than White-rumped Sandpiper (see also juvenile Dunlin (*p. 196*)).
White beneath. Upperparts scaled buff-white (no white 'V's); streaked buff breast-band.

VOICE Call purring "*prreet*".

Vagrant from N America: <500 records, <350 Ireland), all months, most Jul–Nov. Freshwater, estuaries.

DUNLIN

dark flank marks

wings and tail ± equal

JUVENILE

IN FLIGHT, **dark-centred rump** rules out White-rumped Sandpiper.

JUVENILE

broad pale scaly edges above

bold dark spots above

ADULT

wings very long; extend beyond tail

very short legs

JUVENILE

Stilt Sandpiper *Calidris himantopus*
18–23 cm | WS 38–47 cm

Like large Curlew Sandpiper (*p. 199*) or small dowitcher
(*p. 225*) on **longer**, greenish-yellow legs, with **thicker bill**.
Long neck withdrawn or pushed up and forward, bill angled down.
ADULT **barred across underside**; rufous cap, cheek patch.
ADULT WINTER grey and white with dark cap; weak
grey flank streaks. JUVENILE brighter, scaly above.

VOICE Low, single, "*whu*".

JUVENILE

IN FLIGHT, weak
wingbar; white rump.

ADULT SUMMER

faintly
downcurved
bill

rufous
cheeks

barred
below

JUVENILE

Long pale legs

Vagrant from N America: <50
records (<20 Ireland), Apr–Nov,
most Aug–Sep. Freshwater.

Broad-billed Sandpiper *Calidris falcinellus*
15–18 cm | WS 34–37 cm

Small, short-legged wader, size between Dunlin (*p. 196*) and
Little Stint (*p. 201*). Bill **thick at base, downward curve at tip**.
Dark eyestripe; **white band forks above eye** in narrow 'V'.
Head pattern weaker in winter; at other times well
marked. ADULT buff-white fringes wear off to reveal
dark brown, rufous edges, hint of pale 'V'.
Breast streaked, belly white. ADULT WINTER more
difficult: plainer, greyer. JUVENILE brighter, more
striped above.

VOICE Dry, upward buzz or trill, "*brrree-et*".

Vagrant from N Europe:
<300 records (<25 Ireland),
Apr–Oct, most spring on E coast.
Freshwater, estuaries.

ADULT SUMMER

dark streaks,
white belly

head pattern
rather weak

grey above

strong head pattern

bill slightly
kinked at tip

ADULT WINTER

JUVENILE

Rare waders: 'Peeps'

See Temminck's Stint (*p. 200*) Little Stint (*p. 201*)

The five rare 'peeps' can be separated into two groups:

Pale-legged: two species; leg colour as Temminck's Stint but plumage more like Little Stint. Great care needs to be taken to distinguish the rare species from one another.

Dark-legged: three species which must be separated with care from Little Stint and each other. Semipalmated Sandpiper is most frequent, Western Sandpiper very rare and Red-necked Stint extremely unlikely. Look for bill shape, webbing between toes, scapular patterns, head patterns. Most are juveniles in late autumn; greyer winter adults are even more difficult, structure and call being most helpful.

Identification of juvenile pale-legged 'peeps' – summary of key features

Temminck's Stint BACK: **no 'V' on back**; TAILSIDES: **white**; CHEST: unstreaked buff-brown; VOICE: *"tiririririr"*

Least Sandpiper/Long-toed Stint BACK: **'V' on back**; TAIL SIDES: **grey**; CHEST: *see below*; VOICE: *see below*

	Voice	Form	Legs / toes	Head pattern	Breast
Least Sandpiper	*"kreeet"*	Chunky, squat	LEGS: short; TOES: short	STRIPE OVER EYE: unforked, joins over bill; BETWEEN EYE AND BILL: unbroken dark line; CHEEK PATCH: reaches eye	Streaked buff band
Long-toed Stint	Rippled *"chrrup"*	Long-necked; tapered	LEGS: long; TOES: long	CROWN: rufous; STRIPE OVER EYE: forked, falls short of bill; BETWEEN EYE AND BILL: broken dark line; CHEEK PATCH: isolated	Greyish, streaks mostly on sides

Identification of juvenile dark-legged 'peeps' – summary of key features

	Little Stint (*p. 201*)	Red-necked Stint	Semipalmated Sandpiper	Western Sandpiper
Voice	*"stit-tit"*	*"kreet"*	Rolled *"tchrrp"*	Thin *"jeet"*
Toes	Unwebbed		Tiny webs	
Bill	Straight; fine tip	Straight; thick tip	Straight; blob tip	Faintly curved; longer, finer tip than Semipalmated
Crown	dark centre, streaked sides	evenly streaked		
Eyestripe and face	EYESTRIPE: forked; FACE: diffuse; streaked cheek	EYESTRIPE: rarely forked; FACE: diffuse; streaked cheek	EYESTRIPE: unforked, bright; FACE: defined dark cheek patch	EYESTRIPE: unforked, strong, white; FACE: diffuse; streaked cheek
Primary project'n	long	medium	short	very short
Tertials	Blackish, edged rufous	Grey, edged off-white	Grey, edged buff	Grey-brown, edged whitish/buff
Scapulars	CENTRES: dark, round; EDGES: rufous-and-white	CENTRES: upper rows as Little Stint; lower rows pale; dark anchor shapes at tip	CENTRES: dark; blunt anchor shapes; EDGES: scaly, whitish	CENTRES: blackish; pointed anchor shapes; EDGES: bright rufous
Chest	Buff-white, sides pale, few streaks	Grey-buff, extensive fine streaks	White or buff, sides greyer; streaked	Orange-buff wash, sides streaked
Back	White 'V'	Obscure 'V'	Obscure or no 'V'	Obscure 'V'

LITTLE STINT

unwebbed

tiny webs

SEMIPALMATED

Tertial pattern + primary projection

Red-necked
grey, off-white edges

medium

Little
blackish, rufous edges

long

Semipalmated
grey, buff edges

short

Western
grey-brown whitish edges

very short

PALE-LEGGED
Long-toed Stint *Calidris subminuta*
14–15.5 cm | WS 27–29 cm

See table *opposite*.

Least Sandpiper *Calidris minutilla*
13–14.5 cm | WS 27–28 cm

See table *opposite*.

Vagrant from Asia (<5 records (1 Ireland): Jun, Aug; scattered). Marshes

Vagrant from N America: <60 records (<15 Ireland), Jul–Nov. Scattered. Waterside habitats.

DARK-LEGGED

NT **Semipalmated Sandpiper**
Calidris pusilla
13–15 cm | WS 27–29 cm

Vagrant from N America: <350 records (<200 Ireland), most Sep–Oct. Freshwater, estuaries.

Western Sandpiper
Calidris mauri
14–17 cm | WS 27–29 cm

Vagrant from N America: <20 records (<5 Ireland), Sep–Oct. Freshwater, estuaries.

NT **Red-necked Stint**
Calidris ruficollis
13–16 cm | WS 28–30 cm

Vagrant from Asia: <20 records (<5 Ireland), Jul–Sep. Marshes.

RED-NECKED STINT
ADULT SUMMER

long wings but projection beyond tail short

call vital

RED-NECKED STINT
JUVENILE

short bill

elongated body, short legs

'double stripe' over eye

LITTLE STINT
JUVENILE

pale 'V' on back

fine-tipped bill

evenly streaked cap

rufous fringes

dark 'arrowheads'

'blob'-tipped bill

long, fine-tipped bill

SEMIPALMATED SANDPIPER
JUVENILE

tiny web

WESTERN SANDPIPER
JUVENILE

231

Spotted Sandpiper *Actitis macularius*

18–20 cm | WS 37–40 cm

Very like Common Sandpiper; see table for differences.

Vagrant from N America: <250 records, mostly autumn/winter; few in summer. Freshwater, coasts.

Spotted / Common Sandpiper – comparison of key features		
	Common Sandpiper (p. 211)	**Spotted Sandpiper**
Structure	Attenuated body, long tail	Rounder body, **short tail**
Voice	Spotted Sandpiper can be similar to Common Sandpiper but less ringing; often gives a sharp, short, whistled "*peet*" or "*pit-wit*", which Common Sandpiper does not.	
Legs	greenish–brownish-yellow	**yellow** to **pale yellowish**
Behaviour	Spotted Sandpiper more crouched; creeps on flexed legs; bobs head/tail more than Common Sandpiper.	
Summer	UNDERPARTS: plain	UNDERPARTS: **spotted**
Winter	**Best identified on structure/call**: Spotted Sandpiper has greyer/plainer chest sides, bolder eyestripe and unmarked tertial edges (hard to see)	
Juvenile	TERTIALS: edges with pale spots GREATER COVERTS: all barred BILL: usually all-dark	TERTIALS: **edges plain** GREATER COVERTS: barring **on tips** BILL: grey-pink with dark tip

plain edge   short tail

SPOTTED SANDPIPER

pale spots on edge   long tail

SPOTTED SANDPIPER

COMMON SANDPIPER

COMMON SANDPIPER
ADULT SUMMER

SPOTTED SANDPIPER
ADULT SUMMER

strong wingbar on innerwing

no or weak wingbar on innerwing

less white in tail than Common Sandpiper

COMMON SANDPIPER

JUVENILE

darkish bill

long tail

tertial edges spotted

greenish legs

bolder eyestripe

JUVENILE

short tail

pale bill

greyer/plainer chest sides

tertial edges plain

yellow legs

ADULT SUMMER

Wilson's Phalarope *Phalaropus tricolor*
22–24 cm | WS 40–42 cm

Distinctive, biggish phalarope (though smaller than Redshank (*p. 206*)): confusion unlikely (but see other phalaropes (*pp. 216–217*); Wood Sandpiper (*p. 209*), Lesser Yellowlegs (*p. 224*). Also, Spotted Redshank (*p. 207*) can raise false hopes when swimming! **Long, fine, black bill**.
On water, low, long-bodied, upright head/neck. On land, slightly awkward; **forward-leaning**, unbalanced look.
ADULT unique, black band through eye widening into **rufous neck stripe** (female brighter than male). Legs black.
ADULT WINTER pale grey, white below. JUVENILE/1ST-WINTER pale grey; dark-centred, buff-edged feathers above; hint of dark band through eye, on neck, no black mask like smaller phalaropes; otherwise **very white. Legs yellow**.
VOICE Flight call "*chu*".

Regular N American vagrant (<350 records (<100 Ireland): most months, most Aug–Oct). Freshwater

ADULT SUMMER ♀

IN FLIGHT wings plain dark; rump square or 'U'-shaped, white.

JUVENILE

ADULT ♂ SUMMER

plain grey

ADULT ♀ SUMMER

JUVENILE

legs duller, underside whiter, than Lesser Yellowlegs

Terek Sandpiper *Xenus cinereus*
22–25 cm | WS 32–35 cm

Like large, greyish Common Sandpiper (*p. 211*) with hunched neck, **long, forward-thrusting, upcurved bill**. Short, **orange-yellow legs**.
ADULT grey-brown, dark band beside back. ADULT WINTER plain, paler, greyer, bright white below. JUVENILE greyish above with paler fringes.
VOICE Fluty "*dududududu*".

IN FLIGHT, grey rump, wide **white trailing edge to wing** behind black stripe; see Redshank (*p. 206*).

ADULT SUMMER

ADULT SUMMER

Vagrant from Asia: <100 records (<10 Ireland), Apr–Oct, rare winter. Freshwater, estuaries.

233

Hudsonian Godwit *Limosa haemastica*
37–42 cm | WS 67–79 cm

Similar to, but slightly smaller than, Black-tailed Godwit (*p. 213*) with finer bill. IN FLIGHT, **blackish underwing**, white wingbar much less prominent than on Black-tailed Godwit. **VOICE** Descending "*tow-wit*".

ADULT MOULTING INTO WINTER

black underwing

BLACK-TAILED GODWIT

WINTER

white underwing

ADULT ♀ SUMMER

ADULT MOULTING INTO WINTER

Vagrant from N America: <5 records (<5 Ireland), Apr–Jul. Marshes.

Vagrant from Asia: <5 records (Britain), Aug–Sep. Grassland.

Vagrant from N America: <20 records (<5 Ireland,: Apr–Oct. Marshes, estuaries.

Little Whimbrel *Numenius minutus*
29–32 cm | WS 57–63 cm

Like small, pale Whimbrel (*p. 214*) with paler face, shorter bill, **dark rump**.

VOICE Flight call higher, thinner than Whimbrel: a rising "*quip quip quip*".

Hudsonian Whimbrel *Numenius hudsonicus*
37–45 cm | WS 75–88 cm

Like Whimbrel (*p. 214*) with **all-dark rump, bold, brighter head stripes**.

VOICE Whimbrel-like piping trill.

white rump

dark rump

WHIMBREL 1ST-WINTER

HUDSONIAN 1ST-WINTER

LITTLE ADULT

ADULT

1ST-WINTER

PE Eskimo Curlew *Numenius borealis* from N America (not illustrated) has been recorded as a vagrant (<5 historical records Britain, 1 Ireland; last 1887), but is now possibly extinct.

EN **Great Knot** *Calidris tenuirostris*
24–27 cm | WS 58 cm

Like Knot (*p. 195*) with **longer, weightier bill**, smaller head, longer wings. ADULT SUMMER **heavy breast spots**, rusty back patches. ADULT/1ST-WINTER, dull, drab, more **spotted on chest** than Knot.

VOICE Generally silent.

ADULT SUMMER

ADULT SUMMER

JUVENILE

ADULT SUMMER

ADULT WINTER

Vagrant from Asia: <5 records (1 Ireland), Jun–Oct. Estuaries.

Vagrant from N America: <50 records (<10 Ireland), Sep–Oct. Freshwater/brackish marshes.

Solitary Sandpiper *Tringa solitaria*
18–21 cm | WS 50 cm

Like smallish, delicate Green Sandpiper (*p. 210*) but bolder white eyering, more tapered hind end. IN FLIGHT, dark rump.

VOICE High-pitched "*peet-weet-weet*".

Vagrant from Asia: 2 records (Britain), Oct–Dec. Estuaries.

NT **Grey-tailed Tattler** *Tringa brevipes*
23–27 cm | WS 51 cm

Medium-sized, grey wader, most like Redshank (*p. 206*) in shape with colours of winter Knot (*p. 195*); dark bill, **yellow legs**. IN FLIGHT, plain wings; grey rump and tail.

VOICE Piping, melancholy "*tweet-weet*".

SOLITARY

GREEN

1ST-WINTER

1ST-WINTER

1ST-WINTER

1ST-WINTER

1ST-WINTER

LARGE WATERSIDE BIRDS

TYPE ID size | bill size, shape and colour | flight shape, especially neck | underside pattern

All are water or waterside birds, some conspicuous, others extremely skulking.

3 bitterns: one scarce, one rare migrant, one vagrant.

6 herons: one widespread, others vagrants.

5 egrets: one widespread, one colonising, others vagrants.

1 spoonbill: migrant and winter visitor to SW England; rare breeder E England

1 ibis: rare migrant, increasing.

2 cranes: 1 localized breeder and scarce migrant, one extreme vagrant (also escapes).

2 storks: both rare migrants..

Ibis (p. 241)

Glossy Ibis unrelated to herons, large, very dark, with curved bill and long, thick legs; in flight long and skinny with rounded wings. Occasionally small groups on watery marshes.

Spoonbill (p. 249)

Spoonbill large, obviously white, typically standing asleep on one leg or wading in shallow water, sweeping unique spatulate bill from side to side.

Cranes (p. 248)

Crane very large, upright marshland bird, like giant heron with relatively small head and bill, no head plumes, but 'bush' of drooping feathers cloaking tail. Long striding, precise walk, picking food from ground. In flight distinct from herons, very long, more fingered, flatter wings, neck straight out.

Storks (p. 247)

Storks fly with outstretched necks on very big, flat, fingered wings, instantly separable from herons. On ground, also a slow, measured walk, catching food in long, heavy, dagger-like bills.

Waterbird ageing/ sexing

Sexes similar (Little Bittern an exception). Juveniles generally duller than adults but in some species (e.g. Bittern) not obvious. Larger species (e.g. Grey Heron) have intermediate immature stages.

ADULT BREEDING

IMMATURE

GREY HERON

GLOSSY IBIS

SPOONBILL

CRANE

Herons (*pp. 240–246*), **bitterns** (*pp. 242–243*), **egrets** (*pp. 244–246*)

Waterside wading birds, eating fish, frogs, other aquatic creatures, using variety of techniques. All have dagger-like bills, and long toes to take weight on swampy surfaces, grip upright stems and help lean forward when feeding.

Bitterns keep to dense upright vegetation (especially reeds) with hidden watery channels, can be extraordinarily difficult to see. Bittern large, Little Bittern only pigeon-sized.

Herons, such as Grey Herons, are more obvious, even at garden ponds. Rare Purple Herons are more secretive than Grey Herons, preferring reeds. All have long necks (Bittern's is cloaked in a cone of dense feathers) and long legs, standing with heads sunk deep down or stretched high up. Typical herons very large, Night-herons large, but Green Heron very small.

Egrets are like white herons, with varying plumes in summer, important differences between species being bill and leg colour. Little Egrets are by far the commonest, Great White Egrets very scarce and Cattle Egrets rarer still, but all have bred. Great White Egret similar in size to Grey Heron; Little Egret smaller.

Herons and egrets fly with legs trailed, heads withdrawn on coiled necks, ruling out storks and cranes (Grey Herons can fly with necks stretched momentarily, and are surprisingly good fliers on big, broad, arched wings, soaring well around treetop colonies in spring).

There are several rarities, some prone to spring appearances when they 'overshoot' on migration from Africa, others from North America, but all are erratic and unlikely finds. Great White Egret appears to be colonizing S England, with regular breeding in recent years, following the dramatic arrival and spread of the Little Egret since the 1970s. Cattle Egret has also bred but has not yet become established.

Waterbirds in flight

Cranes, storks have straight necks, flat wings; herons and egrets pull heads back, wings more bowed.

CRANE

WHITE STORK

GREY HERON

LITTLE EGRET

BITTERN

WHITE STORK

GREY HERON

LITTLE EGRET

Large waterbirds in flight

HERONS AND EGRETS
(*pp. 240–246*)
Neck held back

STORKS
(*p. 247*)
Neck outstretched; large bill

CRANES
(*pp. 248, 250*)
Neck outstretched; small bill

ADULT ♀

LITTLE BITTERN
(*p. 243*)

ADULT ♂

ADULT

GLOSSY IBIS
(*p. 241*)

ADULT

ADULT

JUVENILE

NIGHT-HERON
(*p. 243*)

BITTERN
(*p. 242*)

GREY HERON
(*p. 240*)

ADULT

JUVENILE

PURPLE HERON
(*p. 241*)

ADULT

ADULT

CRANE

ADULT

WHITE STORK

CRANE
(p. 248)

ADULT

ADULT

BLACK STORK
(p. 247)

WHITE STORK
(p. 247)

ADULT

ADULT

JUVENILE

GREAT WHITE EGRET
(p. 245)

SPOONBILL
(p. 249)

ADULT

ADULT

LITTLE EGRET
(p. 244)

SQUACCO HERON
(p. 246)

ADULT

ADULT

ADULT

CATTLE EGRET
(p. 246)

Grey Heron

Ardea cinerea `529`

84–102 cm | WS 155–175 cm

> Purple Heron,
> Great Blue Heron (*p. 251*)

A common large, long-legged, **long-necked**, pale **grey** waterside bird. Bill dagger-like; neck withdrawn into shoulders or extended, forward-leaning or with 'double bend' allowing sudden lunge.

ADULT blackish shoulder/flank; white head, **black band through eye** to short crest; neck may be faintly pinkish, black notches on front. Bill yellow. In spring, pale plumes on back, bill orange or pink-red. JUVENILE grey head, dark streaks on neck.

VOICE Loud, harsh "*fraank!*" At nest, rhythmic bill clattering, croaks, grunts and challenging screams.

Common resident, occasional migrant (14,000 pairs in Britain and Ireland, >60,000 winter)

from Norway

to France

All kinds of watersides. Breeds mainly in treetop colonies

IN FLIGHT, flight feathers smoky grey-black, forewing pale; white patch on leading edge. **Neck withdrawn** (may briefly be stretched out), legs trailed. Wings very broad, **strongly arched**. Capable of high soaring, and steep, twisting descents to treetop nest.

black crown stripes

pale neck

no trace of brown

ADULT

bill brighter, neck flushed pinkish-grey, in spring

ADULT FEB–APR

dull head and bill

grey neck

JUVENILE

dull legs

Glossy Ibis *Plegadis falcinellus* `529`

55–65 cm | WS 88–105 cm

A wading bird of wet meadows, floods, swamps. Suggestive of thickset, squat, thick-legged Curlew (*p. 215*), with **thicker, arched bill**, but **very dark** overall. ADULT black, green and copper gloss. ADULT WINTER/IMMATURE dark grey-brown, whitish neck streaks, whitish line enclosing eye and base of bill.

VOICE Usually silent.

ADULT

IN FLIGHT, slender; outstretched head, trailing legs, rounded wings.

glossy dark maroon and green

ADULT SUMMER

whitish flecks on head and neck

ADULT WINTER

Rare migrant/winter visitor from SW Europe: sometimes small groups, mostly in S; increasing.

Purple Heron *Ardea purpurea* `529`

70–90 cm | WS 120–138 cm

Secretive heron of reedbeds, marshes; snaky neck, slender bill. Compared with Grey Heron: longer neck; longer, thinner bill; narrower wings.

ADULT steely grey; pale-tipped brown plumes on back; **purple-red bend of wing** and flank. Sinuous **neck striped black, white, chestnut**. JUVENILE paler, browner, streaked. Dark cap, striped face, streaked foreneck (pattern like Bittern (*p. 242*) but much slimmer, long-billed).

VOICE Short, harsh croak.

IN FLIGHT, **long, bowed wings**; narrower than Grey Heron, curved trailing edge; **neck 'coil' deeper**, trailing feet longer.

ADULT

ADULT

tapered neck, head barely wider

rufous neck, black stripes

pale rufous neck

JUVENILE

Rare migrant from S and W Europe: (25–30 per year), spring/summer. Has bred. Marshes.

Bittern

Botaurus stellaris ● 529

69–81 cm | WS 100–130 cm

American Bittern (*p. 250*)

Remarkably cryptic heron-like bird of waterside reed/sedge beds: often very hard to see.

Sexes and ages similar. Big, brown, heron-like, creeps through dense vegetation, occasionally visible in thin patches or crossing open ditch. Walks in low crouch; springy action; may shimmer body from side to side. Stands still for long periods, bill often raised skywards. **Yellowish tawny-brown**, marked with black/brown all over (just like winter reedbed). Black cap, streak from bill; long stripes on foreneck. Legs green.

VOICE Spring call of male unmistakable 'boom' – loud, very deep, "*ah-whump!*"

Rare and local breeder (110 males), winter visitor (600)

from N and C Europe

Extensive reedbeds; smaller marshy areas in winter

IN FLIGHT, wings arched, broad; pale band on coverts. Head hunched back in thick wedge.

legs and huge feet light green

Often senses/searches for fish with bill tip immersed; may squat or raise neck remarkably high. Bitterns are severely affected by icing and must move elsewhere.

Little Bittern *Ixobrychus minutus* 529

33–38 cm | WS 49–58 cm

Very rare migrant, winters E Africa: 3–5 per year, (<100 records Ireland), most Apr–May, occasionally breeds. Marshes.

Elusive heron-like bird of dense waterside vegetation, swamps; small, size of Moorhen (*p. 256*). Best seen in flight, sightings often brief.

May stretch to catch fish, showing **elongated neck**; otherwise dumpy. MALE bright, **peach-buff on neck** and belly; **oval buff wing patch**. Otherwise green-black; pale bill. FEMALE **wing patch** duller; **streaks on neck**. JUVENILE browner, more streaked, slightly so on wing patch.

VOICE Call repeated short croak.

Squacco Heron (*p. 246*), Green Heron (*p. 250*)

IN FLIGHT, quick, wing patches show in blur; legs trailed (see *p. 238*).

black and buff

brown and buff

streaked pale brown and buff

ADULT ♂

ADULT ♀

JUVENILE

Rare migrant from Europe: 10–20 per year, (<100 records Ireland), most spring; some escapes. Marshes, waterside trees.

Night-heron *Nycticorax nycticorax* 529

58–65 cm | WS 90–100 cm

Rather large heron with **short, dagger-like bill**: active at dusk; hidden in foliage by day.

ADULT white face, **black cap**, black back; white plumes from nape. **Upperwing plain grey**. JUVENILE dark brown, **spotted white**; streaked below.

VOICE Call short, croaking "quark".

IN FLIGHT (often at dusk) quicker action than Grey Heron (*p. 240*), regular crow-like wingbeats (see *p. 238*).

buff spots on grey-brown

JUVENILE

hint of a dark cap

smooth grey and black

ADULT

IMMATURE

spots reduced, darker back, paler wings

yellow legs

Little Egret

Egretta garzetta 529

55–65 cm | WS 88–106 cm

Cattle Egret (*p. 246*), Snowy Egret, Little Blue Heron (*p. 251*)

Increasing resident, wanderer; spreading inland and to N following colonization (900 pairs breed; 4,800 in winter)

Pure white heron. Still for long spells, feeds like Grey Heron (*p. 240*), or active, leaping, running, stirring feet.

ADULT white; two long plumes from nape; in spring, long, wispy, but undivided plumes shroud tail and wingtips. **Bill grey-black**; facial skin grey or yellowish, brighter colours in spring. Legs blackish, **bright yellow toes** (obvious in flight, but beware muddy feet). JUVENILE bill dull, legs greenish.

VOICE Call short, deep croak; croaks and growls at nest.

Egrets IN FLIGHT, angular neck withdrawn. Size may be hard to judge: Great White Egret slower than Little Egret, wings longer, broader, more bowed; legs long, darker trailing feet.

LITTLE EGRET

GREAT WHITE EGRET

from Europe

Coastal pools, estuaries, lakes, riversides

The size difference between egrets is significant

GREAT WHITE EGRET   LITTLE EGRET   CATTLE EGRET

JUVENILE

bill greener than adult's or yellow base to lower mandible

legs greenish, yellowish on feet extending up to 'knee'.

Facial colour varies from pink/blue to yellowish in spring.

head plumes reduced, back plumes untidy

two long plumes from nape

ADULT WINTER

ADULT SUMMER

legs blackish, feet yellow

Great White Egret

Ardea alba

85–105 cm | WS 140–170 cm

Large, **all-white** egret; size of Grey Heron (*p. 240*).

ADULT bill black (or yellow and green at base), legs black, yellow or red above joint. Breeding birds have no head plumes, but broad, **long cloak of fine, wispy plumes** on back, widely spread in display. ADULT WINTER/IMMATURE bill typically **bright yellow** (best clue by far, if present); legs and feet dark, often **yellowish above joint**. IN FLIGHT, (see *opposite* and *p. 239*) size and action nearer Grey Heron than Little Egret.

VOICE Dry croak.

Scarce migrant, winter visitor (100–150 per year), rare breeder (2 pairs, increasing)

from Europe

Marshes, wet meadows, floods, lakesides

yellow bill

ADULT WINTER

variable facial colour and long, wispy back plumes

black bill

ADULT SUMMER

Cattle Egret *Bubulcus ibis*   👁 Squacco Heron (*p. 246*)

42–52 cm | WS 82–95 cm

A 'white' egret marked with buff in summer: look for bill and leg colours. Feeds among cattle on muddy/grassy fields (though beware that Little Egrets (*p. 244*) will also feed around cattle!). Less elongated and elegant than Little Egret (but not by much); **bill shorter, always paler**; legs shorter, paler. Head deeper, rounder, throat heavier beneath base of bill. ADULT **rich buff crown**, chest patch, back plumes. **Bill yellow**; bill and face patch variably red in spring. Legs pale. ADULT WINTER/IMMATURE all white; bill yellow, legs dusky **greyish-brown**.

VOICE Coarse croaks.

ADULT
SUMMER

IN FLIGHT, quite quick action, short neck/bill, short legs, but easily overlooked as Little Egret at distance.

ADULT
WINTER

yellow bill

strong buff
patches

ADULT
SUMMER

dark legs

pale legs

Rare migrant from Iberia:
40–45 per year, infrequent
influxes S England, Ireland, most
spring. Has bred

Squacco Heron *Ardeola ralloides*   529

40–49 cm | WS 71–86 cm

Small, white-winged, darker-bodied heron of waterside vegetation, ditches, pools. ADULT clean **peachy-pink or buff** overall; long, black-edged plumes from nape; bill blue and black; legs pinkish. ADULT WINTER/IMMATURE drabber, sandy-brown, whole head and neck finely streaked dark grey-brown. Usually hidden at rest (often hard to see).

VOICE Short, croaking quack.

ADULT
SUMMER

IN FLIGHT,
striking **white
wings and tail**.

ADULT
SUMMER

pale,
streaked

black-tipped
blue bill

immaculate
bright buff

ADULT WINTER/
IMMATURE

Very rare migrant from S Europe:
about 2 per year (<20 records
Ireland), most Apr–May. Marshes.

White Stork *Ciconia ciconia* 529

95–110 cm | WS 180–218 cm

Huge **white** or dirty white bird with **black on wings**, plodding progress in wet meadows, marshes with humanoid walk. Long, heavy, **dagger-like, bright red bill**; legs red, often splashed white.

VOICE Practically mute.

IN FLIGHT, innerwing white, trailing edge and outer half black, meeting over rump. Soars masterfully: **head extended**, legs trailed; wings long, broad, **fingered**, in shallow, taut bow quite unlike any heron (recalls vulture or pelican).

ADULT

Black Stork *Ciconia nigra* 529

90–105 cm | WS 173–205 cm

Obvious stork: slimmer, longer-legged, longer-necked than White Stork. A forest/cliff or woodland stream bird, although also feeds in fields. Head, neck, breast and upperparts **black**. **Legs and bill red**.

ADULT

IN FLIGHT (soars), **black chest, black rump and tail**. Blacker underwing has small **white triangular patch** at base joining across white belly to form large white edge.

JUVENILE

JUVENILE/1ST-YEAR
dull; pinkish-brown to greenish bill and legs

glossy; bright red bill and legs

ADULT

ADULT

Rare migrant from S Europe, winters tropical Africa: about 40 per year (<50 records Ireland), all months, most May–Oct. Meadows, marshes.

Very rare migrant from E Europe, winters E Africa: 5–6 per year, (<5 records Ireland), most May–Jun. Scattered. Streams, forest.

247

Crane

Grus grus 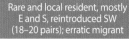 530

96–119 cm | WS 180–222 cm

 Sandhill Crane (*p. 250*)

Sandhill Crane (*p. 250*)

Huge wetland bird,
upstanding on land; flies with **legs and head outstretched**,
on **flat wings** (unlike any heron).

ADULT grey (often stained brown); **black-tipped 'bustle'**
(tertials overlap wingtips and tail). Black face, **white nape**,
red crown. JUVENILE/IMMATURE has plain grey head.

VOICE Loud, ringing or jarring "*krroo*".

Rare and local resident, mostly
E and S, reintroduced SW
(18–20 pairs); erratic migrant

IN FLIGHT, wingtips, trailing edge
smoky black (Grey Heron (*p. 240*)
pattern). Heavy-bellied; thick
foreparts taper into outstretched
neck; wings broad, vulturine/stork-
like, tips upcurved. Migrant flocks
(very rare in Britain) form long
chevrons or 'V's.

ADULT

Marshes, open meadows, floods

ADULT

JUVENILE

Spoonbill

Platalea leucorodia  **529**

80–93 cm | WS 120–135 cm

Big white wading bird, heron-like, not really confusable with elegant egrets. Colonial breeder, sometimes small groups outside breeding season. Stands in shallows (or on tree), head tucked back when sleeping; feeds by marching slowly with long strides, **open bill swept sideways** through water.

ADULT **white**, yellow chin, yellow-buff chest. 'Pineapple' **crest on nape**, drooped, raised or blown aside in wind. Long, dark legs thicker than egret's. Bill extraordinary, unique in Europe: long, broad, with wide, **rounded, flat tip** (black with yellow tip on older birds, pinkish on juveniles, dark with pink beneath on older immatures). JUVENILE drab, has **black wingtip spots**.

VOICE Silent.

Scarce spring/autumn migrant, winter visitor (40–50); rare breeder (10 pairs, recently established). Most on S and E coasts; rare inland

from/to Europe

Lagoons, estuaries, lakes

IN FLIGHT vaguely swan-like (*p. 20*) (but much smaller, quicker), neck outstretched: long legs trail.

JUVENILE

black wingtips

ADULT

On 1ST-WINTER, bill blackish without yellow tip, but pale beneath.

ADULT

JUVENILE

Vagrant North American herons and cranes

Green Heron *Butorides virescens*

45 cm | WS 62–70 cm

Vagrant from N America: <10 records (1 Ireland), Sep–Oct. Near coast. Wetlands.

Very small heron, dark, slaty green above, with deep rufous neck. JUVENILE/1ST-WINTER dark cap, broad rufous and white streaks on chest, chestnut cheeks, pale spots on back.

JUVENILE

1ST-WINTER

bright pale legs show when flying away

Sandhill Crane
Grus canadensis

85–95 cm | WS 160–180 cm

Large, pale grey crane (often stained ochre-brown), **red forehead/cap**, white cheek, dark bill. IMMATURE browner above. Flight feathers paler grey than Crane (*p. 248*).

<5 records (1 Ireland), Apr, Sep–Oct. Fields.

IMMATURE

IMMATURE

American Bittern
Botaurus lentiginosus

59–70 cm | WS 95–115 cm

<75 records (< 25 Ireland), Nov–May, most autumn. Scattered. Marshes.

Like Bittern (*p. 242*) but has browner crown and neck side, longer black moustache, wider rufous streaks on chest, plain greyish wingtips without fine bars.

black cap

brown cap

BITTERN

thinner streaks

wide streaks

IMMATURE

Great Blue Heron *Ardea herodias*
91–137 cm | WS 175–195 cm

Huge heron, like Grey Heron (*p. 240*) but neck pinker/brownish, thighs rufous. IMMATURE more pale pinkish-purplish-brown overall than Grey Heron.

dark back/paler wing more uneven than on Grey Heron

brownish shoulder patch

IMMATURE

brownish thigh often visible on adult

<5 records (Britain): Dec, May. Near coast. Freshwater.

Little Blue Heron ◆
Egretta caerulea
60 cm | WS 95–105 cm

1 record (Ireland), Sep–Dec. Near coast. Marshes/wetland.

Small heron.
ADULT (not recorded) slaty grey. IMMATURE white, like Little Egret (*p. 244*) but develops grey patches as matures; **legs yellow-green**; bill grey with well-defined **black tip**.

Snowy Egret
Egretta thula
60–65 cm | WS 90–105 cm

1 record (Britain): 1st-winter: Sep (long-stayer). Near coast. Marshes/wetland.

Like Little Egret (*p. 244*) but **bright yellow on face**, yellow extending onto lower leg; bushier head plumes or rough crest (two thin plumes on Little Egret). On ADULT, back plumes curl up in wispy filaments (straight plumes on Little Egret).

Difficult white herons	
Little Egret (*p. 244*)	JUVENILE legs green, yellowish stripe inside leg to joint; face greenish; bill blackish, yellow at base
Snowy Egret	Defined pale yellow band extends up back of leg to joint; face yellow; bill greyish-black
Little Blue Heron	Grey-green or yellow-green legs and feet; grey face, bill pale grey with defined black tip

LITTLE EGRET

1ST-WINTER

fan-shaped crest raised in display/aggression

ADULT

yellow face brighter than any Little Egret

SNOWY EGRET

LITTLE BLUE HERON
1ST-WINTER

1ST-WINTER

BUSTARDS

3 species: 1 re-introduction, 2 vagrants.

Bustards are big, stout-legged, short-beaked landbirds. All four species found in Europe are declining, and most are now globally threatened. In the UK, the Great Bustard used to breed quite widely on open downs, but was lost as a breeding species long ago. It is now being reintroduced to Salisbury Plain in Wiltshire. Although wild Great Bustards are rare vagrants, other species are even rarer: famously, a 'Houbara' Bustard (now known as McQueen's Bustard) once appeared in Suffolk, but that is highly unlikely ever to happen again as the bird is on the brink of extinction. The most likely bustard to turn up in Britain (or possibly again in Ireland) is Little Bustard. Since bustards have distinctive white wing patches in flight, other species, especially the odd-looking Egyptian Goose (p. 33), have sometimes been mistaken for bustards by inexperienced observers. In reality, though, bustards are not much like anything else, and Great Bustards so big as to be unmistakable.

VU **PE** **Macqueen's Bustard** (Asian Houbara)
Chlamydotis macqueenii
55–65 cm | WS 130–150 cm

Large, long-necked, long-legged bustard; pale sandy above, white below, grey foreneck. ADULT has thin black cap and black streak on neck.

ADULT ♂

IN FLIGHT, long wings; white flash near wingtip.

ADULT ♀

Vagrant from Asia: 1 modern record (Britain), Nov–Dec.

NT **VU** **Little Bustard** *Tetrax tetrax*
40–45 cm | WS 83–91 cm

Small bustard (size remarkably tricky when isolated bird crouches in vegetation), Pheasant-sized; long legs; long, broad wings. MALE has **black and white neck.** WINTER MALE/FEMALE colours like female Pheasant (p. 270).

IN FLIGHT, unexpected, fast beats, like strange duck, **mostly white wings.**

ADULT ♀

ADULT ♂

Vagrant from S Europe: <250 records (<10 Ireland), most months. Widespread but declining. Arable fields.

530

Crouched bird hidden in tall grass slowly raises round head on slender neck.

ADULT ♀

ADULT ♂

Great Bustard *Otis tarda* `530`

♂ 90–105 cm | WS 210–240 cm
♀ 75–85 cm | WS 170–190 cm

Long extinct UK breeder, being reintroduced (Wiltshire); very rare wild vagrant (150 records (<5 Ireland): most winter, declining). Grassland, fields

Huge, heavy terrestrial bird of extensive open plains; more or less horizontal with erect neck. Despite size, elusive; can hide in tall crops. Looks dull, grey at long range; brighter, richer colours close-up.

MALE whiskered grey head, broad collar of rufous-orange; back barred black and **bright ginger-brown**; white below. FEMALE similar but duller, slimmer, head neat, greyish without 'whiskers'.

IN FLIGHT, **reveals a lot of white** in wing (beware much smaller Egyptian Goose (*p. 33*)). Flying birds dramatic, with long, straight, fingered wings, crane- or stork-like but body heavy, slender neck outstretched, **square tail with no leg projection**.

ADULT ♀

ADULT ♂

cleaner grey on head than any Little Bustard

ADULT ♀

CRAKES and RAILS

CRAKE and RAIL ID   form | bill shape/colour | leg colour | undertail and flank patterns

These are long-toed, short-billed, mostly waterside or water birds, often secretive, quick to run for cover (less likely to fly).
11 species: 15 breed, of which only 3 are widespread; 6 rare vagrants.

Coot and **Moorhen** familiar water or waterside birds, **Water Rail** widespread but far less well known. Other crakes, including summer visiting **Corncrake**, which breeds in northern Scotland and Ireland, are rare and difficult to see.

Coots (*p. 257*) are like blackish ducks with white faces (the bill and bare facial shield, although juveniles also have white on the face and neck). Social, noisy, quarrelsome at times, either on open water or grazing on short grass. Winter flocks can be large, recalling wildfowl. Low-tailed, round-backed, and often dive underwater, reappearing suddenly, as if instantly into swimming position; surface-feeding ducks often associate with them.

Moorhens (*p. 256*) more likely in ones and twos, sometimes up to 50 or so in loose groups on open ground, less often out on open water, frequently in ditches and reedy channels or along riversides – even up in waterside bushes. Diagnostic white flank stripes; swim with cocked tails (revealing big patch of white each side) and bobbing heads, much less round-backed than Coots. Loud calls frequently help locate them.

Water Rails (*p. 258*) generally keep out of sight in dense waterside vegetation, but come out into the open beside ditches and muddy spots, even on woodland pools under trees, or in icy weather: look for the long, slim bill.

Corncrakes are usually merely voices from deep within a hay crop: the loud, ratchet-like double call is unmistakable, but seeing the bird is difficult and requires much patience.

Crake ageing/sexing

Sexes similar, except in some crakes. Juveniles are usually distinguishable but become increasingly like adults by their first winter, with duller bill colours.

COOT

MOORHEN

Moorhens and Coots habitually swim, but look rather different on land: Coots upright, Moorhens often more crouched.

WATER RAIL

SPOTTED CRAKE

Rare crakes are difficult to detect in their densely vegetated habitats, and are often best located by their characteristic songs at night.

Corncrake

Crex crex ● ❶ 530

27–30 cm | WS 42–53 cm

Dry land crake pushed north and west by modernized farming; now rare. Heard more often than seen, usually from hay crop or patches of irises and nettles around fences/stone walls.

Pale, yellowish-brown with **rufous on barred flanks and especially spread wing**. Face and breast **bluish-grey**, flanks barred rufous, overall effect varies according to angle of view (dull grey, or rusty).

VOICE Unique, rhythmic, dry, rasping double "*crairk-crairk*", with open bill, head thrown upwards; at any time, but especially after dark; it is a loud, hard rattle at close range.

Local and rare/scarce summer migrant, Ireland and N Britain (1,400 breeding pairs, including 200 in Ireland, Apr–Sep); reintroduced to East Anglia

to Africa

Hay fields, iris and nettle beds

IN FLIGHT, low, quick; quite slender but rounded rufous wings; head outstretched; legs trailing.

Although seemingly a weak flier if flushed, Corncrakes undertake long-distance migrations to and from Africa.

black streaks above; rusty wing patch

singing male upright, sometimes on rock or wall.

ADULT

ADULT

Moorhen

Gallinula chloropus

30–38 cm | WS 55–60 cm

Purple Gallinule, Allen's Gallinule *(p. 262)*

Rounded, head held low, well forward, on water or land. Longish legs and toes give springy, rhythmic action; bobs head when swimming. Swims, feeds on open grass, clambers in hedges. Often in loose groups but not swimming/grazing flocks as Coot. Typically water/waterside habitats, ready to scuttle off if disturbed (half run/half flight).

ADULT dark with big white patch under tail, white side stripe; unique red-and-yellow bill. JUVENILE paler, browner, whitish throat; similar and under tail. Bill dull olive-brown. By winter, like adult with dark bill.

VOICE Varied, typically bubbling, explosive "*kurrt*"; also abrupt "*ki-yek*" and "*krek-krek-krek*" (often in flight at night).

Common resident, particularly in the lowlands (240,000 pairs; 320,000 in winter)

All kinds of waterside habitats

Often runs across water surface on long, slender toes.

ADULT

Equally likely well-hidden in dense, wet vegetation.

white streaks on flanks

white beside tail

JUVENILE

wingtips/ tail raised

ADULT

red facial shield

big white patch under tail

NT Coot

36–39 cm | WS 70–80 cm

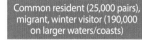
◇ American Coot (*p.262*)

More strictly a water bird than Moorhen, but feeds on adjacent grassy places. Loose flocks may number hundreds (Moorhens scattered; wildfowl more mixed plumage patterns). Less agile than Moorhen; stands more upright, lumpy, rounded, thicker legs set well back.

ADULT has **white facial shield and bill** striking at great range. Duck-like, black at distance, swimming with round head up, **back rounded, high at rear**, but **tail low** (Moorhen forward-leaning with higher tail,). **Dives frequently**. Occasionally puzzling in odd places, such as on sea against light. Closer views show slaty colour, blackest on head. JUVENILE grey-black, **dull white lower face and breast** (see grebes (*pp. 80–83*).

VOICE Loud, sudden "*kowk!*"; various sharp, metallic notes. Young have feeble but far-carrying whistles.

Common resident (25,000 pairs), migrant, winter visitor (190,000 on larger waters/coasts)

from NE Europe

Lakes, pools, reservoirs, rivers, marshes, coastal waters

Often runs across water on flat, broadly-lobed toes.

ADULT

white face and breast

JUVENILE

big white facial shield

ADULT

wingtips/tail held low

no white under tail

Water Rail

Rallus aquaticus `530`

23–26 cm | WS 38–45 cm

Deep-bodied, rounded side-on; compressed and slender end-on, creeps through dense reeds and waterside vegetation. Often heard more than seen. Small, round, long-billed, wetland bird; secretive walk and scuttling run, or short, fast flight to cover. Sometimes more in the open during cold weather/towards dusk.

ADULT appears dark unless close up or in bright light. **Long, red-based bill** distinctive, streaked brown back, **slate-grey breast**. Barred flanks at close range; white-tipped **buff patch under short, raised tail**. Legs pink. JUVENILE browner, paler on breast and over eye; duller bill and legs.

VOICE Piglet squeals, moaning and repeated loud, short, Blackbird-like "*kip*"; song accelerating series of short notes, often at night.

IN FLIGHT, quite small, narrow wings; legs dangle; outstretched head/bill, white mark under leading edge of wing (may also be visible in open-winged run to cover).

Scarce resident (1,100 pairs); fairly common winter visitor (10,000+)

from N and E Europe

Watersides, dense sedge/reed/fen, riverside thickets, woodland ponds, wet ditches

JUVENILE

ADULT

round profile with pointed tail, long spike bill

ADULT

Spotted Crake

Porzana porzana ● ❶ **530**

19–22·5 cm | WS 37–42 cm

👁 Sora, rare crakes (*p. 260–261*)

Small, squat, rounded, dark grey-brown, **short-billed** bird, combining overall impression of Water Rail but short bill of Moorhen (*p. 256*); smaller, harder to see than either. Typically secretive but not necessarily shy: patience may be rewarded if a bird walks onto open mud.

ADULT bill short, straight, stout, **red at base**. Chest spotted white, flanks barred. Big buff patch under tail. **Legs green** (pink on Water Rail). JUVENILE like adult but generally duller.

VOICE Song at night (needs special expedition); sharp, upslurred whistle ending in 'whiplash' or dripping effect, endlessly repeated.

IN FLIGHT, white leading edge to wing catches eye in brief whirring rise from waterside cover.

Rare, erratic summer visitor (25 breeding pairs) and autumn migrant (25–50 per year); declining

Wetlands, coastal pools

rounded profile; short bill

dull bill

JUVENILE

white dots on brown breast

ADULT

bright bill

wavy bars on flanks

white spots on grey breast

Rare crakes

Little Crake *Zapornia parva*

17–19 cm | WS 34–39 cm

Vagrant from E Europe:
>100 records (<5 Ireland),
autumn and spring, most
Mar–May. Scattered. Marshes.

530

Tiny; sharp patterns close up, 'dull and dark' in brief glimpse, **wing projection rather long.** Favours reedbeds/fen and open water in ditches and pools. MALE recalls Water Rail (*p. 258*) but **short bill** green with **red base. Legs green.** Underside **blue-slate.** Back has dark stripes, few small white marks. FEMALE pale buff-brown, darker back, same bill/leg colour. Pale crescentic streak on upper edge of tertials beside often **cocked tail.** JUVENILE weakly barred flanks, white spots above, less red on bill: see Baillon's Crake (shorter wingtips), Spotted Crake (*p. 259*) (greyer chest with white spots).

long wings and tail

minute red gape

JUVENILE

ADULT ♂

red on bill

clean grey beneath

ADULT ♀

red on bill

bright buff beneath

Baillon's Crake *Zapornia pusilla*

16–18 cm | WS 33–37 cm

Vagrant from E Europe: <100 records (<5 Ireland), all months, most Jun–Aug. Scattered; has bred. Marshes.

530

Very small; compare with Little Crake and bigger Spotted Crake (*p. 259*) which favour similar habitat. MALE and FEMALE both like male Little Crake but **short wings**, green bill, **barred rear flanks**. More speckled black and white above. JUVENILE difficult: like small Spotted Crake, more barring/spotting on chest than juvenile Little Crake, more white marks above.

VOICE Spring call nocturnal, a low, dry rattle, 1–2 seconds.

green bill

barred flanks

ADULT

short wings

JUVENILE

no red on bill

Sora Rail *Porzana carolina*

18–21 cm | WS 35–40 cm

Vagrant from N America: <30 records (<5 Ireland), Aug–Apr. Scattered, most near coast. Marshes.

Very similar to Spotted Crake (*p. 259*). ADULT **yellow bill without red**; **black face/throat patch** more extensive, more elongated onto chest, more sharply defined than any dark-faced effect on Spotted Crake. JUVENILE/1ST-WINTER harder: rule out Water Rail (*p. 258*) and tiny crakes, then Spotted Crake – compared with juvenile Spotted Crake, **plain brown chest** (not white spots on grey), browner crown (less evenly streaked black) with thin central dark stripe. At all ages, tertials (cloaking closed wingtips) **plain brown with darker centres** (on Spotted Crake, tertials show broad buff upper edge and several wavy white lines across them).

tertials have pale edges but no white bars

1ST-WINTER

dusky/blackish face

ADULT

Very rare rails

Allen's Gallinule

Porphyrio alleni

22–25 cm | WS 48–52 cm

ADULT like small, green-backed, violet-breasted Moorhen (*p. 256*); red legs; bluish frontal shield. JUVENILE greenish-brown, buff edges (wear off), dull undertail coverts (white on Purple Gallinule), bill and legs reddish-brown.

Vagrant from N Africa: <5 records, immatures (Britain), Jan–Feb. Scattered. Marshes.

ADULT

JUVENILE

(American) Purple Gallinule

Porphyrio martinica

29–33 cm | WS 50–55 cm

ADULT like green-backed, blue-bodied Moorhen (*p. 256*) blue frontal shield, red-and-yellow bill, yellow legs. JUVENILE buffy tan, greenish back, dull bill, dull blue frontal shield, yellowish legs. Undertail plain white without central dark band of Moorhen (buff on Allen's Gallinule).

Vagrant from N America: <5 records, immatures (Britain), Nov–Jan. Scattered. Marshes.

SUB-ADULT

American Coot

Fulica americana

34–43 cm | WS 58–71 cm

Dark, like Coot but **white under tail;** bill has **dark band** near tip; smooth rounded black face against bill, lacks sharp black point where facial shield joins bill.

Vagrant from N America: <10 records (<5 Ireland), Nov–Mar. Scattered. Wetlands.

COOT

sharp black point

no obvious facial shield, but purple/red patch

dark band on bill

white undertail

PHEASANTS, PARTRIDGES, GROUSE and QUAIL

GAMEBIRD ID   size | tail shape and colour | face patterns | leg colour | voice

A small, diverse group of seed-eating, mostly ground birds (some roost and feed in trees). Essentially chicken-like basic form and bill shape, generally rounder bodied. Fly fast and low if disturbed, with bursts of whirring wingbeats between glides on stiff wings. Young birds may fly before fully grown.

10 species: 9 resident, 1 summer visitor; 4 introduced (two close to extinction), plus 1 reintroduced following extinction.

Pheasants (*p. 270*) are released in millions for shooting, some establishing breeding populations. They have rather long, bare legs, short bills and long tails.

Partridges (*pp. 264–265*) include one native species and one long- established introduction, both supplemented by released birds.

Grouse (*p. 266–269*) include four native species, one widespread but declining on heather moors, one restricted to high altitude areas, and two associated with moorland/woodland edge (Capercaillie reintroduced following UK extirpation). They have feathered feet, unlike partridges.

Quails (*p. 272*) unlike the others, are summer visitors. Most detected are singing males.

Gamebird ageing/ sexing

Sexes are dissimilar: in some species markedly. Juveniles look like females and may fly before they are full grown.

GREY PARTRIDGE

QUAIL

BLACK GROUSE

Escapes and introductions

Several related species may occasionally be seen as escapes and introductions: some have bred (Category E* species, covered on *p. 523*).

263

Red-legged Partridge

Alectoris rufa `528`

Fairly common introduced resident in UK (120,000 breeding pairs, extensively released for shooting); rare in Ireland

Farmland, downs, dunes, heaths, sometimes gardens

32–35 cm | WS 47–50 cm

Neat, big-bodied, small-headed partridge with bold colours; introductions persist as wild populations, also tame groups of newly released birds. Often a bird of downland/heath/sandy fields, less restricted to grassy meadows than Grey Partridge.

Sexes alike. Pale sandy-brown; heavy flank bars, **plain back**. **White face edged black**, neck closely streaked black and grey. **Bill and legs red**.

VOICE Curious, puzzling mix of croaks and rhythmic, grating, mechanical chuffing sounds, often "*chu chu chu chu ka-chekchek ca-chekchek cachekchek…*" sometimes delivered from a high perch.

IN FLIGHT, tail shows dark orange sides against grey rump. Glides on flat wings (slightly bowed/drooped on Grey Partridge).

ADULT

○ Chukar Partridge

Note past releases (now illegal) of **Chukar Partridge** *Alectoris chukar* – similar but bigger, plainer on chest without black stripes. These bred and also hybridized with Red-legged Partridge (producing so-called 'ogridges'), some of which may persist.

JUVENILE

ADULT

Grey Partridge

Perdix perdix ● ● **I** 528

28–32 cm | WS 45–48 cm

Increasingly scarce and local resident in UK (170,000 breeding pairs, declining); rare in Ireland

Arable land, meadows, downs

Delicate, beautifully marked, native partridge; small, short-legged bantam-like form. Stretches upwards when alarmed (often just shows head above grass), runs, or flies off low and fast.

Sexes similar; female duller than male. Mid-brown with long black and buff streaks; neck and breast blue-grey; flanks barred rust-brown. **Large orange face patch** (lacks Red-legged Partridge's white face, streaked shawl). Bill, legs horn-brown.

VOICE Male calls during slow, springy, upright walk, a creaky, wheezy "*ke-er-it*" or "*cheevit*", a one-time common countryside sound.

IN FLIGHT, tail spread, **rusty-orange**; barred wings slightly downcurved (straighter on Red-legged Partridge). See Red Grouse (*p. 266*), though grouse are larger, darker, black-tailed, dark-faced; Grey Partridge lacks contrast between back and flight feathers.

ADULT

weak head pattern, grey bill

ADULT ♂

JUVENILE

ADULT ♂

ADULT ♀

dark breast patch biggest on male

Red Grouse

Lagopus lagopus ● **I** 528

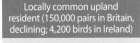

33–38 cm | WS 55–66 cm

Dark, shy, crouching, partridge-like bird: compare with female Black Grouse (*p. 268*). Truly wild and native, not reared and released like introduced Pheasant (*p. 270*). British/Irish race of white-winged European Willow Grouse. Wings dark, **tail black with brown central wedge** of coverts (Grey Partridge (*p. 265*) paler with orange tail and pale brown central wedge).

MALE rich **dark red brown**, fine black and buff barring; **red wattle** over eye (rules out Grey Partridge). **Tail black** (brown on female Black Grouse, orange-red on partridges). FEMALE paler, more yellowish due to copious broader buff bars; small dark eye and bill. Note white-feathered feet.

VOICE Essential moorland sound: loud, abrupt, surprising stutter "*kaa-kaa-kaa – karr-rr-rr-rr-cok cok go-bak go bak bak bak…*"

Locally common upland resident (150,000 pairs in Britain, declining; 4,200 birds in Ireland)

Extensive heather moorland

IN FLIGHT, fast, glides on arched wings, looks very dark except variable **white bars on underwing**.

ADULT ♂

ADULT ♂

can look blackish on moor at long range

ADULT ♀

ADULT ♂

NT Ptarmigan

Lagopus muta race millaisi ‡ see p 525 **528**

see p 525

Scarce and local resident in the Scottish highlands (10,000 breeding pairs, declining)

High, stony peaks and plateaux

31–35 cm | WS 55–65 cm

Small, delicate mountain grouse, rewards hard high climb in most localities but lower down in far north; distinct seasonal colour changes. Has **white wings, black tail** at all times (shared by mainland European race of Red Grouse – Willow Grouse – but unique in Britain).

MALE LATE SUMMER peppered pale grey, **white wings**, belly, feet; small red eye wattle, tiny dark bill. MALE WINTER white except for black tail, patch between eye and bill. In spring patchy change back to grey, often strikingly piebald. FEMALE changes similarly, but summer bird much yellower than male and winter head **all-white**. Slightly bigger Red Grouse has larger bill.

VOICE Varied low, belching, croaking notes, typically "*arr-oo-a-karrrr*".

IN FLIGHT, **white wings** in all plumages.

ADULT ♂ SUMMER

ADULT ♂ WINTER

ADULT ♀ SUMMER

ADULT ♂ SUMMER

ADULT ♀ WINTER

ADULT ♀ MOULTING INTO SUMMER PLUMAGE

ADULT ♂ WINTER

ADULT ♂ MOULTING INTO SUMMER PLUMAGE

Black Grouse
Tetrao tetrix ● 528

Scarce and local resident, mainly in upland areas (10,000 –15,000 (5,000 males)); remnant populations, long-term decline. Absent from Ireland

Moors, plantations, adjacent hill slopes

♂ 49–58 cm | ♀ 40–45 cm | WS 65–80 cm

Big, chicken-like, but 'half size' of Capercaillie; may be obvious on short grass in spring, particularly when males displaying, otherwise elusive.

MALE shiny blue-black with white shoulder spot, **white under tail**. Bluer neck, large red wattle over eye; bill small. In display, long tail raised and fanned, outer feathers **curl outwards**; undertail feathers raised into brilliant white cushion.
FEMALE like small Capercaillie without orange breast; more evenly orange-brown, finer black bars/spots.

VOICE Calls of male far-carrying: rolling, repeated crooning note and 'sneezing' "*tschuwee*".

IN FLIGHT, large, long and flat-backed. MALE prominent **broad white wingbar**; FEMALE tail fractionally **notched** but fanned in flight; not so rufous as Capercaillie, same colour as rump without rufous/grey contrast, not blackish as on Red Grouse (*p. 266*). Shows **weak white wingbar**.

♂ DISPLAYING

ADULT ♂

ADULT ♀

Males display at traditional sites (leks) in spring, with females watching from close by.

ADULT ♂

male may be large and very obvious on open field, or hidden in dense heather/ bracken/plantation or foliage

ADULT ♀

Capercaillie

Scarce and local resident in Scotland (2,000 birds, declining); reintroduced. Extinct Ireland

Pine forests and plantations, adjacent heaths

♂ 74–90 cm | ♀ 54–63 cm | WS 87–125 cm

Huge 'turkey' of forests. Reintroduced historically following UK extinction; elusive and sensitive to disturbance.

MALE dark grey, white shoulder spot, **curved flank streak**. Large, pale, hooked bill. Tail quite long, broad, **rounded**, waxy, blackish with scratchy white marks – held closed and low, or raised in half-circular fan in display. FEMALE big, pale brown, heavily **spotted black**, with clear **orange breast**; compare with Black Grouse. Bill of Capercaillie thicker; tail longer, wider, more rufous against greyer rump.

VOICE Various croaking notes; display song unique series of clicks building into 'popped cork' note.

IN FLIGHT, low, bursting from tree or ground, fast and direct, with quick, deep wingbeats; often just a glimpse of something huge and dark, disappearing.

ADULT ♂

ADULT ♀

ADULT ♂

♂ DISPLAYING

ADULT ♀

FEMALE has blacker barring and more extensive white than Black Grouse.

Males display in ones and twos or, where more common, in groups, at a lek.

Pheasant

Phasianus colchicus 528

♂ 70–90 cm (incl. tail 35–45 cm) | ♀ 55–70 cm (incl. tail 20–25 cm)
WS 70–90 cm

MALE shape and colours unique: big, chicken-like; **long, tapered tail**. Mostly dark red-brown, often richly golden on flank, purple-red on breast, all spotted inky-black. Rump brown, bronze or pale green. Head green-black with bold **red facial wattle**; often broad white collar. Various races intermixed give great variety within basic colour and pattern. FEMALE more obscure, big, long-legged partridge-type, overall pale dusty brown with bold dark spots and 'V'-shapes; **tail long, sharp**, pale brown with dark bars.

VOICE Calls "*kutuk kutuk*" and loud "*kork-kok*" (with thrum of wings).

Abundant and widespread introduced resident (>2 million breed in UK (38 million released annually); 300,000 in Ireland)

Mostly lowlands, close to woods, also heaths, reedbeds

IN FLIGHT, fast and low after initial explosive burst (often scarily from under your feet); long tail obvious (but beware, half-grown young can fly: more pointed tail than on partridges).

ADULT ♀

ADULT ♂

ADULT ♂

newly released birds often in fields, on roadsides, but established populations more secretive; roosts high in trees

ADULT ♀

ADULT ♂
(ring-necked)

Golden Pheasant *Chrysolophus pictus*

♂ 90–105 cm (incl. tail 60–70 cm) | ♀ 60–80 cm (incl. tail 30–35 cm)
WS 65–75 cm

Rare and local introduction
with established breeding
populations in Scotland,
E Anglia; dying out

MALE largely **red and golden-yellow** with long, 'marbled' tawny tail.
FEMALE closely barred black/brown, paler on head and underside
than Lady Amherst's Pheasant.

ADULT ♂

ADULT ♀

Lady Amherst's Pheasant *Chrysolophus amherstiae*

♂ 105–120 cm (incl. tail 75–90 cm) | ♀ 60–80 cm (incl. tail 25–30 cm)
WS 70–85 cm

Rare and local introduction
with established breeding
population in English E
Midlands; virtually died out

MALE largely **black and white** with **yellow rump, long, black-barred
silvery tail**. Female closely barred black/buff, darker than Golden
Pheasant.

ADULT ♂

ADULT ♀

Quail

Coturnix coturnix ● **I** 528

16–18 cm | WS 32–35 cm

An elusive voice: heard much more often than seen.
Small, rounded (stretches to longer shape when singing or
alarmed) partridge-like bird on the ground.

Pale brown with black mottles and **long buff lines** above;
flanks striped (long lines rather than vertical bars).
Head has dark cap with pale central line, dark eyestripe.
MALE also has **black throat markings**.

VOICE Calls (close range) soft "*miaow*" or "*ma-mah*".
Song of male carries far: liquid, rhythmic, low "*quik-wik-ik*"
or "*wit-wi-wit*", usually only clue to bird's presence.

Generally rare (but erratic) and
widespread summer visitor (500
singing males (1,000–2,000) in
'good Quail years'); rare migrant
(Apr–Oct); absent in winter

to
Africa

Downland, cereal fields; migrants
chiefly near coast

IN FLIGHT, long, narrow wings recall crake or
wader, usually a puzzle in brief view or out
of context on migration. May take off with
sudden burst from underfoot, but usually hard
to flush.

ADULT ♂

ADULT ♂

Occasionally seen at edge of open patch in crop or grass.

ADULT ♂

Singing male more upright, still
usually hidden from view.

ADULT ♂

ADULT ♀

PIGEONS, DOVES and SANDGROUSE

PIGEON and DOVE ID   upperwing pattern | upper and under tail pattern | neck pattern

There is no real distinction between a 'pigeon' and a 'dove'. All are short-billed, round-headed, beady-eyed, soft-plumaged birds with broad, tapered wings and wide, round-tipped tails.
7 pigeons and doves: 4 resident, 1 scarce but has abundant feral derivatives; 1 summer visitor; 2 extremely rare vagrants.
1 sandgrouse: extreme vagrant.

Pigeons (*p. 275–276*) are familiar from the ubiquitous street pigeons, descendants of domesticated Rock Doves, especially 'racing pigeons' that have 'gone wild' almost everywhere. True Rock Doves are handsome birds of northern coasts.

The commonest and, in much of the UK, the commonest large bird, is the Woodpigeon: learn it well, to help identify birds of prey and others at a distance, as high-flying pigeons can be mistaken for several other things. Stock Doves are smaller, rounder, bluer, with quicker, deeper wingbeats, without the Woodpigeon's white wing marks, and are usually much less numerous – just keep looking until you see one.

Smaller **doves** (*p. 277–280*) include one that has been in the UK for millennia, the Turtle Dove, in recent decades declining almost to oblivion in most places, and one that arrived naturally only in the 1950s, the Collared Dove. Turtle Doves are rural birds, unlikely in most gardens, whereas Collared Doves are suburban and village birds, and like dockyards, breweries and distilleries, as well as cereal fields and horse paddocks, anywhere where there might be seed and grain.

All have distinctive flight patterns and also special aerial displays. Only the Collared Dove has a 'flight call' but all coo in one way or another, helping identification and location.

Sandgrouse (*p. 274*) Sandgrouse are rounded, short-legged, long-tailed ground birds with short, curved bills. In flight they have long, narrow wings and fly fast with quick wingbeats. They are social birds of semi-arid regions; the one species recorded has occasional 'eruptions' (from Asia) bringing small numbers ('irruptions') into western Europe, but these have become rare and irregular.

Pigeon ageing/sexing

Sexes are alike with no seasonal changes; fresh feathers are purer in colour than faded older ones, which tend to become dull and brownish. Juveniles are distinguishable for a few weeks, being duller, without adult head and neck markings. These develop during the first winter.

WOODPIGEON

ADULT

JUVENILE

TURTLE DOVE

Pigeons and doves in flight

Fast-flying pigeons and doves cross open spaces, often allowing
good views: check size, tail length and pattern, upperwing.
Larger, tighter flocks usually indicate larger
pigeons rather than smaller doves.

STOCK DOVE
(p. 277)

**WOOD-
PIGEON**
(p. 276)

**ROCK DOVE /
FERAL PIGEON**
(p. 275)

**COLLARED
DOVE**
(p. 278)

**TURTLE
DOVE**
(p. 279)

**TURTLE
DOVE**

**COLLARED
DOVE**

RUFOUS TURTLE DOVE

**MOURNING
DOVE**

**PALLAS'S
SANDGROUSE**

ADULT ♂

SANDGROUSE

One species has been recorded, mostly during
'invasions' that now seem to be a thing of the past.

EN **Pallas's Sandgrouse**

Syrrhaptes paradoxus

27–32 cm | WS 60–71 cm

Vagrant from Asia: mostly
historic records (<5 records since
1960), May. Open ground.

ADULT ♀

Pigeon-like, short-legged
ground bird with very **long,
pointed tail**, fast flight. Pale
brown-buff; head orange (like
Grey Partridge (p. 265)); neck
grey; big **black belly patch**.
Upperwing plain but back/
rump strongly barred.

274

Rock Dove / Feral Pigeon

Columba livia **533**

30–35 cm | WS 62–68 cm

Gone-wild descendants of domesticated Rock Doves are the everyday town or Feral Pigeons, but true wild Rock Dove is a handsome pigeon of wilder places in the north.

Wild Rock Dove pale blue-grey, **white rump**, two black bars across wing. **Underwing white**. Breast washed purple, neck glossed green. Compared with domestic/town birds, immaculate; **small** white fleshy patch ('cere') above **slim bill** (big patch, thick bill on many domestics). Domestic birds – racers and tumblers – are released in flocks to 'train' above loft and circle in tight flocks, flickering in sun; racers fly across country in ragged groups; long-necked with slimmer, tapered, swept-back wings in streamlined evolution of basic shape.

Feral Pigeon, common resident in towns (100,000); wild Rock Dove scarce, in north

■ Feral Pigeon
■ Rock Dove

Feral (gone-wild) birds on cliffs very similar but usually include a proportion of darker individuals, more or less dark chequered above, some with patches of white. Town birds, especially, very variable, with rusty/ginger, blue-grey and blackish types, often with black wingbars, but also white flight feathers or other irregularities. However, even the most Rock Dove-like always have a larger cere than is found on wild birds.

Feral Pigeon, towns, quarries, cliffs, adjacent fields, waste ground; Rock Dove near coasts

ADULT
(Feral Pigeon)

fleshy white patch on bill ('cere') small on wild Rock Doves, larger or bulbous on feral/domestic pigeons

large cere

IN FLIGHT **white lower back**, dark tail, white underwing distinctive on wild birds.

ADULT
(Rock Dove)

ADULT
(Feral Pigeon)

ADULT
(Feral Pigeon)

small cere

double dark bar
across hindwing

ADULT
(Rock Dove)

Woodpigeon

Columba palumbus 533

Widespread, abundant resident (2·7 million pairs, plus 2·6 million birds in Ireland), and migrant

Farmland, woodland, parks

38–43 cm | WS 68–77 cm

Most big birds over most of Britain and Ireland will be Woodpigeons. Increasingly bold/tame in towns and gardens.

Big, long-winged, long-tailed, clattering pigeon. Sits upright, motionless, often for hours. Often large flocks, although frequently alone, travelling long distances (often high up). ADULT **white neck patch**, unique **white band across each wing**. **Whitish band** beneath dark tail. Bright neck gloss, pink breast, red and yellow bill. JUVENILE duller, no white neck patches.

VOICE Song loud, rhythmic *"coo, crroo-crroo, cu-coo, cuk crroo-crru, cuk"*. No flight call; various strained cooing, moaning, grunting notes close to nest. Loud wing noise including whistle and clatter in alarm, sudden 'slap'.

IN FLIGHT long, narrow head, long wings taper to blunt point, longish, wide-tipped tail, deep chest. Quick, direct; rises with fast, noisy beats; steady beats over longer distances. Often rises to momentary **'stall'**.

ADULT

very young birds still show wispy down; mottled and unkempt-looking

JUVENILE

adult immaculate; often loses small white feathers in noisy, clattering, aggressive encounters

ADULT

Stock Dove

Columba oenas

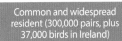

Range of habitats from lowlands to upland moors/cliffs/quarries

28–32 cm | WS 60–66 cm

Neat, blue-grey pigeon; soft, rounded outlines. Often over woodland in fast-moving groups, around old parkland trees, on open fields, sandy heaths; also cliffs on coast and high on hills. Frequently with Woodpigeons, Jackdaws, Rooks.

Like Woodpigeon but bluer grey, emerald on neck, **no striking white**; **two short bars** on innerwing (see Rock Dove (*p. 275*)). Legs bright coral-red; yellow bill tip.

VOICE Song deep, rolling "*oorr-oo*".

STOCK DOVE

ADULT

ADULT

ADULT

WOODPIGEON

IN FLIGHT dull/matt black around **pale grey midwing**; blue-grey rump, black tail-band. Quick, deep beats of arched wings. Compare feral/domestic pigeons: Stock Dove round-headed, broad-winged, tips curved back, slightly rounded; 'racers' longer-necked, sharp-faced, sharper-winged, irregular patterns. Juvenile Woodpigeon has white wing bands, pale tail-band. Display flight has stall and glide like Woodpigeon, but glides/tilts with, innerwing raised, outer half flat (straighter wing on Woodpigeon).

never has juvenile Woodpigeon's white on wing

JUVENILE

ADULT

Collared Dove

29–33 cm | WS 48–53 cm

👁 Mourning Dove (*p.280*)

Neat, elongated, soft-plumaged dove/small pigeon, typically on ground, wires, TV aerials, roofs (not much in trees). Pale beige/sandy-grey. Narrow black collar.

VOICE Diagnostic three-note "*cu-coo-cuk*", middle note strongest, surprisingly varied, with different emphasis, strained or hoarse versions frequent. Flight call nasal, slurred "*kwurrrr*". Wings clatter less than small pigeons but can whistle loudly in short fast flights.

Common resident, following rapid spread in second half of 20th century (285,000 pairs, plus 250,000 birds in Ireland)

Suburbs, gardens, farmland

ADULT

ADULT

IN FLIGHT diffuse grey on upperwing. **Underwing soft pale grey**. Small **black base, wide white tip** to underside of tail. Upperside of tail has diffuse whitish tip – Turtle Dove has white band against black. Strong, fast, direct, less rolling/tilting than Turtle Dove, on bent-back wings; **long tail** catches eye. Display flight steep rise, **long, curving descent**.

upper tail with dark base and broad white tip

lacks collar

JUVENILE

ADULT ♀

slender, pale, delicate dove

sexes very similar, though females tend to be buff-grey and males tend to be pinkish-grey

ADULT ♂

pale plumage overall, except for darker wingtips

Turtle Dove

Streptopelia turtur ● ① 533

25–28 cm | WS 45–50 cm

◉ Rufous Turtle Dove *(p. 280)*

Rufous Turtle Dove (p. 280)

Small dove of woodland edge, thickets, old hedgerows on downs, stubble fields; spring-early autumn only. Compared with Collared Dove, smaller, neater, small-headed, more variegated.

Upperparts **chequered orange-brown**; neck has small streaked patch, no collar. Breast pale pink (**dark against white belly** in flight). JUVENILE paler, duller, greyish, weaker chequering but broad pale feather edges, no neck patch, **more rufous** than Collared Dove.

VOICE Prolonged, purring, soporific *coo*, "*currr-currurrr-curr*".

Increasingly scarce summer migrant (Apr–Sep) (40,000 pairs, continuing dramatic decline)

to W Africa

Bushy downland, hedgerows, fields

ADULT

ADULT

IN FLIGHT, light, agile, **narrow-tipped wings curled back**, tilting or rolling. Wings show small, blue-grey cross-band and dark grey underside Tail grey with dark band, **wide, bright white tip**; underneath more black than Collared Dove, narrower white tip forms striking rim.

upper tail grey with dark band and white tip

slim shape, small head; dull, drab version of adult

often accompanies more distinctive adults

JUVENILE

ADULT

279

Rufous Turtle Dove *Streptopelia orientalis*
30–35 cm | WS 55–60 cm

Like large, heavy Turtle Dove (*p. 279*). Two races: race *orientalis* dark, heavy, pigeon-like; race *meena* paler, smaller than *orientalis* with broader, paler, rufous fringes to wing coverts. Whitish tips to wing coverts create diffuse wingbars.

Vagrant from Asia: <15 Records (Britain), Nov–Feb. Scattered. Gardens/farmland.

Race *orientalis* dark below, undertail greyish. Race *meena* pale belly fades to cream vent/undertail (Turtle Dove has pink breast/ flanks, distinct white belly/ vent/undertail).

RUFOUS TURTLE DOVE
race *orientalis* — rump grey; tip grey-white
race *meena* — rump grey; tip white

TURTLE DOVE
rump brown; tip white

Wingtip (5 tips) equals length of tail projection; distinctly longer, narrower wingtip (6-7 tips) on Turtle Dove

TURTLE DOVE 6–7 tips
short
white
long
5 tips
cream

RUFOUS TURTLE DOVE (race meena)

thin front edge/ring
pinkish brown
JUVENILE *meena* (moulting)
NB adult type feathers

TURTLE DOVE
grey
bare 'diamond' around eye
JUVENILE
grey
3–4 broad black bars on white
ADULT

ADULT
pinkish brown race *orientalis*
from 1st-winter, 5–6 thin black bars on grey patch

Mourning Dove *Zenaida macroura*
28–33 cm | WS 37–45 cm

Small, slim dove with long, tapered tail. Pale olive-brown, pinker on head and chest; few dark spots on wing coverts. JUVENILE black-centred, pale-fringed wing coverts.

Vagrant from N America: <10 records (<5 Ireland), Oct–Jan. Near coasts. Gardens/farmland.

1ST-WINTER

JUVENILE

OWLS and NIGHTJARS

OWL ID   size | head shape | eye colour | wing pattern | voice

NIGHTJAR ID   wingtip pattern | tail pattern | voice

Broadly nocturnal or active at dawn and dusk, but some owls visible by day.
9 owls: 5 resident, 1 historical introduction, 2 also winter visitors; 4 vagrants, 2 extremely rare.
4 nightjars: 1 breeding visitor; 3 extreme vagrants.

Owls (*p. 283*) are birds of prey more or less specialized to life after dark, with thick plumage, large heads and hooked bills largely hidden in deep facial feathers.

TAWNY OWL

Barn and Short-eared (and the exceedingly rare Snowy) Owls hunt by day and Little Owls stand in the open in the daytime, although they feed mostly at dusk. Others, such as the Tawny Owl, are strictly nocturnal and hard to see, unless you find one at roost in a thicket by day. Small birds 'mob' owls, and might help lead you to one.

Short-eared Owls like marshes, moors and rough pasture and can be searched for in the same way as daytime-hunting harriers. Long-eared Owls hunt in such places but roost and nest in trees and are nocturnal. Tawny Owls prefer woodland or heavily-treed parks and gardens: they hoot and call loudly at dusk. Little Owls like old trees in parkland, or tumbledown barns. Barn Owls, farmland or grassland specialists, need several large cavities in trees or buildings for nesting and resting and hunt small rodents in long grass. On a fine afternoon in cold weather, or in the evening in mid-summer when nights are short, they hunt over open fields, marshes and grassy verges.

Owl ageing/sexing

Sexes alike (except in Snowy Owl), with no seasonal variation. Juveniles subtly different, some (such as Barn Owl) may be aged over the next 1-3 years by changing patterns during prolonged moult, but difficult, requiring experience and close examination.

Nightjar (*p. 290*) is a dusk and dawn bird, from late spring to late summer, on heaths, in woodland clearings or near plantations, or on higher bracken-covered slopes. It catches moths in flight, using its long wings and tail to give a uniquely acrobatic, buoyant flight, sometimes spinning around people to give them a close look. The song is the best way to find one: a remarkable wooden churr that can go on for a few minutes. There are two exceptionally rare nightjars and one related 'nighthawk', a vagrant from North America.

Eagle-owl escapes

The huge (larger than a buzzard) Eurasian Eagle-owl *Bubo bubo* is an escape (about 10 per year) and perhaps an illegal introduction, and a few pairs are now breeding. The impact of these birds is being monitored; the species is currently in Category E*, and not on the British or Irish lists.

NIGHTJAR

Owls in flight

With the exception of Short-eared Owl and Barn Owl, views are likely to be brief: concentrate on size, shape (especially length of wing) and the pattern of the hindwing and wingtip.

SHORT-EARED OWL (p. 286)

LONG-EARED OWL (p. 287)

LITTLE OWL (p. 285)

solid

barred

TAWNY OWL (p. 284)

BARN OWL (p. 283)

IMMATURE

SNOWY OWL (p. 288)

Nightjars in flight

Nightjars become active (and males begin to sing) soon after sunset, in good but rapidly fading light, so the potential for good views is small. Nighthawks also fly in daylight.

NB not to same scale as owls

NIGHTJAR (p. 290)

COMMON NIGHTHAWK (p. 291)

RED-NECKED NIGHTJAR (p. 291)

EGYPTIAN NIGHTJAR (p. 291)

Barn Owl

Tyto alba **I** `534`

33–39 cm | WS 80–95 cm

The 'white owl' of farmed countryside, marshes and plantation edges. Narrow body, 'knock-kneed' stance, broad head. Big head, **heart-shaped face** (rounder when relaxed); black eyes, narrow 'V' over bill. Pale **sandy-golden buff** above, dark bars on wings (strongest on FEMALE). 'Pepper and salt' speckling evident close up. **White beneath**, including underwing. IN FLIGHT, head very large, wings sometimes look a little short, broad-based; narrow, with rounded tip. Wingbeats slightly jerky, **hovers briefly before headlong dive** into grass.

VOICE Shrill, bubbly shriek; various hissing, squealing notes.

Dark-breasted races, rare Britain/Ireland (*e.g. guttata* of N, NE and E Europe), orange-buff with dark flecking including underwing coverts and under tail; greyer above; larger dark patch around eye; many difficult intergrades confuse status.

Scarce but widespread resident (4,000 pairs); dark-breasted N European form rare vagrant (probably annual, Autumn–Spring)

Grassland, farmland, marshes

ADULT

ADULT dark-breasted form

colour varies: many paler, yellower, less grey than this individual

ADULT

Dark-breasted birds must be carefully observed, to rule out local Barn Owls with more than normal grey colouring. Check the dark areas around the eyes as well as darker underparts.

Owls in flight *p. 282*

Tawny Owl

Strix aluco ●

37–43 cm | WS 81–96 cm

Most common large owl in Britain but nocturnal, hard to see; voice and silhouette distinctive. Appears pale in car headlights (see Barn Owl (*p. 283*)). Presence can be indicated by small birds noisily mobbing in tree/ivy, or by white droppings under roost (disgorged grey pellets randomly scattered, less helpful).

Woodpigeon-sized (*p. 276*); big, **round head**, short tail. 'Rugby-ball' shape when relaxed. **Rufous** or **grey-brown**, with row of **white spots diagonally along 'shoulder'**, complex cross-barred streaks beneath. **Rounded facial disk, eyes black**. **VOICE** Loud, emphatic "*ke-wick!*", "*wik-wik-wik*" and variations. Pure or breathy hoot – "*hooo! hu – hu- huwoooo-oo*". Occasionally sings during day. Young call – a hissy "*he-wik*" and "*shee-eep*" (see Long-eared Owl (*p. 287*)).

Fairly common resident (19,000 breeding pairs); extreme vagrant Ireland (1 record)

Woodland, parks, large gardens

IN FLIGHT, big head, broad wingtips, quick beats.

ADULT (rufous)

ADULT (grey)

Tawny Owls are mostly rufous in Britain; in the north, and especially farther east in continental Europe, greyer birds are more frequent.

JUVENILE

Watching Tawny Owls at the nest can be dangerous: attacking adults are silent even at very close range.

ADULT (rufous)

Little Owl

Athene noctua

23–27·5 cm | WS 50–57 cm

 Rare owls (*p. 288–289*)

Rare owls (*p. 288–289*)

Small, thickset, big-headed, short-legged owl. Dove- or thrush-sized body, short wings and tail, broad head, low, rounded crown (**pale 'eyebrows' over large yellow eyes** give flatter look). Stands upright, seemingly tiny legs beneath barrel-shaped body, on branch, stump or rock.

Dark brown, paler in front; **white mottling** above, dark streaks beneath. White over eye conspicuous; **eyes yellow**, set in black rings, facial disk weak. Often alert and perched in the open in daytime, but hunts mostly at dusk.

VOICE Loud, clear, nasal whistles – "*kleee-ow*", "*chi-chi-chi*". Song evenly repeated, rising "*keeeah*".

Scarce resident (7,000 pairs), introduced in 19th century

Old trees, parkland, farmland, quarries, rocky islands

On the ground, stands upright on short, pale legs, sometimes running after prey.

ADULT

IN FLIGHT quick, **swooping/ bounding** woodpecker-like before **upward sweep to perch**.

white brows and piercing gaze

ADULT

JUVENILE

285

Short-eared Owl

Asio flammeus 534

33–40 cm | WS 95–105 cm

Breeds on open moors, not in trees. Winter roosts on ground or in low scrub (Long-eared Owl in trees/bushes). Often **flies by day**. Yellowish, some very pale, others dark, more rufous, but whiter belly than Long-eared Owl. Facial disk rounded; broad whitish fan around bill; eyes **pale yellow**, broadly surrounded by black, more striking than Long-eared Owl's. More marbled than streaked above: blobs of buff rather than row of white spots. Closed wing has pale golden-yellow patch.

VOICE Emphatic, tuneless, wheezy "*eeyah!*"; song in flight, deep, booming "*bu-bu-bu-bu*" combined with sharp wing-clap.

Scarce summer (2,300 pairs) and winter visitor (variable numbers, nomadic)

Moors, rough meadows, grassland

Asio owls in flight

Both Long-eared and Short-eared Owls have a similar wing pattern: upperwing (see *p. 282*) has **dark 'wrist' and wingtips separated by contrasting golden-buff patch**; underwing is white with a small black mark and dark wing-tips. They can be differentiated, even at distance, as follows:

Short-eared Owl	WINGTIPS: **black, solid**	
	TRAILING EDGE: **white line**	
	TAIL: **broad bars**	
	BELLY: **pale**	
Long-eared Owl	WINGTIPS: **barred**	
	TRAILING EDGE: **barred grey**	
	TAIL: **narrow bars**	
	BELLY: **streaked**	

IN FLIGHT, **low over open ground**, wavering, harrier-like action, frequent glides.

solid black wingtips

pale belly

no obvious 'ears'

yellow eyes surrounded by black

diffuse feathering around bill

heavy blotches

The 'ear' tufts are rarely obvious, usually only seen when a bird is alarmed, and never as long as those of Long-eared Owl.

ADULT

golden-yellow wing patch

Long-eared Owl

Asio otus **534**

31–37 cm | WS 86–98 cm

Round-headed, upright bird of dense foliage. Winter visitors/migrants appear in thickets, hedgerows near open areas. Nocturnal feeder. Droppings and pellets locate daytime roost.

Oval when relaxed, head round. More olive/yellow than Tawny Owl (*p. 284*). Wide facial disk, white feathering around bill **forms a 'V' above**. **'Ear' tufts long**, wide, often laid flat. **Eyes deep orange**, surrounded by black. Upright when alert; narrows face. Pale shoulder spots; complex streaks and bars beneath. Orange-buff patch towards wingtip.

VOICE Short, moaning, cooing hoot, "*oh*" or "*ooh*". Young bird calls loud, 'squeaky-gate', plaintive "*pee-ee*" or "*pyeee*", louder, sharper, less hissy than young Tawny Owl, most useful call.

Scarce resident (3,600 pairs) and winter visitor

Conifer belts, forests, willow thickets

barred wingtips

IN FLIGHT, slow, wavering action similar to Short-eared Owl but wings marginally broader.

Beware – ear tufts usually not apparent in flight.

See table opposite for plumage comparison with Short-eared Owl.

streaked belly

obvious 'ears'

white 'V' between orange eyes

ADULT

fine freckling

orange-buff wing patch

When alert or alarmed, stretches tall, slender and upright, ears raised and face pattern tightened into a narrower shape.

Snowy Owl
Bubo scandiacus
53–65 cm | WS 125–150 cm

Huge, rounded 'snowman', quite unlike Barn Owl (*p. 283*). Size of Buzzard (*p. 302*), heavier body, big, round head. **Perches upright on ground**. MALE **white**; few marks or none at all. Tiny dark bill tip, **yellow eyes look dark from distance**. FEMALE **grey-black bars** on white above, narrower grey beneath; yellow eyes deceptively dark. IMMATURE more barred, face white.

Vagrant from N Europe: >500 records (<100 records Ireland), mostly N/W Isles, Cairngorms; has bred.

534

IN FLIGHT wingbeats steady, rhythmic with slowish downbeat, quicker upbeat.

ADULT ♂

ADULT ♀

ADULT ♀

ADULT ♂

Rare owls

Only the massive Snowy Owl is at all likely to give good views under normal circumstances: rare smaller owls may be found exhausted or in entirely unsuitable surroundings, such as on remote islands.

Hawk Owl | 534

Surnia ulula

35–43 cm | WS 70–80 cm

Diurnal. Upright, large-headed, **long-tailed** owl. Dark grey-brown with white mottling, white 'V' beside crown, black frame to white face, **yellow eyes**.

> Both European race *ulula* and N American race *caparoch* (on board ship, Cornwall, Mar 1830) have been recorded.

Vagrant from N Europe, N America: <5 records (Britain), most historical, Mar, Sep, Nov, Dec. Woodland/heath.

Tengmalm's Owl | 534

Aegolius funereus

22–27 cm | WS 50–60 cm

Small nocturnal forest owl; upright, big, round head with **high-browed**, 'surprised' expression, bright **yellow eyes**, dark-edged pale facial disk; compare face with Little Owl (*p. 285*).

Vagrant from N+E Europe: <50 records (Britain), most old, summer. Scattered. Woodland.

Scops Owl *Otus scops*

20 cm | WS 47–54 cm

Small, nocturnal, upright, 'eared' owl. Grey-brown or more rufous; row of white spots beside back; bright yellow eyes.

VOICE Call after dusk bright, liquid, ringing "*peoop*" or "*pyup*", repeated every 2–3 seconds.

Vagrant from S Europe: <100 records (<20 Ireland), most old, summer. Scattered. Woodland/gardens.

ADULT

IN FLIGHT, wings and tail closely barred, tail longer than Little Owl's (*p. 285*).

ADULT

ADULT

ear tufts flatten into 'corners' beside crown or raised in points (unlike round-headed Little Owl (*p. 285*)

ADULT (rufous)

ADULT (grey)

24–28 cm | WS 52–59 cm

 Rare nightjars

Dead-branch pattern
marvellous camouflage. Active at dusk.

Usually silhouette at dusk in flight or perched on branch or
log, near-horizontal; **flat, tapered head**, slim body, **long wings
and tail**.

IN FLIGHT **long, tapered wings, tail almost as long**, narrow or
widely spread, twisted; light, floating swoops and glides.
Dives, spins, may approach people. MALE has **white spots on
wingtip** and tail corners (eye-catching in half-decent light)
other detail hard to make out. FEMALE lacks white spots.

VOICE Diagnostic: abrupt, nasal, mechanical "*gooik!*" (beware
Tawny Owl "*ke-wick*"). Song vibrating **churr** for minutes on end
– wooden, hollow, tapping on one note, periodically changing
pitch. 'Runs down' before whiplash clap of wings. (Grasshopper
Warbler (*p. 412*) has prolonged trill, high, metallic, ticking.)

Scarce and local summer migrant
(4,600 pairs, Apr–Sep)

to
Africa

Open heaths, woodland clearings

ADULT ♂

ADULT ♀

ADULT

Rare nightjars

Good views of nightjars in daylight are unusual: seeing a rare one well will be exceptional. Egyptian Nightjar is distinctive, but a silent Red-necked Nightjar will require good fortune. A Common Nighthawk might be active in daylight.

Common Nighthawk

Chordeiles minor

23–25 cm | WS 54–60 cm

Like small, dark Nightjar, whitish marbling on wing, streak of white beside throat. IN FLIGHT (sometimes by day), glides on **wings raised in 'V'. Shallow fork** in tail, blackish shoulder and hindwing outline pale panel, white trailing edge and **white bar across blacker outer half.** MALE white band on tail.

Red-necked Nightjar

Caprimulgus ruficollis

30–34 cm | WS 60–65 cm

Dark nightjar, sharing shape/actions with Nightjar, but rows of pale spots across paler wing coverts (one large row between blacker forewing and plainer hindwing on Nightjar).

Egyptian Nightjar

Caprimulgus aegyptius

24–27 cm | WS 53–58 cm

Pale nightjar; similar shape/actions to Nightjar but paler, buffier, underwing pale with dark tips, white spots absent/insignificant.

pale panel in dark wing

shallow fork in tail

ADULT

pale-tipped primaries on immatures

1ST-WINTER

Vagrant from N America: <25 records (<5 Ireland), Oct. Scattered. Over open ground/urban areas.

ADULT

Vagrant from Iberia: 1 historical record (Britain): 1st-winter, Oct 1856. Open ground.

ADULT

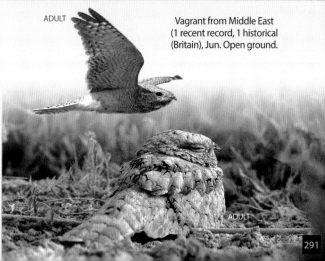

ADULT

Vagrant from Middle East (1 recent record, 1 historical (Britain), Jun. Open ground.

ADULT

BIRDS OF PREY (Raptors)

BIRD OF PREY GROUP ID size | wing shape | tail shape |
underwing pattern | flight action/profile

30 species: 15 breed (4 summer visitors, 2 reintroduced as
breeders, 1 range expanded by introductions), 2 rare migrants;
13 vagrants (3 historic, including 2 vultures); various possible
escapes.

A varied group; falcons not closely related to others but included
here for ease of comparison. Many spend hours perched, mostly
seen more easily when they fly. Size, shapes, attitudes of wings
and tail, and pattern are important. Big soaring birds are not all
birds of prey – Ravens, Rooks, Cormorants, Grey Herons and gulls
are all possible while looking for birds of prey.

Find them by understanding behaviour, range, habitats.
For some, sit well back from a wood, looking for birds flying up
from the trees. Assess likely possibilities.

Raptor ageing/sexing

In most birds of prey, females
are clearly larger than males.
Plumages are often similar,
but Kestrel, Merlin, hawks and
especially harriers show marked
sexual differences. Juveniles
tend to look more like females
but in many species are easily
recognised. One-year-old
(1st-summer) birds can often
be aged, and prolonged moults
on larger species (more or less
continuous in eagles) produce
an obvious patchwork of new,
dark feathers amongst old,
paler ones.

SPARROWHAWK

Harris's Hawk Escape, has bred
*Parabuteo
unicinctus*

tail tip,
undertail,
and rump
white; thighs
and shoulders
chestnut-red

Escaped birds of prey

Some hawks and falcons used by
falconers or for control of pests
may be seen flying free (with
straps on the legs) or escape and
live wild for a short time.
See *pp. 322* and *523* for birds
of prey that are classified as
escapes or of unknown origin).

10 falcons plus 2 'escapes' (*pp. 316–325*): include widespread Kestrel, most likely bird to be seen hovering as
if on a string (Buzzards do so, too). Hobbies feed in the air near water or heaths, with tight manoeuvres and
changes of pace; Peregrine increasingly familiar in urban situations, but a bird of prey capturing a dove on the
lawn is most likely a Sparrowhawk, not a Peregrine (gleaming yellow eye confirms it).

5 eagles in unrelated groups: (*pp. 294–296, 311–312*):
best sought by searching high, distant ridges and
peaks (Golden) or coastal cliffs (White-tailed) in
Scotland: keep looking, but do not expect a close view.

2 hawks (*pp. 313–315*): are woodland/woodland
edge birds that also hunt in open areas
(Sparrowhawk visits gardens). Look for them
displaying over woods in spring.

Osprey (*pp. 299–300*) associated with water, local
breeders but widespread spring and autumn.

2 kites: (*pp. 297, 304, 310*): Red Kite now common and
obvious in many areas following reintroductions.

5 harriers: (*pp. 305–310*): Identification helped by
time of year and location: Hen Harriers on high
moors in summer, lowlands in winter; Montagu's
Harriers only spring–summer in lowlands; Marsh
Harriers most likely over reedbeds, all year in E
England, mostly winter elsewhere.

2 buzzards (*pp. 298, 301–303*): might be seen almost
anywhere on roadside poles and high perches,
year-round;
Honey-buzzard (*pp. 301*): much more elusive and
only spring–autumn.

Birds of prey groups: flight silhouettes

KITE
(pp. 304, 310)

RED KITE

EAGLE
(pp. 294–295)

WHITE-TAILED
EAGLE

OSPREY
(p. 300)

OSPREY

HAWK
(pp. 314–315)

SPARROWHAWK

FALCON
(pp. 316–325)

HOBBY

HARRIER
(pp. 305–310)

MONTAGU'S HARRIER

BUZZARD
(pp. 302–303)

BUZZARD

HONEY-BUZZARD
(p. 301)

HONEY-BUZZARD

RAVEN

CORVIDS *(pp. 464–473)*
(for comparison)

CARRION CROW

Eagles in flight *p. 296*

White-tailed Eagle

Haliaeetus albicilla ●●❙ 530

76–92 cm | WS 200–244 cm

◉ Bald Eagle (*p. 312*)

Massive, heavy eagle, lacks
poise of Golden Eagle but vastly impressive.

ADULT pale brown, whiter on head; huge **yellow bill**; massive
feathered thighs, bare yellow legs. **Tail white**, dull with
wear/staining. IMMATURE browner, streaked black; breast buff with
black lines and 'V's. Tail dark, paler streaks revealed if spread.
IN FLIGHT, very big; **long head**, very **short tail**, long, wide,
'barn door' wings **flat** in glide (not in 'V') or drooped, long
flexible 'fingers' upswept. Deep, powerful beats in longer series
between glides than Golden. Can soar to great height.

VOICE Powerful "*kik-rik-rik*" and "*kee-kee-kee*".

Rare resident, reintroduced
after extirpation (60 pairs: NW
Scotland, Ireland); rare migrant

Coastal cliffs, islands; big lakes

JUVENILE

ADULT

rich brown,
dark eye
and bill

IMMATURE
(2–4 years old)
neat, dark, new feathers; dull
older ones; bleached, worn
older feathers. Pale eye; bill
loses dark tip by 4th-winter

dark head, streaked underside,
unlike Golden Eagle

JUVENILE/1ST-YEAR

upright stance

ADULT

294

Golden Eagle

Aquila chrysaetos ❶ 530

80–93 cm | WS 190–227 cm

◉ Spotted Eagle (*p. 311*)

Spotted Eagle (*p. 311*)

Rare resident (440 pairs: Scotland; reintroduced Ireland); very rare wanderer N England

Big, majestic eagle; see Buzzard (*p. 302*) and White-tailed Eagle. In Scotland, usually long-range bird of peaks/old forest: scan distant skylines!

Huge. Heavily feathered legs, massive yellow feet. ADULT rich brown; **nape paler**, yellowish/orange. IN FLIGHT, blotchy buff band across innerwing. JUVENILE blacker, **white tail with black band**. IN FLIGHT, **white midwing band** (below), small patch above. White reduced with age; immatures retain pale base to tail and primaries. Glides on **raised wings** (like huge, steady Buzzard), circles to great height. Wings relatively longer than Buzzard; tail squarer; longer head. Active flight heavier than Buzzard, deeper beats, short glides. Deep switchback display, wings curved back to blunt 'teardrop'.

VOICE Various short yelps.

Mountains, moors, forests, coastal cliffs

wings, tail and head all proportionately longer than Buzzard; trailing edge more bulging

ADULT

JUVENILE

ADULT has several generations of feathers: dark when new, fading paler

ADULT

IMMATURE

Eagles in flight

Most eagles are large or very large and broad-winged. In Britain and Ireland the choice is usually between the longer-tailed Golden Eagle, which glides on raised wings, and the shorter-tailed, bulky-headed White-tailed Eagle, characteristically flat-winged (like a 'flying door'). Check flight shapes and proportions, underwing and tail patterns.

IMMATURE

IMMATURE

3–4 year-olds have dark forewing, paler flight feathers below

GOLDEN EAGLE
(*p. 295*)

3–4-YEAR OLD

ADULT

IMMATURE

IMMATURE

2-YEAR OLD

WHITE-TAILED EAGLE
(*p. 294*)

ADULT

Kites in flight

Kites must be separated from buzzards, Honey-buzzard and harriers. Slow, relaxed wingbeats and a broad, pale diagonal band on top of the innerwing are good clues. Kites' tails are frequently twisted and have sharp corners: when closed they look forked, when spread, more triangular with a straighter rear edge. They never look rounded. Check tail colour and underwing pattern to separate the widespread Red Kite from the rare Black Kite. Harriers are broadly similar but glide on raised wings, have square/rounded tails and lack large pale patches under the outerwing.

IMMATURE

ADULT

RED KITE
(p. 304)

ADULT

IMMATURE

ADULT

IMMATURE

BLACK KITE
(p. 310)

**CARRION
CROW**

ADULT

IMMATURE

ADULT ♂

ADULT ♀

BUZZARD
(p. 302)

MARSH HARRIER
(p. 305)

Buzzards in flight

Buzzards and similar but unrelated Honey-buzzard can be difficult to tell apart, but usually easy to tell from the slimmer-winged and longer-tailed harriers, kites and bigger eagles (Buzzards can look remarkably eagle-like at times, but size, habitat and location all help, and the Buzzard's patterned underwing usually leaves no doubt). To separate these large, broad-winged, soaring birds, check shape (including the 'set' of the wings, whether in a 'V', flat or drooped) and flight action, tail pattern and underside coloration.

HEAD/TAIL ON **SOARING** PROFILES

BUZZARDS – wings raised

HONEY-BUZZARD – wings level

HEAD/TAIL ON **GLIDE** PROFILES

ROUGH-LEGGED BUZZARD – wings often clearly raised

BUZZARD – wings level or slightly raised

HONEY-BUZZARD – wings down

two dark bands at base, dark tip

ADULT ♂

JUVENILE (dark form)

HONEY-BUZZARD
(p. 301)

broad dark trailing edge

PALE FORM

A variable bird: distinct wing and tail patterns help on typical birds but others look like Buzzard, structure and flight action help more than plumage

two bands at base, dark tip

ADULT ♂

widely spaced tail-bands

ADULT ♀

dark hindwing

widely-spaced tail-bands

JUVENILE

DARK FORM

typical tail

heavy barring on forewing

ADULT ♂

hindwing band diffuse

coverts unbarred

ADULT ♀

hindwing dark

JUVENILE

uniform forewing

few heavy, dark bars across primaries

uniform mid-brown above

greyer; white on tail

ADULT ♀

JUVENILE

white on outerwing;

white tail-band

ROUGH-LEGGED BUZZARD (*p. 303*)

black patches on wing and belly

JUVENILE

BUZZARD (*p. 302*)

ADULT

TYPICAL TYPE dark forewing, pale primaries

fine bars; no tail-band

JUVENILE

ADULT ♀

very pale

black wing patches

ADULT ♂

dark tail-band

black belly patches

IMMATURE

CARRION CROW

JUVENILE

PALE TYPE some extremely pale overall

OSPREY (*p. 300*)

white body

midwing band

299

Osprey

Pandion haliaetus ⬤ `530`

52–60 cm | WS 150–180 cm

◉ Short-toed Eagle (*p. 311*)

Buzzards in flight *p. 298*

Very large, long-winged:
between large eagles and buzzards in size; shape resembles broad- and blunt-winged gull; wingtips upcurved.

Perches upright, tail short. ADULT dark above, **white below** ('front'), dusky breast-band. Head white; **blackish band behind eye**. JUVENILE has bright buff, 'scaly' feather edges all over upperparts. IN FLIGHT, upperwing dark, short tail broadly barred; **white crown** conspicuous. Underwing white at front, central dark band, **black wrist patch**. Flight strong, steady, like Great Black-backed Gull (*p. 128*), relaxed wingbeats and glides on slightly bowed or angled wings. **Hovers** well, body more angled than hovering Buzzard (*p. 302*), wingbeats more forward/back than up/down. **Swoops and dives onto water to catch fish**, resting on surface before flying off.

VOICE High, whistling, "*weilp weilp weilp*" or "*kew kew kew*".

Rare summer visitor (210 pairs: Scotland, locally Wales; introduced C England); rare, widespread migrant (Mar–Oct)

to W Africa

Lakes, rivers, estuaries, adjacent forested areas

tail may look semi-translucent

ADULT

ADULT

JUVENILE

Juveniles look like adults at a distance: their pale feather edges show in a close view.

uniform brown above

ADULT

pale feather edges on immature birds

pale patch on elbow

1ST-SUMMER

Honey-buzzard

Pernis apivorus ● 530

52–59 cm | WS 135–150 cm

Not a true buzzard but very similar.

Much like Buzzard (*p. 302*); very variable (see *p. 299*).
ADULT MALE grey head, greyer back; whiter below; FEMALE browner overall. JUVENILE whiter, with dark mask; more rufous; or very dark. IN FLIGHT (ABOVE), **blackish trailing edge to wing**, broadest on male; tail has **dark tip, two/three bands at base**, **weaker on female**. Pale on top of primaries on female. IN FLIGHT (BENEATH), dark trailing edge, dark bands on rear of wing; **tail as above, or single band at base on male**. Lacks Buzzard's pale breast-band. **Eyes yellow.** juvenile tail may have more weak bars; darker hindwing, heavier barring across inner primaries than Buzzard; dark eye. Shape like juvenile Buzzard; longer, narrow head; longer tail; forewing often angled, hindwing straight. Wingtip hooks back, or broadly rounded. Glides on smoothly drooped wings; soars on flat or slightly raised wings. Display unique: male fluttering wings over back between upward swoops.

VOICE Melodious "*whee-ooo*" or "*whi-whee-oo*".

Rare summer visitor (40 pairs, May–Oct); scarce autumn migrant (100–400)

to Africa

Extensive forests, wooded farmland, parks; coasts in autumn

SOARING

GLIDING

wings held downwards when seen gliding head on/flying away; flat when soaring

ADULT ♂

ADULT ♂

JUVENILE

dark bands on wings and tail –weaker on ♀

widely spaced tail-bands on ♀; single band near base on ♂

compare slim head with chunkier Buzzard; dark hindwing; plain forewing; bars across primaries

yellow eye

ADULT ♂

most whiter beneath than ♀

ADULT ♀

JUVENILE

Buzzard

Buteo buteo 530

48–56 cm | WS 113–128 cm

○ Harris's Hawk (*p. 292*)

Common resident in UK (40,500 pairs); scarce Ireland (200 pairs)

Big, broad-winged, soaring bird; perches on posts, branches, telegraph poles, sits in fields. Close views frequent, unlikely for Golden Eagle (*p. 295*).

Typically mottled **brown**, ADULT **pale 'U' below breast**, barred belly. Creamy-white to very dark. IN FLIGHT, **strongly patterned, whitish beyond dark 'wrist'**. ADULT sharp dark hindwing band and tail tip, JUVENILE streaked belly, uniformly barred tail, ill-defined hindwing band. Quite quick, stiff wingbeats. Soars with **wings usually in 'V'** (juvenile flatter). Straight glides, wings hunched in slight kink; hovers well. Displays in steep switchbacks, dives. Soaring Marsh Harrier (*p. 305*) has longer tail, plainer wing. Honey-buzzard (*p. 301*) flatter wings, smoothly bowed in glide, slower beats.

VOICE Loud, sharp "*pi-yaaa*", explosive close-up. Late summer, wails from juveniles (perched or up high).

Woodland, wooded valleys, heaths, moors, crags, farmland

hovers well

SOARING

GLIDING

wings held level/kinked upwards when seen gliding head on/flying away; raised when soaring

ADULT

ADULT   IMMATURE   JUVENILE (pale)

ADULT

dark trailing edge and tail-band

diffuse trailing edge and tail-band

narrower wings, looks longer-tailed

ADULT

2ND-YEAR has many juvenile feathers, become bleached and faded.

IMMATURE

pale individuals fairly frequent

pale tips to greater coverts form pale bar

JUVENILE (pale)

Rough-legged Buzzard

Buteo lagopus

49–59 cm | WS 120–150 cm

Rare migrant, winter visitor (50 per year, periodically more (185), Oct–Mar; mostly N and E)

Much like Buzzard, breeds Scandinavia; rare Britain/Ireland. Big buzzard, often on bare tree or hovering over open ground.

Typically pale on head and breast. **Blackish belly**, pale thighs; feathered lower leg hard to see. IN FLIGHT, upperside shows **pale band across primaries**, paler innerwing band (kite-like), **broad white tail base** (MALE 3–4 bars at tip; FEMALE narrow, blacker band plus 1–2 fine bars; JUVENILE broad dark band). Beneath, **black wrist patches**, white towards wingtip, black belly, white tail with band. Soars like Buzzard; glides on more 'bent' wings; active flight more 'elastic'. Hovers more than most Buzzards, like giant Kestrel (*p. 316*).

VOICE Silent in winter.

from Scandinavia

Regular race is *lagopus*; N American race *sanctijohannis* (one record (Ireland), Oct) others suspected in N and W Britain; identification requires measurements.

Coastal, open areas, moors, farmland

wings often clearly raised when seen head on/flying away

ADULT ♂

ADULT ♀

dark carpal ('wrist') patches

JUVENILE

dark belly

hovers persistently

dark tail-band broad

JUVENILE

dark tail-band 3–4 bars

dark tail-band 1–2 bars

pale band across primaries

Beware white-tailed Buzzard – usually more bars on tip and sides of tail.

ADULT ♂

JUVENILE

303

NT Red Kite

NT

Milvus milvus 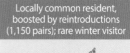 ① 530

61–72 cm | WS 175–195 cm

Black Kite (*p. 310*)

Locally common resident, boosted by reintroductions (1,150 pairs); rare winter visitor

Big, fork-tailed bird of prey, long wings more supple than Buzzard.

ADULT gingery- or **reddish-brown**, dark streaks; paler feather edgings over wings. Head pale; yellow eye. JUVENILE slightly paler beneath, narrower pale feather edges above. IN FLIGHT, **diagonal pale band** across innerwing above; wide, **forked**, dark-tipped, **rusty-red** tail. Underneath, rufous body and forewing contrast with dark midwing panel, big **white patch before black wingtips**. Tail pale beneath, dark corners. Flight supremely elegant, deep flexible beats; soars on **flat/bowed wings** (not Buzzard's 'V' (*p. 302*)) sometimes to great height. Active flight with wide, curved wings well forward, long, notched/forked tail, twisted sideways.

VOICE Wailing, screaming versions of Buzzard-like notes.

Wooded countryside, villages, forests

ADULT

long, flat profile, wings pushed forward, recognisable at long range

shallow tail fork

pale colour

JUVENILE

white tips to coverts create white line on midwing

often forages on the ground in open fields

ADULT

JUVENILE

Marsh Harrier

Circus aeruginosus **530**

43–55 cm | WS 120–135 cm

👁 Black Kite (*p. 310*)

Rare resident (425 pairs, most E England); scarce migrant, winter visitor

Biggest harrier, somewhat buzzard- or kite-like when soaring, otherwise obvious.

Heavier, broader-winged than other harriers (*pp. 306–310*), but typical harrier flight: **low, direct or wavering**, with steady, elastic beats between **glides on raised wings**. MALE strongly patterned, brown with pale head, pale **grey wing, large black tip**; brown back, **grey tail**; underside rusty-buff. FEMALE/JUVENILE strikingly dark. FEMALE **cream cap and throat**, cream patch on forewing, pale streaks on dark breast. JUVENILE blackish-brown, pale crown and throat; dark, plain tail; dark underwing against paler flight feathers. IN FLIGHT, soars high up on raised wings; striking spring display flight, and typical harrier rolling foot-to-foot 'food pass' between male and female. Size, broad wings help rule out other harriers; straighter wings, rounded tail, lack of pale diagonal on upperwing exclude Black Kite (*p. 310*).

VOICE Silent except high chatter over nest in spring.

Marshes, coastal wetlands

spring display flights include acrobatic tumbling between steep undulations

typically seen flying low over marsh: supple flaps between glides on raised wings

ADULT ♂

ADULT ♂

ADULT ♀

MALE may breed in patchy immature plumage

note row of new blackish coverts, rear scapulars and primary feather, against pale older ones – black will fade to brown.

ADULT ♀

ADULT ♂

Harriers in flight

ADULT MALES

PALLID HARRIER
(p. 309)

MONTAGU'S HARRIER
(p. 308)

HEN HARRIER
(p. 307)

MARSH HARRIER
(p. 305)

ADULT FEMALES

PALLID HARRIER

MONTAGU'S HARRIER

HEN HARRIER

MARSH HARRIER

Juvenile harriers with white rumps

All brighter orange-buff below than adult females, upperside feathers edged more rufous.

pale ochre, unstreaked

5-'fingered' wingtip

3–4-'fingered' wingtip

broad wings

dark trailing edge

plain

heavily streaked

unstreaked

MONTAGU'S HARRIER

PALLID HARRIER

HEN HARRIER

NORTHERN HARRIER
(p. 310)

NT Hen Harrier

Circus cyaneus ● ① 530

45–55 cm | WS 99–121 cm

Large, slender bird of prey.

◉ Northern Harrier (*p. 310*), Pallid Harrier (*p. 309*)

Rare resident (780 pairs, including 150 in Ireland); scarce but more widespread winter visitor

IN FLIGHT, **glides with raised wings** between easy, deep wingbeats indicate harrier. Broader wingtip than Montagu's Harrier, slimmer than Marsh Harrier (*p. 305*). MALE eye-catching **light grey, black wingtips**. Whiter belly; white rump; **dark trailing edge to wing**. IMMATURE MALE browner back. FEMALE streaky brown, **white rump**. Pale below, brown streaks. **Tail strongly banded**. Dark cheeks, white around dark eye patch. JUVENILE streaked black on rusty-buff below.

VOICE Calls on breeding area, chattering "*chet-et-et-et-it-it-et*".

from NE and W Europe

Heather moorland, open grassland, marshes

ADULT ♀

JUVENILE

JUVENILE

ADULT ♂

spring display flights include acrobatic tumbling between steep undulations

IMMATURE MALES **often dull, browner-backed** than 'clean and bright' adult

Note on this individual, row of new blackish coverts, rear scapulars and primary feather, against pale older ones – black will fade to brown.

ADULT ♀

ADULT ♂

Montagu's Harrier

Circus pygargus ⬤ 530

39–50 cm | WS 97–115 cm

👁 Pallid Harrier *(p. 309)*

Rare and very local summer visitor (5–10 pairs, most E England; few migrants, Apr–Sep)

Spring–autumn visitor/migrant very like Hen Harrier (resident/winter visitor). Slim harrier, **elongated wingtip** useful clue: tends to glide with tapered tip more swept back, particularly light, airy action.

IN FLIGHT, MALE darker than Hen Harrier, **dark forewing/pale hindwing effect**; large black wingtip; **black midwing bar** unique. White rump weak or absent. Underwing has black bar, chestnut blotches on coverts, unlike immaculate white Hen Harrier. Outer tail lightly barred. FEMALE like Hen Harrier; **dark cheek patch small, more isolated** behind bolder white eye crescents, and pale edge to cheek weak or missing. **Wingtip longer, more pointed.** JUVENILE **buffy-orange below**, without streaks (easier to identify on plumage than older female).

VOICE Calls "*kekekek*" and "*jik-jik-jik*" near nest.

Marshes, rough grassland

1ST-SUMMER ♂ intermediate pattern

ADULT ♀

ADULT ♂

MALE very lightweight, darker plumage than extremely pale male Hen Harrier

ADULT ♀

JUVENILE

ADULT ♂

ADULT ♂

IMMATURE MALES often dull, browner-backed than 'clean and bright' adult

ADULT ♀

ADULT ♂

Head patterns of juvenile harriers with white rumps

Juvenile harriers have white marks above and below the dark eye and dark cheek crescents.
Pallid Harrier has a broad pale collar highlighting the big dark cheek; unstreaked brown neck creating dark shawl.
Montagu's Harrier has strong pattern around eye, weak pale collar; unstreaked throat.
Hen Harrier has weakest pattern, small white marks around eye, streaked neck beneath narrow pale collar.

PALLID HARRIER

MONTAGU'S HARRIER

HEN HARRIER

Juvenile harriers are difficult: structure and plumage must be checked with care and the head pattern is important.

NT **NT** # Pallid Harrier *Circus macrourus* 530

40–50 cm | WS 95–120 cm

Rare, can be difficult to identify. Slim, lightweight, like Montagu's Harrier (*p. 308*), but shorter wingtip.

IN FLIGHT, FEMALE like Montagu's Harrier: plain above, barely a hint of blackish midwing band; underwing darker, plainer dark coverts, darker hindwing.

Vagrant from Asia: <100 records (<10 Ireland), small influxes, Sep–Apr. Scattered. Moors, farmland.

JUVENILE

ADULT ♀

ADULT ♂

ADULT ♀

ADULT ♂

MALE (not recorded in Britain/Ireland) pale grey, white below (including chest). IN FLIGHT, wingtip has narrow black wedge.

Kites in flight *p. 297*

Rare birds of prey

Black Kite *Milvus migrans* 530

48–58 cm | WS 135–155 cm

Compared with Red Kite (*p. 304*), **duller brown**; **tail less forked**, drab brown with short dark bars; underwing less well marked, **dull primary patch** at best. JUVENILE has paler inner primaries.

> Very rare migrant/vagrant from S Europe: 15–25 per year, most Apr–Jun. In S.

ADULT

ADULT

ADULT

IN FLIGHT, less elongated than Red Kite; see Marsh Harrier (*p. 305*); tail triangular, shallow notch when closed. **Pale band across innerwing** (female Marsh Harrier (*p. 305*) has pale leading edge; plain, square tail). Active flight with bowed wings, swooping turns, twisting tail, unlike a harrier.

Eastern race *lineatus* ('Black-eared Kite'), perhaps extreme vagrant to Britain; paler head, dark ear covert patch, slightly paler, barred patch under outerwing.

Northern Harrier 530

Circus hudsonius

45–55 cm | WS 99–121 cm

N American equivalent of Hen Harrier; juvenile similar to Montagu's Harrier (*p. 308*). MALE like Hen Harrier (*p. 307*) but more marked above (sub-adults mottled brown on grey), broader dark trailing edge to wing; hooded appearance; streaked breast, fine bars on underwing, tail. FEMALE (not recorded) darker above, more rufous below than Hen Harrier. JUVENILE broad, five-fingered wingtip like Hen Harrier; usually deeper rufous-buff beneath (closer to Montagu's Harrier), fine streaks restricted to throat. More (5–6) bars on outer primaries than Hen Harrier (best judged on photographs); dark brown neck, pale collar; dark hood.

Vagrant from N America: <10 records Britain (<10 Ireland), autumn–winter. Grassland/marshes.

JUVENILE

streaks only on throat

more (5–6) bars on outer primaries than Hen Harrier

NORTHERN HARRIER   HEN HARRIER

Short-toed Eagle *Circaetus gallicus* `530`

62–69 cm | WS 170–185 cm

A big eagle, bigger than Osprey (*p. 300*), with **large, rounded head** and long, broad wings. Looks pale: sandy brown above, **silvery-white below** with variable fine dark bars (some with dark hood). **No dark 'wrist' patch on wing. Eyes yellow.** IN FLIGHT, broad wings, short wide tail with translucent bars; pale below with no dark wrist patch. Often hovers with heavy, wobbling action.

ADULT

ADULT

JUVENILE

ADULT

no 'wrist' patch

juvenile pale rufous below – dark hood/ streaked breast after 5–6 years, darkest on females

IMMATURE 2–4 YEARS OLD

BUZZARD (pale JUVENILE)

Vagrant from S Europe: <10 records (Britain), May–Oct. S England. Heaths, forest.

VU EN (Greater) Spotted Eagle `530`

Aquila clanga

59–69 cm | WS 157–180 cm

Big, dark eagle, like Golden Eagle (*p. 295*) but wide-winged with broad, blunt tips, **short tailed**. Pale patch at base of primaries and **small pale rump** above, pale 'comma' at base of primaries underneath. IMMATURE variable white spotting on wings.

IMMATURE

IMMATURE

Vagrant from C Europe: 14 records, pre-1915, Oct–Jan. Unlikely now.

Egyptian Vulture *Neophron percnopterus* 530

EN 55–65 cm | WS 146–175 cm

Very large. Fine bill, yellow face, **wedge-tipped tail**; long, rather narrow wings. ADULT **white**, washed yellow/orange, flat wings with **black rear/outerwing** from below. IMMATURE duller, browner.

EGYPTIAN VULTURE

ADULT

ADULT   IMMATURE

IMMATURE

GRIFFON VULTURE

ADULT   IMMATURE

IMMATURE

BALD EAGLE

tail grey, bordered black

whiter underwing than White-tailed Eagle

ADULT   IMMMATURE

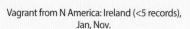
Vagrant from S Europe: (Britain), last 1868, unlikely now.

Vagrant from N America: Ireland (<5 records), Jan, Nov.

Bald Eagle *Haliaeetus leucocephalus* ◆

77 cm | WS 180–200 cm

Huge, short-tailed eagle; flat-winged like White-tailed Eagle (*p. 294*). ADULT (not recorded) black; white head, tail; IMMATURE like White-tailed Eagle; blacker body, whitish underwing bands, tail greyish with blackish tip.

Vagrant from S Europe: 1, Ireland (spring 1842), also Channel Is. (twice).

Griffon Vulture *Gyps fulvus* ◆   530

95–105 cm | WS 240–280 cm

Enormous, wide-winged, very short-tailed. Upperside toffee-brown, flight feathers darker. Brown below, pale lines across wing coverts, flight feathers dark. Soars on raised wings; bulging hindwing, upcurved 'fingers'.

IMMATURE

IMMATURE

Accipiter hawks in flight

Hawks – *Accipiters* – relatively broad-winged, long-tailed; Goshawk can be confused with larger falcons, Honey-buzzard. Check shapes, wingset, underwings, head patterns. Subtleties of shape and size separate Goshawk and Sparrowhawk; falcons are relatively longer-winged, shorter-tailed, with dark eyes. Soaring Gyr Falcon or Peregrine could be taken for a Goshawk.

SPARROWHAWK (*p. 314*)

GOSHAWK (*p. 315*)

note variable shapes of Goshawk, wings swept, flexed or straight out, flat or upswept at tips. Tail broad, often rounded; protruding head, deep chest

ADULT ♂
ADULT ♀
ADULT ♂
ADULT ♂
ADULT ♀

Sparrowhawk smaller, slimmer than Goshawk, hindwing straighter, head shorter, tail slim and square

ADULT ♂
IMMATURE
ADULT ♀
IMMATURE ♀

KESTREL (*p. 316*)

JUVENILE ♀

ADULT ♂
IMMATURE ♂

Sparrowhawk

Accipiter nisus ⓘ 530

♂ 29–34 cm | WS 58–65 cm   ♀ 35–41 cm | WS 68–77 cm

Small, bird-hunting predator; elusive but often soars. Frequent brief presence in gardens. Male smaller, snappier than heavier Kestrel-sized female. **Yellow eye** rules out falcons.

MALE bluish-grey, pink-orange below. FEMALE grey, fades browner; pale stripe over eye. Underside **dull white**, grey bars. Legs slim (Goshawk's thick). JUVENILE rusty-brown. IN FLIGHT, **small head**; broad chest; **long slim tail** (opens in half-fan). Wing broad-based, **outer half short**; spreads to blunt, wide tip, sweeps back to short point (compare Kestrel (*p. 316*), Merlin (*p. 317*)). Quick, deep beats between short, flat glides (**flap-flap-glide** unlike Kestrel's erratic action). Hunts in slanting dive, or short, fast chase; sits and waits in thick cover. Does not hover! Look up if you hear alarm calls from Starlings/tit flocks. In display, fast, bouncing undulations; patrols with slow, deep beats (beware thoughts of Goshawk); headlong plunge into wood.

VOICE Calls chattering "*kewkewkewkewkew*" around nest.

Fairly common resident (48,000 pairs, including 13,000 in Ireland)

Woodland, extensive forest or scattered trees in farmland, parks; hunts over fields, moors, marshes

ADULT ♀

ADULT ♂

ADULT ♀

IMMATURE ♂

ADULT ♀

This is the only bird of prey likely to capture a bird on the average lawn (carries off small prey but may stay to pluck larger birds): takes birds from tits up to Collared Dove size.

ADULT ♂

JUVENILE

Goshawk

Accipiter gentilis Ⓘ **530**

♂ 49–56 cm | WS 90–105 cm   ♀ 58–64 cm | WS 108–127 cm

Big, bird-hunting hawk: see Sparrowhawk, Peregrine (*p. 319*). Female big, long-winged (see Honey-buzzard (*p. 301*)), but 'small Goshawk/large Sparrowhawk' can be problematical.

MALE **crow-sized**; barred below; broad white vent; dark face band. FEMALE **near size of Buzzard** (*p. 302*). JUVENILE brown, **buff** beneath; **streaked black**. IN FLIGHT, **long head**; wide rump; **rounded tail**; **bulging innerwing** with **narrow tip**. Taut 'full stretch' in soar (shape like soaring Kestrel (*p. 316*)), flat wings sweep gently upwards. End-on, 'T'-shape, or wings pointed like Peregrine; side-on, long head, blunt wingtips. Displays with deep undulations; slow flight over wood, headlong plunges. Soars, stoops like Peregrine.

VOICE Call near nest recalls Green Woodpecker (*p. 335*), repeated, shouted "*cha-cha-cha-cha-cha*" and high whine.

Rare, local resident (430 pairs); rare migrant; very small numbers but increasing in Ireland

Woodland, adjacent open areas

N American race *atricapillus* **Vagrant: <10 records (Ireland)** likely escape; reduced barring beneath, accurate assessment only likely from photographs.

JUVENILE

ADULT ♂

blue-grey fades browner by late winter

ADULT ♂

JUVENILE

drop-shaped streaks on bright buff

ADULT ♂

ADULT ♀

Kestrel

Falco tinnunculus ⬤ ⬤ Ⅰ 534

31–37 cm | WS 65–82 cm

👁 Lesser Kestrel (*p. 324*),
Red-footed Falcon (*p. 320*)

Pigeon-size, long-tailed falcon.
Sits upright on wire/post (compare Collared Dove (*p. 278*):
Kestrel bulky up front, tapered to tail). In flight, wings quite
straight (blunt tips) or angled back to point. Tail very slender,
opens to full fan.

Persistent hovering (sometimes very high, often at dusk):
tail spread, wings quiver or flap. **Innerwing pale, outerwing
dark** – contrast unlike other common falcons/hawks.
MALE **black band on grey tail**. FEMALE **ginger-brown** (tail/rump
often greyer). JUVENILE like female; IMMATURE MALE greyer rump/
tail, more spotted above. IN FLIGHT, relaxed, loose beats (not
flap-flap-glide of Sparrowhawk (*p. 314*), not so fast as Peregrine
(*p. 319*) or Merlin, nor so elegant as Hobby (*p. 318*)). Soars well;
wings flat, rather wide. Capable of fast, controlled aerobatics.

VOICE Sharp, whining "*kee-kee-kee-kee*".

Fairly common resident (58,000
pairs, declining)

from
Scandinavia
and the
Low
Countries

Open ground, farmland, heaths,
suburban/waste areas

ADULT ♀/JUVENILE

striking two-tone
effect above

ADULT ♂

ADULT ♀

ADULT ♂

mottled
silvery-buff
below

1ST-YEAR ♂
(one year old)

grey head

ADULT ♂

A Kestrel watches for prey by
hovering, head motionless
relative to the ground.

spotted
chestnut
back

strongly
barred

ADULT ♀

ADULT ♂

Merlin

Falco columbarius race *subaesalon* **534**

26–33 cm | WS 50–67 cm

American Kestrel (*p. 324*)

Smallest falcon, male like male Sparrowhawk (*p. 314*), female close to Kestrel.

Chunky, square-headed. MALE blue-grey, orange-buff below with streaks not bars; head pattern weak like Kestrel. Tail grey with black band. FEMALE/JUVENILE **brown**, less ginger than Kestrel; **no strong upperwing contrast**. Tail barred cream. Dark moustache and rear cheek. IN FLIGHT, fast, low; quick beats, **few glides**; more determined than Kestrel – wings shorter than Peregrine or Hobby (*p. 318*), **wide-based but sharper point** than Kestrel's (see Sparrowhawk, wider wing, shorter tip). Rarely soars, does not hover. Approaches prey with thrush-like **flicked in-out wingtip action** like Hobby, **fast, twisting chase**.

VOICE Sharp "*ki-ki-ki-ki*"; "*week-week-week-week-week*".

Race *aesalon* breeds; larger race *subaesalon* (breeds Iceland) rare winter migrant; race *columbarius* (N America) vagrant (1 record (Ireland): Sep).

Rare summer visitor (1,300 pairs, mostly N and W), migrant; widespread, scarce winter visitor

subaesalon from Iceland

from Scandinavia

Moors, open plantations, bushy hillsides; in winter, wetlands, lowland pastures, coasts

Compact, sharp-winged, fast and direct.

ADULT ♂

race *subaesalon*

ADULT ♀

race *subaesalon*

ADULT ♂

ADULT ♀

JUVENILE

often perches on ground or post

muddier brown than Kestrel; tail barred with cream spots

clear blue-grey with fine dark streaks, grey tail

grey with pale feather edges above; tail barred pale

ADULT ♂ race *aesalon*

IMMATURE ♂

317

Falcons in flight *p. 323*

Hobby

Falco subbuteo 534

29–35 cm | WS 68–84 cm

Red-footed Falcon (*p. 320*),
Eleonora's Falcon (*p. 325*)

Scarce summer migrant, Apr–Sep
(1,200–2,800 pairs)

Aerial, spring–autumn falcon:
see Kestrel (*p. 316*) and especially Peregrine. Delicate, elegant
aerial performer: **changes in pace** evident when hawking insects.

ADULT grey above; plain tail; white below, **thickly streaked** black.
Thighs/vent rusty red, colour elusive. JUVENILE browner; buff
feather edges above, buff cheek; streaked buff below, no red.
IN FLIGHT, patrols on flat/bowed wings, accelerates with **deep,
whippy beats** into upward glide/stall, catching insects. Long,
slanting, flapping dive into fast, swept-wing stoop, after small
birds. **Long-wings** arc to narrow tip, sharper than Kestrel, tail
tapered or half-fanned. **Narrower body, especially rump/tail
base**, than Peregrine, but can be hard to tell; **head small, squat**
into shoulders. Looks **dark** in flight: close view/good light
needed for detail, but **white neck patch** shows well.

VOICE Rather ringing, bright "*kew-kew-kew-kew*".

to
Africa

Open ground, heaths, farmland,
moors, around lakes and marshes

slim tail
base is
a useful
feature

dull dark brown
above

JUVENILE

JUVENILE

ADULT

dark with
white neck

dark,
mottled and
streaked
below

ADULT

streaked below;
rufous rear hard
to see

ADULT

Past reliance on heaths/
pine copses reduced as
Hobbies occupy farmland
and valleys with flooded
gravel pits.

Peregrine

Falco peregrinus **534**

♂ 38–45 cm | WS 87–100 cm
♀ 46–51 cm | WS 104–114 cm

👁 Gyr Falcon (*p. 321*)

Scarce resident (1,800 pairs, including 300 in Ireland): wanders widely in winter

Compare Kestrel (*p. 316*), Hobby, Goshawk (*p. 315*).
Rather heavy, broad-bodied; **rump/tail wider** than Hobby;
protruding head. **Black beneath eye**, **white cheek**.

MALE often bluer, pinker below than female. FEMALE grey and
white; **barred** belly. JUVENILE browner; underside **streaked**.
IN FLIGHT, **wide, pale rump** (Hobby's darker). Wings wide,
tapered (female's blunt tipped, male's sharper) or 'anchor' shape;
short, tapered tail. Flight direct, muscular; **deep, whippy beats**,
often few or no glides. Soars masterfully (wings faintly upswept)
to great height. Chases prey in fast, direct pursuit; rolling swoop
from beneath; or stoop with closed wings. Shapes resemble
pigeon, Raven (*p. 470*), even Fulmar (*p. 90*), at times.

VOICE Around nest: loud, coarse "*haar-haair-haair*",
chattering "*kek-kek-kek-kek*"; various whining sounds.

from
Scandinavia

Cities to wild cliffs, coastal and
inland; winter, almost anywhere

ADULT

broad
tail base

JUVENILE

browner
back

pale tail tip

JUVENILE

streaked
underside

ADULT

barred
underside

bright, pale
shield-
shaped
breast above
bars and
spots

ADULT

ADULT

ADULT

NT **Red-footed Falcon** *Falco vespertinus*   534

NT 28–34 cm | WS 65–76 cm

Very rare migrant from E Europe: (15–20 per year, (<50 records Irelalnd), Mar –Nov, most May. Mainly in S/E. Open spaces, watersides.

👁 Amur Falcon (*p. 325*)

Small falcon, between Hobby (*p. 318*) and Kestrel (*p. 316*) in character. Drifts over open space catching insects, hovers like Kestrel (migrants in Britain/Ireland rarely do so). Wings shorter, tail longer than Hobby.

MALE grey, **rufous thighs/belly** (hard to see in some lights); upperwing **fades to silvery-grey** tip. Red on bill, eyering and legs. IMMATURE MALE (frequent in spring) **rufous on chest**, plainer grey upperwing, **barred/chequered underwing**; old (barred)/new (grey) flight feathers in contrasting patches. FEMALE grey back, barred black, rufous underside. **Buff cap**, **black mask**, white cheeks; orange legs. JUVENILE browner cap, dark mask, white cheeks, underside whiter with black streaks. Very like juvenile Hobby but most have p**ale collar**, **paler underwing** with dark spots, darker trailing edge.

flight often slow, soft, dipping, resembles Black Tern (*page 142*)

ADULT ♀

ADULT ♂

ADULT ♂

1ST-SUMMER ♂

rufous thighs/ belly hard to see in some lights

ADULT ♀

JUVENILE

1ST-SUMMER ♂

ADULT ♂

grey back with soft dark grey bars

bill base, eyering and legs red

underside rufous-buff

ADULT ♂

ADULT ♀

Gyr Falcon *Falco rusticolus* 534

53–63 cm | WS 120–134 cm

Biggest falcon: most British/Irish vagrants 'white'. See Peregrine (*p. 319*), Goshawk (*p. 315*):

Scandinavian Gyr Falcons dark; Icelandic middle-grey; Greenland 'white'.

IN FLIGHT, big, span equals Buzzard (*p. 302*) or female Goshawk, slightly rounded wingtips, broad tail, **deep, heavy belly** reaching back into deep, **broad undertail area**. Slower, shallower action than Peregrine. **Dark coverts/paler flight feathers** below, dark hood but white-face/black moustache weaker than on Peregrine. 'WHITE' ADULT white, copious dark flecks on some, few on others. JUVENILE grey-brown, underwing very dark, underbody heavily streaked; cheeks dark, legs bluish.

> 👁 Beware, escaped Saker (very like juvenile Gyr), Lanner, other falcons and hybrids, which confuse the situation – see *p. 322*

Vagrant from N Europe/ Greenland: <500 records (<150 Ireland), Sep–May. Most winter/ early spring. Moors/cliffs.

JUVENILE

ADULT

JUVENILE

ADULT 'WHITE'

PEREGRINE much smaller. 'moustache' more obvious

JUVENILE

dark cheeks

ADULT (SCANDINAVIAN)

ADULT (ICELAND)

JUVENILE

Escaped falcons

EN **Lanner Falcon**

Falco biarmicus

Long-winged, like huge Kestrel (*p. 316*); rufous cap, rufous/white cheeks. Greyer than Saker, flanks barred, underwing paler; juvenile has densely barred tail.

EN **Saker Falcon**

VU *Falco cherrug*

Sandier-brown, buffier on head/breast, dark streaks below and dark thighs; in flight upperwing has kestrel-like tawny inner/dark outerwing.

Falcons in flight

Compared to *Accipiter* hawks (*p. 313*) falcons are relatively long-winged and short-tailed, dark (not yellow) eyes, but a soaring Gyr Falcon or Peregrine can be taken for a Goshawk. Separating commoner falcons is usually straightforward (Peregrine/Hobby less so), but rarer ones may be difficult: patterns and flight shapes important.

GYR FALCON

LANNER FALCON

ADULT

SAKER FALCON

JUVENILE

dark cheeks

pale cheeks

GYR FALCON
(*p. 321*)

ADULT
(SCANDINAVIAN)

LANNER FALCON

ADULT

SAKER FALCON

ADULT

PEREGRINE (*p. 319*)

ADULT

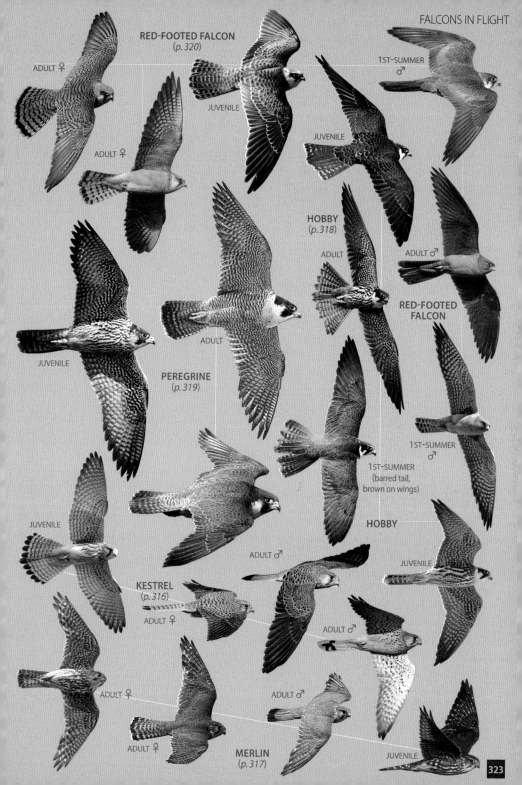

ADULT ♀

RED-FOOTED FALCON
(p. 320)

1ST-SUMMER ♂

JUVENILE

ADULT ♀

JUVENILE

HOBBY
(p. 318)

ADULT

ADULT ♂

RED-FOOTED FALCON

JUVENILE

ADULT

PEREGRINE
(p. 319)

1ST-SUMMER ♂

1ST-SUMMER
(barred tail,
brown on wings)

HOBBY

JUVENILE

JUVENILE

ADULT ♂

KESTREL
(p. 316)

ADULT ♀

ADULT ♂

JUVENILE

ADULT ♂

ADULT ♀

ADULT ♀

ADULT ♂

MERLIN
(p. 317)

JUVENILE

Very rare falcons

Lesser Kestrel *Falco naumanni* 534
27–33 cm | WS 58–73 cm

Like slender Kestrel (*p. 316*).
MALE like Kestrel but bluer head,
**unspotted rufous back, blue-grey
band** across innerwing. Underwing
nearly white, small dark tip, fine
dark specks. FEMALE/IMMATURE hard
to tell from Kestrel; paler cheek/
darker moustache a clue.
IN FLIGHT, shallow, quick wingbeats,
often hovers.

1ST-SUMMER ♂

ADULT ♂

ADULT ♀

unspotted

FEMALE
(not recorded)
very like Kestrel

1ST-SUMMER ♂

ADULT ♂

spotted back
and wing
coverts

KESTREL

ADULT ♂

Vagrant from S Europe: <20
records (1 Ireland), Nov–May,
most spring. Scattered.
Heaths, islands.

American Kestrel

Falco sparverius
23–27 cm | WS 51–61 cm

Tiny kestrel, dumpy, fast
wingbeats. MALE **multi-
coloured head**
(white between black
moustache and rear cheek,
black ear spot), rufous back/
tail, **grey upperwing**.
FEMALE/JUVENILE like Kestrel
(*p. 316*); barred rufous back,
wings, tail, but head like male.

pointed, swept wingtips
in direct flight

ADULT ♂

ADULT ♀

ADULT ♀

ADULT ♂

Vagrant from N America:
<5 records (1 record Ireland),
May–Jun. Scattered. Heaths,
islands.

Eleonora's Falcon
534

Falco eleonorae

36–42 cm | WS 90–105 cm

Large, angular falcon.
DARK FORM **brown-black** with bluish bill and legs.
PALE FORM sooty brown, **rusty below**, streaked dark; **bold black cap/moustache, rounded white cheek/throat** ('hooks' under cap on Hobby (*p. 318*)).

Vagrant from Mediterranean: <10 records (Britain), Jun–Oct. Scattered. Heath/coast.

In both forms, dark forewing/ paler hindwing obvious.

ADULT (dark form)

rusty

rounded white cheek

ADULT (pale form)

1ST-SUMMER like adult, with paler spotted underwing

pale

white 'hook'

HOBBY

ADULT (pale form)

Amur Falcon

Falco amurensis

30–36 cm | WS 65–75 cm

MALE like Red-footed Falcon (*p. 320*) with striking white underwing coverts which may show on immature birds, otherwise difficult/ impossible. FEMALE white beneath with black streaks, crown grey (not buff).

Vagrant from Asia: 1 record (Britain), immature male: Sep.

1st-summer ♂ – barred underwing with tell-tale white adult feathers moulting through

ADULT ♂

ADULT ♂

RED-FOOTED FALCON

1ST-SUMMER ♂

grey

buff

ADULT ♀

ADULT ♂ (not recorded)

ADULT ♀ (not recorded)

KINGFISHERS, CUCKOOS, HOOPOE, BEE-EATERS, ROLLER and PARROTS

This is a group of birds, sometimes called 'higher landbirds', placed together partly for convenience, as not all are closely related to the Passerines, as was once thought. The Passerines are perching birds, the 'highest' order in evolutionary terms, and include more than half the world's birds. They all have three toes pointing forwards, one back, helping them to perch. They are also, less accurately, known as 'songbirds'. Most birds that appear earlier in this book – ducks, waders, birds of prey, gulls – are clearly different. In between are the Near-passerines – from pigeons to woodpeckers. All are land birds, mostly associated with trees; they perch, but many have different arrangements of toes (two forward, two back, or with a more mobile outer toe swinging outwards and backwards). Although many have distinctive voices, they do not 'sing'. This section includes distinctive birds within this intermediate group. Most are related to large numbers of similar species outside Europe.

ID FEATURES   all very distinctive species

Kingfishers (*pp. 327, 521*): 1 widespread resident and 1 rare vagrant. Birds of watersides (kingfishers in other parts of the world include landbirds). The common Kingfisher is mostly a freshwater bird, but visits saltmarsh creeks or rocky coasts, especially in severe weather. It perches quite low, sometimes hovers, and dives to catch fish.

Cuckoos (*pp. 328, 331, 521*): 1 widespread species, 1 vagrant from southern Europe and 2 smaller vagrants from North America. Cuckoos have two toes forwards, two back; small, slightly curved bills; long wings and tails. The common Cuckoo is a widespread but declining summer visitor from Africa, well known for laying eggs in other species' nests.

Hoopoe (*p. 329*): 1 species; a rare or scarce migrant, has bred.
Large fan-like crest combines with broadly banded black-and-white wings to create a unique appearance, but brief views can suggest a woodpecker or Jay.

Bee-eaters (*p. 330*): 2 species, one a scarce visitor that has bred several times in recent years, one very rare vagrant. Bee-eaters perch prominently and fly with graceful swoops and glides, often calling, on straight, outstretched, pointed wings, catching large insects in flight.

Roller(*p. 331*): 1 increasingly rare vagrant from Europe (most species of roller are tropical); like a small pale crow, but showing vivid colours in flight.

Parrots (*p. 332*): 1 regular breeding species introduced (or escaped into the wild), thriving in quite restricted parts of southern England; several other species may be seen as 'escapes' and some breed. See *pp. 332, 523*.

Loud, hissing, cheeping calls draw attention to young Cuckoos demanding food from smaller foster-parents, such as this Meadow Pipit.

VU Kingfisher

Alcedo atthis  race *ispida*¹ see p.525 I **534**

17–19·5 cm | WS 25 cm

👁 Belted Kingfisher (*p. 521*)

Scarce resident (5,000 breeding pairs UK, plus few 100s in Ireland), winter wanderer; temporary declines after freezing winters

Unique colours, stocky shape, dagger-like bill. Smaller than Starling (*p. 372*). Often heard first: **sudden 'plop'** of dive, or **sharp whistle** in fly-by. Can be hard to see despite (or because of) remarkable colours in sun and shade of riverbank.

Greenish to deep blue crown, back and wings, **brilliant blue rump**, white patches behind orange ear coverts, **orange underside**. Vivid electric blue best in bright light, still wonderfully rich even in deepening evening light. Legs orange. MALE has black bill; FEMALE has orange on lower edge. JUVENILE duller, dark legs.

VOICE High whistle "*chi-k-keee*" or "*ki-kee*", and trilled variants.

Freshwater margins, also coasts in winter

IN FLIGHT, blurred wings, **streak of electric blue** immediately obvious (often swings over land to avoid people on bank). Heavy-bellied, but quick flight.

JUVENILE

JUVENILES greener, darker on breast sides, crown has buff edges; legs dull or dark.

ADULT ♀

all black

some orange

ADULT ♂

ADULT ♀

Cuckoo

Cuculus canorus ● 534

32–36 cm | WS 54–60 cm

> **American cuckoos** (*p. 521*)
> **Great Spotted Cuckoo** (*p. 331*)

Long, slim (can look heavy-bodied with drooped wings), **small head, short, downcurved bill**. Tends to perch horizontally on bush, side of tree or wire (browner juvenile, begging for food, more upright). Wingtips often below long, broad tail. Sways tail sideways or up and down. Shape and flight, swooping up to perch, characteristic.

ADULT grey, barred beneath; **white spots** on dark tail. FEMALE buffier on neck/underside (rare rufous form – see *inset below*). JUVENILE greyish or rufous-brown, barred; **whitish patch on nape**. See Kestrel (*p. 316*), Sparrowhawk (*p. 314*) (barred but different shape and posture).

VOICE Soft, far-carrying "*cu-coo*" (loud, penetrating at close range); female has loud, bubbling, chuckling trill. Male also calls low, wheezy, 'dirty laugh' "*gek-eh-eh-eh-eh*".

Scarce summer migrant (Apr–Sep) (14,000 males, plus 12,000 birds in Ireland; declining)

to Africa

Farmland, woodland edge, heaths, in and around reedbeds

wingbeats quick, below body, **slender head raised**

barred underwing has **pale central band**

SPARROWHAWK

no pale band

ADULT ♂

IN FLIGHT, vaguely like pigeon or Kestrel but wings **broad-based, tapered to swept-back tip**; tail wider.

buffy on neck/chest/underside

ADULT ♀

ADULT ♂

grey on chest

ADULT ♀ rufous form

Rare rufous female is red-brown with a black-barred tail

JUVENILE

JUVENILES may be greyish or more rufous, with pale feather edgings and a pale nape spot.

Colourful visitors from Europe

When a high pressure weather system dominates Britain and continental Europe (especially in spring) the associated light southerly winds can create conditions in which migratory species normally found in the Mediterranean and southern Europe reach much farther north than usual. These species are known as 'overshoot migrants' and commonly include Hoopoe and Bee-eater, as well as the less frequent Roller (*p. 331*) and Great Spotted Cuckoo (*p. 331*), amongst others.

Hoopoe *Upupa epops*

25–29 cm | WS 44–48 cm

Rare migrant from S Europe: 100–160 per year, mostly Mar–Oct; has bred. Woodland edge, open ground.

534

Unmistakable, more by pattern and shape than colours (but see Jay (*p. 472*)). **Long, low** on ground; short legs; long, **faintly downcurved bill. Long crest usually flattened into narrow wedge**, briefly raised in broad semi-circular **fan of bright orange-buff**. Upperparts **barred black and white**, blending with shadow and light when feeding unobtrusively on ground; all suddenly revealed as bird takes flight.

VOICE Simple, far-carrying, soft, quick repetition of quite low, hollow "*poo-poo-poo*".

ADULT

IN FLIGHT, erratic, bounding, settling into a springy, rhythmic bouncy series of in-out flicking beats of broad, rounded wings.

ADULT

ADULT

Fan-like crest raised in display or alarm, more often laid flat in backward-pointing spike.

ADULT

Bee-eater *Merops apiaster* `534`

25–29 cm | WS 36–40 cm

Long, slim; elongated tail; curved bill. ADULT bright rusty-brown on back, golden-yellow shoulders and dark rufous head; underneath, soft, rather dull pale blue, with **yellow throat**. JUVENILE duller, square tail without central spike.

VOICE Calls catch attention: deep, throaty, soft, rolling whistles, "*prr-up prr-up*".

Rare migrant from S Europe: 40–70 per year, most spring; very rarely breeds (<70 records Ireland). Dry, sandy, open or bushy spaces.

ADULT

IN FLIGHT, long, triangular wings (like stretched, elegant Starling (*p. 372*)), tail with **sharp central spike**. Deep, quick, rowing beats between **flat, straight-winged, circling glides**, **sudden spurts** to catch flying insects.

ADULT

1ST-SUMMER

dull plumage but develops tail-spike

brown

black 'collar'

golden back

Blue-cheeked Bee-eater

Merops persicus

28–32 cm | WS 35–39 cm

Like Bee-eater but **greener overall**, longer tail spike. Green nape. ADULT blue around eye. JUVENILE duller, lacks blue; shorter tail. Throat has diffuse **red-brown patch** without black border.

VOICE Very like Bee-eater, slightly higher, thinner.

Vagrant from Middle East: <15 records (Britain), summer–autumn. Scattered, near coast.

JUVENILE

IN FLIGHT, underwing similar pale coppery, but black rear edge narrower along full length.

ADULT

green

green back

no black 'collar'

ADULT

Roller *Coracias garrulus* `534`

29–32 cm | WS 35–39 cm

One of Europe's truly spectacular birds: may look dull perched but in flight vivid colours catch the eye. Form like Jackdaw (*p. 466*), but **large, broad head**, longer bill, slim tail. Head and body variably dull or brighter green-blue, greener below; **back pale rufous-brown**. IMMATURE much duller, paler below with subtle streaks, paler areas around the eye and bill and a contrasting dark eyestripe.

VOICE Short, harsh, crow-like, calls.

Vagrant from S Europe: >300 records (<20 Ireland), declining, Apr–Nov, most May–Jun. Farmland/heathland.

IN FLIGHT, quite long-winged, long-tailed, with square, cross-like form. Upperwing bright turquoise, deep blue and blue-black.

ADULT

dark tips to primary coverts, buff-tinged underside may suggest FEMALE or 1ST-SUMMER

ADULT

ADULT

Great Spotted Cuckoo *Clamator glandarius*

35–39 cm | WS 58–60 cm

Cuckoo-like but peculiar gangly shape, with long wings and tail. ADULT **grey above, with white spots**, whitish below; long, dark tail. JUVENILE blackish above, cream below with **rufous outerwing**.

VOICE Unlikely from vagrant; loud, rattling chatter "*cher-cher-cher-cher-che-che-che*".

Vagrant from S Europe: <60 records (<10 Ireland), Feb–May, Jul–Aug. Most in S; scattered. Bushy open areas.

ADULT

JUVENILE

ADULT

Ring-necked Parakeet

Psittacula krameri

37–43 cm (incl. tail 18–23 cm)

Bright green, long-tailed, unlike any European species. **Pale green**, including head, yellower/paler beneath, bluer on tail, with **short, squat, red bill**. MALE black/pink/blue neck ring, black chin.

Alexandrine Parakeet; see also Monk Parakeet (*p. 523*)

Scarce, locally common introduced resident, Britain (established SE England (8,500 pairs), declining except in London parks); communal roosts winter

VOICE Loud, squealing calls, especially in fast, dashing flight.

Parks, gardens, woodland

IN FLIGHT, quite short but pointed, whirring wings, blunt head, elongated tail.

ADULT ♀

female has weaker neck ring than male

ADULT ♂

ADULT ♀

IMMATURE ♂

Alexandrine Parakeet *Psittacula eupatria* Escape, has bred

Easily overlooked as closely resembles Ring-necked Parakeet, but has purplish shoulder patch. Females have a weaker neck ring than males (as Ring-necked Parakeet).

purplish shoulder patch

ADULT ♂

WOODPECKERS

WOODPECKER ID   size | green/pied/brown colour | head pattern | back pattern | call

6 species: 3 breed (and 1 rare migrant may do so sporadically); 1 extremely rare and 1 possible vagrant from N America.

Woodpeckers (*pp. 335–337, 521, 523*) Woodpeckers cling to branches and tree trunks, head-up, tail-down, using the tail as a support. Two are much bigger than a Nuthatch (*p. 452*), less bouncily agile about the trees, but Lesser Spotted Woodpecker is small and more fluttery (it is also now rare).

Green Woodpeckers are as often on the ground or flying up from open grass or heath, taking refuge in nearby trees, but Great Spotted Woodpeckers are birds of trees or at least thick, tall bushes. They are also common garden visitors: the striking ones that flash black, white and red.

The two spotted species call often and 'drum' in spring, making a sudden, short, percussion burst against a resonant branch. Green Woodpeckers have loud, strident, echoing calls.

The **Wryneck** (*p. 334*) is a scarce or rare migrant, mostly near the coast. More like a small thrush or large warbler, its square tail is not used much as a prop. It perches quite still for long spells between bouts of feeding on the ground.

Woodpecker ageing/ sexing

Sexes are almost similar except for head patterns (in particular, position and extent of red). Juveniles duller, more streaked on Green Woodpecker, head pattern different from adults on 'spotted' woodpeckers until autumn moult.

JUVENILE

Great Spotted Woodpeckers are eye-catching, dramatic birds at close range (e.g. on a garden feeder, which is a common sight), but more elusive inside a wood, especially in spring/summer foliage. Lesser Spotted Woodpeckers are rare on feeders, much smaller, and often extremely elusive in a wood: they are most easily located early in spring when they drum and call more frequently. Green Woodpeckers are large, easily seen, but often simply fly up nearby and bound away out of sight. On a garden lawn, they immediately look 'different' and unusual, sloping back to rest on the tail and moving with short, leaping hops.

GREEN WOODPECKER

ADULT ♂

GREAT SPOTTED WOODPECKER

LESSER SPOTTED WOODPECKER

333

Wryneck

Jynx torquilla 534

16–18 cm | WS 25–27 cm

A forest bird; migrants occasionally in unexpected places such as gardens, searching lawns for ants, mostly low scrub beside open spaces on coast. Curious, puzzling, unlike any other woodpecker, nor much like anything else. Sits motionless for long periods in bush or tree, or hops about on ground.

Cryptic, dead wood pattern. Large pale head, **dark central stripe down nape and upper back**, buff throat with fine dark bars. Broad, **pale rump**, longish, **square, pale grey, finely-barred tail** (see Barred Warbler (*p. 424*)). Bill stout, sharp, **quite small**; eye mid-brown, gives staring expression.

VOICE Migrants generally silent; spring song distinctive quick, whining, nasal "*ti-ti-ti-ti-ti-ti*" or "*kyee-kyee-kyee-kyee-kyee*", rather like Kestrel (*p. 316*) or Lesser Spotted Woodpecker (*p. 337*).

Rare migrant, particularly in autumn (300–500 per year); very rare breeder in N (up to 6 males)

from NE Europe

to S Europe and Africa

Woodlands, heaths, open spaces

JUVENILE — dark back/nape stripe 'snakes' as bird turns its head

ADULT

IN FLIGHT, woodpecker-like, shallow undulations, long shooting glides on closed wings.

Wrynecks look unlike anything else, when perched or foraging on the ground, with a small bill, a thin dark eyestripe on the big, round head and dark stripe down the pale grey back.

JUVENILE

Green Woodpecker

Picus viridis

30–36 cm | WS 45–51 cm

Bigger than a thrush; on ground peculiar low, short-legged stance, head raised. Often clings upright on tree or post. Flies with long, deep swoops. Hops/leaps over grass/lawns/anthills, probing with pointed bill, extended tongue.

Unique in Britain: large, **green with glistening red cap, yellow rump**. Dark moustache (black on FEMALE, red-centred on MALE). Pale eye set in black patch gives staring expression. JUVENILE streaked cheek, spotted below, soft pale spots above.

VOICE Very distinctive loud, striking, shouted "*kew-kew-kew*" call; song longer, ringing laugh, sudden "*kyu-kyu-kyu!*", longer "*kyu-yu-yu-yu-yu*".

Common resident in Britain (24,000 breeding pairs, declining); absent from Ireland

Woodlands, heaths, open spaces

IN FLIGHT, rises with burst of quick beats, then bounds away in deep undulations.

ADULT ♂

ADULT ♀

black

ADULT ♂

red

JUVENILE

JUVENILE (JUN–OCT) greyer, barred and streaked, has a 'primitive', almost snaky look, especially when extending long, slender tongue.

typically rests on stiff, notched tail

ADULT ♂

Green Woodpeckers feed mostly on ants and their eggs and larvae, taken from burrows by quick pecks and use of the long, sticky tongue .

Great Spotted Woodpecker
Dendrocopos major

race *anglicus* †
see p.525

I

23–26 cm | WS 38–44 cm

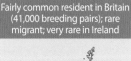
Yellow-bellied Sapsucker (*p.521*)

Thrush-sized; black, white and red; easy to identify but see Lesser Spotted Woodpecker.

Eye-catching, black and white, buff below; unique big **oval white shoulder patches** (easy to see in flight, too). **Vivid red splash under tail** rules out any other bird in Britain. MALE has red nape patch. FEMALE has all black nape. JUVENILE has red cap (extends beyond eye in male), weaker red under tail.

VOICE Loud, sharp, abrupt "*tchik*", occasional squeaky rattle of alarm. **Drums often** in spring: loud, hollow-sounding, fast rattle "*brrrrp*" of about half a second. Young call loudly from nest hole with scratchy, squeaky cacophony.

IN FLIGHT, **zooming undulations**: over a long distance, high, with smooth, even sweeps, bursts of wingbeats – can look small (but not finch-sized) so look for white shoulder patches, red under tail.

Fairly common resident in Britain (41,000 breeding pairs); rare migrant; very rare in Ireland

Woodlands, gardens

ADULT ♂

ADULT ♀

black

red cap
extends beyond
eye in ♂

red

ADULT ♂

JUVENILE ♂

JUVENILE ♂

Northern European race *major*, a scarce migrant, is larger than British race *anglicus*, with shorter bill, whiter underparts.

Lesser Spotted Woodpecker

Dendrocopos minor  534

14–16·5 cm | WS 24–29 cm

Much smaller than Great Spotted Woodpecker, which is bolder in every way, easier to see, more numerous. **Sparrow-sized** (looks bigger due to different shape, wider wings). Unobtrusive, often in tops of trees with dense, thin branches, or in spindly thickets. **Call** best means of locating it.

Black above, **white bars** merge into **whitish patch on back** (no white shoulder patches). **No red under tail.** MALE red crown; FEMALE black crown. Black patch on buff-white cheek.

VOICE Weak "*tchik*" and **distinctive song**, nasal "*pee-pee-pee-pee-pee*" (rare Wryneck (*p. 334*) more whining quality). Drum rattling roll for 1·2 to 1·8 seconds, often twice in quick succession, but Great Spotted Woodpecker (especially female) can give weaker roll than normal, so difficult.

Rare resident (2,000 breeding pairs, declining). Absent from Ireland

Deciduous woodland

red crown

ADULT ♂

ADULT ♂

Flight is fluttery in upper branches (hard to see in full leaf), deeply undulating over longer distance. Relatively large-winged; longer tail than Nuthatch (*p. 452*).

black crown

ADULT ♀

AERIAL FEEDERS – SWIFTS, SWALLOWS and MARTINS

AERIAL FEEDER ID wing shape | underpart colour | rump colour | throat pattern

7 swifts: 1 regular and breeding, others mostly extremely rare vagrants.
8 swallows and martins: 3 breed, 1 rare migrant, 4 very rare.

Swifts (*pp. 339–341*) are exclusively aerial, more so even than swallows and martins; confusion really comes about only through popular misuse of the names. The Swift is a late spring arrival; most are gone by August. A swift's minute legs and forward-pointing toes enable it to hang on to a rough surface but not to grasp a perch; so you will not see Swifts on wires or bare twigs – ever. Look for them in the air: stiff bow-and-arrow shapes, with slender tails and long, scythe-like wings.
They swoop up to nest holes hidden under eaves and in old towers, and dash around in fast, screeching groups.

Swallows and martins (*pp. 342–346*) are the 'hirundines', with elegant, swooping and swerving flights and quiet, chirrupy calls. All are long-distance migrants: the Sand Martin is one of the earliest arrivals, in March; the others a few weeks later.
Sand Martin colonies are groups of holes in earth or sand cliffs. House Martins make mud cups tight under eaves and gables on buildings, Swallows use outbuildings, needing a small shelf or beam for their mud-and-straw nests.
Swallows often perch on wires and television aerials, House Martins on wires and rooftops, Sand Martins on bare branches of waterside bushes, and ropes and wires low over water.
All three join Swifts over water in cold, wet or windy weather, seeking insects where they can, and Swallows feed in the lee of lines of trees and hedges in difficult conditions.

Swift ageing/sexing

Sexes of swifts are alike and have no seasonal changes. Juveniles have white feather edges, obvious when they first fly in late summer. Returning first-summer birds may be identifiable by old, worn flight feathers and pale-edged underwing coverts.

Swallow and martin ageing/sexing

Sexes look alike, but male swallows have longer outer tail feathers than females. Juveniles slightly duller, paler; by following spring, returning birds all have fresh plumage and cannot be aged.

Swallows habitually perch on wires, including fences; martins perch like this but less freely, mostly later in summer/autumn; while Swifts cannot perch and are never seen on wires or bare twigs.

Swift

Apus apus ●● Ⓘ

17–18·5 cm | WS 40–44 cm

👁 Rare swifts (*p. 340–341*)

Rare swifts (*p. 340–341*)

Totally aerial except on nest hidden in cavity. Unlike any other bird (except rarer swifts), but see Swallow (*p. 342*): Swift is bigger, longer-winged than swallows, **all blackish; stiffer, scythe-like wings. Never seen perched** on wire, branch or roof and usually flies directly into nest hole in building, rarely cliff.

Blackish-brown; whitish chin. Underwing flashes paler in sun. Fades browner (see Pallid Swift (*p. 340*)). JUVENILE white lores, fine whitish feather edgings; blacker wings and larger chin patch than adult. IN FLIGHT often high, fast, deep, beats between soaring glides; also slower, erratic, wings almost beating singly. Beware infrequent Swifts with white patches.

VOICE Screeching whistle "*scrrreeee*", female higher pitched than male, often in duet.

Locally common summer migrant, most Apr–Sep (80,000 pairs in UK, declining)

to Africa

Aerial; breeds in old buildings; feeds over open space, woodland, water.

dark

ADULT

white

JUVENILE

larger chin patch

ADULT

dark lores

blacker wings than adult

pale feather edges

ADULT/1ST-SUMMER pale covert fringes and worn, old primaries suggest 1st-summer

JUVENILE JUL–DEC

white lores

face largely pale

Rare swifts

Pallid Swift
Apus pallidus
16–18 cm | WS 39–44 cm

Like Swift (*p. 339*): **scythe-like wings; browner, paler midwing** and **darker 'saddle'** (obscure in poor light). Beneath, paler hindwing, larger whitish throat, dark mask. Pale feather edges give **barred/mottled effect** close-up in good light, otherwise 'muddy' at best. Mottled body vital to exclude pale juvenile Swift.

IN FLIGHT, silhouette like Swift but slightly blunter wingtips; wider head; broader rear body; tail blunter (outer two pairs of feathers nearly equal, outermost longer on Swift).

Vagrant from S Europe: <100 records (<5 Ireland), Mar–Nov, often long after Swifts have gone. Scattered.

Needle-tailed Swift
(White-throated Needletail)
Hirundapus caudacutus
19–21 cm | WS 50–54 cm

Big, stocky, sabre-winged swift; very dark except for pale back, **white throat, white 'U'-shape under tail**.

Vagrant from Asia: <10 records (1 Ireland), May–Jun. Scattered.

Pacific Swift
Apus pacificus
17–18 cm | WS 40–44 cm

Large swift: long, forked tail held in tight point; white throat; **narrow curved white rump**; plain wings.

Vagrant from Asia: <10 records (Britain), Jun–Oct. Most E coast.

PALLID SWIFT

ADULT

large throat patch, **greyish/dark** lores

slightly blunter wingtips

ADULT

more contrast between paler inner and darker outer primaries

PALLID SWIFT

dark mask, stands out against paler head

in good light paler midwing contrasts with darker 'saddle'

ADULT

SWIFT

JUVENILE (JUL–DEC)

large throat patch, **white** lores

ADULT

little contrast

SWIFT

plainer wings/back

ADULT

NEEDLE-TAILED SWIFT

PACIFIC SWIFT

SWIFT (*p. 339*)

white under tail

white rump

forked tail

ADULT

ADULT

ADULT

ALPINE SWIFT

white rump

square tail

ADULT

ADULT

LITTLE SWIFT

Alpine Swift
Apus melba
20–23 cm | WS 57 cm

Shape and flight of Swift but large, powerful bird. Long-winged, broader-bodied than Swift (*p. 339*), more clearly **brown**, with **dark breast-band** above **white belly** (white chin harder to see). Blackish under forked tail. Rump/lower back **broader, paler, brighter brown** than any Swift. Beware infrequent Swifts with patches.

VOICE Loud, mechanical, chattering "*chi-it-it-it-it-it*", unlikely Britain/Ireland.

Vagrant from S Europe: 15–25 per year (<100 records Ireland), most Mar–Jul. Scattered.

Little Swift
Apus affinis
12–13·5 cm | WS 32–34 cm

Small, stocky, blackish swift, with square tail, quite broad, blade-like wings; white throat; wide white rump like House Martin (*p. 343*) (but black beneath).

Vagrant from N Africa: <30 records (<5 Ireland), May–Sep. Scattered.

Chimney Swift 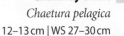NT
Chaetura pelagica
12–13 cm | WS 27–30 cm

Small, chunky swift; broad outerwing, narrow base; short, square-cut tail. Dusky grey-brown, slightly paler throat.

Vagrant from N America: <40 records (<20 Ireland, all in two influxes), Jul–Oct. Scattered, most near coast.

ADULT

ADULT

CHIMNEY SWIFT

Swallow

Hirundo rustica Ⓘ

17–21 cm (incl. tail 3·0–6·5 cm);
juv. 14–15 cm | WS 29–32 cm

◁○▷ Rare swallows (*p. 345–346*)

Locally common summer migrant, Mar–Nov (about 1 million pairs in Britain and Ireland); rare in winter

from/to
N and W
Europe

from/to
S Africa

to
S Africa

Villages, farmland, freshwater, coasts

Sleek, slender, fork-tailed bird with tiny legs; fluent, slinky flight. Perches on branches, wires, TV aerials. **Dark throat** rules out House Martin, **pale underside** unlike quite different Swift (*p. 339*).

Forehead and chin deep red. Tail **deeply forked; white spots** from beneath or when spread. JUVENILE paler throat, shorter tail. IN FLIGHT, often low over fields, water; swerves, wings swept back. In wind and rain, often **in lee of hedgerows or trees**. Action similar to quicker, lighter Sand Martin (*p. 344*), often rises with momentary pause, or sudden sideways twist. On sunny days, chirruping groups at much greater height.

VOICE Calls sharp "*vit vit*", Goldfinch-like chirrupy "*shrrip*", "*tritt-it*"; song rapid musical twitter with quick trill or rattle.

deep blue above, often looks black

long, thin tail streamers

ADULT ♂

ADULT ♀

♀ slightly shorter, broader tail streamers

deep peachy-buff to white beneath

JUVENILE

short tail streamers

ADULT ♂

JUVENILE

Nests in outbuildings, not under open eaves; nest has open top, not side entrance.

House Martin

Delichon urbicum

13·5–15 cm | WS 26–29 cm

Small aerial bird: size between Sand Martin (*p. 344*) and Swallow. **Forked tail**, **triangular wings**, **white rump**.

bar

> **Storm Petrel** (*p. 97*),
> Rare swallows (*p. 345–346*),
> Little Swift (*p. 341*)

From below, **white throat**, **dark underwing**. JUVENILE duller rump (see Red-rumped Swallow (*p. 345*)), blackish areas duller. Short white legs visible when perched, or collecting mud for nest. Round **mud nests under eaves** (Swallow nest usually on support in sheltered situation, Swift (*p. 339*) nests hidden). IN FLIGHT, stiffer than Swallow, less fluent, **more likely circling above house height** (but the two often mix high up or over water). Wings stiffly outstretched in glide; angled back, fluttered in active flight. Comes to puddles, perches on roofs and wires, but less likely on TV aerials, bare branches than Swallow.

VOICE Short, dry, chattering "*trrrit, trri-it*"; twittering song.

Locally common summer migrant, Mar–Oct (379,000 pairs, plus 730,000 birds in Ireland)

from/to N and W Europe

from/to Africa

to Africa

Suburbs, rural areas, lakes

white rump

ADULT

white throat

ADULT

JUVENILE

ADULT

Nest typically under eaves/gable end of building, quarter-sphere with closed top, small entrance.

Small groups gather mud with which they build their nest: a wet patch is essential for successful breeding.

Sand Martin

Riparia riparia ❶ 536

12–13 cm | WS 26–29 cm

👁 Rare swallows (*p. 345–346*)

👁 Rare swallows (*p. 345–346*)

Smaller than Swallow
(*p. 342*), **brown and white**, brown breast-band.

At distance looks dark, darker breast/underwing, **small white belly**; white lower face (breast-band/white throat harder to see). Perches (especially in autumn) along dead branches/wires over water, sometimes swarms on leafy bush or tree.

VOICE Dry, light, short twittering, rasping notes; trill or sharp "*chirr*" if alarmed.

Locally common summer migrant, Mar–Oct (164,000 pairs Britain, plus 600,000 birds Ireland)

to Africa

Near/over water, quarries, earth/sand cliffs

ADULT

ADULT

ADULT

breast-band

Often swoops around nest holes in earth/sand cliff, anywhere from soft cliff above beach or large sand quarry to roadside cutting; uses artificial banks with pipes for burrows.

IN FLIGHT, wings swept back, rather triangular, tail inconspicuous, shortish, slim, forked. Quick, flickery, fluttery arrowhead, upward swoops and twists, quickening rise/stall at intervals, little or no gliding. In poor weather, flocks flutter low over water, head to wind.

ADULT

ADULT

Red-rumped Swallow
Cecropis daurica
14–19 cm (incl. tail 3–5 cm)
WS 27–32 cm

Obvious swallow; pale rump. IN FLIGHT **stiffer, less elegant** than Swallow (*p. 342*), straighter wings, steadier glide; thicker tail streamers often in single 'spike'. **Blue cap surrounded by rufous**, rusty nape useful; **cheeks pale**. Blue-glossed upperparts; tail has white spots. **Rump pale rusty-red** or orange-buff, often whiter against tail. Underside pale (**no dark throat**). **Black patch under tail** square against pale belly, giving 'stuck on tail' look from below. JUVENILE rump whiter and dull; pale nape, black under tail; pale underwings (grey on House Martin (*p. 343*)).

VOICE Call useful – short, hard "*djuit*".

Rare migrant from S Europe, winters Africa: 30–60 per year, (<50 records Ireland), most Mar–May, in S England.

ADULT SWALLOW
dark rump
red chin and forehead
ADULT
ADULT

ADULT
Rufous collar broken by blue nape
Uniform rufous rump
unbroken rufous nape
Streaked below

'Asian Red-rumped Swallow'
race *daurica* or *japonica*
Vagrant: 1 record (Britain), Jun.

ADULT

Crag Martin
Ptyonoprogne rupestris
14–15 cm | WS 27–32 cm

Rather like large, thickset, greyish Sand Martin but underside drab greyish, no breast-band; wide tail has row of square **pale spots across tip**; dark wedge on underwing coverts.

Vagrant from S Europe: <10 records (Britain), Apr–Dec. Scattered.

contrasting dark underwing coverts
ADULT
ADULT
tail spots
all grey, no breast-band
ADULT

345

Vagrant from N America: <15 records (1 Ireland), Oct–Nov. Scattered, near coast.

Vagrant from N America: <5 records (Britain), May, Oct. Scattered, near coast. Freshwater.

Cliff Swallow *Petrochelidon pyrrhonota*
13 cm | WS 28–30 cm

Small, thickset martin; tail shallowly forked, rounded when spread; upperside dark, except pale rufous rump and white collar, pale forehead; underside white, throat and cheeks rufous.

Tree Swallow *Tachycineta bicolor*
15 cm | WS 30–32 cm

Very like House Martin (*p. 343*) but no white rump; more greenish-blue above.

1ST-WINTER

pale rufous rump

JUVENILE/1ST-WINTER

dark rump

1ST-WINTER

JUVENILE/1ST-WINTER

Purple Martin *Progne subis*
20 cm | WS 39–41 cm

Large, swallow-like; perches on wires. JUVENILE dark brown, dark mask, some bluish sheen; paler below, whitish on belly. MALE all iridescent dark purple-blue, paler on flight feathers; FEMALE paler beneath; IMMATURE browner, blue on shoulders, paler, streaked below.

1ST-WINTER

Vagrant from N America: 1 record (Britain), Sep (1 old record Ireland not officially accepted). Near coast.

LARKS, PIPITS and WAGTAILS GROUP ID colour/form | tail length | bill size

Largely ground-dwelling birds that walk, do not hop; larks often crouch low to the ground.
10 larks: 2 resident, 1 winter visitor,1 scarce migrant; the rest vagrants.
11 pipits: 3 breed (2 resident (1 with migrant/scarce breeding race), 1 summer visitor (with migrant races)1 vagrant.
4 wagtails with several distinct races: 2 resident, 1 summer visitor; 1 vagrant.

STREAKY, BROWN (NB the distinctive Shore Lark (p. 350) and Black Lark (p. 353) not streaky brown)

Two unrelated groups of ground birds need to be separated. Streaky brown birds on the ground could include finches, buntings, sparrows (pp. 474–509) and the Dunnock (p. 368) but these all **hop**.
Larks and pipits **walk**, so anything that hops two-footed can quickly be separated from a lark or pipit.

LARK ID head, tail, wing pattern **PIPIT ID** head, back, rump and flank patterns | call	**Lark ageing/sexing**

Lark ageing/sexing

Sexes alike, most with no seasonal change; juveniles distinct but 1st-winter after head/body moult practically indistinguishable unless in the hand.

Larks (pp. 348–353) stockier, bulkier, shorter-tailed than pipits; thicker, more triangular bills; many have at least an impression of a crest (flattened or raised as upstanding triangle).
Most have pale-centred tails, dark each side inside white edges.
Pipits (pp. 354–361) also have white-sided tails, similar to many buntings. **Larks** tend to have larger scapular feathers with slightly drooped, half-dark, half-pale patterns, not so evident on pipits.
Pipits mostly slighter, longer tailed, thin-legged and finer-billed. None have even a hint of a crest.

MEADOW PIPIT

SKYLARK

BLACK/WHITE or COLOURED

WAGTAIL ID head and other plumage details | call	**Wagtail ageing/sexing**

Wagtail ageing/sexing

Sexes differ, and seasonal changes marked; juveniles distinct; 1st-winter after moult may be identifiable, but plumages complex, variable.

Wagtails (pp. 362–365) pipit-like form, strongly patterned, with long/very long black tails with broad white sides. Pied and Grey Wagtails resident, Yellow Wagtail a summer visitor, Citrine Wagtail a rarity. White Wagtail, a race of Pied, is a migrant. Wagtails prefer open spaces often close to water, or around livestock, and walk on the ground; Pied Wagtails are also urban birds.

PIED WAGTAIL

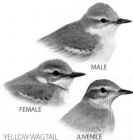

MALE

FEMALE

YELLOW WAGTAIL   JUVENILE

347

Woodlark

Lullula arborea **535**

13·5–15 cm | WS 27–30 cm

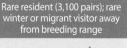

Rare larks (*p. 353*)

Rare resident (3,100 pairs); rare winter or migrant visitor away from breeding range

Small, neat, rounded bird; broad wings, **very short tail**. Feeds in short heather (looks pale against dark vegetation) or cropped grass/clear-felled areas with bare, sandy patches (where very inconspicuous). **Calls** draw attention. Creeps, crouches, leaps up at close range, bounding off before dropping out of sight.

Whitish stripes over eyes meet on nape. Short crest flat or raised as blunt triangle. Cheeks bright, edged darker. **White/black/buff patch on edge of closed wing**. JUVENILE pale, loopy feather edges on upperparts.

VOICE Quiet, or loud: clear "*t'loo-ee*" (emphasis on second syllable, falling at end). Song melodic, pure series of repeated notes: "*loo-loo-loo, leeu leeu leeu, toodl-oodl-oodl, tlui tlui tlui tlui*", from perch or very high, circling song flight before steep, silent plunge; often sings at night.

Heaths, clear-felled forestry

ADULT

IN FLIGHT, tail short; white 'corners'; **no white trailing edge** on rounded wing, dark/pale patch on leading edge easy to see.

patch

ADULT

short tail; white 'corners'

wings rounded

white-black-white patch on edge of wing

scaly forehead/crown

JUVENILE

pale, 'loopy' feather edges

striped crown

ADULT

Skylark

Alauda arvensis  race *scotica* Ⓘ 535

16–18 cm | WS 30–36 cm

👁 Rare larks (*p. 353*), rare 'large' pipits (*p. 360–361*)

Locally common resident (1.7 million pairs Britain, plus 365,000 birds in Ireland), winter visitor

Streaky ground bird (see Corn Bunting (*p. 503*)): almost size of Starling (*p. 372*). **Whitish rear edge to wing**, **streaked breast**, **blunt crest**.

Breast streaked (paler centre, wears whitish in summer); white belly. JUVENILE darker, coarsely marked. **Walks** on ground, in open space away from hedge/trees.

VOICE Call chirruping "*chrrup*" invariably when flushed, thinner with height/distance; winter flocks give high, thin whistles. Song **unbroken outpouring** of fast trills.

IN FLIGHT, wings broad, angular, narrow tips; whitish trailing edge. Tail quite long, dark either side of pale centre, **broad white sides**.

Winter flocks low over fields; migrants high, in long, straggling lines (autumn or snow-driven in winter), revealed by **frequent calls**.

from/to N and W Europe

Wide range of habitats with open ground; winter flocks in lowlands

ADULT

longer tail; white sides

wings with narrow tips

raised crest short and blunt

ADULT

ADULT

Sings in rising hover as if on string before diving to the ground; deeper notes are lost at distance, leaving a thin, silvery thread of sound.

JUVENILE

Widespread race is *arvensis*; race *scotica* sometimes recognised (Scotland, NW England, Ireland); race *intermedia* is a historical vagrant from Asia (Ireland); grey 'Eastern Skylarks', races *cantarella*, *intermedia* or *dulcivox* are suspected but as they intergrade identification in Britain and Ireland unlikely.

ADULT

Shore Lark

Eremophila alpestris 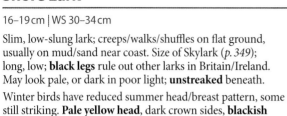 535

16–19 cm | WS 30–34 cm

Slim, low-slung lark; creeps/walks/shuffles on flat ground, usually on mud/sand near coast. Size of Skylark (*p. 349*); long, low; **black legs** rule out other larks in Britain/Ireland. May look pale, or dark in poor light; **unstreaked** beneath.

Winter birds have reduced summer head/breast pattern, some still striking. **Pale yellow head**, dark crown sides, **blackish mask**. Breast-band narrow, browner band beneath, or broader blackish chest patch (clear black in spring/summer).

VOICE Short, simple, squeaky "*eeh*", "*tseep*" or "*ee-du*".

Rare winter visitor (about 75 per year, 25 in Ireland): Oct–Apr

from Scandinavia

Coastal marshes, tidelines, occasionally ploughed fields

IN FLIGHT, like large pipit/small, slender thrush as much as lark: tapered wings; quick, easy, swerving flight. Fairly uniform except tail: pale centre, black sides, white outer edge.

ADULT

ADULT ♂

intensity of yellow and black variable

ADULT OCT–NOV

Short-toed Lark *Calandrella brachydactyla* 535 Rare larks (*p. 353*)

14–16 cm | WS 26–31 cm

Small, pale, round-headed lark; head pattern like female House Sparrow (*p. 476*). Streaked crown, pale wingbar, white underside and thickish, triangular bill.

Yellowish-brown, duller in spring. Dark or rufous **cap above whitish stripe**; small **dark/streaky patch at side of chest** (often hidden unless stretching up; may join as faint streaks across chest). **Unmarked underside. Dark spots across upperwing** (median coverts), thin pale wingbar (greater coverts), long tertials covering closed wingtip (no obvious primary projection). Often pale with contrasted dark/light bands across closed wing, crouched on open ground.

VOICE Calls dry, chirruping "*drit*", "*chrrit*" or "*chirrrip*", recalling House Martin (*p. 343*) or snatch of Linnet (*p. 486*), or a hard, sparrowy "*chip chip*".

Rare migrant from S Europe, winters Africa: 15–25/year (>75 records Ireland), spring and autumn; rarely overwinters. Mainly in E and S, near coast. Sandy ground, short grass.

IN FLIGHT, no white trailing edge unlike Skylark (*p. 349*); tail pale in centre, sides darker, outer edge thinly white.

broad white edge — **SKYLARK**

whitish trailing edge

SHORT-TOED LARK

thin white edge

no white trailing edge

dark median coverts contrast with rest of wing

ADULT

dark neck patch revealed as head is raised

'drooped' streaks typical lark pattern

squats, horizontal, pale and nondescript

neat, rounded feather edges above

long tertials cover closed wing

ADULT

1ST-WINTER

Larks in flight

Larks fly with bursts of wingbeats but flight is much less undulating than finches, and stronger than smaller pipits and buntings. Some have distinctive patterns above or below their broad wings, more useful than most of their tail patterns: look especially for presence or absence of pale trailing edges.

Larks in flight – summary of key features			
	Underwing	Trailing edge	Tail
Woodlark	whitish; NB UPPERWING black/white patch	plain	short; **white 'corners'**
Skylark	whitish	whitish (lacking in some worn birds)	long; white edges
Crested	**rusty**	plain	long; **brownish** edges
White-winged	**black/white**	**white; broad**	long; white edges
Calandra	**blackish**	**white; thick**	short; **white edges**
Bimaculated	**grey**	plain	short; **white tip**

NB Both **Black Lark** and **Shore Lark** are distinctive; the **short-toed larks** both have a plain trailing edge and thin white-sides to the tail

SHORE LARK

rusty

whitish

CRESTED LARK

BLACK LARK

worn plumage

WHITE-WINGED LARK

SKYLARK

whitish

WOODLARK

LESSER SHORT-TOED LARK

SHORT-TOED LARK

Vagrant from Iberia: 1 record (Britain), May. S coast. Grassland.

Lesser Short-toed Lark

Alaudala rufescens

14 cm | WS 26–31 cm

Like Short-toed Lark (*p. 351*) but streaked breast-band, two wingbars; **wingtip projects beyond tertials on closed wing**.

VOICE Distinct fast, buzzing "*d-r,r,r*" call.

SHORT-TOED
none/minimal

long

LESSER SHORT-TOED

ADULT

Vagrant from S Europe: <30 records (Britain), Apr–Jun, Nov. Most in S. Open ground.

Crested Lark

Galerida cristata

17–19 cm | WS 29–38 cm

Like bright, pale Skylark (*p. 349*) with short tail, **longer crest** raised in **pointed triangle**. IN FLIGHT, **plain wings** (rusty beneath); **brownish outer tail feathers**.

SKYLARK
crest never 'pointy'

ADULT

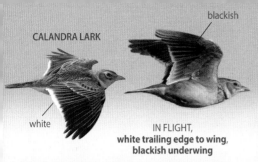

CALANDRA LARK

blackish

white

IN FLIGHT, white trailing edge to wing, blackish underwing

RARE LARKS

IN FLIGHT, **no white trailing edge, greyer underwing**

BIMACULATED LARK

grey

plain

Vagrant from S Europe: <20 records (Britain), Apr–May. Scattered). Open ground.

Vagrant from Middle East: <5 records (Britain), May, Jun, Sep. Scattered. Open ground.

Calandra Lark

Melanocorypha calandra

18–20 cm | WS 38–44 cm

Big, thick-billed lark with pale stripe over eye, dark cheek, blackish neck patch (compare with much smaller Short-toed Lark (*p. 351*); **white sides** to tail.

lores same tone as crown

ADULT

Bimaculated Lark

Melanocorypha bimaculata

16–18 cm | WS 33–36 cm

Like Calandra Lark, but with more contrasting head pattern and more obvious eyestripe; lores darker than crown; **white tip** to tail.

lores darker than crown

ADULT

Vagrant from Asia: <5 records (Britain), Apr, Jun. Scattered). Coastal heath/grassland.

Vagrant from Asia: <5 records (Britain), Oct–Nov. S and E. Coastal grassland.

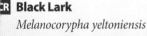

Black Lark

Melanocorypha yeltoniensis

18–20 cm | WS 37 cm

Large, stocky, **blackish**; fresh feathers edged pale; thick, whitish bill. FEMALE (not recorded Britain) dull, pale, grey-brown with blacker wingtips.

IN FLIGHT, dark underwing, blackish coverts.

ADULT ♂

White-winged Lark

Alauda leucoptera

17–19 cm | WS 35 cm

Like rufous Skylark (*p. 349*) with chestnut shoulder. Bright white beneath, white collar. MALE has rufous forehead and shoulder patch.

IN FLIGHT, **broad white band across hindwing.**

ADULT

Tree Pipit

Anthus trivialis ●

14–16 cm | WS 22–25 cm

👁 Rare pipits (*p. 358-361*)

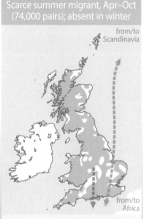

Scarce summer migrant, Apr–Oct
(74,000 pairs); absent in winter

from/to
Scandinavia

from/to
Africa

Heaths, plantations, woodland
edges

Summer pipit: see Meadow
Pipit. Typical of woodland/heathland edge, clear-fell bordering
conifers and adjacent rough grassy areas.

Yellower than average Meadow Pipit; whiter belly; yellowish
breast streaked black, streaks **few and thin on flanks**.
Compared with similar Meadow Pipit: head pattern sometimes
stronger (dark line behind eye, hint of pale ear spot); bill a little
thicker; hind claw shorter (especially long on Meadow Pipit).
IN FLIGHT, song flight like Meadow Pipit but usually **starts and
finishes on perch** (sapling or high branch), also **sings from
tree**, song **ending with long rich notes**.

VOICE Call buzzy, abrupt, vibrant "*teeess*" or "*speeze*", or "*spiz*".
Song richer, more accomplished than Meadow Pipit; canary-like
trills, **long final notes** "*see-a see-a see-a seee-a*" characteristic.

ADULT

more tapered body, longer tail,
finer bill than larks

parachuting
display flight
down to tree

TREE PIPIT
flank streaks
noticeably finer
than breast
streaks

hind claw short
and curved

by autumn, difficult
to tell age

1ST-WINTER

Tree Pipit has
contrasting white belly;
Meadow Pipit more
uniform below

ADULT SPRING

NT Meadow Pipit

NT

Anthus pratensis  ● ❶

14–15·5 cm | WS 22–25 cm   🕐 Rare pipits (*p. 358-361*)

Small, streaky bird, walks on ground. See Tree Pipit, bigger Skylark (*p. 349*). Common all year; often flocks (Tree Pipit never does). Some yellower or more olive; whiter beneath in summer.

Head pattern diffuse, pale eyering often most striking. Back **softly streaked**. Flanks browner than Tree Pipit, with **long, dark streaks** (finer, sparser on Tree Pipit). **White sides to tail** like other pipits. Legs **orange-pink**; **long hind claw**. Keeps to ground, creeping/walking (finches hop/shuffle). IN FLIGHT, rises in **short, springy bounds**; winter flocks circle widely.

VOICE Thin, quick "*seeip-sip-sip*", stronger "*sip sip*". From flocks, short "*pip*" or "*pipit*". Song long, **simple trills**; from ground or in song flight: rises steeply, descends **to ground**, tail and wings in 'shuttlecock' shape.

Locally common resident (1·7 million pairs, plus 1·7 million birds in Ireland); migrant, winter visitor

from/to Greenland   from/to Iceland   from Scandinavia

Scandinavia

NW Africa

from/to NW Africa

Heaths, bogs, moors; in winter more lowland, fields, marshes *etc.*

MEADOW PIPIT
flank streaks similar thickness to breast streaks

ADULT

parachuting display flight down to ground

hind claw long, slightly curved

bright juvenile slightly more boldly streaked than dull, worn adult in summer; median covert centres more pointed, but by autumn usually difficult to tell age

1ST-YEAR [Apr]

overall colour varies individually and as feathers get duller and paler with wear

ADULT [Jun]

1ST-YEAR [Mar]

Rock Pipit

Anthus petrosus  race *petrosus*

15·5–17 cm | WS 23–28 cm ◁◎▷ Buff-bellied Pipit

Small, streaky, walks on
ground; thickset pipit, **dull, dark-legged**; long, **strong bill**;
slurred call. Two races, sometimes distinguishable.

Underside dull, **broad, blurred streaks** less sharp than Meadow
Pipit (*p. 355*). Legs dark red-brown or blackish. Head pattern
weak, except white eyering. In summer, on **rocks, cliffs, grassy
slopes above cliffs**; in winter piers, promenades.

VOICE Song, song flight and call resemble Meadow Pipit; call
'thicker', more slurred, "*feest*" or "*sfeep*", not so often tripled.

Locally common resident (50,000
pairs Britain, Ireland); winter visitor

from
Scandinavia

Rocky coasts; scarce migrant
inland, frequent winter visitor on
coasts beyond breeding range

parachuting
display flight

often
yellow
on bill

WINTER
race *petrosus*

SUMMER
race *petrosus*

greyer than in
winter; becomes
paler with wear

SPRING
race *petrosus*

pale stripe behind eye
short; often weak or
mottled

SPRING
race *littoralis*

SUMMER
race *petrosus*

In winter race
littoralis usually
inseparable from
race *petrosus*.

beware pale
individuals!

Scandinavian race *littoralis* on saltmarsh, lakes/reservoirs (vagrant, Ireland) autumn–spring. By spring, pale stripe
over eye, greyer nape, but vary individually and with extent of moult. Some greyer on head/upper back, flushed pink
on chest with few streaks: these are unlike British/Irish race *petrosus*, but very like Water Pipit.

Water Pipit *Anthus spinoletta*

15·5–17 cm | WS 23–28 cm

Very similar to Rock Pipit; usually shyer, likely to fly off if disturbed (Rock Pipit tends to flit along shore). Alert, wary, more upright.

Dark legs; white tail sides. IN WINTER **white throat between dark streaks**. Browner than Rock Pipit, **whiter below**, fewer streaks. **Dull white wingbars, whitish stripe over eye**. Legs often paler brown than Rock Pipit. IN SPRING, head **grey** with **white stripe over eye**, whitish chin; throat and breast **pale pink**. Few flank streaks; back plain brown. Upright, full-breasted; dark back, pinkish front, surprisingly like Wheatear (*p. 394*).

VOICE Between Rock Pipit and Meadow Pipit, loud "*tsweeep*" or slightly vibrant "*feest*", fuller, thicker, more slurred than Meadow Pipit.

Scarce, very local winter visitor from S/C Europe (190 per year, mostly Sep–Apr). Inland watersides and coastal lagoons or marshes

ROCK PIPIT

lores dark

race *petrosus*
WINTER

race *littoralis*
SPRING

🔊 Buff-bellied Pipit

SUMMER

AUTUMN/WINTER

Buff-bellied Pipit *Anthus rubescens*

15–16 cm | WS 23–28 cm

Like Water Pipit with colours and call of Meadow Pipit (*p. 355*) but **less streaked above** than Meadow Pipit, **more streaked on brighter buff below** than Water Pipit; legs dark. **Pale between eye and bill** (unlike Water or Rock Pipits).

VOICE Similar to Meadow Pipit but sharper, "*p-sip*".

Vagrant from N America: <100 records (<20 Ireland), most months, most Sep–Apr. Scattered). Waterside/reservoirs.

lores pale

AUTUMN/WINTER

Rare pipits

PIPIT FLIGHT CALLS at a glance

MEADOW PIPIT-LIKE

Meadow Pipit – thin, quick "*seeip-sip-sip*", stronger "*sip sip*". From flocks, short "*pip*" or "*pipit*".

Rock Pipit – as Meadow Pipit but more slurred, "*feest*" or "*sfeep*".

Water Pipit – between **Rock** and **Meadow** Pipits: a loud "*tsweeep*" or slightly vibrant "*feest*".

Buff-bellied Pipit – as Meadow Pipit but sharper, "*p-sip*".

TREE-PIPIT-LIKE

Tree Pipit – buzzy, abrupt, vibrant rather than grating, "*teeess*" or "*speeze*", or "*spiz*".

Olive-backed Pipit – "*teess*" or "*tizz*"; similar to **Tree** Pipit.

DISTINCTIVE

Red-throated Pipit – high, long, thin "*p'seeee!*", with strong start and finely-drawn finish, or quiet but explosive "*psee-see-see*".

Pechora Pipit – often silent on migration but occasionally a short, sharp, clicking "*dzep*".

HOUSE SPARROW-LIKE
(large pipits)

Richard's Pipit – throaty "*shrree*"; often softer, flatter or downslurred, "*shrroo*".

Tawny Pipit – harsh, slightly vibrant "*tsreeep*" or "*sfeep*" or shorter "*shilp*", sparrowy "*chwee*" and short "*chup*".

Blyth's Pipit – slightly higher than typical **Richard's Pipit**, less grating or rasping, "*pshiu*" or "*pshee*".

Autumn pipits from behind

Meadow and **Pechora Pipit** have **unmarked rumps**, relatively plain backs and thin wingbars.

Red-throated and **Pechora Pipit** have **marked rumps** and white streaks on the back.

Pechora Pipit has much broader wingbars and also a diagnostic longer wingtip projection.

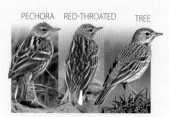

PECHORA   RED-THROATED   TREE

Red-throated Pipit *Anthus cervinus*

14–15 cm | WS 25–27 cm

Very rare migrant from Scandinavia: 8–12 per year, declining, spring and especially autumn. Mostly coastal.

Adults easy, juvenile hard to tell from Meadow Pipit (*p. 355*) except by call. Subtly stockier, broader-bellied, shorter-tailed than Meadow Pipit; bobs tail like wagtail.

ADULT **brick-red to pale red-pink face and throat** all year, weakest on females. More boldly streaked than Meadow Pipit; underside whiter with **black stripes**. **Rump streaked** (plain on Meadow Pipit). Bill **black and yellow**. JUVENILE like well-streaked Meadow Pipit, **greyer above, whiter below** than most, bold black stripes beneath. **Short streaks/spots on rump** useful. Two bright **pale stripes on back**; bolder white stripe over eye than average Meadow Pipit.

VOICE Call distinctive: high, long, thin "*p'seeee!*", or quiet but explosive "*psee-see-see*".

1ST-WINTER

ADULT

Olive-backed Pipit *Anthus hodgsoni*

14–15·5 cm | WS 24–27 cm

Vagrant from Asia: 10–20 per year, occasional larger influxes, mostly autumn. Coastal.

Typically in long grass, close to/under trees. Small, elegant pipit with bold patterns. Bobs tail like small, round wagtail, flying into branches or deep into cover if disturbed.

Upperside **greenish-olive with soft, subtle streaks**. Blackish line beside crown; wide, bright stripe over eye. Black line through eye cuts through drooping end of pale stripe, **creating isolated pale spot at back of cheek**. Breast cream to yellowish, **bold black streaks**. Legs very pale; bill pale at base.

VOICE Call like Tree Pipit's hoarse "*teess*" or "*tizz*".

Tree Pipit (*p. 354*) has a similar, but weakly defined, head pattern. Meadow Pipit (*p. 355*) head pattern weaker still.

TREE PIPIT

1ST-WINTER

isolated pale ear-spot

1ST-WINTER

Pechora Pipit

Anthus gustavi

539

14–15 cm | WS 23–26 cm

Vagrant from Asia: <150 records, Sep–Oct. Islands.

Small, boldly-streaked pipit with **primaries projecting beyond tertial tips**. Two **broad whitish stripes on back**, two white wingbars, buff breast above white belly.

VOICE Short, clicking call "*dzep*" infrequent.

Pechora Pipits can be very difficult to see well as they often spend a lot of time skulking in thick grass.

primaries project beyond tertials

1ST-WINTER

Large pipits

Three large, wagtail-like pipits, rare or very rare; **Richard's Pipit** in autumn the most likely. All fly up boldly, calling (calls exceedingly similar), and drop onto open ground (**Tawny Pipit**) or short grass (**Richard's Pipit** may hover briefly first).

Identification of large pipits – summary of key features	
Richard's Pipit	**Big, upright, long-legged; very long hind claw; pale between bill and eye;** white belly. 1ST-WINTER NEW ADULT-TYPE MEDIAN COVERTS **pointed** blackish centre blurs into browner fringe. VOICE Loud, cheeping, sparrowy "*speew*".
Tawny Pipit	**Wagtail shape;** wagtail-like bill; **short, arched hind claw; dark from bill to eye.** VOICE Thin, vibrant/rasping "*treeze*" or "*tsreep*".
Blyth's Pipit	Smaller, slightly shorter tail; weaker bill and legs, shorter hind claw than Richard's Pipit; buff belly. 1ST-WINTER NEW ADULT-TYPE MEDIAN COVERTS **blunt** blackish centre, sharp whitish fringe. Low, even "*shreeu*", diagnostic "*chup, chup*".

Richard's Pipit *Anthus richardi*

17–20 cm | WS 26–30 cm

Big, upstanding; long, strong legs (see Tawny Pipit). Often exaggeratedly upright, pear-shaped. Some orange-brown; others paler. Streaked like Skylark (*p. 349*); **pale between eye and bill**. Underside white, chest streaks **barely extend onto flanks**, unlike smaller Meadow Pipit (*p. 355*). Dark stripe from bill to blackish neck patch. Bill strong, thrush-like (finer on Tawny Pipit); very **long hind claw**. Walks steadily over grass, clambers through longer vegetation; may bob tail, confusingly like Tawny Pipit. IN FLIGHT, strong, bounding, leaping up and away if disturbed; may hover before settling.

VOICE Calls variable: loud, rough or grating, with rolled 'r'; sparrowy "*shree*" or "*speew*"; softer, flatter or downslurred, "*shrroo*". 'Explosive' shouted notes distinctive; quiet notes from undisturbed birds.

'Large' pipit hind claws

RICHARD'S very long

BLYTH'S medium–short, fine

TAWNY medium, arched

Blyth's Pipit and Richard's Pipit median and greater coverts
Pattern difficult to assess in the field; median coverts shown here:

JUVENILE clear-cut, pointed dark centres, buff sides, white tips.

1ST-WINTER NEW

RICHARD'S: pointed blackish centre blends into brown fringe

BLYTH'S: blunter, more distinct centre

◉ Blyth's Pipit

Vagrant/very rare migrant from Asia: 100–125 per year (>100 records Ireland), most months, mostly Sep–Nov. Occasionally winters. Scattered. Grassland.

ADULT

new median covert

paler birds very like Tawny Pipit

1ST-WINTER

Tawny Pipit *Anthus campestris*   **539**
15·5–18 cm | WS 25–28 cm

1ST-SUMMER

Wagtail-like; big, full-bodied, often on bare open ground, clearly large (stocky wagtail size) but a little smaller than Richard's Pipit, not often so upright or chesty looking. SPRING ADULT **pale, plain plumage**. Upperside dull clay-buff, wings darker with buff feather edges, **black spots across 'shoulder'**. **Blackish line from bill through eye**, dark stripe beside throat. JUVENILE streaked, like Richard's Pipit, soon becomes plainer, scattered streaks. Dark **stripe from eye to bill**. Generally colder, greyish-sandy, less rufous than Richard's Pipit. **Shorter, arched hind claw** (not easy in grass!).

VOICE Calls harsh, slightly vibrant "*tsreeep*" or "*sfeep*" or shorter "*shilp*", sparrowy "*chwee*" and short "*chup*" – some confusingly similar to Richard's Pipit.

Vagrant from S Europe: 7–15 per year, declining (<50 records Ireland), most Apr-May. S coast. Grasslands.

tends to be less upright than Richard's Pipit, more like Yellow Wagtail

1ST-WINTER

ADULT

Vagrant from Asia: <25 records (Britain), autumn. Most coastal, rare winter inland. Grassland.

Note, median coverts all juvenile – no new 1st-winter showing

1ST-WINTER

Blyth's Pipit *Anthus godlewskii*
15·5–17 cm | WS 23–28 cm

Big pipit, like Richard's Pipit; requires patience for identification (see table *opposite*). Slightly shorter legs, weaker bill, slightly shorter tail, more uniform underside, whiter wingbar: all difficult, comparative.

VOICE Crucial but hard to judge: slightly higher than Richard's Pipit, longer, less grating "*shreeu*". **Diagnostic "*chup chup*".**

Pied Wagtail

Motacilla alba race *yarrellii* race *alba*

16·5–19 cm | WS 28 cm

Long black-and-white tail, spindly black legs, white face with **black bib in summer, black chest-band in winter; distinctive calls**. Walks, runs, constantly bobs tail; bounding flight.

Two regular races: **Pied Wagtail** (race *yarrelli* – Britain/Ireland/near Continent) and **White Wagtail** (race *alba* – Continental Europe). Identification easier in spring, can be problematic in autumn/winter. **Rump colour** is the most consistent feature, but best identified to race using a suite of characters (see table and notes). Birds of any age can show mixed and/or intermediate features and are not safely identifiable to race.

👁 Imm. Citrine Wagtail (*p. 365*), Yellow Wagtail races (*p. 364*)

Common resident (290,000 pairs, plus 500,000 birds in Ireland). White Wagtail frequent migrant, most spring; rare breeder (1–5 pairs, northern isles)

alba from/to Iceland and Greenland

from/to Iberia and N Africa

some *yarrelli* to Iberia

Many habitats, including urban

Isolated black breast patch; extensive white face; large white wing patch with grey feather centres.

Asian race *leucopsis* 'Amur Wagtail' Vagrant: <5 records, Britain

♀ **dark grey** ♂ **black**

black

sooty

PIED WAGTAIL race *yarrelli*

WHITE WAGTAIL race *alba*

ADULT MALES MAR–AUG

grey

grey

grey

white/pale grey

border between black nape and grey back defined in ♂, diffuse in ♀

Identification of non-breeding Pied /White Wagtails

PIED race *yarrellii*

RUMP ♂ **black**; ♀ **dark grey**; UPPER TAIL COVERTS **black**; FOREHEAD **broad** white; FLANKS **dark grey**; BELLY white; often subtle grey spots or streaking; CHEST-BAND **wide**.

WHITE race *alba*

RUMP **grey**; UPPER TAIL COVERTS grey to black; FOREHEAD **narrow** white; FLANKS **white to pale grey**; BELLY bright white; rarely any grey markings; CHEST-BAND **narrow**.

ADULT FEMALES AUG–FEB

race *alba*

dark grey, often mottled black

race *yarrelli*

white

black

broad white

mid to dark grey

white (few pale yellow)

1ST-WINTERS JUL–FEB

olive-grey

olive-grey (♂ mottled with black)

narrow white

white to yellowish

race *alba*

dark grey, edged pale grey

pale grey at darkest

mottled olive cheek

dark grey

black, edged white

dark grey

race *yarrelli*

WAGTAIL CALLS AND SONGS at a glance

Pied Wagtail	White Wagtail	Grey Wagtail	Yellow Wagtail	Citrine Wagtail
Cheery, loud, *"tsuwee"*, *"churree"* or *"churee-wee"*; also sharper *"tissick"*	As Pied Wagtail (without sharp *"tissick"*)	Explosive, metallic *"zi-zi"* or *"tsivit!"*; song rapid, sharp *"tiss-iss-iss"* and *"si-si-si"*	Sweet *"tsee"* or *"schlee"*, loud *"sfeesp"* or *"sureee"*; song weak repetition of short, slurred notes	Loud, slightly grating *"zrrip"*, but 'Black-headed' Yellow Wagtail (race *feldegg*) similar

Grey Wagtail

Motacilla cinerea

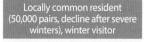

Locally common resident (50,000 pairs, decline after severe winters), winter visitor

17–20 | WS 25-27 cm

Small, elongated, walking, tail-bobbing ground/waterside bird: wagtail with **longest tail**; only one with **yellow found in winter**. Legs **short and pale** (other wagtails' longer, black).

Slate-grey above; very long, **white-sided tail**. **Rump yellow-green; yellow under tail**. Lively, active, bobbing and flirting long tail, often on rocks beside fast-flowing river, tree-lined streams with rapids, weirs *etc.* MALE black chin in summer, yellow underside. FEMALE whiter or mixed black/white throat, paler underside. JUVENILE/1ST-WINTER pink-buff beneath, whiter flanks, **yellow vent**. Flight deeply undulating. Easily disturbed – visits to garden ponds often short, noticed by **distinctive call**.

Clean rivers, mill streams; widely scattered outside breeding season, visiting garden ponds, town-centre rooftop puddles

pale stripe behind eye short; often weak or mottled

♂ WINTER

JUVENILE

some females have dark marks on throat.

ADULT ♂ SUMMER

ADULT ♀

Yellow Wagtail

Motacilla flava race flavissima race flava race thunbergi   538

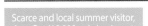
Scarce and local summer visitor, Apr–Oct (19,000 pairs); migrant

to W Africa

Wet meadows, cereal fields; migrant elsewhere; absent winter

 Citrine Wagtail

15–16 cm | WS 25 cm

Slender bird, spring to autumn (Grey Wagtail (*p. 363*)) all year). Several races recorded (*opposite*), which show considerable variation, hybridize and intergrade; but all have same character.

MALE green above, **yellow face and underparts** – no other small bird so **yellow**, without streaks, **walking on ground**. Spindly **black legs** (pale on Grey Wagtail, Yellowhammer (*p. 500*)). FEMALE greyer/browner/olive; pale wingbars; **yellow-buff below**. JUVENILE brownish above, buff below (yellower under tail). Dark moustache, stripes beside throat, narrow bib (see juvenile Pied Wagtail (*p. 362*)). Two whitish wingbars; **long whitish lines on black wing. Shorter tail than Pied Wagtail**, but **broad white tail sides**. IN FLIGHT, easy, quick; **long, deep undulations**.

VOICE Sweet "*tsee*" or "*schlee*", loud "*sfeesp*" or "*sureee*" from perch. Song weak repetition of short, slurred notes.

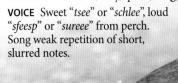

ADULT ♂

ADULT ♀

JUVENILE/ 1ST-WINTER

'Eastern' Yellow Wagtail
Motacilla flava tschutschensis
16 cm | WS 25 cm

Vagrant from Asia: <5 records (Britain): Oct, Dec

possible 'Eastern' Yellow Wagtail

1ST-WINTER

Treated as a race of Yellow Wagtail here, but considered a full species by some authorities. 'Grey' Yellow Wagtails can occur in western races; eastern FEMALE may be contrasted grey-and-white but 1ST-WINTER tinged olive/yellow. Identification not possible without DNA evidence.

Races of Yellow Wagtail
Males in spring can usually be identified. Females/juveniles may look unlike British birds, but most probably not identifiable. Hybrids and intergrades throw up problems.

British
race *flavissima*
summer breeder Apr–Oct.
Green head; yellow over
eye, yellow throat.

Ashy-headed
race *cinereocapilla*
rare, most Apr–May; has
bred.
Cap blue-grey, no white
stripe; chin white.

Blue-headed race *flava*
regular spring; has bred.
Cap grey-blue; cheeks
darker; white over eye; chin
yellow.

Grey-headed
race *thunbergi*
rare spring/autumn.
Cap dark grey, nape paler,
blacker cheek; chin yellow;
back grey-green,
wings browner.

'Channel Wagtail' –
hybrid *flavissima* × *flava*;
rare. Cap and cheeks pale
blue-grey; white stripe over
eye; chin white.

Black-headed
race *feldegg*
vagrant (<25 records,
most May). Cap black; chin
yellow; back bright green.
Call harsh "*tsee-rr*".

Citrine Wagtail *Motacilla citreola*

16 cm | WS 25 cm

MALE obvious: grey above, yellow on head and underside, **black band on hindneck**. FEMALE/AUTUMN JUVENILE/WINTER birds difficult, very like some Yellow Wagtails. Citrine Wagtail has **broader white wingbars** and tertial fringes, pale area between eye and bill, **pale band all round** dark cheek, **white** (not yellowish) under tail.

VOICE Alarm call helps: harsh, loud, slightly grating "*zrrip*", but 'Black-headed' Yellow Wagtail (race *feldegg*) similar.

JUVENILE/
1ST-WINTER

ADULT ♂

ADULT ♀

Vagrant from Asia: <350 records
(<50 Ireland), few spring, most
Sep–Oct. Most near coast.
Marshy fringes.

365

DIPPERS, ACCENTORS, WRENS, ORIOLES, STARLINGS, WAXWINGS

ID   each type has a distinct form and plumage features

A mixture of species that do not fit neatly into other groups.
1 dipper with several distinct races: 2 races resident, 1 race rare winter visitor.
1 wren with several distinct races: 1 mainland, 4 island races; and 1 winter visitor from continent.
2 starlings: 1 resident; one rare but regular migrant.
2 waxwings: 1 irruptive winter visitor; 1 vagrant.

Dippers (*p. 367*) are closely confined to fast, clean rivers. They 'dip' by bouncing up and down as they stand, as if on springs, and are the only small songbirds to walk into water, swim and dive.

Wrens (*pp. 369–370*) are tiny, round, barred brown birds, with short, often cocked, tails, tiny wings and loud, trilling songs. They are widespread, from low scrub to treetops.

Accentors (*pp. 368, 375*) are a small family, only one of which is regular in Britain and Ireland, the widespread Dunnock. They are somewhat chat-like but move more freely on the ground, rapidly flicking their wings and tail.

Golden Orioles (*p. 371*) are exceedingly inconspicuous in dense foliage, but males have a rich, but very short song and are lemon yellow and black.

Starlings (*pp. 372–373*) are pointed-faced, square-tailed, active birds, walking and running more quickly than thrushes, obviously short-tailed. In flight, their triangular wings and short, square tails are distinct: you may see a single bird making a bee-line to a nest, or groups of anything from half a dozen to a million.

Waxwings (*pp. 374–375*) resemble starlings but are short-legged, short-billed and specialist berry-eaters in winter, visiting puddles to drink.

WAXWINGS

Ageing/sexing

Dipper, accentors, wren sexes similar; **orioles, starlings, waxwings** sexes recognisable.

Accentors and wren juveniles very similar to adults; **Dipper, orioles, starlings, waxwings** immatures different

DIPPER

WREN

DUNNOCK

STARLING

GOLDEN ORIOLE

Dipper

Cinclus cinclus ●

17–20 cm | WS 25–30 cm

Dark, dumpy, short-tailed; **white chest**; **always by water**. Blinks white membrane across eye. **Swims**/drifts buoyantly, **frequently dives** or walks into water. Flies off at least disturbance, or dashes past, following stream on jerky, **whirring** wings, **distinctive call**. Typically taut **bobbing** ('on springs') on rock or stony bank by running water. Nests under overhang; often flies through spray/ waterfalls.

ADULT black-brown, browner head, white chest, **rusty band** under belly (race *gularis*, Britain). JUVENILE dull and mottled, dark feather fringes on chest reduce contrast.

VOICE Call (often in flight) hard, thick, oddly rasping "*dzit*" or "*strit*". Song penetrates streamside noise: bright, prolonged, disjointed warble with varied whistles and trills.

Scarce and local resident (13,000 pairs); rare winter visitor from continental Europe

Streams, rivers, rocky lakesides in hilly country. In winter, occasional on lowland rivers, pools, coast

ADULT

IN FLIGHT, low, quick, whirring, slightly jerky; always over water.

ADULT

ADULT
race *gularis*

Race *hibernicus* (Ireland, W Scotland) has blacker back than race *gularis* and reduced rusty breast-band.

ADULT

JUVENILE

Race *cinclus* ('**Black-bellied**' **Dipper**), rare winter visitor from Europe, has black belly; darker head than race *gularis*.

Dunnock

Prunella modularis except races *modularis* and *hebridium* **538**

13–14·5 cm | WS 19–21 cm

👁 Alpine Accentor (*p. 375*)

Small, **dark**, **fine-billed** (see House Sparrow (*p. 476*), pipits (*pp. 354–361*)). **Creeps and shuffles**, legs flexed, tail flicked out-in. Often three/four, waving spread wings; sometimes higher, towards canopy.

Heavily streaked; **greyer face and underside**; dark streaks on flanks. Thin legs orange-brown. Eye reddish. JUVENILE more streaked beneath, spotted above, like juvenile Robin (*p. 388*) but darker, more striped, pale bar across darker wing. Eye dull.

VOICE Bright, even whistle, "*peeeh*" and thin, vibrant "*si-i-i-i-i-i*". Song fast, thin, high, slightly 'flat' warble, even speed and pitch. Shorter, less varied, less rambling than Robin.

Common and widespread resident (2·1 million pairs, plus 1·7 million birds in Ireland)

from W Europe

Clifftop scrub, woods, moorland thickets, to parks and gardens

ADULT
race *hebridium*

Race *hebridium* of Ireland and the Hebrides is browner than British race *occidentalis* (which is darker than race *modularis* (winter visitor from continental Europe)).

ADULT

untidy juvenile soon becomes almost indistinguishable from adult

tiny white tips to coverts (bird above) soon wear off (bird below)

JUVENILE

ADULT

Wren

Troglodytes troglodytes

 races *fridariensis* and *hirtensis*   races *hebridensis, zetlandicus* and *indigenus*   **537**

9–10·5 cm | WS 13–17 cm

Identification simple, but see Dunnock, Cetti's Warbler (*p. 405*). Tiny, rotund, vaguely warbler-like, often low in undergrowth, ditches, garden bric-a-brac, sometimes treetops.

Little variation with age, sex or season: warm brown, **barred crosswise**. **Pale stripe over eye**. Tail narrow, often (not always!) raised. Pops up from cover, calls irritably, dives back.

VOICE Short "*chek*", longer, rolling/rasping "*cherrrr*", irregular scolding rattle. Song loud and vibrant, sudden powerful, ringing, rapid warble with low, quick trill at or near the end.

Widespread and abundant resident (8 million pairs, plus 6 million birds in Ireland)

Anywhere from coastal cliffs to woods, gardens, heaths, moorland thickets; often marshes

WREN RACES
Race *indigenus* found throughout 'mainland' Britain.

Race *troglodytes* (winter migrant from Europe) is brighter and paler.

Local races on outlying islands: Shetland (*zetlandicus*), Fair Isle (*fridariensis*), Outer Hebrides (*hebridensis*) and St Kilda (*hirtensis*) are all more coarsely marked than *indigenus* found throughout 'mainland' Britain and Ireland; Shetland Wren especially so. St Kilda Wren most distinct, largest, palest and most barred and with a longer bill. Island races told by location.
(See p. 370 for races of Wren found in Britain and Ireland.)

JUVENILE/1ST-WINTER not practically separable except in the hand

ADULT

ADULT

A singing Wren is the image of intense effort: tail cocked, its body taut, swaying and vibrating.

The British and Irish races of Wren
6 races of Wren occur, 3 resident on island groups, 1 (Hebridean) migrates to Ireland, 1 (European) arrives from continental Europe in winter.

BRITISH/IRISH WREN race *indigenus*
Abundant: small, rufous; song loud, disjointed, mechanical; long trill

'EUROPEAN' WREN race *troglodytes*
Winter migrant from continental Europe: bright, pale, finely barred

FAIR ISLE WREN race *fridariensis*
Restricted to Fair Isle (10–52 pairs; on cliffs): paler than Shetland race, darker than mainland birds, neatly barred. Prefers sheltered gullies in coastal cliffs.

SHETLAND WREN race *zetlandicus*
Shetland only (common; on cliffs, rocky beaches): rufous, strongly barred, robust; song loud, short.

ST KILDA WREN race *hirtensis*
Restricted to St Kilda (200–230 pairs; around cliffs, rocks, ruins): palest, greyest, longest-billed race; song less mechanical, less shrill than *indigenus*.

HEBRIDEAN WREN race *hebridensis*
Outer Hebrides (common; migrates to Ireland): barred, like *indigenus* but song distinct, fluent, with high, sibilant trills.

Golden Oriole

Oriolus oriolus ● **535**

19–22 cm | WS 44–47 cm

One of Europe's brightest birds but hard to see in leafy canopy. Thrush-like form; more elongated, **longer wings**.

MALE instantly obvious, **pure yellow and inky black**. FEMALE yellow-green, faintly streaked; blackish wing, pale spot near edge; **blackish tail with yellow corners**, green-yellow rump (recalling Green Woodpecker (*p. 335*)). Dull pink-red bill, dark mark to eye (older birds brighter, more like male, but grey between eye and bill). JUVENILE greener, more heavily streaked.

VOICE Strained, harsh, gaspy "*eee-aahk*". **Song unmistakable** (a bit like very short snatch of best Blackbird (*p. 379*)): short, rich, fluty, whistling "*ee-dl-oo*", or "*dl'oo*", or "*ee-deeoo-dli-do*" repeated for long periods.

Very rare summer visitor (and breeder in E/S); rare spring/autumn migrant (100–150/year)

to C and S Africa

Tall leafy trees, especially poplars

IN FLIGHT, direct; steady wingbeats, no woodpecker-like undulations.

ADULT ♂

ADULT ♀

ADULT ♂

ADULT ♀

ADULT ♂

ADULT ♂

ADULT ♀

Starling

Sturnus vulgaris race *zetlandicus* **I** 537

19–22 cm | WS 35–40 cm

Short-tailed, spike-beaked; **walks/runs on ground**. Pre-roost gatherings swirl and dive in co-ordinated manoeuvres. Often hawks insects.

Brown-headed Cowbird (*p.517*), Daurian Starling (*p.523*)

ADULT black, **purple and green gloss**; buff feather edges on wings, around tail. Bill base blue on MALE; pink on FEMALE. In autumn/winter **large white spots overall**. Head whitish, **dark eyestripe**. Legs **orange-brown**. JUVENILE brown; **blackish, spiky bill**; **dark wedge** in front of eye. Develops white spots on black body, as head/neck fade, creating **dark body/pale head**.

VOICE Strident whistles, buzzing "*cheer*". Alarm sharp, clicking "*plik*". Song (puffed-out throat, waving half-open wings) prolonged rattling, whistling, warbling, mimicry; also, on perch or ground, long, rambling subsong.

Locally common resident (about 2 million pairs Britain and Ireland), temporarily abundant in winter (8·5 million birds, plus 2·7 million in Ireland); much decreased

from W Europe

Farmland, urban and suburban areas; also breeds in woodland

IN FLIGHT, **pointed head**, **square tail**, **triangular wings**.

ADULT WINTER

JUVENILE MOULTING

blue

pink

JUVENILE

ADULT ♀ SUMMER

ADULT ♂ SUMMER

Race *zetlandicus* (Shetland) has blacker juvenile plumage than birds in the rest of Britain or Ireland (race *vulgaris*).

ADULT WINTER

JUVENILE MOULTING JUL–OCT

JUVENILE MAY–AUG

black

Rose-coloured Starling *Pastor roseus*

19–22 cm | WS 37–42 cm

Basic starling form, behaviour, but **shorter, blunter bill**, softer, rounder look to head. ADULT unmistakable, **pink and black** with **ragged crest**. In winter pink areas washed brown. JUVENILE moults later than Starling so still unlike adult until late autumn. Pale beige-brown, paler still on rump and underside, buff fringes to all wing feathers. Note pale rump/dark tail/ dark wing contrast in flight (especially when ruling out not-infrequent sandy-coloured young Starling). Bill distinctively yellow with darker tip (blackish on young Starling). Bold dark eye in plain pale face without dark wedge. By late autumn, dull version of winter adult: grey-brown above, pinkish-buff below.

VOICE Calls like Starling but less harsh.

Very rare migrant from C Europe: 40–50 per year (<150 records Ireland), most May–Nov. Adults often in N/W late summer, juveniles coastal in S in autumn. Often with Starlings.

pale belly; short bill

JUVENILE

pale rump, darker wings

ADULT SUMMER

dull bill, pink areas sullied grey
in non-breeding plumage

ADULT WINTER

Summer adult brighter, cleaner pink than winter; pinker bill, legs.

pale brown MAY–OCT/
NOV (later in autumn than
juvenile Starling)

JUVENILE

yellow

Waxwing

Bombycilla garrulus

18–21 cm | WS 32–35 cm

👁 Cedar Waxwing

Scarce, irregular winter visitor, most Nov–Mar; periodic 'invasions' of 100s–1,000s, flocks

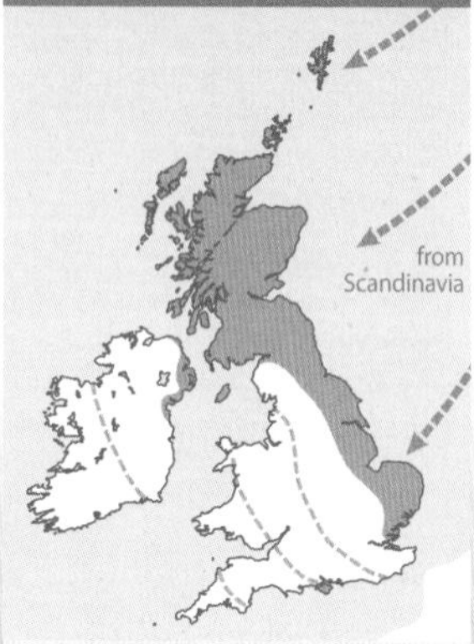

Unmistakable (apart from rare Cedar Waxwing); no other bird has similar crest. Starling (*p. 372*) similar in size, shape and flight action, but Waxwing more sedate (rarely on ground) although **acrobatic when feeding** (eats berries/shoots). Frequently comes to puddles to drink; flocks spend much time inactive in treetops.

Extent of white, yellow and red on wing and tail varies within and between ages and sexes, but **black bib**, black eyestripe, **grey rump** and **rufous under tail** all constant features.

VOICE Helps locate feeding or resting groups: far-carrying, silvery trill, "*sirrrr*". Greenfinch (*p. 483*) and Blue Tit (*p. 446*) can make remarkably similar sounds in spring but Waxwing calls, especially from flock, distinctive.

from Scandinavia

Ornamental shrubs, berry-bearing trees and bushes

IN FLIGHT, quick, dashing or swooping, with longer body profile/ bigger head than Starling.

1ST-WINTER ♂

ADULT ♀

diffuse edge to chin patch

shorter crest

sharp edge to chin patch

1ST-WINTER

ADULT ♂

thin white 'tips' on primaries

'tips' lacking

thick white 'tips' on primaries

Alpine Accentor *Prunella collaris*
16 cm | WS 30–32 cm

Like large Dunnock (*p. 368*), creeping around in similar fashion. **Two white bars** and **blackish band** across wing; yellow base to bill; broad **rufous streaks on flanks**.

Vagrant from C Europe: <50 records (Britain), most Mar–May, Nov–Jan. Most coastal. Rocky areas; on ground.

pale bill can be eye-catching

dark band on wing more obvious than rusty flank streaks

pale, spotted throat inconspicuous

ADULT

Cedar Waxwing *Bombycilla cedrorum*
18 cm | WS 22–30 cm

Like Waxwing, with which may associate: greyer, with **plainer wings**, yellower underparts, **white under tail**.

Vagrant from N America: <10 records (<5 Ireland), Sep–Oct, winter, Jun–Jul. Scattered. Trees/bushes with berries.

drab wing lacks prominent white flashes

JUVENILE/1ST-WINTER

ADULT

yellow beneath (unlike Waxwing)

Easily overlooked amongst Waxwings: pale beneath tail best mark.

THRUSHES, CHATS and WHEATEARS

THRUSH ID   overall plumage | breast pattern | head pattern | call and song
CHAT ID   overall plumage | tail and rump pattern | head patterns | call and song

20 thrushes: 3 common residents, 1 summer visitor,
2 widespread winter visitors that breed occasionally;
14 vagrants, 7 from Asia, 7 from North America.
24 chats and wheatears: 7 breed; 17 rare migrants/vagrants.

True thrushes (*pp. 378–385*) are mostly bigger, longer-tailed,
blunter-billed and rounder-headed than Starling (*p. 372*) and
move with a curious mix of walk and hop, or shuffling leaps,
not running so freely as Starlings. A typical action is the familiar
run–stop–listen–dig for a worm. Flocks are slower, looser, less
tightly coordinated than Starling, on the ground and in flight;
flying birds have shorter heads, rounder wings and longer tails.
While some are resident, Ring Ouzels are summer migrants,
Redwings and Fieldfares arrive in autumn and stay until spring,
and rarities tend to be autumn birds.

New World thrushes (*pp. 386–387*) include one, strikingly
coloured Blackbird-like species and five small, rounded, brownish
birds more or less spotted on the breast, which are more
secretive, and need to be separated from similar Asian chats. All
are very rare vagrants, occasionally in spring, mostly in autumn.

Chats (*pp. 388–393*) and **Wheatears** (*pp. 394–397*) are like very
small, rounded thrushes, with slim bills and rounded heads.
The Robin is a familiar yardstick: it is adaptable, common and
widespread all year in many habitats, whereas the Nightingale
is a summer visitor, with a restricted distribution tied to specific
habitats. Others are much less skulking birds of heath and moor,
preferring more open ground, stones and cliffs, or bushy places.
They tend to have strong patterns, at least on summer males,
although females and juveniles may be less easily distinguished.
Of these, the wheatears form a distinctive group on account of
their form and their black-and-white tail/rump patterns.

NIGHTINGALE

WHEATEAR

SONG THRUSH

REDSTART

Thrush and chat ageing/sexing

In some 'spotted' thrushes, sexes alike, in others they differ, as in most small chats/wheatears (but not Robin).
Some have seasonal changes, others do not.
Juveniles (shown here) distinct, duller, more spotted than adults. 1st-winter and 1st-summer (one-year-old) told from adult by juvenile wing and tail, which become pale and worn.

NIGHTINGALE JUN–AUG

ROBIN MAY–SEP

STONECHAT MAY–AUG
sexes alike in juvenile, plumage; differ by 1st-winter after moult

WHEATEAR JUN–JUL

REDSTART JUN–AUG

Post-juvenile moult
JUVENILE → 1ST-WINTER JUL–SEP: head, body, some wing coverts, from 4–6 weeks, completed at 2–3 months old.

1ST-WINTER ♂ JUL–MAR

1ST-WINTER ♀ JUL–MAR

1st-winter keeps juvenile flight feathers, tail, tertials, many wing coverts, all these browner, more worn than new feathers; difficult to separate from adult by next summer, when heavily worn.

ADULT ♀ SEP–JAN (fresh) JAN–AUG (worn)

ADULT ♂ SEP–FEB (fresh) FEB–AUG (worn)

Adult moult
ADULT: single complete moult (takes 50 days) JUL/AUG – SEP/OCT; fresh feathers have pale tips, lost by spring.

Rare thrushes, chats and wheatears

Rarities mostly have obvious similarity to common groups, so it is usually easy to tell 'a thrush', 'a wheatear' etc., but separating them, especially in 1st-winter plumage, can be challenging.

GREY-CHEEKED THRUSH – one of several similar New World thrushes, quickly bringing to mind 'thrush' (despite smaller size and reduced spotting compared with Song Thrush), but hard to tell apart.

POSSIBLE CONFUSION GROUPS

Dunnock (*p. 368*) fine bill, streaked flanks

Buntings (*pp. 496–509*) thick bill, most have white tail sides, upright on perch or horizontal on ground

Flycatchers (*pp. 438–442*) upright on very short legs; wide bill

Ring Ouzel

Turdus torquatus ●❶ 537

24–27 cm | WS 41–45 cm

Medium-small, dark thrush, recalling Blackbird and Mistle Thrush (*p. 381*). Wings and tail long, narrow. Flight fast, dashing, disappears over skyline. On ground, sleek, flat-backed; head held up, tail often raised. Favours berried bushes/scattered Rowans on heath/moorland edge in autumn.

MALE **black with white chest-band**. Pale edges to wing feathers create **silvery-grey panel on wing**. In autumn/winter pale lacy pattern beneath; white crescent drab. FEMALE duller, **pale feather edges** especially on wings and underside, duller chest-band.

VOICE Scolding, hard "*tuc tuc tuc*", rolling "*churr*". Song wild, loud, recalls Mistle Thrush, based around a few fluty whistles, phrases distinctly separated: "*tuleee tuleee; tiu-lee tiu-lee tiu-lee tiu-lee; schreet schreet*".

Scarce and local summer visitor, Mar–Nov (6,900 pairs, declining); widespread but uncommon on migration spring/autumn

from Scandinavia

to N Africa — to N Africa

Breeds uplands; migrant hills/ downs, coastal areas

underwing dull whitish, usually inconspicuous

1ST-WINTER ♂

1ST-WINTER FEMALE least distinctive; has dull pale wing panel, dull pale scaly feather edges, but only obscure breast-band.

ADULT ♂

ADULT ♀

Blackbird

Turdus merula 537

23·5–29 cm | WS 40–45 cm

👁 Black-throated Thrush (*p. 384*), Siberian Thrush (*p. 385*)

Very common resident (4-6 million pairs, plus 4·9 million birds in Ireland); migrant, winter visitor

Medium-sized, **long tail**.
Run-stop on lawn, edge of field. Double-footed shuffle, run/hop.
Raises tail when stops and after short flight, lowers it slowly.

MALE **black**; **yellow bill** (see Starling (*p. 372*)) and eyering.
1ST-WINTER MALE bill dark, wings brown. FEMALE **much darker** than
Song Thrush (*p. 380*). Throat often whitish, streaked chest but
never black spots on buff as Mistle (*p. 381*) or Song Thrushes.
Bill dark or **yellow with dark tip**. JUVENILE **rustier**, mottled
(male's tail blacker).

VOICE Vibrant, "*srreee*"; soft "*chook*"; loud "*chak*"; repeated
loud "*pink pwink pwink*" especially at dusk. Mild alarm
rhythmic, repeated endlessly; full alarm **clattering, screechy
rattle**. Song best dawn/dusk: long, musical, throaty and
flute-like, falls into rattles and squeaks.

from N and W Europe

Wide range: woods, fields, hedges, parks, gardens, thickets

ADULT ♂

pale outerwing in flight

1ST-WINTER ♂

JUVENILE ♂

dark bill

1ST-WINTER ♂

some juveniles are reddish below; males have blacker tail

1ST-WINTER ♀

NB: 1ST-SUMMER male is like adult but has browner wings

ADULT ♂

ADULT ♀

some individuals have pale breast-band

Song Thrush

Turdus philomelos ● except race *philomelos* **538**

20–22 cm | WS 33–36 cm

👁 Rare American thrushes (*p. 386–387*)

Small, compact thrush (compare with Redwing (*p. 383*), Mistle Thrush). Tends to fly into bush if disturbed (Mistle Thrush goes away over trees). Loud 'slap' of snail-smashing on stone characteristic.

Pale brown, creamy-buff below with **blackish 'V'-shaped spots** (Mistle Thrush bigger; pale-edged wing feathers; sharper, rounder spots). Head pattern weaker than Redwing.

VOICE Thin, sharp "*tik*" or "*sip*"; alarm like weak Blackbird rattle. Song strident: rich, fluty whistles, shouted and squeaky notes, in short phrases, each repeated – even-paced repetition rules out Blackbird and more flowing Mistle Thrush.

Locally common resident (1 million pairs, plus 950,000 birds in Ireland); migrant, winter visitor

from N and W Europe

Gardens, parks, damp woods, hedgerows

ADULT race *hebridensis*

ADULT race *philomelos*

IN FLIGHT, underwing pale orange; tail plain.

ADULT

SONG THRUSH RACES Three races occur in Britain and Ireland but intergrade from south-east to north-west, making it difficult to assign some individuals to race. **Race *philomelos*** (passage migrant and winter visitor from Europe) is the palest. **Race *clarkei*** (resident in Britain and Ireland) is intermediate in tone and markings. **Race *hebridensis*** (resident in the Outer Hebrides/Isle of Skye) is the darkest and also lacks buff on the breast and flanks.

dark cap/pale over eye always very subtle, unlike Redwing

a pale thrush with distinct spots, unlike even palest brown Blackbird

pale spots above

JUVENILE

ADULT race *clarkei*

spots 'V'- or fan-shaped, less crosswise than on Mistle Thrush

Mistle Thrush

Turdus viscivorus ● ❶ 538

26–29 cm | WS 43–45 cm   👁 White's Thrush (p. 384)

Large, often **upright** thrush, obviously pale. Hops with **strong, springy action**. Flies fast, **often high**; small head, long, squared tail, big wings create distinctive shape, especially as family group or small flock streams by, line astern. Aggressive towards intruders near nest.

Paler than Song Thrush. **Dark shoulder spots**, **pale feather edges** on wings; tail has whitish sides and corners. Underside uniform yellowish-cream, **round black spots** often merging on sides of chest. JUVENILE striking, bright and pale; **dark-edged cream spots above**; pale wingbars.

VOICE Call dry, rattling "*tchrrr-tchrrr-tchrrr*". Song similar to Blackbird (p. 379); **less varied**; brief, flowing phrases far-carrying, wild quality, often from high treetop.

Widespread but thinly spread resident (200,000 pairs, plus 25,000 birds in Ireland)

Gardens, parks, woods, hedgerows, moorland trees with berries, windbreaks, pastures

IN FLIGHT, **white underwing** (like Fieldfare (p. 382)) flashes prominently.

ADULT

pale spots and dark fringes above

JUVENILE

markedly bigger, but relatively smaller-headed shape, than Song Thrush

ADULT

pale fringes to wing feathers

Fieldfare

Turdus pilaris ● 538

22–27 cm | WS 40–42 cm

Big, bold, often with Redwings: flocks of tens/hundreds in winter. Typically head-to-wind on ground; also feeds on berries; if disturbed, flies into treetops or next field. Head-on, orange-buff birds across green field; tail-on, scattered grey rumps.

Grey head, brown back, **grey rump/black tail**. Black around eye, yellow on bill give strong expression. Chest pale to deep **orange**, black streaks and spots (blackish flank in spring). Pale grey rump above wide black tail obvious even on ground.

VOICE Low, throaty, chuckling chatter "*chak-chak-ak*" or "*chuk-uk-uk-uk*", often in chorus from flock; nasal "*swee-eep*" (almost like Lapwing (*p. 187*)). Occasional low subsong from spring flocks. Song (rare Britain and Ireland) weak, chattering, repetitive sequence.

Common winter visitor, Oct–Apr (680,000); very rare breeder

from NW Europe

from E and C Europe

Woods, hedgerows, orchards, fields, parks

IN FLIGHT, white underwing (Mistle Thrush (*p. 381*) similar but more elongated, pale tail).

ADULT

ADULT

duller plumage and bill

1ST-WINTER

ADULT

white belly/vent more striking than on other common thrushes

blacker on flank, brighter orange-buff on breast in spring

Redwing

NT

19–23 cm | WS 30–34 cm

Turdus iliacus

Rare thrushes (p. 384–385)

538

except race coburni

Small, dark thrush; bold head pattern. Often flocks with Fieldfares and other thrushes in fields/hedges/orchards. Visits gardens/ornamental shrubberies, especially in severe winters. Flocks usually flighty and wary, slip away through hedge tops. Also feeds deep inside woods.

Darker than Song Thrush. **Cream stripe above eye; dark cheek**, pale moustache. Underside whitish, **lines of dark spots**; flanks **brick-red**.

VOICE Distinctive high, thin "*seeeeh*" (often heard at night); rattling notes. Song rich, fluty phrase. Rambling 'subsong' chorus from roosting flocks.

Common winter visitor, Sep–Apr (650,000); very rare breeder, Scotland (5–12 pairs)

from Iceland

from N and E Europe

Gardens, parks, fields, woods, orchards, hedgerows

ADULT race *iliacus*

IN FLIGHT, **underwing red**. Smaller than Fieldfare: migrant flocks like Skylarks (p. 349), but sleeker, less square, longer-headed.

rear flank spot

ADULT race *coburni*

strongly striped head always characteristic

ADULT race *iliacus*

Icelandic race *coburni* (scarce Britain/Ireland) darker overall than regularly occurring race *iliacus* from N and E Europe; broad streaks almost coalesce on underside.

more streaked than spotted below

Rare Asian thrushes

These large, typical thrushes from the east tend to arrive in late autumn but sometimes overwinter; they may appear in unlikely places, from sand dunes to gardens.

Red-throated Thrush *Turdus ruficollis*

23–25·5 cm | WS 35–39 cm

Like Black-throated Thrush but **sides of tail rusty/red-brown**. MALE has brick-red chest and face, in winter gains reddish gorget. FEMALE streaked grey, buff tinge to chest.

Black-throated Thrush *Turdus atrogularis*

23–25·5 cm | WS 35–39 cm

Favours short grass/berried bushes. Greyish, whiter below, bill **yellow with black tip**. MALE **face/chest black**. FEMALE dull **dark tail** (no rufous); dark mark from eye to bill; **grey mottles on chest and pale streaks on flank**. 1ST-WINTER pale wingbar; streaks on throat and flanks coalesce into blacker breast-band on male.

Vagrant from Asia: 1 record (Britain), Sep–Oct. On coast. Trees/bushes.

RED-THROATED THRUSH
1ST-WINTER ♂

1ST-WINTER ♀

ADULT ♂ WINTER

Vagrant from Asia: <100 records (Britain), Oct–Mar. Scattered. Trees/bushes, often on ground.

White's Thrush *Zoothera dauma*

27–31 cm | WS 35–40 cm

Large, long, large-billed; pale with **crescentic dark barring** (see juvenile Mistle Thrush (p. 381)). Dark bands along upperwing, **black-and-white underwing**, pale tail corners.

Vagrant from Asia: <100 records (<10 Ireland), most Sep–Oct. Most on coast. Trees/bushes; feeds on ground.

1ST-WINTER

Dusky Thrush *Turdus eunomus*

21–24 cm | WS 34–38 cm

Note intergrades with Naumann's Thrush can be impossible to assign to either form.

Dark rusty-brown, white below; dark cap, eyestripe and cheek; bold buff bands above eye and below cheek; blackish spots across chest and 'V'-shapes on flanks; broad rufous wing panel, rufous rump, red underwing. 1ST-WINTER dark centres/paler edges disrupt duller wing panel; head/throat more speckled. 1ST-WINTER FEMALE duller.

1ST-WINTER ♀

1ST-WINTER ♂

Vagrant from Asia: <15 records (Britain), Sep–Mar, May. Widespread. Trees/bushes.

Vagrant from Asia: <5 records (Britain), Dec–Mar. Widespread. Trees/bushes.

Vagrant from Asia: <25 records (Britain), Jun, Sep–Oct. Most on coast; often with Redwings (*p. 381*).

Naumann's Thrush *Turdus naumanni*

21–24 cm | WS 35–40 cm

Warm rufous-brown thrush, pale above, underside closely mottled with diamond-shaped **orange-rufous spots**, rusty rump and tail.

intergrades with Dusky Thrush

1ST-WINTER

Eyebrowed Thrush *Turdus obscurus*

20·5–23 cm | WS 37–40 cm

Pale. ADULT grey on head, chest; **white stripes above and below eye**; orange flanks; IMMATURE browner, **white over eye**; dark eyestripe on grey-brown head; **pale orange flanks**; white belly and vent.

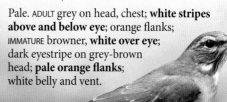

♀/1ST-WINTER

no spots below

Siberian Thrush *Geokichla sibirica*

20–21·5 cm | WS 37–42 cm

Medium-sized thrush; wide **black and white bands on underwing**, white tips on tail. MALE slate grey, **broad white line over eye**. FEMALE brown above, **whitish below with dark bars**, pale above and below dark cheek.

Vagrant from Asia: <15 records (<5 Ireland), most Oct–Jan. On coast. Trees/bushes; on ground.

1ST-WINTER/ ADULT ♀

1ST-WINTER ♂

paler, browner than adult male

385

Rare American thrushes

American Robin and Varied Thrush are large thrushes, clearly similar to British and Irish thrushes. But other North American thrushes (*Catharus*) that have been recorded are smaller, more Nightingale-like (*p. 389*). The most likely species to cross the Atlantic have a large population and wide distribution in eastern North America. Starting their southward autumn migration over the sea they can be caught in strong westerly winds (perhaps resting on an eastbound ship) and make landfall mainly in western Britain, Ireland and the Northern isles.

American Robin
Turdus migratorius
22–25 cm | WS 38–40 cm

<50 records (<15 Ireland), May– Jun, most Oct–Apr. Scattered. Trees/bushes; feeds on ground

ADULT slaty-grey above, paler fringes to wing feathers. Blackish hood, bold **white marks around eye**; throat paler, streaked. Underside pale **brick-red/orange**, darker on male. White with black streaks under tail. Black tail, white corners. IMMATURE paler, with paler edges below.

1ST-WINTER ♂

mottled paler than adult, white tips to wing coverts

Grey-cheeked Thrush *Catharus minimus*
15–17 cm | WS 25–30 cm

Small thrush, uniformly dull olive-brown above; weak eyering, greyish cheeks; diffuse dark spots on buff breast, whiter belly. Underwing dark, white central band.

Swainson's Thrush
Catharus ustulatus
16–18 cm | WS 22–25 cm

Catharus thrushes have banded underwings.

Small, pale thrush, uniformly sandy-brown above; wide, bright, pale eyering, pale line eye to bill; diffuse dark spots on upper breast, plain grey flank. Underwing dark, white central band.

pale line

pale eyering

olive brown

1ST-WINTER

sandy brown

1ST-WINTER

<50 records (<10 Ireland), Jun, Sep–Oct. On coast. Woodland/scrub.

<100 records (<10 Ireland): May, Sep–Nov; most on coast). Woodland/scrub.

Varied Thrush *Ixoreus naevius*
24 cm | WS 35–40 cm

Grey-and-orange thrush, **orange-buff over eye**, on wingbars, **dark cheek and chest-band**; dark underwing with broad pale band. The bird recorded lacked orange – an extremely rare grey-and-white aberration; any future record likely to be as bird shown here.

NT Wood Thrush *Hylocichla mustelina*
17–18 cm | WS 25–30 cm

Rounded, short-tailed thrush; uniformly bright brown above except rustier nape; bold pale eyering, dark-flecked cheek. Large rounded spots all over pale underparts. Underwing dark, white central band.

1ST-WINTER

1ST-WINTER

1 record (Britain), Nov. On coast. Woodland/scrub.

1 record (Britain): Oct; on coast. Woodland/scrub.

Hermit Thrush *Catharus guttatus*
16–17 cm | WS 20–25 cm

Small, dumpy thrush, greyish- or sandy-brown above, rusty tail and wing patch (rufous towards rear); variable eyering; dark spots on throat/chest. Underwing dark, white central band. See Rufous-tailed Robin (*p. 401*), which has pale underwing.

Veery *Catharus fuscescens*
16–18 cm | WS 22–27 cm

Small thrush with thick neck, broad tail; uniformly warm brown above; bland face, greyish cheek; few diffuse spots on buff throat; pale, unmarked flank. Underwing dark, white central band (pale underwing on similar Rufous-tailed Robin (*p. 401*)).

greyish-brown or sandy-brown

rufous tail

1ST-WINTER

warm brown

few spots

plain flank

1ST-WINTER

Rufous-tailed Robin (*p. 401*)

<15 records (<5 Ireland), Oct. On coast. Woodland/scrub.

<15 records (Britain), May–Jun, Oct–Nov. On coast. Woodland/scrub.

Comparison of juvenile chats *p. 377*

Robin

Erithacus rubecula Ⓘ

12·5–14 cm | WS 22–25 cm

Bluethroat (*p. 400*),
Red-flanked Bluetail (*p. 401*)

Familiar garden bird; small chat in mid-level canopy/thickets. Distinctive rounded silhouette (but often quite slim). Curtseys, flicks wings and tail. Hop-and-stop bouncy action, deft flit to ground and up again.

Red-orange face and breast. Late summer adults **very faded**; fresh and bright by autumn. Red not vivid, but 'glows' in dark recesses. JUVENILE no red, pale spots above, dark crescents below, yellowish wingbar, dull tail, pale legs. Compare Redstart (*p. 392*), Nightingale, Dunnock (*p. 368*) – see *p. 377*; develops patchy red on throat/chest during moult.

VOICE Sharp "*tik*"; thin, high "*see*". Song **long**, fluent, melodic, **more or less melancholy** (in spring, strong passages like Garden Warbler (*p. 419*)); **frequent changes in speed**; long-drawn notes characteristic. Often **sings at night** near lights.

Very common resident (5·5 million pairs, plus 5·4 million birds in Ireland); common migrant

from N W Europe

Wide range of habitats: forests, gardens, heaths

ADULT
British/Irish race
melophilus

ADULT
European race
rubecula

Migrants from continental Europe (race *rubecula*) paler, more olive, bluer neck patch; less approachable than resident race *melophilus*.

no red; spotted, but has same character as adult

JUVENILE

Nightingale

Luscinia megarhynchos ●

15–16·5 cm | WS 26–28 cm

👁 Rare chats (*p. 400–401*), Veery (*p. 387*)

Rare, local summer visitor, Apr–Sep (7,500 pairs); rare on migration. Vagrant Ireland (<50 records)

Secretive summer visitor (see Garden Warbler (*p. 419*), Robin). Easy to hear, hard to see in thickets: sings from cover (occasionally exposed perch); typically heard first, then glimpsed on ground or on songpost.

Like large Robin without red: tail often raised and conspicuous. Plain head, dark eye, whitish eyering. ADULT rusty-brown, greyer neck, rufous rump and tail (Redstart (*p. 392*) has dark centre). JUVENILE spotted; mottled darker on chest; pale wingbar (see *p. 377*).

VOICE Low, **grating** "*kerrrr*"; clear, whistled "*wheep*". Song, day or night: **long**, considerable **variation in pace**, pitch and quality; longer pauses than Song Thrush (*p. 380*). Loud, distinctive **deep bubbling**; sudden **change from slow and thin to fast, deep notes** and long **crescendo** "*sseee, ssseee, ssseee seeeee*".

to Africa

Dense thickets, woodland

ADULT

singing bird shows puffy white throat

long tail held down

Eastern race *golzii* vagrant: <5 records (Britain) Sep–Oct greyer than regularly occurring race *megarhynchos*, with rufous tail, pale line over eye, pale tertial fringes, long tail (see Rufous Bush Chat (*p. 398*).

plain and pale, brighter towards tail

ADULT

389

Comparison of juvenile chats *p. 377*

Whinchat

Saxicola rubetra ⬤❶ 538

12–14 cm | WS 22–24 cm

Upright, on bush-top or isolated tall stem. Less squat than Stonechat. May perch high on tree but usually low down. **Pale stripe over eye**, **white at sides of tail** always helpful.

MALE **long white stripes** above and below **black mask**; apricot throat and breast. White patch on outerwing. Looks more black-and-white by late summer. FEMALE duller; long **buff line over eye**; distinctive pale, bright buff with long dark streaks ('dead grass') back. JUVENILE/1ST-WINTER more buff, scalloped; stripe over eye less striking; throat/cheek contrast reduced, approaching some Stonechats.

VOICE Sweet "*siu*" and "*siu-tek tek*". Song variable, sometimes like Robin (*p. 388*) with added rattles and clicks, often dry, ticking sequence before more musical, fast flourish.

Scarce summer visitor, Apr–Oct (20,000 pairs, mainly in N and W, declining); scarce on migration

from/to Scandinavia

to Africa

Grassy heaths, bracken stands, young plantations

black mask bordered by white

ADULT ♂

pale stripe over dark mask

ADULT ♀

head pattern relatively weak but still distinctive

ADULT ♂

1ST-WINTER

Stonechat

Saxicola rubicola ❶

11·5–13 cm | WS 21–23 cm

◉ Siberian Stonechat (p. 402)

Locally fairly common resident (15,000 pairs, plus 120,000 birds in Ireland); scarce migrant/winter visitor outside breeding range; more coastal after hard winters

Like Whinchat but dumpy, pot-bellied; **all-dark tail**. Usually on top of Gorse/Heather, sometimes on wire, tree; can skulk low down.

MALE **black hood**, **black throat**, **white neck patch**, rufous breast, white belly; rump white, finely streaked. White wing patches spread in display. FEMALE/1ST-WINTER browner; **dark hood and throat**; neck patch weaker; pale crescent under throat; rump brown, thickly streaked. JUVENILE pale stripe over eye, whitish chin, more like Whinchat but stripe over eye shorter, whitish crescent under streaked throat, tail dark.

VOICE Sharp whistle with or without hard "*tak*" notes, "*whee-tak*". Song fast, chattering, squeaky warble.

Continental race *rubicola* is presumed migrant: MALE shows less orange on breast, bigger white neck and wing patches, more white on rump, but overlap with British/Irish race *hibernans* makes identification uncertain.

Heaths, scrubby areas

ADULT ♂ race *rubicola*

weak pale line over eye and under throat

1ST-WINTER ♀

dark flank against white vent

big white neck patch

small neck patch

1ST-WINTER ♂

ADULT ♀

ADULT ♂ British/Irish race *hibernans*

Comparison of juvenile chats *p. 377*

Redstart

Phoenicurus phoenicurus **538**

13–14·5 cm | WS 25 cm

Slender, like slim Robin
(*p. 388*), constantly **quivering
orange-red tail**. Elusive in canopy; often around rocks on
wooded slope; heath/woodland edge.

🔊 Rare chats (*p. 400–401*) and small American thrushes (*p. 387*)

MALE **white forehead**; **black throat**, **grey back**, rufous breast.
Rump and tail sides **rusty-orange**. In autumn, white forehead,
black face part-obscured; wings dark, often with pale panel;
wear during winter/spring produces bright breeding plumage.
1ST-WINTER male is browner, and wear produces less bright
1ST-SUMMER plumage, with browner wings. FEMALE orange-buff
beneath, plain face, black eye and pale eyering. JUVENILE spotted,
rusty tail like female. Black legs (unlike Robin, Nightingale
– see *p. 377*).

VOICE Sweet, strong "*sweep*" (similar to Chaffinch (*p. 481*),
Chiffchaff (*p. 426*)); often "*wheet-tik tik*" or fast ticking (like
Hawfinch (*p. 479*)) in alarm. Song stops short: low, indrawn,
vibrant "*srree srree srree*" followed by quick, musical warble.

Locally fairly common summer
visitor, Apr–Oct (100,000 pairs,
declining); scarce on migration

from/to
Scandinavia

to
Africa

Breeds old oak woodland, some
in stone walls near upland fields;
migrants particularly near coasts

1ST-WINTER ♀

pale edges
to wing
feathers

1ST-WINTER ♂

ADULT ♂

ADULT ♀

tail flickered
constantly

Note 1ST-SUMMER
male is like adult but
has browner wings

Black Redstart

Phoenicurus ochruros ● **538**

13–14·5 cm | WS 25 cm

Like Redstart but darker, greyer; behaviour more like Wheatear (*p. 394*), on ground.

MALE **smoky-grey**, **blacker face and chest**, white wing panel. Uppertail coverts/sides of tail rusty-orange. Young male (often breeds) greyer, browner wing. FEMALE/IMMATURE **brownish-grey**, **plain grey head**, pale eyering; wing panel weak. Uppertail coverts and **tail sides rusty-red** (Redstart has more rufous on rump). **Black legs** unlike young Robin (*p. 388*).

VOICE Sharp "*weet*" or "*weet-t'k t'k*". Song far-carrying but not loud, trill followed by curious dry crackle, musical flourish.

Very rare and local breeder (50 pairs); more widespread but scarce migrant and winter visitor

from Europe

Breeds cities, railway stations, industrial sites; migrant/winter mostly on rocky coasts

'Eastern' Black Redstart
1ST-WINTER ♂

BLACK REDSTART RACES
Race *gibraltariensis* is resident and a visitor from Europe.

'Eastern' Black Redstart – races *phoenicuroides/xerophilus/rufiventris* form a group from Central Asia (wintering NE Africa) **vagrant, <10 records (Britain); all 1st-winter ♂**

1ST-WINTER male 'Eastern' Black Redstart has a grey forehead/back; blackish chest more extensive than male Redstart; reddish below. Females impossible to distinguish.

Beware hybrids and S European 'red-bellied' Black Redstarts.

ADULT ♀

ADULT ♂

NB: 1ST-WINTER ♂ may look like ♀ or more like adult ♂

1ST-WINTER

mid-grey, overall

wing panel variable

Wheatear

Oenanthe oenanthe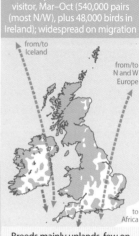

14–16·5 cm | WS 27–28 cm

Rare wheatears (p. 396–397)

Only common wheatear:
ground-loving, repeatedly flying ahead if disturbed, revealing
big white rump, **black 'T' on tail**. All plumages white rump/
tail base, black centre and tip to tail – in flight, white is big, eye-
catching patch unlike anything except very rare wheatears.

MALE pale blue-grey above, pale buff below. **Black mask**, blackish
wings. Variable pink/yellow-buff below, fades whiter in summer.
Large 'Greenland' race *leucorhoa*, mostly late spring: browner
back, stronger orange-buff underside than British/Irish breeders
(race *oenanthe*). FEMALE grey-brown above, buff below; paler
stripe over eye, only slightly **darker ear coverts**, **plain dark
brown wings**. Greyish bloom wears off back, fades to brown
and white by mid-summer; by autumn strikingly different, with
broad, **bright buff edges to wing feathers**. JUVENILE wider pale
tips to primaries (see p. 377).

VOICE Whistled "*wheet*" and hard "*chak*". Song often given in
short **fluttery song flight**, or from low perch, quick-fire phrase
of chattering and ticking notes with musical chirps.

Locally common summer
visitor, Mar–Oct (540,000 pairs
(most N/W), plus 48,000 birds in
Ireland); widespread on migration

from/to
Iceland

from/to
N and W
Europe

to
Africa

Breeds mainly uplands, few on
sandy heaths and downs; migrant
particularly on coast

ADULT ♂
(display flight)

1ST-SUMMER ♂

mask and
wings
brownish

ADULT ♀

ADULT ♂ (SPRING)

Pale; wings form
black horizontal
band along body.

Wheatear tail patterns
Typical tail patterns shown: some variation, and detail can be hard to observe; tightly closed when perched, so pattern hidden.

PIED WHEATEAR	BLACK-EARED WHEATEAR	WHEATEAR	ISABELLINE WHEATEAR	DESERT WHEATEAR
black forms narrow, broken tip, extends onto corners	black forms narrow tip, 'curls' up sides	black forms basic 'T'-shape; tip even width	black forms broad tip, small white basal panels	almost all-black

autumn males show black mask beneath buff fringes

adult female, 1st-winter male and 1st-winter female inseparable in autumn

ADULT ♂ (AUTUMN)

1ST-WINTER/ ♀

'Greenland' Wheatear race *leucorhoa*

brownish ear coverts

brownish back

1ST-WINTER race *oenanthe*

≤7 tips

long wings; shows 7–8 primary tips

buffy underparts

ADULT ♂ race *leucorhoa* (spring)

1ST-WINTER race *leucorhoa*

longer legs

Wheatear tail patterns p. 395

'Western' race *hispanica*

narrow black mask or black face/throat

orange-buff back

♂ SPRING

black wings and shoulders

'Eastern' race *melanoleuca*

whiter above

black mask/throat more extensive; **black above bill**

♂ SPRING

Black-eared Wheatear
Oenanthe hispanica
13·5–15·5 cm | WS 25–26 cm

Vagrant from S Europe: <100 records (<10 Ireland), Apr–Oct. Most on coast. Open ground.

Perches on bushes. White rump; **black tail-band narrow** or broken by white, **curls up onto sides.** Two races, with dark- or pale-throated males and females. Two races, *hispanica* (SW Europe) and *melanoleuca* (SE Europe). MALE (see *inset left* for summer plumages); in autumn usually hint of summer pattern. FEMALE (both races) dark, slender, some have dark throat. **Tail pattern** like male; **blackish underwing.** Race *melanoleuca* tends to have dark back/orange breast; *hispanica* less contrast.

1ST-WINTER ♂

autumn males usually show a hint of the summer pattern

1ST-WINTER ♀ race *hispanica*

♂ SPRING

blackish; whitish cap; white below, buff on breast.

Pied Wheatear *Oenanthe pleschanka*
14–16·5 cm | WS 25–26 cm

White rump, tail sides, **narrow black tail-band extending around corners.** MALE (see inset left). FEMALE/IMMATURE cold grey-brown; **pale scaly bars** on back unlike very closely similar Black-eared Wheatear, some warmer brown like eastern Black-eared Wheatear. Face, throat, breast dusky greyish-brown with soft streaks/mottles.

1ST-WINTER ♀

1ST-WINTER ♂

Vagrant from E Europe: <100 records (<10 Ireland), May–Jul, most Sep–Dec. Most on coast. Open ground.

NT Desert Wheatear *Oenanthe deserti*   538

14·5–15·5 cm | WS 25–26 cm

Vagrant from E Europe: <150 records (<10 Ireland), autumn–spring, most Nov–Dec. Most on coast. Open ground.

Pale wheatear with **all-black tail**, white rump. MALE **black face/throat joined to black wing**. FEMALE/IMMATURE greyish-sandy above, whiter below; pale shoulder, darker midwing, black wingtips. Dark underwing coverts.

Three races recorded: *deserti* (from Middle East) described above; *homochroa* (from N Africa) smaller, paler, pinkish; *atrogularis* (from Asia) larger, browner. Vast majority in Britain/Ireland impossible to assign to race.

1st-winter like adult with pale fringes on wings; male has blackish face obscured by pale tips, wearing off by spring

1ST-WINTER ♂

1ST-WINTER ♀

pale wheatear with small white rump, black tail

1ST-WINTER ♂

Isabelline Wheatear *Oenanthe isabellina*

15–16·5 cm | WS 26–28 cm

Vagrant from E Europe: <50 records (1 Ireland), May, Sep–Nov. Most on coast. Open ground.

Upright, strikingly pale, sandy brown, thick-billed wheatear. Broad black tail-band but short 'T'-stem; plain wings, except **blackish alula**. White line over eye tapers out over cheek, dark line from bill short behind eye.

underwing silvery-grey/ whitish – hard to see

ISABELLINE WHEATEAR

WHEATEAR

WHEATEAR

1ST-WINTER

Underwing coverts white, dark centres (fresh), darker overall when worn

black alula

1ST-WINTER

Rare chats

Warm winds from the south and east in late spring might just bring some exciting arrivals to Britain and Ireland. Along with expected Hoopoes and Bee-eaters, there may perhaps be one of several extremely rare and unpredictable chats (including rock thrushes and wheatears (see *p. 396-397*), most of which are distinctive in spring, but may be more difficult to identify if they arrive in autumn.

Rufous Bush Chat *Cercotrichas galactotes*

16 cm | WS 26–28 cm

Slim, thrush-like. Orange-brown (SW Europe) or grey-brown (SE Europe); dark eyestripe, pale line over eye; **rufous rump; black-and-white tips** to **raised tail.**

ADULT

Vagrant from S Europe: <5 records (Britain), May–Jun. On coast. Open scrub, feeds on ground.

White-throated Robin *Irania gutturalis*

14 cm | WS 25–27 cm

Form like Redstart (*p. 392*). MALE blue-grey above, pale rusty-orange below; white stripe over eye; **black lower face, narrow white throat.** FEMALE/IMMATURE pale; face grey; whitish throat, moustache; **orange flanks; blackish tail**; black legs.

Vagrant from Middle East: <15 records (<5 Ireland), Aug–Oct. On coast. Open scrub, feeds on ground.

Longer-tailed, more thrush-like stance than Red-flanked Bluetail (*p. 401*).

ADULT ♂

1ST-WINTER ♀

Moussier's Redstart *Phoenicurus moussieri*

12 cm | WS 20–22 cm

Small, short-tailed redstart. MALE black above, **long white stripe over eye**, wing panel; orange beneath. FEMALE/IMMATURE grey-brown above, **pale rufous on belly, rump and sides of tail**; white eyering.

Vagrant from N Africa: 1 record (male) (Britain), April. On coast. Open ground.

ADULT ♂

ADULT ♀
(not recorded)

Rock Thrush *Monticola saxatilis*

18 cm | WS 32–35 cm

Small, short-tailed, spike-billed, thrush-like. MALE grey hood, **white patch on back**, rufous underside. FEMALE/IMMATURE brown, close pale bars above and **dark bars on rusty-buff** below. **Rufous tail.**

Vagrant from S Europe: <50 records (<5 Ireland), Feb–Oct, most Apr–Jun. On coast. Rocky areas/cliffs.

ADULT ♀

ADULT ♂

Blue Rock Thrush *Monticola solitarius*

21–23 cm | WS 37–40 cm

Long-bodied, tapered, thrush-like with markedly **long bill**. MALE **slaty blue**, wings darker. FEMALE/IMMATURE **dark brown** above, dusky **buff below with close dark bars**. Tail dark.

Vagrant from S Europe: <5 records (Britain), May, Oct. On coast. Rocky areas/cliffs.

ADULT ♂

ADULT ♀

White-crowned Black Wheatear *Oenanthe leucopyga*

18 cm | WS 26–29 cm

Large **black** wheatear with white rump; white tail with short black centre, **dark spots across tip**, not complete band. Large white vent. ADULT glossy, usually (not always) obvious **white crown**; IMMATURE dull, black crown. **Tail pattern critical.**

Vagrant from N Africa (1 record: Jun; on coast). Open ground. Also June record, either this species or Black Wheatear *O. leucura*, from Ireland.

ADULT

Bluethroat *Luscinia svecica* `538`

13–14 cm | WS 23–25 cm

Rare migrant from Europe: 40–60 per year, (<50 records Ireland), Apr–May, Aug–Oct. Mainly on coast; declining; has bred. Often in reedbeds, willows; on muddy paths.

Small, resembles Robin (*p. 388*); runs/hops, raises and dips **slender tail** with exaggerated action.

MALE **white stripe over eye, electric-blue breast** above black, white, rufous bands. Red spot on race *svecica* (N Europe), white on race *cyanecula* (C and S Europe), rarely all blue. FEMALE/IMMATURE **white stripe** over eye; black and white throat; **rusty across breast**. Most females lack blue; variable on young male. IN FLIGHT, **rusty-red sides at base of tail**.

VOICE Loud, arresting "*shlak*". Song strong, clear whistle with fast, variable flourish, including mimicry.

ADULT ♂
White-spotted race
cyanecula

1ST-WINTER ♂

ADULT ♂
Red-spotted race
svecica

ADULT ♀

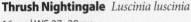
rusty edges
to tail

Thrush Nightingale *Luscinia luscinia*

16 cm | WS 27–28 cm

Very like Nightingale (*p. 389*). ADULT duller, mottled across chest, faint moustachial stripe; wingtip longer, shows eight primary tips (seven on Nightingale); tiny first primary hidden (visible beyond primary coverts on Nightingale); alula may show pale outer/dark inner half (uniform on Nightingale).

ADULT

Very rare migrant from N Europe: <250 records (<5 Ireland), most Apr–May, Sep. Mainly on coast. Scrubby areas.

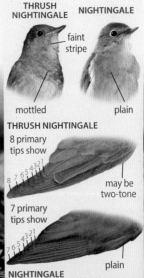

THRUSH NIGHTINGALE   NIGHTINGALE

faint stripe

mottled   plain

THRUSH NIGHTINGALE
8 primary tips show

8 7 6 5 4 3 2 1

may be two-tone

7 primary tips show

7 6 5 4 3 2 1

plain

NIGHTINGALE

Siberian Rubythroat *Calliope calliope*
15 cm | WS 26–27 cm

Pale brown, Robin-like (*p. 388*) bird; **white line over blackish eyestripe**, black and white stripes under cheek. MALE throat vivid red. FEMALE/IMMATURE throat whitish.

1ST-WINTER ♀

rounded, long-legged, often cocks tail

Plain brown tail (eliminates Bluethroat with no blue on face)

1ST-WINTER ♂

Vagrant from Asia: <15 records (Britain), Oct. On coast. Scrubby areas; feeds on the ground.

Red-flanked Bluetail *Tarsiger cyanurus*
14 cm | WS 25–26 cm

Shape like small Robin (*p. 388*); MALE blue above, white below, orange flank. autumn birds olive-brown above, rump and tail **slaty-blue**; pale greyish-buff below, paler throat, **pale orange flank**; white eyering. Female White-throated Robin (*p. 398*) greyer with darker grey breast-band.

ADULT ♂

shape and actions like slim Robin or Redstart (*p. 392*)

1ST-WINTER

Very rare migrant from NE Europe, winters Asia: <150 records (<5 Ireland), most Sep–Nov, extremely rare Dec–May. Most on coast; recent increase. Trees.

Rufous-tailed Robin
Larivora sibilans

👁 Hermit Thrush, Veery (*p. 387*)

14 cm | WS 21–22 cm

Grey-brown robin: pale, scaly spots on mottled throat and breast; white eyering; bright rufous rump and tail. Compare Veery and Hermit Thrush (*p. 387*).

1ST-WINTER

Vagrant from Asia: <5 records (Britain), Sep–Oct. On coasts. Scrubby areas, feeds on the ground.

Siberian Blue Robin *Larivora cyane*
12 cm | WS 20–22 cm

Small, short-tailed robin with sharp bill, pale pinkish legs. MALE (not recorded) dark blue above, white below, FEMALE/IMMATURE brown above, dark scaly feather edges on buff breast, white belly; bluish tail.

1ST-WINTER ♀

Vagrant from Asia: <5 records (Britain), Sep–Oct. On coast. Scrubby areas, feeds on the ground.

Siberian Stonechat *Saxicola maurus*

12–13 cm | WS 22–23 cm

MALE (very rare) like male Stonechat (*p. 391*); bolder white neck patch, smaller orange chest patch, whiter underside, **broad white rump**, underwing coverts and axillaries **black**. IMMATURE like mixture of Stonechat and paler Whinchat (*p. 390*), with Stonechat's blacker tail. Rump distinctly **all pale, unmarked buff to whitish**; underwing coverts black on male, grey on female (more like Stonechat). Pale overall; **pale line over eye** and pale throat; pale, streaked cheeks and nape. Back greyish-brown with dark streaks; pale feather edges on wings and back give black-and-buff effect. Separating races *maurus* and *stejnegeri* often not possible; *stejnegeri* tends to be darker, warmer buff-brown with smaller neck patches and rump patch. 'Caspian' race *variegatus* more white in base of tail.

STONECHAT
ADULT ♂
race *hibernans*

markings on rump

extensive orange

flank sullied grey

Vagrant from Asia: <400 records (<10 Ireland), May, autumn/winter, most Oct. Mainly on coast. Majority W Siberian race *maurus*; 1 E Siberian race *stejnegeri*; <5 Caspian race *variegatus*. Scrubby areas.

ADULT ♂
race *maurus*

smaller orange breast patch than Stonechat

flank pale

dark tail

'CASPIAN' STONECHAT
ADULT ♂
race *variegatus*

white sides to base of tail

STONECHAT
1ST-WINTER
race *hibernans*

SIBERIAN STONECHAT
1ST-WINTER
race *maurus*

'CASPIAN' STONECHAT
1ST-WINTER
race *variegatus*

(OLD WORLD) WARBLERS, CISTICOLAS and CRESTS

GROUP ID general structure and coloration | tail shape | behaviour

Warblers are complex, their relationships still being investigated. All have relatively thin 'insect-eater' bills. They tend to be slender-legged and tapered, unlike the more chunky tits (*p. 443-451*). Some are dull, some bright, some uniform, others patterned;

49 old world warblers (plus 1 identified only to a species pair):
14 breed (1 erratically, 2 resident, 2 others regular in winter) 35 scarce migrants/ vagrants.

1 cisticola: vagrant.

3 crests: 2 resident; 1 (kinglet) vagrant from America.

Warbler ageing/sexing

Sexes alike in most species, differ in others (most but not all *Sylvia* species); juveniles differ slightly and may be identifiable through 1st-winter.

Regulus crests – 2 species (*pp. 436–437*) plus 1 vagrant (*p. 511*): prefer trees, bushes. CALLS: high, thin, sharp notes. SONGS: simple, rhythmic phrase or trill. STRUCTURE: slim, sharp bill; tails square/notched; wings short. PLUMAGE: sexes almost alike; greenish, pale below, unstreaked, wings barred blackish/cream; head patterns important.

ID head pattern

GOLDCREST

Sylvia warblers – 14 species (*pp. 417–425*): prefer thick scrub/hedges/low vegetation. CALLS: short, hard notes. SONGS: fast, irregular, harsh or very musical. STRUCTURE: strong; heavy bill; thick legs; square tails, some long and slim PLUMAGE: sexes differ in most, especially in head pattern; brown/grey above; buff/pale beneath, unstreaked.

ID head pattern | back colour | call and song

SYLVIA
WHITETHROAT

***Phylloscopus* warblers**: – 16 species (*pp. 426–435*): prefer treetop foliage, where they are veryactive, gleaning insects from the leaves (some hover), not seen much on the ground; in scrub/bushes on migration. CALLS: variations on sweet, more or less two-syllable notes. SONGS: musical cadence, or repeated, staccato notes, or metallic trill; no harsh notes. STRUCTURE: slim, sharp bill; thin legs; tails square/notched; under tail coverts short. PLUMAGE: sexes alike; greenish/yellow or brownish; head patterns important: most have stripes over and through eye, some rarer species have wingbars.

ID leg colour | wingbars | head pattern | call and song

PHYLLOSCOPUS CHIFFCHAFF

***Acrocephalus* warblers** – 7 species (*pp. 405–410*): prefer waterside vegetation, often clinging to vertical stem; in bushes/scrub on migration. CALLS: short, hard notes and churrs. SONGS: fast, repetitive, rhythmic phrasing, include musical and harsh notes, mimicry. STRUCTURE: low, sloping forehead, sharp bill, strong legs; tail slightly rounded; undertail coverts medium-long. PLUMAGE: sexes alike; plain or streaked brown above, unstreaked buff below; head patterns and rump colours important.

NB **Cetti's Warbler** (*p. 405*), – different genus found in similar habitat: dark red-brown above, paler below with round wings and a broad square-ended tail (often raised); outburst of abrupt song diagnostic.

ID wing detail | subtle plumage and structure differences

ACROCEPHALUS MARSH WARBLER

***Locustella* warblers** – 5 species (*pp. 411–413*): prefer dense, low vegetation/scrub, creeping, elusive, low down; in bushes/grass on migration. SONGS: remarkable, prolonged, trilling or reeling songs, insect-like, often at dusk or nocturnal. STRUCTURE: sharp bill, flat head, long, rounded tail; wings short, curved outer edge; under tail coverts long. PLUMAGE: sexes alike; brown, plain or streaked; underparts and tail patterns important.

ID subtle plumage differences

LOCUSTELLA GRASSHOPPER WARBLER

***Hippolais* and *Iduna* warblers** – 6 species (*pp. 410, 414–416*): all rare migrants, prefer bushes, trees. CALLS: short, hard notes. STRUCTURE: between *Acrocephalus* and *Phylloscopus*: strong, wide bill; strong legs; wings long- or short-tipped; tails square; under tail coverts short. plumage: sexes alike; greenish/yellow or brown/buff, unstreaked; most pale between eye and bill.

ID wing detail | subtle plumage and behaviour differences

***Cisticola* warblers** – 1 species, rare vagrant (*p. 411*): found in scrub/bushes with a preference for wetlands. SONG: repeated sharp, high note. STRUCTURE: round wings, short round tail. PLUMAGE: sexes alike; pale buff-brown, streaked; spots under tip of tail.

CISTICOLA FAN-TAILED WARBLER

HIPPOLAIS – ICTERINE WARBLER

SETOPHAGA YELLOW-RUMPED WARBLER

American Warblers and Vireos

Vagrants from North America (*pp. 511–515*), mostly brightly-patterned in breeding plumage but predominantly occur in autumn in duller, more difficult, first-winter plumages. North American wood warblers very variable: look for head patterns, wingbars, presence or absence of streaks above and below and white on tail. Vireos (*p. 511*) stockier, with thicker bills: head patterns, wingbars important.

Cetti's Warbler

Cettia cetti **536**

13–14 cm | WS 18–20 cm

Small, dark, dumpy warbler; **easy to hear**, hard to see.
Skulks in dense vegetation: perches briefly in open, sings,
disappears, sings again somewhere else! (Wren (*p. 369*) often
in same watery habitat, flies across open spaces in same way.)

Rufous-brown, darker than Reed Warbler (*p. 407*). Distinctive
whitish throat, **grey cheeks, breast; pale stripe over eye**; dull
underside, otherwise plain. **Tail long, square, dark rufous**;
often held up revealing dark undertail coverts with pale tips.
IN FLIGHT, low, quick; rounded wings.

VOICE Short, hard, sharp "*quilp!*", or "*plit*": loud and distinct
from dense waterside vegetation (especially in winter) but
can be a quiet note. Song **sudden loud outburst**, short notes,
momentary pause, then **fast** series – "*chwee; chwee: chuwee-
wee-wee-wee-wee chwit-it!*" Bold, ringing, musical, upbeat effect
unlike any likely birds nearby.

Scarce and local resident (1,900
singing males, mostly S England).
Vagrant Ireland (<5 records)

Dense waterside vegetation:
overgrown ditches, reedbeds,
scrubby tangles

ADULT

sometimes appears
on edge of thicket,
perched with tail raised

Sings from hidden perch with
great gusto, often moving to
another spot nearby before
delivering the next phrase.

ADULT

may hop across
gaps in reeds,
over leaf-litter

Sedge Warbler

Acrocephalus schoenobaenus

11·5–13 cm | WS 18–20 cm

Aquatic Warbler (*p. 410*),
Fan-tailed Warbler (*p. 411*)

Small, subtly streaked
brownish warbler with white stripe over eye.

ADULT dark cap, eyestripe; wide **white stripe above eye**.
Back olive-brown, **soft streaks**; plain, **pale sandy rump**.
Wings more variegated than Reed Warbler. By late summer,
duller, darker, more uniform. **Silky white throat**; bright buff
rear flanks. JUVENILE slightly yellower or pale gingery; paler
central crown stripe; small, faint, dark streaks on breast.

VOICE Hard "*tuk*" and short, flat "*trrrr*". Song energetic, varied,
scratchy and irritable, or more musical. Less repetitive and
rhythmic than Reed Warbler. Often short whirry **song flight**
(not seen in Reed Warbler). Typically begins with **sweet,
musical notes** often like Yellow Wagtail (*p. 364*) call.

Locally fairly common summer
visitor, Apr–Oct (300,000 pairs,
plus 130,000 birds in Ireland);
uncommon on migration

from/to
Scandinavia

to
Africa

from/to
Africa

Waterside reed/nettle beds,
bramble thickets; damp rushy
moors; scrub on migration

frequently sings in
rising, wing-whirring
song flight, unlike
Reed Warbler

ADULT
(display flight)

ADULT

Sings upright on exposed perch or
hidden in bushy tangle: bright pale
throat often catches the eye.

plain rump
and uppertail
coverts

ADULT

pale feather fringes;
pale centre to crown

1ST-WINTER

Reed Warbler

Acrocephalus scirpaceus ① **537**

12·5–14 cm | WS 18–20 cm

Small, slim, **plain** brown warbler (see Sedge, Marsh (*p. 408*), Garden (*p. 419*) Warblers and Whitethroat (*p. 420*)). Sidles up reed, dives back or dashes across open space, quickly out of sight.

Unstreaked; weak stripe over eye. Slender, **spike-like bill**, tapered shape unlike Garden Warbler (beware autumn migrant Reed Warbler in bushes and summer birds foraging in trees). ADULT mid-brown, pale below. **Pale rufous-brown rump and tail**. JUVENILE more rufous overall. **Puffy white throat**; orange-buff breast and flanks (head-on, singing, deeper creamy white bib than Whitethroat).

VOICE Low, slurred "*tcharr*", softer "*kresh*", grating "*krrrr*". Song invaluable: **rhythmic, repetitive**, each phrase repeated 2–4 times, lower, more even than Sedge Warbler without high trills: "*chara-chara-krrik-krrik-krrik charee charee charee*" etc.

> Rare *Acrocephalus* warblers (*pp. 408–410*), Savi's Warbler (*p. 411*)

Variation in Asian race *fuscus* greater than difference from British/Irish race *scirpaceus*, and usually indistinguishable; majority paler above, nape often greyer; brighter only on rump and uppertail coverts. One record (identified from DNA sample).

Locally very common summer visitor, Apr–Oct (90,000 pairs, uncommon in Ireland); migrants often away from breeding areas

from/to NW Europe

to Africa

from/to Africa

Reedbeds, swamps, adjacent trees; scrub on migration

sings from upright stem; often a chorus before dawn

Reed Warblers are adapted to sidling up vertical perches, but migrants may turn up almost anywhere, looking oddly out of context and uncomfortable.

often well hidden in reeds, but rustle of stems may give it away before short, low flight across open space

ADULT

1ST-WINTER

Marsh Warbler *Acrocephalus palustris*

13–15 cm | WS 18–20 cm

Very rare, erratic summer visitor, England, May–Sep (5–10 pairs), winters SE Africa. Very rare, mostly coastal on migration (30–50 per year), (<10 records Ireland). Marsh vegetation; scrub. **537**

Separating migrants from Reed Warbler (*p. 407*) difficult; summer birds told by song. **Crisp, pale tertial fringes**, more contrasted than Reed Warbler; alula darker; tail rounder; more angular nape. ADULT more sandy-olive than Reed Warbler, rump brighter **but not rusty**. Paler, **lemon-buff** below. Eyering bolder than short stripe over eye.

VOICE Dry, rattling "*terrrr*", soft "*chek*". Song lively, flowing; **great variety of accurate mimicry**. Can give hesitant, quieter, Reed Warbler-like performance during day. Nasal "*tzay-beeee*" distinctive, but many grating notes.

ADULT

pale-tipped primaries (unlike Reed Warbler)

strong tertial pattern

1ST-WINTER

dark alula

strong pale legs and claws

REED WARBLER
1ST-WINTER

Blyth's Reed Warbler

Acrocephalus dumetorum

12·5–14 cm | WS 16–18 cm

Very like Reed (*p. 407*) and Marsh Warblers; may perch with head and tail raised ('banana' shape). Broad **pale stripe from eye to bill** (light 'blob'); short/absent behind eye; **long, pale bill darkening towards tip** (sharper contrast on Paddyfield Warbler); dull grey-olive-brown above with **very plain wings**. Legs dark (pinker on Marsh Warbler).

Eastern Olivaceous Warbler (*p. 415*), Sykes's, Booted Warblers (*p. 416*)

1ST-WINTER

Vagrant from E Europe: <200 records (<10 Ireland), Jun, Aug–Oct. Mostly on coast. Reedbeds, scrub

Plain brown *Acrocephalus* warblers – key features

	General appearance	Head pattern	Tertials	Wingtip	
Marsh Warbler	Olive; barely brighter rump	Weak stripe, bolder eyering'	Sharply edged; just longer than secondaries	Long; 8 obvious pale tips (wear off in summer)	sharply edged
Reed Warbler (*p. 407*)	Warm brown; rustier rump/tail	Weak stripe over eye; white throat	Weakly edged; same length as secondaries	Long; 7 dull obvious pale tips	weakly edged
Blyth's Reed Warbler	Olive; very uniform	Stripe over eye bulbous in front	Very plain	Short; 6 obvious pale tips 1st-winter has smooth 'bronzy' panel on secondaries	plain
Paddyfield Warbler	Bright; sandy/rusty. Long tail	Stripe over eye edged dark above and below	Fringed pale	Short; 5–6 obvious pale tips	pale fringes

Vagrant from E Europe: <150 records (<10 Ireland), most Aug–Sep. Mostly on coast. Reedbeds, scrub.

eyestripe usually bold

yellowish base to short dark bill

pale edges to dark tertials

ADULT

Paddyfield Warbler

Acrocephalus agricola

12–13·5 cm | WS 15–17 cm

Like small, tawny, pale Reed Warbler (*p. 407*), with **short bill, long tail**. **Bold pale stripe over eye**, fading to rear (resembles Sedge Warbler (*p. 406*)), beneath **darker sides** to plain brown crown; dark eyestripe. Bill dark, **yellowish base/sharp black tip**. Wings brown, distinct **darker feather centres** on tertials (plainer on Blyth's Reed Warbler). Wingtip projection short. Rump/uppertail often bright sandy/rusty.

VU **Aquatic Warbler** *Acrocephalus paludicola* ● 　537

VU 11·5–13 cm | WS 16–18 cm

More secretive than very similar Sedge Warbler (*p. 406*): requires close observation to be sure. **Cream stripes on blackish-streaked back. Streaks on rump** and pointed uppertail coverts. ADULT **fine streaks on chest, flank**; legs pale pink. **Cream stripe on blackish crown**; broad buff stripe over eye. **Pale-faced**: dark eyestripe **short of bill**. JUVENILE underparts unmarked; buff marks on crown sides, but contrast still strong.

VOICE Ticking "*chak*" or "*chek*", or deep "*tuk*".

ADULT

unmarked buff

AQUATIC
dark streaks in pale

SEDGE
1ST-WINTER

streaked rump and uppertail coverts

Very rare migrant from N Europe: 7–10 per year; most records juveniles (<20 records Ireland), Aug–Sep. Mostly coastal S, SW England (declining). Reedbeds, tall marshy vegetation.

Great Reed Warbler

Acrocephalus arundinaceus
16–20 cm | WS 25–30 cm

Much too big for Reed Warbler (*p. 407*): **stronger, two-tone bill, crashing movements** in reeds. Bolder **pale stripe above eye**, fading out quickly behind; **thick, dark eyestripe**. Short flights over reeds: long wings; long, broad, slightly raised tail.

VOICE Call hard "*crek*". Song **loud, coarse, repetitive, deeper** notes than Reed Warbler, also high squeaky ones, sometimes hesitant, but unique in full flow – "*krr-krr kreek kreek kreek krrr krr grik grik chweee chweee chweee kerra kerra kerra…*".

Very rare migrant/vagrant from Europe, winters Africa: <300 records (<10 Ireland), most May–Jun. Sometimes sings for a few days. Reedbeds, scrub.

ADULT

Thick-billed Warbler

Iduna aedon
16–17 cm | WS 24–28 cm

Looks like large, plain-brown *Acrocephalus* warbler. Peaked head; short, stout, pale bill; pale area between eye and bill; dark eye in plain, pale face.

big, long-tailed, short-winged, plain warbler; bland head, beady eye, deep bill

Vagrant from Asia: <10 records (Britain), May, Sep–Oct. N Isles. Scrub, dense vegetation.

ADULT

Fan-tailed Warbler *Cisticola juncidis*
(Zitting Cisticola)
10–11 cm | WS 12–15 cm

Tiny, pale brownish warbler, finely streaked on crown; bolder black and buff streaks on back. Short, round tail has **black spots and white feather tips**.

VOICE Song in high, bounding flight, repeated metallic "*dzeep… dzeep…*".

Vagrant from S Europe: <15 records (<5 Ireland), Mar–Nov. Most S, SE England. Coastal grassland/wetlands.

ADULT

1ST-WINTER

Savi's Warbler *Locustella luscinioides* ● 537
13·5–15 cm | WS 16–18 cm

Very rare summer visitor, winters Africa, Apr–Aug (up to 5 pairs), migrant, from Europe (<15 records Ireland). Mostly large reedbeds near coast.

Located by song, from dense reeds. Brownish warbler; paler below with **very long brown undertail coverts** and **broad tail**. Obvious curve to edge of blunt-tipped closed wing. Most like Reed Warbler (*p. 407*), which has shorter, slimmer, whiter undertail coverts. Plumage more **uniform** than Grasshopper (*p. 412*), Sedge (*p. 406*) Warblers.

VOICE Sharp, metallic "*pvit*". Song like Grasshopper Warbler, often at night, but **lower and faster**, more purring or buzzing than ticking/reeling.

ADULT

'thick' rear-end, broad tail

underside browner towards tail

River Warbler *Locustella fluviatilis*
14·5–16 cm | WS 16–18 cm

Resembles Savi's Warbler, but long undertail coverts darker with prominent pale crescentic tips; **throat and breast subtly streaked**.

VOICE Song sharp, metallic, shaking trill, fast, rhythmic or mechanical "*schili-schili-schili-schili-schili-schili . . .*".

Very rare migrant/vagrant from N Europe: <50 records (Britain), May–Sep. Widespread. Damp bushy places.

long, sharp bill

ADULT

streaked throat and breast

broad, plain wing; long, curved outer edge often noticeably pale

Grasshopper Warbler

Locustella naevia ● **536**

12·5–13·5 cm | WS 16–18 cm

🕐 Rare *Locustella* warblers (*p. 411, 413*)

Located by **distinctive song**.
Secretive, rather elongated warbler, creeping, skulking in low, dense vegetation. May flush at close range, flits ahead, dives back down; looks **pale, yellowish, round-tailed**.

Subtly marked. ADULT olive- to yellowish-brown, **soft streaks** on crown and back; some have diffuse flank streaks.
Dark streaks under tail may be conspicuous as bird tilts and drops out of sight. **Undertail coverts long**, extending well down tail. JUVENILE often more yellow; some have slight fine streaking on throat or chest. Sedge Warbler (*p. 406*) has stronger back/rump contrast, bolder stripe over eye.

VOICE Sharp "*tik*" or "*psit*". **Song remarkable**, at dusk or in warm, sultry weather: **prolonged reeling trill**, often for minutes on end; **mechanical**, more like old-fashioned freewheeling bicycle than insect; at distance, thinner, whirring trill on one note (volume changes occasionally). Savi's Warbler (*p. 411*) similar; also see Nightjar (*p. 290*) (quality very different).

Rare and local summer visitor, Apr–Oct (11,000 pairs, plus 24,000 birds in Ireland); scarce on migration, mostly coastal

to Africa

Tall grass, often growing through scrub/brambles; reedbeds

Song helps locate a singing bird in thicket or on low, exposed perch.

ADULT

some 1st-winter birds are quite yellowish overall

1ST-WINTER

tapered both ends; long, low crown profile

1ST-WINTER

Lanceolated Warbler
Locustella lanceolata
12 cm | WS 16–18 cm

Vagrant from Asia: <150 records (Britain), Sep–Oct. Mostly N Isles. Dense vegetation.

Like small, extremely skulking, short-tailed Grasshopper Warbler but more distinctly streaked; **tertials have sharper, narrow pale fringes**; **diffuse streaking beneath** on autumn immatures more extensive than on young Grasshopper Warbler.

Migrant Lanceolated Warblers are usually very skulking, and brief views of small parts at a time are most likely!

broad, pale fringes

GRASSHOPPER WARBLER

striking black tertials with narrow pale fringes

1ST-WINTER

wide plumage variation

1ST-WINTER

Pallas's Grasshopper Warbler   *Locustella certhiola*
13–14 cm | WS 18–20 cm

Vagrant from Asia: <75 records (<5 Ireland), Sep–Oct. Mostly N Isles. Dense vegetation.

Like Grasshopper Warbler and similarly skulking, difficult to observe in low vegetation. Stronger dark cap, pale stripe over eye; sharper white edges/tips on blackish tertials; **white tips beyond blackish band on tail feathers**.

bright, yellow-buff-olive underparts, warm chestnut/rufous rump, contrasting with long, very dark tail

1ST-WINTER

white tips to dark tail

Icterine Warbler
Hippolais icterina
12–13.5 cm | WS 22 cm

Rare migrant: 50–80 per year, (<250 records Ireland), mostly autumn on coast in E/SE England). Trees, scrub.

Slightly bigger, bulkier than Willow Warbler (*p. 428*); stronger bill, legs. Like Melodious Warbler but more lively, less skulking. ADULT pale grey-green and yellow (brightest in spring). JUVENILE usually **paler than Willow Warbler**. Underside white; pale yellow throat and breast. **Pale between eye and bill** (unlike Willow Warbler but same as Melodious Warbler). Differs from Melodious Warbler in wing structure; **pale wing panel** (occasionally worn off on adults, weaker on juveniles).

VOICE Infrequent hard "*tek*" (Reed Warbler (*p. 407*) calls more often).

Melodious Warbler
Hippolais polyglotta
12–13 cm | WS 20–21 cm

Very rare migrant: (20–30 per year, declining (vagrant Ireland <250 records), mostly autumn on coast in S/SW England). Trees, scrub.

Like Icterine Warbler (also see Willow (*p. 428*) and Reed (*p. 407*) Warblers). More skulking, subdued, rounder/pear-shaped than Icterine Warbler. Typically rounder head; **plainer wings**. **Wing structure** crucial. ADULT greener above than Icterine Warbler, more uniformly yellowish below, even in autumn. JUVENILE paler fringes on wing, but striking Icterine Warbler-like pale wing panel not usual.

VOICE Call subdued sparrow-like chattering, and short "*tchret-tret*".

Primary projection half length of longest tertial (**short wing**); usually no pale wing panel.

MELODIOUS short

Primary projection) equals longest tertial (**long-winged** effect); usually prominent pale wing panel.

ICTERINE long

1ST-WINTER

pale

pale edges to wing feathers

plain wing

pale

ICTERINE WARBLER

MELODIOUS WARBLER

ADULT [Aug]

broad, pale bill, a touch smaller than on Icterine Warbler

bill pink-orange; large, pointed, wide-based

ADULT

ADULT [May]

legs browner than Icterine Warbler

legs bluish-grey

Note Willow Warbler has orange-brown legs

Eastern Olivaceous Warbler *Iduna pallida*

12–13·5 cm | WS 18–21 cm

Slim, **long-billed**, square-tailed warbler; very pale brownish-buff, paler beneath. Slight dark line from eye to bill and short, weak pale stripe above. **White-edged tail**. Closed wingtip half tertial length. See larger, greyer Olive Tree Warbler.

Vagrant from SE Europe: <25 records (<5 Ireland), Sep–Oct. On coast. Trees, scrub tall vegetation.

Sykes's, Booted Warb;ers (p. 416), Olive Tree Warbler, Blyth's Reed Warbler (p. 408)

ADULT

long bill broad at base, shows much pale orange-yellow.

plain pale brown; faint or no pale wing panel

particularly bright, pale and clean below

1ST-WINTER

Frequently dips tail downwards (like Chiffchaff (p. 426)); smaller Sykes's Warbler (p. 416) extremely similar.

Olive Tree Warbler *Hippolais olivetorum*   537

16–18 cm | WS 26–28 cm

Slightly larger than Barred Warbler (p. 424); greyer than Eastern Olivaceous Warbler. **Long** wingtip projection, eight primary tips show; **long tail**; weak mark between eye and bill, short pale line above; greyish head and back, darker wings with strong **pale panel**; whitish tail sides.

VOICE Call deep "*tuc*".

Vagrant: 1 record (Britain), Aug. N Isles. Trees, scrub.

long, deep bill orange-yellow at base

ADULT

1ST-WINTER

Pale, grey and heavy up-front, this is a bigger, greyer bird than Eastern Olivaceous Warbler.

Booted Warbler *Iduna caligata*

11–12·5 cm | WS 18–21 cm

Vagrant from Asia: <200 records (<10 Ireland), most Aug–Oct. On coast. Scrub, tall vegetation.

Chiffchaff (*p. 426*) size, pale Reed Warbler (*p. 407*) colours: short, hard call. Short undertail coverts, spiky bill indicate possible Booted/Sykes's Warbler or *Hippolais* warbler (*p. 414*), but see Blyth's Reed Warbler (*p. 408*). Buff- to grey-brown; **short pale stripe over eye**; **weak, dark eyestripe reaching bill**; sides of crown may look darker. **Short, fine bill dark near tip. Tertials dark-centred, tips evenly spaced**; short wingtip. Very thin pale edges to tail; feather tips square. Legs pinkish-brown. Similar Eastern Olivaceous Warbler (*p. 415*) has longer wingtip.

VOICE Call short, dry "*chrek*".

Eastern Olivaceous (*p. 415*), Blyth's Reed (*p. 408*) Warblers

subtly dark between eye and bill

subtle dark 'smudge' near tip below

square tail, short body, short under tail coverts give *Phylloscopus*-like effect, but forages low like *Acrocephalus*

1ST-WINTER

Comparison of Booted and Syke's Warblers			
	Head	Bill and legs	Wing and tail
Booted Warbler	Pale stripe over eye **distinct** **Weak dark line** between eye and bill	BILL: **Short, fine; dark towards tip** LEGS: **pinkish-brown**	TERTIALS: **dark centred** TAIL: **square**
Syke's Warbler	Pale stripe over eye **less distinct** **Pale** between eye and bill	BILL: **Longer, spiky; pale to tip** LEGS: **Longer, dark grey**	TERTIALS: **plain** TAIL: **graduated**

Sykes's Warbler *Iduna rama*

11·5–13 cm | WS 18–21 cm

Vagrant from Asia: <25 records (<5 Ireland), Aug–Oct. On coast. Scrub, tall vegetation.

Very like Booted, Eastern Olivaceous (*p. 415*), Blyth's Reed (*p. 408*) Warblers – subtle features depend on angle and light but strikingly like *Acrocephalus* in shape. Sandy grey; short **pale stripe over eye** less defined than Booted Warbler; **pale between eye and bill** (no stripe); dark sides to lower crown. **Long, spiky bill pale to tip. Tertials plain, tips unevenly spaced**; short wingtips. **Graduated tail feathers visible in frequent flicks; longer body shape than Booted Warbler**; undertail coverts shorter than Blyth's Reed Warbler).

VOICE Call short, dry "*chek*".

Eastern Olivaceous (*p. 415*), Blyth's Reed (*p. 408*) Warblers

compared to Booted, longer bill and graduated tail, looks more like *Acrocephalus* but forages higher like *Phylloscopus*

weakly-defined pale stripe

pale between eye and bill

bil pale

1ST-WINTER

Dartford Warbler

Sylvia undata **536**

13–14 cm | WS 16–18 cm

 Marmora's Warbler (*p. 423*)

Marmora's Warbler (*p. 423*)

Rare and very local resident (3,000 pairs, declines in severe winters); very rare migrant. Vagrant Ireland (<15 records)

Elusive, secretive, long-tailed warbler of heather/gorse. Very small; tail exaggerates size, often but not always raised. Located by call or song, often hard to see well. Flies **low and fast over heather**, tail dipping, swooping into gorse, small pine, or deep heather.

Darker, longer- and thinner-tailed than Whitethroat (*p. 420*); **red eyering**. Long-tailed, short-winged, pot-bellied (but can look slim). MALE dark blue-grey, throat and **breast brownish-red**. FEMALE paler, duller, brownish grey; paler on throat. JUVENILE paler, greyer; browner wings.

VOICE Call distinctive (Whitethroat comes close) **buzzing churr**: low, soft, simple, nasal "*chairrrr*". Song brighter, fast sequence, whistles and buzzy notes in jumbled warble, usually from half- or fully hidden perch in gorse.

Heather/gorse heath (mostly S England, coastal East Anglia; rare S Wales, Midlands)

1ST-WINTER

Dispersing 1st-winter birds appear in coastal brambles, scrub and gorse bushes, but long tail, dark head and back, and rusty flanks should dispel thoughts of rarer species.

classic gorse-top pose, but more often hidden deep inside bush or heather

tail often slightly raised, sometimes flat or held very high

ADULT ♂

ADULT ♀

Blackcap
Sylvia atricapilla

13·5–15 cm | WS 20–23 cm

👁 Western Orphean Warbler (p. 424)

Small, stocky, slightly sluggish woodland bird; heavy movements. Marsh Tit (*p. 450*) superficially similar (but has black bib). Wintering birds visit bird tables.

MALE plain grey-brown, paler below, **round black cap** (falls short of gape). Pale grey collar from rear. FEMALE pale grey-brown, brighter buffish below, pale undertail may show as streak; dull **rufous cap**. JUVENILE has darker rusty cap (immature male in autumn shows mixed brown/black cap).

VOICE Hard, unmusical "*tek*" or "*tak*"; quick, anxious series if alarmed. Compare song with Garden Warbler, which it may mimic – rich, throaty, fast, **fluty warble, vigorous and musical**, typically low start increases in speed and volume, more strident, more forceful than Garden Warbler. Faster, less varied, shorter than Nightingale (*p. 389*).

Common summer visitor (900,000 pairs, plus 260,000 birds in Ireland), passage migrant; small numbers winter

from NW Europe

from C Europe

to Mediterranean

Woodland, thickets, parkland

MARSH TIT (*p. 450*) – possible confusion species – note black nape; more extensive black cap; black in front of eye, black bib

cap brighter rufous than juvenile

ADULT ♀

ADULT ♂

MALES sing from bush-top to tall tree-top height; sometimes two or three together in brief skirmish, with prolonged songs.

ADULT ♂

males show black feathers in cap

1ST-WINTER

Garden Warbler

Sylvia borin `536`

13–14·5 cm | WS 20–22 cm

Small, brown, woodland bird: see Blackcap, Spotted Flycatcher (*p. 439*). No contrasted cap, no green or yellow – a **plain, pale brownish** warbler. Quite skulking, slow and sedate; sits still for lengthy spells, but flies rapidly between songposts.

Upperparts sandy-grey-brown; less rusty than Reed Warbler (*p. 407*) (which has longer head/bill profile, less rounded). **Bland head pattern** with thin whitish eyering, usually faint pale stripe over eye; diffuse greyish neck patch. Large dark eye prominent. Bill dark blue-grey, slightly **thick and stubby** for a warbler; legs dark grey. JUVENILE has crisp, very fine, pale feather edges on wing and tail.

VOICE Call "*chek*" or "*tsak*", a little softer, more wooden than Blackcap's; alarm more 'chuffing' "*chuff-chuff-chuff*" or "*cha cha cha*". Song may be like Blackcap's but generally longer phrases, simpler, more even delivery: **fast, flowing/bubbling tempo** (less acceleration in middle, less forceful finish).

Locally common summer visitor, Apr–Sep (190,000 pairs, scarce Ireland), passage migrant

from/to Scandinavia

to Africa

from/to Africa

Woodland, thickets, scrub

superficial resemblance to Spotted Flycatcher soon lost with skulking behaviour in foliage

ADULT

ADULT ♂

MALES sing from low bramble to tall tree height; inconspicuous but may fly long distance to new song perch.

fresh autumn feathers have immaculate pale fringes

1ST-WINTER

Whitethroat

Sylvia communis

13–15 cm | WS 18–22 cm

⊙ ▶ Rare *Sylvia* warblers (p. 422–425)

Locally common summer visitor, Apr–Oct (930,000 pairs, plus 95,000 birds in Ireland), migrant

Bright, pale warbler; **rufous wings**, **white throat**. Alert, perky; male raises crown, puffs out throat. Frequently raises and swings tail, dives into depths of dense vegetation. **Bouncy song flight**, or sings from exposed wire or twig, or from cover. Compare Lesser Whitethroat.

Broad, **gingery-rufous feather edges** on wings. Tail long, slim, **white-sided**. Legs **pale yellow-orange**. MALE grey head, broken white eyering, white throat (greyish centre if ruffled). FEMALE browner, head greyish-brown, gingery cheeks; some nearly as grey as male. Rufous wing patch conspicuous against duller olive back and rump. JUVENILE neat, bright: strongly contrasted dark feather centres/sandy edges on wing.

VOICE Varied; including nasal, slightly buzzy, breathy "*aid-aid-aid*", longer, buzzy "*churr*", rhythmic "*wichety-wichety*". Song (perched or in wing-waving song flight) fast, **churring, scratchy warble** with fast rise-fall rhythm.

from/to NW Europe

to Africa

from/to Africa

Hedgerows, scrub, thickets, dense bramble patches, nettle beds

ADULT ♂ (display flight)

ADULT ♂

MALES sing from wires or tall perches, or well hidden in dense hedgerow, bramble patch or nettle bed, but periodically rise into fluttery song flight (*right*)

grey head

ADULT ♂

head usually greyish-brown with gingery cheeks

1ST-WINTER

ADULT ♀

Lesser Whitethroat

Sylvia curruca ⓘ `536`

11·5–13·5 cm | WS 17–22 cm

Small, sleek warbler; no bright colours. Skulking, often disappears out of back of bush.

⟨◉⟩ Rare *Sylvia* warblers (*p. 422–425*)

Like compact, short-tailed, grey Whitethroat; head darker, **cheeks contrast more with white throat**. Back dull, **no rufous on wings. Legs blue-grey**; eyes dark. JUVENILE bright, pale; white eyering; dark mark from eye to bill; paler edges to flight feathers. IN FLIGHT, shows **white outer tail feathers**.

VOICE Clicking, hard "*tet*" or "*tuk*", sharper than Blackcap's (*p. 418*); high "*see*". Song low warble before loud, wooden rattle "*tuk-atuk-atuk-atuk-atuk-atuk-atuk*".

Scarce summer visitor, Apr–Oct (64,000 pairs), passage migrant; has bred in Ireland

to
E Africa

Tall, dense hedgerows, thickets

WINTER **presumed 'Central Asian' Lesser Whitethroat**
race *blythi/halimodendri*

1ST-WINTER **presumed 'Central Asian' Lesser Whitethroat**
race *minula/halimodendri*

'Siberian' Lesser Whitethroat – race *blythi* (vagrant, <100 records: Oct–Feb) paler head, whiter line over eye than breeding birds (European race *curruca*). 'Central Asian'/'Desert' Lesser Whitethroat – race(s) *minula/halimodendri* (perhaps vagrant) brown nape, buff flanks, pale lores, short wings/long tail, much white in outer tail; tit-like call.

some individuals have pale stripe over eye

1ST-WINTER race *curruca*

1ST-WINTER

Eastern races sometimes suspected but rarely confirmed, as identification not straightforward, sometimes probably impossible without DNA sample.

ADULT race *curruca*

The Subalpine Warbler complex from S Europe includes four races, three of which have occurred in Britain: **'Western' Subalpine Warbler** (race *iberiae*) and **'Eastern' Subalpine Warbler** (races *cantillans* and *albistriata*), plus a closely similar species, **Moltoni's Subalpine Warbler**.

ADULT MALES
Apart from tail pattern and call differences are subtle and colours vary with light conditions; see table for descriptions.

'Eastern'
SUBALPINE
race *albistriata*

'Western'
SUBALPINE

race *iberiae*

Subalpine Warbler *Sylvia cantillans*

12–13 cm | WS 17–21 cm

MALES greyish above, with white 'moustache'; pinkish below. FEMALES/JUVENILES all paler, browner than male; slight white moustache. Red around eye inside whitish eyering; eyering and pale yellowish legs rule out Lesser Whitethroat (*p. 421*); 'Western' Subalpine Warbler and Moltoni's Subalpine Warbler inseparable without call. See table for summary of key features.

Very rare migrant/vagrant: *iberiae* (from Iberia, S France and Italy) and *cantillans* (from Italy) presumed to form majority (past records mostly unassignable to race), >500 records (>50 Ireland), 25–35 per year, mostly S in spring; *albistriata* from SE Europe <50 records, Apr–Oct. Most on coast. Scrub.

Moltoni's Subalpine Warbler *Sylvia subalpina*

11·5–13 cm | WS 18–21 cm

Very like Subalpine Warbler. See table for differences.

Vagrant from Mallorca, Corsica, Sardinia, N Italy: <5 records (Britain), May–Jun, Oct. On coast. Scrub.

FEMALES/IMMATURES all very similar; tail pattern essential for ID (see table)
IMMATURE 'rufous' *Sylvia* warblers can be difficult to identify – see opposite

ADULT ♀
'Western'
race *iberiae*

MOLTONI'S
SUBALPINE

Identification of 'subalpine' warblers – summary of key features

	MOLTONI'S SUBALPINE WARBLER	SUBALPINE WARBLER		
		'Western' – *iberiae*	'Eastern' – *cantillans*	'Eastern' – *albistriata*
ID Criteria	FROM 'EASTERN' SUBALPINE: tail pattern FROM 'WESTERN' SUBALPINE: call	FROM 'EASTERN' SUBALPINE: tail pattern FROM MOLTONI'S SUBALPINE: call DNA required to confirm race	FROM 'WESTERN' SUBALPINE and MOLTONI'S SUBALPINE: tail pattern DNA required to confirm race	
Call	**Rolling, dry "ttrrrrr"**, like Wren (*p. 369*), fading at end	Soft "*chuk*" and harder "*tek*" or "*tek-tek-tek*"	similar to 'Western' Subalpine	**Dry, hard click, "tet"** or rolling **"trret"**
	Small white tip on 2nd outermost feather (T5) curves **up inner edge, not up shaft**; less white on 3rd outermost feather (T4) T4 T5		White on 2nd outermost feather (T5) extends **up shaft** on inner web forming large white wedge; **much white** on 3rd outer feather (T4) T4 T5	
Spring ♂	UPPERPARTS: pale grey UNDERPARTS: pale brownish or buffish pink extending to belly WHITE MOUSTACHE: intermediate	UPPERPARTS: blue-grey, dusky or purplish; wings browner grey UNDERPARTS: brick-red to deep pink breast and flanks; paler belly WHITE MOUSTACHE: thinner	UPPERPARTS: pale grey UNDERPARTS: pale brownish or buffish pink extending to belly WHITE MOUSTACHE: broader	

'Rufous' *Sylvia* immatures

Juvenile **Subalpine**, **Moltoni's** and **Spectacled Warblers** all look broadly similar to the common **Whitethroat** and care needs to be taken to distinguish between them. The pattern of the tertials is one reliable feature that can be used.

Vagrant from S Europe: <10 records (Britain), May–Jul, Oct. On coast, inland. Low scrub.

Spectacled Warbler *Sylvia conspicillata*
12–13 cm | WS 18–20 cm

Like small, dark Whitethroat (*p. 420*). MALE **black between eye and bill**, blue-grey hood, white throat, dusky pink underparts, unstreaked rufous wing patch. FEMALE/1ST-WINTER like Whitethroat and subalpine warblers; **more extensive rufous** (few/no dark centres) on wing; pointed dark centres to tertials; shorter primary projection; yellower legs, dark tail with broad white sides.

VOICE Call "*tchhh tchhh*". Song short, fast, even warble.

MOLTONI'S SUBALPINE WARBLER
JUVENILE

dark tertials edged **tawny-brown**

wings lacking rufous patch

tertials edged **rufous** with **rounded** dark centres

primary projection **long**

dark centres to rufous feathers

WHITETHROAT

ADULT ♀ / 1ST-WINTER

ADULT ♂

tertials edged **rufous** with **pointed** dark centres

legs yellowish

primary projection **short**

RE **(Asian) Desert Warbler** *Sylvia nana*
11·5–12·5 cm | WS 18–20 cm

Small, pale warbler, like Whitethroat (*p. 420*) with pale, bland face. Pale grey-brown above, **rump and tail rufous** with dark feather centres and white sides; bill and legs pale; **eye yellow**.

VOICE Call fast, nasal, tit-like "*tr-r-r-chair-chair*". Song rich, fluty warble.

ADULT

Vagrant from Asia: <15 records (Britain), May, Sep–Dec. On coast. Scrub.

Marmora's Warbler *Sylvia sarda*   536
13–14 cm | WS 16–18 cm

Resembles pale grey Dartford Warbler (*p. 417*); JUVENILE difficult, but whiter throat and belly, flanks greyer.

VOICE Call short dry "*chr't*". Song like short, fast, churring phrase of Robin (*p. 388*).

ADULT ♂

Vagrant from Mediterranean: <10 records (Britain), May–Jun. Upland/coastal heath.

Barred Warbler *Sylvia nisoria* `536`

15·5–17 cm | WS 22–25 cm

Long, heavy, square-tailed warbler. Tends to move slowly
(or stay still for long spells) in thick scrub. MALE steely-grey;
two white wingbars, **white tertial tips**; grey bars below.
Yellow eye in dark face. Vaguely resembles Wryneck (*p. 334*).
FEMALE more broken bars; duller eye. JUVENILE (most frequent in
autumn) **grey-buff**, paler below. Pale eyering; short pale line
over **dark eye**; thrush-like bill. **Thin wingbars**; pale tertial tips.
Pale bars on rump; tail long, **dark with white sides**. Underside
pale; scaly bars on rear flank, particularly under tail.

VOICE Call long, loud, fading rattle "*trr-rr-rr-t-t-t*".

ADULT ♂

Spring MALE distinctly barred; pale
wingbar; has rising, fluttering
song flight.

big, pale, long-tailed,
heavy warbler with
bold dark eye

JUVENILE

Rare migrant from E Europe,
winters Africa: 150–350 per
year (<200 records Ireland),
most Aug–Oct. Mostly on coast.
Dense scrub.

Western Orphean Warbler *Sylvia hortensis*

15 cm | WS 25 cm

Vagrant from S Europe: <5
records (Britain), May, Sep, Nov.
On coast. Trees, bushes.

Like large, grey, stout-legged Blackcap (*p. 418*) but **dark cap
extends below eye onto cheeks**; pale eye; white throat, underparts
pinkish-white. 1ST-YEAR and 2ND-YEAR birds have dark eyes, paler ear
coverts; like **large, long- and thick-billed** Lesser Whitethroat (*p. 421*).

VOICE Dry, churred "*trr-trr-t*".

all plumages have
diffuse dark hood rather
than sharp cap

bigger than Lesser Whitethroat;
stouter bill with paler base; longer,
wider tail with bolder white side

1ST-WINTER

ADULT ♂

Sardinian Warbler *Sylvia melanocephala*
13–14 cm | WS 18–22 cm

Long-tailed warbler; males easy, females confusing. Compare subalpine warblers (*p. 422*), Whitethroat (*p. 420*). Tends to keep low. Tail long, slender, **blackish with white sides** (white 'corners' or spotted rim in low, fast flight to next bush). MALE grey, **blackish hood** extending over cheeks, white throat; **red eyering**. FEMALE drab, browner: **hood grey**, red eyering paler, throat greyish. JUVENILE even browner; white throat against dark underside (see Rüppell's Warbler).

VOICE Loud, hard "*tsek*" and distinctive longer rattle, varying in pitch and pace, "*tuet-et-et-et-et-et-et*".

Vagrant from S Europe: <100 records (<5 Ireland), mostly spring. Mostly on coast. Low scrub, thickets.

1ST-WINTER ♂

darker grey head than female

All plumages have striking white throat and a red eyering

ADULT ♂

ADULT ♀

Rüppell's Warbler *Sylvia rueppelli* 536
14 cm | WS 23–25 cm

Grey warbler with heavy, curved bill. MALE **black face and throat, white moustache**; red eye. FEMALE/1ST-WINTER pale throat but whiter moustache stands out; pale blue-grey bill; dark tail with white sides; **well-defined pale edges to wing coverts** and tertials. See subalpine (*p. 422*) and Sardinian Warblers.

VOICE Dry, fast chatter. Song slower, deeper rattle than Sardinian Warbler.

Vagrant from SE Europe: <10 records (Britain), Apr–Jun, Sep. On coast. Dense scrub.

ADULT ♂

ADULT ♀

Chiffchaff

Phylloscopus collybita

10–12 cm | WS 15–21 cm

Very small, active, 'tail-dipping' woodland bird.

Iberian Chiffchaff, rare *Phylloscopus* warblers (pp. 430–435)

Compared with similar Willow Warbler (*p. 428*): slightly finer bill, rounder head, shorter wing; frequent **downward tail 'dips'** more obvious than Willow Warbler's tail flourish.

ADULT race *collybita* (majority British/Irish birds) green or dull, **dusky olive** with pale edges to dark wing and tail. Pale stripe over eye; dark eyestripe; **white crescent under eye**. Underside dull, yellowish, whiter under tail. Legs **thin, dark** brown–black. (Willow Warbler's legs typically pale, sometimes dark with paler feet, not so spindly.) Fresh autumn plumage, brighter, yellower, more buff beneath. JUVENILE late summer/autumn greener, yellower below; pale orange bill base.

VOICE Simple "*hweet*", less disyllabic than Willow Warbler, less forceful than similar note of Chaffinch (*p. 481*). In summer/autumn, slurred "*shrilip*" or "*shlip*". Short "*hoot*" in autumn. Song obvious: well-defined, even-paced notes in random sequence, "*chip-chap-chiff-chap-chap-chiff-chee*". Interspersed with low "*grrt-grrt*". Song frequent in autumn.

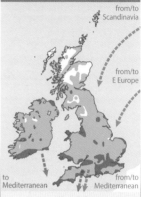

Very common summer visitor, most Mar–Oct (750,000 pairs, plus 300,000 birds in Ireland), migrant; rare winter (few 100s)

from/to Scandinavia

from/to E Europe

to Mediterranean

from/to Mediterranean

Woodland; willows close to water; well-wooded gardens, parks

ADULT (SPRING) race *collybita*

CHIFFCHAFF race *collybita*

dark legs

WILLOW WARBLER

pale legs

Winter birds typically dull, grey-olive, wings and tail darker, unlike 'cleaner' Willow Warbler.

1ST-WINTER race *collybita*

Early March Chiffchaffs like willows close to water, with abundant insects; or sing from open, still-leafless trees – easier to see than in mid-summer foliage.

Chiffchaff races – key features

collybita	COLOUR: 'Olive and yellow'. CALL: a rising "*hweet*"
abietinus	COLOUR: Grey/buff, less olive/yellow, yellow streaks below and on face; others paler, 'colourless', whiter below. CALL: "*hweet*"
tristis	COLOUR: Grey-khaki-brown; buff over eye, breast sides, flanks; yellow only on underwing/bend of wing. CALL: a flat cheep "*eeep*" or "*peet*"

Some autumn/winter birds match N/E European race *abietinus*: greyer or browner, dull grey-buff beneath (same structure, leg colour, eyering, tail-dip as other races).

1ST-WINTER race *abietinus*

1ST-WINTER race *tristis*

1ST-WINTER race *collybita*

'Siberian Chiffchaff' race *tristis* rare (100–145 per year, autumn–winter) (includes browner form *fulvescens* from W Siberia): brown and buff, wing and tail weakly edged greener, no yellow beneath; wider buff line over eye, blackish eyestripe; bill and legs black. Call flat "*peep*".

Iberian Chiffchaff *Phylloscopus ibericus*

11–12 cm | WS 15–21 cm

Vagrant from Iberia: <50 records (1 Ireland), Mar–Jul. Widespread. Woodland.

May be impossible on plumage, but compared with Chiffchaff: upperparts slightly greener, more contrasted buffish-yellow breast/whiter belly, yellowish edges to brown wing feathers. Yellow line over eye /dark eyestripe more like Willow Warbler. Wingtip slightly longer than Chiffchaff.

VOICE Call **slurred down**, not up, "*wee-oo*". Song distinctive: typically three sections, "*djup djup djup wheep wheep chittichittichittichitta*" or "*chop chop wheep wheep chuckachuckachuckachucka*".

Colours, longish wingtip close to Willow Warbler; hard to tell from Chiffchaff without voice (note: southern Iberian populations have shorter wing, like Chiffchaff).

yellow stripe over eye

weak eyering

yellowish base to bill

yellow throat

ADULT (SPRING)

yellow vent

white belly

Willow Warbler

Phylloscopus trochilus  except race *acredula*

11–12·5 cm | WS 15–21 cm

Small, slim, pale 'green' warbler of trees and bushes.

⊙ Iberian Chiffchaff (*p. 427*), rare *Phylloscopus* warblers (*p. 430–435*)

Locally very common summer visitor, Apr–Oct (2 million pairs, plus 1·6 million birds in Ireland), passage migrant

See Chiffchaff (often difficult): slightly longer; flatter head; **longer wingtip**; **paler legs**; does not 'dip' tail frequently.

ADULT brighter, cleaner than average Chiffchaff (*p. 426*) (often subtle). Typically greenish above, pale yellow-cream breast, whiter belly. Quite **strong yellowish line over eye**; weaker eyering above paler cheek than Chiffchaff. Bill more extensively pale. **Legs pale orange-brown**, sometimes darker with pale feet. Wings much plainer than Wood Warbler. JUVENILE stronger yellow stripe over eye, more solidly **yellow** beneath.

VOICE Call more firmly two syllables than Chiffchaff: "*hoo-eet*", like Redstart (*p. 392*). Song immediately distinctive: short, sweet, lilting, whistling cadence, descending overall.

from/to NW Europe

to Africa

from/to Africa

Woods, scattered birches/oaks/ willows on heaths, moors

ADULT (SPRING)

Frequently sings from top or side of bush on exposed perch; allows close views with careful approach.

ADULT (SPRING) race *trochilus*

'clean' and pale compared with Chiffchaff

legs nearly always paler, browner than Chiffchaff's

strong yellow stripe over eye; pale bill

1ST-WINTER race *trochilus*

1ST-WINTER race *acredula*

Scandinavian race *acredula* (scarce migrant) is greyer above, whiter below than British/Irish breeders (widespread European race *trochilus*).

Wood Warbler

Phylloscopus sibilatrix ● ❶

11–12·5 cm | WS 16–22 cm

👁 Bonelli's warblers (*p. 430*)

A bright 'green' warbler of dense woodland canopy above open ground/leaf-litter, most easily **located by song**.

Slightly bigger than Willow Warbler; long, wide-bellied: long wings often drooped beside **short, broad tail**. ADULT greener than Willow Warbler; **long yellow stripe over eye**; broad, dark eyestripe. Lower face, upper breast pale lemon-yellow, against white underside. More contrast than Willow Warbler, but many are pale yellow only on throat. Wings **more contrasted** than Willow Warbler or Chiffchaff (*p. 426*), brown feathers edged yellow-green, blacker-centred tertials.

VOICE Call high, sweet, sad "*siuuh*". Song: rhythmic repetition of call note (resembling Willow Tit (*p. 451*)), between more frequent trills – metallic, ticking firming up into **short, fast trill** (see also Western and Eastern Bonelli's warblers (*p. 430*)).

Scarce and local summer visitor, Apr–Sep (17,000 pairs); rare migrant outside breeding areas

to Africa

Oak, Beech, Larch woods

ADULT (SPRING)

Wood Warbler in early summer is best found by following up the silvery trilled song in woodland without an understorey.

strength of yellow throat varies; some very pale

ADULT (SPRING)

1ST-WINTER

ADULT (SPRING)

long wingtip often drooped beside tail

'clean' white underside; no hint of buff or yellow

Western Bonelli's Warbler *Phylloscopus bonelli*

10·5–11·5 cm | WS 18–20 cm

Vagrant from SW Europe:
<150 records (<20 Ireland),
most Aug–Oct. Mostly on coast.
Trees/bushes.

Slender, pale warbler, Chiffchaff (*p. 426*) size. Grey-green, rump **brighter yellowish-green; silky white below. Head rather plain**; weak line behind eye; short pale stripe over eye. Wing and tail feathers edged pale green. Bill sturdy, pale base, dark tip; legs mid- or dark brown.

VOICE Call long "*tu-eee*". Song fast, soft, **bubbling trill**, even speed and pitch, "*prr-r-r-r-r-r-r-r-r-r-r*" (resembles Wood Warbler (*p. 429*); song of Cirl Bunting (*p. 501*) also similar but more metallic).

Beware 'grey' Chiffchaff
(probably race *abietinus*)
with green fringes on wing.

1ST-WINTER

ADULT (SPRING)

Bonelli's warbler calls	
WESTERN "*tu-eee*"	
EASTERN **short** "*chip*"	

Eastern Bonelli's Warbler *Phylloscopus orientalis*

11–12 cm | WS 18–20 cm

Vagrant from SE Europe:
<10 records (Britain), May, Sep,
Oct. On coast. Trees/bushes.

Small, pale warbler almost identical to Western Bonelli's Warbler; **call** vital. Greyish above, brighter, greener wings and rump; white underside.

VOICE Call **distinctive short "*chip*"**.

Beware 'grey' Chiffchaff
(probably race *abietinus*)
with green fringes on wing.

1ST-WINTER

ADULT (SPRING)

Dusky Warbler *Phylloscopus fuscatus*

10·5–12 cm | WS 16–19 cm

Vagrant from Asia: 15–20 per year (total <15 Ireland), most Sep–Nov. Mostly on coast. Dense scrub, woods.

Slighter, browner than Radde's Warbler, rather like **brown Chiffchaff** (*p. 426*) **calling like Blackcap** (*p. 418*). Upperparts dull grey-brown, paler below, pale creamy/brighter buff undertail. **Long, wide, pale stripe over eye** sharply defined throughout, **buff behind eye**, often thin at front. **Bill fine, sharp**; legs brown.

VOICE Hard "*tek*" or clicking note, sometimes short series (beware Wren (*p. 369*)!) or softer, sucked, "*ch'k*" or "*tsuc*".

small, skulking, brown warbler with marked stripe over eye

1ST-WINTER

Radde's Warbler *Phylloscopus schwarzi*

11·5–12·5 cm | WS 17–19 cm

Vagrant from Asia: 7–10 per year (total <20 Ireland), most Sep–Oct. Mostly on coast. Dense scrub, woods.

Small, stocky, thick-legged warbler; often in thick cover, hard to see. Similar to Dusky Warbler. Olive-brown; yellowish or buff below with brighter flanks, **apricot-buff under tail**. **Long stripe over eye** blurry buff at front, sharply defined cream/white at rear; broad dark eyestripe. Cheeks rather mottled. **Bill quite thick**, pale orange/pink; legs pale orange-yellow.

VOICE Rather soft "*chuc*", subdued or louder, often in long series, "*chrep*" or "*chett*".

bold broad stripe over eye; long, tapering towards nape

1ST-WINTER

Wing-barred warblers

Until recent years, Yellow-browed Warblers were rare 'Siberian' vagrants, but numbers have steadily increased and now several hundred might be expected in an autumn. Some of these penetrate far inland and some remain to winter, but it is still essentially a late September–October bird of coasts, headlands and islands. Only after the main influx of Yellow-browed Warblers might fewer Pallas's Warblers be expected, always much scarcer despite a recent increase. Hume's Warblers remain rare, often later arrivals, sometimes wintering.

Warblers with single wing-bars (shown on *pp. 434–435*) are rather different: Greenish Warbler is the most frequent, usually seen around late August, while Arctic Warbler is scarcer, more northerly, and others remain great rarities, mostly difficult to identify with confidence.

from Siberia

These rare migrants are also typical of northern isles, or prominent coasts and headlands in the east, where large numbers of commoner migrants might be expected.

Pallas's Warbler *Phylloscopus proregulus*

9–9.5 cm | WS 14–16 cm

Tiny, most like Yellow-browed Warbler (also see Firecrest (*p. 437*)). Green above, whitish beneath; short upper wingbar; **broad yellow midwing bar**; tertial edges pale. **Very long pale stripe over eye, black eyestripe**; long, narrow **pale central crown stripe**, green-black bands either side. Diagnostic **pale yellow rump** shows when wings flicked, or when hovers.

VOICE Calls less frequently than Yellow-browed Warbler, softer, rising "*chuee*".

> Vagrant from Asia: 50–100 per year (total <50 Ireland), Oct–Nov, a few overwinter. Mostly on coast. Woods (particularly with Sycamore), scrubby thickets.

Yellow-browed Warbler *Phylloscopus inornatus*

9–10.5 cm | WS 15–16 cm

Active, smaller than Chiffchaff (*p. 426*). Inconspicuous, but often calls. Low thicket to treetop; constant wing/tail twitching. **Long, cream/yellow stripe over eye**, dark eyestripe (see Pallas's, Hume's Warblers). Wing much like Pallas's Warbler: eye-catching, **broad** midwing bar **yellow-cream. Tertials tipped white** (plain on Greenish Warbler (*p. 434*)). Underside silky-white, faintly streaked greyish.

VOICE Sharp, high, loud, rising "*tchu-wee!*", "*tssooee*" or "*tsweest*"; weaker, whispy, at distance.

> Vagrant from Asia: 1,000 per year, recent influxes up to 2,000, Sep–Oct, a few overwinter. Widespread, mostly on coast. Woods (particularly with Sycamore), scrubby thickets.

Hume's Warbler *Phylloscopus humei*

9–10.5 cm | WS 15–16 cm

Some unidentifiable without call; greyer or browner than Yellow-browed Warbler. Stripe over eye **tinged buff**; wingbars more **buff on grey** than yellowish on dark green; tertial tips duller. Bill blacker, legs darker.

VOICE Call essential – dull, flat "*dsweet*" or longish, slightly falling "*dsee-o*".

> Vagrant from Asia: <150 records (<5 Ireland), Oct–Mar. Mostly on coast. Woods,, scrubby thickets.

bold, striking head pattern with central crown stripe

brighter than most Yellow-browed Warblers

yellow rump

1ST-WINTER

A hovering bird may reveal the diagnostic pale yellow rump.

many individuals have a hint of a crown stripe

bright greenish to grey-green; wingbar often the feature initially most obvious

1ST-WINTER

Yellow-browed Warblers hover at times, but less so than Firecrests (*p. 437*) and Pallas's Warblers.

if present, faint crown stripe greyish-green

duller than most Yellow-browed Warblers: call is a vital clue

1ST-WINTER

'Double' wing-barred warbler calls – at a glance

YELLOW-BROWED WARBLER
Sharp, rising "***tchu-wee!***" or "***tsweest***"

PALLAS'S WARBLER
Infrequent soft, rising "***chuee***"

HUME'S WARBLER
Dull, flat "***dsweet***" or longish, descending "***dsee-o***"

Greenish Warbler *Phylloscopus trochiloides*

9·5–10·5 cm | WS 16–18 cm

Small green warbler; **thin pale wingbar**. Very like Arctic Warbler but dark eyestripe **not quite touching bill; cream stripe over eye** thin in front, **stripes meet over bill.** Whitish below. Bill small, lower half **all pale.**

VOICE Bright "*tsi-li*" or "*chilip*". Rare spring/summer migrant may sing: slightly jerky, piercing notes, break in middle and trill at end.

ADULT [May]

Most Greenish Warblers are seen in August–September, but a few arrive in late May or June and are heard singing.

in autumn the wingbar is broader on fresher-plumaged immature birds than on adults with worn plumage

1ST-WINTER [Sep]

1ST-WINTER

Very rare migrant from NE Europe: 15–20 per year (<50 records Ireland), few spring, most Aug–Sep, few Oct. Mostly coastal. Woods, scrubby thickets.

Race *plumbeitarsus* 'Two-barred Greenish Warbler' **Vagrant from Asia: <5 records (Britain): Sep–Oct)** like Green Warbler but stronger upper wingbar, pale stripes over eye fall short of bill (like Arctic Warbler).

Arctic Warbler *Phylloscopus borealis*

11·5–13 cm | WS 17–19 cm

Stocky warbler; green above; greyish breast, paler belly, faintly streaked. **Pale midwing bar**; often shorter upper bar; worn adults may not show any wingbar. Long, **broad, dark eyestripe reaches bill**; mottled cheeks. Long **yellow-cream stripe** over eye to nape **falls short of bill**. Bill strong; **dark tip to lower mandible.**

VOICE Hard "*dzit*".

stripe meets over bill

stripe falls short of bill

GREENISH WARBLER

ARCTIC WARBLER

ADULT [Sep] in worn plumage

1ST-WINTER

In autumn, fresh-plumaged immature birds are brighter and have a broader wingbar.

Very rare migrant from N Europe: 5–10 per year (<10 records Ireland), most Aug–Oct. Mostly on coast. Woods, scrubby thickets.

Vagrant from Asia: 1 record (Britain), Sep. On coast. Woods.

Green Warbler

Phylloscopus nitidus

10–11 cm | WS 15–17 cm

Small, bright greenish warbler, brighter above and **yellower below** than Greenish Warbler and Yellow-browed Warbler (*p. 432*), with **two thin, yellow wingbars**; long pale yellow stripe over eye; yellowish throat and cheeks.

Vagrant from Asia: <5 records (Britain), Oct. Woods.

Eastern Crowned Warbler

Phylloscopus coronatus

12 cm | WS 16–18 cm

Resembles Arctic Warbler: strong bill, two weak wingbars, long stripe over eye; but **dark cap** has **pale central stripe**.

bright green-and-yellow warbler

pale central crown stripe

ADULT

NB sole British record aged as 1st-winter

1ST-WINTER

Pale-legged Leaf Warbler/Sakhalin Leaf Warbler

Phylloscopus tenellipes/borealoides

10–11 cm | WS 18–20 cm

Single record identified only to species pair (near-identical except for song). Greenish above, **darker crown**, **brighter rump**; very long, narrow, pale stripe over eye; pale wingbar, often small/broken upper wingbar; white below; pale pink legs.

VOICE Sharp, metallic "*tip*". See Greenish, Arctic Warblers.

Vagrant from Asia: 1 record (Britain), Oct. On coast. Woods.

SAKHALIN LEAF WARBLER

ADULT

1ST-WINTER

PALE-LEGGED LEAF WARBLER

The two species shown here are extremely similar: confirming identification may require examination in the hand.

Goldcrest

Regulus regulus 🅘

8·5–9·5 cm | WS 14–15 cm

👁 Ruby-crowned Kinglet *(p. 511)*

Minute; like tiny, dumpy, olive-green warbler with well-marked wings, 'plain' face. Can skulk but often high in trees.

ADULT olive-green, whiter beneath, **black/white wing bands**. Face pale, weak **dark moustache** down from bill. Crown has **streak of yellow**, narrow black edge. MALE crown brighter than FEMALE's: more orange, spread in display (see Firecrest). JUVENILE lacks crown stripe.

VOICE Song rhythmic, very high-pitched, with 'di-diddle' element and **slight terminal flourish** (usually lacking in Firecrest): "*si-sissi si-sissi si-sissi sissi-si-siswee-it*" (see Treecreeper *(p. 453)*). Call slightly less shrill, slightly more emphatic, slower than Long-tailed Tit *(p. 445)*: "*ssee-ssee-ssee*" or "*zree-zree-zree*" (3–4 notes, sometimes single, stronger call). Feeding flocks make tiny sharp "*sit*" notes.

Very common resident (770,000 pairs, plus 720,000 birds in Ireland), migrant, winter visitor

from N and W Europe

Woodlands, thickets, hedgerows; migrants often in coastal bushes

yellow

ADULT ♀

Goldcrests and Firecrests both hover to feed, often just outside the foliage of trees and thickets.

ADULT ♂

JUVENILE

more orange

Firecrest

Regulus ignicapilla **535**

9–10 cm | WS 14–15 cm

👁 Pallas's Warbler (*p. 432*)

Minute, like Goldcrest but more richly coloured: **whiter beneath**, with **distinctive head pattern**. Song always a good indication of presence.

ADULT bright green above, sides of breast/shoulder gleams bronzy yellow in good light. Bold **white wedge-shaped stripe over eye**; thin white line beneath; **black eyestripe**, moustache. Crown has **broader black sides** than Goldcrest, striking yellow/orange central line (widens into fan of orange-red in display). JUVENILE lacks crown stripe.

VOICE Song varies, but typical form fast, accelerating, slightly rising, simple trill (without rhythmic 'te-diddle' form or terminal flourish): "*zi-zi-zi-zizizizizizi*". Call like Goldcrest, sometimes single, often 2–3 notes, first longer, "*zee-zi-zi*", but calls often indistinguishable.

from Europe

Woods, thickets, dense evergreens (favours Holly/Ivy/Yew stands)

more contrasted green above/white below than Goldcrest

black and white stripes on head, unlike Goldcrest's bland face

yellow

ADULT ♀

ADULT ♂ displaying

ADULT ♂

more orange

JUVENILE

FLYCATCHERS

FLYCATCHER ID   overall colour | wing pattern | tail pattern

Flycatchers are small, slender or rounded, with long wings, slim tails and short legs; they perch upright and are much less mobile in foliage than warblers. They catch insects in wide-based bills that look slightly thicker than on many warblers.

6 species: 2 breeding summer visitors; others rare migrants/vagrants.

Flycatchers (*pp. 439–442*) are small, woodland, park or garden birds, that sit still on perches for long spells and fly out to catch insects in the air, or drop to the ground to find food. They are less likely to glean food from foliage, as do warblers, robins and small chats. Their small bills are slender when seen from the side, but quite broad-based, with a wide gape. Their wings are long, held alongside the slim tail, sometimes drooped rather low. All are migrants and may be seen outside their normal breeding ranges in spring and autumn.

Flycatcher ageing/ sexing

Male and female differ, except in Spotted Flycatcher; juveniles, 1st-winters and 1st-summer males recognisable.

POSSIBLE CONFUSION GROUPS

Warblers (*pp. 403–437*) have similar slender bills, some (e.g. *Hippolais*, *Iduna*) also similarly wide-based, but short-legged, upright stance is characteristic of flycatchers; bold patterns of 'pied' group unlike any warbler. Small chats (*pp. 388–397*) are also upright, but shorter-tailed, rounder-bodied.

American 'Flycatchers'

Four species of American flycatchers (*p. 520*) have been recorded; although they have a basic similarity of shape, structure and behaviour to Old World Flycatchers they are not closely related. Their large heads and more or less crested appearance separate them. They are all exceptionally rare vagrants.

Spotted Flycatcher

Muscicapa striata ●ⓘ **538**

13·5–15 cm | WS 23–25·5 cm

Typically upright, wide-eyed, alert, short-legged, thickish-billed small brown bird, neither quite like a warbler nor a chat. Quietly alert, mostly inactive. Large head (flattened forehead/rounded nape), large dark eye, **long wingtips** and tail. Quick, jerky wing-flick and/or tail dip. Perches in open on post, fence, branch or wire, **flies out to snatch flying insect** with obvious 'snap', **returning to same perch** or one close by.

ADULT dull brownish (not so plain as Garden Warbler (*p. 419*). **Crown streaked**. Wings have silvery-buff feather edges (see Pied Flycatcher (*p. 440*)). Underside grey-buff or whitish, **grey-brown streaks** on breast; white under tail. **Short black legs**. JUVENILE buff spots over back; yellow-buff wingbar.

VOICE Calls, from perch or in flight, thin, scratchy or slightly vibrant "*sirrr*" or "*tseeet*". Song variable, weak repetition of calls, or longer, more musical, thin, squeaky phrases.

⟨👁⟩ Red-breasted/Taiga (*p. 442*), Brown (*p. 441*) Flycatchers

Scarce summer visitor, most May–Sep (30,000 pairs, plus 40,000 birds in Ireland, declining)

from/to Scandinavia

to Africa

from/to Africa

Woods, parks, gardens; elsewhere on migration (spring, autumn)

ADULT

Upright; pale with spotted breast

small pale bird; flies out to catch insect and returns to perch

ADULT (SPRING)

only trace of wingbar compared with Pied Flycatcher

JUVENILE

1ST-WINTER

Pied Flycatcher

Ficedula hypoleuca ●❶ 538

12–13·5 cm | WS 21·5–24 cm

👁 Collared Flycatcher

Small, rounded woodland bird with much white in wing: see Spotted Flycatcher (*p. 439*), Chaffinch (*p. 481*). Long-winged, short-tailed; big dark eye. **Long wingtips** often drooped. **Short, dark legs**. Frequently inconspicuous, **drops to ground to feed**, returns to new perch.

MALE **black and white**: one or two white forehead spots, **white splash on wing**. 1ST-SUMMER MALE (breeds) plumage browner. FEMALE **brown and white**, blacker on wings; wing panel smaller. Brownish beside throat, more or less joined across chest. AUTUMN MALE like female, except blacker tail. JUVENILE drabber, throat marks darker, less white on wing.

VOICE Sharp "*pwit*", sweet "*huit*", often "*huit-tik*". Song staccato, whistled phrase (less free-flowing than Redstart (*p. 392*)), some mimicry; several variants in irregular sequence.

Siberian race *sibirica* (vagrant, 1 record (Britain): Sep; on E coast) can only be told from regularly occurring breeding race *hypoleuca* when examined in the hand (fractionally larger and less intensely black, but races intergrade).

Scarce to locally common summer visitor in N and W (38,000 pairs, Apr–Aug)

from/to Scandinavia

to Africa

from/to Africa

Breeds mainly in oak woods; mostly near coasts on migration (spring and especially autumn)

no other small bird so plain black above, clean white below

ADULT ♂

1ST-WINTER ♂

narrow patch at base of primaries falls well short of wing edge

variable dark patch beside throat

1ST-SUMMER ♂ brown in plumage

ADULT ♀

very short dark legs

440

Brown Flycatcher
Muscicapa dauurica
12–13 cm | WS 19·5–21·5 cm

Like small, greyish, plain
Spotted Flycatcher (*p. 439*).
Head and breast **unstreaked**;
big eye and **white eyering**;
clearly **broad-based bill**.

white eyering

broad-based bill
with extensive
pale base

1ST-WINTER

**BROWN
FLYCATCHER**

buff eyering

**SPOTTED
FLYCATCHER**

relatively
narrow bill
with restricted
pale base

Vagrant from Asia: <5 records
(Britain), Sep–Oct. On coast.
Woods.

Collared Flycatcher *Ficedula albicollis*   538
12–13·5 cm | WS 22·5–24·5 cm

Vagrant from E Europe:
<50 records (1 Ireland), most
Apr–Jun, few Sep. Mostly on
coast. Usually woods.

Similar to Pied Flycatcher in all plumages; shorter tail may be
evident. Compared to Pied Flycatcher, MALE **broad white collar**,
bigger forehead splash, broader wing panel, wider band across
primaries, **white rump**. 1ST-SUMMER MALE has collar but forehead
and wing very like Pied Flycatcher. FEMALE/1ST-WINTER wider,
longer extension of pale throat onto neck; **larger white patch
on primaries** widens close to edge of wing. SUMMER FEMALE has
subtly whiter rump.

1ST-SUMMER ♂

First-summer (one year-old) males
retain brown wings.

ADULT ♀

primary patch
widens close to
wing edge

white
rump

hint of
pale rump

ADULT ♂ SUMMER

ADULT ♂ WINTER

441

Red-breasted Flycatcher *Ficedula parva* `538`
11–12 cm | WS 18·5–21 cm

Tiny, endearing flycatcher; bold dark eye, eye-catching tail pattern. Perches quietly on low perch, on edge of clearing, or moves about restlessly higher in trees. Often droops wingtips, raises tail; legs very short. Dark rump, black tail with **rectangular white panel each side**. White often inconspicuous on perched bird, eye-catching flash in flight. MALE greyish head; **orange-red chin, throat**; brown upperparts; pale buff to white underside. FEMALE pale olive-brown; **strong white eyering**; pale throat. JUVENILE peachy-buff on throat and breast, whiter beneath; dull, thin, rusty-buff wingbar.

VOICE Soft "*tuc*" or "*tic*"; short, hard "*t't*"; or longer, dry, "*t-trrt*".

Rare migrant from E Europe: 30–100 per year, chiefly autumn. Mostly on coast. Woods.

White sides to base of tail is a key identification feature of Red-breasted and Taiga Flycatchers.

JUVENILE/1ST WINTER

ADULT ♂
SUMMER

Taiga Flycatcher *Ficedula albicilla*
11–12·5 cm | WS 18·5–21 cm

Extremely similar to Red-breasted Flycatcher. MALE has small orange throat patch surrounded by **grey cheek and breast-band**. JUVENILE has **blacker upper tail coverts**, greyer chest.

VOICE Fast rattling chatter like dry, buzzy Red-breasted Flycatcher.

RED-BREASTED FLYCATCHER

pale back and rump, dark tail

pale back, blacker rump and tail

TAIGA FLYCATCHER

Vagrant from Asia: <5 records (Britain), Apr, Oct–Nov. On coast. Woods.

JUVENILE/
1ST WINTER

ADULT ♂
SUMMER

TITS, NUTHATCHES and 'CREEPERS'

TIT ID   overall plumage | head pattern | call and song

Tits are small, rather bulky-bodied, short-winged birds with rounded heads and small, slightly bulbous, bluntly triangular bills (sharper on Bearded and Penduline Tits). They are sociable, often in loose, mixed flocks when not breeding.

6 tits: all resident, 3 common, 2 declining, 1 Scotland only
Long-tailed Tit, Bearded Tit (both resident) **and Penduline Tit** (vagrant) **are similar in form but unrelated to the tit family**, each belonging to their own individual family.

Tits (pp. 446–451) are either green, blue and yellow, or drab brownish with blackon the head. They have a bolder, more stop-start or leaping progress through trees or across spaces than most warblers, pausing to explore, often hanging from slender twigs. Calls are strident, whistling, or buzzing, with many high, thin, contact notes. Marsh and Willow Tits are a very difficult pair to identify: calls and songs are invaluable. Both seem destined to disappear from most of Britain quite soon. CrestedTits are restricted to pine woods in northern Scotland: best discovered by their purring calls.

Long-tailed Tit (p. 445) is not closely related, but has a basic tit-like form, with a very long, slim tail. They are social, vocal and easy to see.

Bearded Tit (or Bearded Reedling) (p. 444) is an also unrelated bird of reedbeds and fen vegetation,discovered by its calls and usually seen flitting over the reed tops.

Penduline Tit (p. 454) prefers poplars and willows in summer, reedbeds and areas of reedmace in winter.

Tit ageing/sexing

Sexes differ slightly (males brighter) or look identical; juveniles are duller and in some species can be separated through the first winter.

IMMATURE

BLUE TIT

LONG-TAILED TIT

BEARDED TIT

PENDULINE TIT

NUTHATCH and 'CREEPER' ID   overall plumage | wing pattern | call and song

Much smaller than woodpeckers, these birds are unlikely to be confused although they spend their lives creeping about on tree branches and climbing tree trunks (Wallcreeper on rock faces).

2 nuthatches: 1 resident;1 vagrant
3 'creepers': 2 treecreepers: 1 resident;1 vagrant, and the unrelated **Wallcreeper** (vagrant – p. 455)

The **Nuthatch** (p. 452) is unique in the UK: small, stout, short-tailed, spike-billed and strongly patterned. It climbs up and down with equal ease, without using its tail, relying on the strength of its feet and claws. It is noisy, especially in spring.

Treecreepers (p. 453) include two nearly identical species, only one at all likely to be seen: Treecreeper is common and widespread; Short-toed Treecreeper very rare. They use their tails for support as they creep upwards or spiral around branches (rarely rocks or walls): they can hang beneath, but rarely come downhill as do nuthatches. They come to the ground much less often, and cannot properly walk or hop.

NUTHATCH

TREECREEPER

443

Bearded Tit (Bearded Reedling)

Panurus biarmicus 535

14–15·5 cm | WS 16–18 cm

👁 Penduline Tit (*p. 454*)

Scarce, local resident (550–600 pairs); winter dispersal

Small, elongated, **long-tailed bird of reeds**, reedmace; succession of calls and movements, but hard to see. Acrobatic among stems; feeds on ground beneath, with double-footed shuffle.

Bright tawny with **black and cream wing streaks**, short, triangular, bright golden-orange bill. MALE striking, narrow-crowned bright **blue-grey head**, big, **drooped 'moustaches'**. Black patch under tail. FEMALE has plain head, pale undertail; **long brown tail has narrow white sides**. JUVENILE blackish on back, black streaks on outer tail; male has yellow bill, black stripe to pale eye, female has dark bill, paler patch to eye.

VOICE Calls are very distinctive, quite loud, metallic, pinging "*ching*" or "*p-chink*".

May fly short distance low over reeds, whirring flight before diving out of sight.

Reedbeds; more widespread in some winters, in varied wetlands

dark bill; faint eye-patch

JUVENILE ♀

yellow bill; dark eye-patch

JUVENILE ♂

ADULT ♂

ADULT ♀

Long-tailed Tit

Aegithalos caudatus race *rosaceus*

13–15 cm | WS 16–19 cm

Easy, obvious: tiny, tit-like; acrobatic; **long, slim tail** often raised. Round, audibly-whirring wings. Often flies single-file across spaces revealing flocks of 10–20 or so. Mixes with tits (*pp. 446–451*), Goldcrests (*p. 436*).

ADULT black and dull white. **Black stripes** beside crown blend into dark back; **pink shoulders**; white-sided black tail. JUVENILE duller, no pink, brown 'face'.

VOICE High, thin, unemphatic "*see-see-see*" or "*si-si-si*" (quicker, less 'body' than Goldcrest); distinctive short, abrupt "*brr-p*" mixed with dry trilled "*ts-rreet*" and metallic "*pit*".

Fairly common resident (120,000 pairs, plus 115,000 birds in Ireland); rare migrant/vagrant

Woodland, hedgerows, thickets, large gardens

In recent years, Long-tailed Tits have become more frequent at feeders and seed put out for garden birds.

ADULT

Northern race *caudatus* (vagrant in autumn/winter) has pure white head; strikingly different from resident British/Irish race *rosaceus*, but status confused by intermediate birds.

once the first autumn moult is completed, young birds are indistinguishable from adults.

JUVENILE

no other small bird in a tree has such a long tail, but beware winter roosts of Pied Wagtails in urban treetops

ADULT
race *rosaceus*

Blue Tit

Cyanistes caeruleus  race *obscurus*

Common, widespread resident
(3·3 million pairs, plus 2·2 million
birds in Ireland)

Woodland, gardens, scrub,
hedgerows, reedbeds

10·5–12 cm | WS 17–18 cm

Tiny, acrobatic feeder in high canopy, on feeders. Leaps/hangs more than warblers, frequent **wing flicks**; strong grip whatever angle or perch. Flight fast, direct, 'stops dead' on perch. Often in mixed flocks. Barrel-bodied, pale bird, 'green' or 'yellow' with white face, depending on view.

ADULT pale blue wings and tail, often dull; some FEMALES faintly greener, often more vivid on spring MALE. **Blue cap inside white band**, white face, black chin obvious marks. Smaller, paler than Great Tit; underside with slight streak in centre, not bold black band; **tail blue** without white sides. JUVENILE greener, with greenish cap; yellow cheeks and throat.

VOICE High, sharp "*si-si-si*", frequent rhythmic "*sisi-du*"; "*tzisi-di-di-di*". Song slurred, trilled "*see-see-si-surrrrr*".

Continental race *caeruleus* (winter visitor – not illustrated) differs so slightly (*e.g.* 10% shorter wing length) that it cannot be reliably distinguished in the field from the sedentary British/Irish race *obscurus*.

pale above eye

JUVENILE

ADULT

weak dark
line
on breast

blue cap

white
forehead

blue tail

dark eyestripe

ADULT

Great Tit

Parus major race *newtoni*

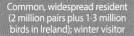

Woodland, gardens

13·5–15 cm | WS 18–20 cm

Small, but bigger, longer-looking, more boldly patterned than Blue or Coal Tit (*p. 449*). Acrobatic feeder, but also moves through low vegetation, explores bark, and feeds on ground.

Big **white cheeks** make identification instant (but see Coal Tit). ADULT **black stripe down centre of belly** (tapers on FEMALE, widens between legs on MALE). Bright pale yellow or buffish-yellow beneath. Green above, bluer wings with white bar. **White sides to tail** (unlike Blue Tit). JUVENILE pale, dull, cap greenish-black, cheeks greenish-yellow. Continental race *major* (irruptive winter visitor) yellowish above, duller below, bill fractionally smaller than resident British/Irish race *newtoni*.

VOICE Very varied, many strident, off-key notes: "*pink*" or "*chink*" (like Chaffinch (*p. 481*)), "*pink-a-tchee tchee*"; "*tsweet*"; "*tsi-uti-uti*". Song loud, see-sawing two- or three-note, whistle, "*tsee-tsoo tsee-tsoo tsee-tsoo*" or "*tchee-tchu*" or "*tchi-too-tcha*". Taps bill loudly.

The continental race *major* tends to have a smaller bill yellower back and duller underparts, but these features are variable and most individuals cannot be safely assigned to race.

Continental race *major*

Partially melanistic birds with black cheeks are occasionally seen, particularly in the home counties.

ADULT ♀

FEMALE: black narrows towards legs

black above eye

ADULT ♂

black forehead

white cheeks

white sides to tail

MALE: black widens between legs

JUVENILE

447

Crested Tit

Lophophanes cristatus ● race *scoticus* **535**

10·5–12 cm | WS 17–20 cm

Tiny, buff-brown tit, no bright colours but **striking head shape**. Listen/look in Scottish pine forests/plantations – nowhere else.

Superficially similar to Marsh Tit (*p. 450*), but sharp **pointed crest** (barred black and white), black eyestripe extending around cheek, black throat continuing as collar. FEMALE has slightly shorter crest than MALE, thinner head stripes. JUVENILE slightly browner on head, crest blunt.

VOICE Useful clue: thin trilling, rolling or purring note with distinct rhythm – "*p'trrr-up*" or "*burrur-ur-eet*". Also high, thin "*seeet*" notes.

Scarce and local resident, N Scotland only (2,400 pairs)

Pine forests

ADULT
Northern race
cristatus

ADULT
European race
mitratus

Central European race *mitratus* (similar to race *scoticus*), and northern race *cristatus* (paler, more 'grey and white') both recorded in 19th century, very rarely since (<10 records), but frequent intergrades make identification in isolation unsafe.

ADULT

In Britain, restricted to native Scots Pine and plantations in Scotland.

cheek pattern and collar as distinctive as upstanding crest

ADULT
British race *scoticus*

Coal Tit

Periparus ater race
britannicus

10–11·5 cm | WS 17–21 cm

Tiny tit, close to Goldcrest (*p. 436*) in size. **No yellow, blue or green**, but summer adults fade drab greenish. Favours conifers, also feeds on the ground. Acrobatic, often in mixed flocks. Visits feeders but takes food away to eat nearby or hide in cache.

Large black head, **white cheeks**, unique **clear-cut white patch on back of head**; large black chin, **buff underside** without streak. Back olive-grey; **two white bars** across wing; plain tail.

VOICE Sharp "*tsooo*" or "*tsee*" and melancholy variations; short, sharp, hard 'spitting' note. Song resembles Great Tit (*p. 447*) in emphatic two-note rhythm, but simpler, sharper, less strident "*see-too see-too*".

Common, widespread resident (600,000 pairs, plus 925,000 birds in Ireland); migrant, winter visitor

Woodland with some pine/ spruce/Larch, scrub, thickets

yellowish tinge
to cheeks

ADULT
race *hibernicus*

Irish race *hibernicus* (vagrant in Britain) slightly browner; yellower on cheeks and underside than race *britannicus*.

bluish-grey above

ADULT
race *ater*

tiny crest

ADULT
race *ater*

Regular visitors from continental Europe (race *ater*) bluish-grey on back and wings, uniform beneath; minute crest on nape.

olive above, flanks darker than belly on British race *britannicus*

ADULT
race *britannicus*

Marsh Tit

Poecile palustris ● **535**

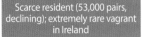

Scarce resident (53,000 pairs, declining); extremely rare vagrant in Ireland

Mature woodland and associated secondary growth, hedgerows, old gardens; comes to feeders

11·5–13 cm | WS 18–19·5 cm

Small, brown, **black-capped** tit; no green, blue or yellow. Very like Willow Tit; identification requires care but **call** invaluable. (See also Blackcap (*p. 418*), which lacks black bib.)

Slightly colder, duller overall than Willow Tit (which is much colder, whiter below in N Europe). Smaller, more defined white cheeks against grey-brown neck; often (not always) glossier black cap and smaller, squarer black bib. Underside often plainer without strong buff flanks (much overlap); usually **plainer wing** with weak lengthwise panel (but some are well-marked). **Bill with pale patch at base of upper mandible** (absent on Willow Tit). A combination of features plus call is ideally needed.

VOICE Bright, cheery, whistled "*pit-chew!*" best instant clue, rules out Willow Tit. Various thin "*si-si*" notes, quick, easy, lightweight "*tsi-tsi-dee-dee-dee*" (clearly related but lacking harsh nasal quality of Willow Tit). Song simple, flat, even rattle, "*chi-ip-ip-ip-ip*" or more ringing "*witawitawitawitawita*".

Marsh/Willow Tit calls compared
MARSH TIT – Whistled "***pit-chew***"; light "***tsi-tsi dee dee dee***"
WILLOW TIT – Deep, buzzy "***tsi-tsi chair chair chair***"

BLACKCAP ♂ (*p. 418*) – possible confusion species – note grey cheeks and nape; smaller black cap; pale in front of eye, no bib

ADULT

Willow Tit

Poecile montana ●

Woodlands, willow/Alder scrub, old hedgerows, woodland edges; comes to feeders

12–13 cm | WS 17–20·5 cm

Small, grey-brown and buff tit; **black cap**, **distinctive calls**. See Marsh Tit: requires careful identification as most features overlap. Increasingly scarce and hard to find.

Dull brown, buffish below. Compared with Marsh Tit, more often dull black cap; often wider inverted-'V'-shaped black chin (but much overlap); thick-necked. Invariably buff flanks, some **rusty-buff** unlike Marsh Tit. Whitish cheeks blend to buff before greyish shoulders. Wings more often have distinct **pale panel** lengthwise along middle. Bill all dark.

VOICE Absence of Marsh Tit's bright, clear "*pit-chew*" helpful. Has deep buzzy "*tsi-tsi chair chair chair*"; basic "*tchairr*" note more buzzing, nasal than lighter notes of Marsh Tit. Short, sharp "*tsi tsi*". Song "*tsew-tsew-tsew*" (like Wood Warbler (*p.429*)) or rare brief, melodic, rich warble.

wider black nape
Less 'bull-necked'
cap often glossy
pale patch on base of upper mandible
black bib often 'neater'
MARSH TIT

ADULT race *borealis*

Northern European race *borealis* (vagrant, <5 records (Britain): Feb–Mar) is relatively distinctive: whiter than resident British race *kleinschmidti*.

WILLOW TIT
bill all dark
ADULT British race *kleinschmidti*
some individuals have rusty-buff flanks

Nuthatch

Sitta europaea

12–14·5 cm | WS 22·5–27 cm

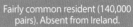 Red-breasted Nuthatch *(p. 454)*

Red-breasted Nuthatch *(p. 454)*

Alert, bouncy, agile, short-tailed woodland bird; hangs upside down; climbs up and down trees, stone walls; feeds on ground.

Unique pale **blue-grey** above, buff below. **Bold black eyestripe**, rusty flanks. Wedge-shaped head and bill. **Tail short, square**, with black-and-white corners. MALE chestnut flanks and undertail. IN FLIGHT, usually over clearings, flitting, straight, no agility, with markedly spike-like bill/heavy body/short tail.

VOICE Distinctive (from treetop to ground level): loud, clear, ringing or shouted whistles, often in fast series – "*ch'wit*"; "*hwit hwit hwit*"; tit-like "*sit*". Song clear "*wheee wheee wheee*".

Fairly common resident (140,000 pairs). Absent from Ireland.

Woodland/parkland; comes to feeders

distinctive flat wedge-shape; short, square tail

ADULT ♂

chestnut flanks and undertail

ADULT ♀

buff flanks and undertail

Treecreeper

Certhia familiaris

12·5–14 cm | WS 17·5–21 cm

Short-toed Treecreeper *(p. 455)*

Common resident (200,000 pairs);
N European race rare vagrant
(most N Isles, NE coasts; autumn)

Creeping, brown-backed bird, white underneath; **pressed to bark** or hanging from below branch. Occasionally on walls; rarely, briefly, on ground (cannot properly walk). **Climbs (often spirals) upwards, using tail as support** even under branch.

Mottled brown; **whitish stripe over eye**; spiky brown tail; narrow bands of blackish and cream across wings. **White beneath**. IN FLIGHT, weak, undulating, hesitant, shows obvious broad **pale band along length of wing** both above and below.

VOICE Thin, long, faintly vibrant "*srreeee*". Song thin, high, quiet but far-carrying, sweet free-flowing phrase with a flourish at the end (compare more rhythmic Goldcrest *(p. 436)*, louder rattling Chaffinch *(p. 481)*).

Woodland

creeps jerkily up trunks and branches, but equally often clings underneath

ADULT
race *familiaris*

ADULT
British/Irish race
britannica

Northern European race *familiaris* (vagrant, status confused by intergrades: N Isles, E coast), bright white beneath, copious white spots above, paler claws compared to resident British/Irish race *britannica*.

453

Penduline Tit *Remiz pendulinus*
10–11·5 cm | WS 16–17·5 cm

Small, acrobatic, tit-like bird with finely pointed bill, black legs. ADULT striking pattern: rusty-brown above, buff below, **pale grey head**, **broad black mask** (like tiny male Red-backed Shrike (*p. 457*)). Rusty band across wing usually distinct. JUVENILE buffier, with paler back, plain buff head; black eye in plain face, **rusty wing band**.

VOICE Call distinctive (beware thin, high Reed Bunting (*p. 502*) notes): long, downward "*tseeeee*".

Vagrant from Europe: >300 records (Britain), most months, some overwinter. Most on coast. Reedbeds, reedmace.

Nest is a hanging pouch of willow/ poplar down and cobwebs with a side-entrance 'porch'; has not bred in Britain but in 1990 a lone male built a nest.

A reedbed bird in winter, but found high in riverside willows/ poplars in summer.

JUVENILE

ADULT ♂

ADULT ♀

ADULT

Red-breasted Nuthatch
Sitta canadensis

11 cm | WS 19–21 cm

Small forest bird: typical nuthatch (*p. 452*) actions. Grey above, bright buff below, **dark cap** and eyestripe, **bold white stripe over eye**.

Vagrant from N America: 1 record (Britain), Oct–May. On coast. Pine woodland.

Short-toed Treecreeper ● 537

Certhia brachydactyla

13 cm | WS 17·5–21 cm

Very hard to separate from Treecreeper (*p. 453*) except by voice. Drabber; whiter throat above dull, soiled **off-white or buff underside**; focus on shape of black against longer 'V'-shaped buff wingbar, and larger pale primary tips, best determined from photographs.

VOICE Call strong, penetrating "*tsoot*"; song has **distinct pattern of individual notes**, staccato, without terminal flourish – "*tseet tseet, tseet-it-eeroit-it*" (some mimic Treecreeper too!).

sharp 'sawtooth' on rear edge of buff 'V'

SHORT-TOED TREECREEPER

black front edge to long, acute buff 'V' forms blunt angle

TREECREEPER

stepped rear edge of buff 'V'

black front edge to rounder buff bar forms sharp, square notch deep into buff

hind claw shorter on Short-toed Treecreeper (right)

Vagrant from Europe: <30 records (Britain), Sep–Apr. On coast. Woodland.

Vagrant from C/S Europe: <15 records (Britain), May–Jun, Sep–Apr. Cliffs/quarries.

Wallcreeper *Tichodroma muraria*

16 cm | WS 27–32 cm

Extraordinary, unique bird, fluttering/climbing around cliffs, rocks; springy, bouncy action, flicks wings. Pale grey; **crimson on wings**; very short, square tail; thin bill. MALE extensive black throat in summer (narrow black line on FEMALE); throat white in winter. IN FLIGHT, bounding, fluttering; very **broad, rounded wings**: **crimson on upperwing**; outerwing black with rows of **round white spots**.

ADULT ♀

Perches with wings tightly closed, but searches for food with frequent rhythmic in-out flicks of outerwing.

SHRIKES

SHRIKE ID head pattern | crown/back/rump colour | wing details | upper/under tail colour

Shrikes are roughly the same size or smaller than common thrushes, (*pp. 378–383*) much smaller than any bird of prey (*pp. 292–325*). They perch quite upright and have round heads, short wings and long tails; their bills are thick and very slightly hooked. In flight, they look round-winged and long-tailed; they may hover momentarily (Great Grey Shrike for 30–40 seconds or more).

9 species: 1 regular migrant (and scarce breeder); 1 regular migrant/winter visitor; 7 rare or very rare vagrants

Shrikes (*pp. 457–463*) are charismatic yet perch quietly doing nothing for long spells and can be very elusive. When they do feed, they behave like birds of prey: dropping to the ground for an insect, reptile or vole, or chasing small birds. They impale prey on thorns, both as a 'larder' and to help dismember larger items.

Red-backed Shrikes used to breed but are now scarce migrants: spring males are beautiful and obvious, females and immature birds are rufous-brown and must be told both from small thrushes and other, rarer shrikes.

Great Grey Shrikes are autumn migrants and winter birds on heaths and open land with bushes or tall trees. A distant 'whitish spot' on a bush top is worth checking: nothing else shares the pale grey, black and soft greyish-white pattern, including a typical shrike 'mask', except for the exceedingly rare Lesser Grey Shrikes, a vagrant in summer. Woodchat Shrikes are the most frequent of the rare shrikes: usually spring adults, black and white with distinctive rufous caps; like all shrikes they tend to perch upright on bush tops or wires, keeping still, often elusive but very obvious once found.

Shrike ageing/sexing

Sexes differ, slightly in 'grey' species, markedly in Red-backed Shrike. Juveniles differ slightly from adults but may become difficult to distinguish by winter.

[Jul]

[Sep]

JUVENILE MAY–SEP

moult suspended before migration

Post-juvenile moult
OCT–FEB completed in winter quarters.

IMMATURE ♀ SUMMER FEB–JUN

[Apr]

Immature moults (1st- and 2nd-summer)
Moults from JUN, suspended before migration, completed in winter quarters – has fresh dark wing feathers contrasted with old, faded primary coverts and inner primaries.

Adult moults
Moults from JUN, suspended before migration, completed in winter quarters – all wing feathers of similar age, without contrast

ADULT ♂

ADULT ♀

Red-backed Shrike

Lanius collurio ●

16–18 cm | WS 24–27 cm

Rare shrikes (*p. 458–463*)

Scarce migrant, mostly coastal in autumn; very rare summer visitor (irregular breeder, <5 pairs).

from Scandinavia and Europe

to E and S Africa

Bushy heaths, thickets

Males unmistakable, other plumages may be puzzling: look for thick, hook-tipped bill; strong feet; upright stance; hint of dark mask; fine 'V'-shaped bars beneath. All point to 'shrike'. Broad, rounded head; thick bill; **long, slim tail** (often spread, flaunted with sideways twist). Perches on exposed twigs or inconspicuous on side of bush/hedge; easily overlooked. See much rarer Isabelline Shrike (*p. 458*).

MALE striking: **blue-grey head**; **black mask**; reddish back; pale pink breast. **White sides to black tail**, against **grey rump**. FEMALE/JUVENILE/1ST-WINTER rufous brown, **greyer nape and rump** (reverse of Isabelline Shrike); whitish below with darker scales; pale patch between bill and large, dark eye; **dark smudge behind eye**. Underside of tail greyish.

VOICE Short, harsh notes.

greyish crown

barred flanks

1ST-WINTER

ADULT ♂

upright, large-headed, slim-tailed

ADULT ♀

ADULT ♂

Isabelline Shrike *Lanius isabellinus*

16·5–18 cm | WS 26–28 cm

Vagrant from Asia: <100 records (<10 Ireland), Feb–Dec (most Oct–Nov). Mostly coastal. Bushy places.

Small shrike, like Red-backed Shrike (*p. 457*) but longer-tailed; shorter primary projection (6–7 primary-tips visible on closed wing; typically eight visible on Red-backed Shrike). **Tail rufous above and beneath**. Two races recorded: *isabellinus* (Daurian Shrike) and *phoenicuroides* (Turkestan Shrike); adults usually distinct, 1st-winter/winter birds difficult/impossible to tell apart.

MALE has black mask, small white primary patch (can be absent on female, and shown by a few Red-backed Shrikes). Race *isabellinus* pale sandy-grey above, pink-buff below; race *phoenicuroides* darker above, more rufous on crown, nape and rump; whiter beneath. FEMALE/1ST-WINTER like young Red-backed Shrike but rusty rump and tail (including underside). Race *isabellinus* pale above, tertials/secondaries fading very pale; **buff below, no upper/underside contrast**; pale/rufous-ginger scaly bars below. Stripe over eye, ear-coverts and throat buff/pale orange. Race *phoenicuroides* pale sandy/greyish, no bars above, but **rufous nape and rump**; more contrasted whiter underside with darker crescents; white stripe over eye; blacker mask.

VOICE Calls and song resemble Red-backed Shrike.

'TURKESTAN SHRIKE'
race *phoenicuroides*

ADULT ♂

ADULT ♀

'DAURIAN SHRIKE'
race *isabellinus*

ADULT ♂

ADULT ♀

Juvenile 'brown' shrikes

Autumn migrant shrikes are difficult and require close concentration: focus on the head, tail, upperside and underside:

RED-BACKED SHRIKE
1ST-WINTER

8 primary tips show

Juvenile 'brown' skrikes – summary of key features	
Red-backed Shrike	Most likely. HEAD: barred; greyish; dark mask. TAIL: brown/rufous above, dull beneath. UPPERSIDE: rusty, barred; greyer nape and rump. UNDERSIDE: whitish; crescentic bars.
'Daurian Shrike'	HEAD: buffish; no strong mask. TAIL: rufous above and below. UPPERSIDE: pale as underparts; nape/rump as back. UNDERSIDE: buff; scaly pale ginger bars.
'Turkestan Shrike'	HEAD: whitish over eye; dark mask. TAIL: rufous above and below. UPPERSIDE: darker than underside; nape/rump rufous. UNDERSIDE: whitish; dark crescentic bars.
Brown Shrike	Least likely. HEAD: brown crown; strong mask. TAIL: long, dark rufous-brown. UPPERSIDE: darker than underside; rump brighter. UNDERSIDE: buff; fine crescentic bars.

'DAURIAN SHRIKE'
race *isabellinus*

1ST-WINTER

'TURKESTAN SHRIKE'
race *phoenicuroides*

1ST-WINTER

Brown Shrike *Lanius cristatus*

18–20 cm | WS 25–28 cm

Resembles female Red-backed (*p. 457*) and Isabelline Shrikes; bigger head, **thicker bill**, shorter wings (five–six primary-tips visible on closed wing); longer, graduated tail. FEMALE/1ST-WINTER more uniformly warm brown from crown to rump; wing coverts/tertials darker with duller fringes; mask more complete, dark grey/black. Underside barred like Red-backed Shrike, but more buff than white. Bill dark, grey-pink base.

Vagrant from Asia: <25 records (1 Ireland), Sep–Jan. Mostly on coast. Scrubby areas, heaths.

short wings: only 5–6 visible primary show tips (6–8 on other 'brown' shrikes)

1ST-WINTER

Great Grey Shrike

Lanius excubitor

VU

21–26 cm | WS 30–34 cm

Thrush-sized, **pale**, grey, white and black bird. Often on obvious bush-top, tree or overhead wire perch, but can be exceedingly unobtrusive. Long, slim tail (spread, tilted or twisted for balance), rather large head, short wings, thick bill. Only rare Lesser Grey Shrike and very rare Southern ('Steppe') Grey Shrike similar. Great Grey Shrike has **longer tail**, shorter wingtips than Lesser Grey Shrike.

ADULT **very pale**; **black mask** (thin white line above it); **black-and-white wings and tail**. Whitish patch above closed wing obvious or part-hidden. FEMALE slightly duller than MALE: greyer below, very faint bars. JUVENILE has crown and back pale grey; underside with faint bars.

VOICE Short harsh calls; sometimes low, rambling subsong.

Scarce autumn migrant, winter visitor (150–300 per year). Vagrant Ireland (<50 records)

from Scandinavia

from Europe

Heaths, forest edge, bushy areas

IN FLIGHT, striking, **long white band** across outerwing, sometimes extending inwards, white sides to tail. Bounding flight, **sweeping up to perch**; if repeatedly disturbed will move far away in long, high, swooping flight.

ADULT

sits on open perches: at a distance an obvious pale 'blob' with black band across middle

crown plain

1ST-WINTER

ADULT

underparts faintly barred

Lesser Grey Shrike *Lanius minor*

19–21 cm | WS 28–30 cm

535

Vagrant from SE Europe:
<200 records (<10 Ireland),
Jun–Oct. Mostly on coast.
Open bushy areas.

Obvious 'grey, black, white' shrike. Compared with Great Grey Shrike, slightly stockier, more bull-necked, often sits bolt-upright. Closed wings **slightly longer, more pointed**, closed tips reach beyond tail base (fall short on Great Grey Shrike). ADULT **darker**, grey above, clearly **pink below**, with white throat. Black mask extends as **broad band across forehead** (best mark). JUVENILE has pale edges to blackish wing feathers. Crown and back pale grey with faint bars; underparts plain; no forehead band; weak, blackish mask. Bill thicker, blunter, paler than Great Grey Shrike.

IN FLIGHT, white wing patches broader than Great Grey Shrike's.

black 'blob' on face at distance

crown and back faintly barred

forehead grey

ADULT SUMMER

JUVENILE

underparts plain

pink flush to underparts

Southern Grey Shrike

Lanius meridionalis

23–25 cm | WS 30–34 cm

Race recorded, *pallidirostris* ('Steppe' Grey Shrike), like pale Great Grey Shrike with **paler bill, weaker mask, bigger white primary patch, longer wingtip.**

'STEPPE' GREY SHRIKE
race *pallidirostris*

pale between eye and bill

longer wingtip and shorter tail than Great Grey Shrike

Vagrant from Asia/Middle East:
<25 records (Britain), Apr, Jun,
Sep–Dec. Most on coast.
Open bushy areas.

1ST-WINTER

Woodchat Shrike *Lanius senator*

17–19 cm | WS 25–27 cm

Rare migrant from Europe: 20–35 per year (100 records Ireland), mostly spring, Mainly on coast. Open bushy areas.

Smallish shrike, **black and white with rufous cap**. Stocky, relatively short-tailed; often perches on wire, bush top. More or less Corn Bunting (*p. 503*) size and shape.

Most records of C/S European race *senator*. MALE black mask; rufous cap, nape; black back. FEMALE mask interrupted by whitish marks, cap paler. Both sexes **white oval each side of back**; broad white wing patch (absent on vagrant W Mediterranean island race *badius*. JUVENILE/1ST-WINTER more difficult: compared with Red-backed Shrike (*p. 457*), colder, **greyish** above; **barred, whitish rump** (plain rufous on Red-backed Shrike); line of **whitish feathers**, each with black crescent, along shoulder (rufous with darker centres on Red-backed Shrike).

IN FLIGHT, white in wings and on rump **striking pied effect**.

ADULT ♂

'scruffy' black mask

ADULT ♀

ADULT ♂

'clean' black mask

IMMATURE ♀ [Apr]

'cold', greyish, scaly; white along shoulders

JUVENILE

ADULT ♂

W Mediterranean island race *badius* (spring vagrant, <15 records (<5 Ireland)) lacks white wing patch.

Vagrant from SE Europe: <5 records (Britain), Sep–Nov.
On coast. Scrub.

Masked Shrike *Lanius nubicus*
17–18 cm | WS 18–20 cm

Slender shrike; long, narrow tail. ADULT (not recorded) black and white, orange-buff flanks. 1ST-WINTER like dark 1st-winter Woodchat Shrike with barred crown, blacker mask, **whiter shoulder patch; slim, blacker tail with white edges.**

Long-tailed Shrike *Lanius schach*
22–27 cm | WS 25–26 cm

Big shrike: combines grey crown/back, black mask and white throat with **brown rump** and **deep buff underside**, and striking **long tail**.

ADULT ♂

1ST-WINTER

1ST-WINTER

Vagrant from Asia:
1 record (Britain),
Nov. On coast.
Scrub.

Crows in flight p. 465

ADULT
'thin-billed' race
macrorhynchos

ADULT
'thick-billed' race
caryocatactes

Nutcracker
Nucifraga caryocatactes
32–38 cm | WS 49–53 cm

Unlike any other crow: dark brown, lines of copious **white spots; white vent and tail tip**, white bars under wing. Two races recorded: 'thin-billed' *macrorhynchos* (most frequent), 'thick-billed' *caryocatactes* (two records); told by bill size, but overlap.

Vagrant from C Europe:
<500 records (Britain), Aug–Mar.
Widespread; infrequent invasions.
Pines; often on ground.

CROWS

CROW ID   overall colour | wing and tail shape | size | calls

Large strongly-built birds with short, arched beaks and feet that are strong but suited to perching rather than grasping prey.
9 species: 6 common residents, 2 less common; 1 rare/sporadic vagrant.

Crows (*pp. 465–473*) are either 'black', with a colourful sheen in the right conditions, or more boldly patterned or coloured, including the Magpie and Jay. All except the Jay and vagrant Nutcracker are obvious birds of open places.

The biggest is the Raven, nesting on cliff ledges or in trees, and uniquely rolls over momentarily in flight. Size may not be obvious, so shape and calls help separate it, especially from the Rook, which is a consistently social bird, breeding in treetop colonies up to hundreds strong.
Rooks and Jackdaws feed, fly and roost together, sometimes in big, noisy flocks. Jackdaws are bold, noisy, inquisitive and excellent fliers. Carrion Crows are frequently more solitary, but gather in scores on beaches and in fields. In the north, in Ireland and on the Isle of Man the Carrion Crow is replaced by the Hooded Crow, once a winter visitor in England but now rare. The Chough is 'finger-winged', square-tailed and glossy with red bill and legs: a cliff bird of coasts and quarries or mineshafts, rare outside its breeding range. Choughs are wonderfully adept fliers, but Jackdaws and Rooks fly over coastal clifftops and may briefly confuse.

Magpies are black and white, glossy, and long-tailed, not confusable with anything else.
Jays, secretive woodland birds, draw attention by their calls and fly overhead in autumn, often carrying acorns.

Crow ageing/sexing

Sexes alike, no seasonal changes; juveniles generally duller but difficult to distinguish beyond first moult.

Crows in flight

Concentrate on size, tail shape, wingbeats and plumage contrasts.

RAVEN
(p. 470)

CARRION CROW
(p. 468)

HOODED CROW
(p. 467)

JUVENILE

ROOK
(p. 469)

CHOUGH
(p. 471)

JACKDAW
(p. 466)

NUTCRACKER
(p. 463)

JAY
(p. 472)

MAGPIE
(p. 473)

Jackdaw

Corvus monedula **535**

30–34 cm | WS 70–75 cm

Small, grey-black crow, resembling a pigeon but stouter, stronger, longer-legged, more upright.

Grey-black, slight gloss; **inky black face and cap** against **pale grey shawl**. **Whitish eye** obvious close-up. **Bill short and stout**, head rounded but broad. IMMATURE duller than adult with less well-defined cap IN FLIGHT, quick, with **flickery beats**; frequently soars, often in large groups, swirling out from trees or cliff, swinging around with noisy outburst and returning. Often mixes with bigger Rooks.

VOICE Metallic "*jak*", "*chak*", "*kya*", but very varied: single bird can create prolonged, rapid, bouncy cacophony, with short, sharp, barked, shouted or squeaky notes. Noisy, quick-fire, staccato chorus from flocks going to roost.

Common resident (500,000 pairs, plus 2·8 million birds in Ireland); rare winter visitor

Town centres to cliffs, farmland, parks, old woodland

ADULT

Wings slightly rounded, often slightly curled back; smoother, rounder, gentler shapes than Rook (*p. 469*) or Chough (*p. 471*).

ADULT

Race *monedula* (often referred to as 'Nordic' Jackdaw) rare/scarce migrant (Nov–May) greyer than resident British/Irish race *spermologus*, with **paler band on side of neck**. Some birds darker above with pale neck band, perhaps from farther east.

white eye

dark cap and chin

grey neck

1ST-WINTER

ADULT

immature duller than adult

Hooded Crow

Corvus cornix **535**

44–51 cm | WS 85–95 cm

Striking **two-tone, grey-and-black crow** (grey faintly washed fawn/pinkish-buff in some lights). Social where common but often isolated pairs on moors. IN FLIGHT, action and shapes like Carrion Crow (*p. 468*), without quicker, more determined impression of Jackdaw, or rounder tail of Rook (*p. 469*), or 'presence' of larger Raven (*p. 470*).

Narrow zone of Hooded × Carrion Crow hybridization crosses N Scotland. Hybrids have 'shadow' of Hooded Crow pattern, but grey areas darker, or streaked black. Occasional hybrid pairs elsewhere, and hybrid patterns may persist for generations.

VOICE Repeated "*kraa kraa kraa*" on even pitch.

Common resident (160,000 pairs, plus 540,000 birds in Ireland); scarce (declined) winter visitor outside breeding range

from Scandinavia

Low-lying coasts, beaches, moors, fields, mountains, woodland edge

ADULT

ADULT

Crow shape combined with pale body easily recognised.

Hybrid Hooded x Carrion Crows are usually obviously intermediate, but subsequent generations may be more or less like one of the parents.

grey with black head and breast

black wings and tail

ADULT

Crows in flight *p. 465*

Carrion Crow

44–51 cm | WS 85–90 cm

Big black bird; see Rook, Raven (*p. 470*). Mixes with Rook (not at colony), less numerous where Rook forms large flocks (but flocks of 100s, *e.g.* rubbish tips, fields spread with manure).

Neater than Rook, smoother plumage. Broad, low crown; **shorter, more arched, black bill** (excited bird raises forehead/crown in steep, smooth dome, less peaked than Rook), **black face**. Hard to tell from young Rook: body plumage tighter; bill less pointed, blacker; basal bristles smoother (less obvious 'bump'); thicker neck and shoulders. IN FLIGHT, soars less than Rook: fairly sedate, straight (unless chasing bird of prey). Some birds have whitish bands across wings (due to deficient diet).

VOICE Hard, rough, "*kraang-kraang-kraang*", "*kraaa*"; soft "*krr-krr-krr*". Other calls varied, not so 'musical' as Rook.

Common resident (790,000 pairs). Generally rare Ireland but locally common in NE

On/near open ground anywhere: woodland edge, fields, beaches

Rook (juvenile): thin, pointed bill; basal bristles prominent; neck relatively slender

Carrion Crow: heavy bill, basal bristle profile smooth; neck thick

Raven: very heavy bill, basal bristles prominent; neck very thick

ADULT

Short head/neck/bill; short, **square tail**; wings oblong, broad at tip, held rather straight.

ADULT

smoother curve to belly profile, less angular than Rook

Rook

41–49 cm | WS 80–90 cm

Common 'crow'; see Carrion Crow, Raven (*p. 470*).
Always social, often with Jackdaws (*p. 466*); nests in **treetop colonies** (Jackdaws mix at colony, but not Carrion Crows).

'Loose' body plumage, **wide, shaggy flank**; steep forehead, **peaked crown**; tapered, very wide-based bill. ADULT black, purple gloss, except **bare grey-buff face**, greyer bill. JUVENILE black face, best told from Carrion Crow by shape, structure (see *annotations below*). IN FLIGHT, capable of acrobatics in wind and much **more likely to soar** to great height, than Carrion Crow. Flocks swirl over colony at any time of year.

VOICE Varied: around colony, deep, 'comfortable' caws and croaks; typical "*craa-craa-craa*". Frequent loud, far-carrying, high "*crroo-crroo-crroo*", choked trumpeting notes, musical squeaks and squeals; deep, mechanical, wooden rattle in flight.

Very common resident (1·2 million pairs, plus 3·7 million birds in Ireland)

Farmland, woodland edge, copses, clifftops, urban areas

Juvenile has black face and is very like Carrion Crow: differences as shown here:

basal bristles form more prominent 'bump'

ADULT

neck and shoulders not as thickset

long, more pointed bill

JUVENILE

ADULT

Long head and bill; **long, round or wedge-shaped tail** (closer to Raven); tapered wingtips often curve back.

from the side, broad head/bill looks long and tapered

Raven

Corvus corax

54–67 cm | WS 125–135 cm

Huge, charismatic crow (size often obvious but can be hard to judge); see Carrion Crow (*p. 468*), especially Rook (*p. 469*). May form flocks (scores) where common.

All black. Very large; crown round, peaked or flattened, smooth profile. Throat raised in 'beard', uniquely bulbous in flight. **Bill long, deeply arched**. IN FLIGHT, size approaches Buzzard (*p. 302*); soars masterfully, diagnostic **momentary roll onto back** with angled wings. May twist primaries to create loud, rasping thrum. Most soaring birds less black (beware high-flying Cormorant (*p. 74*)); Buzzard broader-winged. Moulting ADULTS show gappy trailing edge, swept-back 'fingers'; JUVENILES have shorter, 'complete' wings.

VOICE Carries far: loud, echoing, abrupt, hollow quality "*prruk-prruk-prruk*"; higher, more ringing "*tonk!*" Loud "*quak quak*"; subdued notes, rattles, clicks at close range.

Scarce resident, locally common (12,000 pairs, plus 70,000 birds in Ireland)

Upland areas, chalk downs, forest, coastal cliffs

Long wings with long, narrow tips, slightly bulging trailing edge; straight or angled leading edge. **Tail long, broad; rounded or wedge-shaped**: at times, distinctive 'diamond' (more like Rook's when closed).

ADULT

all black, scaly feather edges close-up

heavy, arched bill

ADULT

Chough

Pyrrhocorax pyrrhocorax 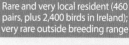 race *pyrrhocorax* ‡ see p.525 **I** **535**

37–41 cm | WS 75–90 cm

Glossy black bird of cliffs and quarries. Similar size to Jackdaw (*p. 466*), with longer, slimmer, curved bill; longer tail; longer, broader, squarer wings. Joyful, extravagant and acrobatic in flight around cliffs, often in small flocks. On ground, bouncy hops and walk; **long wingtips** dipped and raised, head bowed; probes into tussocks/under cowpats. British/Irish birds (race *pyrrhocorax*) are smaller, more purplish, than continental races.

Black, steely-blue sheen. **Slender, downcurved bill and legs red**. JUVENILE shorter, orange bill; narrower wings, faintly notched tail in flight. IN FLIGHT, compare shape with Jackdaw and Rook (*p. 469*) (both also soar and dive around coastal cliffs); often dives with half-closed wings, frequently pulling back up in steep bounding climb.

VOICE Jackdaw-like but longer, more **ringing, piercing**, shouted "*chee-aah*", "*chaaa*", "*chrri*".

Rare and very local resident (460 pairs, plus 2,400 birds in Ireland); very rare outside breeding range

Mostly coastal cliffs, islands, rare inland; feeds on nearby pastures, piles of seaweed on beaches

Broad, **square-tipped** deeply fingered wings (two-tone beneath with **blacker coverts**); head quite long, narrow, tail short, square.

ADULT

inky black body, variable gloss

red bill

triangular shape

ADULT

red legs

Jay

32–35 cm | WS 50 cm

<O> Hoopoe (*p. 329*)

Smallish, wide-winged, contrasted woodland/garden bird: 'big with white rump' as it flies across road or clearing, often followed by another.

Pinkish, greyer back; **black-and-white wings**; **white rump**; black tail. Streaked crown, **black moustache**. Patch of **electric blue** on wing.

VOICE Subdued or loud 'mewing'; more frequent harsh screech of alarm or irritation, hoarse, tearing "*shraairk!*"

Fairly common resident (160,000 pairs); irregular migrant

IN FLIGHT, quick, elusive in dense trees. Flies higher, with springy, elastic beats, between feeding woods and during regular autumn movements.

black-and-white wings

white rump

black tail

ADULT
European race *glandarius*

Woodland, parks

ADULT
Irish race
hibernicus

Irish race *hibernicus* (above) darker, more rufous back and cheeks than resident race *rufitergum*.

Northern/central European race *glandarius* (bird in flight *above*) is greyer; reaches Britain/Ireland in some years;

Scottish race *caledonicus* also greyish: gradation between forms prevents firm identification.

black moustache

grey-pink body

ADULT
British race
rufitergum

Magpie

Pica pica

40–51 cm (incl. tail 20–30 cm) | WS 56–61 cm

Unmistakable, handsome, **long-tailed**, pied bird: often in small bands, equally singly or in pairs; sometimes larger gatherings.

Head and breast dull black; wings glossed blue; **long tail** glossed green, blue and intense purple. **Big white shoulder patch**, **white belly** and wingtips. JUVENILE has shorter tail but cannot be mistaken for anything else.

VOICE Loud, chattering, staccato "*cha-cha-cha*" and variations.

Common resident (590,000 pairs, plus 750,000 birds in Ireland)

Widespread, woods, farmland, bushy areas, suburbs, parks

IN FLIGHT, can be overlooked when seen head-on and tail not obvious, but steady, quick beats and frequent steep, closed-winged dives to ground or perch characteristic.

spread wings reveal streaky white outer half

ADULT

Frequent spring gatherings in bare treetops.

unique black and white pattern

long tail

ADULT

SPARROWS AND FINCHES

SPARROW ID	head pattern | tail pattern
FINCH ID	bill shape/colour | wing and tail pattern | streaking | rump colour | calls and song

4 sparrows: 2 resident; 2 vagrants.
21 finches: 12 resident (2 Scotland only, 1 very rare); 2 winter visitors; 2 migrants; 5 vagrants (plus vagrant sparrows and finches from America).

Finch, Sparrow or Bunting?

Finches, **sparrows** and **buntings** (see *p. 496*) can be told from other perching birds by their triangular bills and short legs.

Sparrows (*pp. 476–477, 495*) all have plain, unstreaked underparts, ruling out most finches and buntings, except Chaffinch, which is easily told by the extensive white in its wings and tail.

Finches (*pp. 478–495*) are distinguished from the similar buntings with more difficulty: many buntings have blackish tails with white outer feathers, while finches have thin, pale feather edges or patches of colour on their tails. There are more detailed differences, such as the shape of the bill (on buntings, the upper mandible often makes a smaller 'lid' on the big, broad lower one) and the pattern of the dark centres on the tertials (a marked 'stepped' shape on buntings). Some finches have fine songs; a few, unlike any bunting, display by using song flights. Many finches are also more acrobatic feeders, on tall stems and in trees, than the buntings. Finches as a group have a remarkable variety of bill shapes, adapted primarily for shelling seeds; from the beech-nut crunching Hawfinch to the pine-seed-extracting crossbills.

upper mandible generally smaller than lower; backward point at gape

REED BUNTING

BRAMBLING (FINCH)

backward point at base

HOUSE SPARROW

Sparrow ageing/sexing

House Sparrows have marked sexual differences but male and female Tree Sparrows are the same, both with a 'male-like' plumage. Juveniles can be separated but look like adults by their first summer.

Finch ageing/sexing Some have marked differences between male and female, and also between breeding and non-breeding plumages. Breeding colours are often obscured by dull feather tips in winter, revealed as these fall away in spring. Juveniles and first-winters are mostly identifiable.

Adults and juveniles have a single moult each year.

Post-juvenile moult	Adult moult
JUL–SEP: flight feathers and some coverts retained for a full year, becoming very abraded.	JUL–SEP (body moult may rarely continue into spring): complete moult after breeding; breeding plumage assumed by abrasion/disintegration of dull feather tips.

JUVENILE
APR–SEP

♀ ♂

ADULT
SEP–JAN (fresh)
JAN–AUG (worn)

The types of finches

Finches fall into several groups and can be told apart by their frequent flight calls, with experience, or by their songs.

CROSSBILL

Greenfinch, **Linnet** and **Twite** all have pale (yellow or white) streaks on the outer edges of their wing and tail feathers. **Greenfinches** are uniquely largely plain, unstreaked green in most plumages. **Siskins** (*opposite*) are green but strongly streaked, with boldly barred wings.

Goldfinch and **Siskin**, and the streaky brown **redpolls**, cling to tall stems and seedheads to feed, while **Linnet** and **Twite** stand on the ground and reach up to seedheads with their bills, or pull them down under one foot. **Siskins**, **redpolls** and **Goldfinches** also feed in treetops. Some species visit bird tables and the ground beneath, while others specialize in artificial feeders, especially **Siskins**, **Goldfinches**, **redpolls** and **Greenfinches**.

Crossbills are treetop feeders, prising open scales of cones with crossed bill tips. When they fly off, they can be extremely vocal.

GREENFINCH

GOLDFINCH

LESSER REDPOLL

Hawfinches are large-billed, capable of dealing with cherry stones and other tough foods, but they also feed a good deal on beech mast under trees. **Bullfinches** are quieter, secretive feeders on soft buds, shoots and berries.

Chaffinch and **Brambling** are remarkably similar in shape, structure and pattern but differ in colour details: **Chaffinches** are widespread all year, **Bramblings** winter visitors. They tend to feed on the ground, or take caterpillars from foliage in summer.

HAWFINCH

BULLFINCH

CHAFFINCH

American Sparrows

Vagrants from North America (see *pp. 518–519*), mainly in spring and probably mostly crossing the Atlantic at least partly on board ships, include sparrows (such as White-crowned Sparrow) and finches (such as Evening Grosbeak, Dark-eyed Junco and Eastern Towhee), as well as 'sparrows' that are more closely related to Old World buntings, such as Savannah Sparrow.

WHITE-THROATED SPARROW

House Sparrow

Passer domesticus ● ⓘ

14–16 cm | WS 18–25 cm

👁 Spanish Sparrow (*p. 495*), Rock Sparrow (*p. 495*)

Small, garrulous, finch-like; **thick bill**, **short pale legs**, **unstreaked beneath**. Very social, family groups to hundreds where abundant, keep loosely together; noisy, squabbling groups in hedges and thickets. Flies from field to hedge in **tight whirring groups**, rather tail-down.

MALE **grey band on crown**, red-brown hindneck. Pale grey cheeks; **black throat and bib**. Underside **unmarked** pale grey. Broad white bar on upperwing. Bill thick, triangular, black. In winter, **small black chin**, bib lost; crown obscured by buff tips; **whitish ring around sides of neck**; bill yellowish. FEMALE less conspicuous, **pale brown**; **broad buff stripe** from eye over cheek. **Unstreaked** pale grey-buff underside. Two pale buff streaks on back. Bill thick, pale buffish.

VOICE Loud chirrups and cheeps, "*cheep*", "*chwilp*", "*shreep*"; song includes calls in prolonged, rich, loud, emphatic but unmusical performance.

Still common resident (6 million pairs, plus 2-4 million birds in Ireland); much decreased, now rare/absent in some areas

Suburban areas, gardens, parks, farmland, coastal grassland/scrub

grey feather edges obscure head pattern and bib in winter

hint of pale collar

ADULT ♂ WINTER

greyish-brown cap over broad pale stripe

ADULT ♀

grey feather edges wear away to reveal colour beneath in spring

unstreaked underside

white cheeks

large black bib

ADULT ♂ SUMMER

Tree Sparrow

Passer montanus ● Ⓘ **538**

12–14 cm | WS 20–22 cm

⟨👁⟩ Spanish Sparrow (*p. 495*)

Scarce, local resident (60,000 pairs, scarce Ireland)

Woods, farmland, waterside thickets

Small, thick-billed, streaky brown: sexes alike, resembles male House Sparrow. Mixes with finches, House Sparrow, buntings, even feeding on waterside 'tideline'. Hops with tail raised; crown feathers often raised, give rounder head, small-billed appearance. Fast, whirring, agile flight.

ADULT **all-brown cap**, white cheek with **black spot**. Black bib always small and neat (not so extensive or streaked as spring House Sparrow). Almost complete white collar. Bill black in summer, buffish/grey in winter. JUVENILE duller, centre of crown diffusely paler/greyer.

VOICE Distinctive hard "*tek*" or "*tet-et-et*" in flight, and cheerful "*tsuwit*". Song higher, more chattering, less dynamic than House Sparrow's.

dull cap, small cheek spot

JUVENILE

domed chocolate-brown crown

yellowish on bill

black cheek spot

small black bib

ADULT WINTER

black cheek spot

brown cap

pale collar

unstreaked below

ADULT SUMMER

Bullfinch

15·5–17 cm | WS 22–29 cm

Thickset, broad-headed finch; big white rump; distinctive call. Blue-black wings, broad **whitish wingbar**. Quiet, reclusive but not necessarily shy. Parrot-like when feeding, often hovers.

MALE **black cap and chin**, grey back, **red-pink breast**.
FEMALE black cap/chin, grey-brown above, grey-buff underside.
JUVENILE no black cap or chin. IN FLIGHT, **white wrap-around rump** (broader than Brambling's (*p. 480*)). Overhead, pale underwing; white vent and square, dark tail distinctive.

VOICE Low, hollow whistle, "*peooo*" or "*heeew*", particularly penetrating in spring. Song quiet, vibrant, reedy ('policeman's whistle'), creaky sounds. 'Trumpet' call sometimes given is distinctive of race *pyrrhula*.

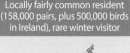

Locally fairly common resident (158,000 pairs, plus 500,000 birds in Ireland), rare winter visitor

Woodland, thickets, hedgerows, orchards

ADULT ♂
race *pyrrhula*

ADULT ♂
race *pileata*

black cap continues onto chin

Northern European race *pyrrhula* (rare migrant: Oct–Mar) larger than British and Irish race *pileata*: MALE **deeper red** beneath, white rump **extends farther** up blue-grey back; FEMALE only identifiable by measurements.

JUVENILE

pale unstreaked underside continues onto cheek

white rump

blue-black wings and tail

ADULT ♀
race *pileata*

JUVENILE has same basic shape and pattern as adult, but browner; head plain; no streaks; broad pale bar across black wing.

Hawfinch

Coccothraustes coccothraustes ●

16·5–18 cm | WS 29–33 cm

👁 Evening Grosbeak (p. 516)

Rare and local resident (4,800 pairs, declining). Scarce winter visitor Ireland (<250 records)

Big, handsome, striking finch, but shy, hard to find; faithful to a few traditional sites. May sit upright on treetop (like Crossbill (p. 492)); feeds on ground.

Bright crown, pale cheeks, black chin; **pale wing band**. Bill large (not grotesquely so), blue and black (yellowish in winter). MALE bright forehead and cheek, darker cap, grey hindneck; rump pale tawny. Wings steely-blue. FEMALE duller, less pinkish below, browner between eye and bill. JUVENILE may be perplexing: pale throat, blackish barring below, but broad white wing panel and **white tail tip**.

VOICE Call hard, dry, clicking or ticking "*tik!*" (often louder than Robin (p. 388) but very like Redstart (p. 392)), or "*tik-ik-ik*". Quiet, variable song.

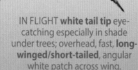

ADULT ♂

Old woodland, parks with lines of tall trees, especially Beech, Hornbeam, cherries

JUVENILE

IN FLIGHT **white tail tip** eye-catching especially in shade under trees; overhead, fast, **long-winged/short-tailed**, angular white patch across wing.

JUVENILE has same basic pattern as adult but dull, pale, marked by mottles and bars beneath.

pattern same but head and bill duller in winter

ADULT ♂ WINTER

bright cap and cheeks

pale band on wing

ADULT ♀

no streaks

ADULT ♂ SUMMER

Brambling

Fringilla montifringilla 539

14–16 cm | WS 25–26 cm

Similar size, structure to Chaffinch but **orange shoulder, white rump**. Often with Chaffinches; feeds under trees, in fields; beneath bird tables on spilled seed.

MALE black hood, orange shoulder and breast, black/white/buff wings, white belly. In winter (most likely), dark cap, dark bands beside grey nape, bright **yellow bill**. Rusty-brown on back, fading whiter; hoary look to head (pale fringes to feathers wear away by spring, revealing black). Pale **orange chest against white belly**; **flanks spotted**. FEMALE subdued but similar pattern: **pale nape between dark bands**; dull orange breast against **white belly**, dark **flank spots**; buff shoulder, wingbar.

VOICE Twangy, 'vulgar', coarse "*tswairk*" or "*tsweep*", harder "*chup*" than Chaffinch. Song (rare) includes deep buzzing note.

Scarce winter visitor (erratic, locally common in some years)

from N and W Europe

Woodland, farmland

IN FLIGHT, narrow **white rump** distinctive.

Flight like Chaffinch: slightly jerky/hesitant; flocks quite loose.

1ST-WINTER ♂

pale feather edges wear away to reveal solid black in spring

1ST-WINTER ♀

orange-buff shoulder

yellow on bill

black head, back, obscured by whitish fringes

grey band on neck

ADULT ♂ SUMMER

ADULT ♂ WINTER

orange 'shoulder'

ADULT ♀

white belly

white belly, dark flank spots, unlike Chaffinch

Chaffinch

Fringilla coelebs race *gengleri*

14–16 cm | WS 24–28 cm

Sparrow-sized, long-bodied finch; white on wings and tail (white shoulders often hidden). In winter in fields, under trees, tame around car parks, picnic sites, pub gardens.

White shoulder, wingbar and tail sides. MALE pinkish with bluish cap and bill; in autumn/winter colours obscured by buff feather edges (wear away by spring). FEMALE/JUVENILE same shape, structure, pattern, but dull, colourless; white bar across midwing. Dark sides to crown. Underside **unstreaked olive-buff**. See Brambling (same structure/feather tracts).

VOICE High, ringing "*pink*"; in flight, "*chup*" characteristic. Spring/summer, monotonous "*huit*" for long periods, slightly like Chiffchaff (*p. 426*). Song bright, rattling "*chip-chip-chip cherry-erry-erry*", accelerating into final flourish.

Very common resident (5-6 million pairs, plus 4-2 million birds in Ireland), winter visitor

from N and W Europe

Woodland, farmland, gardens

IN FLIGHT, striking white on wings and tail; greenish rump; flocks loose, uncoordinated.

European race *coelebs*

ADULT ♀

ADULT ♂ WINTER

European race *coelebs* (winter visitor) slightly paler and 'cleaner' than resident British and Irish race *gengleri*. The difference is subtle and best noted when a mixed flock allows direct comparison.

ADULT WINTER ♂ race *gengleri*

ADULT SUMMER ♂ race *gengleri*

white bar across middle of wing

ADULT ♀ race *gengleri*

481

Goldfinch

Carduelis carduelis race *britannica*

12–13·5 cm | WS 20–25 cm

Small, distinctive finch: **red on face, yellow band on wings**. Feeds on tall seedheads, in trees (Alder, birches). Perches high in tall tree, inconspicuously inside leafy canopy. Often 5–10; sometimes many more in good feeding areas.

ADULT **red, white and black face**, black wings with **broad yellow bands**. Slim; tail deeply notched. Dark breast patches, white belly. Some birds may be sexed: MALE red on face generally extends behind top of eye, patch between eye and bill black; FEMALE red less extensive, patch beside bill greyer. JUVENILE plain greyish head; yellow band on duller wing, buff feather tips.

VOICE Call quite like Swallow (*p. 342*), slurred, sweet, musical "*swilp*", "*swilip*", "*sililip*"; also harsh, churring rasp. Song fast, tinkling trills, chattery notes from tree.

Common resident (300,000 pairs, plus 915,000 birds in Ireland), winter visitor

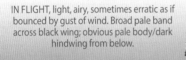

from W Europe

to Low Countries

IN FLIGHT, light, airy, sometimes erratic as if bounced by gust of wind. Broad pale band across black wing; obvious pale body/dark hindwing from below.

Farmland, open spaces, heaths, scrub, areas with seeding thistles

ADULT

greyer between eye and bill

unique black/white/red head

black between eye and bill

ADULT ♀

ADULT ♂

dark breast patch

similar to adult, but paler, and head plain grey

JUVENILE

Greenfinch

Chloris chloris race harrisoni

14–16 cm | WS 24–27 cm 👁 Citril Finch (*p. 485*)

Common resident (695,000 pairs, plus 830,000 birds in Ireland), winter visitor

Big, thick-billed, upright finch; deeply forked tail. Feeds in fields, on feeders, under trees; flocks bunch more tightly than Chaffinch (*p. 481*).

MALE **apple green**; grey on wing. **Big pale bill**, dark 'frown', **yellow streak on wing**. In winter, dull feather tips.
FEMALE narrower yellow streak on wing; back duller, some subtly streaked. JUVENILE soft streaks above and below. Yellow wing flash thin, still characteristic.

VOICE Call short "*jup*"; erratic trill "*jup-jup-up-up*", heavier, louder than Linnet (*p. 486*), less metallic than Redpoll (*p. 489*). Juvenile loud "*chup*", like Crossbill (*p. 492*). Song, perched or in **stretched-winged song flight**, includes loud, nasal "*dweeez*"; **ringing, musical trills**, varying speed, rhythm.

Breeding birds in Britain and Ireland sometimes treated as race *harrisoni*; in N Scotland and winter migrants, race *chloris*.

from Scandinavia

Parks, woods, farmland, open spaces, heathland scrub; winter flocks, even on tidelines

IN FLIGHT, yellow streaks on wing, but **yellow beside base of tail** more striking in rear view. Wingbeats more emphatic than Chaffinch: long undulations.

ADULT ♂

faint streaks on breast

JUVENILE

1ST-WINTER ♂

FEMALE and WINTER MALE can look dark green-grey in dull light.

dark mask

thick pale bill

ADULT ♂

broad yellow streak on wing

ADULT ♀

Siskin

Spinus spinus 539

11–12·5 cm | WS 18–22 cm

Citril Finch, Atlantic Canary (p. 523)

Tiny, slender, streaky, greenish finch with notched tail; fine, pointed bill. Acrobatic feeder in twigs, often with other finches, tit flocks. Often inconspicuous in treetops, giving chorus of soft calls. Disturbed flocks twist and turn tightly together.

Broad **black and yellow bands** across wing, yellow side to tail. MALE **black cap and chin**, yellow over eye, yellow breast, white belly with few streaks; rump yellow. FEMALE paler, duller head, greyer back, whiter below with more dark streaks. JUVENILE duller, streaky, narrower yellow wingbars, but same character.

VOICE Call distinctive, ringing, squeaky "*tluee*", "*tilu*" or "*tzsy-ee*". Also hard, harsh rattle or churr; fast medley from treetop flocks. Song fast, twittery, squeaky with trills and light, buzzy, wheezy notes.

Locally fairly common resident (357,000 pairs), winter visitor

from N and W Europe

Localized breeder; more widely in winter in conifers, Alder, birches; comes to feeders

ADULT ♂

In late winter/spring, males frequently break from feeding to sing.

ADULT ♂

IN FLIGHT, long yellow stripe along blackish wing.

black cap, yellow behind eye

yellow-green bar across blackish wing

ADULT ♂

lacks cap

pale bar on blackish wing

distinct wingbars

streaks beneath

JUVENILE

whitish beneath, streaked black; looks a grey bird on feeders (redpolls brown)

ADULT ♀

Serin *Serinus serinus*

11–12 cm | WS 18–22 cm

◉ Atlantic Canary (*p. 523*)

Very rare migrant from Europe: 30–40 per year (<15 records Ireland), most Apr–May); very rare breeder. Mostly woods, villages near S coast.

Tiny, round-headed, greenish/ yellowish, streaky finch; calls draw attention. **Tiny bill, yellow rump.** Pale crescent under eye; pale lower cheek; dark moustache. See Siskin, beware escaped Atlantic Canary (*p. 523*). Sits upright, hard to see in treetops; crouches/hops on ground. MALE **yellow forehead**, over eye, on throat; **white belly**; flanks streaked. FEMALE greyer, less yellow. JUVENILE buff-brown, streaked; **same face pattern**; no yellow; curved, **buff wingbar**; pale buffish rump (see Linnet (*p. 486*)). IN FLIGHT, light, fast, buoyant, bouncy.

VOICE Call jingling trill; upswept "*tu-wee*". Song fast, 'splintering glass' jingle, often in song flight.

ADULT ♂

539

Males are easy to see in spring when singing from a high perch.

1ST-WINTER ♀

densely streaked; weak wingbars

ADULT ♀

ADULT ♂

yellow rump

two pale bars on dark wing

head more like Linnet than Siskin

JUVENILE

Citril Finch *Carduelis citrinella*

11·5–13 cm | WS 20–22 cm

May feed on the ground like Linnet (*p. 486*).

Vagrant from S Europe: <5 records (Britain) (males), May, Jun. On coast. Woods.

Most resembles Siskin in size/structure, but adults **not streaked; two broad greenish-yellow bars** on blackish wing. MALE yellowish face, **grey nape**, yellow-green underside. FEMALE greyer. JUVENILE slightly browner, wingbars narrower, underside narrowly streaked, rather bunting-like.

ADULT ♂

Linnet

Linaria cannabina ●● race *autochthona* Ⓘ **539**

12·5–14 cm | WS 20–24 cm

○ Serin (*p. 485*),
Common Rosefinch (*p. 491*)

Small, short-billed finch.
Distinct face patterns; grey bill.
Flocks fly high, bounding, co-ordinated, drop into low
vegetation; stand up to feed, not clinging onto stems.

MALE **grey head**, red forehead; **plain red-brown back; white
streaks along wing and tail** sides. Underside plain buff, breast
red (extensive, bright in spring). FEMALE no red; greyish head,
lightly streaked back; fine streaks on breast, belly white.
In dull light, dark, greyish with **whitish face marks**, eyering.
IN FLIGHT white edges to outerwing and tail feathers (see Twite).

VOICE Twittering, dry "*chet-et-et*"; twangy "*tsooee*", less forceful
than Greenfinch (*p. 483*), less hard than Redpoll (*p. 489*).
Song musical sweet warbling.

Scottish race *autochthona* (not illustrated) darker, more slender bill, but
grades into race *cannabina* farther south.

Locally common resident
(535,000 pairs, plus 550,000 birds
in Ireland), migrant, winter visitor

from
Scandinavia

to Low
Countries

Heaths, rough grassland and
'waste' ground; farmland stubbles

JUVENILE

sharp bill

fine dark
streaks
beneath

ADULT ♂ WINTER

colours obscured
by pale feather
edges

peaked
crown

pale crescents above and
below eye; pale cheek
spot in all plumages

ADULT ♀

unstreaked
back

red forehead
and breast

white tail
streak

ADULT ♂

Twite

Linaria flavirostris ● **I** `539`

12·5–14 cm | WS 22–24 cm

Much like Linnet but **buffy plumage** and buff wingbar like redpolls (*pp. 488–490*); **tawny-buff throat**. Flocks feed low down in herbs, often circling saltmarsh before dropping down.

SUMMER MALE boldly streaked; large tawny-buff throat patch; **deep pink rump**. Bill greyish. FEMALE lacks pink. In winter (both sexes), **buff throat patch**, **yellow bill** (grey on Linnet), buff wingbar; long white streak on closed wing and side of tail (more conspicuous than Linnet). Brighter beneath but spread wing, tail similar to Linnet.

VOICE Distinctive: harder flight note than Linnet, closer to redpolls: **twangy, nasal, buzzing** "*twaa-it*". Song fast, twittering, mixing twangy call and rattling trills.

Scarce resident and summer visitor (11,000 pairs); rare winter migrant in S

Breeds uplands/coastal crofts; winters on low-lying coasts

Race *pipilans* of N Britain, Ireland, slightly darker than race *flavirostris* (winter migrant from Scandinavia); birds from the Outer Hebrides ([race] '*bensonorum*') dark and heavily streaked, but differences are slight and not easy to assign individuals to race unless comparison is possible.

ADULT WINTER

1ST-WINTER

yellow bill

in winter both sexes have a yellow bill, and can be distinguished by rump colour (pink on males)

dull, softly streaked

pale wingbar

glimpse of pink rump indicates male

no pink on rump indicates female

pale greyish bill

pale tawny-buff throat

ADULT ♀ SUMMER race *flavirostris*

pale sides to tail

ADULT ♂ SUMMER race *flavirostris*

Redpolls

Redpolls split opinion amongst taxonomic authorities; some regard the complex as comprising several species; some just one or two. Although often difficult to tell apart, the differences between the various forms are appreciable. Here, redpolls are treated as three species.

Redpolls are small, slim, streaky finches with broad **buff or white wingbar**, **red cap** and **black chin**. Distinguished from other finches by dark wings, pale crosswise bar (not streak down wing as Linnet, Twite (*pp. 486–487*)), tiny yellow bill, **short dark legs**. They are active, acrobatic; often with Siskins (*p. 484*), but less addicted to feeders, often feeding on the ground.

From late winter or spring male redpolls become extensively pink or red: some very red on the breast, pink on underparts and rump, almost like rosefinches (*p. 491*). Winter plumages are generally duller – see *p. 490*.

LESSER REDPOLL

1ST-WINTER/ ADULT ♀

legs may be pink

red cap

LESSER REDPOLL

1ST-WINTER/ADULT ♀

neat, rounded tail feathers in winter indicate adult; worn, pointed tips indicate 1st-winter

small black chin

curved pale bar across wing

LESSER REDPOLL

late winter/ spring male can be extensively red-pink from January onwards

ADULT ♂ SUMMER

COMMON REDPOLL

ADULT ♂ SUMMER

Lesser Redpoll

Acanthis cabaret  **539**

11–14 cm | WS 16–20 cm

Common Rosefinch (*p. 491*)

Darkest form; broad **buff wingbar**, shiny **red cap**, **black chin**. MALE pink/red foreparts; in spring many **pink-red all over breast**, pink on rump; less so in autumn/early winter. FEMALE small red cap, black around bill, streak through eye; long **streaks on buff flanks** beside white belly. JUVENILE lacks red cap, sometimes through winter.

VOICE Hard, fast metallic "*chuch-uch-uch-uch-uch*"; twangy "*tsooeee*". Song (often long, bouncy song flight) mixes calls with jingly trill "*trrrreeee*".

Scarce and local resident (25,000 pairs), winter visitor (numbers vary year to year)

Woodland, scrub, heaths, moors; favours birches; widely in winter

Redpolls – summary of key identification features	
Lesser Redpoll	Smallest, darkest; darkest buff wingbar (fades); rump brown/pink; buff edges on wings; streaks under tail.
Common Redpoll	Large, pale; white wingbar; rump grey-white/dark streaks; white edges on blacker wings; streaks under tail.
Arctic Redpoll	Large, pale; large head/neck, tiny bill; white rump or white upper band; white under tail with one streak at most.

Common Redpoll *Acanthis flammea*  race *flammea*
(Mealy Redpoll)

11·5–14 cm | WS 18–20 cm

Two races: *flammea* (N Europe to Alaska); *rostrata* (Greenland/Iceland).

S**lightly larger** than Lesser Redpoll; **paler**, less buff, especially on head; whiter lines on back; **whiter wingbar**. **Rump white/greyish** with short, dark streaks (streaked brown/buff on Lesser Redpoll); blacker wings have whitish fringes (buff on Lesser Redpoll); flanks whiter. Much variation; buff on Lesser Redpoll fades whiter by late winter. Race *rostrata* (rare migrant, has bred) large, broad-winged, like Twite (*p. 487*); brown with blacker streaks, broader flank stripes.

VOICE Much like Lesser Redpoll but variable deeper notes.

Scarce/rare winter visitor from N Europe; mostly N/E Britain. Woodland

streaks on whitish rump

ADULT WINTER ♂ *flammea*

Arctic Redpoll *Acanthis hornemanni*

12–14 cm | WS 20–26 cm

Two races: *hornemanni* (NE Canada, Greenland) and *exilipes* (N Eurasia).

Large head, thick neck; **very short bill**. **Narrow grey streak or all-white under tail** (dark streaks on Lesser and Common Redpolls). Some have **bright buff head** and upper back, whiter body; Male *exilipes* can be obvious 'snowball'; other plumages less distinct. ADULT broad white wingbar, **large white rump**. MALE breast pale pink; rump pink in spring. JUVENILE **unmarked white band on rump**, streaked upper edge, or fine streaks overall, more like Common Redpoll.

VOICE Like other redpolls.

Very rare migrant/vagrant from N Europe, Greenland: 5–35 per year (<10 records Ireland), Oct–Apr, Mostly N, E Britain. Trees.

large white rump

ADULT WINTER ♂ *hornemanni*

Redpolls in winter

Redpolls feed in high tops of birch, alder and other trees, or on fallen seed beneath, sometimes joining finch flocks in fields: they can be hard to see well. Fortunately, they also come to feeders where they can be examined closely.

Plumages vary with age, sex and season and differences between races sometimes overlap, so many will be hard to identify with precision beyond 'redpoll'.

Check size, bulk; bill size.

Look carefully at head and wingbars; pale buff areas tend to fade whiter towards spring.

Examine the rump and undertail coverts if you suspect a scarce or rare redpoll.

Compare with other redpolls nearby if possible.

COMMON REDPOLL

ARCTIC REDPOLL

1ST-WINTER/ADULT ♀

LESSER REDPOLL

looks sleek and slim when alert and active but can be fluffed up, almost round, especially in cold weather

COMMON REDPOLL

ADULT ♂ WINTER race *rostrata*

ADULT ♂ WINTER race *flammea*

winter adult darker than 1st-winter Lesser Redpoll

ARCTIC REDPOLL

Arctic Redpolls have large, round heads and tiny bills seemingly 'pushed in' to the face. Adult males may be obvious, females and juveniles much less so

ADULT ♂ WINTER race *hornemanni*

ADULT ♂ WINTER race *exilipes*

Common Rosefinch *Erythrina erythrina*

13·5–15 cm | WS 24–25 cm

Indigo Bunting (p. 516)

Rare/scarce migrant from NE Europe, winters Asia: 100–250 per year (<10 records Ireland), most Apr–May, Sep–Oct, Mostly N Isles, on coast; has bred. Woodland edge, scrub.

Round-headed, long-tailed, sparrow-like finch with big, slightly bulging bill; bold dark eye in plain face rules out female House Sparrow (p. 476), redpolls (pp. 488–490). Pale tertial edges but all-dark tail rules out most buntings; Corn Bunting (p. 503) bigger with paler bill, more striped head.

MALE **bright deep red on head, breast and rump**, otherwise mid-brown with whiter belly and tertial tips. Raises crown feathers in distinct peak. FEMALE olive-brown, subtly streaked; **two thin, pale wingbars**. JUVENILE brighter, buffier on flanks, slightly sandier above, sharper streaks beneath; **two broader, pale buff, parallel wingbars**. Whitish eyering.

VOICE Call soft, upswept "*tiu-eek*". Rhythmic, whistling song with simple phrases: "*weedy-weedy-weedy-wu*".

ADULT ♂
stout, bulbous bill

ADULT ♀
dark eye in plain, pale face

two thin pale wingbars

1ST-WINTER

pale wingbars and tertial edges

faint, soft streaks

Crossbill

Loxia curvirostra **539**

15–17 cm | WS 27–30 cm

⟨◐⟩ Two-barred Crossbill (*p. 494*)

Scarce and local resident (11,000 pairs); widespread irregular migrant/immigrant elsewhere, occasionally breeding

Big, large-headed finch; **arched** bill, **crossed tips**. Often upright on treetop (see Hawfinch (*p. 479*)); groups fly high above trees. Feeds quietly, parrot-like agility; bursts of calls help locate them. Drinks from puddles. 'Irruptions' irregular. Some long-bodied (so look longer-tailed); others short-bodied, tail looks shorter.

MALE **dull red**, **brighter rump**. IMMATURE MALE greenish, patched orange-red. FEMALE greenish, **rump yellower**; plain wings (unlike Greenfinch (*p. 483*)). JUVENILE dull, streaked; may have white wingbars, thin tertial fringes (see *p. 494*).

VOICE Calls deep purring notes from perch, building to ringing "*jip-jip-jip*" as flies off; forceful "*djeep-djeep-djeep*" generally higher pitched than Parrot Crossbill. Often excited chorus, typical of all crossbills. Song buzzing, trilling, whistled sounds.

from N and C Europe

IN FLIGHT, dynamic, bounding flight over treetops, often over long distances.

Coniferous woods, windbreaks; favours spruce

JUVENILE

JUVENILE ♂

plain wing

finely streaked overall

basically green and grey

ADULT ♀

IMMATURE MALES combine juvenile streaks with adult colour, especially on rump. The amount of adult colour increases with age.

variably orange-red and brown

WINTER ♂

Crossbill identification

Common, Scottish and Parrot Crossbills share similar plumages and general character and are not easily identifiable: concentrate on head, bill and calls. Even Parrot and Common Crossbills can be very difficult, while Scottish Crossbills are intermediate, often impossible without analysis of sound recordings. Look for them in conifers and listen for falling cones; they feed very quietly but may suddenly create an outburst of loud calls, often before flying away.

■ Scottish Crossbill
■ both species
■ Parrot Crossbill

smallest

tip often long, curved

CROSSBILL

bill deep

cheeks 'bulging'

SCOTTISH CROSSBILL

bill deepest, roundest

tips barely cross

PARROT CROSSBILL

Scottish Crossbill   *Loxia scotica* 539

16–18 cm | WS 27–30 cm

Size and structure more or less intermediate between Crossbill and Parrot Crossbill. Found in same forests, including planted conifers. Plumages as Crossbill but underwing typically paler. **Bill deep**, heavy; head rather **fat-cheeked**.

VOICE Between Crossbill and Parrot Crossbill: best confirmed by analysis of sound recordings.

fat, 'bulging' cheeks

ADULT ♀

ADULT ♂

Rare and local resident (<5,000 pairs) restricted to Scottish Highlands; movements obscure. Pine forest, particularly Scots pine

Parrot Crossbill   *Loxia pytyopsittacus* 539

17–18 cm | WS 30–33 cm

Biggest crossbill, feeds on seeds from large pine cones. FEMALE smaller bill than MALE, but on average Parrot Crossbill has **bigger, deeper, blunter bill**, wider head (thicker neck, often shows 'ruff' when hunched), smaller eye than Crossbill. Bill deep, **bulging** (like ball pressed into face), slightly 'hanging'.

VOICE Like Crossbill, but typically deeper, harder quality, "*tup*" (rather than "*klip*" or "*jip*") – "*tup-tup-tup-tup…*".

'flat' cheeks   ADULT ♀

ADULT ♂

Very rare and local breeder in Scottish Highlands; erratic vagrant Britain from N Europe (<10 per year). Conifer forest or coastal conifers

Two-barred Crossbill *Loxia leucoptera* `539`

14–16 cm | WS 25–29 cm

Small crossbill, slender bill; white wingbars, broad tips to tertials. See Crossbill (*p. 492*).

MALE **raspberry-red**; **blackish wings**, **two broad white wingbars**. Tertials have **white, shield-shaped tips**. FEMALE pale grey-green, smaller tertial tips. JUVENILE olive-grey, dull wings, fine white wingbars. Occasional Crossbill with thinner white wingbars lacks obvious white tertial tips.

VOICE High, sharp "*chip-chip-chip*". Vibrant piping "*feet*" distinctive.

Very rare, irregular migrant from N Europe: 8–10 per year (<5 records Ireland), most Sep–Mar. Widespread. Coniferous woodland, particularly Larch.

1ST-SUMMER ♂
dark tips

CROSSBILL shows variable very thin pale wingbars on fresh feathers but not a broad double bar nor obvious white tertial tips.

ADULT ♀

double white wingbar; tertial spots

broad white wingbars and large tertial spots

thin wingbars; white on tertials

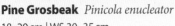

JUVENILE

ADULT ♂

Pine Grosbeak *Pinicola enucleator*

18–20 cm | WS 30–35 cm

Very large, bulky (in cold weather) or rather slender, slim-tailed finch with **rounded bill**; **white wingbars**. MALE pale red and grey, blacker wings. FEMALE greenish and grey. JUVENILE male like adult female but gradually develops orange red, recalling young male Crossbill (*p. 492*).

Vagrant from N Europe: <15 records (Britain), Oct–May. Widespread. Woods, gardens.

Round (cold, inactive) or slim (active) shape; bulbous bill.

ADULT ♂

ADULT ♀

Spanish Sparrow *Passer hispaniolensis*
14–16 cm | WS 22–24 cm

Vagrant from SE Europe: <15 records (Britain), Oct–May. Widespread. Usually with House Sparrows.

MALE like dark male House Sparrow (*p. 476*), but **cap all red-brown**, big **white cheek**, broad black streaks on back, black bib breaks into broad **black streaks over whole underside**. FEMALE often indistinguishable from House Sparrow; sometimes faint streaks below.

ADULT ♂ SUMMER

grey cap

HOUSE SPARROW

ADULT ♂ SUMMER

brown cap, white cheeks

bold black streaks above and below

Pattern obscured by pale feather fringes but crown still brown; underside heavily streaked.

ADULT ♀

ADULT ♂ WINTER

very like House Sparrow

Vagrant from N Africa: <20 records (Britain), May–Jun, Aug–Sep. Widespread. Bare ground; rocks.

Trumpeter Finch *Bucanetes githagineus* 539
11·5–13 cm | WS 22–26 cm

Small, pale, round-headed finch; like unstreaked Linnet (*p. 486*) with bulbous bill. MALE orange-red bill; pink on wings, rump. FEMALE/JUVENILE paler, no pink; bill pale pink.

VOICE Call nasal, grating "*tchep, tchairp*"; song short, vibrant buzz "*airr*".

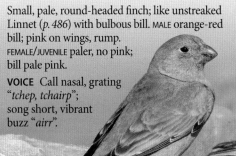

ADULT ♂

Vagrant from S Europe: 1 record (Britain), Jun. On coast. Open, rocky/stony areas.

Rock Sparrow *Petronia petronia*
14–16 cm | WS 28–32 cm

Like female House Sparrow (*p. 476*) but bolder **dark band each side of crown**, broad pale band over eye; long **brown streaks on whitish underside**; white spots at tip of tail.

VOICE Nasal/twangy "*pee*", harder "*pi-eet*", quick twitter.

ADULT

BUNTINGS

BUNTING ID head, wing, rump and tail patterns | streaking | leg colour | calls and song

19 species: 5 resident –1 local SW England, 1 rare breeder Scotland (also a winter visitor);
1 scarce migrant, 13 rare migrants/ vagrants.
NB the vagrant American sparrows are currently classified as buntings – see p. 475, 516–519

Buntings (*pp. 497–509*) look much like finches (see *p. 474* for more information) but have slightly longer, slimmer tails, and different detailed bill shapes, with a narrow upper mandible fitting like a lid on a broader, deeper lower one, adapted for feeding on seeds, particularly grasses.

The shape and pattern of the tertials also differs from finches, often with a distinctly 'stepped' black central patch. Many have bold white tail sides, not unlike some larks and pipits (see *p. 347*). However, buntings hop and shuffle; larks and pipits walk. The most lark-like in other ways, the Corn Bunting, is easily told from them by its plain tail. Some are farmland birds, Reed Bunting is a marsh or wetland bird, while the two non-*Emberiza* species (Snow and Lapland Buntings) are found mainly around the coast in winter. Unlike some finches, buntings have simple songs, with monotonous, rather unmusical phrases given from a low perch.

An impressive list of buntings, including many rare species from Europe and Asia, have been recorded in Britain and Ireland – they can, however, be difficult to identify. Throughout this book, simple, everyday language has been used wherever possible to describe the parts of a bird, but with buntings learning a few technical terms helps to improve precision when looking for the key, often subtle, identification features of some species. This 1st-winter Little Bunting, with its component parts pointed out, aims to clarify the meaning of these terms.

Bunting ageing/sexing In most species, males and females differ and have distinct breeding and non-breeding plumages. Juveniles are often identifiable through the first winter. **Adults and juveniles have a single moult each year.**

Post-juvenile moult
JUL–SEP: usually retaining most secondaries, primaries and tail feathers and some coverts. Unmoulted juvenile primary coverts dark brown, edged rufous, worn and frayed. Iris dark grey-brown, slowly becoming chestnut.

Adult moult
JUL–SEP: complete moult after breeding. Fresh primary coverts have firm grey tips. Iris dark chestnut. Fresh plumage has pale feather tips obscuring pattern beneath. Tips break away or wear off in spring to give bolder breeding season patterns.

1ST-WINTER
SEP–MAR

ADULT (fresh)
SEP–MAR

ADULT (worn)
APR–AUG

REED BUNTING

line over eye
eyestripe
nape (hindneck)
pale cheek spot
cheek
back
lesser coverts (shoulder)
median coverts (upper wingbar)
greater coverts (lower wingbar)
tertials
rump [obscured]
wingtip
vent
flank
outer tail feather

crown
side of crown
eyering
throat
dark line by throat
moustache
chest
breast

Lapland Bunting

Calcarius lapponicus ●

Scarce, local winter visitor (700 birds); has bred Scotland

from Greenland

from Scandinavia

Winters saltmarsh, adjacent rough fields, stubble; on migration, also rocky coastal grasslands; breeds moorland

15–16 cm | WS 24–27 cm

Rustic Bunting (*p. 505*), N American sparrows (*p. 518–519*)

Low-slung bunting, always on ground: see Snow Bunting (*p. 498*), Reed Bunting (*p. 502*). Autumn/winter birds (most likely) dull, obscure; breeding male (rare) striking.

MALE black cap, face, bib; white line on neck. NON-BREEDING MALE broad pale stripe over eye curving under cheek; **black line around cheek**, rusty-red hindneck; **mottled blackish bib**, breast-sides; **striped flanks**. FEMALE/1ST-WINTER subdued (see Reed Bunting): **pale central crown** with darker sides. Reddish-buff face, triangular **blackish 'corners' to cheeks**; nape dull or dusky rufous. Back has long blackish streaks, long creamy stripes; two thin **white wingbars outline reddish panel**.

VOICE Dry, hard, low rattling trill "*trrr-r-r-r-t* or *trr-r-r-t'k*" (lighter "*ticky-ticky-tik*" at distance); soft, or longer, loud "*teu*".

IN FLIGHT, long-winged, more like Snow Bunting than Reed Bunting; best told by call.

streaks on side of breast extend onto flank

crown with pale centre and dark sides

ADULT ♂ WINTER

whitish upper and lower wingbars enclose bright chestnut greater coverts

1ST-WINTER

ADULT ♀

ADULT ♂ SUMMER

Snow Bunting

Plectrophenax nivalis 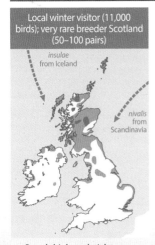 **539**

Local winter visitor (11,000 birds); very rare breeder Scotland (50–100 pairs)

insulae from Iceland

nivalis from Scandinavia

Breeds high peaks/plateaux; winter, coastal shingle/marsh, also peaks/moors inland

15·5–18 cm | WS 32–38 cm

Short-legged bunting, always perches on ground (or low roofs around ski lifts *etc.*). **Unstreaked below**, **white on wings in flight**. Often tame, inconspicuous.

MALE **black and white**. FEMALE back buff streaked black. In winter both sexes **tawny-brown** on crown, cheeks, breast; **yellow bill**; **black legs**. Tawny feather tips wear off by spring. 1ST-WINTER paler buff tertial tips than adults, more pointed tail feathers.

VOICE Characteristic rippling, rhythmic "*til-lil-il-it!*"; bright, whistled "*peu*", often combined.

Two races breed and winter: *nivalis* (Scandinavia eastwards to Greenland), *insulae* (Iceland; usually commoner in Britain). Winter *nivalis* back frosty greyish centre with browner sides, pale rump; *insulae* back uniformly darker and browner, darker rump and breast-band. Summer male *nivalis* has white rump; *insulae* shows dark feather tips on rump.

ADULT ♀ SUMMER race *nivalis*

ADULT ♀ SUMMER race *insulae*

ADULT ♂ SUMMER race *nivalis*

unmarked white rump

ADULT ♂ SUMMER race *insulae*

IN FLIGHT, MALE has **white wings**, black tips; FEMALE shorter white band on wing; 1ST-WINTER less white in wing than adults.

Determining the age and sex of winter birds can be difficult, due to subtle differences between races. White in outer primaries indicates male, but extent depends on age and race. Blunt dark centres to scapulars = male; pointed centres = female. On females, >60% white on base of the second innermost primary indicates race *nivalis*; <40% white is diagnostic for race *insulae*.

ADULT ♀ WINTER
race *insulae*

ADULT ♂ WINTER
race *insulae*

ADULT ♂ MOULTING
INTO SUMMER PLUMAGE
race *insulae*

1ST-WINTER ♀
race *nivalis*

ADULT ♂ MOULTING
INTO SUMMER PLUMAGE
race *nivalis*

Yellowhammer

Emberiza citrinella ● ● ❶ 540

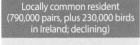

Locally common resident (790,000 pairs, plus 230,000 birds in Ireland; declining)

to/from Scandinavia

Heaths, downs, farmland, moorland edge; more widely in winter

16–17 cm | WS 23–29 cm

👁 Cirl, Pine (p. 509), other rare buntings (p. 504 –509)

Long, slim, sharp-billed 'yellow' bunting. Feeds on ground, perches freely, very upright. See Cirl Bunting, Corn Bunting (p. 503).

Rufous-orange rump, blackish tail with white sides. MALE **yellow head** and breast; blackish lines on head; orange-brown on breast, flanks. In winter, head more striped. FEMALE streaked black; thin pale wingbars. Pale **yellowish** below, dark flank streaks. **Yellowish crown with dark sides**, dark cheek with pale spot. Yellow tinge, **rusty rump**, **black-and-white tail** help identification. JUVENILE/1ST-WINTER duller, but hint of yellow beneath, same rump and tail: age/sex difficult to tell.

VOICE Call clicking "*tswik*", "*tik*"; rasping "*tzu*". Song high, metallic notes, one or two high/low at end – "*sip-ip-ip-ip-ip-ip-seee-u*" or ending "*-seeee*". Also faster, trilling version.

ADULT ♂ WINTER race *citrinella*

ADULT ♂ SUMMER race *citrinella*

1ST-WINTER

Race *caliginosa* in N/W darker, more greenish on head, rufous on breast/flanks than race *citrinella* of S/E, but races intergrade.

ADULT ♀ race *citrinella*

ginger/ chestnut rump

1ST-WINTER ♂ race *citrinella*

1ST-WINTER ♀ race *citrinella*

Cirl Bunting

Emberiza cirlus ●

16–16·5 cm | WS 22–25 cm

👁 Pine Bunting (*p. 509*), other rare buntings (*p. 504 –509*)

Slim, reddish/yellowish bunting. Resembles Yellowhammer but **dull olive rump**. Black-and-white tail rules out sparrows, finches.

MALE green breast-band, **black-and-yellow face**, black throat (obscured in winter). FEMALE/JUVENILE like female Yellowhammer, but **rump dull olive-grey**; chestnut more confined to shoulders; underside has finer streaks, more around upper breast; plainer dark crown, dark line behind eye and dark edge to cheek with prominent whitish spot; pale eyering.

VOICE Call distinct but elusive: high, thin, quiet "*si*" or "*zit*". Song locates male (see Yellowhammer, Lesser Whitethroat (*p. 421*)) – short trill on one note; fast, thin and metallic "*ts-r-r-r-r-r-r-r-r*" or slightly slower, more distinct "*tsi-tsi-tsi-tsi-tsi-tsi-tsi-tsi*", without Yellowhammer's usual flourish. Less wooden, hollow or rattling than Lesser Whitethroat.

Rare local resident (860 pairs); rare migrant/vagrant elsewhere. Extreme vagrant Ireland (1 record)

Farmland, old meadows, tall hedgerows

ADULT ♂ SUMMER

ADULT ♂ WINTER

1ST-WINTER ♀

olive-grey rump

ADULT ♀

Reed Bunting

Emberiza schoeniclus ● **540**

14–16 cm | WS 21–28 cm

Slim, streaky, thick-billed bunting; **long blackish tail with broad white sides**, revealed in out-in flicks.

👁 Lapland Bunting (*p. 497*), rare buntings (*p. 504 –509*), N American sparrows (*p. 518 –519*)

MALE **black head**, **white neck and moustache**; upperparts black. In winter, buff/brown tips obscure pattern but wear away by spring to reveal black (variable intermediate stages). FEMALE like winter male; back often has two cream stripes; rump browner. Crown all dark, **pale band over eye**; cheek dark with **blacker surround** ('mask' effect); black stripe from bill beside white throat. 1ST-WINTER drab; buff band over eye, paler cheek; long dark stripes on face reach bill; grey-brown rump; dark legs. White in tail rules out Corn Bunting (*p. 503*), sparrows, most finches.

VOICE Call simple "*tseup*", high, thin "*tseee*". Song, monotonously repeated from low perch, disjointed, short, simple, slow phrase "*sup-jip-chilee-up*".

Locally common resident (185,000 pairs plus 220,000 birds in Ireland), migrant

from Scandinavia

from N Europe

Watersides, wet heaths, moors; gardens in winter

ADULT ♀ SPRING

ADULT ♂ SUMMER

changes from winter to summer through wear of dull feather tips; summer plumages wear gradually darker

female rumps generally browner than male's

1ST-WINTER ♀

1ST-WINTER difficult to separate from adult female except by more worn wing and shape and wear of tail feathers.

autumn adult rump dull olive; by spring, male's wears to brighter, pale grey

ADULT WINTER ♂

1ST-WINTER ♀

1ST-WINTER ♂

Corn Bunting

Emberiza calandra ● 540

16–19 cm | WS 26–32 cm

Large, brown, streaked, **plain-tailed** bunting; no bold colours. Keeps low, **hops** (unlike larks); often on fence, mound of earth in big field, isolated bush on grassy downland, or sings from overhead wire (long, lumpy, tail tilted down, head tipped back).

Pale buff-brown, streaked dark. Streaks merge into central patch on whitish breast. **Big pinkish-buff bill, plain brown tail, plain wings** rule out Skylark (*p. 349*). Age, sex, seasonal differences insignificant, but some more striped on head than others; breeding birds of W Scotland most heavily streaked and darker above, yellower below. IN FLIGHT, if disturbed, groups fly up hurriedly to hedge or wires (Skylarks fly off higher up).

VOICE Call loud, full "*quik*" or "*plip*". Song highly characteristic: short, monotonous, crunching glass/shaking keys quality – **short** notes followed by rising, straining trill "*tuc-tuc-tuc-tss-rr-rreeeee*", given in upright, open-billed pose.

Scarce and local resident (10,000 pairs, declining). Now only vagrant in Ireland

Farmland, grassy downs

ADULT ♂

Singing male distinctive even at long range: head back, bill open; on exposed perch in open landscape.

ADULT

streaks on breast often merge to form dark patch

forehead slopes to thick, pale bill

no bright colours or strong pattern

closely streaked all over

plain tail

ADULT

ADULT

503

Little Bunting
Emberiza pusilla

◉ N American sparrows (p.518–519)

12–13·5 cm | WS 18–20 cm

Small, neat bunting, subtle but distinctive (see Rustic Bunting). Resembles female Reed Bunting (*p. 502*) except: small, sharp, **straight-edged bill**; distinct **white eyering** in plain face; **rusty cheeks** with whitish spot at rear; **pale/rufous between eye and bill**; dark eyestripe, blackish edge of cheek **does not reach bill**; dull lesser coverts; two thin, whitish wingbars; pale **pink legs**. MALE rufous central stripe on black crown, rufous face. FEMALE duller, face less red. 1ST-WINTER may have rufous nape, usually rufous cheeks, central crown and nape between darker sides – typical bill, eyering, plain face all useful.

VOICE Call important: sharp, clicking "*zik*" or "*tik*".

Rare autumn migrant/winter visitor from NE Europe: 30–50 per year (vagrant Ireland <50 records), most Sep–Mar; mostly in N. Coastal grassland, bushes.

REED BUNTING – common species most likely to cause confusion in the autumn plumages shown here. Note bill shape and long dark streaks on cheek and throat reaching bill.

ADULT ♂ WINTER like Rustic Bunting

1ST-WINTER ♂ like Black-faced Bunting

ADULT ♀ like Little, Pallas's Reed and Black-faced Buntings

sharp, straight-edged bill

WINTER

pale eyering

dark surround on rear cheek

1ST-WINTER

Chestnut-eared Bunting *Emberiza fucata*

15–16 cm | WS 20–22 cm

Much like Little Bunting: similar chestnut cheeks with **pale buff spot**, **bright pale eyering** – but **lacks dark eyestripe and dark cheek edge**. Yellowish breast; dark streaking on chest, hint of chestnut band below; chestnut lower back and rump (dull on Little Bunting); longer tail.

VOICE Call explosive "*tzic*" similar to Rustic Bunting.

◉ N American sparrows (p.518–519)

Vagrant from Asia: <5 records (Britain), Oct. On coast. Scrub.

pattern like Little Bunting but weaker pale stripe over eye, stronger eyering and less black on cheek edge; also resembles larger Ortolan Bunting (*p. 508*)

1ST-WINTER

Rustic Bunting
Emberiza rustica
13–14·5 cm | WS 20–24 cm

N American sparrows (p.518–519)

Very rare migrant/vagrant from NE Europe: 6–8 per year, declining (<20 records Ireland), May–Jun, most Sep–Oct. On coast, mostly in N. Marshy scrub, thickets, woods.

Neat, peak-crowned bunting. Migrants inconspicuous. See Little Bunting. Bold face pattern, **rufous flank stripes**. Unstreaked **red-brown rump** (redder than Yellowhammer (*p. 500*), brighter than Reed Bunting (*p. 502*)). Thin white wingbars. Bill pink with dark tip (grey on Reed Bunting). MALE **black head, white stripe over eye**, white nape, cheek spot, throat. FEMALE head pattern slightly obscured; streaked red-brown below. 1ST-WINTER **pale crown with blacker streaks on sides**; long, **broad buff stripe behind eye**; black eyestripe, edge of cheek; white cheek spot. Rufous streaks across breast; broader **red-brown streaks** on flanks.

VOICE Call sharp "*zit*".

ADULT ♀

pale stripes above and below dark cheek

1ST-WINTER

ADULT ♂ SUMMER

brick-red rump

white underside

Pallas's Reed Bunting *Emberiza pallasi*
13–13·5 cm | WS 20–25 cm

1ST-WINTER ♂

Vagrant from Asia: <10 records (Britain), Oct, Mar. Widespread. Scrub.

Like **small** Reed Bunting (*p. 502*); straight-edged bill, long tail. Black streaks on grey-buff upperparts, paler rump, dull grey patch on lesser coverts. Weak head pattern: pale brown cap without dark sides or dark eyestripe; **pale cheek above black spot**. 1ST-WINTER almost **unmarked** below but some migrate in JUVENILE plumage, streaked blackish on breast, browner lesser coverts and rump, **two whitish wingbars**; pink-based bill.

VOICE Call sparrow-like "*chee-ulp*".

Only likely in autumn at migration watchpoint: look for 'small dull Reed Bunting' with pale rump.

1ST-WINTER ♀

grey

paler rump

REED BUNTING
1ST-WINTER ♀

bright rufous lesser coverts

brown rump

streaked

505

Black-headed Bunting *Emberiza melanocephala*

14–15·5 cm | WS 20–23 cm

MALE red-brown above, **yellow below**, **black hood**. FEMALE dull, hood greyish, throat and underside pale yellow, **rump rusty** (greenish/yellowish on Red-headed Bunting (p. 522)). 1ST-WINTER duller, greyish-buff below, **yellow under tail**; brown tail lacks white. May be impossible to separate from escaped/possible vagrant Red-headed Bunting unless rusty rump and finely streaked crown of Black-headed Bunting can be seen.

VOICE Call fine high "*psip*".

👁 Red-headed Bunting (p. 522)

Vagrant from Asia: <250 records (<15 records Ireland), spring/summer, most May–Jun. Scattered. Grassland, bushes.

ADULT ♂ SUMMER

ADULT ♀

1ST-WINTER

rusty coloured rump

Yellow-breasted Bunting *Emberiza aureola*

EN
CR

15 cm | WS 20–22 cm

MALE (very rare) chestnut, yellow below; white shoulder, black face. 1ST-WINTER **yellowish**, closely streaked; two pale bands down back; **pale central stripe on dark crown**; yellowish cheek spot, yellow-buff band beneath black-edged greyish cheek; **two white wingbars**. Rump grey-brown, streaked; white tail sides.

VOICE Call high, sharp, metallic "*tsip*".

Very rare migrant from NE Europe: <250 records (<10 Ireland), fast declining, Sep–Oct. On coast, most N Isles. Scrub, stubbles.

ADULT ♂ SUMMER

1ST-WINTER

Yellow-browed Bunting

Emberiza chrysophrys

13–14 cm | WS 20–25 cm

Small bunting, recalls Little and Rustic Buntings; small, sharp bill. 1ST-WINTER black crown, **white stripe on nape**; broad band over eye rufous in front, **yellow, fading out to white** behind; chestnut cheek with white spot. Narrow black streaks on pale underside.

VOICE Call thin, high "*sip*".

◉ N American sparrows (*p. 518–519*)

Vagrant from Asia: <10 records (Britain), Oct. On coast. Scrub.

1ST-WINTER

Black-faced Bunting

Emberiza spodocephala

14–15·5 cm | WS 20–23 cm

Slim bunting; white tail sides. 1ST-WINTER MALE grey on head (black on face from December); resembles Dunnock (*p. 368*). ADULT/1ST-WINTER FEMALE like dull olive-grey Reed Bunting (*p. 502*) with greyer neck, greyish rump; dark stripe beside throat beneath pale moustache; dull greyish or yellowish underside.

VOICE Call quiet, thin, metallic "*tip*".

Vagrant from Asia: <10 records (Britain), Mar–Apr, Sep–Oct. On coast. Scrub.

ADULT/1ST-WINTER ♀

Adult ♂ blacker on face

1ST-WINTER ♂

Chestnut Bunting

Emberiza rutila

14–15 cm | WS 20–21 cm

Small bunting; domed head, small bill. 1ST-WINTER streaked black and grey above, wings rustier with two whitish bars. Whitish stripe over eye; whitish face, throat and band under grey-centred cheek; **yellow** beneath with fine flank streaks; **rump chestnut, tail lacks prominent white sides**.

VOICE Call sharp "*zik*".

Vagrant from Asia: 1 record (Britain (under review)), Oct. On coast. Status confused by occasional escapes. Scrub.

1ST-WINTER ♂

Ortolan Bunting *Emberiza hortulana*

15–16·5 cm | WS 21–27 cm

Slender, delicate, pale bunting; soft, pastel shades, distinctive expression; black-and-white 'bunting tail'. Yellowhammer (*p. 500*) shape, slim bill, notched tail. White or **yellowish eyering in plain face**; yellow chin and throat; rather sharp, pointed **pinkish bill** and pink legs. Feeds on the ground.

MALE **pale green head; yellow throat and line under cheek**; pale orange underside, browner upperparts (no great contrast). FEMALE similar but duller, finely streaked on crown and breast. 1ST-WINTER like female, with **yellowish eyering**, more streaks below, hint of grey-green on the head and pale orange beneath.

VOICE Metallic "*chip*" or "*sli*" alternating with fuller "*plit*".

👁 Cretzschmar's Bunting · 540

Very rare migrant from Europe, winters Africa: 20–30 per year, declining (<150 records Ireland), most Apr–Oct. On coast. Grasslands, bushes.

1ST-WINTER

ADULT ♂ SUMMER
unique green/yellow/orange combination; look for eyering, pink bill

pink bill 'droops' from greenish head; yellow chin

ADULT ♀

'cold' brown rump

Cretzschmar's Bunting *Emberiza caesia*

14–15·5 cm | WS 23–26 cm

Closely resembles Ortolan Bunting. MALE head **blue-grey** (not greenish); throat **rusty** (not yellow). 1ST-SUMMER more buffish-chestnut, less olive, than Ortolan Bunting; chin orange.

VOICE Call metallic "*tchip*" or "*schip*".

1ST-WINTER

'warm' brown rump

540

Vagrant from SE Europe: <10 records (males) (Britain), Apr–Jun. On coast. Grassland, rocky areas.

rusty throat

blue-grey head

ADULT ♂

Pine Bunting *Emberiza leucocephalos*

16–17·5 cm | WS 25–30 cm

Shape, size of Yellowhammer (*p. 500*).
MALE **white crown, cheek, breast-band;**
black-edged chestnut over eye, chestnut throat;
rufous streaks beneath (see Rustic Bunting
(*p. 505*)). 1ST-WINTER like pale Yellowhammer,
lacking yellow; wingtip feathers edged white.
Beware infrequent pale Yellowhammer and
hybrids/intergrades, which have pale yellow
feather edges on wings.

VOICE Sharp "*tswik*" notes, like Yellowhammer.

pale Yellowhammers have some yellow, most reliably on the wing feathers

YELLOWHAMMER 1ST-WINTER ♀

PINE BUNTING 1ST-WINTER ♀

ADULT ♂ WINTER

1ST-WINTER ♂

Vagrant from NE Europe/Asia:
<75 records (<5 Ireland), most
months, most Oct. Widespread.
Farmland, scrub.

compared with Yellowhammer, whiter beneath with rufous streaks, pale orange flanks; wing feathers narrowly edged white, never yellow

Rock Bunting *Emberiza cia*

16 cm | WS 20–27 cm

Slim, ground-loving bunting; rusty-brown with
black streaks above, **plain orange-brown below**.
MALE head/breast grey, **black bands** beside crown,
through eye and under cheek. FEMALE duller;
JUVENILE drabber still, crown streaked brown,
head stripes less distinct.

VOICE Call thin, high, short "*si*".

Vagrant from S Europe: <10 records (Britain),
Feb–Jun, Oct. Widespread. Grassland, rocky areas.

ADULT ♂

VAGRANT LANDBIRDS FROM NORTH AMERICA

Rare birds from North America are exciting to see in Britain and Ireland. Some species are regular visitors from the Canadian Arctic, but from Canada and the USA a remarkable total of 133 North American (Nearctic) species (excluding pelagic seabirds) have occurred as vagrants in Britain and/or Ireland.

More than 80% of all individual American landbirds have been recorded in autumn, centred on mid-October. In south-west England more than 95% are in autumn; in the Northern Isles autumn arrivals predominate, but more than 35% have been in spring. In autumn, eastbound transatlantic weather systems bring small birds across quickly: in spring, when seed-eaters are more frequent, such conditions are rare. Consequently, birds that arrive in the autumn (including the insectivorous warblers, vireos, thrushes, cuckoos and flycatchers) are very likely to have made the Atlantic crossing without stopping, although spring arrivals, particularly the granivorous American sparrows (especially those records close to British and Irish ports), may have made all or part of the crossing on board vessels. Birds that are thought to have arrived in this way are often termed 'ship-assisted' vagrants.

In the past, south-west England – including renowned areas such as the Isles of Scilly – was favoured by American landbirds, although they have been widely spread across islands and headlands from south-west Ireland and Dyfed to North Wales. More recently, the Western Isles, Orkney and Shetland have earned a special place for such birds. In the north, autumn arrivals tend to be earlier than in the south, and there is a greater proportion of seed-eating birds – finches, buntings, sparrows – in the overall mix. Yet American landbirds turn up at widely scattered sites across Britain and Ireland, even on bird feeders in gardens.

The following table summarises the Nearctic bird species that have been recorded (the figures do not include European species with a Nearctic race that has been recorded (e.g. Brent Goose (Black Brant), Bewick's Swan (Tundra Swan) and Iceland Gull (Thayer's Gull)). Green shading indicates those 51 species covered in the following section; buff shading indicates species covered elsewhere in the book.

'Type' of bird	Species	Pages
Wildfowl	14	44–45, 52–54, 68–69
Divers	1	79
Cormorants	1	85
Frigatebirds	1	99
Herons and egrets	5	250–251
Grebes	1	85
Large birds of prey	2	310, 312
Rails	3	262
Cranes	1	250
Waders	23*	186, 191, 223–235
Auks	3	172
Terns	4	152–154
Gulls	6	112–113, 116, 136, 138–140
Doves	1	280
Cuckoos	2	519
Nightjars	1	291
Swifts	1	341
Kingfishers	1	519
Woodpeckers	1	519
Falcons	1	324
American flycatchers	4	518
Vireos	3	511
Kinglets	1	511
Swallows and martins	3	346
Waxwings	1	375
Nuthatches	1	454
Mimids (mockingbird, thrasher, catbird)	3	519
Thrushes	7	386–387
Pipits	1	357
Finches (Evening Grosbeak)	1	516
Tanagers	2	517
Grosbeaks and buntings	2	516
Nearctic sparrows (incl. Eastern Towhee, Dark-eyed Junco)	8	516–519
Icterids (American orioles, Brown-headed cowbird, Bobolink)	3	517
American warblers	20	512–515

* including Eskimo Curlew (now probably extinct)

Vireos

Like sluggish, heavy-moving warblers; round head, thick, wide bills, stout legs.
They inhabit forest and undergrowth in North America. Look for precise head patterns, overall colour and presence or absence of wingbars. They have occurred widely in Britain and Ireland, mostly near coasts.

Red-eyed Vireo *Vireo olivaceus*

13–14 cm | WS 22–24 cm

AUTUMN ADULT red eye, worn primaries.
1ST-WINTER/WINTER dark brown eye until late winter, unworn primary tips.

grey cap with blackish sides

bold white stripe over eye

1ST-WINTER

plain wings

Most regular North American landbird (3–4 per year). <200 records (>50 Ireland), Sep–Nov. Scattered (most on coast).

Yellow-throated Vireo

Vireo flavifrons

14 cm | WS 20–24 cm

1 record (Britain), Sep. On coast.

1ST-WINTER

pale yellow 'spectacles'

two white wingbars

yellow throat

white underside

Philadelphia Vireo

Vireo philadelphicus

13 cm | WS 20–23 cm

<5 records (1 Britain), Oct. On coast.

1ST-WINTER

plain grey crown

diffuse pale stripe over eye

plain wings

dark from bill through eye

dull underside, yellowest towards rear (duller chest sides)

Crests

Kinglets or crests are like tiny warblers (see Goldcrest (*p. 436*)): one species has occurred, not frequently enough to establish any pattern; future occurrences are most likely in late autumn.

Ruby-crowned Kinglet *Regulus calendula* ◆

9–11 cm | WS 16–18 cm

Tiny, like greyish juvenile Goldcrest (*p. 436*). ADULT has small red nape, usually hidden.

1 record (Ireland), Oct. On coast.

white eyering

black-and-white wingbars

1ST-WINTER

dull greyish face, no moustache or eyestripe

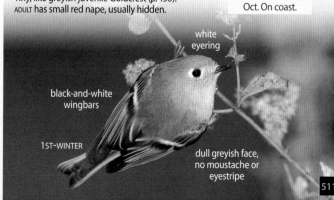

North American Warblers

Not related to Old World warblers, but similar looking small, slender, slim-billed birds that prefer trees and dense foliage. They arrive, particularly after strong winds from the west, most often on western headlands and islands. Summer adults (very rare) are brightly coloured but autumn juveniles are much duller and more difficult to identify.

LOOK FOR head patterns | wing and tail markings | upperpart/underpart streaking

Blackpoll Warbler
Setophaga striata
13–15 cm | WS 20–25 cm

👁 Bay-breasted Warbler

<60 records (<15 Ireland), Jun, Sep–Dec (most Oct). On coast.

ADULT ♂

white edge to outer tail feathers

white undertail

Full black cap, white cheeks; wingbars

1ST-WINTER

olive head/back

faint dark streaks on back

long wings

breast yellowest at front

faint streaks

two long, curved white wingbars

orange legs

Yellow-rumped Warbler
Setophaga coronata
12–15 cm | WS 19–24 cm

<40 records (<20 Ireland), Jan, May, Jun, Oct, Nov. Mostly on coast.

ADULT ♂

two long white wingbars

pale yellow rump

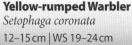

white crescents above and below eye

yellow rump, chest sides and crown; eye crescents, wingbars

1ST-WINTER

dark streaks on flanks

black legs

Cape May Warbler
Setophaga tigrina
12–14 cm | WS 19–22 cm

<5 records (Britain), Jun, Oct–Nov. Scattered.

plain greyish head/back or yellowish neck patch

greenish wings, diffuse pale wingbars

olive rump

white crescents above and below eye

ADULT ♂

1ST-WINTER

yellow collar, chestnut cheeks, black cap, wingbar

darkish legs, yellow soles to feet

faint streaks on flanks or underside streaked grey, centre line white

Nearctic warblers – preferred habitats

Trees	Blackpoll, Yellow-rumped, Cape May, Bay-breasted, Blackburnian, Magnolia, Canada, Tennessee, Golden-winged, Black-and-white Warblers, American Redstart, Parula	Bushes	Wilson's, Blue-winged, Yellow, Yellow-rumped Warblers
		Wet vegetation	Hooded Warbler, Yellowthroat
		Ground	Waterthrush, Ovenbird

Bay-breasted Warbler
Setophaga castanea
13–15 cm | WS 20–23 cm

1 record (Britain), Oct. On coast.

two long, curved white wingbars

faint dark streaks on back

buff undertail

strong bill

1ST-WINTER

unstreaked

Blackburnian Warbler
Setophaga fusca
11–13 cm | WS 20–22 cm

<5 records (Britain), Sep, Oct. On coast.

pale yellow band over eye

dark, triangular cheek patch

two wide, white wingbars

1ST-WINTER

long dark streaks on flanks

orange-yellow throat

Chestnut-sided Warbler
Setophaga pensylvanica
10–14 cm | WS 16–21 cm

<5 records (Britain), Sep, Oct. On coast.

lime-green crown/back

unstreaked grey-white underparts; at least hint of **chestnut on flanks**

grey cheeks

1ST-WINTER ♀

'pot-bellied'

Magnolia Warbler
Setophaga magnolia
11–13 cm | WS 16–20 cm

<5 records (Britain), Sep. On coast.

Clear view of the tail most important.

scarcely streaked back

white eyering

two narrow white wingbars

white band across tail

1ST-WINTER

yellow underparts; few soft streaks

American Redstart
Setophaga ruticilla
13 cm | WS 16–23 cm

<10 records (<5 Ireland), Oct–Nov. Scattered.

yellow sides to tail

flanks yellow (♀) or **orange** (♂)

pale yellow **band** on wing (may be absent)

1ST-WINTER ♀

Northern Parula
Setophaga americana
11–12 cm | WS 16–18 cm

1ST-WINTER ♂

brighter

green-yellow patch on back

1ST-WINTER ♀

white crescents above and below eye

pale yellow throat, chest

blue-grey wings; two wingbars, lower long and wide

<20 records (<5 Ireland), Sep–Nov. On coast.

Preferred habitats *p.513*

Hooded Warbler
Setophaga citrina
13 cm | WS 18–20 cm

<5 records (Britain), Sep. On coast.

wide yellow patch above large dark eye

long white spots under tail visible from below or when tail fanned

very pale legs/feet

1ST-WINTER ♀

Wilson's Warbler
Cardellina pusilla
10–12 cm | WS 16–20 cm

<5 records (1 Ireland), Sep, Oct. On coast.

black eye in yellow face

dark cap

1ST-WINTER ♀

relatively long tail; no white markings

pale legs/feet, yellow soles

1ST-WINTER ♂

Yellow Warbler
Setophaga petechia
12–13 cm | WS 16–20 cm

<10 records (<5 Ireland), Aug–Nov. On coast.

pale-fringed tertials

plain face

yellow edges to tail; no white markings

yellow underparts – may have chestnut streaks

1ST-WINTER ♀

Common Yellowthroat
Geothlypis trichas
14 cm | WS 20–22 cm

<15 records (1 Ireland), Jan–Feb, May–Jun, Sep–Dec. On coast.

black cheeks yellow throat

1ST-WINTER ♂

yellow throat

1ST-WINTER ♀

pale brownish underparts

1ST-WINTER ♀

Black-and-white Warbler *Mniotilta varia*
11–13 cm | WS 20–22 cm

<20 records (<5 Ireland), Mar, Sep–Dec. Scattered.

Unmistakable tiny, black-and-white-striped warbler; behaves like Nuthatch/Treecreeper. Pale crown stripe rules out adult Blackpoll Warbler (*p.512*). FEMALE/1ST-WINTER have paler ear coverts than MALE. Looks blue-grey in flight or quick glimpse.

black crown with white central stripe

black and white stripes all over

1ST-WINTER ♂

Canada Warbler *Cardellina canadensis* ◆
13 cm | WS 19–21 cm

1ST-WINTER ♀

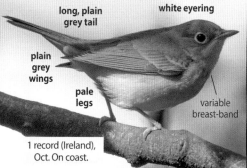

long, plain grey tail

white eyering

plain grey wings

pale legs

variable breast-band

1 record (Ireland), Oct. On coast.

Tennessee Warbler *Oreothlypis peregrina*
11·5 cm | WS 18–20 cm

Small, greenish warbler, like Arctic Warbler (*p. 434*) but **yellower**.

faint wingbar

weak stripe over eye

white undertail

fine, grey-based bill

<5 records (Britain), Sep. On coast.

1ST-WINTER

NT Golden-winged Warbler
Vermivora chrysoptera
11·5 cm | WS 18–20 cm

1 record (Britain), Jan. Inland.

Blue-winged Warbler ◆
Vermivora cyanoptera
11·5 cm | WS 18–20 cm

1 record (Ireland), Oct. On coast.

broad black mask and throat

yellow on wing

bluish-grey wings, two pale wingbars

dark stripe from bill to eye

1ST-WINTER ♂   1ST-WINTER ♂

Northern Waterthrush
Parkesia noveboracensis
12–15 cm | WS 21–24 cm

<10 records (<5 Ireland), Aug–Oct. On coast.

Small, pipit-like; **walks on ground**, **bobbing tail** like wagtail. VOICE loud, sharp "*chinK*".

very long pale stripe over eye tapers to nape

1ST-WINTER

dark streaks on buff/white underparts

Ovenbird
Seiurus aurocapilla
11–14 cm | WS 19–26 cm

<10 records (<5 Ireland), Sep, Oct, Dec. Most on coast.

Small, rounded warbler, **walks on ground** with deliberate steps; bobs tail, tosses leaves aside.

rusty crown stripe, edged black   **white eyering**

1ST-WINTER

long black stripes on white breast

Tanagers, Finches, Buntings and 'New World Blackbirds' (icterids)

A mixed group, some species resembling Old World finches and buntings. **Tanagers** are slender, finch-like, thick-billed, fruit-eating species of forest canopy; '**New World Blackbirds**' (icterids) include sharp-billed orioles, cowbirds and Bobolink. They find what cover they can where they arrive on coasts and islands, most favouring trees and bushes.

Rose-breasted Grosbeak
Pheucticus ludovicianus
18–22 cm | WS 29–33 cm

thickset; finch-like

striped crown

<40 records (<10 Ireland), May, Sep–Dec. On coast. Trees/bushes.

two bars of white spots on wing

1ST-WINTER ♂

ADULT ♂

Unique; striking black-and-white plumage

Indigo Bunting
Passerina cyanea
11–15 cm | WS 18–23 cm

<5 records (1 Ireland), May, Oct. On coast. Trees.

Note: ADULT MALE blue; ADULT FEMALE **scattered hints of blue**.

black eye in plain head

sharp, conical bill

two weak wingbars

faintly mottled; nondescript

1ST-WINTER

Evening Grosbeak
Hesperiphona vespertina
20 cm | WS 30–33 cm

<5 records (Britain), Mar. On coast. Trees.

broad yellow stripe over eye

1ST-WINTER ♂

large, heavy finch

black-and-white wings

big pale bill

Dark-eyed Junco
Junco hyemalis
13–17 cm | WS 18–25 cm

<50 records (<5 Ireland), Nov–Feb, Apr–Aug. Scattered. Trees; feeds on ground.

MALE slate grey. FEMALE/1ST-WINTER slightly browner.

small; finch-like

ADULT ♂

white tail sides

very pale bill

white belly

Eastern Towhee
Pipilo erythrophthalmus
17–23 cm | WS 20–28 cm

1 record (Britain), Jun. On coast. Scrub/woodland; feeds on ground.

stout; long white-sided tail

warm dark brown head, breast, back

white in wing

ADULT ♀

orange flanks

Scarlet Tanager *Piranga olivacea*
16–19 cm | WS 25–30 cm

1ST-WINTER ♂

1ST-WINTER
olive-green above

wings dark (FEMALE)
black (MALE)

underwing
white

pale
yellow
below

<15 records (<5
Ireland), Sep–Oct.
On coast. Trees.

Summer Tanager *Piranga rubra*
17 cm | WS 25–27 cm

1ST-WINTER

1ST-WINTER brownish or
orange-brown above

**wings plain
olive**

underwing
yellow

**dull
orange-yellow
below**

1 record (Britain),
Sep. On coast.
Trees.

Bobolink
Dolichonyx oryzivorus
16–18 cm | WS 19–26 cm

dark crown with
buff central line

bunting-like

**two cream
stripes down
back**

1ST-WINTER

pointed tail
feathers

<40 records
(<5 Ireland),
Sep–Nov. On coast.
Grassland, bushes.

Baltimore Oriole
Icterus galbula
17–22 cm | WS 23–30 cm

Note: ADULT MALE black head.

<30 records
(<5 Ireland),
May, Sep–Jan.
Scattered.
Trees, gardens.

long, sharp,
triangular bill

**dark wings;
two white
bars**

**orange
chest**

pale
orange
rump

1ST-WINTER ♂

Brown-headed Cowbird
Molothrus ater
16–22 cm | WS 34–36 cm

sleek, stocky mainly
terrestrial

MALE glossy black;
dull brown head

thick, triangular
bill

FEMALE/1ST-WINTER dark grey-
brown, **paler head** (see late
summer juvenile Starling (p. 372))

slim tail
often raised

ADULT ♀

ADULT ♂

<10 records
(Britain), Apr, May,
Jul. On coast.
Grassland, bushes.

517

American Sparrows

A varied group, some strikingly patterned, others presenting real identification problems as there are several similar species and races in North America. Ground birds, they are likely to be found in varied open habitats: some records are close to dockyards, indicating likely 'ship-assisted' Atlantic passage.

Summary of favoured habitats and key features of American sparrows					
Lark Sparrow	Savannah Sparrow	Fox Sparrow	Song Sparrow	White-throated Sparrow	White-crowned Sparrow
Grassland			Scrub		
Unstreaked underparts; unique head pattern	Small, pale, streaked; short-tailed, rather 'neckless'; pale line over eye (usually yellowish in front)	Bunting-like; striking rufous-streaked plumage; grey band over eye	Variable; grey over eye, grey cheek; heavily streaked; long, rounded tail	Yellow-and-white band over eye; white chin	Black-and-white striped crown; grey beneath

Lark Sparrow
Chondestes grammacus
15–17 cm | WS 28 cm

<5 records (Britain), May, Jun. On coast.

**bold stripy head pattern;
crescent under eye;** dark spot on chest

ADULT

Fox Sparrow ◆
Passerella iliaca
15–19 cm | WS 26–28 cm

1 record (Ireland), Jun. On coast.

broad grey band over eye

rufous cheek

grey and rufous
streaks on upperside

small bill

ADULT

white underparts,
**heavily streaked
rusty-brown**

Savannah Sparrow
Passerculus sandwichensis
11–17 cm | WS 18–25 cm

<5 records (Britain), Apr, Sep, Oct. On coast.

Two races recorded: *oblitus* and larger, paler *princeps* which has narrower, browner streaks.

chunky, neckless shape

pale central crown stripe

pale band over eye may be yellow at front

short, slim tail

ADULT

heavy dark streaks on pale breast

Song Sparrow
Melospiza melodia
11–18 cm | WS 18–25 cm

<10 records (Britain), Apr, May, Oct. On coast.

dark, rusty streaks on upperside

grey cheek

broad grey band over eye

long, rounded tail

ADULT

white underparts with rusty-black streaks

White-throated Sparrow
Zonotrichia albicollis
18 cm | WS 24–25 cm

ADULT

white band over eye, bright yellow at front

white throat (edged black)

two white wingbars

<50 records (<5 Ireland), Sep–Jul. Scattered, mostly near coast.

White-crowned Sparrow
Zonotrichia leucophrys
18 cm | WS 24–25 cm

ADULT

1ST-WINTER crown stripes grey and rufous

narrow white crown stripe in black cap; white band over eye

underparts grey-brown, unstreaked

<10 records (1 Ireland), Jan, May, Oct. On coast.

underparts grey, unstreaked

Mockingbirds and Thrashers (mimids)

A very varied group of long-tailed, thrush-like birds: those that have occurred being relatively distinctive (although there are other species in North America that are closely similar).

Northern Mockingbird
Mimus polyglottos
21–28 cm | WS 31–38 cm

<5 records (Britain), May, Aug. Coasts.

long-tailed; pale grey above, whitish below; **two white wingbars** and **white patch on spread wing; white-sided tail**

NORTHERN MOCKINGBIRD   ADULT

Brown Thrasher
Toxostoma rufum
23–30 cm | WS 29–33 cm

1 record (Britain), Nov. Coastal thicket.

Grey Catbird
Dumetella carolinensis
20–24 cm | WS 22–30 cm

<5 records (1 Ireland), Oct, Nov. Coastal thicket.

large; **long tail; rufous above**, two white wingbars; buffy-white below with **blackish streaks**

BROWN THRASHER

1ST-WINTER

smoky-grey, with **long, often raised tail** (when shows **dark rufous undertail); black cap**

GREY CATBIRD

1ST-WINTER

Tyrant Flycatchers
These birds, with no close equivalent in Britain and Ireland, include various upright, large-headed, big-billed flycatching birds of woods and bushes. The smaller flycatchers in autumn sometimes pose almost insuperable identification problems, as they are extremely similar and best separated in North America by their songs and calls in spring.

Eastern Kingbird *Tyrannus tyrannus* ◆
19–23 cm | WS 33–38 cm

Upright, big-headed, long-tailed, 'tapered' grey-and-white bird.

<5 records (Ireland), Sep–Oct. On coast. Bushes, trees.

strong, wide bill

dark head

greyish upperparts

1ST-WINTER

white underparts

long, black tail with white tip

Eastern Phoebe *Sayornis phoebe*
14–17 cm | WS 26–28 cm

Upright, **big-headed** flycatcher; **pumps tail up and down.**

1 record (Britain), Apr. On coast. Exposed perches.

dark 'hood'

all-dark bill

no eyering

grey-brown upperparts

two indistinct buff wingbars

white throat

grey breast, underparts buffish

ADULT

Alder Flycatcher *Empidonax alnorum*
13–14 cm | WS 18–22 cm

Small, olive-and-yellowish flycatcher. Alder/Willow *E. traillii* Flycatchers (latter not recorded) very difficult, even when trapped and measured.
VOICE Call "*pip*" (Willow Flycatcher "*whit*").

<5 records (Britain), Sep–Oct. On coast. Bushes.

round, dusky head

greyish back

pale tertial fringes

white throat

two white wingbars

1ST-WINTER

short closed wing point

Acadian Flycatcher *Empidonax virescens*
12–13 cm | WS 17–20 cm

Large-headed, stout-billed flycatcher; white wingbars, **long wing point** crucial.

1 record (Britain), Sep. On coast. Bushes.

olive-green head and upperparts

thin eyering

bill long, pink at base

grey wings with two white bars

underparts yellowish

pale tertial fringes

grey legs

long closed wing point

1ST-WINTER

North American cuckoos, kingfishers and woodpeckers

<10 records (<5 Ireland),
Oct–Feb. Scattered. Rivers.

ADULT ♂

Belted Kingfisher

Megaceryle alcyon

31–34 cm | WS 48–58 cm

Big, crested, grey-and-white
kingfisher with dark chest-
bands. **VOICE** Piercing,
squeaky, chattering rattle.

ADULT ♂

grey
chest-band

ADULT ♀

grey/rufous band;
lower rufous band
onto flanks

1 record Britain, 1 Ireland, Sep–Oct. On coast.
Woodland.

Yellow-bellied Sapsucker

Sphyrapicus varius

18–21 cm | WS 35–40 cm

Small woodpecker: black-and-white;
long white band on wing.
adult red forehead and black-and-
white striped head, throat red (♂),
white (♀); black chest;
back black mottled with
white. juvenile as adult but
drabber, lacks obvious red
on crown and black on
chest; contrast reduced by
pale feather edges;
♂ with reddish tinge
to throat.

IMMATURE ♂

JUVENILE

Black-billed Cuckoo

Coccyzus erythrophthalmus

28–31 cm | WS 40–44 cm

Duller than Yellow-billed Cuckoo,
wings less bright. Long grey-brown
tail with small white tips on outer
feather tips, appearing dull from
below. Bill grey. White chest but
throat, undertail buff.

<20 records (1 Ireland), Sep–Oct.
Scattered, coastal.

BLACK-BILLED CUCKOO

JUVENILE/
1ST-WINTER

In flight the bold tail pattern and
rufous wing flash are striking.

**YELLOW-BILLED
CUCKOO**

Yellow-billed Cuckoo

Coccyzus americanus

29–32 cm | WS 38–43 cm

Grey-brown and white cuckoo;
rufous patch on wing; long tail with
brown centre, large white tips to
blackish outer feather tips, making
bold black-and-white from below;
white edge to outermost tail feather
from above. White from throat to
tail. Bill yellow and black.

JUVENILE/1ST-WINTER

<80 records (<15 Ireland), Sep–
Oct. Scattered, mostly coastal.

521

Birds of uncertain origin and escapes/introductions

The official British and Irish Lists (see *p. 524*) are subdivided into Categories A, B and C. Not forming part of the Lists are Categories D (birds of uncertain origin) and E (those known to have escaped from captivity). Category D is a 'holding' category for species that have been reliably identified, but for which a truly wild origin is questionable. Category D species may be upgraded to A if further evidence comes to light or new records are acceptably of wild birds, or demoted to Category E, if there is no likelihood that birds recorded were wild.

At the end of 2015, 12 species were placed solely in Category D in Britain, although Bald Eagle is in Category A in Ireland. There are 12 species in Category D in Ireland, of which four (Red-breasted Goose, Red-legged Partridge, Bridled Tern and Purple Martin) are on the British list. Overall, 20 species are in Category D in either Britain or Ireland.

Following is an annotated list of all the birds currently in Category D in Britain (■) and/or Ireland (■), together with any other category code relevant to that species.

The nine Category D species included elsewhere in the book, either because they are also on the official British List or Irish List, or in order to highlight potential identification pitfalls as they occur frequently, are listed below. The remaining 11 species are shown here.

Category D

Red-breasted Goose *Branta ruficollis*   (*p. 25*)   `A` `D1`

<5 records Ireland (vagrant (<100 records) Britain)

Ross's Goose *Anser rossii*   (*p. 16*)   `D`

<50 records. Usually recorded with Pink-footed Geese (*p. 25*) autumn–spring (status unclear due to escapes from captivity, which have bred)

Wood Duck *Aix sponsa*   (*p. 47*)   `D1`

<50 records Ireland (1 possible vagrant) (British birds considered escapes from captivity; has bred)

White-headed Duck *Oxyura leucocephala*   (*p. 48*)   `D`

<5 records Ireland (vagrant (<100 records) Britain)

Red-legged Partridge *Alectoris rufa*   (*p. 264*)   `C1` `D4`

Unsuccessful introductions in Ireland (common, established introduction Britain)

Bald Eagle *Hieraaetus pennatus*   (*p. 312*)   `D` `A`

<5 records Britain (vagrant <5 records Ireland)

Bridled Tern *Onychoprion anaethetus*   (*p. 155*)   `A` `D3`

1 record Ireland (vagrant (<25 records) Britain)

Saker Falcon *Falco cherrug*   (*p. 322*)   `D`

Infrequent records; status confused by falconers' escapes

Purple Martin *Progne subis*   (*p. 346*)   `A` `D1`

Historical record Ireland, early 1840 (vagrant (1) Britain)

Falcated Duck   `NT`
Anas (Mareca) falcata
46–53 cm

<20 records (1 Ireland): (status unclear due to escapes from captivity)

`D` `D1`

drooping tertials

ADULT ♂

FEMALE like brown Wigeon (*p. 302*)

long, dark grey bill

long, dark tertials

ADULT ♀

Booted Eagle *Hieraaetus pennatus*   `530`
45–55 cm | WS 110–130 cm

`D` `D1`

ADULT pale form

size of Buzzard (*p. 302*), dark brown or whitish below, white rump, pale band on upperwing

1 in Ireland and Britain (Mar): considered to be an escape

Red-headed Bunting
Emberiza bruniceps
16 cm

Infrequent: status confused by likely escaped cagebirds

`D` `D1`

FEMALE **unmarked pale yellow** below. JUVENILE duller, greyish-buff below, **yellow under tail**; brown tail lacks white; may be inseparable from Black-headed Bunting (*p. 506*).

MALE **yellow below, red-brown hood**.

Great White Pelican
Pelecanus onocrotalus
140–180 cm

D

Occasional: most known escapes, none acceptable as being of wild origin

529

peaked forehead
pale neck

House Crow
Corvus splendens
41–43 cm

D2

long bill

black cap, face and throat

<5 records Ireland: likely ship-assisted

Greater Flamingo
Phoenicopterus ruber
120–145 cm

D **D1**

530

pink legs

NB Most flamingos in Britain/Ireland escaped Chilean race/species *chilensis*: **legs grey, pink joint.**

Infrequent: no proof of wild origin

Northern Flicker
Colaptes auratus
30–35 cm

D2

1 record Ireland: Oct: arrived on board ship

Daurian Starling
Agropsar sturninus
17 cm

D

<5 records: May, Oct: possible vagrant – status confused by possible escapes

Mugimaki Flycatcher
Ficedula mugimaki
13 cm

D

1 record: Nov; potentially escaped bird

American Goldfinch
Carduelis (Spinus) tristis
11–13 cm

D1

resembles female Chaffinch (p. 481), yellow on face.

Historical record Ireland, Sep 1894

Yellow-headed Blackbird
Xanthocephalus xanthocephalus
22–26 cm

D

<10 records when commonly sold as cagebird: unlikely vagrant

Category E*

These species have been recorded 'free' but are mostly obvious escapes from captivity and have bred. They are of importance, as they may become established and self-sustaining over time. They could potentially compete with native species or be damaging to commercial crops, and records of these species are therefore maintained more carefully. Introductions of non-native species are always unwise, and unlicensed releases are illegal. Species can be categorized as E* as well as other categories (*e.g.* Quail – see table *pp. 527–540*), but there are 26 solely in Category E*. Those that are similar to wild species or are regularly encountered are illustrated.

Helmeted Guineafowl *Numida meleagris*
Chukar Partridge *Alectoris chukar* (p. 264)
Silver Pheasant *Lophura nycthemera*
Reeves's Pheasant *Syrmaticus reevesii*
Wild Turkey *Meleagris gallopavo*
Indian Peafowl *Pavo cristatus*
Black Swan *Cygnus atratus*
Trumpeter Swan *Cygnus buccinator* (p. 16)
Swan Goose *Anser cygnoides*
Bar-headed Goose *Anser indicus* (p. 16)
Emperor Goose *Chen canagica* (p. 16)
Upland Goose *Chloephaga picta*
South African Shelduck *Tadorna cana*
Muscovy Duck *Cairina moschata*
Wood Duck *Aix sponsa* (p. 47)
Cinnamon Teal *Anas cyanoptera* (p. 16)
Speckled Teal *Anas flavirostris*
Harris's Hawk *Parabuteo unicinctus* (p. 292)
Budgerigar *Melopsittacus undulatus*
Rosy-facedLovebird *Agapornis roseicollis*
Alexandrine Parakeet *Psittacula eupatria* (p. 332)
Blue-crowned Parakeet *Aratinga acuticaudata*
Monk Parakeet *Myiopsitta monachus*
Eurasian Eagle-Owl *Bubo bubo* (p. 281)
Red-winged Laughing-thrush *Garrulax formosus*
Atlantic Canary *Serinus canaria*

Monk Parakeet
Myiopsitta monachus
29 cm (incl. tail 10 cm)

Atlantic Canary *Serinus canaria*
10–14 cm

resembles Serin (p. 485) but longer tail, larger bill; weaker pattern with dark streaks on yellow below

British and Irish Lists, and status and legislation

This table, for the first time in a popular book, gives the official lists of species recorded in Britain and in Ireland, together with a summary of their status and the legislative protection afforded them. The species are listed in taxonomic order, reflecting natural relationships between species and genera. This ordering of species has changed dramatically in recent years with the development of new scientific techniques, such as DNA sequencing, elucidating evolutionary relationships, and further changes are likely. Political response to conservation status is also subject to change, but current EU frameworks provide a logical, evidence-based and robust set of directives that shape national bird and habitat protection laws. The legal situation in the UK (and in England, Wales, Scotland and Northern Ireland where appropriate), and in the Republic of Ireland is outlined here.

LIST CATEGORIES and BoCC STATUS

LIST CATEGORIES

Britain

The British Ornithologists' Union (BOU) (www.bou.org.uk/british-list) maintains a list of the birds recorded in Britain. There are five broad categories, the first three of which, combined, constitute the official 'British List':

CATEGORY A	Recorded in an apparently natural state at least once since 1 January 1950.
CATEGORY B	Recorded in an apparently natural state at least once between 1 January 1800 and 31 December 1949, but not subsequently.
CATEGORY C	Introduced species with self-sustaining populations. There are six sub-categories: **C1** (naturalized introduced); **C2** (naturalized established); **C3** (naturalized re-established); **C4** (naturalized feral); **C5** (vagrant naturalized (no species currently)); and **C6** (former naturalized).
CATEGORY D (see *p. 522*)	Species that would otherwise appear in Category A except that there is reasonable doubt that they have ever occurred in a natural state. This is a holding category and is not intended to be a long-term assignment of any species. The species concerned are reviewed regularly with a view to assigning them to either Category A or E.
CATEGORY E	Species recorded as introductions, human-assisted transportees or escapees from captivity, and whose breeding populations (if any) are thought not to be self-sustaining. Species in Category E that have bred in the wild in Britain are designated as E*. Category E species form no part of the British List (unless already included within Categories A, B or C).

Ireland

The Irish Rare Birds Committee (IRBC) (www.irbc.ie) maintains a separate list of the birds recorded in Ireland. As with Brtitain, Categories A, B and C constitute the official 'Irish List':

CATEGORIES A, B, D and E – as equivalent BOU categories.

CATEGORY C	Introduced species with self-sustaining populations. There are two sub-categories: **C1** (self-sustaining established feral breeding populations); and **C2** (originated from established naturalized populations outside Ireland).
CATEGORY D (see *p. 522*)	Four sub-categories: **D1** (species that would otherwise appear in Categories A or B except that there is a reasonable doubt that they have ever occurred in a natural state); **D2** (species that have arrived through ship or other human assistance); **D3** (species that have only ever been found dead on the tideline); and **D4** (species that would otherwise appear in Category C1, except that their feral populations may not be self-supporting).

Species listed only within either Categories D and E or E* are included in the table and shaded purple ■ . Species that have not been recorded in a country are shaded grey ■; birds that could not be assigned to species are coded N/A, shaded pale grey ■.

At the end of March 2016, three species that would be new for the Irish List, and three that would be new for the British List were still under review. They have been included in the table and are coded (A). Figures or dots in brackets indicate that the listing relates to certain races only.

BoCC STATUS

Birds of Conservation Concern (BoCC) codes species as **Red**, **Amber** or **Green** according to conservation status, and is reviewed by leading conservation organizations every five years (Britain in 2015; Ireland in 2013). Species that are Red or Amber listed in Britain and/or Ireland are indicated by red (■) or amber (■) shading – all other regularly occurring species are 'green'. In Britain, races have been independently assessed and some are Red or Amber listed in their own right. These are indicated by a red (●) or amber (●) dot respectively; where appropriate, details of the races concerned are given in the relevant species account. In a few instances, races are Green listed, even though the species as a whole is Red or Amber listed; these are indicated with a green dot (●)[‡]. Details may be found in *British Birds* 108 (December 2015), pp. 708–746 (britishbirds.co.uk/wp-content/uploads/2014/07/BoCC4.pdf).

The criteria for Red and Amber listing are as follows:

RED LIST: Species are categorised as **Red** if they meet one or more of five criteria:
GLOBALLY THREATENED – listed by BirdLife International as Probably Extinct, Critically Endangered, Endangered or Vulnerable (*see IUCN RED LIST below*).
HISTORICAL DECLINE – severe decline in UK/Ireland between 1800 and 1995, without substantial recovery.
BREEDING POPULATION DECLINE – decline in UK/Irish breeding population of more than 50%, over 25 years or since the first BoCC review in 1969 ('longer-term').
NON-BREEDING POPULATION DECLINE – similar severe decline in UK/Irish non-breeding population.
BREEDING RANGE DECLINE – similar severe decline in the UK/Irish range.

AMBER LIST: Species are categorised as **Amber** according to eight criteria:
SPECIES OF EUROPEAN CONSERVATION CONCERN (Endangered world-wide or in an Unfavourable conservation state in Europe).
HISTORICAL DECLINE – RECOVERY – red listed for Historical Decline in a previous review but recent recovery (more than doubled in the last 25 years).
BREEDING POPULATION DECLINE – moderate decline (by more than 25% but less than 50%).
NON-BREEDING POPULATION DECLINE – moderate decline (by more than 25% but less than 50%).
BREEDING RANGE DECLINE – moderate decline (by more than 25% but less than 50%).
RARITY – UK breeding population less than 300 pairs (Irish population less than 100 pairs), or non-breeding population less than 900 individuals.
LOCALISATION – at least 50% of the UK breeding or non-breeding population found in ten or fewer sites.
INTERNATIONAL IMPORTANCE – at least 20% of the European breeding or non-breeding population found in the UK or Ireland.

SPECIES

All species on the official British or Irish Lists (categories A, B or C) are highlighted in the table in **Bold Text**. The names recommended by the British Ornithologists' Union Records Committee (BOURC) (also adopted for the Irish List) are used in this book, as they are best known to most people. This means that diver and skua (rather than loon and jaeger), for example, and simple names such as Avocet, Knot and Swallow (instead of Pied Avocet, Red Knot and Barn Swallow) have been used, in keeping with centuries of popular usage in Britain and Ireland.

‡ **Note:** although only single races of Fulmar, Ptarmigan, Kingfisher and Chough have been recorded in Britain, the BoCC status for these races differs from the overall species-level assessment.

IUCN RED LIST STATUS [Europe]

BirdLife International (the official International Union for Conservation of Nature Red List authority for birds) determines the global conservation status of birds, including: **EX** (Extinct); **PE** (Possibly Extinct); **CR** (Critically Endangered); **EN** (Endangered); **VU** (Vulnerable) (species categorised as **PE**, **CR**, **EN** and **VU** are termed 'Globally Threatened') and **NT** (Near Threatened). All other species are officially categorized as Least Concern (**LC**), although this is not coded in the table in order to highlight the Globally and Near Threatened birds. The 2015 global Red List status and European Red List status [in square brackets] is given. (NB [**RE**] = Regionally Extinct.)

EU LEG BD Ann (EU Biodiversity Legislation indicating relevant Annex)

Species listed in **Annex 1** or **Annex 2** of the European Union (EU) Wild Birds Directive 2009 are indicated. Annex I of the Directive lists 194 species and subspecies (races) which are: in danger of extinction; vulnerable to specific changes in their habitat; considered rare because of small populations or restricted local distribution; requiring particular attention for reasons of the specific nature of habitat. Of these, 117 occur in Britain and Ireland. Annex 2 lists species that can be shot within specified seasons.

LEGAL PROTECTION

Most species of wild bird in Great Britain are afforded a certain level of protection under the Wildlife and Countryside Act 1981 (as amended) (WCA 1981) (exceptions are, for example, poultry and game birds). Although there are slight variations between the various countries (in particular Scotland has a greater suite of offences to protect wild birds), the following is common to England, Scotland and Wales:
(a) it is an offence to kill, injure or take any wild bird;
(b) it is an offence to take, damage or destroy the nest of any wild bird while the nest is in use or being built;
(c) it is an offence to take or destroy the egg of any wild bird.

In England and Wales these three above offences are only triggered if committed "intentionally", whereas in Scotland they may be committed either "intentionally" or "recklessly."

SPECIAL PROTECTION – SPECIAL PROT'N (Sched. 1) (GB and Northern Ireland (NI))

Wild birds listed on Schedule 1 of the WCA 1981 are afforded a higher level of protection in that, for them, it is also an offence (in England, Wales and Scotland) to intentionally or recklessly (a) disturb any wild bird included in Schedule 1 while it is building a nest or is in, or near a nest containing eggs or young; or (b) disturb the dependent young of such a bird. There are further offences in Scotland to protect Schedule 1 birds. In Northern Ireland protection is afforded under Schedule 1 of the Wildlife (Northern Ireland) Order 1985 as amended by The Wildlife and Natural Environment Act (Northern Ireland) 2011, and in the Republic of Ireland under The Wildlife Act 1976 as amended by The Wildlife (Amendment) Act 2000. In Great Britain and Northern Ireland, species on Schedule 1, Part 2 of the relevant Act are afforded special protection during the breeding season but can be killed outside a specified close season. These are shown in the table by a grey-shaded circle (◉).

In all UK countries and the Republic of Ireland, the EU Wild Birds Directive 2009 has been adopted and transposed into national law. This Directive gives protection to wild birds and their habitats (and provides for exceptions when wild birds may lawfully be harmed) and also requires classification of Special Protection Areas and other special conservation measures for wild bird species listed in Annex 1 and which are regularly occurring migratory species.

This section has been written as a non-technical summary. Anyone requiring legal advice regarding the protection of birds should consult a qualified legal professional.

BIODIVERSITY LISTING

Under the UK Biodiversity Action Plan, species and habitats are highlighted for conservation action, and lists have been drawn up for each country. Lists of these habitats and species are published as a requirement of Section 41 (England) and Section 42 (Wales) of the Natural Environment and Rural Communities (NERC) Act 2006, Section 2(4) of the Nature Conservation (Scotland) Act 2004, and Section 3(1) of the Wildlife and Natural Environment Act (Northern Ireland) 2011. They are used to guide decision-makers, such as local and regional authorities, in their duty "to have regard to the conservation of biodiversity in the exercise of their normal functions". A dot indicates that the species is included on the relevant country's Biodiversity List: England (EN); Wales (WA); Scotland (SC) and Northern Ireland (NI). Specially protected species in the Republic of Ireland are detailed in the Wildlife Act 1976 and Wildlife (Amendment) Act 2000. In the Republic of Ireland Biodiversity Action Plans are largely based on counties or local authority areas.

LIST CATEGORIES & BoCC STATUS — Britain (BoCC 2015)	Ireland (BoCC 2013)	KEY TO SPECIAL PROTECTION ● Sched. 1 ○ Sched. 1, Part 2 — SPECIES	IUCN GLOBAL RED LIST STATUS [Europe]	EU LEG BD Ann	SPECIAL PROT'N Sched. 1 GB	NI	BIODIVERSITY LISTING NERC EN	WA	Biod. List SC	NI	Page
A, C2	A, C1	Mute Swan		2							17
A, E ●	A	Bewick's Swan	[EN]	1	●	●	●	●	●	●	18
A, E*	A	Whooper Swan		1	●	●			●	●	19
A, E ● ●	A	Bean Goose		2					●		28
A, E*	A	Pink-footed Goose		2							29
A, E* ●	A	White-fronted Goose		1,2†			●	●	●	●	30
A, E*	A	Lesser White-fronted Goose	VU [EN]	1							31
A, C2, C4, E* ●	A, C1	Greylag Goose		2	○						27
A, C2, E*	A, D1	Snow Goose									31
D, E*		Ross's Goose									16
A, C2, E*	A, C1	Greater Canada Goose		2							22
A, E	A	Cackling (Lesser Canada) Goose									23
A, C2, E*	A, C1	Barnacle Goose		1					●		26
A, E ●	A	Brent Goose		2			●	●		●	24
A, E*	D1	Red-breasted Goose	VU [NT]	1							25
C1, E*		Egyptian Goose									33
B, D, E*	B, D1	Ruddy Shelduck		1							33
A	A	Shelduck									32
C1, E*	C1	Mandarin Duck									47
E*	D1	Wood Duck									47
D, E	D1	Falcated Duck	NT								523
A, E*	A	Wigeon		2		○					37
A, E	A	American Wigeon									44
A, C2	A	Gadwall		2		○					40
A, E	A, D1	Baikal Teal									45
A ●	A	Teal		2							42
A	A	Green-winged Teal									45
A, C2, C4, E* ●	A, C1	Mallard		2							38
A	A	Black Duck									44
A, E	A	Pintail		2	○	○				●	41
A	A	Garganey		2	●	●			●	●	43
A, E*	A	Blue-winged Teal									45

† Greenland White-fronted Goose race *albifrons* on Annex 1
White-fronted Goose race *albifrons* on Annex 2

Britain (BoCC 2015)	Ireland (BoCC 2013)	SPECIES	IUCN GLOBAL RED LIST STATUS [Europe]	EU LEG BD Ann	GB	NI	EN	WA	SC	NI	Page
A	A	Shoveler		2		○				●	39
A, C2, E*	A	Red-crested Pochard		2							46
A, E		Canvasback									54
A, E*	A	Pochard	VU [VU]	2		○			●	●	49
A, E	A	Redhead									54
A, E	A	Ring-necked Duck									53
A, E	A	Ferruginous Duck	NT	1							53
A	A	Tufted Duck		2						●	50
A ●	A	Scaup	[VU]	2	●	○	●		●	●	51
A	A	Lesser Scaup									52
A ● ●	A	Eider	NT [VU]	2							64
A		King Eider									66
A		Steller's Eider	VU	1							67
A		Harlequin Duck									68
A	A	Long-tailed Duck	VU [VU]	2	●						60
A	A	Common Scoter		2	●	●	●	●	●	●	63
A		Black Scoter	NT								69
A	A	Surf Scoter									68
A	A	Velvet Scoter	VU [VU]	2	●						62
A		White-winged Scoter									69
A, E	A	Bufflehead									54
A, E	A	Barrow's Goldeneye	[NT]								67
A, E* ●	A	Goldeneye		2	○	○				●	56
A, E	A, D1	Hooded Merganser									54
A	A	Smew		1					●		57
A	A	Red-breasted Merganser	[NT]	2							58
A	A	Goosander		2			●				59
C1, E*	C1, C2	Ruddy Duck									48
D, E		White-headed Duck	EN [EN]	1							48
A, E* ●	A	Quail		2	●	●				●	272
C1, E*	D4	Red-legged Partridge		2							264
A ●	A	Red Grouse	[VU]	2			●	●	●	●	266
A ●‡		Ptarmigan	[NT]	2							267
A, E ●		Black Grouse		2			●	●	●		268
C3 ●	B	Capercaillie		1,2	●				●		269
A, C2, E* ●	A, C1	Grey Partridge		2			●	●	●		265
C1, E*	C1	Pheasant		2							270
C6, E*		Lady Amherst's Pheasant									271
C1, E*		Golden Pheasant									271
A	A	Red-throated Diver		1	●				●		76
A ●	A	Black-throated Diver		1	●				●	●	77
A	A	Pacific Diver			●						79
A	A	Great Northern Diver	[VU]	1	●				●		78
A	A	White-billed Diver	NT [VU]		●						79
A	A	Black-browed Albatross	NT								98
A		Yellow-nosed Albatross	EN								98
A ●‡	A	Fulmar	[EN]								90

KEY TO SPECIAL PROTECTION
● Sched. 1
○ Sched. 1, Part 2

Britain (BoCC 2015)	Ireland (BoCC 2013)	SPECIES	IUCN GLOBAL RED LIST STATUS [Europe]	EU LEG BD Ann	Sched. 1 GB	Sched. 1 NI	NERC EN	NERC WA	NERC SC	Biod. List NI	Page
A	A	Fea's Petrel	NT	1							100
A		Capped Petrel	EN								100
A	A	Cory's Shearwater		1							93
A		Scopoli's Shearwater									93
A	A	Great Shearwater									93
A	A	Sooty Shearwater	NT							●	91
A	A	Manx Shearwater				●			●		95
A		Yelkouan Shearwater	VU								95
A	A	Balearic Shearwater	CR [CR]	1		●	●		●	●	95
A	A	Macaronesian Shearwater									95
A	A	Wilson's Petrel									97
B		Frigate Petrel	[EN]	1							100
A ●	A	Storm Petrel		1		●			●		97
N/A	B	Cape Verde Storm Petrel or Madeiran Storm Petrel or Monteiro's Storm Petrel	NT / VU [VU]	1							101
A ●	A	Leach's Petrel		1	●				●		97
A	A	Swinhoe's Petrel	NT								101
N/A		White-bellied Storm Petrel or Black-bellied Storm Petrel									101
A		Red-billed Tropicbird									99
A	A	Gannet									89
A ●	A	Cormorant									75
A	A	Double-crested Cormorant									85
A ●	A	Shag									74
D, E		Great White Pelican		1							523
A		Ascension Frigatebird	VU								99
A		Magnificent Frigatebird									99
A ●	A	Bittern		1	●	●	●	●	●	●	242
A	A	American Bittern									250
A	A	Little Bittern		1	●						243
A, E*	A	Night-heron		1							243
A	A	Green Heron									250
A	A	Squacco Heron		1							246
A, E	A	Cattle Egret									246
A		Snowy Egret									251
	A	Little Blue Heron									251
A	A	Little Egret		1		●					244
A	A	Great White Egret		1							245
A	A	Grey Heron				●					240
A		Great Blue Heron									251
A	A	Purple Heron		1	●						241
A, E	A	Black Stork		1							247
A, E	A	White Stork		1							247
A, E	A	Glossy Ibis		1							241
A, E ●	A	Spoonbill		1	●						249
A	A	Pied-billed Grebe									85

KEY TO SPECIAL PROTECTION: ● Sched. 1   ◐ Sched. 1, Part 2

Britain (BoCC 2015)	Ireland (BoCC 2013)	SPECIES	IUCN GLOBAL RED LIST STATUS [Europe]	EU LEG BD Ann	Sched. 1 GB	NI	NERC EN	WA	Biod. List SC	NI	Page
A	A	Little Grebe									84
A	A	Great Crested Grebe									80
A ●	A	Red-necked Grebe							●		81
A ●	A	Slavonian Grebe	VU [NT]	1	●				●		83
A ○	A	Black-necked Grebe			●	●			●	●	82
D, E	D1	Greater Flamingo		1							523
A	A	Honey-buzzard		1	●						301
A, E	A	Black Kite		1							310
A, C3, E*	A, C2	Red Kite	NT [NT]	1	●	●					304
A, C3, E	A, C2, D4	White-tailed Eagle		1	●	●			●	●	294
D, E	A	Bald Eagle									312
B, D, E		Egyptian Vulture	EN [EN]	1							312
	B	Griffon Vulture		1							312
A		Short-toed Eagle		1							311
A ○	A	Marsh Harrier		1	●	●			●		305
A ●	A	Hen Harrier	[NT]	1	●	●	●	●	●	●	307
A	A	Northern Harrier			●						310
A	A	Pallid Harrier	NT [NT]	1	●						309
A	A	Montagu's Harrier		1	●						308
A, C3, E*	A	Goshawk			●	●				●	315
A	A	Sparrowhawk				●					314
A, E*	A	Buzzard				●					302
A, E	A	Rough-legged Buzzard									303
B	B	(Greater) Spotted Eagle	VU [EN]	1							311
A, E	A, D4	Golden Eagle		1	●	●			●	●	295
D, E	D1	Booted Eagle		1							523
A, E ○	A	Osprey		1	●	●			●		300
A	A	Water Rail		2							258
A	A	Spotted Crake		1	●				●		259
A	A	Sora Rail									261
A	A	Little Crake		1							260
A	A	Baillon's Crake		1							261
A, E*	A	Corncrake		1	●	●	●	●	●	●	255
A	A	Moorhen									256
A		Allen's Gallinule									262
A		Purple Gallinule									262
A	A	Coot	[NT]	2							257
A	A	American Coot									262
A ●	A	Crane		1							248
A	B	Sandhill Crane									250
A	B	Little Bustard	NT [VU]	1							252
A		Macqueen's Bustard	VU [PE]								252
A, E*	B	Great Bustard	VU	1							253
A ●	A	Stone-curlew		1	●		●				177
A	A	Black-winged Stilt		1	●						181
A	A	Avocet		1	●						180
A ●	A	Oystercatcher	NT [VU]	2							178

LIST CATEGORIES & BoCC STATUS		KEY TO SPECIAL PROTECTION ● Sched. 1 ◐ Sched. 1, Part 2	IUCN GLOBAL RED LIST STATUS [Europe]	EU LEG BD Ann	SPECIAL PROT'N Sched. 1		BIODIVERSITY LISTING NERC			Biod. List	Page
Britain (BoCC 2015)	Ireland (BoCC 2013)	SPECIES			GB	NI	EN	WA	SC	NI	
A	A	American Golden Plover									191
A	A	Pacific Golden Plover									191
A	A	Golden Plover		1,2		◐	●	●	●		190
A	A	Grey Plover		2							189
A	A	Sociable Plover	CR [CR]								192
A		White-tailed Plover									192
A	A	Lapwing	NT [VU]	2		●	●	●	●	●	187
A	A	Little Ringed Plover			●						182
A ● ●	A	Ringed Plover						●			183
A	A	Semipalmated Plover									186
A	A	Killdeer									186
A	A, E	Kentish Plover		1	●						184
A	A	Lesser Sand Plover									185
A		Greater Sand Plover	[VU]								185
A		Caspian Plover	[RE]								185
A	A	Dotterel		1	●	●			●		188
A	A	Upland Sandpiper									226
A		Little Whimbrel									234
B	B	Eskimo Curlew	PE								234
A	A	Hudsonian Whimbrel									234
A ●	A	Whimbrel		2	●	●				●	214
A ●	A	Curlew	NT [VU]	2	●	●	●	●	●	●	215
A ● ◐	A	Black-tailed Godwit	NT [VU]	2	●	●	●		●	●	213
A	(A)	Hudsonian Godwit									234
A ●	A	Bar-tailed Godwit	NT	1,2			●	●			213
A ●	A	Turnstone									179
A	A	Great Knot	EN								235
A ●	A	Knot	NT	2					●		195
A	A	Ruff		1,2	●	●			●		202
A	A	Sharp-tailed Sandpiper									227
A	A	Broad-billed Sandpiper									229
A	A	Curlew Sandpiper	NT [VU]								199
A	A	Stilt Sandpiper									229
A	A	Red-necked Stint	NT								231
A	A	Long-toed Stint									231
A	A	Temminck's Stint			●				●		200
A	A	Sanderling									194
A ● ●	A	Dunlin				●			●	●	196
A	A	Purple Sandpiper			●				●		198
A	A	Baird's Sandpiper									228
A	A	Little Stint									201
A	A	White-rumped Sandpiper									228
A	A	Least Sandpiper									231
A	A	Buff-breasted Sandpiper	NT								226
A	A	Pectoral Sandpiper									227
A	A	Western Sandpiper									231
A	A	Semipalmated Sandpiper	NT								231

LIST CATEGORIES & BoCC STATUS		KEY TO SPECIAL PROTECTION ● Sched. 1 ◐ Sched. 1, Part 2	IUCN GLOBAL RED LIST STATUS [Europe]	EU LEG BD Ann	SPECIAL PROT'N Sched. 1		BIODIVERSITY LISTING NERC		Biod. List		Page
Britain (BoCC 2015)	Ireland (BoCC 2013)	SPECIES			GB	NI	EN	WA	SC	NI	
A	A	Wilson's Phalarope									233
A	A	Red-necked Phalarope		1	●				●	●	216
A	A	Grey Phalarope									217
A	A	Terek Sandpiper		1							233
A	A	Common Sandpiper									211
A	A	Spotted Sandpiper									232
A	A	Green Sandpiper				●			●		210
A	A	Solitary Sandpiper									235
A		Grey-tailed Tattler	NT								235
A	A	Spotted Redshank		2							207
A	A	Greater Yellowlegs									224
A	A	Greenshank		2	●	●					208
A	A	Lesser Yellowlegs									224
A	A	Marsh Sandpiper									222
A	A	Wood Sandpiper		1	●				●		209
A ●	A	Redshank		2		●				●	206
A	A	Jack Snipe		2							219
A	A	Short-billed Dowitcher									225
A	A	Long-billed Dowitcher									225
A	A	Woodcock		2					●		220
A ●	A	Snipe		2							218
A	A	Wilson's Snipe									223
A	A	Great Snipe	NT	1							223
A	A	Collared Pratincole		1							193
A		Oriental Pratincole									193
A	A	Black-winged Pratincole	NT [VU]								193
A	A	Cream-coloured Courser	[NT]	1							192
A	A	Pomarine Skua									159
A	A	Arctic Skua							●	●	158
A	A	Long-tailed Skua									160
A	A	Great Skua									161
N/A		South Polar Skua / Brown Skua									161
A		Tufted Puffin									172
A	A	Puffin	VU [EN]			●					168
A		Long-billed Murrelet	NT								172
A ●	A	Black Guillemot									169
A		Ancient Murrelet									172
A ● ●	A	Razorbill	NT [NT]								167
B	B	Great Auk	EX								165
A		Little Auk									170
A ●	A	Guillemot	[NT]								166
A		Brünnich's Guillemot									172
A		Aleutian Tern									154
A	A	Sooty Tern									155
A	D3	Bridled Tern									155
A ●	A	Little Tern		1	●	●			●	●	148
A	A	Gull-billed Tern		1							150

Britain (BoCC 2015)	Ireland (BoCC 2013)	SPECIES	IUCN GLOBAL RED LIST STATUS [Europe]	EU LEG BD / Ann	GB	NI	EN	WA	SC	NI	Page
A	A	Caspian Tern		1							150
A	A	Whiskered Tern		1							150
A	A	Black Tern		1	●						142
A	A	White-winged Black Tern		1							142
A		Cabot's Tern									153
A	A	Sandwich Tern		1		●			●		147
	A	Elegant Tern	NT								152
A	A, D3	Royal Tern									153
A	A	Lesser Crested Tern									152
A	A	Forster's Tern									154
A ●	A	Common Tern		1		●			●		144
A ●	A	Roseate Tern		1	●	●	●	●	●	●	146
A	A	Arctic Tern		1		●			●		145
A	A	Ivory Gull	NT								111
A	A	Sabine's Gull									109
A ●	A	Kittiwake	[VU]								108
A		Slender-billed Gull		1							137
A	A	Bonaparte's Gull									113
A	A	Black-headed Gull		2			●	●	●		106
A	A	Little Gull	[NT]		●						110
A	A	Ross's Gull	[EN]								111
A	A	Laughing Gull									112
A	A	Franklin's Gull									113
A	A	Mediterranean Gull		1	●	●					107
A		Audouin's Gull		1							139
B		Great Black-headed Gull									137
A ●	A	Common Gull		2							114
A	A	Ring-billed Gull									116
A ● ●	A	Lesser Black-backed Gull		2							126
A ● ●	A	Herring Gull	[NT]	2			●	●	●	●	124
A ●	A	Yellow-legged Gull									130
A	A	Caspian Gull		2							131
(A)	A	Slaty-backed Gull									138
A	A	American Herring Gull									140
	(A)	Vega Gull									141
A ●	A	Iceland Gull									135
A		Glaucous-winged Gull									138
A ●	A	Glaucous Gull									134
A	A	Great Black-backed Gull		2							128
A	A	Pallas's Sandgrouse	[EN]								274
A, C4, E*	A	Rock Dove / Feral Pigeon		2							275
A ●	A	Stock Dove		2		●					277
A	A	Woodpigeon		2							276
A	A	Collared Dove		2							278
A ●	A	Turtle Dove	VU [VU]	2		●	●	●	●	●	279
A		Rufous Turtle Dove									280
A	A	Mourning Dove									280

533

Britain (BoCC 2015)	Ireland (BoCC 2013)	SPECIES	IUCN GLOBAL RED LIST STATUS [Europe]	EU LEG BD Ann	Sched. 1 GB	Sched. 1 NI	NERC EN	NERC WA	NERC SC	Biod. List NI	Page
A	A	Great Spotted Cuckoo									331
A●	A	Cuckoo				●	●	●	●	●	328
A	A	Black-billed Cuckoo									521
A	A	Yellow-billed Cuckoo									521
A, E*	A	Barn Owl			●	●			●	●	283
A	A	Scops Owl									289
A	A	Snowy Owl		1	●	●					288
A		Hawk Owl		1							289
C1	A, C2	Little Owl									285
A●	(A)	Tawny Owl									284
A	A	Long-eared Owl				●					287
A●	A	Short-eared Owl		1		●			●	●	286
A		Tengmalm's Owl		1							289
A●	A	Nightjar		1	●	●	●	●	●	●	290
B		Red-necked Nightjar									291
A		Egyptian Nightjar									291
A	A	Common Nighthawk									291
A	A	Chimney Swift	NT								341
A	A	Needle-tailed Swift									340
A●	A	Swift							●	●	339
A	A	Pallid Swift									340
A		Pacific Swift									340
A	A	Alpine Swift									341
A	A	Little Swift	[VU]								341
A	A	Hoopoe			●						329
A		Blue-cheeked Bee-eater									330
A	A	Bee-eater			●						330
A	A	Roller		1							331
A●‡	A	Kingfisher	[VU]	1	●	●			●		327
A	A, D1	Belted Kingfisher									521
A	A	Wryneck			●				●		334
A	A	Green Woodpecker									335
A	A	Yellow-bellied Sapsucker									521
A●	A	Great Spotted Woodpecker									336
A●		Lesser Spotted Woodpecker					●	●			337
	D2	Northern Flicker									523
A	B	Lesser Kestrel		1							324
A●	A	Kestrel				●		●	●		316
A, E	A	American Kestrel									324
A	A	Red-footed Falcon	NT [NT]	1							320
A		Amur Falcon									325
A●●	A	Merlin		1	●	●			●		317
A	A	Hobby			●	●			●		318
A		Eleonora's Falcon		1							325
A, E	A	Gyr Falcon		1	●	●					321
A, E	A	Peregrine		1	●	●			●		319
D, E		Saker Falcon	EN [VU]								322

Britain (BoCC 2015)	Ireland (BoCC 2013)	SPECIES	IUCN GLOBAL RED LIST STATUS [Europe]	EU LEG BD Ann	SPECIAL PROT'N Sched. 1 GB	NI	BIODIVERSITY LISTING NERC EN	WA	SC	Biod. List NI	Page
C1, E*		Ring-necked Parakeet									332
	A	Eastern Kingbird									520
A		Eastern Phoebe									520
A		Alder Flycatcher									520
(A)		Acadian Flycatcher									520
A		Yellow-throated Vireo									511
A	A	Philadelphia Vireo									511
A	A	Red-eyed Vireo									511
A ●	A	Golden Oriole			●						371
A	A	Brown Shrike									459
A	A	Isabelline Shrike									458
A ●	A	Red-backed Shrike		1	●			●	●		457
A		Long-tailed Shrike									463
A	A	Lesser Grey Shrike		1							461
A	A	Great Grey Shrike	[VU]								460
A		Southern Grey Shrike									461
A	A	Woodchat Shrike									462
A		Masked Shrike									463
A, E* ●‡	A	Chough		1	●	●		●	●	●	471
A	A	Magpie		2							473
A ○	A	Jay		2							472
A		Nutcracker									463
A	A	Jackdaw		2							466
	D2	House Crow									523
A	A	Rook		2							469
A	A	Carrion Crow		2							468
A	A	Hooded Crow							●		467
A	A	Raven									470
	A	Ruby-crowned Kinglet									511
A	A	Goldcrest									436
A		Firecrest			●						437
A		Penduline Tit									454
A ○	A	Blue Tit									446
A ○	A	Great Tit									447
A ○		Crested Tit			●						448
A ○	A	Coal Tit									449
A ●		Willow Tit					●	●	●		451
A ●	A	Marsh Tit					●	●	●		450
A	A	Bearded Tit			●				●		444
A	A	Woodlark		1	●		●	●			348
A		White-winged Lark									353
A ● ○	A	Skylark		2			●	●	●	●	349
A, E		Crested Lark									352
A ● ○	A	Shore Lark			●						350
A	A	Short-toed Lark		1							351
A		Bimaculated Lark									353
A		Calandra Lark		1							353

‡ See p. 525.

Britain (BoCC 2015)	Ireland (BoCC 2013)	SPECIES	IUCN GLOBAL RED LIST STATUS [Europe]	BD Ann	GB	NI	EN	WA	SC	NI	Page
A		Black Lark	[CR]								353
A		Lesser Short-toed Lark									352
A	A	Sand Martin				●					344
A		Tree Swallow									346
A	D1	Purple Martin									346
A		Crag Martin									345
A,E	A	Swallow									342
A ●	A	House Martin									343
A	A	Red-rumped Swallow									345
A	A	Cliff Swallow									346
A	A	Cetti's Warbler			●						405
A ●	A	Long-tailed Tit									445
A		Eastern Crowned Warbler									435
A		Green Warbler									435
A	A	Greenish Warbler (includes **Two-barred Warbler**)									434
N/A		Pale-legged Leaf Warbler or Sakhalin Leaf Warbler									435
A	A	Arctic Warbler									434
A	A	Pallas's Warbler									432
A	A	Yellow-browed Warbler									432
A	A	Hume's Warbler									432
A	A	Radde's Warbler									431
A	A	Dusky Warbler									431
A	A	Western Bonelli's Warbler									430
A		Eastern Bonelli's Warbler									430
A	A	Wood Warbler				●	●	●	●	●	429
A	A	Chiffchaff									426
A	A	Iberian Chiffchaff									427
A ● ●	A	Willow Warbler									428
A	A	Blackcap									418
A	A	Garden Warbler				●					419
A	A	Barred Warbler		1							424
A	A	Lesser Whitethroat				●					421
A		Western Orphean Warbler									424
A		Desert Warbler	[RE]								423
A	A	Whitethroat									420
A		Spectacled Warbler									423
A ●	A	Dartford Warbler	NT [NT]	1	●						417
A		Marmora's Warbler		1							423
A		Rüppell's Warbler		1							425
A	A	Subalpine Warbler									422
A		Moltoni's Subalpine Warbler									422
A	A	Sardinian Warbler									425
A	A	Pallas's Grasshopper Warbler									413
A		Lanceolated Warbler									413
A ●	A	Grasshopper Warbler					●	●	●	●	412

Britain (BoCC 2015)	Ireland (BoCC 2013)	SPECIES — KEY TO SPECIAL PROTECTION: ● Sched. 1 ◐ Sched. 1, Part 2	IUCN GLOBAL RED LIST STATUS [Europe]	EU LEG BD Ann	Sched. 1 GB	Sched. 1 NI	NERC EN	NERC WA	Biod. List SC	Biod. List NI	Page
A		River Warbler									411
A ●	A	Savi's Warbler			●		●				411
A		Thick-billed Warbler									410
A	A	Booted Warbler									416
A	A	Sykes's Warbler									416
A	A	Eastern Olivaceous Warbler									415
A		Olive Tree Warbler		1							415
A	A	Icterine Warbler									414
A	A	Melodious Warbler									414
A	A	Aquatic Warbler	VU [VU]	1			●	●			410
A	A	Sedge Warbler									406
A	A	Paddyfield Warbler									409
A	A	Blyth's Reed Warbler									408
A	A	Marsh Warbler			●		●				408
A	A	Reed Warbler				●			●		407
A	A	Great Reed Warbler									410
A	A	Fan-tailed Warbler									411
A	A	Cedar Waxwing									375
A, E	A	Waxwing									374
A		Wallcreeper									455
A		Red-breasted Nuthatch									454
A		Nuthatch									452
A	A	Treecreeper									453
A ◐		Short-toed Treecreeper			●						455
A ● ◐	A	Wren		1†					●†		369
A, E		Northern Mockingbird									519
A		Brown Thrasher									519
A	A	Grey Catbird									519
A ● ◐	A	Starling		2			●	●	●	●	372
A	A	Rose-coloured Starling									373
D, E		Daurian Starling									523
A ◐	A	Dipper									367
A	A	White's Thrush									384
A		Varied Thrush									387
A		Wood Thrush	NT								387
A	A	Hermit Thrush									387
A	A	Swainson's Thrush									386
A	A	Grey-cheeked Thrush									386
A		Veery									387
A, E	A	Siberian Thrush									385
A ●	A	Ring Ouzel				●	●	●	●	●	378
A	A	Blackbird		2							379
A		Eyebrowed Thrush									385
A		Dusky Thrush									385
A		Naumann's Thrush									385
A		Black-throated Thrush									384

† Wren race *fridariensis* (Fair Isle Wren) is listed on Annex 1;
  races *fridariensis* & *hirtensis* (St Kilda Wren) are on Scottish Biodiversity List

LIST CATEGORIES & BoCC STATUS		KEY TO SPECIAL PROTECTION ● Sched. 1 ◐ Sched. 1, Part 2	IUCN GLOBAL RED LIST STATUS [Europe]	EU LEG	SPECIAL PROT'N		BIODIVERSITY LISTING				
Britain (BoCC 2015)	Ireland (BoCC 2013)	SPECIES		BD Ann	Sched. 1		NERC		Biod. List		Page
					GB	NI	EN	WA	SC	NI	
A		Red-throated Thrush									384
A	A	Fieldfare		2	●					●	382
A ● ●	A	Song Thrush		2			●	●	●	●	380
A ● ●	A	Redwing	NT [NT]	2	●				●	●	383
A ●	A	Mistle Thrush		2							381
A, E	A	American Robin									386
A	A	Rufous Bush Chat									398
A		Brown Flycatcher									441
A ●	A	Spotted Flycatcher				●	●	●	●	●	439
A	A	Robin									388
A		Siberian Blue Robin									401
A		Rufous-tailed Robin									401
A		White-throated Robin									398
A	A	Thrush Nightingale									400
A ●	A	Nightingale									389
A	A	Bluethroat		1	●						400
A		Siberian Rubythroat									401
A, E	A	Red-flanked Bluetail									401
A	A	Red-breasted Flycatcher		1							442
A		Taiga Flycatcher									442
A		Collared Flycatcher		1							441
A ●	A	Pied Flycatcher				●		●			440
D		Mugimaki Flycatcher									523
A ●	A	Black Redstart				●					393
A ◐	A	Redstart				●					392
A		Moussier's Redstart									398
A	A	Rock Thrush									399
A, E		Blue Rock Thrush									399
A	A	Whinchat				●					390
A	A	Siberian Stonechat									402
A	A	Stonechat									391
A	A	Wheatear									394
A	A	Isabelline Wheatear									397
A	A	Desert Wheatear	[NT]								397
A	A	Black-eared Wheatear									396
A	A	Pied Wheatear									396
A		White-crowned Black Wheatear									399
A		Alpine Accentor									375
A ● ●	A	Dunnock					●	●	●	●	368
A ●	A	House Sparrow					●	●	●	●	476
A		Spanish Sparrow									495
A ●	A	Tree Sparrow					●	●	●	●	477
A		Rock Sparrow									495
A ● ◐	A	Yellow Wagtail					●	●	●	●	364
A	A	Citrine Wagtail									365
A ●	A	Grey Wagtail									363
A ◐		Pied Wagtail									362

LIST CATEGORIES & BoCC STATUS		KEY TO SPECIAL PROTECTION ● Sched.1 ○ Sched.1, Part 2	IUCN GLOBAL RED LIST STATUS	EU LEG	SPECIAL PROT'N		BIODIVERSITY LISTING				
Britain (BoCC 2015)	Ireland (BoCC 2013)	SPECIES	[Europe]	BD Ann	Sched.1 GB	NI	NERC EN	WA	Biod. List SC	NI	Page
A	A	Richard's Pipit									360
A		Blyth's Pipit									361
A	A	Tawny Pipit		1							361
A	A	Olive-backed Pipit									359
A ●	A	Tree Pipit			●		●	●	●	●	354
A	A	Pechora Pipit	[VU]								359
A ●	A	Meadow Pipit	NT [NT]								355
A	A	Red-throated Pipit									358
A ●	A	Rock Pipit									356
A ●	A	Water Pipit									357
A	A	Buff-bellied Pipit									357
A	A	Brambling			●				●		480
A, E ●	A	Chaffinch									481
A		Evening Grosbeak									516
A ●	A	Hawfinch					●	●	●	●	479
A	A	Common Rosefinch			●				●		491
A, E		Pine Grosbeak									494
A ●	A	Bullfinch					●	●	●	●	478
A, E		Trumpeter Finch		1							495
A, E ●	A	Greenfinch									483
A ● ● ○	A	Linnet					●	●	●	●	486
A ●	A	Twite				●	●	●	●	●	487
A	A	Lesser Redpoll					●	●	●	●	489
A ●	A	Common Redpoll									489
A	A	Arctic Redpoll									489
A	B	Two-barred Crossbill			●						494
A	A	Crossbill			●	●					492
A		Scottish Crossbill		1	●				●		493
A		Parrot Crossbill			●				●		493
A ●	A	Goldfinch									482
A		Citril Finch									485
A	A	Serin			●						485
	D1	American Goldfinch									523
A	A	Siskin							●		484
A ●	A	Snow Bunting			●				●		498
A ●	A	Lapland Bunting			●						497
A		Summer Tanager									517
A	A	Scarlet Tanager									517
A	A	Rose-breasted Grosbeak									516
A, E	A	Indigo Bunting									516
A		Eastern Towhee									516
A		Lark Sparrow									518
A		Savannah Sparrow									518
A, E	A	Song Sparrow									518
	A	Fox Sparrow									518
A, E	A	White-crowned Sparrow									519
A, E	A	White-throated Sparrow									519

Britain (BoCC 2015)	Ireland (BoCC 2013)	SPECIES	IUCN GLOBAL RED LIST STATUS [Europe]	EU LEG BD Ann	GB	NI	EN	WA	SC	NI	Page
A, E	A	Dark-eyed Junco									516
A, E		Black-faced Bunting									507
A	A	Pine Bunting	[VU]								509
A ●	A	Yellowhammer				●	●	●	●	●	500
A	A	Cirl Bunting			●		●				501
A		Rock Bunting									509
A, E	A	Ortolan Bunting		1							508
A		Cretzschmar's Bunting		1							508
A		Yellow-browed Bunting									507
A	A	Rustic Bunting	[VU]								505
A		Chestnut-eared Bunting									504
A	A	Little Bunting									504
A	A	Yellow-breasted Bunting	EN [CR]								506
(A), E		Chestnut Bunting									507
A ◐	A	Reed Bunting					●	●	●	●	502
A		Pallas's Reed Bunting									505
A, E	A	Black-headed Bunting									506
D, E	D1	Red-headed Bunting									523
A ●	A	Corn Bunting					●	●	●		503
A	A	Bobolink									517
A		Brown-headed Cowbird									517
A, E	A	Baltimore Oriole									517
D, E		Yellow-headed Blackbird									523
A	A	Ovenbird									515
A	A	Northern Waterthrush									515
	A	Blue-winged Warbler									515
A		Golden-winged Warbler	NT								515
A	A	Black-and-white Warbler									514
A		Tennessee Warbler									515
A	A	Common Yellowthroat									514
A		Hooded Warbler									514
A, E	A	American Redstart									513
A		Cape May Warbler									512
A, E	A	Northern Parula									513
A, E	A	Magnolia Warbler									513
A		Bay-breasted Warbler									513
A		Blackburnian Warbler									513
A	A	Yellow Warbler									514
A		Chestnut-sided Warbler									513
A, E	A	Blackpoll Warbler									512
A	A	Yellow-rumped Warbler									512
	A	Canada Warbler									515
A	A	Wilson's Warbler									514

Key to header: LIST CATEGORIES & BoCC STATUS — Britain (BoCC 2015), Ireland (BoCC 2013). KEY TO SPECIAL PROTECTION: ● Sched. 1; ◐ Sched. 1, Part 2. SPECIAL PROT'N: Sched. 1 (GB, NI). BIODIVERSITY LISTING: NERC (EN, WA), Biod. List (SC, NI).

Acknowledgements and photographic credits

Many people have contributed, directly or indirectly, to the production of this book since its inception ten years ago. Our sincere thanks go to everyone who has influenced the final product. We particularly acknowledge the efforts of enthusiastic birdwatchers across Britain and Ireland who provide much data on the status and distribution of birds, upon which we have drawn heavily. By the same token, we acknowledge the contribution of the British Ornithologists' Union Records Committee (BOURC) and Irish Rare Birds Committee (IRBC) as the official authorities regarding lists and records, and the journals *British Birds* and *Irish Birds* in which annual reports of rare birds and periodic summaries of scarce migrants are published. In addition, much information has been obtained from the surveys and other studies undertaken by the Royal Society for the Protection of Birds (RSPB), British Trust for Ornithology (BTO) and Wildfowl & Wetlands Trust (WWT).

A special mention goes to Rachel and Anya Still for their invaluable contributions behind the scenes which helped to bring this book to fruition. We also extend our particular thanks to Brian Clews for his commitment and dedication in sourcing hundreds of images, and his keen eye in proof-reading. Thanks, too, go to Tim Hounsome at Biocensus and Jess Chappell at the RSPB for their assistance with the status and legislation section; to Mark Balman at Birdlife International for his help in preparing the distribution maps; and to Dani López Velasco for his comments on some key identification issues. We also thank Robert Kirk, Publisher, Field Guides & Natural History, at Princeton University Press, for his encouragement and help throughout this project.

The production of this book would not have been possible without the generous support of the many photographers who kindly supplied their images. In total, 3,298 images are featured, representing the work of 251 photographers. Collating these images proved to be a monumental task and we would like to express our gratitude to Marc Guyt and Roy de Haas at the Agami photo agency in the Netherlands (agami.nl) for their invaluable help in this process.

A number of photographers generously provided access to their entire portfolio of images. Their work is featured extensively throughout the book and their skill is clear to see. All of them spend many hours with a camera, using their technical expertise, extensive local knowledge and understanding of wild birds in pursuit of the perfect picture. We particularly thank Martin Bennett, who travels widely in search of birds and is out in the field almost daily studying the wildlife of the New Forest; Roger and Liz Charlwood (worldwildlifeimages.com); Mark Darlaston, whose special expertise is in seabirds; Greg and Yvonne Dean (worldwildlifeimages.com), Michael McKee (michaelmckee.co.uk), who enjoys photographing his local wildlife but also travels widely in search of rare birds; and Marcus Varesvuo (facebook.com/markus.varesvuo), an award-winning photographer from Finland whose photographic artistry is highlighted in several books.

The contribution of every photographer is gratefully acknowledged and each image is listed in this section, together with the photographer's initials, as follows (images sourced via Agami are indicated with an ^A after the photographer's initials):

Andrew Adams (andrewa.zenfolio.com) [AA]; Andrew M Allport [AMA]; Jim Almond (shropshirebirder.co.uk) [JAl]; Amar-Singh HSS [A-S HSS]; John Anderson (pbase.com/crail_birder) [JAn]; Tormod Amundsen (biotope.no) [TA]; Dave Appleton [DA]; Jem Babbington [JBa]; Danny Bales [DBa]; Sue Barth [SB]; Bill Baston/Agami [BB^A]; Roy & Marie Battell (moorhen.me.uk) [RMB]; Sam Bayley [SBa]; Tom Beeke [TB]; Ken Behrens [KB]; Amir Ben Dov (gull-research.org) [ABD]; Martin Bennett [MB]; Alex Berryman [AB]; Richard Bonser (rothandb.blogspot.co.uk) [RB]; Han Bouwmeester/Agami [HB^A]; Colin Bradshaw [CB]; Dermot Breen (dermotbreen.blogspot.co.uk) [DBre]; Dave Bryan [DBry]; Simon Buckell [SBu]; John Burnside [JBu]; butterflyonmyshoulder.ca [B.ca]; John Caddick (johncaddick.co.uk) [JCa]; Mark Carmody (flickr.com/photos/drcarmo) [MCa]; John K Cassady (jkcassady.com) [JKC]; Graham Catley (pewit.blogspot.co.uk) [GC]; Mikael Champion [MCh]; Keith Chapman [KC]; Roger & Liz Charlwood (worldwildlifeimages.com) [RLC]; Trevor Codlin [TC]; Pete Coe [PC]; David Cooper [DCoo]; John Cooper [JCo]; Daniel Couch (flickr.com/photos/25915567@N00) [DCou]; D Cuddon [DCu]; Stephen Daly (andalucianguides.com) [SDa]; Mike Danzenbaker/

CREDITS

Agami [MDan^A]; Mark Darlaston [MDar]; Tony Davison [TDa]; Kit Day (kitday-uk.com) [KD]; Roy de Haas/Agami [RdH^A]; Raymond De Smet [RDS]; Greg & Yvonne Dean (worldwildlifeimages.com) [GYD]; Jaap Denee/Agami [JD^A]; Iosto Doneddu (flickr.com/photos/38480380@N05) [ID]; Adrian Drummond-Hill [AD-H]; Kevin Du Rose [KDR]; Tony Duckett [TDu]; Steve Duffield [SDu]; Matt Eade [ME]; Dean Eades (Birdmad.com) [DE]; Graham Ekins (flickr.com/photos/graham_ekins_world_wildlife) [GE]; Ralph Eldridge (lightrae.ca) [RE]; Ivan Ellison [IE]; Ashley Fisher [AF]; Ian Fisher [IFi]; Charlie Fleming (parrotletsuk.typepad.com/wldlife_in_a_suburban_gar) [CF]; Richard Frèze [RF]; Steven Fryer (reservoirbirder.blogspot.co.uk) [SF]; Ian Fulton (pbase.com/ianfulton) [IFu]; Steve Gantlett (sgbirdandwildlifephotos.co.uk) [SG]; George Gay [GG]; Hans Gebuis/Agami [HGeb^A]; Hans Germeraad/Agami [HGer^A]; Chris Gibbins (gull-research.org) [CG]; Doug Gochfeld (flickr.com/photos/29840397@N08) [DG]; Lee Gregory [LG]; Antonio Gutiérrez [AG]; Pablo Gutiérrez Varga [PGV]; Marc Guyt/Agami [MG^A]; Marlin Harris [MH]; Hugh Harrop (hughharropwildlifephotography.blogspot.com) [HH]; Russell Hayes (birdmanbirds.blogspot.co.uk) [RHa]; Jeffrey Hazell [JH]; David Hemmings/Agami [DH^A]; Brian Henderson [BH]; Ron Hindhaugh (flickr.com/photos/16309940@N05) [RHi]; Michael Daniel Ho (MichaelDanielHo.com) [MDH]; Mike Hook (flickr.com/photos/58239862@N02) [MHo]; Tim Hounsome [TH]; Richard Howard [RHo]; Jean-Claude Jamoulle [J-CJ]; Garry Jenkins [GJE]; Tom Johnson [TJ]; Gareth Jones (pixelbirds.co.uk) [GJo]; Steve Kolbe [SK]; Maxim Koshkin [MK]; Hannu Koskinen [HK]; Paul Lawrence [PL]; Vincent Legrand/Agami [VL^A]; Tony Leukering (flickr.com/photos/tony_leukering) [TL]; Wil Leurs/Agami [WL^A]; Martin Lofgren (wildbirdgallery.com) [ML]; James Lowen (pbase.com/james_lowen) [JL]; Bruce Mactavish [BM]; Michael Malpass [MMa]; Phil Mann (flickr.com/photos/46796989@N02) [PMa]; Karel Mauer/Agami [KM^A]; James McCormick [JM]; Michael Mckee (michaelmckee.co.uk) [MMc]; Arnold Meijer/Agami [AM^A]; David Monticelli/Agami [DM^A]; Galicia Monticelli [GM]; Nial Moores [NM]; Denzil Morgan (pinterest.com/janeymo50/denzil-morgan-photography) [DM]; Pete Morris/Agami [PMo^A]; Tomi Muukkonen/Agami [TM^A]; Jerry O'Brien [JO'B]; Daniele Occhiato/Agami [DO^A]; János Oláh (sakertour.com) [JO]; Rob Olivier/Agami [RO^A]; Arie Ouwerkerk/Agami [AO^A]; Vincent Palomares (oiseaux.net/photos/vincent.palomares) [VP]; José M Pantaleón [JMP]; John Pelechaty (flickr.com/photos/johnpelechaty) [JPe]; Jari Peltomäki/Agami [JPel^A]; Joe Pender (wwwsapphirepelagics.blogspot.co.uk) [JPen]; Yoav Perlman [YP]; Christopher Plummer (pbase.com/cplummer) [CP]; Jeff Poklen [JPo]; Seppo Pollanen [SP]; Mike Pope [MP]; Brian Rafferty (flickr.com/photos/brianrafferty) [BR]; Rob Riemer/Agami [RR^A]; George Reszeter (birdphotography.co.uk) [GRe]; Ghislain Riou (oiseaux.net/photos/ghislain.riou/photos.html) [GRi]; Dave Roach [DR]; Laurie Ross [LR]; Juan Sagardia Pradera [JSP]; Ran Schols/Agami [RS^A]; Reint Jakob Schut/Agami [RJS^A]; Ray Scott [RSc]; Will Scott [WS]; Glyn Sellors (glynsellorsphotography.com) [GS]; Dubi Shapiro/Agami [DS^A]; Tom Shevlin (wildlifesnaps.com) [TS]; Brian Small/Agami [BSm^A]; Dave Smallshire [DSm]; Bryan J Smith [BJS]; Steve Smith (birdingpooleharbourandbeyond.blogspot.co.uk) [SS]; Walter Soestbergen/Agami [WS^A]; Laurens Steijn/Agami [LS^A]; Robert Still [RSti]; Richard Stonier (birdsonline.co.uk) [RSto]; Brian Sullivan [BSu]; Andy & Gill Swash (worldwildlifeimages.com) [AGS]; Tom Tams [TTam]; Paul Tatner [PT]; Tim Taylor (wildimaging.co.uk) [TTay]; Marc Thibault [MT]; August Thomasson (augustthomasson.weebly.com) [AT]; Roger Tidman [RTi]; David Tipling (davidtipling.photoshelter.com) [DT]; Ralph Todd [RTo]; Chris Upson [CU]; Mitchell Vanbeekum (mitchvanbeekum.com) [MV]; Arnoud van den Berg [AvdB]; Jacques van der Neut [JVDN^A]; Harvey van Diek/Agami [HvD^A]; Menno van Duijn/Agami [MvD^A]; Paul van Hoof (paulvanhoof.nl) [PvH]; Chris van Rijswijk/Agami [CvR^A]; Colin Vanner [CV]; Markus Varesvuo/Wild Wonders (facebook.com/markus.varesvuo) [MVa]; Alex Vargas/Agami [AV^A]; Martijn Verdoes/Agami [MV^A]; Mike Watson (birdquest-tours.com) [MW]; Ian N White (flickr.com/photos/ian_white) [INW]; Kristin Wilmers/Agami [KW^A]; Wim Wilmers/Agami [WW^A]; Peter J Wilson [PJW]; Rob Wilson (robwilsonphotos.co.uk) [RWi]; Phil Winter (flickr.com/photos/philwinter) [PW]; Michelle & Peter Wong [MPW]; Roger Wyatt [RWy] and Steve Young (birdsonfilm.smugmug.com) [SY].

A number of images have been sourced through the generous terms of the Creative Commons Attribution-ShareAlike 2.0 Generic license. These are indicated by "/CC" after the photographer's name in the list. Other images sourced via the photographic agencies FLPA (flpa-images.co.uk) and Shutterstock (shutterstock.com) are credited in full.

The following codes are used: M = male; F = female; Juv = juvenile; Imm = immature; 1w = 1st-winter (*etc.*); 1s = 1st-summer (*etc.*); non-br = non-breeding; Ad = adult; spr = spring; sum = summer; aut = autumn; win = winter; (st) = standing/perched; (sw) = swimming; (fl) = flying (up = upperwing; un = underwing); (h) = head.

Cover: **Robin** [DT].

Title page: **Barn Owl** [BR].

INTRODUCTION **p8: Swans** both [AGS]; **Geese** (sw) [MB], (fl) [GYD]; **Shelduck** (sw) [HH], (fl) [DT]; **Ducks (dabbling)** M (sw) [AGS], (fl) [MVa], F (fl) [AOᴬ]; **Ducks (diving)** M (sw) [DOᴬ], (fl) [HH], F (fl) [MVa]; **Ducks (sea)** all [HH]; **Cormorants** (sw) [RdHᴬ], (fl) [AGS]; **Divers** (sw) [RSto], (fl) [HH]; **Grebes** (sw) [MB], (fl) [RScᴬ]. **p9: Herons** (st) [AGS], (fl) [DT]; **Bitterns** (h) [DT]; **Egrets** (st) [AGS], (fl) [HH]; **Spoonbills** (st) [HH], (fl) [MVa]; **Ibises** (h) [AGS]; **Cranes** (st) [HBᴬ], (fl) [HH]; **Storks** (h) [DOᴬ], (fl) [AGS]; **Gannet** [HH]; **Shearwaters** [HH]; **Storm Petrels** [MDar]; **Auks** (sw) [HH], (fl) [AGS]; **Gulls (larger)** all [AGS]; **Gulls (smaller)** (st) [MVa], (fl) [RdHᴬ]; **Terns** (st) [RE], (fl) [AGS]; **Skuas** (st) [HH], (fl) [MDar]. **p10: Snipe** [HH]; **Plovers (smaller)** (st) [HH], (fl) [MVa]; **Plovers (larger)** (st) [DOᴬ], (fl) [DOᴬ]; **Stone-curlew** [GYD]; **Sandpipers** [AGS]; **'Peeps'** both [HH]; **Waders (larger)** (st) [MB], (fl) [JPelᴬ]; **Curlews/Godwits** (st) [MB], (h) [AGS]; **Avocet** (st) [DT]; **Stilt** (h) [HH]; **Oystercatcher** (st) [AGS]; **Turnstone** (h) [HH]; **Phalaropes** both [HH]; **Pratincoles** (fl) [RScᴬ]; **Coursers** (st) [MMc]; **Moorhen & Coot** both [AGS]; **Rails** [DT]; **Crakes** [CvRᴬ]; **Corncrake** [MW]. **p11: Eagles** [HH]; **Kites** [RScᴬ]; **Osprey** [MVa]; **Harriers** [DOᴬ]; **Buzzards** (fl) [AGS], (st) [HBᴬ]; **Hawks** (fl) [MVa], (st) [HH]; **Falcons** (fl) [HH], (st) [RJSᴬ]; **Cuckoos** (fl) [DT], (st) [MB]; **Owls** [JPelᴬ]; **Nightjars** (fl) [DT], (st) [MB]; **Swifts** [DT]; **Swallows** [RScᴬ]; **Pheasants** [DT]; **Grouse** [Giedriius/Shutterstock]; **Partridges** [AGS]; **Bustards** [MVa]. **p12: Kingfishers** [DOᴬ]; **Parakeets** [AGS]; **Doves** [AGS]; **Pigeons** [AGS]; **Bee-eaters** [HH]; **Rollers** [AGS]; **Sandgrouse** [MDanᴬ]; **Hoopoe** [HH]; **Oriole** [MGᴬ]; **Woodpeckers** [MB]; **Wryneck** [MB]; **Jay** [DT]; **Crows** (fl) [AGS], (st) [Erni/Shutterstock]; **Magpie** [AGS]; **Shrikes** [MVa]. **p13: Larks** [AGS]; **Pipits** [MVa]; **Wagtails** [MB]; **Dipper** [DT]; **Wren** [MB]; **Accentors** [HH]; **Starlings** [MB]; **Thrushes** [AGS]; **Nuthatches** [GYD]; **'Creepers'** [HH]; **Waxwings** [HH]; **Chats** [AGS]; **Warblers ('reed')** [DT]; **Warblers (other)** [AGS]; **Crests** [HH]; **Flycatchers** [MB]; **Tits** [HH]; **Sparrows** [MB]; **Finches** [MB]; **Buntings** [DOᴬ].

WILDFOWL **p14: Swans** all [AGS]; **Geese** (skein) [HH], **Greylags** [MB], **Canada** [AGS]; **Shelduck** (sw) [HH], (fl) [JPelᴬ]. **p15: Garganey** [DOᴬ]; **Shoveler** [MDanᴬ]; **Gadwall** [MB]; **Merganser** [HH]; **Tufted Duck** [AGS]; **Goldeneye** [DT]; **Mallard** [AGS]. **p16: Mallard** Juv [MVa], M [AGS], M (eclipse) [DT], F [DT]; **Cinnamon Teal** both [Richard Seeley/Shutterstock]; **Trumpeter Swan** [MVa]; **Ross's Goose** [MVᴬ]; **Bar-headed Goose** [AGS]; **Emperor Goose** [Bildagentur Zoonar GmbH/Shutterstock]. **p17: Mute Swan** (sw) [DT], others [AGS]. **p18: Bewick's Swan** (flock) [HH], Ad (h) & (sw) [AGS]; **Tundra Swan** [Paul Reeves Photography/Shutterstock]; **Whooper Swan** [AGS]. **p19: Mixed flock** [HH]; **Whooper** Ad [DOᴬ], Juv (h) [AGS]; **Bewick's Swan** Juv (heads) both [AGS]. **p20: Mute Swan** Ad (up) [AGS], (un) [DT], Imm [MB]; **Bewick's Swan** Imm [AGS], Ad [DT]; **Whooper Swan** [RdHᴬ]. **p21: White-fronted Goose** Juv [HH], Ad (un) [MVa], (up) [HH]; **Pink-footed Goose** both [DT]; **Bean Goose** (un) [HH], (up) [MVa]; **Greylag Goose** (un) [HH], (up) [MVa]; **Barnacle Goose** (un) [MVa], (up) [MVa]; **Brent Goose** both [DT]; **Snow Goose** [HH]; **Greater Canada Goose** [AGS]. **p22: Greater Canada Goose** (fl) [GYD], (skein) [MVa], (sw) [HH], (h) [AGS]; **Cackling Goose** (sw) [BSmᴬ]. **p23: Todd's** [BH]; **Lesser** [HH]; **Atlantic** [AGS]; **Richardson's** (inset) [AGS] (sw) [BSmᴬ]; **Ridgway's** (sw) [DT]. **p24: Brent Goose** (flock) [DT], (fl) [RScᴬ], *bernicla* [AOᴬ]. **p25: Brent Goose** *hrota* Ad [HH], Juv [HH]; *nigricans* [AOᴬ]; *bernicla* [MvDᴬ]; **Red-breasted Goose** (st) & (fl) [DT]. **p26: Barnacle Goose** (skein) [AGS], (fl) & (flock) [DT]. **p27: Greylag Goose** all [HH]. **p28: Bean Goose** Ad (st) & (sit) [HH], (fl) [MVa]; **Tundra** (h) [MVa], **Taiga** (h) [MVa]; **Pink-footed Goose** (h) [DT]. **p29: Pink-footed Goose** Ad (fl) [DT], [others HH]. **p30: White-fronted Goose** Greenland [DT], others [HH]. **p31: Snow Goose** (fl) & Ad white [HH], dark [Dennis W Donohue/Shutterstock]; **Lesser W-f Goose** Ad (st) [MVa], (h) [HGebᴬ], Juv (h) [HH]; **White-fronted Goose** (heads) both [HH]. **p32: Shelduck** M (st) [MGᴬ], (fl-un) [AGS], (fl-up) [JPelᴬ], Juv [DOᴬ]. **p33: Egyptian Goose** Ad (fl) [AGS], (st) [Maciej Olszewski/Shutterstock], Grey (h) [Tristram Brelstaff/CC], Juv (inset) [Charles Sharp/CC]; **Ruddy Shelduck** M [DOᴬ], F [HH]. **p34: Shelduck** [DT]; **Mallard** M [MVa], F [AOᴬ]; **Shoveler** M [DOᴬ], F [MVa]; **Pintail** M [JPelᴬ], F [MVa]; **Garganey** both [DOᴬ]; **Teal** M [DOᴬ], F [MVa]; **R-b Merganser** M [HH], F [MVa]; **Goosander** M [DT], F [MVa]; **Gadwall** M [AB], F [RTi]; **Pochard** M [JPelᴬ], F [Maciej Olszewski/Shutterstock]; **Wigeon** M [RScᴬ], F [RTi]; **B-w Teal** both [MDanᴬ]; **Am Wigeon** M [AGS], F [MDH]. **p35: Smew** both [MVa]; **Surf Scoter** [MDanᴬ]; **Velvet Scoter** both [MVa]; **Goldeneye** both [MVa]; **Long-tailed** both [HH]; **King Eider** M & F [HH], 1wM [MVa]; **Eider** M & F [HH], 1wM [MvDᴬ]; **Ferruginous Duck** [JPelᴬ]; **Tufted Duck** both [MGᴬ]; **Scaup** both [MVa]. **p36: Teal** [DT]; **Shoveler** (fl) [MDanᴬ], (st) [DOᴬ]; **Mallard** (fl) [Ana Gram/Shutterstock], (st) [MVa]; **Pintail** (fl) [MVa], (st) [CvRᴬ]; **Gadwall** both [MVa]. **p37: Wigeon** F (fl) [AGS], (Dec) [RScᴬ], (Mar) [DOᴬ], M (fl) [AOᴬ], (May/Oct) [DT], (Nov/Apr) [RdHᴬ]. **p38: Mallard** F (fl) [AOᴬ], (sw) [HH], M (fl) [MVa], (Jun/Sep) & (Oct/May) [AGS]. **p39: Shoveler** M (fl) [DT], (h) [Steve Byland/Shutterstock], (May/Aug) [DT], (Sep/Apr) [HH], F (fl) [AGS], (sw) [HH]. **p40: Gadwall** (fl) M & F [RTi], (sw) [AGS], (May/Sep) [HBᴬ], (Oct/Apr) [AGS]. **p41: Pintail** F (fl) [MVa], (sw) [AGS], M (fl) [JPelᴬ], M (h) [HH], M (sw) [AGS]. **p42: Teal** pair (st) [HGerᴬ], F (fl) [MVa], (sw) [HH], M (fl) [DT], (sw) [HH], (inset) [AGS]. **p43: Garganey** M (fl) [DOᴬ], (h) [HH], (sw) [DT], (inset) [DT], F (fl) [DOᴬ], (sw) [HH]. **p44: Am Wigeon** F (sw) [MMc], (fl-un) [MDanᴬ], (fl-up) [MDH], M (fl-up) [AGS], (sw) [HH], 1wM (fl-up) [MDanᴬ]; **Wigeon** F (h) [DOᴬ], (fl-un) [MVa], (wing) [AGS]; **Black Duck** both [AGS]; **Mallard** (wing) [DOᴬ]. **p45: G-w Teal** M (sw) [HH], (fl) [MVa]; **Teal** M (fl) [DT], F/Juv (wing) [MVa], F (h) [DT]; **B-w Teal** F (sw) [AGS], (h) [MvDᴬ], M (sw) [HH], F/Juv (wing) [MDanᴬ]; **Baikal Teal** M (sw) [RdHᴬ], F/Juv (wing) [TB], F (h) [Wang LiQiang/Shutterstock]; **Garganey** F/Juv (wing) [DOᴬ], F (h) [HH]. **p46: R-c Pochard** M (fl) [MVa], (h) [Timothey Kosachev/Shutterstock], (sw) [DT]; F (fl) [JMP], (sw) [DT]. **p47: Mandarin** F (fl) [MB], (sw) [Maciej Olszewski/Shutterstock]; M (fl)

[MB], (st) [AGS]; **Wood Duck** F [AGS], M [MG^]. **p48: Ruddy Duck** F (fl) [MDan^], F (sw) [AGS]; M (fl) [KB], M (sw) [MV^], (inset) [Tom Reichner/Shutterstock]; **W-h Duck** both [AGS]. **p49: Pochard** F (fl) [Maciej Olszewski/Shutterstock], (sw) [DO^]; M (fl) [JPel^], (h) [RdH^]; Juv [HH]. **p50: Tufted Duck** (inset) [WL^]; M (fl) [MG^], (Jun-Oct) [MVa], (Sep-May) [AO^]; F (fl) [MG^], (sw) & (h) [AGS]. **p51: Scaup** (flock), M (fl) & F (fl) all [MVa]; F (Mar-Sep) (h) [HH], (Sep-Mar) [AM^]; M (Sep-Jun) [HH]; ImmM [MVa]; Juv (h) [DT]. **p52: Lesser Scaup** M (top left & bottom left) [HH], (bottom right) [AGS]; F (sw) [DT], (h) [HH]; **Scaup** (h) [HH], (wing) [MVa], (sw) [HH]; **Tufted Duck** (h) [MVa]. **p53: R-n Duck** M (fl) [Rck_953/Shutterstock], (sw) M & F [HH]; **Tufted Duck** (wing) [MG^]; **Ferruginous Duck** (fl-un) [Webloqiq/Shutterstock], (fl-up) [JPel^]; (st) both [HH]. **p54: Bufflehead, Hooded Merganser, Redhead, Pochard, Canvasback** all [HH]. **p55: Mallard x Pintail** [TJ], **Shoveler x Gadwall** [MDan^], **Wigeon x Am Wigeon** [DBa], **Tufted x Pochard** [TDu], **Tufted x Ferruginous** [AT], **Pochard x Ferruginous** [CP], **Tufted x Ring-necked** [SY], **Scaup x Tufted** [AGS]. **p56: Goldeneye** (fl) M & F [MVa], F (sw) [HH], M (sw) [AGS]. **p57: Smew** (fl) M & F [MVa], F (sw) [MMc], M (sw) [WS^]. **p58: R-b Merganser** (inset) [AO^]; F (fl) [MVa], (sw) [HH]; M (fl) [HH], (sw) [DO^]. **p59: Goosander** (inset) [JCa], others [MVa]. **p60: Long-tailed Duck** Juv (fl) [DT], others [HH]. **p61: Long-tailed Duck** (flock with scoter) [MVa], others [HH]. **p62: Velvet Scoter** M (sw) [MMc], others [MVa]. **p63: Common Scoter** all [MVa]. **p64: Eider** 1s [MVa], others [HH]. **p65: Eider** Nearctic (h) [DH^], others [HH]. **p66: King Eider** all [HH]; **Steller's Eider** [HH]. **p67: Goldeneye** F (wing) [MVa], others [HH]; **Barrow's Goldeneye** M (sw) [HH], others [MVa]; **Steller's Eider** all [HH]. **p68: Surf Scoter** M [HH], (h) & (fl) [MDan^]; F [HH], (fl) [MDan^]; **Harlequin Duck** F (fl) [MMc], F (sw) [HH], M (fl) [MvD^], M (st) [MMc]. **p69: W-w Scoter** *deglandi* all [HH]; *stejnegeri* 1wM [TA], F (h) [DCo]; **Black Scoter** all [HH]; **Velvet Scoter** both [MVa]; **Common Scoter** M [MVa], F [AGS].

CORMORANTS, DIVERS & GREBES p70: Cormorant (st) [TTay], (h) [AGS]; **Shag** (fl) & (dive) [HH], (leap) [AO^]. **p71: R-t Diver** Ad sum & (fl) [HH], Juv [DO^], Ad win [RSto], (moulting) [DT]; **G C Grebe** Pair [AGS], (fl) [RSc^], Juv [Maciej Olszewski/Shutterstock], Ad win [MB]. **p72: Cormorant** Imm & (fl-un) [HH], Ad (fl-up) [AGS]; **Shag** all [HH]; **G C Grebe** Ad (fl) [RSc^], (sw) [HvD^]; **R-n, Slavonian & B-n Grebes** all [HH]; **Little Grebe** [DO^]. **p73: R-t Diver** Ad sum (fl-un) & (fl-up) [HH], win (fl) [DO^], (sw) [RSc^]; **G N Diver** win (fl) [MH], sum (fl) & (sw) [HH]; **B-t Diver** sum (fl-un) & (fl-up) [MVa], win (fl) [RSc], (sw) [AO^]; **W-b Diver** Ad sum (fl) [MVa], win (fl) [PC], (sw) [DSm]; **Pacific Diver** (fl) [MV^]. **p74: Shag** Ad sum (fl), (h), (sw) & Juv (sw) all [HH], Ad non-br [MDar], Juv (st) [KM^]; **Cormorant** Juv (h) [HH], (sw) [RdH^]. **p75: Cormorant** Ad (h) & (st) [MvD^], (fl) [AGS]; Ad non-br [DO^]; Imm [Erni/Shutterstock]; (inset) *sinensis* [DT], *carbo* [MDar]. **p76: R-t Diver** (fl) & 1w [DO^], Ad sum [HH], 1w [DO^], Ad win [RSto]. **p77: B-t Diver** (fl) [RSc], 1w [GYD], 1w [AO^], Ad win [CvR^]. **p78: G N Diver** (fl) [MH], others [HH]. **p79: Pacific Diver** [BJS]; **B-t Diver** [CvR^]; **W-b Diver** Ad sum [Bering Land Bridge National Preserve/CC], 1w [HH]; **G N Diver** [HH]. **p80: G C Grebe** Juv [Maciej Olszewski/Shutterstock], 1w [DT], Adults both [HH]. **p81: R-n Grebe** Juv [HH], Ad win [DO^], Ad sum [MvD^]. **p82:** Black-necked Juv [Bildagentur Zoonar GmbH/Shutterstock], Ad sum [RSc^], Ad/1w [DO^], (h) [HH]; **Slavonian Grebe** (h) [HH]. **p83: Slavonian Grebe** Juv (h) [MVa], Ad sum [MvD^], Ad/1w [HvD^], (h) [HH]; **B-n Grebe** both [HH]. **p84: Little Grebe** Juv (h) [Erni/Shutterstock], (sw) [AGS], Ad/1w [MVa], Ad sum [MB]. **p85: D-c Cormorant** (h) [AGS], Ad [HH], Imm [KB]; **Cormorant** [DO^]; **Shag** [HH]; **P-b Grebe** 1w [DO^], Ad sum [DT].

SEABIRDS p86: Gannet (colony) & (fl) [HH], (sw) [MDar]. **p87: Cory's Shearwater** [HH]; **Fulmar** all [HH]; **Sooty Shearwater** [DM]; **Manx Shearwater** [MDar]; **Great B-b Gull** [AGS], (sw) [HH]; **Storm Petrel** [MDar]. **p88: Gannet** Ad (fl-up) [AGS], others [HH]. **p89: Gannet** all [HH]. **p90: Fulmar** (fl-up) [AGS], others [HH]. **p91: Sooty Shearwater** (fl) top left 4 birds [MDar], others [HH]. **p92: Great Shearwater** (up) [DT], (un) [MG^]; **Cory's Shearwater** both [HH]; **Scopoli's Shearwater** both [DO^]. **p93: Great & Cory's Shearwaters** [DO^]. **p94: Manx Shearwater** (flock) & (up) [MDar], (side) & (un) [MDan^]; **Balearic Shearwater** all [MDar]; **Macaronesian Shearwater** (up) [TJ], (un) [JSP]; **Yelkouan Shearwater** [DO^]. **p95: Manx Shearwater** [MG^]; **Balearic Shearwater** [MDar]. **p96: Storm Petrel** (bottom left) [DM^], others [MDar]; **Leach's Petrel** (un) [VL^], (up) [SY]; **Wilson's Petrel** (up) [MG^], (un) [HH]. **p98: Black-browed Albatross** Ad (up) [MG^], (un) [DT], Imm [MG^]; **Yellow-nosed** Ad [MG^]; Gannet [HH]. **p99: Magnificent Frigatebird** Ad [CvR^], Juv [AGS]; **Ascension Frigatebird** [MG^]; **Tropicbird** [AGS]. **p100: Fulmar** [HH]; **Desertas Petrel** [MVa]; **Zino's Petrel** [JSP]; **Fea's Petrel** all [HH]; **Capped Petrel** both [MDan^]; **Frigate Petrel** [RB]. **p101: Madeira Petrel** both [HH]; **Swinhoe's Petrel** [RB]; **Leach's Petrel** [TJ]; **Black-bellied Storm** (fl-up) [Andrew M Allport/Shutterstock], (fl-un) [MG^].

GULLS & TERNS p102: Common Tern both [HH]; **Black Tern** [MDar]. **p103: Herring Gull** 1w (fl) [HH], Ad sum (st) [MVa], others [AGS]; **Great B-b Gull** [AGS]; **Little Tern** [MVa]. **p104: Herring Gull** Juv & 1s [AGS], 1w & 2w [HH]; **Black-h Gull** Juv (fl) [AO^], 1w & 1s (fl) [DO^], others [AGS]. **p105: Herring Gull** 3w & 3s [HH], others [AGS]; **Black-h Gull** 2w [DO^], Ad win [AGS], Ad sum (fl) [RdH^], (st) [HH]. **p106: Black-h Gull** (fl) 1w [DO^], Ad sum [RdH^], Ad win [HH], (h) Ad win [AGS], 1s [MVa]; Juv [AGS]; (st) 1w [DO^], Ad sum [MVa]. **p107: Mediterranean Gull** (fl) 1w [SY], Ad sum [MVa], Ad win [DO^], 2w [SP]; Juv [CvR^]; (h) Ad moulting to win [AGS], Ad sum [HH], Ad win [AGS]. **p108: Kittiwake** Juv (fl) [AGS], others [HH]. **p109: Sabine's Gull** 1s & Ad win [MDar], Ad sum [DM], Juv [RJS^]; (sw) Juv [MDar], Ad [BB^], (h) [Crossley ID Guide/CC]. **p110: Little Gull** (fl) Ad sum [HH], Ad win [MvD^], 1w-up [MDan^], 1w-un [JH]; (st) Juv & Ad sum [MVa]; (sw) 1w & Ad win [HH]. **p111: Ross's Gull** (fl) 1w [SY], Ad sum [BM], Ad win (un) & (up) [HH], 1w (sw) [MMc], Ad win (st) [SY]; **Ivory Gull** (fl) Ad [MG^], 1w [SY]; (st) both [MW]. **p112: Laughing Gull** (fl) 2s [HH], Ad win [MDar], 1w [SY], (st) all [AGS]; (h) [HH]. **p113: Bonaparte's Gull** Ad win & 1w [BSu], (st) [HH], (h) [Bruce MacQueen/Shutterstock]; **Black-h Gull** [AGS], (wing) [DT]; **Franklin's Gull** (st) [MMc], others [BSu]. **p114: Common Gull** *heinei* [YP]; (h) top [DT], bottom [HH]; (st) [DT]. **p115: Common Gull** (fl) Juv [MVa], 1w & 2w [AGS], Ad sum [HH]; (st) 2w & 1w [HH], Juv [CvR^]. **p116: Ring-billed Gull** (st) Ad win & 2w [HH], 1w [VL^]; (h) [HH]; (fl) Ad win [HH], 1w [MDan^]; **Common Gull** (wings) both [HH], Ad win (h) [DT], Ad sum & 2w (h) [HH], (st) [AGS].

p117: Little Gull 1w (un) [MHo], 1w (up) [HH], Juv (un) [MVa], Juv (up) [DT], Ad win [MDar]; **Sabine's Gull** 1s [MDar], 1w [TDu], Juv [RJS^]; **Kittiwake** 1w (un) [AGS], 1w (up) & Ad win [HH]; **Black-h Gull** Ad win [HH], 1w [DO^]; **Mediterranean Gull** 2w (wing) [MVa], Ad win [JPel^], 1w [SY]; **Common Gull** 1w & Ad win [AGS], 2w (wing) [HH]. **p118: Glaucous Gull** 3w (fl) [MVa]; all others [HH]. **p119: Lesser B-b Gull** (fl) [MDar], (st) *graellsii* & *intermedius* [AGS]; **Great B-b Gull** (fl) [HH], (st) [AGS]; **Herring Gull** (fl) [HH], (st) [AGS]; **Yellow-l Gull** (fl) [JAI], (st) [AO^]; **Caspian Gull** (fl) [DO^], (st) [GYD]. **p120: Lesser B-b** & **Herring Gulls** [AGS]; **Caspian Gull** [AM^]; **Yellow-l Gull** [DO^]; **American Herring Gull** [MDan^]; **Thayer's Gull** [MMc]; others [HH]. **p121: Lesser B-b, Herring** & **American Herring Gulls** [AGS]; **Yellow-l Gull** [DO^]; **Caspian Gull** [MMc]; **Thayer's Gull** [MDan^]; **Slaty-backed** & **Glaucous-winged Gulls** [PMo^]; others [HH]. **p122: Yellow-l Gull** all [DO^]; **Herring Gull** (fl) [PT]; **Caspian Gull** (fl) [CG], (st) [ABD]; **Great B-b Gull** (fl) & (st) [HH]; **Lesser B-b Gull** (fl) [JKC], (st) [SY]. **p123: Yellow-l Gull** (fl) [DO^], (st) [AG]; **Herring Gull** both [HH]; **Caspian Gull** (fl) [SY], (st) [CG]; **Great B-b Gull** (fl) [HH], (st) [AGS]; **Lesser B-b Gull** (fl) [SY], (st) [AGS]. **p124: Herring Gull** Juv & 3w [AGS], 2w & Ad sum [HH], (h) [DT], (st) [AGS]. **p125: Herring Gull** *argenteus* (wing) [DT], Juvs [AGS], others [HH]. **p126: Lesser B-b Gull** (fl) 1s [GJo], 2w [SY], Ad sum [MDar], others [AS]. **p127: Lesser B-b Gull** *fuscus* [HK], 2w [BM], others [AGS]. **p128: Great B-b Gull** (fl) 1w & 2w [MDar], 3w & Ad win [HH], (h) [CvR^], (st) [AGS]. **p129: Great B-b Gull** 3w [JPo], 2w & Juv [HH]. **p130: Yellow-l Gull** Ad (fl) [MB], others [DO^]. **p131: Caspian Gull** (fl) 1w [AM^], 2w [CG], 3w [SY], Ad [DO^], (st) [GYD]. **p132: Yellow-l Gull** all [DO^]; **Caspian Gull** (wing) [DO^], (fl-up) [AM^], (st) [CvR^], (tertials) [MMc]; **Herring Gull** (wing) & (fl-side) [HH], (h) & (tertials) [AGS]. **p133: Thayer's Gull** 1w [VL^], Ad win [DM^]; **Kumlien's Gull** all [HH]; **Iceland Gull** 1w & Ad win [HH], 2w [AM^], 3w [MMc]; **Glaucous Gull** Ad win [MG^], others [HH]; **Glaucous-winged Gull** both [MDan^]. **p134: Glaucous Gull** 3w [RTo], others [HH]. **p135: Iceland Gull** 1w & 3w [MMc], others [HH]; **Thayer's Gull** [DM^]. **p136: Iceland Gull** both [HH]; **Kumlien's Gull** all [HH]; **Thayer's Gull** Ad win (fl) [GM], (sw) [MDan^], 1w (fl) [VL^], 1w (st) [MDan^]; **Herring Gull** (wing) [AGS]. **p137: Great Black-headed Gull** 1w (fl) [MVa], 1w (st) [AO^], Ad win [HH], Ad sum [JPel^]; **Slender-billed Gull** Ad sum (fl) [DO^], 1w (fl) [MMc], Ad sum [HH], 1s [DO^]. **p138: Slaty-backed Gull** Ad win [MG^], others [PMo^]; **Glaucous-winged Gull** 1w [PMo^], 3w & Ad win [HH]. **p139: Glaucous-winged Gull** both [MDan^]; **Glaucous Gull** (wing) [HH]; **Slaty-backed Gull** both [MG^]; **Lesser B-b Gull** (wing) [SY]; **Audouin's Gull** Ad sum (st) [DO^], 1s (st) [SS], Juv [TH], others [AGS]. **p140: American Herring Gull** Ad win (h) [DT], others [AGS]; **Herring Gull** Juv [AGS]. **p141: American Herring Gull** 3w [KB], 1w [MDan^]; **Herring Gull** all [HH]; **Vega Gull** all [PMo^]. **p142:** Black Tern [SY], W-w Black Tern [RdH^]. **p143: Black Tern** Ad sum (fl-up) & (fl-un) [MDar], Ad (moult) [MG^], Ad win [MDar], Juv (fl-un) [MVa], *surinamensis* [AGS], Juv (st) [WL^]; **W-w Black Tern** Ad sum (fl-up) & (fl-un) [HH], Ad (moult) & Ad win [RLC], Juv [SY], Juv (st) [RazvanZinica/Shutterstock]. **p144: Common Tern** (fl) 1s & Juv [MDar], Ad sum [HH]; (st) Juv (fresh) [HH], Juv [MG^], Ad sum [RE]. **p145: Arctic Tern** 1s (fl) [MDar], others [HH]. **p146: Roseate Tern** (fl) (un) [MVa], (up) [MVa], (juv) [GS]; (st) Juv (old) [GS], Juv [GS], Ad (st) & (heads) [SY]. **p147: Sandwich Tern** (fl) Ad win [AO^], Juv [DO^]; (st) Juv [DO^], Ad sum [HB^], (h) [WL^]. **p148: Little Tern** (fl) (up) [Georgios Alexandris/Shutterstock], (un) [AGS], Juv [AO^]; **Least Tern** (inset) [AGS]; (st) Juv [GS], Ad sum [TDa]. **p149: Little, Gull-billed, Arctic** & **W-w Black Terns** [HH], **Sandwich Tern** [SY], **Common** & **Whiskered Terns** [AGS], **Roseate** & **Black Terns** [MVa], **Caspian Tern** [DO^]. **p150: Black Tern** [MB], **Whiskered Tern** [MVa], **W-w Black Tern** [SY]. **p151: Whiskered Tern** Ad win (st) [AV^], others [AGS]; **Caspian Tern** Ad sum (fl) & (st) [HH], 1s [RSto]; **Gull-billed Tern** Ad sum (fl) [AO^], Ad win [HH], (st) [DO^]; **Sandwich Tern** Ad sum [SY], Ad win [MDar]. **p152: Elegant Tern** (fl) [DT], (st) [BSm^], (h) [RdH^]; **Lesser Crested Tern** (fl) [AD-H], (st) [KD], (h) [AGS]. **p153: Royal Tern** (st) [Feroze Omardeen/CC], (fl) *albididorsalis* [Hugh Lansdown/Shutterstock], (h) *maxima* sum [AGS], (h) *maxima* win [MMc], (h) *albididorsalis* [VL^]; **Caspian Tern** [HH]; **Cabot's Tern** (st) & (h) [WL^], (fl) [AGS]; **Sandwich Tern** Ad win (h) [WL^], Ad sum (h) [HH], (wing) [SY]. **p154: Forster's Tern** Ad sum (fl) [WL^], Ad win (fl) [KB], (st) [MMc], (h) [AGS]; **Common Tern** (tail) & (h) [HH]; **Aleutian Tern** both [PMo^]. **p155: Sooty Tern** all [MMc]; Bridled Tern (fl) both [TTam], (st) [WS].

SKUAS p156: Arctic Skua (fl) [MvD^]; **Pomarine Skua** Juv [DBre], 1s [LS^]. **p157: Arctic Skua** pale, intermediate & dark [HH], (flock) [MDar]; **Pomarine Skua** 2s [JPen], Ad [LS^]. **p158: Arctic Skua** (fl) [MDar], Juv [KM^], others [HH]. **p159: Pomarine Skua** (fl) [LS^], Ad sum dark and pale [CvR^], (fl) [Erni/Shutterstock], Juv [AO^]. **p160: Long-tailed Skua** Juv [MMc], others [HH]. **p161: Great Skua** (fl) (up) & (un) [HH], (h) [IE], (sw) [MDar]; **South Polar Skua** (fl) [JSP]. **p162: Long-tailed Skua** pale [AO^], dark [CvR^]; **Arctic Skua** pale [AO^], intermediate [MvD^]; **Pomarine Skua** [AO^]; **Great Skua** [IE]. **p163: Long-tailed Skua** pale (un), (up) & intermediate [JPen], dark [SY]; **Arctic Skua** pale [MVa], dark (un) [MDar], (up) [SG]; **Pomarine Skua** all [DBre]; **Great Skua** (up) & (un) [AO^]. **p164: Long-tailed Skua** all [HH]; **Arctic Skua** intermediate (HH), others [MDar]; **Pomarine Skua** (up) & dark [MDan^], (un) [MDar], (side) [LS^]; **Great Skua** all [HH].

AUKS p165: Puffin [Mark Caunt/Shutterstock], **Guillemot** colony [DT]. **p166: Guillemot** (fl) [AGS], Ads (h) [DT], others [HH]. **p167: Razorbill** (inset) [AGS], others [HH]. **p168: Puffin** juv (h) & Adw [RE], others [HH]. **p169: Black Guillemot** Adw (fl) [TS], others [HH]. **p170: Little Auk** win (fl) [TJ], sum (fl) & (st) [GYD], others [HH]. **p171: Black Guillemot** sum [HH], win [TS]; **Puffin** [HH]; **Little Auk** sum [GYD], win [TJ]; **Guillemot** sum (un) & (side) & win [HH], (up) [AGS]; **Razorbill** sum (un) & (side) [HH], (up) [MVa], win [GRi]; **Brunnich's Guillemot** all [HH]. **p172: Brunnich's Guillemot** both [HH]; **Guillemot** [HH]; **Razorbill** [HH]; **Tufted Puffin** (fl) [DM], (sw) [MV^]; **Ancient Murrelet** [MDan^]; **Long-billed Murrlet** [MMc].

WADERS p173: Sanderling Ad win [DT], others [HH], (flock) [MVa]. **p174: Curlew Sandpiper** (fl) [JPel^]; **Little Ringed Plover** (fl) [RSc^]; **Greenshank** (fl) [MVa]; **Common Sandpiper** (st) [AV^]; **Cream-coloured Courser** [Carl Day/Shutterstock]; **Curlew** (h), **Black-tailed Godwit** (h), **Grey Plover** (h), **Curlew Sandpiper** (h), **Greenshank** (h), **Stone-curlew, Oystercatcher, Avocet, Black-winged Stilt** & **Collared Pratincole** all [Erni/Shutterstock].

Bittern [DT]. **p238: herons** [DT]; **storks** [AGS]; **cranes** [HH]; **Glossy Ibis** [AGS]; **Little Bittern** F [DO^A], M [DO^A]; **Night-heron** Juv [MVa], Ad (up) [DO^A], Ad (un) [DO^A]; **Bittern** [DT]; **Grey Heron** [HH]; **Purple Heron** Juv [HH], Ad [MVa]. **p239: White Stork** [AGS]; **Crane** (un) [HH], (side) [HH]; **Black Stork** [RdH^A]; **White Stork** [AGS]; **Great White Egret** [HH]; **Spoonbill** Juv [DO^A], Ad [MVa]; **Little Egret** [HH]; **Cattle Egret** [AGS]; **Squacco Heron** [MG^A]. **p240: Grey Heron** (fl) [HH], Ad (st) [AGS], (h) [MvD^A], Juv [HH]. **p241: Glossy Ibis** (fl) & Ad sum [AGS], Ad win [MMc]; **Purple Heron** (fl) & Ad [HH], Juv [HB^A]. **p242: Bittern** all [DT]. **p243: Little Bittern** all [DO^A]; **Night-heron** Juv & Imm [DO^A], Ad [HH]. **p244: Little Egret** Ad win [MG^A], Ad sum [AGS], (inset) [HH], (fl) juv [DO^A], (fl) (top left) [HH]; **Great White Egret** both [HH]; **Cattle Egret** [HB^A]. **p245: Great White Egret** win [HB^A], sum [HH]. **p246: Cattle Egret** all [AGS]; **Squacco Heron** (fl) [MG^A], Ad win/Imm [DO^A], Ad sum [GYD]. **p247: White Stork** (fl) [AGS], Ad [DO^A]; **Black Stork** (fl) [HH], Juv (h) [HB^A], Ad [AGS]. **p248: Crane** Ad & Juv [HB^A], (fl) [HH]. **p249: Spoonbill** (fl) Juv [DO^A], others [HH]. **p250: Green Heron** Juv [MG^A], 1w [MMc]; **Sandhill Crane** both [MW]; **Bittern** (h) [JPel^A], **American Bittern** [DT]. **p251: Great Blue Heron** Imm [MMc]; **Little Blue Heron** [AGS]; **Little Egret** 1w [HH]; **Snowy Egret** both [AGS].

BUSTARDS p252: Macqueen's Bustard both [AGS]; **Little Bustard** F (st) [MVa], F (fl) [AGS], M (st) [GYD], M (fl) [AO^A]. **p253: Great Bustard** (fl) [MMc], others [MVa].

CRAKES & RAILS p254: Coot (Ad) [MB], (h) [AGS]; **Moorhen** [Abi Warner/Shutterstock]; **Spotted Crake** [MG^A]; **Water Rail** [MB]. **p255: Corncrake** (fl) [JO], Ad (left) [JPel^A], (right) [MW]. **p256: Moorhen** (fl) [MG^A], Juv & Ad [AGS], (inset) [DCou]. **p257: Coot** (fl) [MG^A], Juv & Ad [AGS]. **p258: Water Rail** (inset) & Juv [MVa], Ad [DT]. **p259: Spotted Crake** Juv [TTay], Ad [CvR^A]. **p260: Little Crake** Juv [JD^A], M [AGS], F [MVa]. **p262: Baillon's Crake** Juv [DO^A], Ad [MG^A]. **p261: Sora Rail** 1w [MMc], Ad [AGS]. **p262: Allen's Gallinule** Juv [INW], Ad [DM^A]; **Purple Gallinule** [DM^A]; **American Coot** [HH]; **Coot** [HH].

'GAMEBIRDS' p263: Black Grouse [DT]; **Pheasant** M & F [AGS]; **Grey Partridge** [DT]; **Quail** [MVa]. **p264: Red-legged Partridge** Ad [AGS], Juv [RTi], (fl) [MDH]; **Chukar** [AGS]. **p265: Grey Partridge** (fl-up) [MVa], (fl-un) [DT], Juv [IE], M [CvR^A], F [RSc^A]. **p266: Red Grouse** (fl-up) [BR], (fl-un) [Paul Miguel/FLPA], M [Giedriius/Shutterstock], F [DT]. **p267: Ptarmigan** (fl-up) [MVa], (fl-un) [HH], F sum & M sum [RTo], M transitional [Dave Pressland/FLPA], M win [Paul Hobson/FLPA], F win (h) [MVa], F moult (h) [DT]. **p268: Black Grouse** (inset) [DT], M (fl) & F (fl) [MVa], M (st) [HB^A], F (st) [Lisa Louise Greenhorn/Nature in Stock/FLPA]. **p269: Capercaillie** M (fl) & F (st) [MVa], others [HH]. **p270: Pheasant** M (st) [DT], (h) [AGS], M (fl) [Costas Anton Dumitrescu/Shutterstock], F (st) [DT], F (fl) [Budimir Jevtic/Shutterstock]. **p271: Golden Pheasant** M [Erni/Shutterstock], F [AGS]; **Lady Amherst's Pheasant** M [Erni/Shutterstock], F [J-CJ]. **p272: Quail** (fl) [MVa], (inset left) [HvD^A], (inset right) [HGeb^A], M (st) & F (st) [DO^A].

PIGEONS, DOVES & SANDGROUSE p273: Woodpigeon Ad [HH], Juv [AGS]; **Turtle Dove** [HH]. **p274: Stock Dove** (up) [RSc^A], (un) [DT]; **Woodpigeon** (up) [RSc^A], (un) [AGS]; **Rock Dove/Feral Pigeon** (up) [HH], (un) [GG]; **Collared Dove** (up) [AGS], (un) [RTi]; **Turtle Dove** [RSc^A], (un) [RSc^A]; **Mourning Dove** [TS]; **Rufous Turtle Dove** both [RSc^A]; **Pallas's Sandgrouse** both [MDan^A]. **p275: Feral Pigeon** (inset top and bottom) [AGS], (h) [DT], (fl) [HH]; **Rock Dove** [MMc]. **p276: Woodpigeon** all [AGS]. **p277: Stock Dove** (fl) both [MVa], Juv [MvD^A], Ad (st) [DT]; **Woodpigeon** [RSc^A]. **p278: Collared Dove** (fl-up) [MDan^A], (fl-un) [RTi], M (st) [AGS], Juv (h) [DO^A], F (h) [DT], (tail illustration) [RSti]. **p279: Turtle Dove** (fl) both [RSc^A], Juv (st) [DT], (tail illustration) [RSti]. **p280:** (tail illustrations) [RSti]; **Rufous Turtle Dove** Ad orientalis [RWy], Juv meena [HH]; **Turtle Dove** Ad (h) [AGS], Juv (h) [HH], (wing) [DT]; **Mourning Dove** 1w [MMa], Juv [MG^A].

OWLS & NIGHTJARS p281: Tawny Owl, Nightjar & **Eurasian Eagle-owl** [DT]. **p282: Short-eared Owl** (up) [AGS], (un) [MB]; **Long-eared Owl** both [HH]; **Tawny Owl** both [MB]; **Little Owl** [PW]; **Barn Owl** [DT]; **Snowy Owl** [MVa]; **Red-necked Nightjar** [PvH]; **Nightjar** [DT]; **Common Nighthawk** [TJ], **Egyptian Nightjar** [JBu]. **p283: Barn Owl** (fl) & (st) [DT], dark (inset) both [HH]. **p284: Tawny Owl** (fl) [MB], rufous [MB], grey [PW], Juv [AGS]. **p285: Little Owl** Ad (fl) [PW], Ad (st) [DT], Juv [GYD], (inset) [BB^A]. **p286: Short-eared Owl** (fl) & (inset) [BB^A], (st) [JPel^A]. **p287: Long-eared Owl** all [HH]. **p288: Snowy Owl** F (st) [HH], others [MVa]. **p289: Hawk Owl** (fl) [MVa], (st) [HH]; **Tengmalm's Owl** [MVa]; **Scops Owl** rufous [HH], grey [CvR^A]. **p290: Nightjar** M (fl) & F (fl) [DT], Ad [MB]. **p291: Common Nighthawk** (fl) [BSm^A], (st) [DM^A], **Red-necked Nightjar** (fl) [PvH], (st) [SDa], **Egyptian Nightjar** (fl) [JBu], (st) [AvdB].

BIRDS OF PREY p292: Sparrowhawk [AGS]; **Harris's Hawk** [Kojihirano/Shutterstock]. **p293: Red Kite, Sparrowhawk, Hobby, Raven & Carrion Crow** [AGS]; **Montagu's Harrier** [DT]; **White-tailed Eagle, Buzzard** & **Honey-buzzard** [HH]; **Osprey** [RdH^A]. **p294: White-tailed Eagle** Ad (fl) [DT], Ad (st) & Imm [HH], Juv (fl) [MW], Juv/1w (h) [MVa]. **p295: Golden Eagle** Ad (fl) [HH], Ad (st) [MVa], Juv (fl) [MVa], Imm (st) [CvR^A]. **p296: Golden Eagle** Imm (un x2) & (up) [MVa], Ad [HH]; **White-tailed Eagle** Imm (un) [RR^A], Imm (up) [MVa], Ad & Juv [DT]. **p297: Red Kite** Imm (up) & (un) [AGS], Ad (up) [RSc^A], (un) [RSc^A]; **Black Kite** Imm (up) & (un) & Ad (up) [DO^A], Ad (un) [HH], **Carrion Crow** [AGS], **Buzzard** [AGS], **Marsh Harrier** both [HH]. **p298: Honey-buzzard** Ad (up) [DO^A], Juv (up) [MVa], pale M [DT], pale F & pale and dark Juvs [DO^A], dark M [MMc], dark F [MVa], (flight profile illustrations) [RSti]. **p299: Buzzard** (top left) [RTi], Ad [MVa], Juv & pale Juv [MVa], Imm [AGS]; **Rough-legged Buzzard** F (up) & F (un) & Juv (up) [MVa], Juv (un) [RSc^A], M [JPel^A]; **Osprey** [MVa]. **p300: Osprey** (fl-up) [MVa], (fl-un) [DO^A], Juv (inset) [SY], Ad [MVa], 1s [VL^A]. **p301: Honey-buzzard** Juv (fl) [MVa], others [DO^A], (flight profile illustrations) [RSti]. **p302: Buzzard** (hover) [WW], (fl-up) [SY], Juv (st) [KW^A], others [MVa], (flight profile illustrations) [RSti]. **p303: Rough-legged Buzzard** M (fl) [JPel^A], F (fl) [MVa], Juv (un) [RSc^A], (hover) [KM^A], Juv (up) & (st) [HH], Ad (st) [AO^A], (flight profile illustrations) [RSti]. **p304: Red Kite** Ad (fl-up) & Ad (fl-un) [RSc^A], Juv (fl-un) [AGS], Juv (fl-up) [DT], Juv (st) [HGer^A], Ad (st) [MMc]. **p305: Marsh Harrier** M (fl-up) & M (fl-un) [DT], others [DO^A]. **p306: Hen Harrier** M (un)

[JPel^], M (up) & F (un) [DO^], F (up) & Juv [MVa]; **Marsh Harrier** M (un) [JPel^], M (up) [DT], F (un) [DO^], F (up) [RTi]; **Montagu's Harrier** M (up) [DO^], Juv [SDa], others [MVa]; **Northern Harrier** [MMc]; **Pallid Harrier** M (un) & Juv (un) & Juv (up) [HH], M (up) [LS^], F [KB]. **p307: Hen Harrier** Juv (fl-un) [DO^], Juv (fl-up) [HH], F (fl) [MVa], M (fl) [MB], F (st) [John Hawkins/FLPA], M (st) [Bildagentur Zoonar GmbH/Shutterstock]. **p308: Montagu's Harrier** 1sM (fl) & F (fl-up) [AGS]; M (fl-un) [MB]; M (fl-up), F (fl-un) & F (st) [HH]; Juv (fl) [MDan^]; M (st) [DT]. **p309: Pallid Harrier** (h) [HH]; **Montagu's Harrier** [MVa]; **Hen Harrier** (h) [Malcolm Schuyl/FLPA]; **Pallid Harrier** F (fl) [DO^], Juv (fl) [HH], M (fl) [KB], F (st) [William S Clark/FLPA], M (st) [RLC]. **p310: Black Kite** (fl-un) [DO^], (fl-up) [MVa], (st) [MVa]; **Black-eared Kite** [AGS]; **Northern Harrier** Juv (fl-un) & (fl-up) [MMc], (st) [BSm^], (wing) [MMc]; **Hen Harrier** (wing) [DO^]. **p311: Short-toed Eagle** Ad (fl-left) [DO^], Ad (fl-right) [HH], Juv (fl) [AM^], Imm (pale) [KDR], Ad (st) [RF]; **Buzzard** Juv (pale) [MVa]; **Spotted Eagle** (st) [MW], (fl-un) & (fl-up) [DO^]. **p312: Egyptian Vulture** Ad (st), Imm (st) & Imm (fl-up) [DO^]; Ad (fl-un) & Ad (fl-up) [HH]; **Bald Eagle** Imm [DH^], (fl) [TJ]; **Griffon Vulture** Imm (st) [GYD], Imm (fl-un) [MVa], Imm (fl-up) [HH], Ad (fl-un) [HH]. **p313: Sparrowhawk** M (side) [MVa], M (un) [MB], M (up) [MVa], F (side) [AO^], F (un) [JPel^], Juv F (up) [AO^], Imm [MVa]; **Kestrel** (un) [AGS], (up) [HH]; **Goshawk** (side) [RSc^], F (un) [MDar], others [MVa]. **p314: Sparrowhawk** F (fl-up) [AO^], M (fl) & F (st) [MVa], F (inset) [RO^], others [MB]. **p315: Goshawk** (fl-un) [MVa], M (fl-side) [RSc^], Juv (fl) [MVa], M (st) & F (st) [WS^], Juv (st) [HB^]. **p316: Kestrel** M (fl-un) & M (fl-up) [JPel^], F (fl-up) [HH], F (st) [WS^], M (st) [RJS^], others [DT]. **p317: Merlin** Juv (fl) [AO^], F (st) [MB], Imm (st) [AO^], others [MVa]. **p318: Hobby** Ad (fl-up) [DT], Ad (fl-un) [AGS], Juv (fl-up) & Ad (st) [MVa], Juv (fl-un) [DO^]. **p319: Peregrine** Ad (fl-up) & Juv (fl-un) [AGS], Juv (fl-up) [MVa], Ad (fl-un) [MVa], Ad (st) both [AO^]. **p320: Red-footed Falcon** 1s (fl-up) [MG^], 1s (fl-un) [RSc^], Juv (fl) [RHa], others [HH]. **p321: Gyr Falcon** white (fl) [Steve Byland/Shutterstock], Ad white (st) [TM^], Juv (inset) [Ómar Runólfsson/CC], others [MVa]; **Peregrine** [DO^]. **p322: Gyr Falcon** both [MVa]; **Lanner Falcon** (fl) [DO^], (st) [MVa]; **Saker Falcon** (fl) [DO^], (st) [DS^]; **Peregrine** (st) [AO^]. **p323: Red-footed Falcon** F (up) & F (un) & M [HH], Juv [RHa], 1sM (up) [MG^], 1sM (un) [RSc^]; **Peregrine** Ad (un) [MB], Ad (up) & Juv [AGS]; **Hobby** Juv (up) [MVa], others [DT]; **Kestrel** Juv [DT], Ad F [HH], M (up) & M (un) [JPel^]; **Merlin** Juv [AO^], others [MVa]. **p324: Lesser Kestrel** 1sM (fl-un) [MVa], 1sM (fl-up) [AGS], M (fl-up) [AGS], M (fl-un) & M (fl-up) & F (fl-un) [HH], F (st) [DO^], 1sM (inset) [JO], M (st) [AGS]; **Kestrel** M (fl-up) [MVa]; **American Kestrel** M (fl) [BH], M (st) [AGS], F (fl-up) [DH^], F (fl-un) [BSu], F (st) [BSm^]. **p325: Eleonora's Falcon** dark (fl) & pale (fl) [AGS], (st) [ID]; **Hobby** [MB]; **Amur Falcon** M (fl) [RSc^], M (st) [DS^], 1sM (fl) [DBry], F (st) [WL^]; **Red-footed Falcon** both [HH].

'HIGHER LANDBIRDS' p326: Cuckoo & Meadow Pipit [MB]. **p327: Kingfisher** M (st) [DO^], F (st) [PW], F (fl) [DO^], Juv [AGS]. **p328: Cuckoo** M (fl-up) & M (fl-un) [DT], M (st) [Erni/Shutterstock], F (h) [CF], F rufous (inset) [JSP], Juv (inset) [MVa]; **Sparrowhawk** (inset) [MMc], (fl-up) [DO^], (fl-un) [MVa], (st) [HH]. **p329: Hoopoe** (inset) [MMc], (fl-up) [DO^], (fl-un) [MVa], (st) [HH]. **p330: Bee-eater** Ad (fl-up) [MG^], Ad (fl-un) [GYD], 1s (fl) [MVa], (st) [HH]; **Blue-cheeked Bee-eater** Juv (fl) [RdH^], Ad (fl) [JPel^], (st) [MVa]. **p331: Roller** (fl-up) [MVa], others [AGS], **Great Spotted Cuckoo** all [AGS]. **p332: Ring-necked Parakeet** (flock) [D^], (fl) [KC], F [HH], M & Imm M [AGS]; **Alexandrine Parakeet** [Skierx/Shutterstock].

WOODPECKERS p333: Green Woodpecker M [MB], Juv (h) [RLC], **Lesser Spotted & Great Spotted Woodpeckers** [MB]. **p334: Wryneck** Juv (inset) [HH], (st) [MB], (fl) [AGS]. **p335: Green Woodpecker** M (fl) [RMB], M (inset) [AGS], M (st) [MB], F [PW], Juv (inset) [RLC]. **p336: Great Spotted Woodpecker** M (fl) [Victor Tyakht/Shutterstock], M (st) & F (h) [MB], Juv M (h) [RLC], Juv M (inset) [HH]. **p337: Lesser Spotted Woodpecker** M (st) & (inset) [MB], F [MMc].

AERIAL FEEDERS p338: Swifts [AGS], **Swallows** [DT]. **p339: Swift** Ad (side) & Juv (head on) [HH], others [DT]. **p340: Pallid Swift** all [DO^]; **Swift** (un) [MVa], others [DT]; **Needle-tailed Swift** [BSu]; **Pacific Swift** [MDan^]. **p341: Alpine Swift** [DO^]; **Little Swift** both [MG^], **Chimney Swift** both [BSu]. **p342: Swallow** M (fl) [JPel^], F (fl) [MG^], Juv (fl) & Juv (st) [DO^], M (st) [WL^], (nest) [Phototr/Shutterstock]. **p343: House Martin** Ad (fl-un) [RSc^], Ad (fl-up) & Juv (fl) [DT], (st) [MB], (nest) [Erni/Shutterstock], (group) [AGS]. **p344: Sand Martin** (colony) [RR^], (fl-up) [MVa], (fl-un) [RSc^], Ad (st) both [DO^]. **p345: Red-rumped Swallow** (fl-un) [MVa], (fl-up) [MMc], (st) [RLC], *daurica/japonica* [IFu]; **Swallow** [JPel^]; **Crag Martin** (fl) both [AGS], (st) [HH]. **p346: Cliff Swallow** (st) [DO^], others [BSu]; **Tree Swallow** all [BSu]; **Purple Martin** (st) [JPe], (fl-up) [TL], (fl-un) [VL^].

LARKS, PIPITS & WAGTAILS p347: Skylark [HH]; **Meadow Pipit** [MB]; **Pied Wagtail** [MB]; **Yellow Wagtail** M (h) [HGeb^], F (h) [TTay], Juv (h) [RLC]. **p348: Woodlark** (fl-up) [JO'B], (fl-un) [RSc^], Ad (on branch) [Menno Schaefer/Shutterstock], Ad (on ground) [DO^], Juv [GYD]. **p349: Skylark** (fl-up) [RSc^], (fl-un) [RSc^], (st) (inset) [MVa], (h) [DT], Juv (st) [HH], Ad (st) [AGS]. **p350: Shore Lark** (fl) [MVa], (st) both [HH]. **p351: Short-toed Lark** (fl) [AF], Ad (h) [MMc], Ad (st) [RLC], 1w (st) [HH]; **Skylark** [RSc^]. **p352: Woodlark** (fl-un) [RSc^], (fl-up) [JO'B]; **Skylark** (fl-un - tail spread) [DO^], (fl-un - tail closed) [RSc^], (fl-side) [DT], (fl-up) [RSc^], **Skylark** (h) [DT]; **Crested Lark** (fl-un) [MG^], (fl-side) [MVa], (st) [AGS]; **Short-toed Lark** (fl) [AF], (wing) [AGS]; **Lesser Short-toed Lark** (fl-up) [RHo], Ad (st) [MMc], (wing) [AGS]; **Black Lark** [MK]; **White-winged Lark** [HvD^]; **Shore Lark** [MVa]. **p353: Calandra Lark** (fl-up) [AGS], (fl-un) [HH], Ad (st) [Erni/Shutterstock]; **Bimaculated Lark** (fl-un) [VP], (fl-up) & Ad (st) [DO^]; **Black Lark** [MDan^]; **White-winged Lark** [MDan^]. **p354: Tree Pipit** Ad spr [AGS], 1w [MVa], (fl) [RSc^], (inset) [DT]. **p355: Meadow Pipit** (fl) [RSc^], 1s (Apr) [HGeb^], 1s (Mar) [MG^], Ad (Jun) [MVa], (inset) [DT]. **p356: Rock Pipit** (fl) & *petrosus* spr [AGS], *littoralis* spr [MMc], others [HH]. **p357: Water Pipit** sum & aut/win [DO^]; **Rock Pipit** *petrosus* (inset) [HH], *littoralis* (inset) [MMc]; **Buff-bellied Pipit** [HH]. **p358: Red-throated Pipit** Ad [HH], 1w [DO^], (inset) [HH]; **Pechora Pipit** (inset) [HH]; **Tree Pipit** (inset) [DO^]. **p359: Olive-backed Pipit** [MMc]; **Tree Pipit** (h) [HH]; **Pechora Pipit** (st) & (inset) [HH]. **p360: Richard's Pipit** Ad [MVa], 1w [RLC]. **p361: Tawny Pipit** 1w [PJW], Ad [DO^], 1s [MMc]; **Blyth's Pipit** [MVa]. **p362: Pied Wagtail** *yarrelli* M sum [MPF/CC], F sum [AGS], 1w [MB]; **Amur Wagtail** [RSc^];

White Wagtail *alba* M sum [Andreas Trepte/CC], F sum [MVa], 1w [HH]. **p363: Grey Wagtail** Juv [HH], M [DO^], M win (h) [MVPhoto/Shutterstock], F (h) [DO^]. **p364: Yellow Wagtail** M & F [TTay], Juv/1w [RLC]; Eastern [MMc]. **p365: Yellow Wagtail** *flavissima* [TTay], *cinereocapilla* [DO^], *flava* [Bildagentur Zoonar GmbH/Shutterstock], *thunbergi* [MG^], 'Channel' [RHa], *feldegg* [AGS]; **Citrine Wagtail** Juv/1w & F [HH], M (h) [Dmytro Pylypenko/Shutterstock].

DIPPERS, ACCENTORS, WRENS, ORIOLES, STARLINGS, WAXWINGS p366: Waxwings [MB], **Dipper** [DT], **Wren** & **Dunnock** [MB], **Starling** [HH], **Golden Oriole** [MG^]. **p367: Dipper** (fl) [HH], Ad *gularis* [DT], Juv [DM], Ad *hibernicus* [MCa], Ad *cinclus* [MMc]. **p368: Dunnock** Ad (on ground) [HH], (singing) & Juv [DT], hebridium [MC^]. **p369: Wren** Ad [MB], (inset) [DT]. **p370: Wrens** *indigenus* [DT], *troglodytes* [MVa], *fridariensis* & *zetlandicus* [HH], hirtensis [JM], *hebridensis* [GC]. **p371: Golden Oriole** F (st) [MVa], others [MG^]. **p372: Starling** (fl) both [PMo], Ad win [MB], *zetlandicus* [HH], others [AGS]. **p373: Rose-coloured Starling** Ad win [HH], Ad sum [DO^], Juv (st) [MMc], (fl) both [PMo]. **p374: Waxwing** (flock) [MB], others [HH]. **p375: Alpine Accentor** [MMc], **Cedar Waxwing** Juv/1w [Kelly Colgan Azar/CC], Ad [Dennis W Donohue/Shutterstock].

THRUSHES & CHATS p376: Song Thrush, Nightingale & **Wheatear** [MB]; **Redstart** [HH]. **p377: Nightingale** Juv [RTi]; **Robin** Juv [MVa]; **Wheatear** Juv [AO^]; **Redstart** Juv [AGS]; **Stonechat** 1w M [DT], others [AGS]; **Grey-Cheeked Thrush** [HH]. **p378: Ring Ouzel** (fl) [MG^], 1w M [JL], M & F [MVa], (inset) [MB]. **p379: Blackbird** M [DT]; F, Juv (h) & 1w F (h) [HH]; M (fl) [RSc^], 1w M (fl) [MG^]; 1w M (h) [MvD^]. **p380: Song Thrush** (fl) [AO^], Ad *clarkei* & Juv [AGS], *hebridensis* [SDu], *philomelo*s [HH]. **p381: Mistle Thrush** (fl) [MVa], Ad [HH], Juv [JAn]. **p382: Fieldfare** (fl-up) [MG^], (fl-un) [MVa], 1w [HH] & Ad [HH]. **p383: Redwing** (fl) [MG^], *iliacus* [HH], *coburni* [RTo]. **p384: Red-throated Thrush** [RWi]; **Black-throated Thrush** [MMc], 1w F [HH]; **White's Thrush** [HH]. **p385: Dusky Thrush** 1w M [CvR^], 1w F [CU]; **Naumann's Thrush** [Old Apple/Shutterstock]; **Eyebrowed Thrush** [Nitat/Shutterstock]; **Siberian Thrush** F [PMo^], 1w M [HH]. **p386: American Robin** [MMc]; **Grey-cheeked Thrush** [HH]; **Swainson's Thrush** 1w [HH]; (fl) [SK]. **p387: Varied Thrush** [MV^]; **Wood Thrush** [AGS]; **Hermit Thrush** [AGS]; **Veery** [HH]. **p388: Robin** Ad [MB], Juv [MVa], *rubecula* [DO^]. **p389: Nightingale** Ad (sing) [HH], Ad (bottom) [HH], *golzii* [JBa]. **p390: Whinchat** M (top) & F [AGS], M (bottom) [DO^], 1w [HH]. **p391: Stonechat** M *rubicola* [MVa], others [AGS]. **p392: Redstart** 1wF [WL^], 1wM [MVa], M & F [AGS]. **p393: Black Redstart** M, F & 1w [HH], Eastern (inset) [MMc]. **p394: Wheatear** [DO^], M spr [DT], 1s M [AGS], (fl) [MVa]. **p395:** (wheatear tail pattern illustrations) [RSti], **Wheatear** M aut [HH], 1w/F [CvR^]; 'Greenland' Wheatear M spr [TC], 1w [DO^], *oenanthe* (wing) [CvR^]. **p396: Black-eared Wheatear** 1w M [RWi], 1w F *hispanica* [RSto], M *hispanica* both [HH], M *melanoleuca* both [AGS], (tail illustration) [RSti]; **Pied Wheatear** 1w F [VL^], 1w M [AM^], M spr [AGS], (tail illustration) [RSti]. **p397: Desert Wheatear** 1w M (st) [TTay], 1w M (h) [DO^], 1w F [MMc], (tail illustration) [RSti]; **Isabelline Wheatear** (fl) [AGS], 1w [DO^], (tail illustration) [RSti]; **Wheatear** 1w [DT], (fl) [MVa], (tail illustration) [RSti]. **p398: Rufous Bush Chat** [MVa]; **White-throated Robin** M [DO^], 1w F [MMc]; **Moussier's Redstart** M [AGS], F [GE]. **p399: Rock Thrush** M [GYD], F [DO^]; **Blue Rock Thrush** M [BB^], F [DO^]; **White-crowned Black Wheatear** [DO^]. **p400: Bluethroat** F [MVa], others [HH]; **Thrush Nightingale** Ad [MVa], (h) [HH], (wing) [MVa]. **Nightingale** [AGS], (wing) [HH]. **p401: Siberian Rubythroat** 1w F [IFi], 1w M [HH]; **Red-flanked Bluetail** 1w [HH], M [MVa]; **Rufous-tailed Robin** [HH]; **Siberian Blue Robin** [MDan^]. **p402: Siberian Stonechat** *maurus* M & 1w [AGS]; *variegatus* M [DO^], 1w [RB]; **Stonechat** M [AGS], 1w [CV].

(OLD WORLD) WARBLERS, CISTICOLAS & CRESTS p403: Goldcrest [MB]; **Whitethroat** [AGS]. **p404: Chiffchaff** [DT]; **Marsh Warbler** [HH]; **Grasshopper Warbler** [MVa]; **Icterine Warbler** [HH]; **Fan-tailed Warbler** [DO^]; **Yellow-rumped Warbler** [HH]. **p405: Cetti's Warbler** Ad [MB], (inset) [DT]. **p406: Sedge Warbler** 1w [DO^], others [DT]. **p407: Reed Warbler** Ad [DT], 1w & (inset) [HH]. **p408: Marsh Warbler** 1w [MMc], others [HH]. **p409: Paddyfield Warbler** (st) [HH], (wing) [DO^]; all other wings [HH]. **p410: Aquatic Warbler** Ad [HvD^], (h) [HGeb^]; **Sedge Warbler** (h) [AGS]; **Great Reed Warbler** [HH]; **Thick-billed Warbler** [HH]. **p411: Fan-tailed Warbler** 1w [MVa], Ad [DO^]; **Savi's Warbler** [HGeb^]; **River Warbler** [MvD^]. **p412: Grasshopper Warbler** Ad [DT], 1w [HH], 1w (h) [MMc]. **p413: Lanceolated Warbler** (left) & (right) [MMc], (inset) [HH]; **Grasshopper Warbler** (wing) [MMc]; **Pallas's Grasshopper Warbler** [MMc]. **p414: Icterine Warbler** Ad [MVa], 1w & (wing) [DO^], **Melodious Warbler** Ad (May) [DO^], Ad (Aug) & (wing) [HH]. **p415: Eastern Olivaceous Warbler** Ad [AGS], 1w [HH]; **Olive Tree Warbler** Ad [DO^], 1w [HH]. **p416: Booted Warbler** 1w [HH]; **Sykes's Warbler** 1w [HH]. **p417: Dartford Warbler** all [MB]. **p418: Blackcap** M [DT], M (inset) [AGS], F (h) [DO^], 1w [HH]; **Marsh Tit** (h) [HH]. **p419: Garden Warbler** Ad & (inset) [AGS], 1w [DO^]. **p420: Whitethroat** M & (inset) [DT], (fl) [AGS], F [GYD], 1w [DO^]. **p421: Lesser Whitethroat** *curruca* Ad [DO^], 1w (h) [MB], 1w [HH]; *blythi/halimodendri* (left) [CB], (right) [MMc]. **p422: Subalpine Warbler** *albistriata* M [HH]; *iberiae* M & F [HH]; **Moltoni's Subalpine Warbler** M [DO^]; (tail pattern illustrations) [RSti]. **p423: Moltoni's Subalpine Warbler** Juv [DO^]; **Whitethroat** Juv [MB]; **Spectacled Warbler** M & F/1w [DO^]; **Desert Warbler** [DO^]; **Marmora's Warbler** [MMc]. **p424: Barred Warbler** Ad [MVa], Juv [HH]; **Western Orphean Warbler** M [DO^], 1w [MMc]. **p425: Sardinian Warbler** all [DO^], **Rüppell's Warbler** M [AGS], F [GRe]. **p426: Chiffchaff** Ad [RSc^], 1w & early March (inset) [AGS], *collybita* (inset) [DO^], **Willow Warbler** [AM^]. **p427: Chiffchaff** *abietinus* & *collybita* [HH], *tristis* [DO^], **Iberian Chiffchaff** [JL]. **p428: Willow Warbler** (inset) [DT], Ad [AM^], 1w *trochilus* & *acredula* [HH]. **p429: Wood Warbler** (inset) [HH], Ad (front) [MB], Ad (side) [RSc^], 1w [HH]. **p430: Western Bonelli's Warbler** Ad [DO^], 1w [HH]; **Eastern Bonelli's Warbler** Ad [AGS], 1w [MMc]. **p431: Dusky Warbler** [HH]; **Radde's Warbler** [HH]. **p433: Pallas's Warbler** 1w & (h) [HH], (inset) [AGS]; **Yellow-browed Warbler** 1w & (inset) [MVa], (h) [HH]; **Hume's Warbler** 1w [AM^], (inset) [HH]. **p434: Greenish Warbler** 1w & (h) [HH], Ad (inset) [MVa], *plumbeitarsus* [TTam]; **Arctic Warbler** Ad & 1w [HH]. **p435: Green Warbler** Ad [DO^]; **Eastern Crowned Warbler** 1w [MMa]; **Pale-legged Leaf Warbler** [MPW]; **Sakhalin Leaf Warbler** [DCoo]. **p436: Goldcrest** M & F [HH], (fl) [MVa], Juv (h) [SBa]. **p437: Firecrest** Juv (h) [SBa], others [HH].

549

FLYCATCHERS p438: Pied Flycatcher [AGS]; **Alder Flycatcher** M [MMc]. **p439: Spotted Flycatcher** Ad spr [MB], Ad (inset) & 1w [HH], Juv [AGS]. **p440: Pied Flycatcher** Ad M [Martin Fowler/Shutterstock], 1s M [DO^], 1w M [HH], F [AGS]. **p441: Brown Flycatcher** 1w & (h) [AGS]; **Spotted Flycatcher** (h) [AGS]; **Collared Flycatcher** Ad M [MVa], others [HH]. **p442: Red-breasted Flycatcher** all [HH]; **Taiga Flycatcher** M [RdH^], others [HH].

TITS, NUTHATCHES & 'CREEPERS' p443: Blue Tit both [MB]; **Long-tailed Tit** [Erni/Shutterstock]; **Bearded Tit** [DT]; **Penduline Tit** [HH]; **Nuthatch** [MB]; **Treecreeper** [MB]. **p444: Bearded Tit** Ad M [Bildagentur Zoonar GmbH/ Shutterstock], Juv M & Ad F [MVa], Juv F (h) [MvD^], (fl) [AGS]. **p445: Long-tailed Tit** (flock) [MB], Ad [HH], *caudatus* [Piotr Krzeslak/Shutterstock], Juv [PL]. **p446: Blue Tit** Ad (top) & Juv [AGS], Ad (bottom) [HH]. **p447: Great Tit** M & *major* (h) [HH], F [AGS], Juv [MVa], melanistic (inset) [CvR^]. **p448: Crested Tit** (inset) [HH], *scoticus* [DT], *mitratus* (inset) [DO^], *cristatus* (inset) [CvR^]. **p449: Coal Tit** *hibernicus* (inset) [MC^], *britannicus* [HH], *ater* (inset top) [MVa], *ater* (inset bottom) [RLC]. **p450: Marsh Tit** [Erni/Shutterstock]; **Blackcap** [HH]. **p451: Willow Tit** *kleinschmidti* [SY], *borealis* [HH]; **Marsh Tit** (h) [HH]. **p452: Nuthatch** M [GYD], F [MB]. **p453: Treecreeper** both [HH]. **p454: Penduline Tit** Juv & F [DO^], M [MMc]; **Red-breasted Nuthatch** [HH]. **p455: Short-toed Treecreeper** Ad & (wing) [HB^], (claw) [MVa]; **Treecreeper** (wing) [HH], (claw) [DT]; **Wallcreeper** F [GJe], (inset) [MVa].

SHRIKES p456: Great Grey Shrike [MB]; **Woodchat Shrike** Juv (Jul) [John Navajo/Shutterstock], 1w (Sep) & 1s F (Apr) [HH], M & F [DO^]. **p457: Red-backed Shrike** Ad M (fl) [TM^], 1w & F [HH], M [Erni/Shutterstock]. **p458: Isabelline Shrike** *phoenicuroides* M & F [AGS]; *isabellinus* M [DO^], F [HH]. **p459: Isabelline Shrike** *isabellinus* (fl) [HH], (st) [DT], *phoenicuroides* [DO^]; **Red-backed Shrike** 1w [RSc^]; **Brown Shrike** [MMc]. **p460: Great Grey Shrike** Ad [MVa], (fl) [HH], 1w [HGeb^]. **p461: Lesser Grey Shrike** Ad [DO^], Juv [CvR^]; **Southern Grey Shrike** [MMc]. **p462: Woodchat Shrike** F & F [DO^], M (fl) [MVa], Imm F [HH], Juv [John Navajo/Shutterstock], *badius* [TTam]. **p463: Masked Shrike** M [AGS], 1w [HH]; **Long-tailed Shrike** [MG^]; **Nutcracker** *caryocatactes* [HB^], *macrorhynchos* [CvR^].

CROWS p464: Rook (flock) [HH], (rookery) [SY]. **p465: Raven** (left) & (centre left) [HH], (centre right) & (right) [AGS]; **Hooded Crow** (up) [MG^], (un) [MVa]; **Carrion Crow** (un) [AGS], (up) [JL]; **Chough** (up) [DT], (un) [AGS]; **Rook** Juv [DT], (un) [AGS], (up) [HH]; **Nutcracker** both [MVa]; **Jay** (up) [MVa], (un) [DT]; **Jackdaw** (left) [HH], (centre right) [AGS], (right) [DT]; **Magpie** (up) & (un) [AGS]. **p466: Jackdaw** Ad & (fl) [MB], 1w [AGS], *monedula* [HH]. **p467: Hooded Crow** Ad & (fl) [HH], hybrid [HvD^]. **p468: Carrion Crow** Ad [Erni/Shutterstock], (fl) [AGS], (h) [DT]; **Rook** (h) [HH], **Raven** (h) [AGS]. **p469: Rook** Ad [AGS], (fl) & Juv [HH]. **p470: Raven** Ad [AGS], (fl) [HH]. **p471: Chough** Ad [Erni/ Shutterstock], (fl) [AGS]. **p472: Jay** *rufitergum* [DT], *glandarius* (fl) [MVa], *hibernicus* (inset) [MC^]. **p473: Magpie** (flock) [PMa], Ad [AGS], (fl) [DT].

SPARROWS & FINCHES p474: Reed Bunting, Brambling & **House Sparrow** [MB]; **Siskin** Juv/1w & F [HH], M [RJS^]. **p475: Crossbill, Goldfinch, Lesser Redpoll, Hawfinch, Bullfinch** & **Chaffinch** [MB]; **Greenfinch** [DCu]; **White-throated Sparrow** [HH]. **p476: House Sparrow** M sum & win (h) [AGS], F [HH]. **p477: Tree Sparrow** Ad sum [RLC], Ad win [HH], Juv [MG^]. **p478: Bullfinch** M & F [AGS], Juv [Andy Morffew/CC], *pyrrhula* [HH]. **p479: Hawfinch** M sum & F [DO^], M win (h) & Juv [HH], (fl) [MB]. **p480: Brambling** (fl) both [MVa], (flock) [AGS]; M sum (h), 1w M & F [HH], M win [DT], 1w F [MMc]. **p481: Chaffinch** (fl-up) [MVa], (fl-un) [RSc^]; *gengleri* F & M win [AGS], M sum [DT]; *coelebs* F [MvD^], M [RJS^]. **p482: Goldfinch** (fl) [JCo], others [AGS]. **p483: Greenfinch** M Ad [HH], Juv [AGS], others [DO^]. **p484: Siskin** M (fl) [MVa], M (st) [RJS^], others [HH]. **p485: Serin** M [AGS], M (inset) [HH], F & 1w F [MVa], Juv [DT]; **Citril Finch** [MMc]. **p486: Linnet** M win [DT], others [AGS]. **p487: Twite** 1w (inset) [SDu], others [HH]. **p488: Lesser Redpoll** all [MB]; **Common Redpoll** [HH]. **p489: Common Redpoll** [HH]; **Arctic Redpoll** [HH]. **p490: Lesser Redpoll** 1w/F [MB]; **Common Redpoll** (tail) [MVa], others [HH], **Arctic Redpoll** all [HH]. **p491: Common Rosefinch** M & F [DO^], 1w [HH]. **p492: Crossbill** (flock) & Juv M (inset) [DT], F [CvR^], M [Erni/ Shutterstock], Juv (inset) [AO^]. **p493: Scottish Crossbill** all [DE], **Parrot Crossbill** M [MVa], F & (h) [DE], **Crossbill** (h) [HH]. **p494: Two-barred Crossbill** all [HH], **Crossbill** (inset) [Erni/Shutterstock], **Pine Grosbeak** both [HH]. **p495: Spanish Sparrow** M win [HH], M sum [AGS], F [DO^]; **House Sparrow** [AGS]; **Trumpeter Finch** [MMc], **Rock Sparrow** [DO^].

BUNTINGS p496: Reed Bunting M 1w [AGS], M win [DO^], M sum [MB], F 1w [HH], F win [DT], F sum [MB]; **Little Bunting** [MMc]. **p497: Lapland Bunting** (fl) [RHa], others [HH]. **p498: Snow Bunting** *nivalis* F [GYD], M [MVa]; *insulae* F [MVa], M [RTo]. **p499: Snow Bunting** (flock) [MVa], *insulae* F & M win [HH], M moulting to sum [DT]; *nivalis* 1w F [AGS], M moulting to sum [RO^]. **p500: Yellowhammer** M win (h) [AGS], M sum [DO^], 1w M [MG^], F [RdH^], 1w F [HH], *caliginosa* [MMc]. **p501: Cirl Bunting** M sum & F [DO^], M win [PGV], 1w F [Mike Lane/FLPA]. **p502: Reed Bunting** M sum & win & 1w F (inset) [DO^], 1w M [AGS], F spr [DT], 1w M F [HH]. **p503: Corn Bunting** (h) [AGS], others. **p504: Little Bunting** win & 1w [HH]; **Reed Bunting** M win [DO^], 1w M [HH], F win [MB]; **Chestnut-eared Bunting** both [HH]. **p505: Rustic Bunting** 1w [DT], M & F [MVa]; **Pallas's Reed Bunting** both [DCoo]; **Reed Bunting** 1w F [HH]. **p506: Black-headed Bunting** M [AGS], F [GYD], 1w [MMc]; **Yellow-breasted Bunting** 1w [HH], M sum [RSc^]. **p507: Yellow-browed Bunting** [RWi], **Black-faced Bunting** 1w F [VL^], M [MT]; **Chestnut Bunting** [SG]. **p508: Ortolan Bunting** M & F [DO^], Juv [AO^]; **Cretzschmar's Bunting** M [MMc], 1w [MVa]. **p509: Pine Bunting** M win [DO^], 1w M [HH], 1w F [VL^]; **Yellowhammer** 1w F [MVa]; **Rock Bunting** [HH].

VAGRANT LANDBIRDS FROM NORTH AMERICA p511: Red-eyed Vireo [SY]; **Yellow-throated Vireo** [AGS]; **Philadelphia Vireo** [DM^]; **Ruby-crowned Kinglet** [Kelly Colgan Azar/CC]. **p512: Blackpoll Warbler** M [AGS], 1w [MMc]; **Yellow-rumped Warbler** M & 1w [HH]; **Cape May Warbler** M [Lee Kensinger/USFWS/CC], 1w [HH]. **p513: Bay-breasted Warbler** [Seabamirum/CC]; **Blackburnian Warbler** [BSu]; **Chestnut-sided Warbler** [GYD];

Magnolia Warbler [MMc]; **American Redstart** [Kelly Colgan Azar/CC]; **Northern Parula** 1w M [DM^], 1w F [LG].
p514: Hooded Warbler [AGS]; **Wilson's Warbler** 1w M [ME], 1w F (h) [USFWS Mountain-Prairie/CC]; **Yellow Warbler**
1w F [HH]; **Common Yellowthroat** both [BSu]; **Black-and-white Warbler** 1w F [DO^], 1w M [AGS]. **p515: Canada**
Warbler [KD]; **Tennessee Warbler** [Neil Bowman/FLPA]; **Golden-winged Warbler** [DM^]; **Blue-winged Warbler**
[DO^]; **Northern Waterthrush** [MMc]; **Ovenbird** [Dennis W Donohue/Shutterstock]. **p516: Rose-breasted**
Grosbeak Ad M [AGS], 1w M [MMc]; **Indigo Bunting** [DM^]; **Evening Grosbeak** [MV^]; **Dark-eyed Junco** [HH];
Eastern Towhee [Kelly Colgan Azar/CC]. **p517: Scarlet Tanager** [MMc]; **Summer Tanager** [AGS]; **Bobolink** [MMc];
Baltimore Oriole [MMc]; **Brown-headed Cowbird** both [AGS]. **p518: Lark Sparrow** [AGS]; **Fox Sparrow** [Steve
Byland/Shutterstock]; **Savannah Sparrow** [HH]; **Song Sparrow** [HH]. **p519: White-throated Sparrow** [HH];
White-crowned Sparrow [DM^]; **Northern Mockingbird** [Kelly Colgan Azar/CC]; **Brown Thrasher** [Robert L
Kothenbeutel/Shutterstock]; **Grey Catbird** [AGS]. **p520: Eastern Kingbird** [B.ca]; **Eastern Phoebe** [Alan Murphy
BIA/Minden Pictures/FLPA]; **Alder Flycatcher** [MMc]; **Acadian Flycatcher** [DM^]. **p521: Belted Kingfisher** M (fl)
[MDan^], M (h) Tim Parker/CC, F [Robert L Kothenbeutel/Shutterstock]; **Yellow-bellied Sapsucker** Imm M [MDan^],
Juv [Steven Russell Smith Photos/Shutterstock]; **Black-billed Cuckoo** [MCh]; **Yellow-billed Cuckoo** both [MMc].

Birds of uncertain origin and escapes/introductions **p522: Falcated Duck** both [AGS]; **Booted Eagle** both
[AGS]; **Red-headed Bunting** M [DM^], 1w/F [DCo]. **p523: Great White Pelican** (fl) [DO^]; **Greater Flamingo** Ad
[AGS]; **Northern Flicker** M [Wplynn/CC]; **House Crow** [AGS]; **Daurian Starling** [A-S HSS]; **Mugimaki Flycatcher**
[AV^]; **American Goldfinch** [Fyn Kyn/CC]; **Yellow-headed Blackbird** [AGS]; **Monk Parakeet** [Vladimir Kogan
Michael/Shutterstock]; **Atlantic Canary** [RLC].

Finally, the authors would like to express their own personal debts of gratitude.

Rob Hume thanks his wife Marcella for frequent valuable discussion, and apologises to her, and
to Noah and Charlotte Holt, for so often coming second to the laptop for several months. Long
inspired by Peter Hayman, Rob refers frequently with profit and pleasure to Peter's beautiful and
meticulous work in *The Complete Guide to the Birdlife of Britain & Europe* (Mitchell Beazley, 2001).

Rob Still gives a big shout to Charcz 'n' Bobs Design & Catering and the 'Shetland', as well as everyone,
past and present he has enjoyed birding with, whether still in touch or not, you will know who you
are – thank you for the inspirations. Oh and that Muscovy Duck that 'bit' me when I was aged about 5
– which led me to start drawing and describing details of plumage, in order to recognise and avoid...

Andy Swash would like to thank his wife Gill for her unstinting support over the many months
of solitude during the final stages of production, and for her insightful comments on the text.
He would also like to make special mention of John Sage, who inspired his interest in birds from
a very early age, and thank his parents, Bob and Mary, for their constant encouragement.

Hugh Harrop would like to thank Mum for buying him his first pair of binoculars and Michelle and
Cerys for sharing his love of birds. Special thanks go to Richard Smith and to both the late Richard
Harrop and the late Ken Lloyd for being such wonderful mentors in his teenage years.

David Tipling would like to thank all the photographers and birders, who over the years, have
facilitated photographic opportunities. Many of the results are reproduced in this book. A special
mention goes to Jake Jones, who invited him into his garden to photograph the singing Robin that
adorns the cover.

Male Sparrowhawk
by Martin Bennett

Index

This index includes the English and scientific (*in italics*) names of all the birds in this book.

Bold text highlights main species accounts.

Italicized figures indicate page(s) on which key comparative photographs appear.

Blue figures relate to the entry in the status and legislation table.

Regular text is used for species and races that are not subject to a full account, and to indicate pages where comparative tables appear.

552

About the authors

This book has been several years in the making: an ambition of **WILD***Guides* only now made possible by advances in digital photography and graphic design.

Rob Hume, freelance writer and editor for 35 years and editor of RSPB publications from 1983 to 2009, was Chairman of the British Birds Rarities Committee, and has led wildlife holidays in the UK, Europe and Africa.

Robert Still, co-founder and publishing director of **WILD***Guides*, is an ecologist and widely travelled naturalist. His design philosophy and exceptional skills in computer graphics have been crucial to the concept, development and production of the **WILD***Guides Britain's Wildlife* series.

Andy Swash has been involved professionally in nature conservation since 1977 and is managing director of **WILD***Guides*. A renowned photographer, he leads photographic tours worldwide, and has devised, co-authored and edited many other books.

Hugh Harrop founded the ecotourism business, Shetland Wildlife, and is one of Shetland's top birders and naturalists. His award-winning photographs have been published throughout Europe and North America.

David Tipling, one of the world's most widely published wildlife photographers, is author or commissioned photographer for many books and writes for leading wildlife and photographic magazines.